Alias David Bowie

Alias David Bowie

a biography

Peter and Leni Gillman

Hodder & Stoughton
LONDON SYDNEY AUCKLAND TORONTO

For Danny and Seth,
children of the 1970s

British Library Cataloguing in Publication Data
Gillman, Peter
   Alias David Bowie: a biography.
   1. Bowie, David   2. Rock musicians –
   England – Biography
   I. Title   II. Gillman, Leni
   784.5'0092'4   ML420.B754

   ISBN 0-340-36806-3 HB
   ISBN 0-340-40290-3 PB

Contents

Family Tree

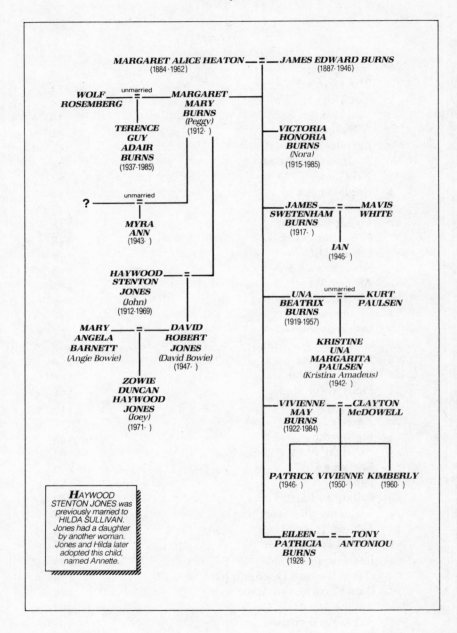

MARGARET ALICE HEATON — = — JAMES EDWARD BURNS
(1884 - 1962)   (1887 - 1946)

WOLF — = — MARGARET
ROSEMBERG   unmarried   MARY
            BURNS
            (Peggy)
            (1912-)

TERENCE
GUY
ADAIR
BURNS
(1937-1985)

VICTORIA
HONORIA
BURNS
(Nora)
(1915-1985)

? — = — MYRA
  unmarried   ANN
             (1943-)

JAMES — = — MAVIS
SWETENHAM   WHITE
BURNS
(1917-)

IAN
(1946-)

HAYWOOD — = —
STENTON
JONES
(John)
(1912-1969)

UNA — = — KURT
BEATRIX   unmarried   PAULSEN
BURNS
(1919-1957)

MARY — = — DAVID
ANGELA   ROBERT
BARNETT   JONES
(Angie Bowie) (David Bowie)
              (1947-)

KRISTINE
UNA
MARGARITA
PAULSEN
(Kristina Amadeus)
(1942-)

ZOWIE
DUNCAN
HAYWOOD
JONES
(Joey)
(1971-)

VIVIENNE — = — CLAYTON
MAY   McDOWELL
BURNS
(1922-1984)

PATRICK   VIVIENNE   KIMBERLY
(1946-) (1950-)   (1960-)

*Haywood
STENTON JONES was
previously married to
HILDA SULLIVAN.
Jones had a daughter
by another woman.
Jones and Hilda later
adopted this child,
named Annette.*

EILEEN — = — TONY
PATRICIA   ANTONIOU
BURNS
(1928-)

Introduction

This book could not have been written without David Bowie. We should like to thank him for being the inspiration of a task that has fascinated and preoccupied us for almost three years. We came to it as outsiders, knowing almost nothing of the music world or of David Bowie. We depart from it with a sense of wonder at the ways of that world and at the achievements – often despite the music world – of David himself.

That is, however, the extent of David's contribution to this book. According to his New York office, he has made it a firm rule that the only biography he will assist with is "the one he writes himself". For a while, it seemed as though we might prove the exception. After dispatching an outline of our book, we received a letter from David's aide, Corinne Schwab, who said that ours sounded "a little less mischievous, a little more mature" than any other book about David in existence or in preparation.

Any prospect of cooperation was ended in April 1985, when the London *Sunday Times* published three articles based on our research thus far. David, we learned, was outraged. In particular, he objected strenuously to the suggestion that there was any link between the content of his work and the traumas that have afflicted his family and, especially, his half-brother Terry.

The only formal response we received came from David's record company, EMI, who objected to the quotations in the articles from David's lyrics, on the grounds that they violated their copyright, and demanded that all copies of the book should be destroyed. The *Sunday Times* responded that the amount quoted from David's lyrics did not violate the 1956 Copyright Act, which permits the use of reasonable extracts for "criticism or review", and our publishers, Hodder and Stoughton, added that since no books had yet been printed it was pointless arguing whether or not they should be destroyed.

Informally, David responded in other ways. Later that year he reacted angrily to a question about the articles posed by an American television reporter: he refused point-blank to answer, saying he had heard enough on the topic of his family over the previous twenty years. In 1986 he took up the same point when he complained to the British newspaper *Today* of biographers who "drag out long-lost aunts to supply all the details, aunts I've had absolutely no contact with for maybe twenty years – who have no knowledge of me – and absolutely unbelievable, blatant lies are told . . ."

We would not dream of arguing, as a Freudian psychiatrist might, that the very strength of David's reaction makes our case; we are content to let our readers come to their own judgment. But it was certainly made clear to us that for David, we have ventured into forbidden territory. That in itself would have made any cooperation far less likely; in any case, we also learned that the only basis on which David might have answered our questions was on seeing a draft of our manuscript first. That is a condition we would never have been prepared to accept.

To research this book, therefore, we conducted interviews with over 150 friends, relatives and colleagues, listed on pages 495–6, who had known or worked with David. Some were exceptionally helpful, patient, and forthcoming; others were more cautious. To all, we are immensely grateful. But from those who were cautious, and from the people we approached who declined to be interviewed, we became acquainted with another aspect of the music world that was new to us: the question of power.

A performer as successful as David has immense personal power: the power to dispense patronage, the power to make others want to be liked by him. It was undoubtedly a fear of this power that made some people unwilling to talk to us, lest they jeopardise their position and their prospects. David has also managed to extend his power more formally, for a number of requests we made for photographs were refused on the grounds that our book had not received his official approval.

David's attitude helps to illustrate another aspect of the music world: its extreme rapaciousness. Where every facet of a performer's life can be bought and sold – as David's once was – it is understandable that he should try to retain as much control over it as possible. And where a performer believes – as David does – that he has been unfairly exploited in the past, it is also natural that he should be hostile towards those attempting to profit from his renown.

But we believe that David's desire for control goes further. A central theme of this book is David's fascination for the media game, as he learned how to create and manipulate a succession of images of himself. Today, he is the master of that process, rarely allowing more than restricted glimpses of himself to be made public. The activities of biographers, particularly those with no allegiances or obligations in the music world, challenge both his power and the view he has established of himself. They also threaten some of the myths he has so skilfully laid down – and when those myths meet personal as well as professional needs, David appears even more at risk.

It could be argued, as David does, that such biographies are unduly intrusive. We do not accept that view. We believe that a performer who has posed such enigmas as David, who has paraded illusion and paradox to such effect, can only be described and understood by knowing the truth behind the myths he has established. We also believe that the force and complexity of his songs and lyrics can not be fully appreciated unless examined against his personal history. Only then does the full extent of his artistic achievement become clear.

Our narrative begins with the moment when the first of David's family myths was laid down, and ends with David's accomplished appearance at the Live Aid concert at Wembley Stadium in July, 1985. David's next major performance, as polished and professional as ever, came in the British film *Absolute Beginners*, which had its London première in April, 1986. David wrote several songs for the film, including the title track. We believe that this song, although tailored to the needs of the film, contained, as always, a strong personal element. One line in particular intrigued us, especially as it could be read – as so often – in different ways. Was it a parting shot? Or pre-emptive strike?

I am absolutely sane . . .

1

The Hero of Archangel

*Wembley Stadium has never seen such an occasion. Its gaunt
towers and austere stone walls are usually the setting for such
august national rituals as the English soccer cup final, played out
on Wembley's immaculate turf each spring. Now, on July 13th,
1985, the 70,000 people at Britain's Live Aid concert have abandoned the bleak concrete terracing into which they were first
corralled and have occupied that hallowed turf. For six hours they
have stood under a flawless summer sky to applaud the succession
of musical idols who have paraded before them. They are already
clapping again, their bare arms extended above their heads, in
expectation of the next performer to appear.*

*A tall, slender figure, wearing a pastel-grey suit, its close-fitting
jacket cut to the top of his buttocks, its loose trousers falling over
his angular legs, set off by a white shirt and a cream patterned tie,
steps through the canvas awning at the side of the stage. He surveys
the audience with a grin, gives a brief, amiable wave and heads
towards the centre of the stage. At first his gait is a good-humoured
saunter; within a few steps he is moving to the beat of the music,
elbows and shoulders pumping, the quiff of his auburn hair bob-
bing over his forehead. As he reaches the microphone he waves to
the audience again, more expansively this time, accompanied by a
broad, flashing smile. He retreats momentarily and then dances
forward, tapping the stage twice with each pointed toe. He takes
the microphone in his right hand, balances it elegantly between his
thumb and first two fingers, and starts to sing.*

*In his eighteen minutes on stage, David Bowie performs four
numbers, each stemming from a different phase of his turbulent,
episodic career. The first, 'TVC 15', comes from his time in Los
Angeles in 1975, a year which saw him embroiled in litigation
with his manager, prey to paranoia, close to physical and mental
breakdown, and indulging in cocaine. The second, 'Rebel Rebel',
belongs to the raucous period of the early 1970s when, with his
career seemingly stalled, he decided that the only way to become
a rock and roll star was to act the part of one, thus adopting the
first of the series of personas which threatened to dominate him*

off the stage as well as on. The third, 'Modern Love', comes from the 1980s, when, by now the cool and accomplished international star, he showed his mastery of changing musical fashion by producing a fast-driving rock number that fitted easily into his disco album, 'Let's Dance'.

The audience greets each number with a surge of applause, a recognition of the historical tour that David is providing. Warming in turn to their response, David first undoes the three buttons on his jacket, then loosens his tie. He garnishes his act with a skilful pastiche of performing styles, providing first a quick knee-shimmy in the manner of Elvis Presley, next a brief sequence of mincing steps borrowed from Mick Jagger, then two flagrant pelvic thrusts in the style of the least inhibited black performers, like James Brown. He bounds on to the catwalk beneath the stage and beckons to the audience to join him in the choruses. They clap and wave their arms with still greater fervour, a sea of votaries urging him to give them more.

His fourth and last number is '"Heroes"'. It is one of his most triumphant songs, composed during a recuperative two-year so-journ in West Berlin, and bringing resolution to some of his most anguished dilemmas. It thus serves as a fitting tribute to the beneficent spirit of this afternoon at Wembley. As the band plays its tense but celebratory opening chords, David offers the dedication: "to my son, to all our children, and to the children of the world . . ."

David Bowie's first hero was his grandfather, Jimmy Burns. The tales of Jimmy Burns's military exploits around the world were related countless times throughout his family, and David loved to hear them from his older half-brother Terry when they were still together in the narrow terraced house in Brixton where David was born. He was a professional soldier who survived four years on the western front in the first world war and went on, so it is told, to even greater feats of valour. Renowned in the family for his proud and upright bearing and his fine military moustache, he first appeared in one of his grandson's songs in 'Rubber Band', which David wrote and recorded when he was nineteen:

> In 1910 I was so handsome and so strong
> My moustache was stiffly waxed and one foot long.

The story of Jimmy Burns and his family provides a number of clues to the enigmas David Bowie presents, from his complex and often obscure lyrics, to the contradictory statements he has made about his past and the bewildering succession of public faces he has displayed. It also shows the importance of fantasy and imagination in the troubled saga of David's family, and in the life and career of David himself.

Jimmy Burns's parents were poor Irish immigrants who had settled in Manchester; they had eight sons, all of whom joined the British army. Jimmy enlisted in the Highland Light Infantry in 1903, when he was just sixteen, and two years later was posted to India.

It was a time of calm in the rule of the British Raj. The regiment was posted to Meerut, a garrison town close to Delhi, and known in the army as the pig-sticking capital of India. While the officers spent most of their time riding down wild boars and impaling them on their lances, for Jimmy Burns and the other foot solders there was little to relieve the tedium beyond occasional foot patrols to show the flag.

After two years in Meerut, Jimmy Burns applied to join a cavalry regiment, the 3rd King's Own Hussars, which was then serving in the Punjab, and contained two of his brothers. He was transferred in May 1907 and soon became an accomplished cavalryman with his own horse, a sprightly black stallion named Bob. The story of how he and Bob had once danced before a Maharajah was also told in the family, and also how, one evening when he and his brothers got wildly drunk, he had a picture of Bob tattooed on his back. The tattoo was so large that the horse's front legs extended over his shoulder to touch his collar-bone, and later Jimmy used to delight his children by removing his shirt and flexing his muscles, so that Bob appeared to dance.

In December, the 3rd Hussars were posted to South Africa, sailing to Durban and reaching their garrison at Roberts Heights, close to Pretoria, just before Christmas. Just as in India, it was a tranquil period in the history of British rule. The rebellious Dutch settlers had been subdued (the regimental history observes that they were "sullen and aloof") and the sole signs of the recent Boer wars were the clusters of soldiers' graves in the dusty countryside. The regiment took its pleasure in the dance halls, roller-skating rinks, and silent cinema of Pretoria. With still no military action to speak of, Jimmy sought a further diversion by joining the regimental band and learning to play the clarinet.

Jimmy Burns also resolved that life in South Africa would be improved if he were to take a wife. Ever since being posted overseas he had been writing to a young woman he had known in

Manchester. Her name was Margaret Heaton, and her father was a professional soldier too. Jimmy now wrote to her again and boldly asked her to come out to South Africa and marry him. Margaret declined: she told Jimmy that she was unable to leave England in case she had to help look after her mother.

The 3rd Hussars returned to Britain just before Christmas, 1911. By then Margaret, who was twenty-seven, had moved south to Margate, where she was working as a nursing auxiliary at the Royal Seabathing Hospital. Jimmy sought her out immediately, and was entranced by her flowing tresses and gentle eyes, captured in a family photograph which shows her with the pious stare of a madonna. Margaret found that, at twenty-four, Jimmy had a soldier's physique, with jet-black hair, a strong moustache, and — as she later described them — "the bluest of eyes". When Jimmy proposed to her again she accepted. They were married at All Saints Church, Margate, on January 22nd, 1912.

The next eighteen months comprised the most peaceful period of their married lives. The regiment was installed at its home base of Shorncliffe Camp near Folkestone on the Kent coast, and they were allocated married quarters at Cheriton, on the edge of the Downs. They decorated their new home with the trophies Jimmy had brought back from overseas: from Africa, an ostrich egg and a pair of ebony elephants with ivory tusks; from India, ornate brass candlesticks and an engraved chest lined with camphor-wood.

Jimmy had occasional spells away from home when the regiment went on manoeuvres in Cambridgeshire or on Salisbury Plain. He also perfected his skills with the clarinet at the army musical college at Kneller Hall, and played with the regimental band at the Royal Tournament in June 1912. It was a propitious time to start a family, and their first child was born in the hospital at Shorncliffe Camp on October 2nd, 1913. They christened her Margaret Mary, but both then and later, as David Bowie's mother, she was known as Peggy.

The idyll came to an end in August 1914. Two weeks after Britain and Germany went to war, the 3rd Hussars were sent to France and a week later rode into battle at Mons. The cavalry had been rendered obsolete by a newer weapon of war, the machine-gun, and the regiment beat a chaotic retreat. That winter the 3rd Hussars were held in reserve, their men stricken with frostbite, the horses up to their hocks in mud. In the spring they moved up to the front at Ypres, and stood in wait as the infantry tried to punch holes in the German lines for the cavalry to burst through. The infantry were repelled by rolling banks of chlorine gas, which cost the British 65,000 casualties, and the regiment withdrew.

The war brought hardship to Margaret too. She had become pregnant only days before Jimmy left for France, and her second daughter was born at Shorncliffe Camp on April 30th, 1915. With Jimmy then at Ypres, Margaret named her baby Victoria Honoria, in hope of an early victory. Soon afterwards the regiment's married quarters were commandeered for the recruits flooding into the Channel ports, and Margaret and her children had to move inland to the village of Southborough in the Weald of Kent. There she shared a tiny cottage at 25 Taylor Street with another soldier's wife, Mrs Neale.

At other times, Southborough would have been a reassuring place to live. A rural community of white weatherboard cottages and orderly red-brick houses, overlooked by the reassuring granite tower of St Peter's Church, it lies among the lush pastureland, mellow orchards and tangy hopfields that give Kent its title as the Garden of England. But in 1915, it bore all the signs of war. Midway between London and the Channel ports, it was an ideal place to billet soldiers on their way to the front. Bugles sounded through the streets each morning, summoning the troops to parade on Southborough Common, and the army's horses were exercised on the common too. The surrounding woods were festooned with telephone wires, and Southborough's gravel pit became a firing range.

For Margaret Burns there were constant reminders of the ordeals her husband faced. When some titanic new offensive was launched in France, she could feel the ground tremble from the firing of the guns. She saw the injured men who were brought back to be nursed in the local hospitals, and who ringed the common in the summer in their wheelchairs. She watched the funerals which made their way to the cemetery at St Peter's Church, accompanied by the lament of the Dead March. Each week she scanned the roll of honour in the *Kent and Sussex Courier* which listed the forty or fifty men from the Weald who had been injured, captured, or killed.

Two years passed before Jimmy Burns, by then a lance-corporal, came home on leave. He arrived in Southborough in August 1916 and during his brief stay helped Margaret and her two children move to a new home at 15 Meadow Road. It was a rented house at the end of a short terrace, with four small square rooms, and a lavatory – but no bathroom – in the tiny back yard. By the time Jimmy returned to France, Margaret was pregnant again. Her third child – and only son – was born at Meadow Road on May 28th, 1917, and she christened him James.

In January 1918, Jimmy Burns took part in the regiment's costliest battle of the war, when it lost more than a hundred men in an attack on a spinney known as Rifle Wood. He survived, and was promoted to corporal soon afterwards. By the summer he was one of only three dozen men who had been with the regiment from the start of the fighting. In September, he was spared the slaughter of the closing months of the war when he was selected as a potential commissioned officer and was sent back to England to join an officers' training course.

Armistice Day, November 11th, was celebrated in Southborough and the other communities of the Weald with bonfires, bunting, and impromptu parades of soldiers through the streets. But no one doubted that Britain would still need an army and so Jimmy Burns remained on his officers' training course. A photograph of his class, posed before a monumental beech tree, shows him to be a mature man of thirty-one, with a fine moustache and confident stare, immaculate in breeches and puttees. He completed the course successfully, and on March 5th, 1919, was awarded his commission as a second lieutenant. He was assigned to the 2nd Battalion of the Manchester Regiment, then part of the allied occupation forces in Germany but shortly due to return to Britain.

It was the climax of Jimmy Burns's military career. For a man of his social background to become an officer after sixteen years in the ranks was an achievement of which he was immensely proud. His pride was short-lived. The War Office announced that the Manchester Regiment would be reduced in size and told Second Lieutenant Burns that his services were no longer required. Jimmy returned to Southborough with the bitter feeling that his qualities as an officer had been questioned and found wanting. But Margaret felt only relief that the years of hardship and anxiety she had endured were over at last.

In the spring, Jimmy Burns saw a chance to prove his military prowess after all. The British government was calling for men to join an expeditionary force to Russia. Its aim was to support the anti-Bolshevik forces trying to overturn the communist revolution, and the War Office offered a bounty of £50 to all who would take part. Jimmy volunteered, and was assigned to the 46th Battalion of the Royal Fusiliers. He did so even though his officer's training was discounted and he had to return to the ranks as a private.

The echoes of Jimmy Burns's decision still reverberate among his children today. His son Jimmy, who served with distinction in the second world war, believes that it stemmed from his father's anger at seeing his ambitions thwarted and a desire to prove his worth after all. "I know he was a bit chocker with being in the army all those years, and getting his commission which was a big thing in those days," he says. "I think that was the reason he joined up again, thinking to himself, 'I was good enough to be an officer in the war . . .' Probably that was something I would have done myself."

The Burnses' daughter Pat – their sixth child, born in 1928 – is also aware of the high place the episode holds in the canon of family grievances. "My father was very impetuous," she says. "All he wanted was adventure." Pat is sure that the £50 bounty was a powerful lure, as the family was so poor. But what was conveyed to her above all was her mother's anger that her father should have gone to war again. "She was very bitter after bringing up three children by herself with the constant worry that he would be killed in France," she says. "After all that, he went off again. She never forgave him."

And so, in June 1919, Jimmy Burns left Southborough once more. His departure awoke in Margaret all the fears and anxieties she had suffered; she was also pregnant again. When Southborough held a "day of peace" on the common in July, with a service, an afternoon of races, and a forty-foot bonfire that blazed away into the night, she felt unable to share the general rejoicing. But when her husband came home in October, his decision appeared to be vindicated. For Jimmy Burns was a hero.

The story was told by the *Kent and Sussex Courier* of October 31st, 1919. It bore the headline: "Southborough Man Wins the Military Medal in Russia". Below it was a photograph of "Pte. J. E. Burns", his dark locks parted around his forehead, his moustache more bushy and resplendent than ever.

The *Courier* reported that the British expeditionary force had landed at the port of Archangel, just below the Arctic Circle, and pushed inland along the Dvina River. But it soon encountered superior enemy forces and was compelled to retreat to "a place called Ivanofskaze". There Jimmy Burns was one of sixteen volunteers "who offered to stay behind and endeavour to hold up the Bolsheviks while our forces were retiring".

The story continued: "With rifle fire, supported by two Lewis guns, these sixteen men kept back the enemy long enough for our force to retire in order, but thirteen out of the sixteen were killed, and the three survivors, the officer, Pte. Burns, and another private, were wounded, Pte. Burns being in charge of the party part of the time. It was discovered from prisoners taken the following day that they had held up a Battalion. Pte. Burns assisted his wounded comrade, though wounded himself, and they both managed to escape on ponies."

The *Courier* congratulated Private Burns – "of 15, Meadow Road, Southborough" – on being awarded the Military Medal "for bravery in Russia", adding that he was "the first Southborough man to gain this distinction on the Russian front". It reminded its readers that he had been made an officer on March 5th, had then been demobilised, but had volunteered to join the Russian Relief Force as a private. It concluded: "He is now home on leave."

It was an extraordinary tale of courage and daring, which makes the award of a Military Medal, at the lower end of the range of honours, seem distinctly churlish (a Distinguished Conduct Medal would have been far more appropriate). The story has been passed down through the successive generations of his family, and is still related by them more than sixty years later.

There is just one flaw: the story is untrue.

The fullest account of the actions of the 46th Royal Fusiliers at Archangel is contained in the battalion's official war diary at the Public Records Office at Kew. The diary is twenty-eight pages long, and consists of a day-by-day account of the battalion's actions between disembarking in Russia on July 1st, 1919, and sailing for home on August 31st. The diary contains nothing which remotely fits the action described in the *Kent and Sussex Courier* "at a place called Ivanofskaze".

Neither is any trace of Jimmy Burns's Military Medal to be found. It is not cited in the battalion war diary, which lists all medals won by its officers and men during the expedition. Nor is it recorded in the volumes of the *London Gazette*, which publishes every gallantry award made to the British forces. The Army Medal Office of the Ministry of Defence is more specific still: "There is no trace in records held of an award of the Military Medal."

Even members of the family who told the story, assuming it to be true, remained uneasy over some of the details. The Burnses' daughter Pat says that although she was told that her father was shot through the calf, she could not remember ever seeing scars from the wound. Her brother Jimmy says that he never saw his father's medal – and he knew what a Military Medal looked like, since he was awarded one himself in the second world war.

The only plausible explanation for the story that appeared in the *Kent and Sussex Courier* is that it was concocted by Margaret Burns. It enabled her to resolve the intolerable conflict her husband had created, loving him dearly while deeply resenting the anguish he caused her. Her solution was to sanctify her suffering by making her husband a hero. That required his tacit collusion; by his children's accounts, it was given. Although Jimmy Burns often told his daughter Pat about his life as a soldier in India and South Africa, he never mentioned his supposed exploits in Russia at all. "That all came from my mother," Pat says.

Pat had always believed that her father had talked to her brother about the episode. But Jimmy denies that and says that all he knew about "the Archangel do" came from his mother. "She always did have a strong imagination," he adds.

The heroism of Jimmy Burns nonetheless came to occupy a vital place in the mythology of the Burns family, providing a landmark to cling to as storms broke around them. For Margaret Burns the episode became an emblem of her struggle to preserve her family in the face of a malign fate. She largely managed to do so until war returned, bringing separation, illegitimacy, madness and death. Finally she proclaimed that there was a curse on the Burns family that would not be laid to rest until the last member had died.

The story of her family can therefore be seen as the story of its struggle against that curse. For some the outcome was insanity. For David Bowie, it was one of the impulses in a career that touched both madness and genius.

2

The Dogs of War

It was without enthusiasm that Jimmy Burns surveyed the jobs offered in the *Kent and Sussex Courier* at the end of 1919:

> General farm hand, help with
> milking, able to plough.
>
> All round workman for small
> fruit and hop farm, wife tie hops.
>
> General handyman for quiet
> Christian household – ten
> shillings a week.

A litany of pleas by other army veterans offered even less encouragement:

> Discharged soldier seeks
> employment as firm's representative
> or any light capacity.
>
> Demobilised soldier, married, 14 years'
> experience as grocer's assistant,
> requires situation in Tunbridge Wells –
> willing, faithful, and energetic;
> gilt-edged testimonials.

All wars end with the promise that those who fought in them will be rewarded for their sacrifice; rarely is that promise kept. In Southborough after the first world war it was clear that Britain was still a nation of poverty and social divisions. Destitute families walked through the streets singing for alms, and Southborough council posted a notice warning vagrants that they could only spend one night there before moving on. And Jimmy Burns discovered that neither his training as an officer nor his new status as hero could provide him with a job.

His predicament was to be incorporated in his grandson's song, 'Little Bombardier', about a soldier returning from the war: "Peace left him a loser," David wrote, for he had "unskilled hands that knew no trade". In 1920, Jimmy turned to the one non-military skill he possessed. One morning he pulled on his army greatcoat and walked into Tunbridge Wells, the genteel spa town two miles from Southborough. He took up position on a street corner, laid his cap on the pavement, and played his clarinet. Only that evening did he reveal to Margaret what he had done. Yet there was a note of pride in his voice when he told her that a woman had stopped to tell him how beautifully he played.

Busking, sometimes by himself, sometimes with other former soldiers, was Jimmy's main source of income for more than three years. He eventually found a job as a lorry-driver with a local building firm; later he worked for the Tunbridge Wells Electrical Company, helping to lay power cables as the company's supplies radiated further and further into the Weald. It was both a dirty and dangerous task, and two of his colleagues were electrocuted and killed as they worked in a ditch. But he still took a soldierly pride in his appearance, placing his trousers in a press each night and polishing his shoes fiercely in the morning, before departing in his official company overcoat, its brass buttons gleaming.

Meanwhile the family continued to grow. The baby conceived before Jimmy left for Archangel was born on November 27th, 1919, and christened Una Beatrix; the Burnses' fifth child, Vivienne May, was born on February 17th, 1922; Eileen Patricia, their sixth and last child, on April 24th, 1928. By now space at Meadow Road was at a premium. The new baby slept with her parents at the back of the house, while the four older girls shared the bedroom in the front. Their brother Jimmy slept in the front room downstairs, which also served as the family living room.

The children have alluring memories of those early days. Their father taught Nora (her name had been shortened from Honoria) to play the clarinet, Vivienne the dulcimer, Jimmy the drums. Peggy, Una and Pat all learned to sing, and the family gathered for musical evenings, in the Victorian manner, around the living-room fire. Jimmy also entertained the children with stories of his days in India and South Africa. They would beg him to take off his shirt and show them the tattoo of Bob on his back, crying: "Make him dance, Daddy, make him dance!"

Jimmy and Margaret Burns were strict parents too, and kept careful watch over their children's doings. They were forbidden to bring their friends into the house, and even in their teens had to be home by ten o'clock. Margaret told her daughters that she did not like them "running around with young men", and instructed them to be "honest and true". She also told them they must be "clean inside as well as out", and every Saturday made them stand in line to receive a spoonful of syrup of figs. In case they protested, their father was always on hand to ensure that they swallowed it down. To the children, it was only natural that their parents should present a united front. "My father adored my mother," says Pat. "And she was very proud of him. She was always telling us how smart and handsome he was."

Yet conflicts within the marriage, if less visible to the children for a while, remained. There were inevitable clashes over religion, for Margaret was an Anglican, Jimmy a Catholic. This led to a dispute over the children's education in which Jimmy, at first, had his way. The three oldest girls – Peggy, Nora and Una – all attended St Augustine's Convent School in Tunbridge Wells. Their father also woke them on Sunday mornings to take them to mass at St Augustine's Church, where he was a verger, leaving Margaret at home.

There were sharp contrasts between their personalities too. Jimmy was overtly affectionate; Margaret was not. Jimmy was fond of demonstrating his physical prowess and liked to take Margaret by the waist and lift her up; embarrassed by displays of intimacy, she always demanded to be put down. Her daughter, Pat, found that the only way she could induce her mother to display affection was by putting her arms around her, so that she would be compelled to respond. Pat was also fond of sitting on her father's knee to listen to his stories, but as she grew up her mother remonstrated that she was "too old for that sort of thing".

The neighbours in Meadow Road found Margaret aloof and uncommunicative. Long after the end of Jimmy's military career, they still called her "the officer's wife". Margaret, in fact, relished the disguised social compliment the epithet contained. At the same time she felt increasing resentment that her husband had not achieved more in his life. Her disappointment became more acute when Jimmy Burns's brother Tom and his wife arrived in Southborough. They moved into a house, number 106, at the top end – the *good* end – of nearby Springfield Road.

It was far grander than 15 Meadow Road, with a flight of steps, a porch and, if one included the semi-basement, three floors; later Thomas Burns acquired some riding stables on the common at Modest Corner. And if Margaret Burns had social pretensions, that was even more true of her brother-in-law and his wife, as

Argile Skinner, a neighbour at Modest Corner, recalled almost sixty years later. "They held themselves superior to the others," he says.

Margaret's envy was heightened by the family's excursions to Mount Ephraim, the most desirable part of Tunbridge Wells. Jimmy was secretary of the local branch of the army's veterans association, the Old Contemptibles; a retired general named Soady invited Margaret and her children to take tea with his wife at their mansion overlooking Tunbridge Wells Common. He sent his chauffeur to collect them, and they sipped tea from bone china on the general's lawn, waited on by maids in uniform.

Margaret also visited Mount Ephraim to clean the house of a doctor whose wife she had known as a nurse while working at the Royal Seabathing Hospital in Margate. One Christmas, the doctor and his wife went away and asked Margaret and her family to stay there to look after the house. They spent a week there, wondering at the new world so suddenly revealed: the younger Jimmy Burns remembers a bedroom that contained "top hats, hockey sticks, and cricket balls". It all served to sharpen Margaret's feelings of frustration. "She felt that she deserved better," says Pat. "She felt let down."

Gradually, it seemed, Margaret Burns withdrew into a private world. Every Sunday Jimmy Burns went through the ritual of asking her into Tonbridge for afternoon tea; every Sunday she refused. Pat was delighted, for her father usually took her instead. They caught the bus to Tonbridge Castle and walked in its grounds, then had tea at a local cafeteria. Margaret stayed at home, immersed in books. "She was always reading, reading, reading," Pat says. "She was very fond of Shakespeare, and could remember reams."

Margaret also sought recourse in her imagination, as she had done in 1919. In the 1930s, she took to writing poetry, an activity which she came to pursue with almost religious devotion. She kept a notebook in the pocket of her apron, and would break off from her kitchen duties to dry her hands and inscribe a new couplet that had just come to mind. Later her poems were transcribed into a small, loose-leaf notebook with a black cloth cover, each signed with the date and the three initials M.A.S.: M for Margaret, A for Alice, and S for Swetenham, an old family name of which she was fond. Her poems told of love and regret, parting and nostalgia. They reveal the extent of her feelings of loneliness and longing, and her belief in the therapeutic powers of fantasy.

In 'Bruised', Margaret wrote:

Alias David Bowie

A broken blossom dropped by some careless hand
Lay by the wayside.
I stooped, and its fragrance filled the air,
To me brought memories, long cherished in my heart,
Poor broken life . . .

'Musing' conjured a romance of bygone times:

I wish I'd lived in the days of Old
When maids were fair, and Knights were bold
Awaiting for my Hero, in armour shiny bright
To take me on his charger
And bear me thro' the night . . .

'Calumny' reveals feelings of loneliness and isolation, brought
about by some unnamed scandal:

That lonesome monster calumny
It whispers words o'er cups of tea
And then it goes from mouth to mouth
It travels then from North to South
Where'er it goes, you're shunned by all
Then you find yourself against the wall . . .

A number, like 'The Flowers' Ball', 'Tiny Folks', and 'The Pixies'
Interlude', summoned childhood fantasies, of gnomes and fairies
and flowers that talk, but who disappear with the dawn. Other
evoked childhood memories and sensations, like 'Christmas Eve'
and 'Jack Frost':

Old Jack Frost has come again
He's busy on the window pane
Look around and you will see
He traces birds and flowers with glee . . .

Some were even more explicit in their longing to return to the
warmth and security of childhood, like 'The Erring One':

A woman sat amidst the gloom
And all was silent as a tomb
For her thoughts were far away
The thought of childhood's happy days
And wished they'd come again . . .

Other paid tribute to the power of the imagination, either to conjure fears and nightmares, or to escape those fears, as in 'Land Of Make Believe':

> In the land of make believe
> Children love to play
> In the land of make believe
> All the lovers stray
> Young and old, rich and poor
> Pass right thro the magic door
> In the land of make believe
> All our dreams come true . . .

Margaret used to recite her poems to her daughters. But they were becoming puzzled or embarrassed by her behaviour, and tried to ignore her. Jimmy also regarded her poetry as "strange" and paid it little heed. Their themes nonetheless informed the family mythology, for what is most striking is the clear similarities with some of David's earliest lyrics.

David also incorporated his grandfather's reaction in another early song, 'Little Bombardier'. Regarding his wife as increasingly eccentric, Jimmy turned for companionship to the public bar of the Bell in the London Road. He acquired a considerable capacity for its beer, drinking ten pints in an evening, and coming home aggressive and rude. Then Margaret would be at her most self-righteous. "James," she would complain, "you're just like a beast in a field." In 'Little Bombardier', the former soldier who cannot find work seeks solace in drink, thereby becoming a prototype for the isolated and alienated figures of David's universe:

> Frankie drank his money, the little that he made,
> Told his woes to no man, friendless, lonely days.

The first of the calamities to overwhelm the Burns family seemed, at first, to have been initiated by dreadful chance. On June 5th, 1929, which happened to be Derby Day, Una, then aged ten, was waiting for the bus in London Road to take her to school. A car skidded and mounted the pavement, driving her against a hoarding that was advertising Bisto gravy. The car's mudguard impaled her thigh and police and firemen took over an hour to cut her free. She was still clutching her bus-fare when she was taken to hospital, where more than a hundred stitches were needed for her wounds.

The immediate consequence of the accident was that Margaret

had her way over the children's education. She told Jimmy that since the journey into Tunbridge Wells was manifestly so hazardous, they would now attend St Peter's School, a Church of England foundation, on Southborough Common. He had no alternative but to agree.

The accident also seemed to estrange Una from the rest of the family. Pat recalls her as "quiet and refined, and always very withdrawn. She was very ladylike and you never heard her shout." Later Pat learned that Una had felt apart from the rest of the family from an early age. "Right from a tiny child she used to say that she didn't belong to us. She said she was adopted."

Then it was Peggy who became the focus of her parents' anxieties. As the eldest child she was the first to leave home, responding, when she was twenty-two, to the ceaseless advertisements for domestic servants in the *Kent and Sussex Courier* and becoming a nanny to the children of the owners of the Culverden Park Arms Hotel in Tunbridge Wells.

Although Peggy "lived in" at the hotel, she paid regular visits to Meadow Road. She brought the children with her and still wore her striped nanny's dress and felt hat. "She was lovely-looking," says Pat, "with quite a lot of bearing about her." Peggy also modelled corsets and lingerie for the ladies of Tunbridge Wells in a dress shop near the hotel. Jimmy Burns was immensely proud of her, and when Margaret, as always, refused to partner him to ladies' night at the Old Contemptibles, he took Peggy instead.

It was thus a doubly painful blow for Jimmy Burns when he learned of Peggy's political activities, of such notoriety that they were remembered in Southborough fifty years later. "Two of the girls," said Argile Skinner at Modest Corner, "joined the Fascists."

The girls in question were Peggy and her cousin Marjorie, the daughter of Jimmy's brother Tom in Springfield Road. They were attracted by the strutting figure of Oswald Mosley, who combined radical economics with talk of racial superiority, and adopted a declamatory style of oratory that aped Adolf Hitler. They attended a meeting at Fiveways Corner in Tunbridge Wells and then joined a march through Southborough to Tonbridge where, so Argile Skinner recalls, "it was smashed up by the police". Pat believes that her sister was attracted less by Mosley's policies than by the black uniforms his henchmen wore. Whatever the lure, Jimmy Burns was incensed. He told Peggy: "If you ever do that again, don't come back to this house." Peggy obeyed.

In Southborough, Peggy's political flirtation came to appear a minor affair against the next drama in which she was involved.

Among the staff at the Culverden Park Arms Hotel was a barman, Wolf Rosemberg, the son of a prosperous Paris fur dealer, who had come to England in a youthful search for adventure. Known by the rest of the staff as Jack, he had Latin good looks and a debonair manner that Peggy found enthralling. She fell passionately in love with him, and said later that he had been the only true love of her life.

Nothing in Peggy's upbringing had prepared her for the outcome of such a relationship. In the Burns family, sex was the great unmentionable, never to be discussed. Almost inevitably, in the spring of 1937, Peggy became pregnant. When she told her parents, her worst fears about their reaction were confirmed. Her father raged that she had brought disgrace on the family and her mother spent a day in tears. Afterwards they relented and promised to help. On their instructions, Peggy brought Rosemberg to the house where they asked him to marry her. To Peggy's joy, he agreed. Soon afterwards, he disappeared.

Peggy's baby was born in Pembury Hospital, near Tunbridge Wells, on November 5th, 1937. She named him Terence Guy Adair. Guy came from a nurse who pointed out he had been born on Guy Fawkes Day; Adair was an old family surname on her mother's side; and Terence – soon shortened to Terry – was Peggy's own idea. She brought Terry home to Meadow Road and nursed him through an attack of bronchitis. But it was her mother who increasingly took care of him, and when he was six months old Peggy went back to work in Tunbridge Wells.

In Southborough's tight-knit community, the episode provided a fruitful talking point, to be dissected in shops, pubs and kitchen parlours throughout that winter. Perhaps Margaret Burns would now display fewer airs and pretensions; perhaps her husband would spend less time in the Bell. The member of the Burns family who suffered most directly from the gossip was their son Jimmy, twenty that year. Having won a scholarship from St Peter's to Skinners', the public school in Tunbridge Wells, he appeared to have a promising future, perhaps in one of the professions. He was also a prominent local sportsman: a strong swimmer, like his father, and a member of the local cricket team which played on Southborough Common. But he was subjected to so much banter over Peggy from his friends and colleagues that he left Southborough and joined the army. Even though he enlisted in his father's old regiment, the 3rd King's Hussars, his father was appalled. "He said I was a bit of a fool," the younger Jimmy Burns says today.

Almost fifty years on, Terry's relatives were united in the warmth of their memories of him. "He was a lovely kiddy, very attractive, I liked Terry a lot," his uncle Jimmy said. His aunt Vivienne recalled: "What a handsome boy Terry was – he had a beautiful face, eyes like my father, navy-blue eyes." Pat remembered his "lovely sunny disposition, laughing, happy and affectionate". She felt especially drawn to him because, having been born six years after the rest of her sisters, she – like Una – felt something of an outsider in the family. "We were both loners," she says. "He came into my life and filled a gap."

Terry's grandfather, Jimmy Burns, doted on him too, dandling him on his knee and providing another source of affection. Much later, as Terry despairingly surveyed the wreckage of his life, that time in Southborough assumed the nature of an enchanted dream. "Why can't we go back to how it was then?" he would ask Pat. "They were the happiest days of my life."

At 11.15 a.m. on Sunday, September 3rd, 1939, the Burns family gathered round the wireless set in their front room to hear the mournful voice of Neville Chamberlain announce that Britain and Germany were again at war. Margaret Burns said that her son Jimmy would have to go to war, and began to cry. The inhabitants of Meadow Road came out into the street to discuss the news but then the siren on the roof of Southborough fire station signalled Britain's first air-raid alert and drove them back indoors.

Having seemed to be in the front line twenty-five years before, Southborough now felt that to be so again. In the summer of 1940, it watched the RAF joust with the German Luftwaffe overhead; that winter, fifteen bombs fell on or near the village, though causing no deaths. Later Southborough found that it lay in "doodlebug alley", the path of the German flying bombs and rockets that were hurled at London. Six V-1s, falling far short of their target, crashed around the village, as well as a V-2, a monstrous rocket that plummeted to earth so fast that the noise of its fall was heard only after it had exploded.

The Burns family survived these onslaughts physically unscathed. But the return of war revived all Margaret Burns's fears of twenty-five years before. This time, she watched helplessly as the misfortunes she had known were visited on her children.

What precisely occurred during that period is one of the topics about which David is most sensitive: as those who wish to write about him discover, "the family" is now a taboo subject. In the past, David has responded to such questions in a glib manner that reflected his own estrangement from his relatives. "Most of them are nutty," he said in an interview with *Playboy*, published in 1976. "In, just out of, or going into an institution. Or dead." Although the matter has rested there until now, David's answers did at least convey the extent of the devastation his family had suffered. Of his mother's generation alone, three of the six children were diagnosed as mentally ill and had long periods receiving medical treatment in hospital and mental institutions. The first victim was Una.

Una was nineteen when the war began, a pretty young woman with a retroussé nose and long, golden hair. But her distracted air was more marked and she was spending little time at home. In response to the government's campaign to persuade women to assist the war effort, she joined the servicemen's supply organisation, the NAAFI, and was posted to a canteen in the garrison town of Aldershot. There she fell in love with a Canadian soldier, Kurt Paulsen, a handsome and powerfully built man whose Norwegian origins showed in his striking fair hair. Una was as unprepared as her sister Peggy for the outcome of sexual relationships, and quickly became pregnant. On July 5th, 1942, she gave birth to a baby girl in Aldershot Hospital, and named her Kristine.

With the dire example of Peggy before her, it was in some trepidation that Una debated what to tell her parents. Not only was her baby illegitimate; Paulsen had a wife and four children in Canada. She decided to lie to her parents, telling them that she and Paulsen were married instead, and changing her name to Paulsen to add credibility to her story. Her parents believed her. "They thought Kurt Paulsen was a very nice chap," says Pat.

Meanwhile Paulsen had promised Una that he would divorce his wife and marry her. They stayed together for a year, supplementing Paulsen's army pay with a compensation payment for her childhood road accident that had been placed in trust for her until she was twenty-one. But by late 1943, Una no longer believed Paulsen's promises and went back to Southborough. Paulsen followed her and persuaded her to come back and live with him in Guildford. They were parted again when Paulsen went to Europe after the invasion of France in 1944.

By now Margaret Burns, who had become increasingly suspicious about Una's story, had discovered the truth about Paulsen. But when she confronted Una with the news of Paulsen's wife and family, Una still maintained that she had married Paulsen herself, and so her family concluded that he must be a bigamist. Eventually Una succumbed to the strain of the fiction she was trying to maintain, and to the pressure of caring for her baby alone. She suffered a mental breakdown and spent several months in hospital.

When Una left hospital and returned to Southborough, her family were baffled and disturbed. Once so meticulous about her appearance, she was now dishevelled and unkempt. She was alarmingly volatile, sometimes hostile and aggressive, sometimes dejected and withdrawn. She told her sisters that she had heard voices instructing her and Kristine where to go. At times she spoke in a strange, disjointed way so that her sisters could hardly understand her at all.

These were among the classic signs of schizophrenia, but no one in the family had even heard the word before. In the 1940s, even more than now, the subject of mental illness was shrouded in ignorance and taboo, and Una's family was unaware of the terror that she had suffered, with feelings of persecution, ethereal voices, and visions of heaven and hell. In her bewilderment, Margaret Burns could only say that her daughter seemed "unwell". Finding little comfort or solace in Southborough, Una returned to Guildford with her baby. She stayed in a lodging house and found a variety of jobs, hoping all the time that Paulsen would return.

Nora too was a victim of the despairing liaisons that are made in times of war, and her illness followed a remarkably similar course to Una's. The Burnses' second child, twenty-four when the war began, she was a stocky woman with a healthy outdoor appearance, a broad smile and dimpled cheeks. At the start of the war she joined the Land Army and worked in a market garden near Southborough. She also became engaged to a soldier from Wales. When he was sent overseas, she promised to wait for him but he was captured and became a prisoner of war. When he was finally repatriated at the end of the war he told Nora that he wanted his freedom and broke off their engagement. From then on, says her sister Pat, Nora was "completely changed".

Pat, then sixteen, had little sympathy for Nora at first. Pat was still living at home, having left school at fourteen to work in a sweetshop in the London Road, later becoming a telephonist at the Tunbridge Wells exchange. "I used to come home from work and hand over my money to my mother, and there was Nora having tantrums and smoking her head off all day," Pat says. Pat was irked when her mother tried to excuse Nora by saying that she was a "war baby", having been born during her husband's absence during the first world war. The only other explanation Margaret Burns could offer was that Nora suffered from "bad nerves".

Then Nora fell in love again, this time with a Polish refugee who was staying in a displaced persons' camp near Southborough. Named Jan, he was desperately thin, could speak hardly any English, and had a row of false teeth made of steel. "He was like something out of Belsen," says Pat. "Poor devil, he must have suffered, but he was completely crazy."

He and Nora lived together for a time in a dank bed-sitting room in the Portobello Road in West London, but then Nora returned to Southborough. Jan pursued her on foot, walking the thirty miles from London wearing his pyjamas beneath his clothes against the cold and carrying his spectacles in a jam jar. He then asked Nora to go back to Poland with him. With Poland in ruins from the war and gripped by political struggles with the USSR, it seemed a hopeless proposal, but Nora agreed.

Before long Nora was sending letters to her family in Southborough complaining of the bitter cold and the desperate shortage of food, and imploring them to get her home. After lengthy negotiations conducted via the Foreign Office, the family succeeded. When Nora returned to Meadow Road she had deteriorated even more. "She used to scream and break windows," Pat says, "and fly into terrible rages."

Nora was taken into hospital where she was diagnosed as suffering from manic-depressive psychosis. Her doctors recommended a lobotomy, a drastic operation – no longer performed today – to sever the nerves in the disordered segment of the brain. Her mother signed forms giving her consent, although Pat is certain she was not aware what she was agreeing to. "She still thought Nora just had bad nerves, and she just hoped the operation would make her better." Although the operation moderated Nora's behaviour, she still suffered from depression, and she went to live in a mental hostel near her brother Jimmy in Yorkshire.

For a long time it seemed that Vivienne, the Burnses' fifth child, had survived the family affliction. Just 4 feet 10 inches tall, she was witty and vivacious, and the only one of the Burns children to inherit their father's jet-black hair. At the start of the war, when she was seventeen, Vivienne and her sister Peggy moved to West London to work on an assembly line in a munitions factory. Later she transferred to the women's Auxiliary Territorial Service, or ATS, and was stationed at an anti-aircraft battery in Stanmore. There she met an American serviceman and in December 1944 became a GI bride. After the war, she and her husband Clayton McDowell, returned to the US and settled near Washington, DC.

Not even the distance of the Atlantic, nor the space of a decade, could spare Vivienne. In 1957 she suffered a schizophrenic attack that was all the more devastating to her family for appearing to come out of a clear blue sky. But to Vivienne, as she later recounted, displaying the fractured syntax and logic that are characteristic of her illness, it seemed that all her misfortunes stemmed from the war.

"I just wanted someone to believe me," she said. "Things happen, certain things leading to other things . . . then I cracked up. The war – it was horrible. All those people . . . I tried to do what I could. I've got to forget the past, that's what they tell me, but you can't forget some things, can you? Nobody can.

"How strange – how can things happen like that in a small place to one family? Sometimes I wonder why it has been so bad on me, I didn't start that horrible war. How could we deal with that maniac Hitler? Those doodlebugs used to come right over where I lived. I used to watch those things. But I never dreamed it would happen to me."

Of the Burnses' six children, that left Peggy, Jimmy and Pat. And it was Peggy who provided her parents with further shocks during the war. When Vivienne transferred to the ATS, Peggy remained at the munitions factory where they had been working together. After a brief affair with a married man she became pregnant again. She gave birth to her second child at the Kent and Sussex Hospital in Tunbridge Wells on August 29th, 1943. The baby was a girl, and Peggy named her Myra Ann.

Whereas Peggy's parents had said they were prepared to forgive her when Terry was born, this time they did not. Margaret Burns told Peggy that she was irresponsible, and that one man – Jimmy Burns – had been enough for *her*. She also told Peggy that she could not keep her baby in Meadow Road. When Myra Ann was three months old, Peggy handed her over to a couple in Tunbridge Wells who had agreed to become her foster-parents.

Margaret Burns's behaviour towards Peggy was made more harsh by the extent to which she had contributed to Peggy's misfortunes. She had never discussed either personal relations or sex with her daughters, while at the same time her increasingly cold and withdrawn personality had impelled them to look for affection outside the home. Peggy herself later remarked that she had mistakenly believed she could find affection through sex.

The last word was with Peggy. When Myra Ann was nine months old, her foster-parents asked Peggy if they could adopt her, and Peggy agreed. Before the formalities were concluded, Peggy brought

Myra Ann home to Meadow Road for the last time. Her father was asleep but Peggy woke him to look at the baby, telling him he would never see her again. "That broke his heart," says Peggy's sister Pat. "He cried and cried."

Terry, meanwhile, remained at Meadow Road. With Peggy living and working in Tunbridge Wells again, it was his grandmother who brought him up, helped by his grandfather, who continued to lavish attention on him, and by his aunt Pat. Pat taught him to read from the comic album *Film Fun*, taking him on her lap and turning the pages while he pointed to the words and asked what they said. While Terry's grandparents paid for his upkeep, Peggy supplied all his clothes, which were invariably the best available: tweed trousers, Fair Isle jumpers, and best-quality leather shoes.

Sometimes Terry seemed confused over the roles of those around him. When his mother was due to visit Meadow Road he would stand at the window watching for her, occasionally turning to ask: "Where's Peggy?" When she arrived she usually had a soldier on her arm who would be introduced to him as "uncle".

Then came another dramatic event: the return of Jack Rosemberg. Soon after Terry was born, in her distress at being deserted, Peggy had sent a photograph of Terry to Rosemberg's parents in Paris. They had responded to her implicit appeal for help by offering to look after Terry themselves, but Peggy refused. Then Rosemberg came to Britain as a member of the Free French forces led by Charles de Gaulle. Immaculately dressed in his uniform, he arrived without warning one afternoon at Meadow Road. Margaret Burns asked him into the kitchen where he reached into his pocket and pulled out handfuls of money, which he put on the kitchen table. Then he asked if he could take Terry away.

Margaret refused. She told Rosemberg that she could not possibly agree, as Peggy was not there to give her consent. Rosemberg pleaded and pleaded, but she was adamant – although she did say that she would accept the money to help pay for Terry's upkeep. Rosemberg told her that she could keep the money, and left. He never saw his son again.

By the end of the war, Margaret Burns was herself displaying increasingly alarming behaviour. One visitor to Meadow Road who witnessed it was Una's daughter Kristine, who was with her mother as she looked for comfort with her family in Southborough. After a life as traumatic as any other in the family, she lives today in the US, where she has changed her name to Kristina – by which she is referred to throughout this book. She remembers her grandmother as "a very cruel woman – she took her anger out on everyone around her".

Although Kristina experienced this at first hand, it was Terry who suffered most. Once when Terry was rebuked for some misdemeanour, he smirked in nervousness. "Nanny said, 'Go on, laugh again,' and he smirked again and she smacked him across the ear and said, 'That'll teach you to laugh at me.'"

The most distressing incident concerned the lavatory in the Burnses' back yard. It was too large for young children to use with ease, and on one occasion Terry smeared the seat. "Nanny took him out and rubbed his nose in it," Kristina says. "He was very upset by that, and cried a lot." Kristina believes that her grandmother's cruelty had a damaging effect on Terry. Whereas her aunts were struck by Terry's sunny disposition as a baby, Kristina remembers him as "a gentle soul – he was very quiet and sensitive, and didn't laugh a lot".

At times, the family has wondered to what extent Margaret Burns herself was responsible for the misfortunes it suffered. By now, it could be said, she was displaying many of the signs of a schizophrenic personality. True, she never crossed the divide into full mental illness, and thus did not enter the world that for schizophrenics is only tenuously related to reality. But she found it hard to express affection or emotion, disliked physical contact with others, had feelings of envy and alienation, had become isolated and remote, and showed increasing hostility and even violence to others. But did this mean, her descendants wondered, that her children had somehow acquired their illness from her? "It can't be a coincidence," says Kristina.

In the 1940s there was stark disagreement over the origins of mental illness. The argument was summarised as "nature versus nurture": some experts believed that mental disorder was inherited through the genes, others that it resulted from the victim's upbringing. (Since then the theories have merged, with most experts agreeing that the causes of mental illness contain elements of both.) Although the Burns family were unaware of the academic debate, they unwittingly touched on these issues at times. After the war Peggy had a furious row with her mother, telling her that the family's misfortunes were all her fault. Her mother retaliated by saying that Peggy had been "bad seed" from the start. And it was in her attempt to explain all that had gone wrong that Margaret Burns declared that there must be a curse on the family, which would persist until every member had died.

These imprecations, like the story of Jimmy Burns, were disseminated throughout the family, and were still being repeated forty years later. For later generations, the implications were awesome. If mental illness is solely inherited and will strike without warning, then, as Margaret had implied, there is little point in trying to escape. But if it depends on what happens in the lifetime of those who are vulnerable, then a great deal depends on an ability and determination to resist. Margaret's grandson David was to be brought face to face with the family misfortunes through the fate of both his aunt Una and his half-brother Terry. Not surprisingly, concern about madness was to become a major influence on his creative life.

In July 1946, the six children of Jimmy and Margaret Burns came together for the last time. It was a time of both pride and mourning. During the war, the younger Jimmy Burns had won a Military Medal with Montgomery's "desert rats" in North Africa, and a Distinguished Conduct Medal at the siege of Cassino in Italy, the citation praising his "coolness, courage and disregard for his own safety". On July 25th, he went to Buckingham Palace to be awarded his two medals by King George VI, watched by his sister Peggy and his nephew Terry. When they came home Margaret Burns announced: "We've got two heroes in the family now."

Terry was equally proud, telling his cousin Kristina: "I saw the King." When he wrote a school composition about the occasion, however, his teacher refused to believe him and accused him of lying.

Jimmy Burns senior never saw his son's medals. He had contracted leukaemia and died, at the age of fifty-nine, just four days before his son's investiture. All six of his children attended his funeral, at Tunbridge Wells cemetery on July 26th. His coffin was draped with a Union Jack, and his former comrades in the Old Contemptibles Association stood to attention when it passed by. The event was reported in the *Kent and Sussex Courier*, which recalled that Jimmy Burns had been a member of the Russian Relief Force to Archangel, and for his bravery had been awarded the Military Medal.

3

The London Boy

At the end of the war, Peggy Burns was working as a waitress in the restaurant at the Ritz cinema in Tunbridge Wells, a hushed upstairs room where the ladies of the spa town could take a sedate afternoon tea. One of her regular customers was a slight man in his early thirties with glasses and receding, sandy hair, who had recently returned from the war. His name was Haywood Stenton Jones, though everyone knew him as John.

John Jones was born in the grimy Yorkshire town of Doncaster in 1912. His childhood was lonely and without affection, for both his parents – his father was a prosperous boot and shoe dealer, his mother the daughter of a foreman in a woollen mill – died when he was young. He was brought up by a relative who sent him to endure the rigours of an English public-school education at Skipton, fifty miles away. He emerged a withdrawn and emotionally stunted young man who found it hard to display his feelings. But beneath his impassive exterior, he was laying plans that would shape his life and that of his son David. For John Jones wanted to break into show business.

At twenty-one, John was due to receive a legacy from his parents that had been placed in trust for him until he came of age. The amount was £3,000, and John had decided to use this as capital to launch his career as a show-business entrepreneur. In the spring of 1933, six months before his inheritance was due, he travelled to London to reconnoitre his plans. There he fell in with a resourceful band of performers, promoters and club owners, among them an Irishman named James Sullivan, whose career ranged from music-hall artiste to circus clown. Sullivan had a daughter named Hilda who was an entertainer too. When John met her he was convinced that she could fulfil his dreams.

Hilda had a delightfully cosmopolitan background. Her mother was an Italian acrobat who had died in a circus accident when Hilda was five. She had seen little of her father since that time, for she had been brought up by her grandmother in France. In 1933, the year Hitler came to power in Germany, she was in Vienna, where she was singing in night clubs and was known as the

Viennese nightingale. When Nazi thugs appeared in the streets of Vienna, Hilda fled to Britain. Her father met her at Charing Cross Station, accompanied by John Jones, who was immediately entranced. "He asked me to go and have a cup of tea with him at the Lyons Corner House in the Strand," she says. "And he fell madly in love with me."

John saw in Hilda everything he was not. She was vivacious and outward-going; a handsome woman with high cheekbones, wavy golden hair, and a tantalising smile. She was also a witty singer and an accomplished pianist. John made her a twofold proposition: he would launch her show-business career in England, and he would marry her too.

At first, Hilda contemplated John without enthusiasm. She had left the love of her life, the son of a wealthy Italian banker, in Vienna. They had been desperate to marry but his parents disapproved of her theatrical background and refused their consent. John, by comparison, seemed colourless and dull. "He was very taciturn, nothing made him laugh," she says. "You never saw his lips move and you never saw him smile."

As John pressed his attentions, Hilda came to appreciate his "English" qualities of courtesy and gentleness. "I never did love him, but I was very fond of him," she says. And, as she admits, John was offering a powerful lure. "He wanted to see my name in lights. That was his dream. He wanted to make me a star." Hilda accepted John's offer and they were married on December 19th, 1933, just three months after John had come into his inheritance.

John put his plans into action almost at once. He joined forces with a theatrical producer and asked him to set up a revue to be called *11.30 Saturday Night*. Hilda was to receive star billing, and it cost John £2,000 of his £3,000 inheritance. The producer booked it to play for a week each in Dudley, Croydon and Chelsea. There, Hilda believes, lay the fatal mistake. "They were dead places," she says. The show flopped.

John made a desperate bid to recoup his losses by bringing the show to London and attempting to stage it at a theatre in the Strand. But the producer told John it was a lost cause and pulled out. Worse, he told John that to cover his own costs he was taking possession of all the props and equipment John had bought. When John protested, the producer flourished an open razor in his face and told him, "You're finished." John backed down.

With just one-third of his inheritance left, John gambled the entire £1,000 on opening a piano-bar in Charlotte Street. He called it the Boop-a-doop, and Hilda was to be the resident performer.

John hoped the club would attract a sophisticated West End crowd: to Hilda, he was the last person to achieve such an aim. He was not in the least gregarious, and did not even drink or smoke. "He didn't make people welcome," she says. "You could introduce someone to him and he'd turn his back and read the paper." Within a year, the Boop-a-doop had closed and John's £1,000 was gone.

With his dreams in ruins, John took a job as a porter at the Russell Hotel. He spent his evenings writing applications for office jobs and was eventually offered the post of clerk at Dr Barnardo's, the respected charity, founded in the nineteenth century to care for destitute children, with a chain of orphanages throughout Britain. John started work at Dr Barnardo's head office at the Elephant and Castle on September 4th, 1935. Hilda's own dreams of stardom were reduced to becoming an usherette at a cinema in Kentish Town.

A year later, their marriage seemed over. The failure of John's ambitions left him moody and depressed; at times he was sulky and withdrawn, at others he lost his temper, usually in clashes with Hilda over money. "He'd ask, 'How much money you spent, how much money you got left?' I say, 'Look, I went out with a pound, I got nothing. That's it, I spent a pound!'" Hilda would storm out and go to stay with her father, who by then had abandoned his own show-business career and was working as the caretaker at Somerset House, where he occupied a tiny flat in the basement.

Against all the odds, the marriage was revived two years later. John's work took him to Birmingham, where he had an affair. His lover became pregnant and in January 1938, she gave birth to a baby daughter. When John told Hilda what had happened, he assumed she would ask for a divorce. Instead, deep longings stirred within her, for she had always wanted a baby of her own, and she suggested that they should bring up John's daughter themselves. John's lover agreed, and she handed over the baby to him at Euston Station. "He brought the child to me," Hilda says. "He just put the bundle in my arms and said, 'This is Annette.'"

Hilda was overjoyed, and formally adopted Annette not long afterwards. She and John were reunited and set up home again in Camden Town. But Hilda was distressed to find that John expected her to raise the baby alone. "He never gave me any money for her. He didn't want to know her."

In 1939 the war separated John and Hilda once more. John already belonged to the Territorial Army – he was a keen marksman, and took part in shooting competitions at Bisley – and so he was recruited into the regular army immediately. He joined the

Royal Fusiliers and, like the younger Jimmy Burns, fought in North Africa, Sicily and Italy. When he came home on leave, Hilda found that her husband had become "human". He now drank and smoked, and liked to join her in staying up late with her friends. "If he had stayed like that, he would have been a nice person," she says.

Hilda, meanwhile, was aiding the war effort too. She had resumed her show-business career, adopting the stage name Chérie – the name she was still using forty-five years later, when she sang and played at the Queen of Hearts pub in the London suburb of Kingsbury. She joined the forces entertainment service, ENSA, and performed at camps and garrisons throughout Britain, while Annette stayed at a convent boarding school in Hertfordshire. Then Hilda met another man on her travels and set up home with him in Bloomsbury. When John returned from the war, their marriage was over, this time for good.

As Hilda and John considered how to reorganise their lives, Hilda made one request. She and John had both accumulated savings from their wartime pay, and they agreed to invest it jointly in buying a house. "I didn't need anything for myself," Hilda says today. "But my idea was to provide something for Annette."

They found a terraced house at 40 Stansfield Road, Brixton, a tall, narrow street close to the main railway line. Housing in the inner-city areas of South London, which had suffered from the rain of V1s and V2s at the end of the war, was then exceptionally cheap, and it cost them no more than £500. It was left undecided whether John would live in the house himself, but Hilda and he agreed that if it was ever sold, the proceeds were to go to Annette; otherwise, Annette was to take possession of the house when she was twenty-one.

When John was demobbed he returned to his job at Dr Barnardo's. His work took him to Tunbridge Wells, where he met Peggy Burns. At thirty-two, in her black waitress's dress with its white pinafore, she cut a trim and lively figure, and he returned to court her over tea and scones at the Ritz cinema restaurant. He saw in her some of the qualities that had attracted him to Hilda: she was handsome and vivacious, and had a sense of fun.

Peggy's reaction to John was similar to Hilda's. She too cherished memories of her first love, Jack Rosemberg; she too was impressed by John's courteous and cultivated bearing. When she took John to meet her parents at Meadow Road, he wore a tweed overcoat, with the collar turned up, and a neat cravat at his neck; her family concluded that he was "a gentleman".

Soon afterwards John asked Peggy if she would come to live with him, with a view to getting married once he and Hilda were divorced. Peggy agreed. After the earlier traumas of her life, she welcomed the stability that he offered; she explained later that she hoped he would "take over" and look after her.

Hilda, meanwhile, was living in a flat in Hilldrop Crescent, Kentish Town. She was considerably taken aback when John arrived at the flat with Peggy, making it clear that he intended to live there too: John even carried Peggy over the threshold as if they had just got married. Although they managed to co-exist, Hilda told John she expected him to find a place of his own soon.

In July 1946, Peggy travelled to Southborough for her father's funeral – the last occasion when all six of his children were together. Only later did Peggy reveal to her family that she was pregnant again. When her mother heard the news, she took Vivienne with her and visited Peggy in Hilldrop Crescent. She remonstrated with Peggy once more, but Peggy told her to mind her own business; her mother retaliated by saying that she was "washing her hands" of her. By now Hilda had laid down an ultimatum: either John left Hilldrop Crescent, or she would. There was only one solution: John and Peggy moved into the house in Stansfield Road. Since they had no furniture, Hilda gave them most of hers.

In 1946, Brixton still bore the scars of war. Its long rows of terraced houses had a gap-toothed air, with fireweed and buddleia adorning the bombsites. Memories of the blackouts were sustained by a ban on illuminating advertising and window displays, and most food and clothing remained "on the ration". Long queues formed when the first bananas to arrive in Britain after the war reached Brixton's bustling street market; spivs and the black market reigned. Yet there was a pioneering spirit in the air, shown in the faces of the young and idealistic MPs in army uniform who had been elected in 1945. With a majority of almost 200 seats, the Labour government headed by Clement Attlee prepared to take ownership of transport, steel and coal for the nation, and to provide free health care, education and welfare for all.

In Stansfield Road it was hard for Peggy to forget her family's troubled past. Una and her baby Kristina, then aged four, had gone wandering again, and John and Peggy offered to take them in for a time. Una was more disturbed than ever, and seemed incapable of caring for Kristina: Peggy would find her shivering where Una had laid her on top of her bed, instead of tucked beneath the bedclothes. Then Kurt Paulsen pulled up outside Stansfield Road in an army jeep; beribboned with medals from France and Germany, he had come to say goodbye. When he returned to Canada he told his wife about his affair with Una. His wife forgivingly suggested that they should bring up Kristina themselves, and they wrote to Una to offer her a home. But Una turned the offer down.

Peggy's third child – John's second – was born at 9 a.m. on January 8th, 1947. They named him David Robert: John chose the name David, and Peggy had always liked Robert, which was in any case the name of John's father. The baby made an immediate impression on the midwife attending Peggy at Stansfield Road. Invoking mystical as well as medical powers, she told Peggy that he had "been here before", since he had such "knowing eyes". David received his first intimation of the family tensions almost at once, when Kristina smeared excrement from his nappy on the wall. "I was jealous," she says. "I tried to pretend he had done it. I couldn't understand why nobody would believe me."

If the infant David registered these strains, it would hardly have shown. When Pat visited Brixton she found "a lovely-looking baby – always smiling and very placid. He never got into a temper. He took after his father. I liked him a lot when he was little. He used to sit on my knee, and he was very quick."

David's birth had left one important administrative matter unresolved. Hilda had applied for a divorce but it did not become absolute until August 1947. On September 12th, John and Peggy were married at Brixton Register Office, with Peggy's mother, relenting from her previous intransigence, acting as one of the witnesses.

Soon afterwards Una left Stansfield Road. Her illness was worsening, and Kristina's jealousy of David was becoming more acute. She punched David to make him cry, and the first time he stood up, she screamed with laughter and pushed him down. "I intended to be the only one who walked," she says. Una and Kristina returned to Southborough where Margaret was perplexed by her daughter's increasingly bizarre behaviour. In her ignorance she could only remark: "Una doesn't seem well."

When Una had gone, Peggy told John that she wanted Terry to join them in Stansfield Road. Although Terry visited his mother in Brixton from time to time – Kristina remembers how they would "kick ball" in the narrow garden behind the house – Terry was still living in Southborough. He had proved an exceptional pupil at St Peter's, passing an entrance examination for Judds School in Tonbridge at the precocious age of nine. But his grandmother, Margaret Burns, had become more eccentric since her husband's death, and Peggy felt that she should look after Terry herself.

It was an explosive proposition, for John was plagued with jealousy over Peggy's love for Jack Rosemberg. With his blue eyes set in a broad, confident face, and his thatch of dark hair, Terry was a visible reminder of his father's dashing good looks and Peggy's chequered past. But Peggy insisted, and John deferred to her demand.

Terry, then aged ten, moved to Stansfield Road early in 1948. That autumn he started at Henry Thornton, a well-regarded grammar school a mile away beside Clapham Common. He was registered there as Terry Jones, for John had changed his name from Burns by deed poll. (Later in life, Terry changed his name back to Burns.) Terry was to remember Henry Thornton with affection. "Everyone was very kind to me there," he recalled.

The school seemed warmer still in contrast with the chill household Terry now inhabited. Like both her mother and her husband, Peggy seems to have found it hard to display emotion towards anyone but young children. Her sister Pat had observed that she was affectionate and confident in her handling of babies – "but when they get to a certain age she can't communicate", Pat says. "I don't know what it is." It was Terry who now suffered most in this respect. "I never saw her kiss him or put her arms round his shoulders or touch him, nothing."

Terry also had to contend with the overt jealousy of his stepfather, and it was this, above all, that left scars which marked the rest of his life. He was a physically awkward child, and John Jones would mock his attempts to learn to ride a bicycle. Terry's discomfort was witnessed by John's daughter Annette, who spent almost a year living at Stansfield Road, after her parents' divorce. Annette was very fond of Terry – "he was very much a brother to me" – and so felt for him when he incurred the hostility of John Jones. "He was always in trouble with my father, for nothing," Annette says. "There were quarrels, things blew up, someone answered back, the way things do in a troubled house." David, by contrast, was "the be-all and end-all – he was the god of the house".

Terry suffered further because there was no one at hand to whom he could express his feelings of frustration and rejection. "He could never speak to anyone," Annette says. "He couldn't speak to Daddy and I don't think he felt free to speak to his mother because of Daddy and David." Terry's one confidante, on her visits to Stansfield Road, was his aunt Pat. "He was a beautiful child, so intelligent and bright," she says. "His spirit was broken within about a year. He would put his arms around my neck when I went to see him there and he had great big blue eyes and he used to whisper to me, 'I hate him, I hate him, I hate John Jones.'"

Peggy did her best to shield David from the family's travails, hushing her sisters to silence should one of them raise the subject in his presence. But young children are usually more alive to the tensions around them than their parents give them credit for. And David was drawn, ineluctably, towards the focus of those tensions at Stansfield Road. The fondest relationship in the household at that time, so Pat believes, was between David and Terry. They shared a bedroom on the ground floor, and on cold mornings David would snuggle into Terry's bed. "He worshipped Terry," says Pat. "And Terry idolised him."

In interviews throughout his career, David has provided colourful accounts of his childhood in Brixton. He has told how he was born in a "houseful of blacks", and how, as he walked to school past Brixton prison, he wondered about the fate of the miscreants incarcerated behind its high, forbidding walls. He described Brixton as "a very rough area – like Harlem", adding: "I was very butch in those days. I was in street brawls and everything." He has also talked of visiting Brixton's "ska and bluebeat clubs", and asserted that by the time he moved from Brixton it had left "great, strong images" in his mind.

David's account of his childhood has usually been faithfully relayed by the writers and publishers of the entertainment world, who tend to live in symbiotic relationship with their subjects, jointly nurturing the myths vital to sustain them all. These versions have contributed powerfully to the image of David as a street-wise performer, moulded in a tough, raw neighbourhood. They also stood to confer artistic credibility upon his music, through the implication that he had, almost mystically, absorbed black influences in his childhood.

The truth is far more prosaic.

As the electoral register for Brixton shows, there was no "houseful of blacks" at 40 Stansfield Road. There was, in fact, just one other person living there in 1947, when David was born – one Ann McLachlan. Nor is David's description of Brixton as London's equivalent of Harlem remotely accurate. It is true that Brixton is known as one of Britain's densest black communities today, even though the ratio of black to white is only one in three, as against the uniformly black population of Harlem itself. But in 1947 there were virtually no black inhabitants in Brixton at all. The first influx of West Indians did not arrive until 1948, when immigrants who had been brought to Britain on the liner *Empire Windrush*, and were housed in tents on Clapham Common, gravitated to Brixton in search of cheap accommodation. And in the early 1950s, when David was growing up in Brixton, they still formed only a tiny and passive minority.

David's account of walking past Brixton prison on his way to school each morning is equally inventive. It has, however, been assisted until now by the mystery surrounding precisely which primary school he did attend – even council officials hoping to publicise David's local origins when he performed at a Benefit for Brixton concert in 1983 were unable to find out. The answer is to be found less than a hundred yards from Stansfield Road at Stockwell Infants, a former Victorian board-school building, with tall windows and high grey walls, in Stockwell Road.

The school register records that David began his education at Stockwell Infants on November 12th, 1951, six weeks before his fifth birthday. David was evidently nervous that day, for he has since described how he peed on the floor, and was so embarrassed that he did not dare tell his teacher. But it would have been quite impossible to make the journey past Brixton prison that David later described, for the prison is almost a mile to the south.

In painting so fanciful a picture, David was fulfilling an implicit contract to provide the chroniclers of the music world with the stuff of which myths are made. Indeed, he became so intuitively sensitive to this process that he would suit his responses to the expectations of his interviewers and the circumstances of their encounters. Thus the version of his childhood that has him surviving street brawls in some British Harlem was served to the exotic American show-business writer Rex Reed one night in 1976, as they sped in a Cadillac across the New Mexico desert.

These considerations might not have been ignored for so long if another of the received truths about David's childhood had been questioned. David has frequently asserted that he lived in Brixton until he was eleven, whereupon his family moved to the suburb of Bromley. In fact, the public records show that the move had taken place by early 1953, when David was just six. It follows that David was a child not of the inner city, but of the emollient suburbs.

David's imaginative account of life in Brixton has thus served as a racy alternative to circumstances more banal than rock stars are supposed to spring from. But it has also helped to conceal a childhood overshadowed by the spectre of the family's misfortunes.

*

Eight miles to the south-east of Brixton, on the border between the London outskirts and the county of Kent, Bromley was a new world. In the nineteenth century it was a neat and placid town whose most famous inhabitant was the writer H. G. Wells. Wells sought to escape the confines of Bromley by spinning fantasies like *The Time Machine* and *The War of the Worlds*, books which helped to invent science fiction. Wells was drawn back to the spirit of Bromley with *Love and Mr Lewisham* and *The History of Mr Polly*, archetypal accounts of life among the straitened middle classes.

Between the two world wars, builders and architects sought to create a new Bromley. They dreamed of *rus in urbe*: of country and town combined, with houses standing in tiny green enclaves as if a city had been set in parkland. The fingers of suburbia spread ever outwards, long roads of semi-detached houses, their progress marked by fresh-planted cherry trees set in the pavement, snaking into the countryside. Their purchasers were the new commuting classes who rode into central London on the clicketing green trains of Southern Railway. At weekends they mowed their lawns and dug their vegetable patches, and watched the world from behind a veil of lace curtains. Bromley was transmuted from a separate town into a satellite of the metropolis: a property-owning, conservative, middle-class haven.

These were among the features that attracted John and Peggy Jones to Bromley, although a further impetus came from John's dislike of the West Indians who were moving into Brixton. "John was very prejudiced towards coloured people," says his first wife Hilda, firmly: "*very*."

John and Peggy bought a house at 106 Canon Road, a tiny cottage in a terraced street in the Bickley district of south Bromley, arriving – as the electoral register records – around New Year, 1953. With a looming gas-works in the next street, it was not quite arcadia. Even so, there were cricket fields and recreation grounds close at hand, and woods and golf courses nearby. A year later they sold that house and bought another at 23 Clarence Road, a more imposing Edwardian semi-detached in a leafy street a short distance away.

The aspirations held by John and Peggy in moving to Bromley were further revealed by the upbringing they conferred on David. At first, they sent him to a small private school, before John, ever watchful over the family finances, concluded that its fees were beyond their resources, and David was admitted to a local council school, Raglan Infants, a little more than a quarter-mile from

Clarence Road. Thereafter – in utter contrast to David's own account – his life was as secure and conformist as his parents could make it. He was a demure child with a neat side parting and a ready smile, who sang in school choirs and joined the local Wolf Cubs.

But there was one member of the Jones family who was at first unable to share the delights of middle-class Bromley. That was Terry, who, at the age of fifteen, had been left behind in Stansfield Road.

From its promising start, Terry's career at Henry Thornton school in Clapham had ground to a halt. His teachers had no doubt of his intelligence, and he was an expert chess-player. He was a keen sportsman too, as a boxer and a member of the school cricket team. But he found no support for his endeavours in the tense atmosphere at home. "My sister was always criticising, criticising," says Pat. The stress Terry was under showed when he suffered fainting fits at school and had to be brought home. Then John declined to support Terry at school beyond the minimum leaving age of fifteen, and Peggy did not intercede on his behalf. Terry left Henry Thornton several months before his fifteenth birthday with no academic qualifications to his name.

That summer, Terry found a job as a clerk at Amalgamated Press, publishers of smudgy comics and undemanding women's magazines. He worked in the company's costings department in Southwark, a short ride by bus or tube from Brixton. When the family prepared to move to Bromley, Terry assumed that he would be going with them. But Peggy told him that it would be far more convenient if he stayed in Brixton. She found lodgings for him at 42 Stansfield Road, next door to their own former house.

The family's departure to Bromley deepened Terry's feelings of bitterness and envy. Before long, his battered psyche suffered a new blow, when his landlord made homosexual advances towards him. Terry punched him in the face and found refuge with a neighbour, Mrs Cripps, whose kindness he remembered for the rest of his life.

Peggy had little choice but to agree that Terry could rejoin the rest of the family in Bromley after all. His return rekindled all the old antagonisms that Peggy had hoped to escape. Terry was exposed once again to the jealousy and criticism of John Jones, and his isolation within the family increased. As before, Peggy did her best to shield David from the family tensions. But her task was made harder by the reappearance of another reminder of the family past, in the hapless figure of David's cousin, Kristina.

For five years, as her mother's illness worsened, Kristina had followed a nightmare odyssey around institutions and surrogate homes. Most distressing of all, she was often the victim of her mother's deranged fears: Una attacked her with a knife, locked her in cupboards, and, in the most horrific incident of all, dangled her by the legs from the top of a building. Complaints of Una's behaviour reached the police and she was taken to court. Kristina was questioned too but she was so distraught at seeing her mother in the witness box that she burst into tears and refused to answer.

Soon afterwards, Una abandoned Kristina in a hotel. Kristina was taken into care by the local welfare department and placed in a children's home in Bournemouth named Milton House. Una found her there and smuggled her out inside a suitcase, but the police tracked her down. On September 25th, 1950, Una was sent to Park Prewett, a towering Victorian mental hospital near Basingstoke. She was diagnosed as schizophrenic and given a range of treatment that included electro-convulsive therapy and doses of insulin. They had little effect.

Kristina forgivingly remembers her mother today as "a very gentle person who just couldn't cope". She also believes that her mother's deranged perceptions, like Vivienne's, focused on the war: random and violent, it became the paradigm of insanity. "She would talk about blood a lot," Kristina says. "She was very concerned with blood and death."

Kristina spent fifteen months in Milton House. Like the other children, she was constantly smartened up for the visits of prospective parents. She was mortified when a woman declared: "She's not very pretty, is she?" although the matron loyally responded, "No, but she's very bright." She left Milton House in 1951 and spent two years with foster-parents in Bournemouth. In 1953, when she was eleven, an elderly couple named Mr and Mrs Bell agreed to give her a home in Bromley. They lived at 45 The Chase, a mere quarter-mile from John and Peggy Jones.

It was no coincidence that the two homes were so close. Bournemouth's child welfare department had been in contact with Peggy, finding her "very sensible and level-headed" (a later report noted that Peggy's husband was "connected with Dr Barnardo's" and that "they had a son David aged 7 years"). The department's officials hoped that Kristina would benefit from living near her aunt and she spent two weeks with the family in the summer of 1953, before joining the Bells in September.

Kristina soon justified the faith shown in her by the matron of Milton House by winning a place at Bromley Grammar School for

Girls. The Bells were ambitious for her too, attempting to correct her table manners and sending her to elocution lessons every week. But Kristina made clear her distaste for these social graces. As a report of the Bournemouth child welfare department observed, "She complained they wanted to make a lady of her and she didn't want to be a lady." She also argued with Mr Bell over the meaning of words and, when challenged, would produce a dictionary to prove her point.

The Bells' most significant complaint concerned the time Kristina was spending with the Jones family. She often made a detour to visit them after school, and stayed with them at weekends too, attracted by a family that was, to appearances at least, united and intact. Kristina hoped that her aunt would invite her to live with them. "It was the only family that I really knew," she says.

David was then seven. Kristina remembers him as "polite and well-bred – he adored me and followed me around". But she was still prey to violent jealousy, stirred above all by David's skill at extracting new possessions from his parents. "Every time I went there David would say, 'Look at my new gramophone' or 'Look at my new something or other' . . . He used to infuriate me because we would go somewhere together and I'd see something I liked and I'd say, 'Can I have that?' and they'd say, 'No, pipe down.' David would stand there and say, 'That's so nice, may I touch it if I'm very careful?' and they'd let him touch it, and end up giving it to him."

As before, Kristina gave vent to her feelings by punching David. She also told him that if his guinea pigs were held up by their tails, their eyes would fall out. This time she was in no doubt that her feelings had been conveyed. "He cried bitterly. He was very naive and trusting as a little child."

On her visits to Bromley, Peggy's sister Pat discerned another David, one already taking a strong interest in his personal appearance. "He had beautiful blue eyes and lovely blond hair," Pat says. "He always liked to comb it his way, forward, with a quiff by his ear. If you combed it he always had to do it again himself. He looked at himself a lot in the mirror. He was a vain child, and he always liked to look different."

Here, as Pat observed, was another source of tension within the family: Peggy was determined that in this respect too David should be as conventional as possible. "David was always clean and tidy and spotless – my sister made a thing of that. Every five minutes she would say, 'Pull your sock up', 'Have you washed your face?'"

Grandfather Jimmy Burns, "so handsome and so strong," at his ill-fated officers' training course in 1918.

Left: Grandmother Margaret Burns with three of her six children: (left to right) Margaret Mary, known as Peggy, David's mother; Victoria Honoria, known as Nora, David's aunt; James Edward, known as Jimmy, David's uncle.

Below: Jimmy Burns junior, winner of the Military Medal in the Second World War: "two heroes in the family now."

Above: David's aunt Una with the Canadian serviceman, Kurt Paulsen, and their daughter Kristine (David's cousin) photographed in 1946. Una was diagnosed as schizophrenic.

Far left: Aunt Vivienne, a GI bride, with her husband Clayton McDowell. Vivienne was also diagnosed as schizophrenic.

Left: Aunt Nora, photographed in 1950. She was diagnosed as manic-depressive.

Below: Aunt Pat with her doomed nephew Terry, David's half-brother, in the halcyon days of Southborough.

Top: David (left), with his father, John Jones; beside him, enjoying the family feeling, his cousin Kristine.

Above: John Jones during the Second World War. Left: Kristine – now named Kristina Amadeus – today.

Above: Pat Burns on her wedding day in 1959, flanked by her husband Tony (centre) and her nephew Terry (left), her "surrogate child".

Below left: David's mother, Peggy, in 1962.

Below right: David's long-lost half-sister Annette, now living in Egypt, with her mother Hilda, John Jones's first wife, photographed in 1985.

At seventeen, Terry was growing into a lean and good-looking young man, with clean-cut features that reflected those of his father. Like David, Terry was meticulous about his appearance too, looking in the mirror to check that his tie was straight and his hair in place. His main pleasure came from the company of David and Kristina. He would crouch for hours with them over David's Monopoly board, and afterwards delight them with beautifully woven stories, among them the tales of the exploits of grandfather Burns that he had heard in Southborough. But even at the age of twelve, Kristina could discern the extent of Terry's true loneliness. "I don't think that was a very happy time for him," she says. "He didn't fit in."

There was no doubt who was the most privileged member of the family. John and Peggy owned a television, the first Kristina ever watched, and it was always David who decided which channel they should view of the two then available. He invariably chose the children's programme *The Flowerpot Men* – "everything had to stop for *The Flowerpot Men*," says Kristina – and, later in the evening, the science-fiction series, *The Quatermass Experiment*.

Equally, there was no doubt that Terry felt excluded from the family proceedings. Even towards David, John was as undemonstrative as Peggy – "no hugging and kissing," recalls Kristina. But when he came home in the evening, he invariably took David into the living room and told him what he had done that day. Peggy would stay in the kitchen, leaving Terry to retreat disconsolately upstairs.

Terry's isolation was also witnessed by John's daughter Annette who also stayed with the family in Bromley for a time. Aged sixteen, she was training to be a nurse, and when Peggy went into hospital for an operation she helped to look after David. She particularly noticed how, if Terry ventured to express his opinion, he was instantly contradicted by John. "Sometimes with people you feel that if you say something's right they'll say it's wrong. It was that sort of atmosphere – no actual shouting rows, just edginess."

Terry was also beginning to display an ominous volatility, sometimes happy and exuberant, sometimes plunged into sombre moods. Only to Pat, once again, did Terry reveal the strength of his feelings towards his step-father. "When I grow up," he vowed, "I'm going to kill John Jones."

By now, David too had become sensitive to the tensions swirling through the family. As in Stansfield Road, Terry was his main source of physical contact, playing tickling games and ruffling his hair. But John actively discouraged signs of affection towards Terry from both David and Kristina – "even though," Kristina adds, "we both adored him." Kristina observed the damaging effect his father's edict had on David. "I think he felt very responsible, as children do, for the fact that he was the favourite child because of his father, and he was given attention by his father and Terry wasn't." In consequence, she believes, David learned to suppress all signs of his own feelings, and to retreat within a protective mental shell.

In 1955, the erosive atmosphere in the Jones household was at last eased. First, Kristina left Bromley, a move succinctly recorded by Bournemouth's tireless child welfare department: "The Bells give up." The Bells had announced that they no longer felt able to cope with her: "We feel we have utterly failed," they admitted, "but we do not see why our lives should be made a misery on that account." But they hoped that "she may yet learn to fit herself into a household somewhere." Bournemouth's officials took her back, and in April found her new foster-parents in Dorset.

Then Terry prepared to leave Bromley too. He was approaching his eighteenth birthday, which meant undertaking the chore of National Service. That entailed spending two years learning, first, boot-polishing and square-bashing, then, how to avoid boot-polishing and square-bashing. The only chance of excitement lay in joining some unlikely post-colonial adventure, such as Suez.

It was, of course, compulsory; only those who could point to a university course, a disabling illness or a widowed mother could escape. However, those liable for National Service had one other choice: they could sign on for three years instead of two and thus acquire enhanced status, a better chance of going overseas, and a few shillings a week extra pay. Most young men saw the offer as a ploy to deprive them of their liberty for an extra year; but Terry succumbed. He told his aunt Pat that he did so because he was "utterly fed up" at home and wanted to go as far away as possible.

The prospect of Terry's departure offered an immediate benefit. John, wary as ever, was finding Clarence Road too expensive to maintain: now they would be able to move into a smaller house. They searched in the less fashionable northern part of Bromley and eventually found what they needed in the tight cluster of Edwardian streets around Sundridge Park station. It was at 4 Plaistow Grove, a small terraced house with two rooms plus a cramped kitchenette downstairs, and two bedrooms, and a tiny boxroom, upstairs.

The family moved to the new house in June. John and Peggy

took the bedroom at the front and gave David the one at the back, overlooking the rear of the Crown public house; for the six months before he was due to begin his National Service, Terry was allocated the boxroom alongside.

Terry left Plaistow Grove in November. He had enlisted in the Royal Air Force and was posted first to Malta, which he enjoyed, then to Tripoli in Libya, where in those roseate days before Colonel Gaddafi the British still had a military base. He found life on the edge of the Sahara unremittingly tedious, brightened only by the occasional boxing tournament.

The move to Plaistow Grove relieved the pressure on the family budget that John Jones had been feeling. But the house was undeniably cramped, and John and Peggy felt that David should have more space. Not long after Terry had gone, John knocked down the wall of his bedroom and amalgamated it with David's.

4

A Happy Land

The move to Plaistow Grove – which was to be David's home for the next ten years – was a major landmark in the family's life. It took David to a new school and neighbourhood, and brought him a new set of friendships, some of which persisted through his career. But this event is another David has chosen at times to obscure. In 1967 he told the music reporter George Tremlett, then writing for the *New Musical Express*, that when he was eight he moved not to Bromley but to Yorkshire. There he spent two years living with an uncle in an ancient farmhouse, "surrounded by open fields and sheep and cattle"; the house had a seventeenth-century monk's hole where Catholic priests hid during times of Protestant persecution. Although David added that he was essentially a child of the city, Tremlett helpfully observed that it was indeed "a romantic place for a child to grow".

Most of David's previous biographers have readily accepted this account, even though it directly contradicted David's simultaneous assertion that he had lived in Brixton until he was ten or eleven. As in Brixton, the truth of the matter is not hard to establish. In Rangefield Road, Bromley, just five minutes' walk from Plaistow Grove, stands Burnt Ash Juniors, a typical red-brick suburban school, built between the wars, with two storeys and a large asphalt playground. The Burnt Ash register unequivocally records that David entered the school upon being transferred from Raglan Infants on June 20th, 1955, when he was eight, and that he remained there until July 24th, 1958, when he was eleven.

What is initially more puzzling about David's claim that he lived in Yorkshire is that it negates his Brixton fantasy which was so apt to his career as a rock-star. But David's story contains one detail of overriding potency, confirming the extent to which David's rewriting of his childhood served his deeper personal needs. For David told Tremlett that Terry had moved to Yorkshire with him too. The significance of that further inventive touch becomes clear from the course of events at Plaistow Grove, where Terry had effectively become a non-person.

*

As an otherwise unremarkable school in the London suburbs, Burnt Ash had one claim to fame. Its headmaster, George Lloyd, had a passion for what was known as "movement training". He taught it to every class in the school, dividing the pupils into four groups and equipping them with a percussion instrument, such as a tambourine or triangle, and instructing them to move to its rhythm.

The classes were considered so successful that they were filmed for the benefit of teacher-training colleges, and their renown even reached across the Atlantic, for on David's first day at Burnt Ash a delegation of teachers from the US had come to observe the classes in person. David himself proved a most suitable pupil. George Lloyd – who died in 1980 – once told a colleague, Mrs Pat Mountford, of the impression David had made on him. "He said that David was quiet, artistic and self-effacing – not a great personality, but a sensitive and imaginative boy," Pat Mountford recalls.

David's closest friend at school was Dudley Chapman, a tall, large-boned child from a secure middle-class home in Lake Road, halfway between Burnt Ash School and Plaistow Grove. Physically he and David could hardly have been less alike, for David was then "as skinny as a rake and very angular and bony", Dudley says. He also recalls that David was spectacularly double-jointed, and could sit on the floor with both feet lodged behind his neck.

Dudley's friendship with David was formed when they arrived together in the A-stream of their second year at Burnt Ash. (Dudley had come to the school late, after spending two years in a sanatorium with tuberculosis.) It was an alliance forged in fear, for their teacher was the awesome Mrs Baldry.

David and Dudley knew Mrs Baldry as "the Bulldozer". "She was dreadful, a real dragon," says Dudley. "She would stalk up and down with her cane under her arm." Both disciplinary offences and failures of learning were punished – although David's greater tactical skills ensured that he suffered less than Dudley. With the magnanimity that comes with the hindsight of decades, Dudley concedes that Mrs Baldry "probably meant ever so well".

Now retired, and living in Dorset, Mrs Baldry's principal memory of David is of "a very nice boy, perfectly cheerful", with "a broad smile showing all those big teeth", sitting in the front row of her class. Dudley denies the implication that David's place in the front reflected some favoured status in Mrs Baldry's eyes. When he and David first entered her class, they appropriated a prized pair of seats at the back of the room. One day they discovered the

53

pleasant twanging noise that can be obtained by flicking a ruler inserted under a desk lid. To the Bulldozer, that was virtually a capital offence. "We were brought down to the front so we sat under her nose and she could keep an eye on us," Dudley says.

Thus the friendship between Dudley and David flourished most vigorously outside Mrs Baldry's classroom. David spent "hours and days" at Dudley's house, especially enjoying its extensive garden, a dozen times the size of the narrow strip behind Plaistow Grove. "Ours was a big, close family, affectionate," Dudley adds. "For two years, probably, David spent most of his time at our house."

From Dudley's description of the rare occasions when he and David visited Plaistow Grove, it is not hard to see why David preferred Dudley's home. Peggy would open the door and stand aside as David entered without exchanging a word. "It was a very cold household," Dudley says. "She'd feed him, clothe him, do all the mother's things, but there was no cuddling, nothing like that. I don't ever recall if he asked his mother if I could come or anything like that. She'd be sitting there reading. It was just as if he was there but not there. There was no sign of affection at any time. I don't think it was a family. It was a lot of people who happened to be living under the same roof."

In itself, Dudley's account appears to explain why David should conjure an alternative version of his first two years at Plaistow Grove, sparing him both Mrs Baldry's eagle eye and the coldness of his home. But there is another, more compelling reason that emerged during our interview with Dudley Chapman, today a successful insurance loss adjuster, at his Oxfordshire home. Throughout their friendship, David had kept a secret which Dudley was astonished to learn twenty-five years later. "I never knew," Dudley said, "that David had a brother."

Nor did Mrs Baldry. Towards the end of David's time at Burnt Ash, as its pupils prepared for the examination which would decide their next school, his parents were asked to complete a form stating whether he had any brothers and sisters. In 1984, Mrs Baldry – who although devoted to her memory of David, had taken only a general interest in his life – could still remember that his parents had recorded that he had a half-sister, John's daughter Annette; but they had not mentioned a brother, or half-brother, at all. She too was astonished to learn of Terry's existence.

The truth was that the family history had been sanitised by David's parents, and Terry expunged. The effect of this edict – spoken or otherwise – on David can only have been devastating.

Forced to suppress or deny the existence of someone who had been his main source of physical affection, he must have been subject to overwhelming feelings of confusion and guilt. And, just as his grandmother, Margaret Burns, had resolved her conflicts by creating a fantasy, David did so too, spinning an alternative child-hood in Yorkshire which disposed of Dudley Chapman and re-united him with Terry.

Like other stories David told, it did contain a germ of truth. David, in fact, had not one but two uncles in Yorkshire. One was his Uncle Jimmy, who had moved to Doncaster after the war. He is emphatic today that David and Terry never lived with him. On one occasion, David and his mother Peggy did stay with him "for two or three weeks" while John was working for Dr Barnardo's at Harrogate.

David's second uncle was on his father's side, for John had a sister, Rhona, who had married a farmer in the Dales country north of York. David and his parents did visit her on occasion — but never with Terry. Terry was to point out that in any case he could not have lived with David at the relevant time, in Yorkshire or anywhere else, since he was away in the RAF.

George Tremlett remains unabashed today at his part in retailing David's fantasies so unquestioningly. In the 1960s, he says, "there was an immense amount of untruth in the music business. People used to tell the most impossible stories . . . the whole thing was a sort of charade." Yet David's Yorkshire tale will also help explain the preoccupations of some of his earliest lyrics. They too were concerned with an idealised childhood, alongside other themes from the family mythology. David's account of his childhood came closer to the truth than Tremlett ever knew.

David's friendship with Dudley offers other pointers to his develop-ing interests. First, there was Japan and the East. "David was very keen on the martial arts, oriental things," says Dudley; David talked avidly of Japan. The interest was expressed principally in endless wrestling matches in Dudley's house: "We would wrestle for hours all over the living-room floor, knocking over the chairs." The bouts usually ended even, with David's excessive wiriness balancing Dudley's superior weight. They also provided the physi-cal contact that David lacked at home, particularly after Terry's departure. In view of subsequent developments, Dudley is anxious to deny that there was an homosexual element involved. "David was just sort of normal. He showed the same kind of interest in little girls as other boys."

Second, there was the west, and America. David and Dudley played long-drawn-out games of cowboys and Indians, ranging through the house and into the garden. For boys of eight or nine, that was hardly exceptional. But Dudley again remembers that David took a closer interest in the wild west than any of their friends.

Third, there was music.

Before the mid-1950s, teenagers did not exist. Children were supposed to progress to adulthood with no awkward transitional period in between. The image they were to aspire to was embodied in the popular performers of the day: crooners and balladiers like Ronnie Hilton, Dickie Valentine, Alma Cogan and Anne Shelton. In their sleek, unruffled hairstyles, their neatly tailored clothes, they seemed to have been grown-up all their lives.

Simultaneous revolutions in style and technology altered that for ever. From across the Atlantic came sinewy figures to replace the cut-out adults and to mirror the stirrings and tribulations of adolescence: Johnnie Ray, Bill Haley, the climactic Elvis. The spread of television liberated the family wireless, permitting children to tune into the mutinous new sounds on Radio Luxembourg, waxing and waning on the ether, while the BBC went on as if nothing had changed. As Britain's economy expanded, encouraged by the proclamation of prime minister Harold Macmillan that the nation had "never had it so good", it was found that young people suddenly had money. Portable electric record players supplanted the unwieldy gramophones, with clockwork motors, that their parents owned.

Young people also discovered that musicians could be lured from their pedestals. In the unlikely person of Lonnie Donegan, a banjo player from Glasgow who first performed with Chris Barber's traditional jazz band, the new art form of skiffle was born. Its appeal now seems utterly perverse, for its biggest hits – 'Rock Island Line', 'Bring A Little Water Sylvie' – were facsimiles of the bitterest laments of Negro chain-gangs, hardly apposite to the spreading affluence of post-war Britain. But its advent meant that music was no longer a remote, technical pursuit, but could be re-created by anyone who could lay their hands on a tea chest, a broom handle and a washboard – still a common household item, for washing machines remained a luxury in Britain in the 1950s. In Bromley, at the earliest age when they could make an impact, David Jones discovered all of these things.

Dudley Chapman already had some musical expertise. Like many other middle-class children, grinding out scales in chill living rooms at their mothers' behest, he had taken piano lessons since he was three. He and David also listened to his parents' large pre-transistor wireless. When Lonnie Donegan's recordings scaled the hit parade, Dudley and David were among the many who tried to simulate them. They too procured a tea chest, carved a hole for the broom handle, and fastened a string from the top of the handle to the edge of the chest. "I used to play the piano," says Dudley, "and we used to fool about."

The young David Jones did not instantly reveal himself as a musical prodigy: far from it. "He had no inbuilt talent," says Dudley: "he never struck me as being at all musical, not a gifted child." For all her fond memories of David, Mrs Baldry agrees. She taught Dudley and David the recorder, deterring them from intoning the wrong note with the threat of punishment. "I would never say that David outshone everybody else," she says. "He didn't."

Mrs Baldry was also in charge of the Burnt Ash Junior School Choir, and in a photograph taken in 1958 – the date is chalked on a small blackboard, held up by the two girls in the front row – David appears as a demure eleven-year-old, hair brushed to one side, wearing a fresh white shirt. The choir sang the songs that all English school choirs sang: 'The Ash Grove', 'Linden Lea', 'Londonderry Air'. Again, Mrs Baldry is careful not to overstate David's abilities. "He was no spectacular singer. You'd never have picked him out and said, 'That boy sings wonderfully.'"

It was not the painfully learned tunes of Mrs Baldry's recorder class, or the airs of the Burnt Ash School Choir, that fired David's musical imagination: it was Elvis Presley. Later, David described the precise moment: "I saw a cousin of mine dance when I was very young. She was dancing to Elvis's 'Hound Dog' and I had never seen her get up and be moved so much by anything." 'Hound Dog' burst into the British hit parade in September 1956; and the cousin was Kristina, who at the age of fourteen had reappeared in David's life once again.

After joining her new foster-parents in Dorset in 1955, further misfortunes had piled upon her. She was unjustly accused of theft and questioned by the police; removed to an orphanage; and then – after a display of entirely justifiable truculence – consigned to a home for disturbed children in Devon. But Peggy had continued to take a kind-hearted interest in Kristina and in 1956 invited her to spend Christmas at Plaistow Grove.

By now, Kristina discovered, David had succeeded in extracting from his parents both a "little tin guitar" and a record player, "when no one else had a record player". This time she restrained herself from taking physical retribution. The copy of 'Hound Dog' which so entranced David was hers. David owned 'Love Me Tender' but he disliked its slow tempo and Kristina generously agreed to swap it for 'Hound Dog'.

Kristina was also present when David had his first enticing glimpses of stardom. It came by way of his father, who had at last found a way to live out his show-business dreams of thirty years before. John Jones was still working for Dr Barnardo's, and in 1950 had been promoted to the post of secretary to its management committee. His colleagues found John difficult to know; one commented later that he viewed his staff "something like an army sergeant major sees those under him", and that he was "meticulous in his appearance which together with his bearing probably reflected his service in the army during the war".

These were evidently qualities valued by Dr Barnardo's, for in 1956 John Jones was promoted to head its publicity department. The department had long been moribund, for the staff of Dr Barnardo's had a defensive attitude towards the outside world, believing that their good works should stand for themselves. John went at his new task with gusto, reorganising the department and exhorting the Dr Barnardo's staff to help spread the word abroad.

He also initiated a bold new policy to capitalise on the goodwill that existed towards Dr Barnardo's in the entertainment world, where a number of its alumni were to be found, by staging charity concerts to raise funds. His colleagues now saw a new face to the unsmiling sergeant major: "He was particularly happy when dealing with 'theatrical people'," one says. John especially enjoyed mingling with the performers in the greenroom after the shows; even if vicariously, his show-business dreams had been fulfilled at last.

Almost from the start, John took his son to these occasions – and at Christmas, 1956, Kristina saw the effect they had on an impressionable nine-year-old boy. John took both her and David to a show at Catford town hall, where they saw Tommy Steele perform. Afterwards Kristina went backstage with John and David, and heard John relate how his own son had "aspirations as a performer" too. "Uncle John," she observed, "enjoyed all the celebrities and the whole world, that touch of glamour." John had given David an autograph book which he worked assiduously to fill. He did so, Kristina says, because he knew "that Uncle John really wanted him to be a star". In that moment, she believes, David's own ambition was born.

Kristina returned to Plaistow Grove for the last time at Easter, 1957. Her mother Una had contracted cervical cancer and in April lay dying in Kingston Hospital. Kristina travelled up from Devon to visit her – the first time she had seen her mother in four years – and afterwards stayed at the Joneses'. On April 15th, she and David went to the cinema to see *The Hunchback of Notre Dame*. When they came home, Peggy told Kristina that her mother had died. By now, Kristina was numb to life's onslaughts. "David was very sweet," she says. "He gave me a hug and a kiss and told me that I still had him."

Peggy had remained in contact with Kristina's father, Kurt Paulsen, and wrote to tell him of Una's death. Paulsen replied to say that although it would be "difficult to fill the gap" caused by Una's death, he felt he should "shoulder the responsibility which is rightly mine". Early in 1958 Kristina left England for North America, where further trials awaited her. She was not to see David again for fourteen years.

In September 1957 David, together with Dudley Chapman, began his final year at Burnt Ash. Their relationship with Mrs Baldry now entered its most apocalyptic phase. One morning Mrs Baldry stumbled over one of Dudley's legs, splayed out beyond his desk. She told Dudley that he was "wicked and uncontrollable" and complained to his parents that he had tripped her up deliberately. Then she marched Dudley and David into George Lloyd's office and demanded that he set them more work. Lloyd told Dudley and David: "I think you're ripe to go and see my sister."

Marjorie Lloyd ran the 18th Bromley Wolf Cub pack, attached to St Mary's Church opposite the end of Plaistow Grove. David and Dudley visited the pack in its wooden hut, decorated with charts of the Cub badges and a Union Jack, and joined up soon afterwards. Marjorie Lloyd remembers David as "a good lad, neat and willing – a very reserved, clean and polite boy, who got on well".

David was a dedicated Cub too, and his green Cub jersey soon bore a good selection of badges; he also became a "sixer". The highlight of the year was the summer camp, held on a farm near Bognor Regis in Sussex. "We had a tremendous time, really superb," Dudley remembers. Among the star attractions were the pies – "real steak pies" – served at a time when memories of meat-rationing were still strong.

It was through the acquisition of the techniques of guerrilla warfare, learned on the *maquis* of the Sussex Downs, that Dudley and David finally felt they had obtained the upper hand over Mrs

Baldry. Only a small diversion on their way to Cub meetings on Friday nights took them past her front door, which became the target for a hail of missiles. "Stones, lumps of mud, anything, bangers come firework night – throw it and run," says Dudley. "We were just kids."

Not for much longer. In January 1958, David's eleventh birthday heralded the dramatic intersect known as the eleven-plus. A set of examinations taken in a single day determined not only the children's next school, but also, because of the segregated educational system, the probable course of the rest of their lives.

For the boys of Burnt Ash, there were four possible outcomes. Firmly at the top in order of preference was the independent school, Dulwich College; but only one or two each year from Burnt Ash would enter its exalted gates. Next came Bromley Grammar School, within reach of most of Mrs Baldry's class. Below that was Bromley Technical High School – "the Tech". At the bottom, came Quernmore: the local secondary modern, intended to supply the nation with its factory workers, clerks, and shop assistants. The pressure from parents, on both children and teachers, was intense. "They all wanted their children to go to the grammar school," Mrs Baldry says. "I was supposed to be a sort of magician who could wave a wand and get them in."

David sat the examination in January, shortly after his eleventh birthday. The results were announced by Easter. He had missed the grammar school but won a place, respectably enough, at Bromley Tech. By the lights of his parents, however, he had failed. With the examples of Terry and Kristina before them, they felt that he too should have gone to a grammar school. His aunt Pat recalls the fraught atmosphere in Plaistow Grove that ensued. "They were very upset and so was David, because he felt he had let them down."

Dudley Chapman really did fail. He was consigned to Quernmore, thereby sundering his friendship with David for ever. On July 24th, 1958, Mrs Baldry's class met for the last time. There was a rather surprising ceremony, for the boys of her class had clubbed together to buy her a present (the girls gave her individual gifts). The idea had come from Dudley's mother, and it was David who was nominated to make the award.

"David Jones came out with a big parcel all wrapped up in paper and said, 'This is from all the boys to you,'" Mrs Baldry recalls. Inside was an outdoor seat which has pride of place in her garden today. Dudley remembers the occasion too. "This was a new woman," he says. "She cried."

5

Bromley Rebel

On the opening day of the new school year, in September 1958, David caught the number 410 bus outside Bromley North station for his first journey to Bromley Technical High School. The bus took him to Keston on Bromley's southern borders, where the parks and gardens of suburbia give way to authentic farms and woodland, and deposited him fifty yards from the school entrance in Oakley Road. His first sight of the school can hardly have been encouraging. Its gates were set among spiked iron railings whose penitentiary appearance was only partly mitigated by the trim privet hedge behind. Beyond, amidst expansive green playing fields unknown in the inner cities, rose a brisk example of utilitarian 1950s design, with red walls and long windows, relieved only by the modest flourish of a brief flight of steps leading to the glass doors of its main entrance.

The school's principal aim was equally brisk and utilitarian. It was to provide the nation with its artisans: designers, technicians, engineers. Its pupils were not to be fuelled by too much ambition; much better that they should leave school at sixteen, work diligently in the offices and workshops of South London and northern Kent, and take their place in the uncomplaining life of the suburbs.

At first, it seemed that David had accepted his lot. Alan Gonzalez, who was in the same class as David throughout their five years at Bromley Technical High School, recalls the mostly uninspired teaching they first received: "Put it on the blackboard, copy it in your books." David dutifully did so. At the end of his first year, the school recorded that David was "reliable and quiet"; at the end of the second, that he was "a good steady worker who should do well".

A school photograph taken at the end of his first year shows a placid if unsmiling child, his hair conventionally brushed to one side, his tie neatly disappearing behind a grey pullover, and a pair of pens tucked into the top pocket of his blazer. But that calm exterior – just like the smiling face shown to Mrs Baldry – served to conceal further conflicts, caused by Terry's return from the RAF.

*

Terry had completed his three-year stint in the RAF in November 1958, just two months after David began at Bromley Tech. His return to Plaistow Grove was marked by an eruption of feeling made more devastating by its contrast with the family's habitual determination to suppress its emotions. For when Terry, RAF kitbag on his shoulder, had returned to Plaistow Grove, and – so he thought – to home, Peggy told him abruptly: "You can't stay here."

Peggy asked Terry in and made him a cup of tea. She explained how, during his absence, John had demolished the wall between David's bedroom and the boxroom Terry had regarded as his, which meant that there was nowhere for Terry to sleep. "Anyway," she added, "John doesn't want you here."

Later that day, Terry arrived at the home of his aunt Pat. She was now engaged to be married – her fiancé, Tony Antoniou, was a chef who had come to Britain from Cyprus several years before – and they were living together in a two-room flat over an optician's shop in Finsbury Park. In visible distress, Terry told Pat what had happened. She invited him to stay, and Tony lent Terry £50 to buy some clothes.

A day or so later, Terry went back to Plaistow Grove to collect his belongings. John Jones was there. As Terry related afterwards, John was "ever so nice" and asked how he was. But Terry was consumed with rage over his latest rejection and, with his childhood oath to kill John surging through his mind, grabbed his jacket and pushed him against the wall.

"I had wanted this moment to come," he told Pat afterwards. "I said I was going to pay him back for the way he had treated me all those years. But he was terrified, shaking like a leaf, and I felt sorry for him. I thought to myself, 'Is this the man I've hated all these years?' I thought to myself, 'I can't be bothered, he's nothing,' and I walked out."

Terry returned to Finsbury Park where Pat told him he could stay for a while, sleeping on the put-you-up in her living room. He also went back to work for Amalgamated Press, this time as an accounts clerk at their offices in Farringdon Road, close to Fleet Street. There he was befriended by an engagingly bluff fellow-worker, Bill Berks, who for a time provided Terry with a semblance of the family life he craved.

Bill Berks was the closest equivalent to be found in British trade unionism to a power boss. He came from an East End family, and worked in the East Enders' preserve of the national newspaper printing industry. Like his father, Bill belonged to the British

Communist Party, and was an official of the print union NAT-
SOPA. It was through politics that Terry first came to Bill's notice,
for Terry was acquiring radical ideas of his own. He read the *New
Statesman* and often spoke at the union's chapel meetings. They
had a second point of contact through sport, for Bill was also
captain and manager of the works soccer team.

According to Bill, who later left the printing industry and moved
to Cornwall, Terry "begged" him to let him play. Bill put him in
the team's defence at right-back, alongside Bill at centre-half. "He
had no confidence in himself at all," Bill says. "He wasn't that
good either, and I used to have to cover for him. But he gave 101
per cent."

It was in the same protective spirit that Bill watched over Terry
at work, allocating him a generous share of the casual shifts in
Fleet Street by which print workers would earn the fat of their
living. But Terry proved an unreliable protégé. By then he had left
Pat's flat and was living by himself in a bed-sitter in Notting Hill.
He often overslept and so Bill would drive to Notting Hill to fetch
him. Soon Bill suggested that Terry should come and live near him.

Bill and his wife Madeleine – her name was always shortened
to "Mad" – had a house in South London, at Forest Hill. Bill's
parents owned a house in nearby Herne Hill containing a small
attic flat, with its own kitchen and a view over the South London
rooftops, which Terry rented for 35 shillings a week. Bill's mother
Florence remembers Terry as "a smart and handsome chap. He
always wore a nice suit and a tie, and I always remember his lovely
teeth. He was no trouble at all – he was the best tenant I had."

Mad has fond memories of Terry too. "He was lovely. He had
black hair, blue eyes, gorgeous teeth, he was about six feet tall, a
handsome man." Mad helped him equip his kitchen, going on a
shopping expedition with him to buy a tin opener and other
utensils, and stocking his cupboards with tins of food. This act of
home-making was a potent one for Terry. "He was thrilled to have
his own possessions," says Mad. "He clasped them to his chest,
and said: 'These are mine.'"

The truth was that the Berkses were providing Terry with the
nearest version he had known to a warm and responsive family
life since leaving his grandparents' home in Southborough. He
lived at his flat during the week, but at weekends stayed with Bill
and Mad. On Friday nights, Bill and Terry, with several friends,
would indulge in the male pursuit of visiting Soho to make a round
of drinking and gambling clubs. On Saturdays, they stayed at
home. Bill relished the intellectual stimulus Terry offered: as well

as the political interests they had in common, Terry had an encyclo-
paedic knowledge of subjects that ranged from 1940s movie stars
to the history of cricket. They also stayed up into the small hours
to play long, attritional games of chess.

"Our games were very stubborn and competitive – no one
wanted to give an inch," Bill says. When Mad complained to her
mother that Bill's interest in her was being so far diverted, her
mother gave Bill a Scrabble set. The Scrabble contests extended
even further into the night than chess. "Mad could have throttled
her," says Bill.

Mad developed her own friendship with Terry. When Bill
worked a Sunday-afternoon shift in Fleet Street, Terry would
confide to her his feelings about himself and other people. Mad
knew that during the Friday-night jaunts to Soho Terry sometimes
went with prostitutes, and was puzzled why so handsome a man
should do so. "He said that he couldn't afford the luxury of falling
in love. He didn't mean he couldn't afford the money, but at that
time I didn't know what he meant."

Later, Mad acquired a better insight into Terry's needs. Terry
used to stay in the spare bedroom in Forest Hill, but after Mad's
first child was born there was no longer any room for him. One
Saturday night the Scrabble session lasted even longer than usual,
and Mad invited Terry to sleep on their settee. "I found some
blankets and slung them at him. But he laid down and said, 'Go
on, tuck me in.' He just wanted me to tuck him in like a mum,
although I was only two years older than him." Terry snuggled
expectantly beneath the blankets. "So I stood there and tucked
him in and he went to sleep."

Terry also showed Mad a battered photograph that he always
carried in his wallet. It depicted a handsome and smiling middle-
aged man, if also somewhat overweight, wearing a silk shirt. Terry
told Mad that his name was Wolf Rosemberg, and that he was his
father.

Terry had acquired the photograph as the result of a dramatic
intervention by Pat. Increasingly angered by the treatment Terry
had received from John Jones, she had resolved to appeal to
Rosemberg for help. She traced him via the International Red Cross
to the city of Oran in Algeria and telephoned him there, asking if
there was any way he could assist Terry. Rosemberg told her that
he always kept a photograph of Terry as a baby on his desk – it
was the one Peggy had sent to his parents – and said: "I always
wanted him." Rosemberg then wrote to Terry, enclosing a photograph of himself, and asking him to come and live in Oran.

As Terry told Mad, he had turned his father's invitation down. "I don't know him," he said. "He's never contacted me over all these years, and he's a stranger to me." Yet he still carried Rosemberg's photograph and often showed it to Bill and Mad. He also revealed his feelings towards his step-father, describing how John Jones had mocked him when he tried to ride a bike. "Terry loathed that Jones bloke," says Mad.

Through all these conflicts, there was one respect in which Terry's feelings never wavered. That, as Bill reports, was his affection for David. "I remember him saying at work, 'My brother's got a guitar,' and he thought that was terrific. He was very proud of David, and he used to go and see him all the time."

After his confrontation with John Jones, Terry had stayed away from Plaistow Grove for a time, and saw little of David. Upon his return to South London, with Bromley a comfortable three-mile bus ride from Forest Hill, he began to see David regularly again. And if that provided one fixed point in Terry's life, for David there was an equivalent gain. David had absorbed Terry's clash with his father with his customary impassivity. But he was now able to enjoy the protective friendship of an elder brother who, having departed for the RAF a wan and uncertain teenager, had returned a man, handsome and muscular, witty and worldly-wise.

Terry helped David discover a new world beyond the drab confines of the suburbs. He took David to jazz clubs in the West End, buying him Coca-Colas while he drank beer. He also introduced David to the writings of the beat authors like Jack Kerouac, with whose lonely existential journey through life he naturally empathised; David enjoyed reading them too. "I thought the world of David," Terry said later, "and he thought the world of me."

The resumption of his relationship with Terry, and the broadening of his horizons that it brought, led David to reconsider the possibilities offered at Bromley Tech. In place of the conformist pre-adolescent, a restless teenager emerged who was determined to test the boundaries of the adult world. No longer would David win praise for his quiet reliability and steady work; instead, says his classmate Alan Gonzalez, there appeared a David "full of ideas and a very strong character. There was no way the school system was going to mould him."

At the start of his third year at Bromley Tech, David was fortunate in coming under the aegis of a man who also rejected the limitations the system imposed. The head of the school's art section, which David had joined, was an enthusiastic teacher named Owen Frampton.

Frampton had taught art in the borough since the war and rejected the customary distinctions between the "academic" and "creative" aspects of educational endeavour. At Bromley Tech he had merged art, design, and technical skills, and equipped a studio with the tools for drawing, painting, photography, pottery and plastics alongside each other. "I wanted T-squares hanging next to paintbrushes," he says. He also had the confidence to tolerate behaviour that more orthodox staff regarded as outright rebellion. His charges "damn well knew that if they got into trouble, old Frampton was there to get them out".

Frampton's colleagues looked askance at this state within the state and would ask sarcastically if he considered himself part of the school or not. His former pupils have almost universal respect for his aims. Alan Gonzalez says he was "someone who didn't talk down to you". Another contemporary, Colin Clark, remembers him as "a very good arts master". A third, Trevor Blythe, regarded him as "a bumptious little sod", but adds: "I liked him though."

And so David began to spread his wings. Owen Frampton says, without showing undue ardour, that David "worked well at his art – he always enjoyed his art work." As with his first music lessons at Burnt Ash, David equipped himself with the *lingua franca* of the subject. His contemporaries remember him more for the skill with which he stretched the school rules, always stopping short of their breaking point. "He was bloody clever," says Alan Gonzalez. "He could balance on a knife-edge."

All schools that enforce the wearing of school uniform contain a dissident group determined to modify it as far as possible. It was David who wore a slim-line version of the school tie by folding over its sides and stitching them down at the back. It was David who dressed in shirts with button-down collars and the tightest of drainpipe trousers.

When pointed "winklepicker" shoes came to Bromley as part of a sudden incursion of Italian styles into Britain, David wore them too. He became an outright style leader by being the first boy at Bromley Tech to own a pair of chisel-toe shoes – "while everyone else," says Alan Gonzalez, "was still in winklepickers and trying to wear them out".

David's stylistic innovations became increasingly bold. Three years after the photograph in which he appears as the model pupil looking straight to camera, the school posed for its photographer again. This time David is casting an impertinent sideways glance, while his hair, in marked contrast to the sea of trim heads around him, is brushed upwards and marked by a garish blond streak.

David's hairstyle was, in fact, the result of an experiment that had misfired, although, characteristically, he could not resist dramatising the circumstances. Several weeks beforehand, he had attempted to cut his hair himself, with predictably disastrous results. In the morning he met Colin Clark. He told Colin: "I've got to go to the hairdresser and get this tidied up," and asked him to cover for him at school. But – as an alternative to revealing his own botched job – he also claimed that he had been at a party where a group of boys had taken such objection to the length of his hair that they had held him down and hacked it off.

At home, David's parents regarded his rebelliousness with weary resignation. Another schoolfriend, Brian Brough, often stayed to tea, which usually consisted of tinned spaghetti – "David always chopped his up into little pieces," Brian recalls – and he remembers Peggy as "a tidy, practical, mumsy sort of person, making sure he had clean shirts and ate properly and that sort of thing". Alan Gonzalez says that Peggy fussed over David continually: "Have you got this, have you got that?" Her efforts were often in vain. "David took full rein – unlike mine, his parents couldn't control him 100 per cent."

That was exemplified most notably by the occasion when David decided to repaint his bedroom, assisted by Alan Gonzalez. "He got a load of black paint and we spent the afternoon decorating it with cave-paintings – bison, men with bows and arrows, that sort of thing – that we copied from an encyclopaedia." Alan judiciously left for home before the storm broke. "It wasn't appreciated, I know," he says.

David's closest friend at Bromley Tech, and the replacement for Dudley Chapman in his affections, was George Underwood. The son of a local greengrocer, George was another of the school's style leaders, wearing an Elvis Presley haircut whose quiff tumbled over a face sadly despoiled by spots. For a long time he and David were inseparable. They were invariably among the group of boys who hid behind the school cycle sheds to smoke or play cards, out of sight of the school physics master who scanned the grounds for miscreants with a telescope.

They were also at the centre of the legendary event when they performed impersonations in the playground of several of their less effectual teachers, watched by almost every boy in the school. "It was one of those rare occasions when an incident attracts the whole school, like lemmings," says Alan Gonzalez. "It took more than one master to break it up."

It was in partnership with George that David's musical interests, from the seeds planted by his father and by Dudley Chapman, began to grow. While Dudley had left the 18th Bromley Wolf Cubs on going to Quernmore, David had stayed for one more year. George was a member too, and in 1958 they had attended a final camp together on the Isle of Wight.

Marjorie Lloyd was in charge as usual. (She has particular reason to remember the occasion, for she drove as far as the Isle of Wight ferry before realising that she had forgotten the tent poles, and had to return to Bromley to fetch them.) David, she recalls, insisted on taking the single-string bass he and Dudley Chapman had made from a tea chest. George had a guitar, and the pair of them performed during the pack's sing-song by the traditional campfire. They chose the Lonnie Donegan hit of the previous year, 'Hang Down Your Head Tom Dooley', and 'Sweet Little Sixteen', the Chuck Berry number which had also reached the British hit parade. "The Cubs thought they were marvellous," Marjorie Lloyd says.

Since then, their greatest shared enthusiasm had become Elvis Presley. David had inveigled his father into buying him a guitar – the one that so delighted Terry – and he and George took their instruments to school, strumming them in the playing fields or on the art-block stairs. They were sometimes joined by Owen Frampton's son Peter, who was also a pupil at the school, and who later played with the Herd and Humble Pie. David played his guitar on the school steps during the school's summer fête in 1962, and George organised an impromptu group – George and the Dragons – for a concert soon afterwards. But David was not included, and his contemporaries felt that of the two, George was the more likely to achieve fame as a musician.

David's friendship with George at school did, however, leave an important – and visible – mark on David's career. For it was George who caused the injury that left David with his eyes startlingly at odds with each other, imparting an appearance that proved so fitting to the dissonance of some of his later personas. It has been written that the injury resulted from a bitter fight between David and George over a girl – or, more sensationally, a boy. As the school secretary, Mrs Sheila Cassidy was the first to attend to David when he was led into the headmaster's office. She sat him in a chair and applied a cold compress to the damaged eye. "My recollection is that they were in fact good pals and it was a simple argument over a girl," she says. "George didn't intend any real harm, but he had a ring on that caught David's eye."

The headmaster, Frederick French, took David in his car to the accident department of Farnborough Hospital, half a mile away. There it was found that the sphincter muscles in his left eye had been damaged, so that the pupil, instead of dilating and contracting with the light, remained open, permanently impairing his sight.

While David has usually made light of his injury, at times he has told a more melodramatic story, asserting that he was in hospital "for months". The point can be resolved through David's continuing passion for things American. The story of his interest in American football has been widely told: how he would recite the latest scores to his friends, and how, on writing to the US Embassy, he was rewarded with a helmet and a pair of shoulder-pads, which he triumphantly brought to school.

David also spent one summer playing baseball. A mile from Plaistow Grove, at Beckenham Place Park, were the headquarters of the Beckenham Blue Jays, a baseball team formed by Canadian ex-servicemen after the war. In 1962 its manager was Harry Laing, whose son Philip was the team's star batter. David attended practice sessions throughout that summer, although making less of an impression as a player – "he wasn't one of the better ones", says Harry Laing, politely – than as the owner of a brand-new catching glove, supplied as usual by John Jones. "That was quite remarkable," says Philip. "You could only buy them at Lillywhites and they came expensive because it was a minority sport. Most of us had old hand-me-down equipment, usually cadged from US bases."

David never made the team. "He didn't seem to have much natural ability," says Philip. "I think he liked the game because it was associated with the United States. He was also attracted by the uniform." But it appears that David's eye injury, sustained that spring, did nothing to impair his modest talent. "I simply wasn't aware of it at all," Philip says.

The most lurid story concerning David's school days is contained in an interview published by *Playboy* magazine in 1976. The interview began, predictably enough, with the question of sex, and David did not disappoint *Playboy*'s readers. He said that sex had first become important to him when he was fourteen: "It didn't really matter who or what it was with, as long as it was a sexual experience. So it was some very pretty boy in class in some school or other that I took home and neatly fucked on my bed upstairs."

This is not a David recognised by his contemporaries at Bromley

Tech. Brian Brough was often admitted as an honorary member of the Jones/Underwood partnership, and he spent a summer holiday with David and his parents in a caravan at Great Yarmouth. There, he and David consorted with "a couple of thick girls from Blackpool". David's girl was several years older than him, "fitting his whole pattern of wanting things earlier than he should have done". But David, says Brian, never showed sexual interest other than in girls, even if the friendships in Great Yarmouth went sadly unconsummated: "It never got remotely as far as that."

At the end of David's fourth year at Bromley Tech, in the summer of 1962, the staff recanted from their previous optimism about his prospects. He was, they concluded, "a pleasant, friendly idler but perhaps capable of better work with maturity". Although David continued to idle during the fifth year, there was one startling moment when his imaginative powers suddenly flowered. David had been manifestly bored during English lessons, until he surprised his teacher and his friends with a brilliantly evocative composition relating the thoughts of a condemned prisoner on the eve of his execution. "We were astounded," Trevor Blythe says. "The English master loved it and read it out. It was streets ahead of anything he had ever done."

For the time being, the composition remained a solitary exception to the verdict of his teachers. In the summer of 1963 David took his GCE examinations, the school magazine recording that he obtained a single O-level pass, in art. By contrast, eleven of his colleagues, among them Trevor Blythe, Brian Brough and George Underwood, passed art at A-level. The school's final judgment reflected this inglorious result. David was "a complete exhibitionist – if he was capable of continuous effort his ability would have been put to better use."

That view was supported by the school games master, Ted Ward. At sixteen, David had grown into a tall, spindly youth, 5 feet 11½ inches tall but weighing only 8 stone 13 pounds. His physique was ideal for basketball and he became reasonably proficient at the sport, and he was also a competent hurdler. But Ted Ward was forced to conclude that David was "an extrovert who likes playing about – he has wasted quite a lot of his ability."

Did the school but know it, David was by then proving that he was indeed capable of continuous effort. He had also resolved not to waste his ability and to put it to good use. It may not have been the purpose that the school had in mind; and it did not accord with his school friends' judgment that it was George Underwood

70

who was more likely to become a star. David was already determin-
edly committed to a musical career.

David's West End visits with Terry, and his increasing fascination
with jazz, had led him to ask his father to buy him an alto
saxophone. John Jones, as always, succumbed. The model David
chose was made of acrylic, which lacked the resonance of a metal
version and had the further disadvantage that if dropped it shattered into hundreds of pieces. But the band leader John Dankworth
used one and David was further attracted by its gaudy appearance:
white, with gilt keys.

At first, David tried to learn his instrument by himself. It was
Terry who, on hearing his first discordant efforts, suggested that
he take lessons, and recommended the saxophonist Ronnie Ross
as a tutor, whom they had seen playing on their excursions to
the West End. Ross had a considerable reputation in the jazz
world: he had performed at the Newport Jazz Festival and had
played with Woody Herman and the Modern Jazz Quartet
on British tours. He also happened to live near David, in Orpington.

In the spring of 1962, Ross thus received a phone call from a
diffident fifteen-year-old schoolboy asking to teach him to play the
alto sax. Ross responded cautiously at first, as he only took on
pupils he felt were serious about wanting to learn. "For the time
it takes to teach somebody," he says, "I'd rather do some practice
myself." But David persisted, and Ross agreed to give him lessons,
once a week for the first three weeks, once a fortnight thereafter,
for which the fee was a modest £2 an hour.

Ross enjoyed teaching David. "He arrived highly motivated and
was well prepared for the learning," Ross says. "He was quite shy,
but he had a good sense of humour. He definitely showed an
aptitude for music, and he was very interested in jazz." Ross was
impressed that David knew the differences between traditional,
mainstream and modern jazz, whose followers were then in a state
of civil war. Ross himself revered the American saxophonist Charlie
Parker, who virtually invented modern jazz. He told David: "It's
no good just playing the saxophone, you must have something in
your head you're trying to achieve. Listen to various people and
try to get that sound into your head."

David unhesitatingly chose Parker as his mentor and played his
records over and over again at home. Ross admired David both
for his audacity and his perseverance. "You notice when people
work at things, because some people when they come back they
give excuses, they've been busy," Ross says. "But he always came

back and he'd done what I'd given him to do. He was a student and he wanted to learn."

After three months David had learned a handful of scales, the basic rhythms of his instrument, and the rudiments of musical notation. The next step was to learn harmony, and beyond that lay the promised land of improvisation. But in August 1962, David came for his last lesson. Ross remembers the occasion well, for David was bursting to impart some news. Before even removing his saxophone from his case, he revealed to Ross what it was.

"He told me he had joined a group."

6

A Dream or Two

The gathering place for aspiring musicians in Bromley was Vic Furlong's record shop, near Bromley South station. In 1962 it had a busy and expectant air, like the newsroom of a newspaper, as its customers awaited the latest Elvis Presley release and followed its inevitable ascent to the top of the British hit parade. It also served as the local equivalent of London's Denmark Street – Tin Pan Alley – where musicians congregated, like casual labourers, in search of work, for Vic Furlong had supplied a noticeboard where groups in search of members, and members in search of groups, could offer their wares.

The shop's further attraction was that it stood opposite a Wimpy bar. No matter that its hamburgers consisted then of a scrawny tissue of minced beef between two lifeless halves of a bun, or that its coffee had the aroma of stewed acorns. In the suburbia of the early 1960s Wimpy bars had, in the jargon of the advertising world, a Unique Selling Proposition. They provided young people with a warm, dry and moderately comfortable place to meet.

Among those attracted to this dazzling social ambience in 1962 was a twenty-year-old merchant seaman, recently retired, who had just arrived in Bromley. In due course, he too placed an advertisement on Vic Furlong's noticeboard which stated that as an "ex Cliff Richard drummer" he was looking for work. His claim was – just – true. But his brief encounter with Cliff Richard was only one stop in an eventful passage through the first two decades of his life.

Dave Hadfield was born in Lancashire in 1941. His mother was a barmaid, his father disappeared before he was born, and he had two step-fathers, one of whom Dave had long believed to be his natural father. He spent his childhood in South Africa but returned as a teenager to Hertfordshire where he attended Cheshunt High School. Among his contemporaries was a guitar player named Harry Webb. Dave did "a few tiny gigs" with Harry before the latter soared to stardom as Britain's response to the new sounds arriving from America, Cliff Richard.

At sixteen, Hadfield joined the merchant navy and became a

fourth officer sailing on passenger liners. Four years later, having concluded that he was wasting his life, he quit the navy and went to live with his grandmother in Bromley. He spent £90 of his £100 savings on a drum kit, pinned his advertisement to Vic Furlong's noticeboard, and waited to see if his grandmother's telephone would ring in response.

The person who called said his name was Neville Wills. He immediately impressed Hadfield by speaking in the languid drawl that marks out the alumni of Britain's public (though really private) schools. Wills said that he belonged to a "little group" called the Kon-rads that was looking for a drummer. Soon afterwards, Hadfield met the other two members of the group. One was Alan Dodds, a young man with strong religious tendencies from Shirley, yet another featureless southern suburb on the borders between Bromley and Croydon. The other was a tall and remarkably thin schoolboy named David Jones.

Dave Hadfield learned that the group had only just been formed, and gathered that its members had met one another in Vic Furlong's and/or the Wimpy bar. As for its curious name, he was told that it derived from a solitary appearance on stage with the singer Jess Conrad who had introduced them as "my Conrads". Apart from making an obscure alteration to the spelling, they had been unable to think of anything better.

It was not long before Hadfield, who was several years older than anyone else in the group, became the Kon-rads' new leader. More surprisingly, it was David Jones, five years his junior, who joined him as its driving force. The two Davids quickly discovered that they shared a determination to graduate to a full professional career. "David and I were very very serious about it," says Hadfield. "David showed more or less total commitment. Of all of us, he had the most positive view of becoming successful. He had no doubts that he was going to do it, no doubts at all."

The Kon-rads at first comprised Alan Dodds and Neville Wills on guitars; Dave Hadfield on drums; and David Jones on a metal tenor saxophone, with which he had replaced his acrylic alto. The group played at church halls, youth clubs, dances and socials along the suburban fringe, with their greatest appeal lying in their renditions of current hits.

It was still the time when the Musicians Union ruled the British airwaves, insisting that only a limited amount of recorded music could be broadcast, so enabling its members to retain their privileged employment within the BBC. The BBC tried to pretend that the journeyman musicians who formed bands like the Northern

Dance Orchestra had become young and vibrant overnight, even though they still ground out lifeless travesties of the hits of the day. But this meant that in 1962 there was no shame in being a band which attempted to perform its own versions of top-twenty songs with greater pizazz than the BBC could muster.

A list of the numbers performed by the Kon-rads at Cudham village hall on November 17th, 1962, issued by Dave Hadfield with instructions on how they were to be played, tells its own story. It contains 58 titles, ranging from classic swing to current hits: from 'In The Mood' ("twist") and 'China Doll' ("swing"), to 'The Young Ones' ("mod") and 'Sweet Little Sixteen' ("fast") – the first song David had ever performed in public, at the 18th Bromley Wolf Cubs' camp.

At first the group rehearsed at the home of any member with parents tolerant enough to allow them to use their front room – David's never did – but later graduated to a church hall on Bromley Common, charging their fans two shillings each to watch. The two Davids worked hard to improve the group's presentation by designing and building their own scenery, constructing a rostrum, and carrying their own lighting. They also daubed fluorescent paint on their hands and guitars so that they glowed in an ultra-violet light which they had also installed. "We had a great affinity on the theatrics," Dave Hadfield says.

The group expanded as it became more popular, taking on a guitar player who said he was called Rocky Shahan and came from Brazil: only much later did the Kon-rads discover that his name was Chaudhari and he came from Pakistan. The Kon-rads also enlisted two sisters, Stella and Christine Patton, as singers. The Pattons had one vital extra attribute: a mother with a driving licence, who used to take them to their venues in a converted newspaper van, until Dave Hadfield passed the driving test himself.

Stella Patton, who came from a church choir in Orpington, never felt easy in her role. "I could sing all right, but I didn't enjoy it very much – I was rather shy," she says. But she enjoyed being part of the Kon-rads. "What made them stand out from most of the groups in the area was that they were good musicians and they weren't satisfied unless their sound was perfect – they had a very professional attitude right from the start." She especially admired David: "He was always playing to the crowd, he was a good showman and went down well."

The Kon-rads' rewards were hardly exorbitant: around £15 per gig between them, although this was vastly boosted when they managed to win bookings on the "Bar mitzvah circuit", playing to rich Jewish households on the celebration of their sons' adulthood. These occasions paid between £40 and £60 but remained, in the terminology of the profession, "bread gigs". "They were a bit conservative and strained," Dave Hadfield explains. "You'd do a number and get polite applause. Not like our local boys and girls, yelling and jumping up and down and having fun." David, he adds, "thought they were awful".

By the spring of 1963, Dave Hadfield felt that the Kon-rads had done all that could be expected. "We used to play a lot of material and get absolutely mobbed – we were even signing autographs, which was ridiculous. We were very good at what we did." But there was one member of the group for whom that was not enough: David Jones. Even so early in his career he became impatient with the restrictions the group's success imposed, displaying a drive to experiment and to expand beyond the limits of convention.

David's first dissatisfaction was with the group's clothes. The Kon-rads wore grey lounge suits, white shirts, diagonally striped ties and elasticated suede shoes: the acme of suburban respectability. For a more casual appearance, they would wear brown corduroy jackets and green corduroy trousers. "They looked very smart," says Stella Patton. But David felt that the group should be bolder. To show what he had in mind, he painted a picture of an American-style zoot suit with triangular shoulders and broad lapels. As an alternative – and following his American theme – he suggested a wild-west outfit.

Neville Wills in particular was horrified at the notion that he should dress up in boots and leather. "It was totally alien to us at the time," says Hadfield. "Our image was appealing to the youth clubs where the kids were fairly straightforward and conservative and middle-class. It was the wrong timing. We just couldn't see that it would improve what we were doing."

David also considered the group's name. There he was on safer ground since no one else liked it either. His most imaginative suggestion was the Ghost Riders, but that did not win approval and so they remained the Kon-rads. He and Dave Hadfield discussed alternatives to their own names too. Hadfield toyed with "Tony Heath" but did not feel convinced enough to change. David complained that his surname, Jones, was "boring" and "didn't have any magic". For a time David called and signed himself Dave Jay.

Then David revealed that he was considering a new name, which derived from his deepening fascination for the mythology of the American west. He talked about a Texan adventurer who had died at the battle of the Alamo and who had given his name to a frontier hunting knife. "He had become his hero for some reason – I don't know what turned the key," says Hadfield. "But he couldn't decide whether to call himself after Jim Bowie or not."

The most serious conflict between David and the rest of the group concerned the material the Kon-rads were performing. Although David could parrot the stream of hit-parade material as effectively as the others, he was also writing his own songs, copying them out on exercise-book paper and asking Neville Wills to help him compose the music. Sometimes he would elaborate a tale from a brief item he had read in a newspaper, and occasionally would produce a song that was intended to be half-recited, something like a talking blues, rather than sung.

Here, especially, David was fighting the commercial climate of the times, when hits were predominantly manufactured by the Svengali figures at the apex of the business, and performers were treated like obedient ciphers. "Writing your own material in those days was like reaching for the heavens," Hadfield observes. "David kept coming up with these songs with Neville but they weren't really very good."

Some of David's songs were performed by the Kon-rads' most consistent singer, Roger Ferris; George Underwood deputed for him once or twice, and sometimes David sang his songs himself, in his wavering, untrained voice. As group leader, Hadfield tried to slip David's compositions among the reproduction hits, telling the audience: "This is one of our original numbers and we're going to play it especially for you." But they aroused little enthusiasm, which made Hadfield anxious in turn. "They used to fall quite flat. I was extremely worried when we used to get to those points. Probably we didn't have the courage to take the risk. We were so popular playing cover versions and I didn't want to lose our popularity."

The conflict came to a head in August 1963. By then, David had left Bromley Tech, speeded by the careers master's farewell advice: when David said he wanted a career in music, the master suggested that he apply to work in a local harp factory. Owen Frampton found David a job as a graphic artist in an advertising agency in Bond Street, the Design Group Ltd, with which he persevered for about six months. But there were already greater prospects with the Kon-rads, for the group had been offered a studio test with Decca Records.

That summer, Decca was known as The Company That Turned Down The Beatles. Having been rejected by Decca, the Beatles had signed a contract with EMI, and their first number one, 'From Me

To You', had just occupied the top of the hit parade for seven weeks. Decca were desperately searching for new groups that would restore both their nerve and their face. In June Decca had released a record, 'Come On', made by the unknown group the Rolling Stones, which reached number twenty-six in the hit parade. The man who introduced Decca to the Rolling Stones was the agent Eric Easton, who was now hoping to repeat the trick. Easton's assistant Bob Knight saw the Kon-rads perform in Bromley and approached Dave Hadfield. "He said he thought we were quite good," Hadfield says, "and we fixed up the audition."

The news threw the group into consternation, and there was intense discussion over which number they should play. Dave Hadfield argued strongly for one of David's own compositions, for he felt that if the Kon-rads were ever to become well known they needed a record that would establish their own identity. David naturally supported him, and the others agreed. They considered three or four of David's songs and chose one with a strong refrain: 'Chorus verse chorus verse, fade after two minutes," Hadfield says. It was one of David's elaborations on a news item which, so far as Hadfield recalls, concerned an air crash.

On August 30th, the Kon-rads drove to Decca's recording studio in Broadhurst Gardens, West Hampstead, where they were led into a room that felt, to Hadfield, the size of an aircraft hangar. He remembers "three or four guys looking at you through a glass panel with a 'well-get-on-with-it' sort of attitude. The whole nervousness was quite appalling, we were literally shaking, and I was almost physically sick."

After a brief warm-up they performed David's song, with David himself taking the vocals. In two minutes it was all over. Soon afterwards the recording came thundering back at the Kon-rads through Decca's giant speakers. "We smiled a bit and felt like the pictures we had seen of the Beatles listening to their playbacks," says Hadfield. "We thought this is it, it's tremendous. But it never materialised."

Eric Easton and Bob Knight were as gentle as they could be in breaking the news that the Kon-rads had been turned down. "They said they thought we were quite good," says Hadfield. "The story we were given, true or untrue, was that they felt we had some sort of potential, they weren't sure what, but they would like to keep us on ice for the time being and take us back to the studio at a later date."

The Kon-rads held an anguished post-mortem – had they chosen the right song, after all? – and the most downcast by far was David.

"He had set his sights on it," Hadfield says. David's disappointment led him to reconsider whether his path to stardom could be achieved with the Kon-rads after all. "That sparked the point where he realised he wasn't going to get anywhere with us," Hadfield adds. Not long afterwards, David left the group.

David's departure set a pattern which was to be repeated several times in the next few years. Each time, David became restless at being restricted by the conventions of taste and commerce, and sought to expand beyond them; each time, he was thwarted. His greatest frustration lay in the lack of enthusiasm that met his attempts to purvey *his* songs – and *his* message. As Hadfield remarked of his stint with the Kon-rads, the time was not yet right.

In 1963, Hadfield thought the schism was all for the best. "If we had got the contract I think there would have been even more problems, frankly," he says. "It would have shattered the group with David taking over the whole thing with three or four of us feeling left out." The Kon-rads, minus David, persevered on the suburban circuit, achieving the zenith of their career when they toured as the opening act with the Rolling Stones.

Occasionally they bumped into a disconsolate David at Vic Furlong's or the Wimpy bar. "We were rather nasty in a way. He wouldn't say much, he'd say he'd formed another group, and he'd ask what we were doing." Triumphantly, the Kon-rads would reply: "We're touring with the Stones."

That autumn, Terry was adrift in London too. He had made an attempt to find a new life 300 miles away, in Cornwall. It had ended in disappointment and rejection.

Early in 1962, the measure of stability Terry drew from his friendship with Bill and Mad Berks had seemed about to end. Bill was tiring of working in the print, and so he and Mad decided to buy a newsagents' shop in Falmouth, a friendly harbour town with a thriving summer tourist industry on Cornwall's south coast. In April they sold their house in Forest Hill and moved into premises in Falmouth's winding main thoroughfare, Arwanack Street. Soon afterwards, Bill's parents moved down to Falmouth to join them.

The Berkses' departure presented Terry with a painful dilemma. Should he remain in London, where he could still see David? Or pursue his substitute family to Falmouth? The Berkses dropped hints that, with their business debts to pay off and a growing family to look after, they would have less time for Terry than before. Terry chose to ignore the hints and followed them to Falmouth that summer.

The Berkses' warning proved all too accurate. "We were up to our neck with the mortgage and we were working very hard," says Bill. "He wanted us to spend time together as we had done in London but I couldn't."

Mad, who now had two young children, was equally preoccupied. Before he left for Cornwall, Terry's mother Peggy had telephoned and asked Mad to let her know how Terry was faring: "He won't get in touch with me himself," Peggy said; "he's a boy with a chip on his shoulder." But Mad had no time to act as Terry's surrogate mother, and there was nowhere in the Berkses' flat above the shop for him to stay.

Terry lodged a quarter-mile away with a landlady whose son had recently left home and so was glad of a young man she could fuss over. But Terry also had to find work, and without Bill to watch over him, his first attempts ended disastrously. His first job was as barman at the Norway Inn at Perranarworthal, three miles out of Falmouth on the Truro road. Having worked in London according to a strict union rule-book, Terry found the Cornish attitude to employees' rights more than irksome. When the bar closed in the afternoon he would retire to his room for a sleep. As often as not the landlord would wake him to ask him to help unload a delivery of beer. "He got really bolshie and turned that job in," says Bill.

Terry's next job was even shorter-lived. He became a waiter at the Royal Hotel in Falmouth but on his first night smashed a bottle of wine that he had been struggling to open. He felt so humiliated by his old clumsiness that he walked out. He was finally hired as a barman at the King's Head in Arwanack Street, and was lucky that the job lasted into the winter, when the tourists depart and Falmouth drifts into hibernation.

With the loss of the Berkses' hospitality, Terry was fortunate to find a new friend in John Garwood, another former London print-worker. Although Garwood says now that he feels he never came to know Terry "deep down", he found him witty and companionable, and enjoyed the evenings they spent drinking together. They also indulged in young men's escapades, most notably after a lunchtime spent drinking when they and several friends set off into Falmouth bay in a small and unreliable motor-boat. The engine broke down and the boat was rapidly swamped; Terry, who could not swim, was wearing the only lifebelt. Luckily they had been spotted by one of the pleasure boats that plied from Falmouth pier. After they had clambered aboard the astonished passengers stared as they sat giggling in their saturated suits. (The episode is significant in another way, for David was later to claim that Terry was a merchant seaman who had twice sailed round the world. The sinking in Falmouth Bay – and an occasion when Terry and Bill Berks were photographed in Customs uniform, borrowed from a friend in the Falmouth Custom house – were the nearest he came to such a feat.)

For a time, it suited Garwood to join Terry in the pursuit of women for one-night stands. They formed a successful team, for Terry was an effective predator: quick-witted, lean and good-looking. One of his captures was a local Cub mistress, with whom he had congress on a heathery hillside outside Falmouth. But, as Mad observed, Terry still fought shy of any longer commitment, and she remembers an art student, "who thought the world of him", crying bitterly because he had abruptly broken off their relationship.

Gradually the delights of Falmouth wore thin. John Garwood found a steady woman friend and no longer wished to partake of the bachelor life; when Terry looked to the Berkses again he found them as busy as ever. With evident bitterness, Terry told them they had reneged on their socialist principles and were set on becoming capitalists; but his accusation was motivated less by ideology than by the rejection he once again felt.

As the summer of 1963 came and went, and the tourists departed once more, Terry foresaw a dull and comfortless winter, against which life in London regained its lustre. In the autumn he told John Garwood and the Berkses that he was leaving Falmouth. They made little attempt to dissuade him. Since he had no savings, Garwood took him to the station and bought his ticket. He shook hands with Terry, said goodbye, and saw him on to the train. As the train prepared to pull out, Terry looked at him through the window as if in mute supplication, then turned his head away.

7

No Game

Leslie Conn's introduction to music gave a strong foretaste of the confusion that seemed to beset his life. He came from a Jewish family in Stamford Hill, and was ten when he was evacuated to Cambridgeshire at the start of the war. There he was brought up by a Christian family who sent him to Sunday school and enrolled him in the choir of Ely Cathedral.

Conn's first job in show business after the war was the less saintly post of record plugger. It entailed an endless, deferential pursuit of the lords of the industry, chief among them the producers and disc-jockeys of the BBC, which meant by turns cajoling and exhorting them to play his clients' records. On one occasion in London he wined and dined a BBC producer who then refused to take the record Conn offered him. The producer was due in Plymouth for a broadcast that evening and so Conn drove there ahead of him, to be holding out the record as the producer arrived. (This time, it was accepted.)

Conn's efforts to create interest in his clients won praise and damnation in equal measure. Max Bygraves called him "the only man who could set fire to a bucket of sand". A manager named Phil Solomons, invoking those innocent pre-decimal days, said that he was "the only Jew who could turn half a crown into a two-bob bit".

From plugging records, Conn turned to managing, but here his record was less equivocal. Among the singers he failed to turn into stars were the Barry Sisters, Shirley Sands and Derry Hart. True to the Jewish habit of telling stories against oneself, Conn calls himself "the most successful failure in show business". Among his failures was David Jones.

In the autumn of 1963, Conn was working with Dick James: and if Conn could claim to be the unluckiest man in show business, Dick James was one of the most fortunate. Once a crooner who recorded such titles as 'Tenderly' and the theme from the ITV series *Robin Hood*, he became a music publisher in 1961. The following year a blushing young man brought a demonstration disc of a song entitled 'Please Please Me' into James's office in Denmark Street.

The young man was Brian Epstein, and James promptly became part-owner of a company, Northern Songs, which held the rights to publish songs written by John Lennon and Paul McCartney. Now James had asked Conn to see if he could help direct a second shaft of lightning to land in the same place. If that could be arranged, the two men agreed to share the proceeds, fifty-fifty.

As if to encourage him, Conn first heard about David Jones by a chance almost as miraculous as his partner's discovery of the Beatles. After David had left the Kon-rads, his father had been searching for ways to use his expertise as publicity officer on his behalf. At his prompting, David wrote to seek the assistance of a washing-machine manufacturer, John Bloom.

Bloom's story, it seemed then, was the paradigm of the British dream: ambitious entrepreneur makes and sells washing machines, undercutting the major manufacturers to achieve savings for consumers and profits for himself. He was also a figure for the age. Under the benign eye of Harold Macmillan, the Conservative government had just begun its twelfth year in charge of Britain's still-buoyant economy, where brash go-getters like Bloom could reap ample rewards. David's letter caught the spirit of the times. If Bloom would furnish "several hundred pounds" for new equipment, they could both get rich.

By then, in fact, Bloom's dream was beginning to fade, and bankruptcy loomed; for the Conservatives, too, time was running out. To Bloom's credit, he did not ignore David's letter. He had known Leslie Conn as a boy in Stamford Hill, and sent David a telegram with Conn's telephone number, suggesting he get in touch. David duly did.

When David met Conn, he said that he belonged to a group called the King Bees, which had five members. One was George Underwood, who had resumed his partnership with David on graduating from Bromley Tech to Ravensbourne College of Art. They had teamed up with three other musicians, several years older than themselves, whom they had met in Bromley: Roger Bluck, who played lead guitar; Dave Howard, bass guitar; and Bobby Allen, who, like David, worked on the lowest stratum of a West End advertising company, and played the drums. The three were schoolboy friends from Fulham who had formed a group in the skiffle days and used to practise in the garage at Allen's home.

The clue to the group's musical approach, and to the style David had lately adopted, lay in their title. It was taken from the blues lyric 'I'm A King Bee' — "I'm a king bee, baby, buzzin' round your hive" — which was the best-known composition of the Louisiana blues singer Slim Harpo. For the blues, and their urban successor, rhythm and blues, had infiltrated the British hit parade. Their most effective proponents were currently the Rolling Stones. Slim Harpo was a hero of the Stones too: 'I'm A King Bee' was one of their favourite numbers, and they included it on their first album. It was typical of their repertoire for its coded references to sex and sexuality, thereby deceiving those unworldly custodians of taste, the BBC.

As the Rolling Stones strengthened their grip on the British hit parade, they had no shortage of imitators. Among them were the King Bees, who like them sang of passion and desire, of sexual athletics and impotence, of alcohol and drugs, all concealed in the black man's *argot*. The King Bees especially liked to emulate the songs of Muddy Waters and Little Richard, further salutations to uninhibited sexuality.

When Conn first saw David and the King Bees perform, he was pragmatic enough to see that where the Rolling Stones were heading, the King Bees might follow. He says that he also perceived enormous promise in David, then approaching his seventeenth birthday. "He had natural charisma," Conn says. "He had magic. He was as broke as any of the kids in those days but he walked around like a star. He had that quality, that star quality, right from the very first minute I met him." Even discounting the element of hindsight in Conn's judgment, he had identified some of the propitious qualities observed by Dave Hadfield. "David believed in himself absolutely," Conn says, "and he was prepared to work very hard for success."

The most generous gloss on Conn's first action on behalf of David and the King Bees is that his enthusiasm for their potential led him to misjudge their market. It happened that John Bloom was about to hold a wedding-anniversary party in a Soho club named the Jack of Clubs, and Conn recommended that the King Bees should provide the music. Before a dinner-jacketed audience that included not only Adam Faith and Lance Percival, but also senior Jewish dignatories such as Lord and Lady Woolfson, the King Bees sang first Muddy Waters's penile exultation, 'Got My Mojo Working', and then his celebration of home-distilled alcohol, 'Hoochie Coochie Man'. "The noise was deafening," Conn recalls. "People had their hands over their ears. I told Davie, 'Cut it, cut it!'"

David was in tears. But Conn told him not to worry about "these people" and reassured him, "You impressed me." He offered to become David's manager, and David agreed. Conn visited Plaistow

Grove and secured the approval of David's parents for a contract which made him David's manager for the next five years, with the option to renew for a second five.

Conn now set about his task of providing Dick James with the next Beatles. He aimed to do so via the method he knew best: a record, which could be plugged to success. He asked Decca to loan him one of their studios in Broadhurst Gardens for the afternoon, in return for first option on the record the King Bees made. Decca, who did not connect Conn's protégé with the lead singer of the group they had turned down six months before, agreed.

For the session, the King Bees chose a Negro spiritual, 'Liza Jane', which – in George Underwood's words – they had "played around with". What emerged was a standard British R and B (rhythm and blues) number that lasted just two minutes thirteen seconds and had little to distinguish it, apart from a few virtuoso squeals from David's tenor sax, from numerous similar offerings.

For the B side, they recorded 'Louie Louie Go Home', which consisted of an unashamed attempt to reproduce a composition by the US group Paul Revere and the Raiders. A version recorded by a second US group, the Kingsmen, was a hit in the US in the summer of 1963, although the Kingsmen had introduced several obscene lines that led to it being banned by numerous radio stations. The King Bees' version was seemly enough, apart from one reference to a woman's moans. Its main interest lay in the King Bees' decision that, having tried to emulate the Rolling Stones on one side, they might as well copy the Beatles on the other. David did his best to imitate a John Lennon blues-shout in the vocals, supported by yodelling cries from the rest of the group.

The session lasted for seven hours, much of it taken up by the efforts of the engineers to obtain the requisite amount of sound from Bobby Allen's drums: they were, he said later, "real cheap", and patched with tape. Allen nonetheless felt that it had been a "very spontaneous session", claiming that this was mostly due to himself and his two Fulham colleagues.

Conn took the demonstration record to Decca's subsidiary, Vocalion, who agreed to produce 3,500 copies. Now he was in his element. He had photographs taken in which David and George at last fulfilled David's aim of wearing leather boots, even if they were soft suede versions in the style of the ITV series, *Robin Hood*. Conn also issued a publicity notice – "from the press room of the Dick James organisation" – which hailed David as "a handsome six-footer with a warm and engaging personality" who had "all it takes to get to the show business heights". 'Liza Jane' was "a beaty, action-packed disc which features the direct no-holds-barred Davie Jones vocal delivery", with "a hard-core, R & B backing".

The record was released on June 5th, 1964, and Conn's greatest coup was to have it played the next day on *Juke Box Jury*, the BBC's latest attempt to engage the attentions of that alien breed, young people. While each new release was played, four "personalities" – usually anything but young – alternatively looked studious, perhaps ostentatiously making notes with the pencil the BBC had provided, or beamed into the camera.

The jurors on June 6th were Diana Dors, Britain's nearest equivalent to a cinema sex symbol in the 1950s; Jessie Matthews, who occupied the title role in the BBC's middle-class soap opera, *Mrs Dale's Diary*; the comedian Charlie Drake; and Bunny Lewis, a promoter and manager whose best-known client was Dave Whitfield, a ballad singer of the pre-rock era. Of the four, only Charlie Drake voted the record a hit.

But David's father was still working hard on his behalf, using the contacts he had developed at Dr Barnardo's. Among them was the novelist Leslie Thomas, himself a former Dr Barnardo's boy, who was then working as a music columnist on the London *Evening News*. John Jones called to tell him that his son David was a pop singer who had just produced his first record. According to Thomas, John's personal verdict on the record was unenthusiastic. "He said, 'I think it's awful, just terrible,'" Thomas says. John added: "On the other hand, Decca have just given him a contract, so would you listen to it please?" Thomas obliged by writing a charitable paragraph about the record in his column.

Conn now judged that the time had come to present David to Dick James. He decided to do so in company with another ambitious young client in his charge, one Mark Feld, who later became Marc Bolan. As Conn describes it, the meeting was a culture clash between the generations: on the one hand, David and Mark, "very abrasive, very aggressive, passionately believing in themselves and doing the big star thing when they were broke"; on the other hand, Dick James, who had been in show business for over thirty years and believed in the old-fashioned virtues of deference and hard work. According to Conn, James's conclusion was brisk and to the point: "You're wasting your time."

James, who died in 1986, disputed Conn's account. He admitted that he had no recollection of meeting David at all, pointing out that a steady stream of hopeful young men were passing through his office at the time. However, he denied that he would have spoken so dismissively to Conn: "I wouldn't dream of addressing anyone like that."

Either way, Conn's failure to convince Dick James of David's worth ended their joint search for the next Beatles. Conn says that he resigned from their partnership on principle: "I didn't see any point in staying after that." James put a different gloss on Conn's departure. "No one in my organisation would have tried to stop him leaving," he said.

Conn moved into a room at 23 Denmark Street, lent by a neighbourly publishing company, rent-free. He remained David's manager, and helped the King Bees to find dates at clubs and colleges, mostly around Bromley. Since their earnings were minimal – "literally peanuts", Conn says – Conn took no commission from them: "They weren't earning enough to make it worthwhile." David and Mark repaid Conn by painting his office instead.

'Liza Jane' made no impression on the hit parade. And, as with the Kon-rads' abortive recording session, its failure served to crystallise David's growing dissatisfaction with the King Bees. He had left his design job with the Bond Street advertising agency, and music was his sole means of support. "It's all right for you," he complained to George Underwood. "You're at college. I'm in this up to my neck." In the summer of 1964, David told Conn that he had left the King Bees and was looking for another group. In that case, Conn told David, he had precisely what he was looking for.

The group in question, the Manish Boys, came from Maidstone, a place distinguished by very little save its chance status as Kent's county town, and the looming walls of its prison that greet visitors who have driven the forty miles from London. In 1964 the group had existed, in one guise or another, for four years. It began as a skiffle group, doing its best (like everyone else) to copy Lonnie Donegan's hits. Next it became a traditional jazz band. Then it called itself the Jazz Gentlemen, occupying the hinterland between jazz and the dance music of the 1930s, made suddenly popular by a group named the Temperance Seven.

In 1963 it changed again, to become Band Seven, hailed in the *Kent Messenger* as "Kent's Newest Rock Band with that BIG (note the baritone sax) Sound". The *Chatham Standard* talked of Kent's "new powerhouse beat septet" and wondered if the "Medway Beat" could challenge Liverpool's leadership of the British record market. In January 1964, encouraged by such accolades, the members of Band Seven decided to become full-time professionals.

The most enthusiastic advocate of the move was Paul Rodriguez, then nineteen, who had learned the French horn at school and played bass guitar and tenor sax. "We wanted to escape from being just a Kentish band," he says. Paul gave up his job as a local newspaper reporter to concentrate on his new career. The group's baritone sax and harmonica player, Woolf Byrne, a twenty-two-year-old industrial chemist, acknowledges that it was all "a tremendous gamble". But, he adds, "musically we felt we had found a goal."

The band's bookings remained all too local – the Royal Star Hotel in Maidstone, the Central Hotel in Gillingham, the East Farleigh Women's Institute Hall – and so they decided to change their style and their name again. They were heavily swayed by their organist, Bob Solly, a devotee of the American blues, with an astonishing collection of the renowned 'Blue Note' LPs imported from the US. In no time at all, says Woolf Byrne, Band Seven had been "totally converted", and Kent's powerhouse beat septet became a blues group.

For a new name, they followed the Rolling Stones in looking to the repertoire of Muddy Waters. They chose his 1955 hit 'Manish Boy', the story of a youth who boasts of his manhood, and thus became – faithfully observing the original misspelling – the Manish Boys.

At this point, the Manish Boys decided to go to London in search of work. Like every other musician from the "provinces" – the disparaging term used by Londoners to describe anywhere outside London – they headed for Denmark Street. There, behind the steamed-up windows of a coffee bar named the Giaconda, the rulers of the popular music industry conducted a large proportion of their business over an espresso coffee and a cheese sandwich. It was at the Giaconda that the Manish Boys met Leslie Conn. He agreed to become their agent and found them bookings at London's leading R and B venues, such as Eel Pie Island at Twickenham and the Flamingo Club in Wardour Street.

By August, the Manish Boys felt that their professional career was safely under way. They were earning £15–£20 a week each and owned a Bedford Dormobile to transport them to gigs. (To be strictly accurate, Woolf's father had loaned them the purchase price, which they were repaying week by week.) The group had settled down at six: Paul Rodriguez, Woolf Byrne and Bob Solly; plus Johnny Flux, on lead guitar; Mick White on drums; and John Watson, a singer who also played guitar. "We felt quite positive about things," says Paul.

It was at precisely this time that David told Leslie Conn that he had left the King Bees and was looking for a new group. It took only a short stretch of imagination for Conn to conclude that David and the Manish Boys should be conjoined to the advantage of all. Conn called the Manish Boys to impart the news that appeared to herald a further advance in their career. He told them he had found a new singer who would be ideal for their group. "He's someone you must have," Conn added. "His name is David Jones."

The only David Jones anyone in the Manish Boys had heard of was a black American singer who – so Bob Solly said – was building a reputation on the European night-club circuit. He sounded ideal, and so they suggested that he should come to their next rehearsal, to be held at Paul's house the following night.

The Manish Boys gathered at Paul's home with an expectant air. They had just started to rehearse when Conn arrived, together, says Paul Rodriguez, with "this Belsen-like refugee figure with blondish hair down to his shoulders". He was patently not the celebrity Bob Solly had described. "We were somewhat disappointed," Paul adds, "at his pallor."

The Manish Boys contemplated their prospective new member, who also carried a saxophone, without enthusiasm. But they were now offered a powerful lure. "We were given this terrific story about how they had got this American tour lined up," Paul says. "Without that, I don't think we'd have taken him. We were happy enough as we were."

So David joined the group, with the idea – at least in the minds of the Manish Boys – that he would be subsumed into their collective personality in the same manner as Mick Jagger and the Rolling Stones. For the moment, that appeared to satisfy David too. He took part in their rehearsal and by the end of the session the Manish Boys had warmed to their recruit. "He had a hell of a good voice and he was a very good sax player," says Paul. "He was a better musician than any of us."

David also extended the group's awareness of American music, bringing them news of James Brown, whose hip-pumping R and B act was electrifying black audiences in the US. When the Manish Boys heard his album *The James Brown Show Live At The Apollo*, it was, Paul says, "as if heaven had been opened up to us". David also performed a dramatic impersonation of James Brown himself. "He had got the American thing off so nicely and that was what we really wanted."

The Manish Boys thus graduated from the blues to rhythm and

blues and were soon playing at towns and resorts throughout southern England. Conn also secured a series of bookings at the prestigious Marquee Club in Wardour Street, a former jazz club that had become a popular venue for R and B groups, who enjoyed its friendly, intimate atmosphere. David soon established a strong rapport with its audiences. "They reacted more to him than to anything else we did," says Paul.

It was largely through David's manifest appeal that he now assumed a curious, unspoken dominance within the Manish Boys: as Paul Rodriguez says, "We all fell under his influence." The immediate effect was on the group's hairstyles. Before David's arrival they were a moderately trim group of young men. David's hair, by contrast, reached his shoulders – and by the end of the year both Woolf Byrne and John Watson were wearing theirs almost as long. John Flux dyed his hair the same custard colour as David's, causing consternation among his colleagues when it grew out at the roots.

To Conn, these excesses were manna, and he was soon telephoning his Fleet Street contacts to offer them a "story". Among them was Leslie Thomas, who obligingly wrote a report in the *Evening News* of November 2nd on the formation of "The International League for the Preservation of Animal Filament". David, described as the organisation's "Founder and President" – and as leader of the Manish Boys – explained that "the League" was intended for "the protection of pop musicians and those who wear their hair long . . . Anyone who has the courage to wear his hair down to his shoulders has to go through hell."

Conn's next coup was an appearance for David on the BBC TV magazine programme *Tonight*, on November 12th. David – now described as president of the Society for the Prevention of Cruelty to Long-Haired Men – told Cliff Michelmore: "For the last two years we've had comments like 'darling' and 'Can I carry your handbag?' thrown at us and I think it just has to stop now." John Watson was interviewed too, and when he claimed that they were planning CND-style protest rallies, David made the quick-witted interjection: "Baldermaston." He and John were even paid five guineas each for taking part.

The Manish Boys were naturally delighted that David's position as the group's style leader brought such advantageous results. But there was another, more controversial respect in which he was making his influence felt: he had introduced an element into his stage act that was best described, in Paul Rodriguez's words, as "camping it up". As Paul explains: "He was doing outrageous things for the time. He was affecting mannerisms that were decid-edly camp. He was making a great thing of it, mincing around on stage."

In Britain in 1964, sexual relations between men were still against the law and homosexuality was virtually a taboo subject. The entertainment industry colluded in the silence. Only once had the word homosexual been spoken in the cinema, in the film *Victim*, starring Dirk Bogarde, which was released in 1961; while the radio series *Round the Horne* sent coded homosexual messages, in the mouths of the characters played by Kenneth Williams and Hugh Paddick, that were accessible solely to the *cognoscenti*.

In the theatre, homosexuality was represented only by the per-formances of female impersonators and pantomime dames, which in any case misleadingly implied that homosexuals found their main pleasure in dressing as women. These performances also appeared safe by remaining within the bounds of dramatic conven-tion, and it was in this light that the Manish Boys viewed David's behaviour on stage. While the current stereotype of homosexuals was, in Woolf Byrne's words, one of "nasty old queers in raincoats that we used to meet in Soho", Paul Rodriguez adds: "We didn't think David was 'queer' just because he was putting on this act. We just thought it was theatrical."

Here, too, the Manish Boys fell under David's influence, emulat-ing his camp mannerisms on stage. Only Paul Rodriguez remained aloof: "I just couldn't see that this was a way to develop an audience," he says. "That poofy camping around didn't seem to work, it was obviously wrong for the time." Paul felt that his objections were vindicated when they performed at the staid Nor-folk resort of Cromer, where the promoter told them they were "obscene" and warned them not to come back. And they had to make a rapid departure from Luton when their audience, predomi-nantly composed of motorcyclists belonging to the emerging stylis-tic tendency known as rockers, took vociferous exception to their act. "We left on the run," says Paul, who was playing trumpet that night. "The general feeling of the audience appeared to be that the trumpet player was all right but the rest were a lot of fucking poofters. In greasy Luton that was not the image to portray."

Although the Manish Boys have wondered since then how far David's behaviour *was* merely "theatrical", and how far it reflected his sexual orientation in a more fundamental way, this was not a question that arose at the time, even in the mind of Woolf Byrne, who usually shared a room with David while on tour. "He never worried me in the slightest," Woolf says now. "I honestly do not remember having any fears."

Any lingering doubts the Manish Boys may have had were further dispelled by David's conspicuously heterosexual behaviour with not one, but two women. The first was with a very pretty, short, dark girl who was enviously rumoured to be infertile, and thereby offering, at a time when the notoriously fallible condoms were the most-used contraceptive, *angst*-free sex. The second was with Dana Gillespie.

In the 1970s, Dana was to achieve some success in the entertainment world, appearing as Mary Magdalene in *Jesus Christ Superstar*, and Mahler's mistress in the biographical film by Ken Russell. But the highest echelons of stardom eluded her, and the reason lay partly – at least, so Dana believed – in her treatment by show-business writers, who could rarely resist the temptation to allude to her most prominent physical attributes, as the headlines showed: "Dana Gillespie is a big girl now." "Dana puts on a brave front." "Dana is all woman – every 44-26-37 inch of her."

Dana's background could hardly have been less like David's. She came from a minor line of the Austrian aristocracy – her full name was Dana Richenda Antoinette de Winterstein Gillespie – and her father was a prosperous Wimpole Street radiologist. As a sensuous fourteen-year-old, with dewy brown eyes and waist-length hair, she was already attending the Marquee Club when she saw the Manish Boys there. She was irresistibly drawn to their lead singer: "He had dyed blond hair down to his shoulders, one of the first men I had noticed like that. He looked great."

The next time the Manish Boys appeared she insinuated herself into the Marquee – "I was a very *forward* fourteen-year-old" – before the rest of the audience. "I was at a mirror brushing my hair and David came up and took the brush from my hand and carried on brushing, saying could he take me home that night, and I said 'absolutely'."

Home was an elegant Georgian house in South Kensington. "I sneaked him up past my parents' bedroom to the top floor and he stayed the night," Dana says. If she was left in no doubt as to David's sexual orientation the same could not be said for her parents. "My father said that he didn't know whether David was a man or a woman until he actually opened his mouth."

Soon they were seeing each other regularly, meeting in Denmark Street and drinking "endless cups of coffee" in the Giaconda. Intent on a show-business career, Dana was studying dancing and music. David would meet her after her evening drama classes: "He would

talk me home and we'd creep upstairs past my parents' bedroom."
Later, Dana moved into her own flat in the basement, which
became a port of call for David between tours. David taught Dana
to play her first guitar chords, followed by the song 'Love Is
Strange'. Dana remembers him as "determined, talented, and *different* – he knew what he wanted, and he wanted to do well".

On one occasion, David invited Dana to visit his parents in
Plaistow Grove. For her, the train journey to southernmost London
was an expedition to an unknown land. "I'd never been into a
working man's house before," she says. "We sat down and had
tuna-fish sandwiches, and the chairs had all those crocheted things
to soak up the Brylcreem and those little arm-rests and it was a
very cosy little room – absolutely tiny."

There was another characteristic that Dana assumed to be an
attribute of working men's houses. "He was one of the first people
I'd met where I had a feeling I was in a house where he didn't love
his parents like I loved mine, and I realised people lived in a
different way. I had a really strong culture shock from going down
and meeting David, not only because he came from a family where
they spoke with an accent whereas I speak the Queen's English,
but the whole kind of life. I knew nothing of it, I was completely
ignorant of it, and it didn't seem like a house with love in it."

The upward progress of the Manish Boys, meanwhile, had stalled.
Somehow, the American tour never materialised. Leslie Conn
introduced them instead to a German promoter who had connec-
tions in Hamburg, the city that had provided an apprenticeship
for the Beatles, and who promised them a German tour. The
Manish Boys were delighted: "Germany was the place to go to
tighten up your act," says Paul. "It was what everybody craved."
They cancelled all their British bookings, only to be told at the last
moment that the tour had fallen through.

Conn did manage to secure them a place on a British concert
tour, part of a package which included Gerry and the Pacemakers,
the Kinks, and Marianne Faithfull. It was the closest they had yet
come to stardom, whose rewards, they discovered, included the
salty porridge they were served in Scotland, digs where they were
charged two shillings for a bath, and groupies who insisted on
coming to bed with them but refused to remove their clothes. They
felt pleased with their reception and confidently awaited their next
invitation to tour. None ensued.

Their next hope lay in making a record, but this too proved a
dispiriting process. It began promisingly, when Conn persuaded

the producer Mickie Most to watch them perform. The Manish Boys were delighted, for Most had just produced 'The House Of The Rising Sun' for the Newcastle group, the Animals. "We did a cracking audition," says Paul. "Afterwards Mickie Most came bounding up and said, 'So – do you want to make records with me?'" Disappointment quickly followed. Most was working for EMI, David was still under contract to Decca, and the problem could not be resolved.

Then the Manish Boys did make a recording for Decca at the Regent Studios in Denmark Street, presided over by producer Mike Smith. But the recording, 'Hello Stranger', was never released because the singing voices of David and John Watson refused to "jell". They also recorded 'Love Is Strange' but that was not released either, largely because the Manish Boys themselves did not like it. "We all had mixed feelings whether it would work," says Woolf. "A few months later the Everly Brothers had a massive hit with it."

The next producer to try was the American Shel Talmy, who was working for Decca, and had produced a series of hits for the Bachelors, a trio of cleancut Irishmen who were quickly lionised by the BBC. For that reason the Manish Boys viewed Talmy with suspicion, and were in an unenthusiastic mood when they gathered at the IBC studio at 35 Portland Place.

For the A side, Talmy chose the song 'I Pity The Fool', which had reached the top of the American R and B hit parade in a version performed by the soul singer Bobby Bland. While the rest of the group was nervous, David appeared at ease – "He was definitely slipping into a very professional gear," Paul says – and produced an accurate facsimile of Bland's overwrought style. There was a polished contribution on lead guitar from Jimmy Page, who had been hired as a session man for the day.

But the Manish Boys were bitterly disappointed with Talmy's contribution. "We raunched it up," says Paul. "But Shel ignored some of the best bits in the original which was *tragic*, and we thought the way he did the whole brass riff was crude in the extreme. It had a counter-riff which Shel destroyed and it sounded crude and tasteless compared to the original."

For the B side, the Manish Boys recorded one of David's own compositions, 'Take My Tip'. Musically it owed much to the group's appearances at the Flamingo Club, with its brassy jazz backing reminiscent of Georgie Fame. Jimmy Page played rhythm guitar and there was an intricate bass line which David taught John Watson, note by note. David's tongue-twisting lyric told of the unrequited love for a woman who was variously a tiger with a scowl and who had more than one fish in her "back garden scene".

Once again there was disappointment. The bass guitar was badly distorted, as its amplifier had blown up. At the end of the session, the Manish Boys had a depressing sense of anti-climax. "It wasn't what we had wanted to do," says Woolf Byrne. "It didn't sound like we wanted it to sound and it certainly didn't seem the sort of stuff we were performing. It was an awful downer instead of a great upper which it should have been."

To add to the frustrations, a lengthy wrangle now ensued over whether Decca or EMI should release the record after all. The hiatus served to bring certain underlying conflicts within the group to the surface, for the rest of the Manish Boys were no longer quite so happy to follow David's example as before. They especially resisted his attempts to press his own material on the group – 'Take My Tip' was one of the few exceptions.

"We were not particularly impressed with David as a composer," says Paul. "He never seemed to come up with anything we wanted to play." Like the Kon-rads before them, the Manish Boys felt at their happiest when performing well-tried cover versions. "Doing original songs wasn't nearly so strong," says Woolf Byrne. "It wasn't what everyone was trying to do."

There was now also open disagreement over David's status within the Manish Boys. To outsiders, it must have seemed that David was happy to be an equal member of the group, particularly when he was quoted in the magazine *Beat '64* as saying: "I would sooner achieve the status as a Manish Boy that Mick Jagger enjoys as a Rolling Stone than end up a small-name solo singer." But that was all part of the skirmishing, for *Beat '64* was edited by Johnny Flux, and Paul Rodriguez had fabricated the quote to counter David's drive for a separate identity.

"When David got publicity it always seemed to say, 'Davie Jones and the Manish Boys', so any publicity we got, we made damn sure it didn't," Paul says. When their single was at last released in March 1964 – by the EMI subsidiary, Parlophone, after all – they also ensured that the only individual credit David received was as writer of the B side, 'Take My Tip'.

Despite the group's disenchantment, David himself was pleased with the record. The next time he met Dana in Denmark Street he took her into a record shop and asked to hear it. "He said, 'Listen, this is mine, I've just had it out this week,' and it was proudly played to me." It also presented Leslie Conn with a new chance to display his prowess; this time, he surpassed himself.

For an entire week, the national press was full of news of an astonishing row over plans for David and the Manish Boys to appear on the BBC TV pop programme *Gadzooks! It's All Happening*. The appearance was scheduled for March 8th. On March 4th, the *Daily Mail* reported that the BBC had banned David from appearing because his hair was too long. David was majestically quoted as saying, "I wouldn't have my hair cut for the Prime Minister, let alone the BBC," with the BBC's producer, Barry Langford, responding: "I'm not against long hair, but kids don't want it any more in their shows."

On March 6th, the *Daily Mirror* announced that the BBC would permit David to appear after all, provided that, if viewers protested afterwards, he would donate his fee to charity. On March 8th, the *Evening News* published a photograph of David having his hair set in preparation for the programme. And on March 9th – the morning after David had appeared – the *Daily Mirror* disclosed that he would have to wait two weeks to learn whether he would be paid. The *Mirror*'s reporter made his own feelings clear: long hair for males was "nauseating", evidence of "a sickness in the air".

No hint appeared in any of the reports that the events described were other than authentic, and they have been presented in unquestioning terms since. In fact, the entire episode was fabricated by Leslie Conn, with the BBC's producer, Barry Langford, happy to concur. "It was one of my promotional things," says Conn. "Of course Barry Langford was a great friend of mine and he loved the idea because it gave his show a lot of publicity." Paul Rodriguez confirms that the affair was "a planned stunt, totally preplanned". Unrepentantly, he adds: "It takes work to get those stories into newspapers – and that's what Les was so good at."

Sadly, Conn's stunt could not make 'I Pity The Fool' into a hit. One of the newspapers which publicised the long-hair imbroglio dutifully observed that it was "a nice record", but otherwise it disappeared almost without trace. So, soon afterwards, did the Manish Boys.

The catalyst was not the dispute over David's standing within the Manish Boys. It was the group's Dormobile. As they were unable to afford professional repairs, Woolf Byrne – on the strength of his expertise as industrial chemist – had been deputed to keep it on the road. He had been fighting a losing battle all winter. He once had to change its engine in a snowstorm, and the question of whether it was working "had become the most important factor in my life". When the Dormobile broke down yet again he announced that he was prepared to toil with it no longer. He left the group and took a job as a lorry-driver.

His defection proved decisive. The group had run out of both money and parents prepared to subsidise them. The other members looked for jobs too, with only Paul Rodriguez maintaining a foothold in the music world when Shel Talmy agreed to pay him £10 a week to write songs. But although there were "bitter feelings" in the group, Paul adds, there was no terminal row. "We just drifted apart."

The Manish Boys have often wondered about the American tour they were offered to persuade them to accept David into the group. On the worst interpretation, Paul Rodriguez says, it was a complete fabrication, and David "would tell any story and go through any tear-jerking act to achieve what he wants". Paul, however, is not inclined to quite so harsh a judgment. "There is a faint chance that it was true, or half-true. I feel there must have been *something* there."

As David contemplated his third successive failure in the spring of 1965, Terry was also in distress. On returning to London from Falmouth, he went to live with Pat, now married and living in a small semi-detached house in the West London suburb of Ealing. He found a job in the oven room of a local bakery, and seemed to enjoy his work. But Pat found him volatile, aggressive, and — having once been so fastidious — quite unconcerned about his personal appearance.

At first Pat assumed that Terry was in "an angry young man phase — rebelling against everything". But his moods became more abrupt and violent. "I used to have a row with him and say if he was going to behave like that, he'd have to find somewhere else to live, and then I'd ring him up at work and say I didn't mean it, and he'd say he knew I didn't."

Terry's behaviour, and Pat's dogged loyalty to him, did nothing to assist her marriage. To her husband's annoyance, she would stay up until two o'clock waiting for Terry to come home. "I used to treat him as my surrogate child," she says. It was a candid revelation of the important place Terry had assumed in her life, for she was unable to have children herself. Sometimes Terry would return drunk, or with his clothes torn from fights. "My husband was getting very funny about it and would say *he* didn't come in like that," Pat says.

Pat did not know that Terry's outward decline marked the onset of mental illness, nor was she aware of the extent of his deterioration. Only later did she learn that on some mornings Terry felt so unwell that he would wait for her to go out before creeping back home and returning to bed.

"I said to him so many times, 'If only you had told me, Terry.' I could kick myself. If only I had known, maybe I could have done something to help."

8

Bright Lights

There are uncanny similarities between the story of the Manish Boys, the group David had just left, and the Lower Third, the group he was about to join. They too were from Kent; they too, in search of fame and fortune, headed for London, and the Giaconda.

The Lower Third came from Margate, on Kent's north-east tip. The area is known as the Isle of Thanet, even though it is firmly attached to the rest of Britain; offshore, the English Channel merges with the North Sea, and the jaws of the Thames estuary beckon. With a row of fading seafront shops, an amusement arcade poignantly named Dreamland, and the skeleton of a pier ravaged by a fire, Margate does its best to present itself as a sunny seaside resort. In the winter, when the shops are shuttered against the wind, the arcade is closed, and the grey sea lashes at the wreckage of the pier, the illusion cannot be maintained.

It was from this bleak habitat that, like the Manish Boys, the Lower Third advanced their claims to be "one of Kent's top rock groups". Formed in 1963, with five members, their name was a confused attempt to capitalise on Thanet's sole literary asset, a brief relationship with Charles Dickens, who had written *David Copperfield* while staying at Broadstairs. They first called themselves Oliver Twist and the Lower Third, adding the second part because its Victorian public-school associations seemed somehow appropriate too.

Denis Taylor, the lead guitarist, a tall, angular young man who had left school at fifteen to work on the assembly line of a local electrical factory, is careful to explain that the group's name was not to be taken too literally. "It didn't mean we were schoolboys," he says. "A lot of groups had silly names in those days. We used to wear these silly little peaked caps too." The group soon jettisoned Oliver Twist from their name and then abandoned the peaked caps as well.

In 1964, the Lower Third won second prize in the East Kent Rock Group Competition, held at Dreamland. Soon they were venturing beyond Thanet, to appear at Sheerness and Sittingbourne at one end of the county and Folkestone at the other. Then they succumbed to the ubiquitous spread of R and B and changed their act, and were hired to play at an all-night session every Saturday at an R and B club in Wardour Street named La Discothèque. Upon returning exhausted to Margate on Sunday afternoon they would share out their earnings: £15, split five ways.

In April 1965, the Lower Third decided, on a 3–2 vote, to turn professional and to move to London. The two dissidents departed, leaving Les Mighall, the drummer and group leader, Graham Rivens, the bass guitarist, and Denis Taylor. They rented a flat in Pimlico for £12 a week and then, in the search for work, made for the Giaconda.

At first they were impressed with the apparent dedication of its denizens to the pursuit of wealth, seeming to fix endless deals over their cups of coffee. "Being a small-town group this was all a big wow to us," Denis says. "We thought if we were going to survive we'd better come to this place every day. We drank tea and coffee and talked to people. But it didn't do us much good."

Feeling handicapped by having only three members, the Lower Third recruited two saxophonists and a singer at the Giaconda. They secured only two bookings in the next three weeks, and the three recruits left. The Lower Third returned to the Giaconda to announce that they were looking for one new member, preferably a singer, and that they would be holding an audition at La Discothèque that afternoon.

One of those who attended, carrying his alto saxophone, was David. When he started to play he was joined by a group of musicians who had come to watch, among them Steve Marriott of the Small Faces, and the audition became an impromptu jam session.

"It went along very nicely," says Denis. "All the right sounds came out, it was James Brown sort of music, big American darkie type of music, but we were still wondering who we could get to sing. That was when we discovered that Davie was a singer and he started singing himself. We were quite impressed. Then we went back to the Giaconda for a cup of tea and egg and chips and we told him we wanted him for our singer. He was very pleased."

Like the Manish Boys, the Lower Third assumed that they had enlisted a new member who would rank as their equal. But David soon took a decisive hand in the affairs of the group, issuing a press statement which clearly showed how he saw his relationship with his new colleagues. "This is to inform you," David announced, "of the existence of Davie Jones and the Lower Third."

The statement continued in a similarly bullish vein. "Reputation-wise, Davie has a spotless chart. Having picked up the gauntlet in the now legendary 'Banned Hair' tale, he stormed into BBC2's *Gadzooks*, leaving such an impression that he has been contracted for yet another appearance this month." The Lower Third – clearly relegated to second place – would be providing "brilliant backings".

Even before the press statement was released, Les Mighall felt so disgruntled that David had usurped his role as group leader that he returned to Margate. It was David who chose his successor, Phil Lancaster, a short, stolid man, aged twenty-two, from a working-class family in North London, who had once played as a stand-in with the Dave Clark Five.

After Phil had placed an advertisement in the *Melody Maker* which read: "Drummer looking for a group," Graham Rivens telephoned and asked Phil to meet David at the Giaconda. There, Phil found "this bloke as skinny as a rake with a double-breasted jacket and shoulder-length blond hair which had been bleached and was growing out. I thought, 'Blimey, he looks a bit trendy' – but that was great."

Phil was expecting to be auditioned but David awarded him the job there and then. "We had a cup of tea together and I think we hit it off because we had the same ideals musically and a lot of the same tastes," Phil says. "I mentioned Bob Dylan and he immediately gave me a perfect impression of Bob Dylan singing. After that we just talked for a bit more and that was it, I was in."

David also dictated the new style of music the group adopted. British groups were finding a domestic context for the American idioms, conveying the concerns of British youth rather than those of American blacks. Foremost among them was The Who, whose first record, 'I Can't Explain', was released in January 1965. Soon afterwards The Who appeared on the ITV programme *Ready Steady Go*. Pete Townshend smashed his guitar, Keith Moon overturned his drums, and the new musical style of heavy rock was established. David and the Lower Third saw The Who at the Marquee, and were enthralled: "It was an absolutely fantastic experience," says Denis, "and Davie thought so too."

Largely at David's prompting, the Lower Third followed The Who's example. "We had a lead guitar making as much noise as possible, a drummer thrashing hell out of the drums, and the bass player looking moody," says Denis. "It really worked." David himself copied the extravagant mannerisms of Roger Daltrey, smashing his microphone against Phil's drums. Phil's fear that this was not all for the best was confirmed when David broke one of his cymbals, but Denis considered David "absolutely brilliant". And Phil could not help being swayed by the unwavering assurance with which David spoke of their collective future.

"He talked about his ambition," Phil says, "but it was always as a group. *We* were going to make it, *we* were going to be in the money. This was a dead cert."

For all David's optimism, bookings remained sadly hard to come by. In theory, Les Conn remained David's manager, but he appeared to have run out of ideas. David and Phil made the dispiriting round of Denmark Street offices themselves, to little avail. One promoter tried the familiar ploy of holding "live auditions" to induce them to play without a fee. David retorted: "We're professionals," and turned him down.

David now announced to the group that their best chance of advancement lay in making a record. He asked Conn to make the arrangements, telling the others: "At least he can do that for us." Conn booked the IBC studios and engaged Shel Talmy as producer. The Lower Third, unaware of Talmy's problems with the Manish Boys, were delighted, for Talmy had produced The Who's 'I Can't Explain'. The group was augmented by a pianist, Nicky Hopkins, for the session, and Glyn Johns was the engineer.

It was David who decided which songs to record, and he confidently chose two of his own compositions. Both resumed the theme of 'Take My Tip', on the frustrations and penalties of love. The message of the A side, 'You've Got A Habit Of Leaving', was straightforward enough. The B side, 'Baby Loves That Way', was more complex, with an early hint of the disconnected and exotic sexuality that later marked David's work. David sang of his lover who

> Treats me good each and every night

while at the same time she "fools around" with other boys

> Who treat her like a modern toy

Musically, 'You've Got A Habit Of Leaving' was strongly reminiscent of The Who — "the sort of thing we let rip with on stage", Phil says — while 'Baby Loves That Way' sounded like the British group Herman's Hermits. It included a repetitive four-note chorus that was supposed to resemble a monks' chant: the "monks" included both Talmy and Conn, with Conn – according to Phil, who was standing next to him – "really out of tune".

When the session was over, few present, it seemed, held out much hope that the record would bring the boost they needed. Phil for one was happy merely to have taken part, and even David was defensive about the record's prospects. He and Phil had just collected an advance copy when they met the singer Chris Farlowe in Denmark Street. Farlowe asked if he could hear it but David replied: "You won't like it." Parlophone evidently shared David's pessimistic feelings, for they showed no urgency in releasing the record.

The delay spelled the end of David's partnership with Leslie Conn: denied this final chance to display his promotional talents, he and David agreed to go their separate ways. It was, Conn insists, an "amicable" parting. "I simply said, 'Listen, David, I've tried everything in my power, why don't we just shake hands and split like good friends?'"

David retains warm memories of his friendship with Conn. In 1982, invoking one of his early American passions, David wrote an inscription in one of Conn's books. It read: 'For Les, from 1st base to home run!! Love David."

Conn's replacement, as manager to both David and the Lower Third, was Ralph Horton. In his late twenties, with a pudgy face, sandy hair and spectacles, he spoke with the nasal and slightly querulous accent of the English Midlands. He had begun his career in the music business in Birmingham, working as an assistant at an artists' agency that went bankrupt. He then came to London to work in Denmark Street and later became a road manager for the Moody Blues, the Birmingham group whose record 'Go Now' was a number-one hit in January 1965.

Horton met David in the Giaconda, and when David complained about the shortcomings of Conn, offered to take over as manager. That, at least, was the explanation David gave the Lower Third. "He wants to hear us," David added, "and we're going to do an audition."

The audition was held in a back room at the Roebuck, a pub in Tottenham Court Road. Horton, who wore a suit, was accompanied by a young blond-haired man, named Neil Andersen, said to be another singer. After David and the Lower Third had played two numbers David announced, without preamble, that Horton was to become new manager, and that the group's headquarters would henceforth be at 79A Warwick Square, near Victoria Station, where Horton shared a two-bedroom basement flat with a Denmark Street agent named Kenny Bell.

The Lower Third greeted this news without enthusiasm. Phil found Horton "a cold fish – I was suspicious of him. I wouldn't have called him a charmer. I didn't warm to him until later and then it was only luke-warm." Denis was even more hostile. "To be blunt, I didn't like the guy when I first met him, and when I left I didn't like him either."

Horton's first management decision concerned the group's appearance. David was still sporting the shoulder-length hair that had been so assiduously exploited by Leslie Conn, while the rest of the group had long hair too. Now David reported that Horton had decreed that they must have an "image". From an indeterminate appearance best described by Denis as "long-haired scruffs", they became "raving mods".

The mods comprised one of the most distinctive stylistic groupings in Britain since the war. Mods had short and elegantly cut hair. They wore brief post-Italianate jackets accurately dubbed bum-freezers, trousers with creases, and a variety of fashion shoes. In youth's tribal divisions, their great adversaries were the rockers, who clung to an image of grease and leather that had begun with the Teddy-boy era of the 1950s and was reinforced by the early Elvis Presley. Rockers rode motorbikes and travelled in packs with as much Hells-Angel bravura as they could muster; mods had Italian motorscooters and wore green anoraks to protect their clothes. From time to time the two factions would gather in ritual confrontation at some seaside resort, winning outraged headlines in the national newspapers, but rarely inflicting serious damage on each other.

Commercially, Horton's decision that the Lower Third should become mods made sense, for the mods were devoted to The Who. Horton escorted them to Carnaby Street, the mods' spiritual headquarters, and equipped them with light blue shirts, floral ties, dark blue hipster trousers, and chisel-toed shoes. He also took them to Charles of Queensway, where their hair was blow-waved into bouffant hives.

For the wary Phil Lancaster, these were unsettling events: the notions of decoration and display carried disturbing implications. Then came an incident at Warwick Square which, Phil says, "frightened me to death". Horton asked him to go out and buy a can of hair lacquer.

"To me, that was very effeminate," says Phil. 'I'd never known blokes to put hair lacquer on. I said I wouldn't go – to me it was being queer, or whatever. Ralph tried to persuade me. He said, 'You'll be all right, say it's for your sister,' and I said, 'I haven't got a sister.'"

But Horton prevailed, and when Phil returned, demonstrated how the lacquer would keep their hair in place when they went on stage. Phil gamely tried it himself. "It wasn't so bad after all," he admits.

Meanwhile, Horton's Denmark Street contacts were bringing work at last. He secured the group a regular Saturday-afternoon appearance in the *Inecto Show* at the Marquee. This was a product of the era of pirate radios, as the BBC refused to acknowledge the arrival of youth culture, and bands of renegades beamed the new music to Britain from wartime forts or fishing vessels in the North Sea. One station, Radio London, had arranged to record sessions at the Marquee sponsored by the makers of Inecto Shampoo.

For the Lower Third it was less than the glamorous occasion it sounded, for they merely played in the intervals between established performers and their contributions were not broadcast. It nonetheless helped David and the group to build a rapport with a regular audience for the first time. It also offered an ideal opportunity to perform David's own songs, now flowing more prolifically than ever.

David would present them to the Lower Third during their rehearsals at the Roebuck or the Marquee, singing the lyrics to a simple melody line on his guitar. Since he could not write music, he and the group then arranged the songs together. "Denis would try something on his guitar and David would say, 'I like that, keep that,'" Phil says. "We all put our own phrasing in and shaped the songs. We all had to like it and approve it, although David definitely took the lead."

Their repertoire included several songs by the Kinks, the unlikely Mary Poppins number 'Chim-Chimenee', and, to close, a thunderous rendition of 'Mars' from Holst's Planet Suite – the theme music from David's once-favoured television serial, *The Quatermass Experiment*. But it was David's own songs which the Marquee audiences applauded most. "We used to have a great following," says Denis Taylor. "People screaming, autographs, it was incredible – I really did feel like a star."

David and the Lower Third now embarked on the task of winning fans beyond London. For transport they had acquired a converted London ambulance, paid for by Graham Rivens's father. Since only Graham had a driving licence, he was appointed honorary chauffeur, and negotiated zig-zag itineraries the length and breadth of Britain. It was also Graham who had to hitch to the nearest garage when they ran out of petrol, a far from uncommon occurrence.

A warm camaraderie developed in the ambulance as it drummed along the motorways, Denis sitting in front with Graham, David and Phil stretched out in the back. David would frequently ask the others how they could make themselves "more sensational". One of his proposals concerned their closing number, 'Mars'. "David wanted to make it terrifically powerful, with world war two sirens and explosions," says Phil. "But it never came off."

David also suggested that they should all wear make-up when they performed. Like the Manish Boys, the Lower Third could not help noticing that David was becoming somewhat "effeminate" on stage, mincing his arms and sashaying his hips – although, Phil observes, "what was thought effeminate then is probably normal today". Despite his previous alarms, Phil was prepared to experiment with David's idea: "He meant clown's make-up, and as that was a normal thing in show business, I thought that was all right." It was Graham Rivens who vetoed the proposal from the driver's seat. "When we put it to him," says Phil, "we got a very duff response."

In general, it appeared that provincial audiences were not yet ready for David. "We'd be blowing our heads off and the locals would turn up and wonder what it was all about," says Phil. "It didn't go down at all well." The exceptions were venues where, as at the Marquee, they could build a regular audience who became accustomed to their style and repertoire. Thus they were most successful at Bournemouth, where they appeared every Friday and Sunday throughout the summer at shows promoted by Horton's flatmate Kenny Bell, and at Ventnor on the Isle of Wight, where they performed on the Saturdays between.

During these weekends, it was easy to feel that success was close. There was a pleasantly gregarious atmosphere on the Isle of Wight ferry, as the Lower Third mixed with groups like the Pretty Things and Johnny Kidd and the Pirates. David especially relished the sense that he was among his peers, and a series of photographs taken by Denis, on the quayside or on board the ferry, shows him confidently acting the star. While the other musicians look stoically to camera, David has a forefinger cocked under his chin, like Rodin's *Thinker*; or tilts his hips, like a call-girl; or poses like a dancer, arms outstretched, at the end of a routine.

Then came an encounter which revealed how remote their aspirations remained. One weekend at Bournemouth the Lower Third were exhilarated to discover that they were sharing the bill with The Who. Pete Townshend heard them rehearsing and came over to ask: "Whose stuff is that you're playing?" When David replied, "Mine," Townshend told him: "That's a bit of a cheese-off – it sounds like mine." Townshend did not press the issue but later that evening he touched on another sensitive matter. Evidently seeking reassurance over his own earnings, he asked Phil how much money he was making.

Phil found it an embarrassing question. "I didn't want to tell him because we were working for virtually nothing," he says. "We probably ended up with about twelve quid each for the weekend if we were lucky and I was just about paying the HP on my drums and I wasn't giving my mum anything. But he said, 'We're on fifty quid a week each, what do you reckon?' So I just said, 'That sounds all right to me.'"

The reality was that their live performances were bringing them barely enough to live on. Any faint hopes they had for their single 'You've Got A Habit Of Leaving' were dashed when it was released on August 20th. They heard it played on the radio two or three times but then it disappeared without trace.

Ralph Horton now embarked on an urgent search for other sources of income. He looked first among the music publishers of Denmark Street. In the 1960s, these were in danger of becoming a supernumerary breed, for their original role as the publishers of sheet music had been usurped by the explosive growth of the recording industry. Some sank into decline; but the more resourceful among them found a new role as middle-men between performers and their recording companies, enabling them to extract what was termed a "mechanical royalty" – 6¼ per cent of the retail price, to be shared with their clients whenever one of their records was sold. They also collected a performing royalty each time one of their songs was broadcast.

The most astute publishers were those who persuaded unknown performers or composers to sign contracts with them in return for modest advances – or even no advances at all – and then watch the proceeds multiply as their fame grew. The scale of the available rewards was shown when Dick James sold his 23 per cent holding in the Beatles' publishing company, Northern Songs, which he had acquired for next to nothing, for £1 million; and when Lew Grade who later acquired the company for £10 million, refused an offer from Paul McCartney and Yoko Ono in 1981 to buy it back for £21 million.

The first publisher to place David under contract was Hal Shaper, owner of a publishing company named Sparta Music, who first saw David perform at the Marquee. David was developing an alluring manner towards those he thought might benefit him: Shaper was impressed by the vulnerability of his act and a beguiling uncertainty in his off-stage persona. However, the "exclusive writing agreement" which David signed with Sparta on September 14th was hardly generous. It ran for one year, with Shaper holding an option to renew it for a second year, and promised David an advance of £10 against a fifty-fifty share of royalties each time a recording of one of his songs was released. For that, Shaper eventually acquired the copyright of sixteen of David's songs which were still bringing him appreciable rewards twenty years later.

The Sparta contract could do little to relieve the immediate financial pressures, and so, on September 15th, Horton visited a publicist and manager with an office in Marylebone, Ken Pitt. Pitt's standing in the music business at that time was high, for he had recently steered the Manfred Mann group to its first major success. Horton asked Pitt if he would help finance David and the Lower Third. Pitt turned Horton down, telling him that he was less interested in groups than in solo performers who would be a "long-term proposition".

Yet Pitt offered one significant piece of advice. He pointed out that there were several established performers named David Jones, including the actor who had recently appeared in Lionel Bart's musical *Oliver* – and later became the token Englishman in the Monkees – and said that it would be sensible if David changed his name.

When Horton passed on Pitt's recommendation, David already had an alternative to hand. No one in the Lower Third thought much of his proposal: Denis Taylor said it would "never catch on". Most disparaging of all was Horton's flatmate, Kenny Bell. "I came in and Ralph and David were in the lounge, and Ralph said, 'We've got a name for him,' so I said, 'What's that then?', so he said 'Bowie, David Bowie,' so I said, 'Well, that sounds fucking stupid' – Bowie knife, you know, fucking potty – and I went out and made a cup of tea."

(Inaccurate as these predictions proved, several misconceptions have persisted over the Bowie name. The first is that the man who invented the Bowie knife was named Jim, the Texan adventurer who died at the battle of the Alamo in 1836. In fact it was designed by Jim's brother Rezin, after he had lacerated three of his fingers with an orthodox hunting knife. Rezin's knife, usually around fifteen inches long, had a strong finger guard between the blade and the hilt, and was balanced so that it could be thrown. It was Jim who made the knife popular after using it in a fight on a Mississippi sandbar in 1827.

The second misconception concerns the name's pronunciation. David himself elected to pronounce it "bo", to rhyme with go. Others pronounce it "bough", to rhyme with cow. Ironically, as an adopted Texan, the original Bowie would have pronounced it "boo", to rhyme with blue.)

Then came a more substantial coup, when Horton, assisted by the record producer Tony Hatch, secured a six-month recording contract with Pye. Soon afterwards David and the Lower Third gathered for a recording session at Pye's Marble Arch studios. They felt immensely optimistic about their prospects, for they were to record one of the most popular numbers from their Marquee repertoire, 'The London Boys'.

David's lyric told of a teenager who left home and headed for London's West End, describing his search for friendship, the lure of the lights, the excitement gained from amphetamine pills, the depression and loneliness that follow. It was a notably prescient statement, for the dominant note of the age was still that of Carnaby Street and miniskirts, of the youth culture heralded by the Beatles and the Stones, of enjoyment, confidence and style. David, by contrast, had identified a new cross-current in the mood of the decade.

Britain was now governed by the Labour Party led by Harold Wilson, whose left-wing rhetoric had helped to end the Conservatives' thirteen years of power the previous autumn. Yet Wilson proved to be the ultimate pragmatist, proclaiming that the future lay with the "white heat of a technological revolution", thus diverting his party's idealism into a matter of computers and microchips. 'The London Boys' showed that David was not to be deceived by any such promises, or the surface glitter of the 1960s. It also displayed his growing gifts as a contemporary observer and his ear for street jargon, and was the clearest statement of personal alienation he had yet made.

The producer, Tony Hatch, was notably diffident in the face of David's uncompromising message. He had just achieved his first major hit with 'Where Are You Now, My Love?', a cloyingly sentimental ballad sung by Jackie Trent that was in utter contrast to David's song. Hatch admitted he had not been in the pop world long – "This is all new to me," he told the Lower Third – and encouraged them to play 'The London Boys' in the style that had appealed to their audiences at the Marquee and Bournemouth.

David sang the lyric with considerable poignancy and they were all "well pleased", says Phil, with the result. Then came bitter disappointment: Pye refused to release 'The London Boys'.

It was David who conveyed this news to the rest of the group. "He said it was because it was about taking pills," Phil says. "I was choked, and David was as well." Hatch's later verdict was that David wrote "too much about London dustbins", while Pye were patently not ready to be purveyors of grainy realism about the subculture of London's disaffected youth. As the fate of 'The London Boys' showed, David's time had not yet arrived.

Rather unexpectedly, someone who did perceive the worth of 'The London Boys' was Horton's flatmate, Kenny Bell. He had attended the audition at the Roebuck and had at first been "not overimpressed" with David. He now changed his view and, aware of Horton's search for finance, offered a half-share in his Bournemouth promotions in return for a half-share in David. But Horton was not interested in Bell's offer. "He rejected it," says Bell. "He wanted Bowie entirely for himself."

Bell's suspicion that Horton was becoming unduly possessive towards David was shared by the Lower Third. No longer did they enjoy the conviction that their fate would be collectively decided; and instead of riding in the group's ambulance, David usually travelled with Horton in his Mark Ten Jaguar. "Dave," says Phil, "was spending more and more time with Ralph, and less with us."

The blond singer, Neil Andersen, was uneasy too. He had come to the early gigs with Horton, and sometimes sang with the group. The Lower Third liked him – Phil found him "a nice friendly bloke" – and enjoyed his talent for "camping it up", as Phil explains. "We used to camp it up too, putting on the typical queer voice. It was all on the surface, we were only mucking about. But Neil was really good at it, he had us all in stitches."

Then Andersen disappeared; and the Lower Third next learned that David had moved into Horton's flat in Warwick Square. Space was at a premium, because Kenny Bell was still living there; for a time, Graham Rivens was staying there too. He and Denis had given up their flats in Pimlico, and he lodged in Warwick Square for a month, sleeping on Horton's living-room settee.

The Lower Third were puzzled that David and Horton had become so close. "I never really sussed it out," says Phil. "But I probably liked to think the best of people." Graham pondered the matter too. "I didn't particularly like his relationship with Ralph, not so much because he was being taken off and away from us –

I tried to ignore that – but more for the other side of his situation with Ralph.''

In November, Horton and David made a new effort to find financial backing. Although his bid for a half-share in David had been turned down, Kenny Bell introduced them to a businessman, Ray Cook, who owned a heating company and was part-owner of a mobile discothèque. When they visited Cook at his flat in Wimbledon, Horton spoke of David's immense promise: not only had he made three records already, but he had another lined up, to be produced by Tony Hatch. It was an effective name to wield, for following 'Where Are You Now, My Love?' Hatch had produced a single for Petula Clark, 'Downtown', which was rapidly climbing the hit parade. Cook was impressed, and felt that David had charisma: he particularly noticed his "striking and sharp features".

David and Horton asked for £1,500, for which Cook would acquire 10 per cent of David's monthly earnings above £100. Upon reflection, Cook decided it was a reasonable gamble, and agreed. On November 15th, a somewhat amateurish agreement confirming the agreement was drawn up. To make absolutely clear that Horton was ceding none of his control, it specified that "Raymond Cook does not become a partner to the management of David Bowie and that Ralph Horton remains the sole manager of the artist."

Cook's first payments followed at once. On November 19th, he settled five outstanding bills totalling £70, and gave Horton £25 cash. On November 20th, he gave Horton £25 to buy a microphone and by the end of the month had handed over a further £70. On December 6th came the biggest payment so far: £410, for a set of amplifiers and speakers.

The new equipment was needed for the forthcoming recording session with Tony Hatch. Once again, David chose two of his own songs; and the A side, 'Can't Help Thinking About Me', represented another advance in his writing. It was notable first for the shaft of light it cast on David's life at home, as glimpsed by the Lower Third during their own occasional visits to Plaistow Grove. "His mother didn't like us at all," says Denis Taylor. "She thought we were leading her boy astray. In fact it was the other way round."

In David's lyric, the tensions and disagreements between himself and his mother were revealed. The song told of a son who had brought unexplained dishonour and shame on his family; she "can't stand the neighbours talking", so he has to pack his bags and leave.

The song introduced another important theme, including a nostalgic yearning for childhood. For David, this held contradictory memories, from lying awake "terrified of school" – and, presumably, of Mrs Baldry – to finding his friend at the nearby recreation ground. Then he says, unambiguously:

> I wish I was a child again
> I wish I felt secure again.

But, David regrets, such memories belong "in never-never land": and the use of evocative nursery language would become another important trait.

Other new themes followed. The boy says goodbye to his girlfriend on a cold railway station: travelling, parting and impermanence were linked notions that would frequently reoccur. Travelling would also become an extended metaphor for the self-examination, the quest for identity, that marked David's creative life.

Like most authors, David ritually disclaimed any notion that the song was about himself, saying in an interview that it described "incidents in every teenager's life". But he left enough clues to show the identity of the teenager concerned, clearest of all being the girlfriend's greeting: "Hi, Dave".

The B side, 'And I Say To Myself', described – like many of David's earlier lyrics – the frustrations and contradictions of love, this time for a "playgirl" who was also the "wrong girl". It was notable for continuing the introspective theme of the A side, and for David's trick of switching perspective, sometimes talking in the first person, sometimes addressing himself in the third person. Changes of stance and role were also to become vital in his life and work.

The recording session – watched from the control room by Ray Cook, anxious over the fate of his investment – lasted for two days. Tony Hatch came fresh from his triumph with 'Downtown', which had just reached second place in the hit parade, and he took a stronger hand than before. He asked David to play the tambourine that had been used on 'Downtown', while he performed the melody on a piano. When the Lower Third sang the backing vocals, Hatch told them that they sounded "like a Saturday night at the old Bull and Bush", and asked them to try again. When the recording was replayed through the studio loudspeakers, the Lower Third were delighted, and believed it would at last bring financial success.

It was in a buoyant mood that David and the Lower Third now

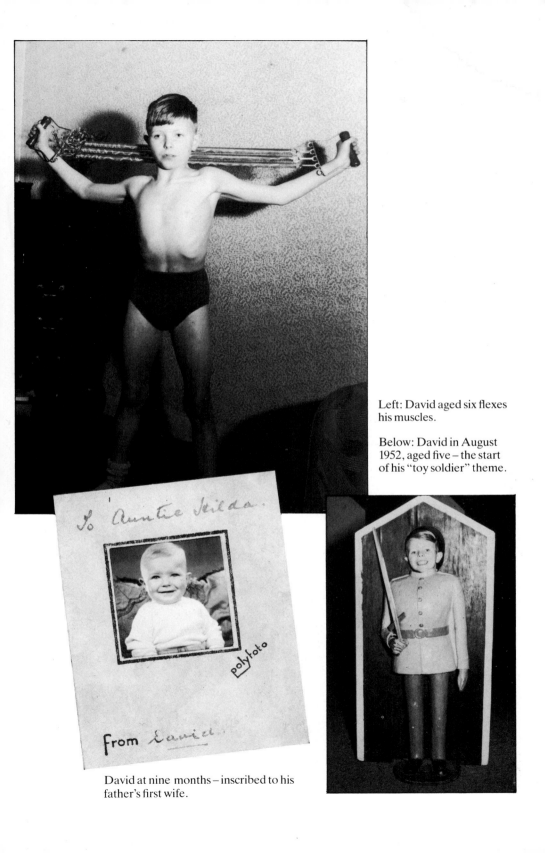

Left: David aged six flexes his muscles.

Below: David in August 1952, aged five – the start of his "toy soldier" theme.

David at nine months – inscribed to his father's first wife.

David – "no inbuilt talent" as singer or recorder-player – with the Burnt Ash Junior School Choir (second row right, next to end).

David with the 18th Bromley Cub Pack: at ease with the camera, at the centre of the group.

Above: David's birthplace – 40 Stansfield Road, Brixton.

Above centre: Growing up in the suburbs – 4 Plaistow Grove, Bromley.

Right: The missing years in Bromley – 1953 was spent at 106 Canon Road, above; 1954 at 23 Clarence Road, below.

Terry's father, Wolf Rosemberg (right), in Morocco in 1952. Terry refused to join him there.

Left: Terry aged 3½, "the happiest days of my life".

Above: Terry (right) with Bill Berks in Falmouth, posing in Customs' uniform. But he never sailed round the world, as David claimed.

Above: Cane Hill mental hospital in Coulsdon, Surrey, Terry's home before he died in January 1985.

Left: Terry and his wife Olga on their wedding day at Croydon in 1972.

embarked on their first foreign tour. It took them to Paris, where Horton had secured them three appearances at a club named the Golf Drouot, starting on New Year's Eve. As they headed for Dover, with David joining them in the ambulance, the warm atmosphere they had previously shared and enjoyed seemed to have returned.

The Channel ferry revived memories of the Isle of Wight; in France, they indulged in shared horror at the raw steaks, the hamburgers they were convinced were made from horsemeat, and the lavatories that consisted of fly-infested holes in the ground. At the Golf Drouot – where David was announced as a "vedette du Marquee Club", and the group was billed as "les Luwers third" – the packed teenage audience besieged the stage and afterwards pounded at the dressing-room door. "It was a little bit frightening," says Phil, "but it was great really."

Then the rift between David and the Lower Third opened up again. Horton flew to Paris to watch their last performance and announced that David was needed urgently in London. He and Horton flew back together, leaving the Lower Third to return in the ambulance. "We were a bit cheesed off with that," says Phil.

The failure of 'Can't Help Thinking About Me' widened the schism. The record was launched at the Victoria Tavern near Hyde Park on January 6th, 1966 – the occasion costing Ray Cook a further £100. When the record was released on January 14th the reviews ranged from encouraging to tepid, with Hatch's arrangement most under fire. Jonathan King wrote: "The performance is impeccable and the lyrics outstanding," but criticised the backing as "monotonous". *Record Retailer* concluded: "Words worth listening to but arrangement not all that original."

Within the group, the most pronounced response was a dispute over the credits. On 'You've Got A Habit Of Leaving', the Lower Third, to their anger, had been omitted from the label entirely. This time they insisted on being credited, but still felt betrayed when Horton produced a billing that read: "David Bowie *with* the Lower Third", instead of "and". They were further angered when both David and Horton suggested they consider "doing stuff on your own".

The final rupture was brought about by Horton. On January 29th, a Saturday, David and the Lower Third had two engagements: the usual afternoon session at the Marquee, followed by an appearance at the Bromel Club in Bromley, where a number of David's school friends would be in the audience. As the Lower

Third were packing away their instruments at the Marquee, Horton announced: "By the way, boys, you're not getting any money tonight." When Phil demanded to know why, Horton said he needed it for "expenses". The Lower Third confronted Horton in Bromley that evening. When Horton repeated that they were not to be paid, Phil told him: "In that case, we're not playing."

A petulant dispute ensued. When Horton told the Lower Third he was taking possession of their equipment, Denis responded: "Well, you can bleeding come and get it." What distressed the Lower Third most was that David, who was watching the proceedings while walking up and down a low garden wall nearby, did not intervene.

"It was a real choker moment," says Phil. "We realised that Dave wasn't backing us up. I walked over and said, 'Ta-ta, Dave,' because I couldn't just walk away. But he wouldn't answer me and that hurt me and then off we went, and that was the end of David Bowie and the Lower Third."

In retrospect, Horton's claim that he had no money to pay the Lower Third appears deliberately provocative. Only the day before, Ray Cook had paid him £300, the last instalment of his investment of £1,500. Nor had that source of finance run dry, for a day or so later David and Horton visited Cook to ask for a further £1,500.

This time, David and Horton purported to bring important financial news. "They said they were negotiating to take over Wimbledon Stadium," Cook says, "and there would be a lot of money coming." Cook was impressed, and agreed to provide the £1,500 they had asked for. David promised that when he was successful, he would buy Cook "a row of houses". Cook paid Horton the first instalment of £300 at once. Only later did Cook reappraise the story he had been told. "I believed it then," he says. "I don't believe it now."

For their part, the Lower Third came to accept that any "shortage of money" was the excuse for David's departure, not its cause. "Looking back," says Phil Lancaster, "it was absolutely right that we should have split up. That is how it was meant to be. David was the bloke with the song-writing ability and the individuality and the performing skills. It was absolute destiny that he was going to go off on his own."

In the summer of 1965, Terry reappeared in Falmouth. To the astonishment of both John Garwood and the Berkses, he arrived in a brick-lorry, having agreed to help the driver unload in return for the lift. "He had always taken great care of himself, always looked after his clothes and was well turned out," Garwood says. Now, instead, "he looked thoroughly dirty and dishevelled".

Terry's flight to Cornwall was an attempt to escape the growing tension in Pat's household. Pat's husband was becoming more hostile, and warned on several occasions that Terry must leave; Terry decided to resolve the situation himself. He was hardly more welcome in Falmouth. Bill and Mad Berks took him to a party that evening but were embarrassed by his crass behaviour. "He was saying loud things," says Mad. "He was openly contemptuous of the people there and you can't do that to the Cornish, they're very closed."

When Mad left the party early, Terry followed her. Feeling rather frightened, Mad told him to go to bed upstairs, while she sat up to wait for Bill. In the morning she found Terry in their living room, staring out into the street. He told her that the human race was worthless, adding: "Not one of them is worth saving, not one of them. What are we here for, what's it all about? It's all a load of crap."

Despite misgivings, Bill and Mad invited Terry to stay for a while. But when Bill attempted to discuss politics, as before, Terry was no longer interested in the possibility of change, talking instead of his despair at the wars and famines that threatened to engulf the human race. He also touched on his own predicament, warning darkly: "I've read Freud and I've read Jung, and I know exactly where I'm heading." When he was asked if he meant that he was going to end up in a dosshouse, he replied, enigmatically: "Oh no, I've got my pride."

After a week in Falmouth, Terry returned to London, and went to stay with Pat again. Although the atmosphere had not eased, the winter passed without further alarms. But early in 1966, at about the time that David left the Lower Third, Terry was involved in another pub fight in the West End. The police arrived, and Terry was hit over the head by a truncheon and arrested. In court the next morning he pleaded guilty to a minor offence and was fined £10. When he came home, Pat's temper snapped. "I told him that I couldn't cope with all this. I said that if he was going to behave like that, he would have to find somewhere else to live."

Pat suggested to Terry that if he found himself a room nearby, she would do his washing and he could eat with them at weekends. She came home from work that evening to find that he had left his doorkey and a farewell note on the kitchen table.

Pat rang Peggy at once and asked if Terry had been in touch

with her. "I don't know where he is," Peggy replied. Besides, she added, "Terry's a man. He's old enough to stand on his own two feet."

9

Pretty Thing

David's severance from the Lower Third presented an immediate problem: he was booked to appear at the Mecca Ballroom in Leicester on February 10th, 1966, less than two weeks time. In the urgent search for a new group, Ralph Horton placed an advertisement in *Melody Maker*. This time there was to be no risk of confusion over who was to have the dominant role. Musicians were required, the advertisement spelled out, "to accompany a singer". It further noted that the singer in question "had a record in the charts – and climbing".

For Derek Fearnley, a twenty-six-year-old bass guitarist from the London suburb of Sutton, the advertisement held immediate allure. A former grammar-school boy whose first ambition in life had been to become a policeman, most of his musical experience had been with bands touring US military bases in West Germany, playing dance tunes that ranged from foxtrots to modern jazz. With its reference to "the charts", Horton's advertisement hinted at a new and exciting world that Derek had hitherto watched from afar: a world of packed concert halls and screaming fans, of disc-jockeys and television shows, of battles for supremacy between the Beatles and the Rolling Stones, whose records had alternated at the top of the hit parade throughout 1965.

In reality, the only "chart" David's record 'Can't Help Thinking About Me' had reached was the one broadcast by the pirates of Radio London, subject as much to the whims of its compilers as to performances in the marketplace. But when Derek called the number in *Melody Maker*, he was immediately impressed when the person who answered said that his name was Spike and that he was the musician's assistant manager. Derek was less impressed when Spike told him that the musician in question was David Bowie, of whom Derek had never heard. And he was totally thrown when Spike asked him: "What's your image?"

It had never previously occurred to Derek that he even had an image – either you could play your instrument or you couldn't – and he cautiously asked Spike what he meant.

"Are you," Spike asked, "a mod or a rocker?"

Aware that his fate could turn on his answer, Derek concluded that his best choice lay in compromise.

"Er, in between."

Derek was asked to attend the audition at Warwick Square on February 3rd. He was greeted by Spike – a friend of Horton's, his full name was Spike Palmer, and he had once been a roadie with the Rolling Stones – who took him into Horton's bedroom. Horton was there – wearing a suit – and so, lying on a bed, was "a pale, frail weedy-looking bloke with a bouffant hairstyle". David looked at Derek with unnerving steadiness while Ralph questioned him about his musical experience. When Horton asked how old he was, Derek, fearing that twenty-six might appear dangerously close to pensionable age, lied and said he was twenty-one.

Then David said he had written "a couple of songs". He demonstrated the chords on his guitar and asked Derek to accompany him. "So he started to sing," Derek says, "and I started playing, and the first thing that struck me was that it was so *different*. Chord changes and melody lines in pop music were always so predictable and all of a sudden here was a bloke singing songs that weren't predictable, and I thought, Christ, this is good stuff, this is really different, this is really good. His voice was different too, his songs were different, he was different. Halfway through that first number, I just wanted to play in this frail-looking bloke's band."

Horton dampened Derek's enthusiasm by assuming an official tone and asking if, "in the event of your getting the job", he would be prepared to change his image. Since Derek's hair had a greasy quiff and his main musical taste was for 1950s' rock and roll, he was forced to concede that he was probably a rocker after all. Horton said he would have to alter his clothes and his hair, which left Derek, like Phil Lancaster of the Lower Third, uneasy: "Only women had their hair done then." But he replied that he liked David's songs so much that he was ready to do anything.

Horton told Derek that, in the time-honoured phrase, they would "let him know". After a week, Derek assumed he had been turned down. Then Horton telephoned and said that David would like him to join his band. "I was thrilled – absolutely thrilled."

Derek returned to Warwick Square to discover he was now part of a four-piece band. The drummer, John Eager, aged eighteen, came, like Derek, from a staunchly middle-class family, and had learned classical music at Harrow High School. He had turned professional the year before and had been considering a job playing to the transatlantic passengers on the *Queen Elizabeth* when he saw the *Melody Maker* advertisement.

The remaining two members were from Yorkshire. John Hutchinson, twenty-one, was a singer and guitarist from Scarborough who had spent the previous year in Sweden. At his audition David had asked him to play a Bo Diddley rhythm but had also sized him up in the same informal manner as he had Phil Lancaster: "We sat down and talked and we liked each other and I'm sure that was just as important." John had then recommended a Scarborough friend, Derek Boyes, as keyboard player, whom David and Horton accepted as soon as they heard him play.

The band fell naturally into two pairs: the two southerners, from middle-class backgrounds; and the two Yorkshiremen, who had both left school at fifteen, who spoke with the broad musical vowels of their county, and displayed the forthright attitudes that Yorkshiremen take to other parts of Britain. Although Yorkshiremen are often patronised as country cousins, especially by southerners, they found no condescension on David's part. "He was dead honest and dead good to get on with," says Derek Boyes, "and he took me for what I was." Undoubtedly influenced by his father's origins, David was to show a liking for Yorkshire musicians throughout his career.

When he met his new colleagues, Derek Fearnley found that they had already been transformed from journeymen musicians into birds of plumage. Like the Lower Third, they had been taken to Carnaby Street to be equipped with checked shirts and flared green trousers. They also sported the same bouffant hairstyles, imparted at a nearby unisex salon, Him 'n' Hers.

Derek was dispatched to Carnaby Street, but with their first gig due the following day there was no time for Him 'n' Hers. Instead, Horton bent Derek over the washbasin in the corner of his room and rinsed the Brylcreem out of his hair, rearranged it with a dryer and finally sprayed it with lacquer. "I was a bit sickened by the smell and I didn't like the look of me either," Derek says. "But the others were all chuffed. I had been transformed from rocker to mod in about five minutes and they all thought that was great — especially David."

David completed the transformation by renaming the members of his group: Derek Fearnley became Dek, John Eager was Ego, Derek Boyes, Chow, and John Hutchinson, Hutch. At the suggestion of a Radio London disc-jockey, the new group was called the Buzz.

As events at Warwick Square showed, David had assumed a

decisive new relationship with his musicians. Four times previously he had joined existing bands and tried to mould them to his needs. Now he had stamped his authority from the start, not least through the respect he commanded for his own burgeoning talents; in future, every group of musicians David played with would be recruited in the same way. The pattern was confirmed when the Buzz assembled for their first performance, at the Mecca Ballroom in Leicester, on February 10th. David indicated the territory at the front of the stage that was his, and the area to the rear that was theirs. "From day one," says Ego, "we knew this was David and a backing band."

David also gave the band sheets of paper containing the numbers they were to play, most of them his own compositions. Dek was in some difficulty since he had taken part in only one rehearsal: he placed the paper on his amplifier and followed the chord sequences as best he could. "I remember feeling a little bit disappointed at the sound of the band," he says. "We coped with it technically but you can't just put four blokes together and expect them to jell." But his initial enthusiasm for David remained undiminished. "It was the way he moved his arms or put his hands on his hips or strutted about. David Bowie was nobody then but after the first ten minutes he was somebody to me."

Three weeks later, Ralph Horton announced that he would be holding a party in the basement at Warwick Square, and he asked Dek if he would help to run the bar. Dek liked Horton, finding him amusing and being impressed with his apparently extensive contacts, and agreed. On the night of the party, Dek took up his position in an alcove off the living room which had been equipped as a bar, and prepared to offer the first arrivals their drinks. A shock was in store.

"In came a couple of people and I gave them a drink, and then in came another couple, and then another. They were all blokes, you see, but I didn't realise at first, until about fifteen had turned up and I thought, Wait a minute, it's all blokes, and I asked Ralph, 'When's the crumpet coming?'"

Horton made it clear that no "crumpet" would be forthcoming. The alcove was guarded by a low gate behind which Dek retreated, locking it firmly. Before long he was receiving approaches from Horton's guests. At first he rebuffed them as diplomatically as he could. "But in the end I got so fed up that when I got chatted up I just said, 'I'm sorry, you're under an illusion, you're just wasting your time.'"

Chow was another to become aware of the new world that the Buzz inhabited. David was not at the party – "Ralph wouldn't put him on show like that," Chow says – but Chow observed the fascination with which homosexuals clustered around him on other occasions. One suitor was an actor who plied David with barley wines at the Marquis of Westminster, the pub close to the flat in Warwick Square; another was a journalist who managed to insert regular items about David in *Melody Maker*; a third was a commercial radio disc-jockey who played his records with embarrassing frequency. But Horton was always hovering nearby: "He wove this web around David and nobody could get near him," says Chow.

In their frustration, some of David's suitors turned to members of the Buzz, and Chow was approached on numerous occasions. He was no more interested than Dek: "But there was no point in getting uptight. In the business, agents, impresarios, 99 per cent of them were bent anyway."

Dek was relieved when Horton eventually appeared to accept the sexual status quo, evidenced by a chance encounter in the West End one night. Dek and Chow were in the company of two women when they met Horton. Horton looked at them and their companions and told them: "What a waste." But the Buzz still felt that Horton was reluctant for them and David to become too close, and they never knew the intimacy the Lower Third had enjoyed. "I always thought Dave was a bit hard," says Dek, "with an emotional shell around him."

Against Horton as manager, the Buzz had no complaints, at least at the start. He found them two or three bookings a week at cities and towns within a 100-mile radius of London: Crawley, Bournemouth and Southampton in the south; Nottingham, Peterborough and Newmarket to the north. And instead of relying on a share of the proceeds, they were paid a regular £12 a week each. The two southerners thought this acceptable, since neither was paying any rent: Ego was still living with his parents, while Dek was staying with his brother. Hutch and Chow, who were both paying for lodgings, found it harder to make ends meet. But their prospects appeared to improve when David told the Buzz that they were going to make a record.

David's previous single, 'Can't Help Thinking About Me', made with the Lower Third, had risen no higher than 34th in the *Melody Maker* chart. (Even that position may have exaggerated its true appeal, for Ray Cook had given Ralph Horton £250 to help "buy" it into the hit parade.) It seemed to receive a new boost when

Horton secured an appearance for David and the Buzz on *Ready Steady Go* on March 4th, with David singing live while the Buzz mimed to a backing track they had recorded the previous day. Finding themselves in the company of the Yardbirds, the Small Faces, and Manfred Mann, the Buzz felt that fame and success must soon be theirs, but the record dropped from sight soon afterwards.

It was nonetheless with strong expectations that the Buzz arrived at the Pye studios at Marble Arch on March 7th to make the new single – the Buzz's first, and David's fifth. It was to be produced, once more, by Tony Hatch. His reputation as a creator of hits was now high, and David ceded most of the authority to him.

It was perhaps understandable, given the failure of 'Can't Help Thinking About Me', that Hatch should have tried to repeat the successful formula of his own hit, 'Downtown'. But the two lyrics he chose displayed little of David's earlier inventiveness or ambiguity. The A side, 'Do Anything You Say', continued the theme of loss of affection, and the B side, 'Good Morning Girl', beyond describing a passing encounter with the girl of the title, was almost meaningless. Whatever individuality they possessed was further submerged by Hatch's arrangements, and when the record was released on April 1st it made no impact.

The Buzz were as disappointed with the failure as David: Dek for one felt that Hatch had been a damper on the proceedings, and they were hardly consoled when they received only a £10 session fee and were not even billed on the record label. Yet Dek's loyalty remained undiminished. "I was not after individual acclaim," he says. "I was just a bass player and all I wanted was to carry on playing with Dave."

The next venture, an expedition to Scotland, seemed more promising. Riding in a Transit van which Ray Cook had rented on their behalf, they made a round trip of over 1,000 miles, appearing at Dundee on April 3rd and Hawick on April 4th. Ego noted in his diary: "Screaming Scots girls are wild," and felt certain that their reception boded well, although, in truth, almost any band reaching Scotland was ensured a welcome for merely having arrived.

When they returned, they began to play regular Sunday-afternoon sessions, billed as *The Bowie Showboat*, at the Marquee, where Horton had renewed his contacts. The Marquee audience was delighted at David's return and the girls who regularly occupied the front three or four rows cheered 'The London Boys' more eagerly than ever. The Buzz also acquired their first official fan club, founded on the initiative of one of David's most devoted local supporters.

Shirley Wilson, who was sixteen, came from Bromley, and had seen David play the saxophone with the Kon-rads three years before. Because of the informality of the Marquee sessions, where David and the group chatted to the audience between perform-ances, she got to know them well. The group was delighted when she suggested starting a fan club, and she became its first secretary. It cost nothing to join: Shirley merely asked its members to give her stamped addressed envelopes, so that she could send them news of forthcoming dates and – later – signed photographs.

Shirley found David invariably friendly and helpful, never object-ing when she rang him for information. She visited him in Plaistow Grove and sometimes rode to gigs with the group in their ambu-lance. She felt certain, she says now, that David was destined for fame: "He had an aura about him." But somehow the fan club never quite acquired the impetus she thought it deserved, and for that she held Ralph Horton to blame. He seemed to resent her friendship with David; and although he would make promises to help, they often went unfulfilled.

For the Lower Third, the acquisition of a fan club was another token of the success they felt sure would soon be theirs. As he surveyed the cheering Marquee audience, Dek fondly assumed that it contained promoters and managers who would soon be coming forward to offer them more lucrative work. But familiar problems were looming. Ray Cook had finally become disillusioned over his investment, which by April stood at over £3,000. He had given Horton £2,536, paid £300 to hire cars and vans, and guaranteed a £200 overdraft for Horton as well. When Horton asked for more, Cook refused.

Life at Warwick Square became distinctly uncomfortable, with creditors and bailiffs, bearing unpaid bills and writs, beating a regular path to the door. One even brought a court order taken out by Pye Records, who, apparently unaware that David was one of their performers, had sued for payment for some of his own records. As often as not it was a reluctant member of the Buzz who was sent to the door to deny that Horton was at home. Then the basement was plunged into darkness when the electricity was cut off. Horton, who boasted some knowledge of such technological matters, reconnected it himself, but when the London Electricity Board found out they severed it again, this time terminally.

Horton now paid a second visit to seek the help of Ken Pitt. Pitt was still cautious, pointing out that he had enough work to occupy him already. But when Horton renewed his pleas, Pitt promised to come to watch David at the Marquee on April 17th.

What Pitt saw left him transfixed. He was struck by David's slender figure, accentuated by a skin-tight yellow sweater, and by the confidence with which he moved on stage. David sang his own songs mixed with a selection of R and B standards, and finished on the classic Judy Garland number, 'When You Walk Through A Storm', performed, in the halo of a single spotlight, to full bravura effect. It was, Pitt thought, a "daring and delightful" performance.

That evening Pitt returned with David and Horton to Warwick Square. After a long talk, during which he increasingly warmed to David, he offered his help after all. He agreed to take over administrative matters, such as contracts, bookings and accounts, while Horton would remain David's artistic manager.

Ralph sent Pitt the first batch of overdue bills within days. The group was also in urgent need of transport, and on May 16th Pitt paid £125 for a converted ambulance on their behalf. By the end of the month, despite his earlier protestations that he would not be a source of funds, he had paid out £630, against an income of £147.

Although Pitt's intervention brought some respite, it was not enough to retain Hutch, who left the Buzz on June 15th. He was replaced by Billy Gray, a fresh-faced Scotsman who was rapidly "poofed up", as he termed it, and christened "Haggis". The three other original members stayed, with Dek above all convinced of David's talent. He looked forward to rehearsals and found them immensely stimulating, for David would produce a sheaf of new songs, and ask the Buzz, as he had the Lower Third, to help with the arrangements. "He was so creative and overflowing that I was able to think of things I would never otherwise have thought of," Dek says.

On July 5th, David made his third and last attempt to record a hit with Tony Hatch. By now Hatch had concluded that it was the Buzz themselves who were the weak link, and he replaced them with a group of session musicians. The loyal Dek was deeply disappointed: "That affected me personally," he says. Yet the outcome was no different. Hatch made an even more determined effort to fit David to his mould but David's lyrics were among the least distinguished he ever wrote.

The tone of the A side was set by the modish hippy jargon of the title, 'I Dig Everything'. Although it contained some nice details hinting at loneliness – David's cigarettes glow in the dusk as he stands in a window to watch passers-by, he makes friends with "the time-check girl at the end of the phone" – it lacked focus or coherence. The B side, 'I'm Not Losing Sleep', which resumed the theme of love for a woman who considers herself superior, was less convincing still. Hatch's arrangements were equally banal and when the record was released on August 19th it was almost entirely ignored.

At their live performances, the Marquee apart, the Buzz were finding it hard, like the Lower Third, to win attentive fans. A bare handful would gather by the stage but the majority, finding the music unsuitable for dancing, would turn their backs and talk. Dek could barely restrain himself from shouting to them: "Why don't you just stop and *listen* to this bloke?"

Yet David still searched for ways of capturing his audiences' attention. His most imaginative proposal, and a precursor of the theatricality he would one day bring to the staging of his concerts, was to present a mix of live and recorded music. Horton designed an electronic console to house a recording deck, amplifier and echo chamber, and David told the Buzz that they would record some backing tapes. He also planned to address the audience, through the console, in a ghostly, echoing voice.

The console was launched at the Coronation Ballroom in the Ramsgate Pleasurama on August 26th, heralded by a report in the *Kent Messenger* which proclaimed that David and the Buzz had developed a "completely new act". The publicity was vastly premature. David and the Buzz had not yet managed to record any backing tapes and when they carried the console in from the ambulance they found it impossibly awkward and unwieldy. Then, as David tried to speak to the audience, the microphone failed.

There was an attempt to resuscitate the console at the Starlite Ballroom, Wembley, the following night, but it failed again and was abandoned. Then came a further blow. The radio disc-jockey who was one of David's most ardent admirers was arrested for importuning young boys and lost his job.

On September 6th, David went to see Ken Pitt again. This time, he went without Horton. He told Pitt how disappointed he was at the failure of the recordings he had made with Tony Hatch and complained that 'The London Boys', which he considered one of his best songs, had not even been released. When Pitt heard the recording he told David it was "brilliant".

Pitt now took matters into his own hands. He had already recommended that Horton should ask Pye to release David from his contract; since Pye had no wish to make any further records with David either, that had been easily arranged. Pitt now advised David that his best course lay in making his own recording of 'The London Boys' and offering it to another company. On October 18th, David, the Buzz, and two session musicians went to the R. G. Jones studio in Morden to record 'The London Boys', together with two of David's other compositions. In striking contrast with the songs he had recorded with Tony Hatch, they revealed the extent to which his imagination had developed.

One was 'Rubber Band', which marked the reappearance of David's grandfather, Jimmy Burns. In 1910 "so handsome and strong", with his moustache "stiffly waxed and one foot long", Jimmy Burns provided the model for an Edwardian figure who, together with a lady friend, watched a band play "tea-time tunes".

Employing the shift of perspective he had already experimented with in 'And I Say To Myself', David also used his musical grandfather as the basis of a second character, the leader of the band. The story then became the familiar one of estranged or frustrated love. The first character departs to fight, like Jimmy Burns, "in the '14–'18 war". He returns only to find that his girl has married the band leader, and the song ends with a cry of rage: "I hope you break your baton."

David's other new title – which he performed as a recitative rather than a song – was 'Please Mr. Gravedigger'. It was a macabre tale. A churchyard is hit by a bomb during the war, and a gravedigger guards the remains. He steals a golden locket from the grave of a young girl who has been murdered, but is observed by the murderer himself. To ensure that he remains silent, the murderer prepares a grave for the gravedigger too. What was especially notable about the lyric was the appearance of the Burns family's most potent concerns, those of war, destruction and death. Together with 'Rubber Band', it showed the extent to which David had absorbed his family mythology, now emerging with astonishing force.

Although Dek never asked where the inspiration for 'Please Mr. Gravedigger' came from – "David was always producing interesting things, so I was never really surprised" – he was aware of the strong personal basis of David's lyrics. "He said he got all the ideas from his own life and people he knew." Dek believed that 'The London Boys' was the most personal of all: "It was the story of what happened to him."

*

At the end of October, Ken Pitt took David and his recordings to Decca House, an office block beside the Thames on the Albert Embankment. Four years had passed since David's failure with the Kon-rads to impress Decca. Despite Decca's success with the Rolling Stones, it remained a staid and unimaginative company, presided over by its unsmiling founder Sir Edward Lewis, who devoted most of his attention to Decca's classical output, particularly its lucrative cut-price label the Ace of Clubs. Sir Edward had taken little interest in the launching of a division named Deram which was intended to feature contemporary British performers, and which Pitt considered ideal to display David's talents.

At Decca House, Pitt and David met Hugh Mendl, Decca's artists' manager for album recordings, and Mike Vernon, a young producer on Decca's staff. When they listened to David's three tracks, they were instantly impressed, not least because David was writing his own songs. "He obviously had talent," Vernon says. "No two ways about it."

Displaying a decisiveness that was rare for the British record industry, Mendl offered to buy all three recordings for £150, and promised that Decca would release 'Rubber Band' and 'The London Boys' as a single. Mendl also offered an advance of £100 for an album containing twelve of David's songs, which Vernon would produce. It was a far-sighted proposal at a time when it was unusual for popular singers to write their own material, and Pitt readily accepted.

David's own response was strangely muted, giving Pitt his first intimation that, to him at least, David "very very rarely expressed his emotion about anything". But Pitt adds that he is sure "David's heart missed a beat and something inside him went 'thump thump thump' for a while." When the Buzz heard the news about 'The London Boys' their delight was far less inhibited. "We were so bloody excited," says Dek, "because we felt that was going to be the one that would do it."

Following the breakthrough at Decca, a fierce battle ensued for David's allegiance. By securing a contract for a single and an album from Decca, Pitt had accomplished in weeks what Horton had conspicuously failed to do in the preceding eighteen months. What was more, Pitt had a more solid record of achievement and a calmer nature than the anxious Horton. Sensing the danger that David might transfer his loyalty to Pitt, Horton became more possessive still.

It was Chow who was best placed to observe these emotional

tremors. He had moved into the first-floor flat at Warwick Square, which he shared with an obligingly sensual nurse. Chow heard furious rows emanating from the basement, and sometimes David would emerge in tears. Chow also knew that David was still seeing Dana Gillespie, telling Horton when he departed for her flat in Kensington that he was going to visit his parents in Bromley. When Horton found out about Dana, "there was all hell let loose", Chow says. Horton raged that Dana was "a bad influence" who would ruin David's career.

On another occasion that autumn, Chow and David spent an evening with two women in the West End. They were spotted by one of Horton's friends. On returning to London, Horton interrogated Chow about David's companion. But he was near the end of his tether, and told Chow: "I'm washing my hands of him." Soon afterwards he took Chow out for a meal and, close to tears, lamented: "David won't listen to me."

Yet Horton did not yield David easily – and it was the Buzz who were the first victims of the struggle. David and the Buzz were still making regular appearances together, with thirteen bookings in September – their busiest month ever – and ten in October. Then, abruptly, the bookings ceased. "I could never understand that," says Chow. "When all the gigs dried up I thought, there's something funny going on here."

Chow was right. Knowing that Pitt believed that David should become a solo performer, Horton had provoked a crisis to achieve that aim himself: that at any rate is the best explanation for the sudden absence of bookings that so puzzled the Buzz. Soon afterwards, on November 25th, Horton summoned the Buzz to a meeting in Pitt's office (Pitt was away on business in the US and Australia). David, sitting in Pitt's chair, told the Buzz they were fired, blaming the state of the group's finances. "I'm sorry," David said, "but we've got to pack up. We just can't afford to keep you on any more."

Just as when the Lower Third were disposed of, money was the excuse, not the reason, for the demise of the Buzz. It was Dek, by his constancy, who unwittingly exposed the subterfuge. With his faith in David as strong as ever, he said that money was not important to him. "We know you're going to make it," Dek told David, "and we'll hang on." Ego added that since he had "a few quid" he too could manage, "for a bit".

David sat in silence and tears welled into his eyes. Then he rushed out of the office. Dek was amazed: "That was the first sign I had seen of any softness or emotion at all." Then Horton came in and announced: "I'm sorry about that, lads, Dave's really upset. He says thanks for offering but we've decided that we've got to change our tack."

The Buzz had three more engagements to fulfil, ending at Shrewsbury on December 2nd. There were no lamentations: "We just did the gig and packed up," Dek says. Ironically that was also the day Decca released 'Rubber Band' and 'The London Boys'. While the others accepted that their partnership with David was at an end, Dek hoped that he would be able to continue to work with him. By then the Buzz had undertaken two recording sessions for the Deram album but it was not yet complete, and David had asked Dek to help him with the arranging. "As I was still close to David, I hoped that if anything came of the singles or the LP I might be involved."

With Pitt still away, Horton redoubled his efforts on David's behalf, and turned his attention to David's publishing contract. David's contract with Hal Shaper of Sparta Music had been renewed in September, but Horton decided to try to do better. The publisher David Platz, the head of Essex Music, agreed to put up an advance of £500, a considerable improvement on Shaper's terms. Shaper sportingly waived his rights and David signed a contract with Platz on December 7th, countersigned by his father. Horton gave David £300 and kept the remaining £200 for himself.

Substantial though £500 may have seemed, Horton had blundered. Pitt had also been negotiating with Platz and had already secured an offer of £1,000 which he said he would consider while he was away. Platz did not tell Horton of his dealings with Pitt, and naturally concluded the agreement with some alacrity. Pitt returned to London on December 16th, to find the Essex contract signed and the £500 disbursed.

Pitt met David's father the next day and asked what had happened. John Jones told him he thought that the Essex contract had already been approved by Pitt. But Pitt brought still worse news. He told John Jones that while in New York the Broadway publishing company, Koppelman and Rubin, had offered him $30,000 for David's publishing rights, with $10,000 up front. Pitt and John Jones agreed that it would be kinder not to tell David that; but they did tell him about Pitt's earlier negotiations with Platz.

The revelation spelled the end of David's relationship with Horton. On January 18th, he asked to be released from their contract, and Horton agreed. Two weeks later, David asked Pitt to become his manager. On February 10th, Pitt wrote to John

Jones, announcing that he intended to do all he could "to make up for lost time and get David's affairs in proper order and his career going along the right lines".

10

Living the Dream

Ken Pitt was not one of the gregarious managers and promoters who thronged Denmark Street and the Giaconda. He was a solitary figure, tall and softly spoken, who did not even like pubs. He lived and worked in Marylebone, a refined world where befurred dowagers emerge from their apartments to exercise their poodles, and Rolls-Royces await their owners outside the private clinics of Harley Street and Wimpole Street. His office and his flat occupied the top two floors of number 39 Manchester Street, one of the elegant thoroughfares laid out as London expanded in the late eighteenth century.

The décor betokened the man: orderly, discreet, with shelves of books that revealed a taste for the mannered and aesthetic life of the late nineteenth century. Among them were Aubrey Beardsley, Lord Alfred Douglas, and – his favourite – Oscar Wilde, with valued first editions of *The Happy Prince*, *The Picture of Dorian Gray*, and *The Ballad of Reading Gaol*.

The last work held special appeal for Pitt. He saw Wilde's bitter epic poem, spelling out the dire consequences of being imprisoned for homosexual behaviour, as a story with powerful modern parallels. Pitt had strong sympathy for the plight of homosexual men in post-war Britain, still stigmatised for their sexual preferences, and still liable, even at the beginning of 1967, to legal penalties for indulging in them. He collected the writings of Rupert Croft-Cook, who was sent to prison for two years for homosexual offences. And he had been outraged by the "absolutely extraordinary" trial of Lord Montagu, sentenced to twelve months for homosexual offences in 1954, and condemned to furnish the name "Monty" to stand alongside "queer" and "bent", as expressions of popular opprobrium. A cousin of Pitt's was found guilty alongside Lord Montagu and sentenced to eighteen months.

In the 1970s, Pitt was to become active in the Campaign for Homosexual Equality. In the 1980s, although relieved that the "dreadful" days of legal persecution were past, he complained that the barriers facing homosexuals were still enormous, exemplified by the prosecution of contact advertisements in *Gay News*, the seizure of imported books on homosexual themes, the moral panic over AIDs. At the same time, his political attitudes were firmly of the right. He called himself a "high Tory" and believed that the British left had harmed homosexuals by espousing their cause.

In the 1960s, before the law was changed, Pitt was less outspoken. His colleagues were perplexed by what they saw as a withdrawn and secretive personality, and speculated on the clues that, perhaps mischieviously, he would drop. One who puzzled over them was Malcolm Thomson, who had previously worked in the publicity department of MGM, and joined Pitt as his assistant in the early 1960s. "He would give us bits of a story to intrigue us," Thomson says. "He always liked to have a secret and he had a particular smile that said, 'I've got a secret and I'm not telling you any more.'"

Thomson nonetheless admired Pitt for the professional standards he maintained in a not very ethical world. "He never did shabby promotional tricks and always dealt fairly with the press," Thomson says. Thomson also concluded that he knew the mystery of Pitt's past. Since Pitt could speak German, had served in the war, and had ended up as a captain, Thomson deduced that he must have belonged to British Intelligence.

The truth was more straightforward. From a prosperous grocering family in Southall, Pitt had first wanted to become an artist. The war interrupted his plans and he became a communications officer with the Royal Signals Regiment. He landed in France on D-Day and fought through to Germany, acquiring enough German en route to become an army interpreter. He was sent to Palestine when the war in Europe ended and was demobbed in October 1946.

Still hoping to become an artist, Pitt joined the design department of J. Arthur Rank, the company that dominated the British film industry after the war. But he was soon transferred to the publicity department and given the task of escorting Rank's stars and starlets to the West End. In 1951, he was sent to Hollywood with Alan Dean, the leading British male recording star of the day. He took the opportunity to introduce himself to every star he could find and suggest that he should handle their publicity if they came to Britain. In due course; after leaving Rank, he worked for Frankie Laine, Louis Armstrong, Duke Ellington, Gerry Mulligan and Frank Sinatra.

Pitt's first client as manager was the US singer Mel Tormé. But as a rule, he preferred taking unknown performers and guiding them "up each step of the ladder". One was a gypsy he saw busking in the West End in 1954. Pitt named him Danny Purches and persuaded a promoter named Hymie Zahl to put him top of the bill in Middlesbrough, a ploy known in the trade as a "fake top". Pitt equipped Purches with a plunging blouse, a fake campfire, and a cut-out caravan that folded small enough to fit into the guard's van of a train. Purches won massive publicity and a recording contract worth £10,000.

For Pitt, the satisfaction came from "taking rough diamonds, taking people right from their roots, sizing up their potential and building them up to fulfil it". He played a major part in the success of the Mann-Hugg Blues Brothers, whom he first saw perform in March 1963. He became their manager and suggested that they record 'Do Wah Diddy Diddy' which became the first number one of the renamed Manfred Mann group in the summer of 1964. That, too, says Pitt, was an example of "classic management: they were taken from scratch, given an opinion of what I felt they should do, they did it, and it worked."

When Pitt came upon David, he hoped that the same formula would prove effective. David, Pitt says, was "searching up every by-way to see if it led to what he wanted, but it never did". By careful guidance, Pitt believed, David could reach his goals. But they could not be achieved overnight. Unashamedly traditionalist in his views, Pitt looked askance at the speed with which reputations could be made in the 1960s, and liked to warn that they could be lost just as quickly. He told David it was far better to establish a solid foundation so that when success came it would not prove ephemeral, and for that there was no substitute for hard work. "I came to the conclusion that what I had to do was to try to show him that his horizons were much further away than he thought."

Pitt also told David that he defined a truly successful performer as "someone who could top the bill at the Palladium for a month". The remark has been held against Pitt since, for some critics have interpreted it to mean that Pitt felt that David should become, in the despised phrase, an all-round entertainer, perhaps a latter-day Tommy Steele. Pitt protests that he intended it solely as an indication of the scale of popularity David could achieve. He adds that, in any case, David agreed with his plans.

However, Pitt also wonders at times how much he truly knew of David's thoughts and feelings. "Looking back," Pitt says, "I begin to realise how very unexcited he was about *everything*. He was obviously a person who did listen very carefully and take everything in and mull it over and was either with you or against you on a particular thing. Certainly we did have long conversations about this – and I think he went along with it."

Pitt's uncertainty illustrates a key aspect of David's personality at that time, for he was becoming adept at taking his cues from others and displaying those attributes he believed they would most approve of. Since Pitt was quiet, undemonstrative and hard to fathom, David would be too. David was also developing considerable skills of dissimulation, hiding his true feelings and sparing himself awkward personal confrontations. In the end, it was Pitt who was most hurt, with his bewilderment at the abrupt ending of their relationship adding to the pain he felt.

Pitt formally became David's manager on April 25th, 1967, after he, David and John Jones had signed a one-year contract, with Pitt holding options to renew it for a further four years. It gave Pitt 25 per cent of David's earnings, a standard proportion at the time; later on Pitt's share was improved to 30 per cent, although for that, as Pitt points out, David was receiving his services as both publicist and manager.

From the start, Pitt faced the financial pressures which had dogged David's career. The crudely kept accounts he inherited from Ralph Horton showed that in 1966, David and the Lower Third had earned £2,204 from performances, and had a further unearned income of £3,000 contributed by Ray Cook. As Pitt now learned, Cook was pressing Horton to return his investment, but Horton, after offering him £5 per week, had disappeared and never repaid the debt. Pitt had no wish to become embroiled in their dispute, not least because his own account with David was already in deficit. By the beginning of 1967 he had spent £1,525 on David's behalf and had recouped only £553.

The first signs were encouraging. David's first Deram single, 'Rubber Band' and 'The London Boys', released in December, had been winning promising reviews, the best of them in *Disc*, which judged David "a name to reckon with, certainly as far as songwriting is concerned". Now in the offing was the Deram album, which David had been working hard to finish. He and the Buzz had held two recording sessions before they broke up, and they had reconvened at the Decca studios on January 26th and February 25th.

For Dek Fearnley, whom David had offered £50 to help with the arrangements, these were bitter-sweet occasions; although saddened at the end of the Buzz, his admiration for David was as high as ever. "He would come along with the songs," Dek says. "We'd take the first one off the top of the pile and say, 'What can we do with this?' He had a song in its basic form, and we would just work it out. He would say, 'I'd like to have a violin,' and I'd say, 'Yes, let's keep a soulful feel, let's have a trombone,' and he'd say that'd be a great idea. He was so bloody inspiring . . . he spurred me on to things I could never otherwise have done."

For the final session, the Buzz were augmented by members of the London Philharmonia Orchestra, whom the producer, Mike Vernon, had hired for the day – one of the first occasions in the pop world when classical musicians were employed on any scale, and predating the Beatles' *Sergeant Pepper* album by some months. For David and Dek, it was a daunting occasion. They had bought a copy of the *Observer's Book of Music* to unravel the mysteries of musical notation, but their knowledge remained scant. When they distributed their scores they were politely informed that the trumpet part was far too high or the trombone impossibly low. It was Dek who had to ask the musicians to make the necessary corrections. "It was awful," says Dek, "and David left all that to me."

The producer, Mike Vernon, thought the sessions "a lot of fun"; David "was the easiest person to work with". Vernon was especially impressed by the standard of David's compositions. "Some of the melodies were extremely good, and the actual material, the lyrics, had a quality that was quite unique." It was an accurate judgment: most notable of all, although Vernon was not in a position to fully appreciate it, was the view the lyrics offered of David's mental landscape which now lay fully exposed. Their apparent simplicity served to deceive: many were complex and ambiguous, displaying creative gifts that, even at the age of nineteen, lifted him beyond most of his contemporaries. David had already touched on some of the themes in his singles; others appeared for the first time, and presaged his later dominant concerns.

Fully half the fourteen songs on the album reveal, directly or otherwise, David's yearning for an idealised childhood. In some David used the imagery and language of fairy tales, like the castle, golden horse, wicked giants and dragon in 'When I Live My Dream'. 'Come And Buy My Toys' tells of "smiling girls and rosy boys" who meet a pedlar selling:

> Monkeys made of ginger-bread
> And sugar horses painted red.

'There Is A Happy Land' describes "a secret place" where "adults aren't allowed".

A number contain a second familiar theme, the search for affection: in David's fantasy world, love is no longer uncertain and
ephemeral, but pure and whole. This is the thread that runs through
'Sell Me A Coat' and 'Love You Till Tuesday', and is most explicit
in 'When I Live My Dream'. In living his dream, David sang:

> I'll forgive the things you told me
> And the empty man you left behind.

Several songs contrast the protected world of childhood with
the threat of adulthood. David's images were most graphic and
menacing in 'Come And Buy My Toys', where the children's father
ploughs his fields "with a ram's horn" and carves furrows "with
a bramble thorn". 'Uncle Arthur' presents a neat converse: the
story of a thirty-two-year-old man who is unable to abandon his
childhood, and "likes his mummy, still reads comics, follows
Batman". He attempts to break his domestic bonds by getting
married; but the family ties reassert themselves and he returns
home. There was a strong clue to the dynamics of David's own
family in the line

> Back to mother, all's forgiven

– a further glimpse of the guilt-laden atmosphere David described
in 'Can't Help Thinking About Me'.

David's skill as observer of street life, shown in 'The London
Boys', was seen again in 'Maid Of Bond Street' and 'Join The
Gang'. The jargon of the drug culture reappears – "acid" and
"joints" – as does the deceptive glitter of London's nightlife, with
clubs that charge "fifteen bob a Coke". Both, too, were concerned
with loneliness and alienation, dreams and disillusion. Joining the
gang may be

> A big illusion – but at least you're in.

And the Bond Street girl who is

> ... made of lip-stick, powder and paint

is also made of "loneliness" and a "broken heart".

The album also introduced themes that were to become central
to David's work, such as homosexuality and sexual ambiguity. In

'Little Bombardier', the ex-soldier is suspected of a homosexual interest in two children, and is driven out of the town. 'She's Got Medals' describes a woman who passes herself off as a man and joins the army; eventually she resumes the feminine role, discarding her uniform for "dresses silk and green", and settling down to an orthodox life.

A second new theme was hinted at in 'When I Live My Dream':

> Tell him that I've got a dream
> And tell them that you're the starring role.

It appeared more emphatically in 'Maid Of Bond Street':

> This girl is made of flash-lights and films,
> Her cares are scraps on the cutting-room floor.

David's lyrics often predicted the course of action he would take; and these two provide the first intuitive suggestion that he would try to resolve his personal and his creative problems by playing the role of star – the device that lay at the heart of the astonishing succession of personas he presented in the early 1970s.

The same concept helps to explain 'Silly Boy Blue', which, with its references to "mountains of Lhasa" and a "child of Tibet", ostensibly pursued a fascination for Buddhism that David had acquired after briefly meeting a Buddhist priest named Chime Rimpoche. David's interest had brought him an immediate practical benefit, for he discovered that he could induce a meditative trance that helped inspire him when embarking on a bout of song-writing. His companions found that he was almost impervious to others in such states: so much so, as Derek Boyes of the Buzz once witnessed, that he appeared to lose consciousness.

David was also intrigued by a vital aspect of Buddhism's central belief in reincarnation. Buddhists believe that human beings have a continuing and infinite existence, and that when they die they are merely shedding one identity and taking on another. The idea reinforced David's growing intuition that he could find salvation through role-playing and adopting new persona. Unlike the Buddhists, however, he was not content to wait for death to do so; and therein lay the explanation for the final lines of 'Silly Boy Blue':

> You'll never leave your body now
> You've got to wait to die.

The most striking feature of David's lyrics was the extent to which they revealed the grip of his family mythology. His grandfather Jimmy Burns appears, as soldier and bandsman, in 'Rubber Band', and in 'Little Bombardier', which tells of the war veteran who cannot find work and consoles himself through drink. The related family themes of war, destruction and death also appear in 'She's Got Medals' and in the lugubrious 'Please Mr. Gravedigger', and, most starkly, in 'We Are Hungry Men', an apocalyptic view of a world facing catastrophe from famine and totalitarianism – and a trailer for David's epic sequence of albums of the early 1970s, culminating in *Diamond Dogs*.

The extent to which David's lyrics paralleled the poetry of David's grandmother, Margaret Burns, was quite uncanny. She too had been concerned with lost childhood, forsaken love and the power of wish-fulfilment. Some of the similarities were astonishing. She had used fairy-tale imagery, like knights in armour, as David did in 'When I Live My Dream'; she talked of Jack Frost, as David did in 'Sell Me A Coat'; she wrote of "the land of make believe", where "all our dreams come true" – a major theme of the entire album.

Margaret Burns had died in 1962, having remarried some five years before, and many of the family mementoes, particularly from her husband's army career overseas, were thrown out before her children could retrieve them. But her volume of poetry survived, and was looked after by her son Jimmy in Doncaster. So far as Jimmy Burns is aware, David never read his grandmother's poems. Yet the resonances in David's own lyrics show how her attitudes had informed the family mythology, as if it had become a collective unconscious, bearing down on the generations to come.

On a number of occasions, in fact, David was to hint that his inspiration drew from a creative fount whose precise nature and location remained a mystery even to him. "All I try to do in my writing is assemble points that interest me and puzzle through it, and that becomes a song," David said in one interview. In 1972, even more candidly, he admitted: "I'm the last one to understand most of the material I write."

In musical terms, the quality of the album was variable; perhaps most noticeable was the difficulty in categorising it at all. The melodies were inventive without being memorable, and David showed himself open to a range of sources, from the jazz piano in 'Maid Of Bond Street', to the folk guitar of 'Come And Buy My Toys'. David's singing style covered considerable ground, with the strongest influence the maverick British entertainer Anthony

Newley, a former boy-actor whose lyrics, sung in a slightly mocking and distanced manner, appealed strongly to David's own sense of the surreal. As producer, Mike Vernon did not feel that Newley's influence was for the best, and David admitted that he was a "fan".

Vernon served David well, helping to provide witty settings that played to the strength of the lyrics. The most imaginative touch was provided by the sound effects for 'Please Mr. Gravedigger', which included a distant chiming clock, the pitter-patter of rain, and the echo of thunder, to which Vernon, David, Dek Fearnley and the engineer, Gus Dudgeon, all contributed. "We were all learning at each other's expense – as Bowie was too," Vernon says. What struck him above all was the immense certainty with which David approached his task. "He knew what he was doing with the songs and he knew the qualities he wanted to get."

The album was entitled, simply, 'David Bowie', and bore a straightforward cover showing David with post-Mod style, his hair less stiff than before and curling forward over his cheeks. The photograph was taken by Dek Fearnley's brother Gerald. For Dek himself, the album really did mark the end of his partnership with David. For a while Dek tried to find a comparable band, but then took a job in the credit control department of a small company in Sussex. After David, he says today, "everything was such an anti-climax. I don't want to do credit control. I want to be a musician. The most satisfying thing I have done in my life is that LP with Dave."

Early in 1967, at about the time David was finishing the Deram album, Terry returned to Ealing and called at Pat's. The door was opened by strangers who told him they had bought the house the previous November, and that Pat and her husband Tony had gone away. That afternoon Terry went to see his mother in Bromley. A neighbour was there, but Peggy asked him in and made him a cup of tea. Terry asked her what had happened to Pat.

"She's in Australia," Peggy replied.

The blood drained from Terry's face so that he appeared, Peggy later said, "as white as a sheet". Peggy told him that Pat and Tony had emigrated to Australia, where they hoped to go into business with Tony's brother, running a garage and taxi service. Although Pat later explained that she had been unable to tell Terry herself as she did not know where he was, to Terry it appeared the latest in the series of rejections he had suffered. Abruptly, he walked out of Plaistow Grove.

On leaving the house, Terry crossed the bridge over the main railway line at the end of Plaistow Grove and kept on until he found himself at Chislehurst Caves. The caves comprise a network of chalk caverns that were a local tourist attraction and also housed pop concerts: David had played there with both the Kon-rads and the Manish Boys. Terry stopped and looked at the locked and deserted entrance to the caves and at the bare trees alongside. Suddenly, as he later described, he heard someone call his name.

"I heard a voice saying to me, 'Terry, Terry,' and I looked up and there was this great light and this beautiful figure of Christ looking down at me, and he said to me, 'Terry, I've chosen you to go out into the world and do some work for me.' He said, 'I've picked you out.' And the light of his face was so intense that I fell to the ground. I was on my stomach resting on my hands looking down and when I looked around me there was this big burning, a big ring of fire all around me, and the heat was intense, it was terrible. And then it all disappeared."

The moment when schizophrenics suffer their first full attack is one of utter terror. It is the moment when their minds renounce the struggle and escape into another world. But they find no comfort there. They see burning light, feel blazing heat, and hear voices telling them to do their will. They see God and Christ, or Satan and devils. It is a simultaneous vision of heaven and hell.

When his vision had receded, Terry picked himself up and continued blindly walking until he reached the countryside beyond Orpington. There he collapsed beneath a hedge and fell asleep. He spent the next eight days living rough, begging or stealing food from farms and sleeping in outhouses or under trees. Finally he stumbled into a greengrocer's and asked for an orange. Seeing Terry's dishevelled and bewildered state, the greengrocer called the police.

The police took Terry to Plaistow Grove, where Peggy railed at him for coming back in such a state. Terry shouted back at Peggy, and there was a furious row. David was at home, and witnessed the whole episode.

That afternoon, David travelled up to Ken Pitt's office in Manchester Street. He told Pitt: "Terry came home this morning." David had not previously mentioned Terry to Pitt. He now explained that Terry was his brother; and that he was a sailor in the merchant navy who had twice sailed round the world, which was of course untrue. He did not tell Pitt that Terry was mentally ill; nor was he to do so in the three years that Pitt remained his manager.

If the incident provided another example of David's fear of facing his family's past, his father, John Jones, showed a remarkable change of attitude. John was now stricken with remorse for his former jealousy towards Terry, and told him that he was welcome to stay at Plaistow Grove. Thereafter Terry would spend the week having treatment at Farnborough Hospital, and stay at Plaistow Grove at weekends. In later years, Terry had nothing but praise for John's kindness. "He told me how sorry he was for the way he had behaved," Terry said. "There was nothing he would not do for me."

Terry's return to Plaistow Grove was followed by David's departure. He had been spending an increasing amount of time at Manchester Street, and now told Pitt that his "domestic situation" was getting worse. Once again, he did not tell Pitt the whole truth, saying only that the late hours he liked to keep were disturbing his father, who had to get up at seven each morning to go to work. Pitt could tell that David was under pressure, for he looked pale and strained, and suggested that he move into Manchester Street. With visible relief, David agreed.

On June 11th, John Jones took David and his belongings to Manchester Street in his tiny Fiat 500. John inspected the flat and told David approvingly: 'It's very masculine." It was indeed a suitable bachelor flat, with a sitting room, kitchen, and two adjacent bedrooms. Pitt soon found that the meticulous order in which he preferred to live had been violated by the clothes, books and sheaves of paper littering the floor of David's room. After failing to mend David's ways, he simply ensured that David's door was kept shut and tried to forget the chaos behind it.

Pitt now embarked on his self-appointed task of improving David's mind. He dismissed the beat writers Terry had recommended as "juvenilia", and showed him the more cultivated authors on his bookshelves: among them André Gide, Antoine de Saint Exupéry, and Oscar Wilde. David was captivated by both *The Picture of Dorian Gray* and *The Little Prince*, which he read again and again. Pitt looked upon him disapprovingly as a product of the first television generation, and often took him to the theatre, from the classics to pantomime – "the good, the bad, and the indifferent," Pitt says, "allowing him to make up his own mind as to which was which".

Pitt describes the year David spent living with him in Manchester Street as "one of the most stimulating periods of my life". Their relationship was close and relaxed: David would walk around naked, "his big dick swaying from side to side", says Pitt, which prompted him to paper over the kitchen window to block the view obtained by the women living in a neighbouring flat. Once when

Ken emerged from the bathroom without any clothes, David produced a ruler to measure his penis and exclaim, in mock-awe, "Ye gods." How much closer the relationship became, however, Pitt declines to say: "That is something that belongs to him and me." He agrees that it was "strong and affectionate", adding: "I think most people who knew us accept that."

For all the intimacy, David, then twenty, retained a large degree of control over the relationship. "He had a way of sitting in a chair and looking at you with a certain intensity," Pitt says. "He managed to look at you as though his eyes were slightly closed but then you realised that they were in fact wide open and you got the impression that, as you were talking to him, he was analysing and dissecting every word you said and forming an opinion in his mind."

A friend of Pitt's, the actor Michael Armstrong, was franker still. "He seemed always to be playing a cat and mouse game with you," he told Pitt later. "He flirted, he really did."

The Deram album was released on June 1st. It was preceded by another single, 'The Laughing Gnome' and 'The Gospel According To Tony Day', which was issued on April 14th: 'The Laughing Gnome' was a delightful children's record, with David showing his mastery of the pun, enhanced by further ingenious sound effects from Mike Vernon; 'The Gospel According To Tony Day' was the first of a sequence of lyrics in which David reviewed the progress in life of his friends, imagined or otherwise. They attracted little attention at the time – although 'The Laughing Gnome' sold over a quarter-million copies when it was reissued at the height of David's fame – but the Deram album brought some encouraging reviews, the most favourable that by *New Musical Express*, which considered it "intelligent", "refreshing", and "promising", particularly as David had written all fourteen songs himself.

Beneath David's impassive exterior, Pitt believed he could discern a measure of optimism that he was making progress at last. David was heartened by a letter from the film director Bryan Forbes, who told Pitt that the record had "a most unusual quality", and asked him to congratulate David on his behalf. Pitt redoubled his own efforts, buying 100 copies of the record which he distributed to disc-jockeys, producers, music writers. He also placed a half-page advertisement for the album in *Record Retailer*.

Yet neither Pitt nor David could help feeling that their bid to arouse interest in the album was being stifled by apathy on the part of Decca itself. The feeling was shared, within the company, by Mike Vernon, who felt that Decca had never truly adjusted to the new market for popular music and would in fact prefer to have nothing to do with it. "It was a real marble legs and stiff upper lips company and it was very hard to persuade them that they were in the pop record industry," Vernon says. He doubts whether Decca's chairman, Sir Edward Lewis, was even aware that the record had been released; certainly he had no intention of spending money promoting it. Nor did Vernon have any opportunity of altering the chairman's view: in seven years of Decca, Vernon encountered Lewis just once, as he came out of a lift.

Vernon gamely persevered on David's behalf, producing new recordings of 'Love You Till Tuesday' and 'Did You Ever Have A Dream' which were released as David's third Deram single on July 14th. The reviews were the most complimentary yet: "This boy really is something different" (*Record Mirror*); "a mature and stylish performance" (*Record Retailer*); "very funny, and deserves instant recognition" (*Melody Maker*).

In the US, too, interest was stirring. Decca had a subsidiary company in New York, London Records, which was well aware of their chairman's limited tastes and had won considerable autonomy in its operations. It released both 'Rubber Band' and 'Love You Till Tuesday' as singles, *Cashbox* selecting the latter as its Newcomer Pick on September 2nd. London also distributed copies of the album, which was played by radio stations in New York and Philadelphia. Although few material benefits accrued, the American connection brought a new and significant name into David's life: the record producer Tony Visconti.

Of Italian ancestry – and of discernibly Mediterranean good looks – Visconti was born in Brooklyn in 1944. He learned the ukelele at the age of five and by thirteen was playing the guitar at Italian weddings. He graduated to jazz, and played the double-bass in New York night clubs; then he became a song-writer and record producer at a New York music company, the Richmond Organization, whose owner, Howie Richmond, was a partner of David's British publisher, David Platz. Richmond was hugely impressed by David's Deram album, and gave away several hundred copies in the US, together with a thirty-two-page printed collection of his songs which Platz had published.

In 1967 Visconti came to Britain to work as a staff producer with another of Platz's companies, Straight Record. He worked successfully with Georgie Fame and Joe Cocker, and established a reputation for coping with such supposedly unmanageable figures as Marc Bolan. Platz then proposed that Visconti should work with David, suggesting that since David seemed uncertain what musical style he should adopt, Visconti could help him decide.

When Visconti met David, he found him "very young and very wide-eyed". David warmed to Visconti instantly – not least, Visconti suspected, because he was the first American he had worked with. Visconti thought David "a nice, well-mannered Englishman", and certainly not "the bizarre person he was made out to be – or would later become. We became very close in a very short space of time."

That meeting was the start of what was probably the most fruitful musical collaboration of David's entire career. By 1986, Visconti had produced nine of David's albums, taking him from the 1960s to the 1980s. He developed a matchless ability to interpret David's intentions and make his own contribution, skills vital as the techniques of record production became ever more sophisticated and complex.

By the late 1960s it was no longer a matter of going into a recording studio and belting out an entire album in the space of a day or so, as the Beatles had done five years before. It was a question of "laying down tracks" on separate recording channels and mixing and remixing them, over a period of weeks or months. The equipment Mike Vernon used for the Deram album had eight channels; ten years later, thirty-two channels would become commonplace, and some of David's later albums were even compiled in different continents, with the backing tracks recorded in Europe, and David's melody and vocal lines added in the US. A partner like Visconti who could keep control over what was happening while still supplying his own creative input deserved recognition almost on a par with David's own.

David's partnership with Visconti also marked the extension of what might best be termed his twin-track strategy of human relations. Not only was he skilled in being all things to all men – and to all women – he was also becoming adept at separating out the diverse strands of his life.

David suspected, correctly, that Visconti was not someone Pitt would approve of: Pitt had little liking for the young, confident American, of left-wing sympathies, unafraid to speak his mind. Pitt was also nervous of those of David's colleagues he feared could threaten their own close friendship; later, in a rare display of invective, he called Visconti "a draft-dodging anarchist".

Visconti denies that he was either a draft-dodger or an anarchist: "I was," he says, "a flower-child." He also denies that it was ever his intention to come between David and Pitt; thanks to David's skill in keeping the two men apart, he says, he was hardly aware of Pitt at all. "The point is, I never got the impression that Ken Pitt was managing David," Visconti says. "He was not presented to me as David's official manager by David. He was somebody David never talked about."

On September 1st, David made a further attempt to find a hit-record formula when he recorded a new single at the Advision Studios at Bond Street. It was Visconti's production début with David, for he replaced Mike Vernon at the request of David Platz. The A side, 'Let Me Sleep Beside You', displayed considerable confidence in both its lyrics and its arrangement. David had written it as a conscious attempt to produce commercial material that would appeal to Decca, but it was better than that. The lyric, resuming some of the themes of the Deram album, showed David putting aside childhood preoccupations and advancing into the adult world.

It was also the most overtly sexual lyric David had yet written, depicting a woman reaching maturity and sharing her new pleasures with her lover. The tune was sensuous and evocative, sketched on a twelve-string guitar against a background of cellos, with the expert assistance of John McLaughlin on rhythm guitar and Andy White on drums, both recruited by Visconti.

The B side, 'Karma Man', was a further exploration of Buddhism, although it left Visconti sceptical, for one: he saw David's interest in Buddhism as no more than a passing craze, typifying his habit of pursuing a newly discovered subject with sudden and passionate intensity, before moving abruptly to the next.

The first response from Decca was ominous: recoiling from the mildly suggestive title of the A side, they ordered it to be changed to 'Let Me Be Beside You'. Then, on September 18th, the record was presented to Decca's selection panel. It was notorious for the apparent boredom with which its members, their heads immersed in the *Daily Express* and *Daily Telegraph*, gathered each Monday morning to hear the latest offerings. "It was a joke," says Mike Vernon. "They were idiots. But that's the way the company was run." The panel turned the record down.

Ken Pitt, meanwhile, firmly believing that David should develop a wide range of talents, had been searching for other routes to popularity. He met the actor, Michael Armstrong, who had ambitions of becoming a film director. Armstrong had written a screenplay of Offenbach's opera, *Orpheus in the Underworld*, and suggested to Pitt that David would be ideal to play Orpheus himself, since in Armstrong's version he was a pop singer who is torn apart by his fans.

The film went no further: there was a strong homosexual under-current to Armstrong's script, which called for two naked men – one of them David – to kiss. The British Board of Film Censors, to whom Armstrong had submitted a script, advised that it could never be shown, and Armstrong shelved his plans. In the summer, Armstrong wrote a script for a new film, *The Image*. He showed it to David, explaining that it was intended to explore the relationship between reality and illusion in the artist's mind at the moment of creativity, and asked if he would like to play the part of an artist's model who appears to be killed time and again, only to rise on each occasion. David found intriguing similarities with some of the themes he had been exploring himself, and agreed.

David spent most of the first day's filming being soaked with a hosepipe while clinging to the window-sill of a derelict house in Paddington, and that night he developed a chill. Fortunately the rest of the film was shot indoors: David performed ably enough, given his lack of acting experience, but the film – just fourteen minutes long – was awarded an X certificate and was rarely shown until released as a video in 1984.

As Pitt had hoped, the experience stimulated David's imagination in other fields, and he wrote a television play which he hammered out on a venerable typewriter in Pitt's flat. Called *The Champion Flower Grower*, it portrayed a culture clash between a Yorkshire gardening enthusiast and a group of hippies whom he meets in London. David drew on his family background once more: this time on his father's side, for he named the gardener Haywood Kettlewell – Haywood being his father's first name. David also used the character to voice an acerbic commentary on the pretensions of hippies, calling them "a handful of weirdies who wouldn't know one end of a bullock from t'other".

Before submitting the play to the BBC, David pencilled in the names of possible actors for the leading roles, nominating Hywel Bennett for the part of Haywood Kettlewell. He reserved for himself the part of Sammy Slap, a character who, David stipulated, should be "a little backward", with a speech impediment and a loping walk: an intriguing prototype of the "outsider" characters David was later to play.

The BBC returned David's script with a brief note explaining that it displayed a "total lack of dramatic development". Doing his utmost to conceal his disappointment, David assured Ken that he understood why the BBC had returned his play. Then came an episode which revealed the strain he was under.

Early in October Pitt made a fresh approach to Decca, suggesting that they release 'When I Live My Dream' with 'Karma Man'. Both were duly played to the Decca selection panel; both were turned down. When he learned the news, David maintained his usual impassive exterior, but soon afterwards he complained of stomach pains. Pitt sent him to see his doctor who, after a thorough examination, including X-rays, reported that there was nothing physically wrong, and concluded that the pains were caused by nervous tension. Whether that was a result of the continued rejections David was suffering, or of the crisis caused by Terry's return to Plaistow Grove, the doctor was in no position to say.

11

Counting Down

As a lover of the exotic and the bizarre, the dancer Lindsay Kemp has never felt inhibited about the parts he has played. In 1977 his company staged his interpretation of Oscar Wilde's *Salomé*, in which Salomé is portrayed as a fourteen-year-old virgin who is driven to demand the head of John the Baptist by her demented sexual desires. Kemp, a short, muscular figure then approaching forty, took the part of Salomé himself. All the other female roles were danced by men, and the cast was completed by a pair of live pythons.

The orthodox dance critics have never quite taken to Kemp. They have found it hard to categorise his mélanges of decadence, transvestism and wit, and they greeted his next production after *Salomé*, a no less flamboyant interpretation of the life of the Spanish poet Lorca, with hostile reviews. Kemp, who is much given to the theatrical gesture, was so outraged that he left Britain the next day and did not perform there again for six years.

When he returned to London in the autumn of 1983, to stage three new works at Sadler's Wells, it was to a triumph. A younger generation of critics were so unstinting in their praise that even Kemp was taken aback. Nor was he ready for the flattering interest displayed in his relationship with David. He was "terribly nervous", he says, when he addressed a gathering of Bowie fans. "How," he felt them wondering, "can this bald-headed old queen have been Bowie's boyfriend?"

In 1967, Kemp was still struggling for recognition. Born in Liverpool in 1938, he had so alarmed his parents by his enthusiasm for dancing that they sent him to a naval college in Surrey. His interest in dance survived and his first public performances were at working men's clubs in northern England. Thereafter he appeared in cabaret in Brussels with Marlene Dietrich and studied mime with Marcel Marceau in Paris. In the mid-sixties he formed a dance company at the Little Theatre in Covent Garden and became prominent in the heady days of the "arts lab" movement, when it seemed that the barriers of convention had been swept aside and the higher arts stood at the threshold of widespread popular acceptance. But Kemp still found it hard to break free of the customary stereotypes: "I was either cast as a tarty drag queen, or something that was very arty and elite," he said. After yet another performance to a barren auditorium, he lamented: "Why will no one come to see poor Lindsay?"

One of the few people who did go to see Kemp in the autumn of 1967 was David. He was enthralled, and telephoned Kemp to ask if they could meet. Kemp was duly flattered, for he had heard David's Deram album, and had been "terribly moved" by his voice. "It was something fresh that I hadn't heard before but at the same time I felt that I knew it very well. I recognised it from my own experience, my own life. I saw my own heart reflected there."

Even so, Kemp was not prepared for the David who came to his flat in Soho. "I expected him to be not in the least bit physically attractive, with a voice as beautiful as that. I was expecting a very pimply youth to be standing at the door. I was overwhelmed on opening the door to find an angel there."

That encounter was the start of a relationship that was to have a decisive effect on David's career. Kemp became both David's tutor and lover, helping him to shed his inhibitions and discover new possibilities of theatricality and display. David also used his growing skills of manipulation and dissimulation to good effect – until their affair met a dénouement as melodramatic as anything Kemp had ever staged.

Kemp was holding dance and movement classes in Covent Garden which David started to attend, doing his best to improvise to Kemp's trilled single-word instructions – "bird", "wind", "birth". Kemp found David stiff and inflexible at first: "He was considerably more inhibited than he is now and considerably less confident."

David showed little enthusiasm for formal teaching; and Kemp points out that his classes did not include, as has been widely written, instruction in mime. But David was learning wider lessons from Kemp, who encouraged him to be as flamboyant as he was himself. Kemp also taught David the use of make-up, but did not – as has also been widely written, largely because Kemp himself first made the claim – spray David's hair with red lacquer, foreshadowing one of his later stage personas. That was David's own work, and even Kemp was taken aback when David arrived for classes after dyeing his hair red himself that morning. "I didn't mean he should go that far," Kemp says.

David often stayed with Kemp in his Soho flat, and in due course introduced him to Ken Pitt. It was an awkward occasion: "Ken is the kind of guy who suffers in silence," says Kemp, "and David was a bit clumsy in those days." Before long, Kemp composed a new dance about their affair. Entitled *Pierrot in Turquoise*, it had just three parts. David, as Cloud, was the "golden-haired swain", and Kemp, the Pierrot, was his suitor. The third part, Harlequin, was taken by Jack Birkett, a tall and imposing man, known otherwise as the Great Orlando, who was remarkably adept at overcoming the seemingly fatal handicap, for a dancer, of being almost totally blind.

Pierrot in Turquoise had its première at the Oxford Playhouse on December 28th. Kemp made his entrance by descending in a white hammock that represented the moon, while David, as Cloud, flitted about him. David wore a papier-mâché mask modelled on Kemp's face, and the Great Orlando held up the frame of a mirror so that Kemp could paint himself with moonbeams. David sang several of his own songs, including 'When I Live My Dream'. The performance won generous reviews, with David singled out for mention. *Stage* called him an "inventive composer", and the *Oxford Mail* praised his "haunting songs, which he sings in a superb, dreamlike voice".

After a brief rest in London, the show prepared to depart for the Lake District, where it was to appear at the Rosehill Theatre near Whitehaven. The theatre was the personal indulgence of the silk manufacturer Sir Nicholas Sekers, who had converted a barn in the grounds of his eighteenth-century mansion. It held barely 100 people, and its interior walls were lined with pure silk. Sekers's powers of patronage enabled him to lure artists of international standing to Whitehaven, where they played before audiences who had often been imported on special trains from London.

Such lavishness was a natural lure to Kemp, and he had persuaded Sekers to stage *Pierrot in Turquoise* on three successive nights, January 3rd–5th, 1968, and to contribute a generous subsidy to his company into the bargain. "I was in heaven," Kemp says. "I had sponsorship that I had never had before. I had a new show opening. I was in love with an angel who loved me. I had everything – or so I thought."

The party that set off on the 270-mile journey to Whitehaven in a rented Transit van numbered seven. As well as David, Kemp and the Great Orlando, there was the accompanist Michael Garrett, the director Craig San Roque and his wife, and – at the wheel of the Transit – the costume and set designer, Natasha Kornilof. She was a short, effervescent woman, who had been brought up in India by her Russian father and English mother, and who had been working with Kemp for several years. It was largely a labour of love. Kemp would ask her to make "something wonderful" and she would do her best to oblige: "I was never paid," she says.

Natasha was nominated to drive the Transit for the familiar reason that she was the only member of the company with a driving licence. But she was happy to be making the journey in David's company, for she too was having an affair with him. It had begun after they had been introduced by Kemp, who had told her of "this very curious young man" he had met. "I thought, Yes he is, and he's lovely, and it started almost instantly."

David came to her flat in Greenwich and between times helped her to paint the backcloths for *Pierrot in Turquoise*. She found herself curiously vulnerable to David's demands: apparently incapable of looking after himself, he would only have to announce that he was hungry and she would hasten to prepare him a meal. Yet, she says, their affair was "a wonderful experience. He was a wonderful lover, absolutely without qualification, over anyone." David divided his time between Greenwich, Soho and Manchester Street. Kemp and Natasha were unaware that they were rivals; when David felt that an explanation for his absence was called for, he said that he was visiting his mother in Bromley.

After covering the last part of the journey to Whitehaven on roads deep in snow, the entire company was lodged in a freezing cold farmhouse with uneven floorboards and thin plaster walls. David spent the early part of their first night there with Kemp, who had a four-poster bed. Then he slipped away.

"I remember that he said, 'I won't be long,'" Kemp recalls. "I nodded off and then I heard voices, what shall I say, *noises*, coming through that old farmhouse wall. When I went out, Natasha's room was across the way, and his shoes were lying on the floor outside her door. It's horrible to wake up when you expect someone to be there and they're not, they're wrapped up in bed with some woman, and then you hear the music coming through the wall."

Kemp confronted Natasha in the morning. "He's *my* boyfriend," he told her.

"No, he isn't," Natasha replied. "He's mine."

David was summoned and there was a furious row between all three. David seemed little affected at the chaos he had wrought: "He was a bit like Stan Laurel," says Kemp, "very pale and slightly puzzled, with knitted eyebrows." That afternoon, with preparations for the first night under way, Kemp tried to provoke a reaction from David. The story is taken up by the Great Orlando.

"Suddenly I heard this scream from the dressing room," he says.

"Nobody paid any attention, we thought it was someone practising something, and I continued doing my stretches and bounces." Then he was called to the dressing room to find Kemp lying on the floor with blood trickling from his wrists. "I said, 'Check to see if it isn't Kensington Gore,' but it wasn't."

The Great Orlando removed his garters and applied a tourniquet to Kemp's arms. He and the accompanist, Michael Garrett, rolled Kemp into a cape and carried him out of the theatre, passing a bewildered Sir Nicholas Sekers who had just arrived in his Rolls-Royce to check that all was well. Kemp was rushed to Whitehaven Hospital where it was discovered that his injuries were rather less than terminal. "It was a *gesture*," Kemp admits. "Enough to produce plenty of blood. They put Elastoplast on my wrist and told me not to be so daft."

Kemp returned to the theatre just as the audience, in dinner jackets and evening dress, were settling into their seats. Even by Kemp's standards, the performance attained new dramatic heights. As Kemp was lowered in his hammock, the wrists of his Pierrot costume were stained red with blood. David was at last sufficiently moved to cry, his tears saturating his papier-mâché mask and causing it to disintegrate. The audience hailed the performance as a triumph.

Later that night, it was Natasha's turn to occupy centre stage, when she gulped down a handful of sleeping pills. She denies now that this was a serious suicide attempt: "My gesture wasn't as big as Lindsay's," she says. "It was purely that I was in such a state that I kept on swallowing more and more pills. I couldn't get to sleep and it was freezing cold."

In the morning, both Natasha and Kemp observed that David was rather subdued. He spent the remaining nights sleeping alone on a couch in the farmhouse's entrance hall. "We were both beastly to David for a long time afterwards," Natasha says. "He looked cold and tired and we were shouting at him, 'Go on, do that, get that.'" If David complained that he was hungry, Natasha ignored him.

There were times in the summer of 1968 when to be young was truly heaven. To the youthful protesters who choked back the peardrop fumes of CS gas in Paris or dodged mounted police outside the American Embassy in London, it briefly seemed that they were part of a political uprising that could alter the old order for ever. The previous year the adherents of flower power, with their kaftans and psychedelia and talk of universal love, had filled the streets; now the protests had acquired a sharper, political edge. In the end, of course, the old order reasserted itself. But for those involved, the year would always have a resonance to rank with the true turning points of European history, such as 1848 and 1917.

So far as Pitt could see, David took no interest in the summer's political events. Given Pitt's right-wing views, and David's propensity for displaying only those aspects of himself which would be approved of, that was hardly surprising. But there was one way in which, David showed that he was suffused with the spirit of 1968: his growing distrust of any proposal that he considered – the word is best spoken with a sneer – "commercial".

In 1967, David had earned just £322. His appearances with Lindsay Kemp in early 1968, including two weeks at the Mercury Theatre, Notting Hill, and a further week at the Intimate Theatre in Palmers Green in March, brought him precisely nothing. Pitt renewed the publishing contract with Essex Music for an advance of £1,500: the sum sounded handsome enough, but its true value was much reduced if, as Decca seemed determined to ensure, none of his records were released. Only small sums accrued from playing a periwigged dancer in a BBC2 production of a Chekhov play, *The Pistol Shot* – Lindsay Kemp had helped him secure the part – and from three songs David recorded in Hamburg for German television.

Pitt's next proposal was that David should start performing in cabaret, and he told David he was certain he could secure him bookings in the West End by which he could earn £100 a week. At first David seemed tempted, and cooperated in drawing up a list of songs he might perform. A few were his own but most were modern standards like 'Trains And Boats And Planes', 'Sonny', and 'What Kind Of Fool Am I?' Then David changed his mind, and told Pitt that he was only prepared to sing his own songs.

David's vacillation was undoubtedly influenced by Tony Visconti, who believed firmly that David should not compromise his musical principles. On March 12th, he and David went to the Decca studios in West Hampstead in yet another attempt to pass the Decca selection board. They recorded David's lyric, 'In The Heat Of The Morning', which continued the theme of the Deram album by telling of the search for affection against a background of childhood concerns, such as tin soldiers, butterflies and rainbows. The B side, 'London Bye Ta Ta', was another sharp piece of social observation, starting with a snatch of West Indian patois that David had overheard at a railway station, and telling of a farewell to London, a "strange young town" that "brought me down." Four weeks later, Decca turned both recordings down.

Soon afterwards Pitt asked Decca to release David from his contract. With no sign of regret, Decca agreed. David had now been rejected by four different record companies: Vocalion, Parlophone, Pye and Decca. While Pitt wondered whom to approach next, to David there was one obvious contender, precisely because it seemed free of the stigma of being "commercial". That was Apple, the company set up by the Beatles in a bid to wrest control from those malevolent figures John Lennon called "the men in suits".

Since Apple's chief publicist, Derek Taylor, had promised to consider "anyone with something creative to offer", Pitt sent Apple a copy of David's Deram album. Three months later, as Pitt learned in a graceless letter from Gordon Waller, who after achieving passing fame as a pop star had become Apple's head of A and R, they too turned David down. "Apple Records is not interested in signing David Bowie," Waller wrote. "The reason is that we don't feel he is what we're looking for at the moment. Thank you for your time."

By now, John Jones was beginning to wonder whether his ambitions for David were as doomed as his own venture into show business forty years before. On June 3rd, David did make a solo appearance at the Royal Festival Hall, in a bill topped by Tyrannosaurus Rex, for which he received £20. Soon afterwards he auditioned for the stage musical *Hair*, but was turned down. He also auditioned for a part in the film of *The Virgin Soldiers*, by Leslie Thomas – Thomas, who remembered his father's approach at the time of the King Bees, spotted him "sitting in an anteroom, looking half starved" – but failed that too. He then took a part-time job operating a Xerox machine at a printing firm near Fleet Street, for which he was paid £6 a week. To his father, it seemed that he was rapidly losing interest in a musical career.

On July 17th, John Jones wrote to Pitt to express his anxieties over David. "His earnings from show business," he complained, "do not give him sufficient income to pay for his Social Security stamp." Pitt responded by pointing out that David had a "backlog of debts" from the Ralph Horton days and that the Essex advance was not to be sneezed at. He also took the opportunity to press his proposal that David should go into cabaret. Pitt's arguments struck home, and on David's next visit to Plaistow Grove his father took up Pitt's cause. David phoned Pitt that evening and asked: "When do we start?"

The next day, Pitt drew up another list of songs for David to perform, roughly half of them David's own. Even now David resisted. When Pitt said he would have to address the audience between each song, David protested that he wouldn't know what to say. Pitt offered to write a script, reassuring David it would "ooze with sincerity". He then arranged for David to give auditions to several prominent booking agents.

David gave the auditions as if he had never had doubts, and the agents were amazed at the confidence with which he performed. But one of them, believing he was conveying the ultimate accolade, said that David was "better than Cliff Richard". A second applied the *coup de grâce* by telling Pitt: "It's a marvellous act, but where can I book it? It's too good!" David looked witheringly at Pitt, who never mentioned cabaret again.

In August, David moved out of Manchester Street. As he told Pitt, his new address was 22 Clareville Grove, South Kensington. There, he was sharing an attic room, at the top of a narrow staircase, with a singer and actress who went by the stage name of Hermione Farthingale. Although he did not yet tell Pitt, David was in love.

From an archetypal middle-class family in the home counties, Hermione was a young woman of classic English good looks, tall, willowy and self-possessed. She and David had met at Lindsay Kemp's dance centre and had started an affair soon after the Whitehaven débâcle. Although his affair with Natasha Kornilof was over, David was still seeing Kemp, and, as before, wove convoluted tales to explain his absences. When David went to see Hermione, he told Ken Pitt that he was visiting Kemp, sometimes adding the refinement that Kemp needed him because he was ill; he told Kemp, as before, that he was visiting his mother.

It was Pitt who punctured David's stories by telephoning to ask Kemp, with a show of innocence, if he had recovered from his illness. And it was Kemp, his suspicions aroused, who discovered the full truth when he attended rehearsals for *The Pistol Shot* at the BBC. Hermione was David's dancing partner, and they were entwined off the set as well as on. "I can remember the agony of the journey back from Television Centre when he was tagging along with her," Kemp says. "I was livid . . ." Soon afterwards David put an end to all speculation by moving in with Hermione at Clareville Grove.

The person who saw most of them at this time was John Hutchinson, one of the Yorkshire members of the Buzz, who had teamed up with David again. Hutch found Hermione "a nice lass, but a bit posh for me — more like the daughters of my parents' friends. I was always very careful not to swear in front of her."

He enjoyed visiting their attic bed-sitting room, even if it was rather cramped: "There weren't any chairs so we always used to sit on the floor, and David would pop out for a take-away curry. There were grasses and fringed things on the bed, and it had a nice feel about it."

Hutch saw, and approved, a new David, and attributed that to Hermione. "They seemed to suit each other very well. It made David very different. He was completely recovered from the Ralph Horton period. He was fine."

Hutch had resumed his partnership with David as a consequence of David's attempt to resolve the impasse his career seemed to have reached. David and Hermione, who also sang and played guitar, had formed a multi-media trio with a guitarist, Tony Hill. They named it Turquoise but it had just one engagement, at the Round-house on September 14th, before Hill withdrew. Having spent the summer working at a Butlin's holiday camp, Hutch had come to London in search of work, and telephoned David to see if he had any ideas. David invited him to Clareville Grove and asked what style of music he was playing. "I said, 'I'm into Leonard Cohen songs.' I sang him a couple and he asked me if I wanted to take over from Tony."

The new trio was called Feathers. For David, it represented a further step away from commercialism. Its repertoire consisted mostly of David's songs, interspersed with others by the Belgian singer Jacques Brel, and augmented with tape-recordings. David also performed mime, which he had taught himself after watching Lindsay Kemp. Hutch – still the down-to-earth Yorkshireman, at least in David's eyes – saw Feathers as "trying to be arty, trying to be highbrow", but enjoyed it all the same. "There was a folksy feel to the music, it was all a lot less hassle."

Feathers scored a notable accolade when they were interviewed by *The Times*, who, discerning that something was stirring in that distant territory known as "youth", published a three-part series entitled 'The Restless Generation'. The occasion provided an early example of David's obliging readiness to supply journalists with the material they were looking for. He told the interviewer, Sheila More: "We feel our parents' generation has lost control, given up, they're scared of the future . . . I feel it's basically their fault that things are so bad." Sheila More wrote that Feathers typified "the pop world's dismissal of the rest of society" at whose roots lay "a hatred of hypocrisy".

David also lifted a corner of the curtain with which he had veiled his family life, saying that he found it hard to communicate with his father. "He and his friends were all in the army during the war, an experience I can't imagine, and he takes naturally to iron discipline. Discussing religion embarrasses him, and to get emotional about something, well, that's only fit for the servants' quarters" – here David offered a comparison so improbable that it spoke volumes – "like mental illness".

Ken Pitt had little sympathy with a projection of David as youthful revolutionary, and regarded Feathers, he later said, as "an innocuous divertissement that nobody wished to pay for". In three months, Feathers secured just three bookings, netting £56. Pitt meanwhile continued his search for more orthodox outlets for David, the most lucrative being two further appearances on German television, for which he received £280.

In the autumn, David tried once again to make a single. The impetus this time came from the publisher, David Platz, who agreed to finance the session, held on October 24th at the Trident Studios, with Tony Visconti acting as producer. It was not a success. Accompanied by both Hermione and Hutch, David recorded a wistful ballad he had written entitled 'Ching-A-Ling', with another original composition, 'Back To Where You've Never Been', on the B side. But Visconti was dissatisfied with Hutch, who felt in turn that he had been asked to sing in too high a key. Even when Visconti remixed the recording and Platz sent it to several record companies, none was interested.

Pitt meanwhile made a fresh approach to Mickie Most, who had been thwarted in his attempt to record David in the days of the Manish Boys, and had since become a successful purveyor of hits with his own company, RAK Records. The David of 1968 did not impress him, for having asked Pitt to send him the Deram album, he did not respond.

In November, David made a brief foray into the cinema. Although he had been rejected for a major part in *The Virgin Soldiers* he managed to secure a week's work as an actor, for which he received the Equity minimum of £40. However, all but a glimpse of him – as he flashes past the camera during a bar-room fight – ended up on the cutting-room floor. This time he did not bother to conceal his disenchantment from Pitt. "If that's Hollywood," David declared, "you can stuff it."

As the end of 1968 approached, David's prospects appeared more dismal than ever. Pitt calculated that David's income from all sources would not reach £1,000; and since he had not remotely recouped the advance from Essex Music, David Platz exercised his right to extend the contract for six months without further payment. Concluding that a bold move was required, Pitt decided to take a most uncharacteristic risk.

During his visits to Germany, Pitt had sounded out a television producer, Günther Schneider, on the idea of a programme featuring David. Schneider was enthusiastic, and proposed a half-hour special to be recorded in colour. Once back in Britain, Pitt decided to make the programme himself, reckoning that it would act as a showcase for David's talents, as well as earning some useful revenue. It would cost between £7,000 and £8,000 which could be recovered through sales in Britain, Germany and Scandinavia; with Pitt retaining the copyright, everything above that would be clear profit.

To direct the film, Pitt turned to his assistant from the Manfred Mann days, Malcolm Thomson. Thomson was keen to break into films and had been looking for backers for a scheme to produce low-budget, soft-porn pictures. While Pitt regarded that project with due distaste, he believed that Thomson had both the enthusiasm and expertise required.

David at first took little interest in the project, unwilling to commit himself to yet another abortive scheme. When Pitt concluded a contract with Thomson in January 1969, David revealed both his scepticism and his relief, asking Pitt: "So that's definitely on, is it?" He, Pitt and Thomson selected the songs that he would play, and David agreed to perform a mime. Pitt also told David that the film was an ideal opportunity to present a new song. "If you've got anything up your sleeve," he told David, "now's your chance."

A few days later, David called at Manchester Street. He nestled, cat-like, in the elegant chaise longue in Pitt's living room and tuned in his twelve-string guitar. Then, after strumming a brief introduction, he started to sing:

Ground control to Major Tom . . .

12

Lifting Off

By Malcolm Thomson's account, the writing of 'Space Oddity', the song that was to bring David the success he craved, was a communal affair. Thomson and his friend Susie Mercer, the film's production assistant, would meet David and Hermione in Clareville Grove where the song "built up over three or four evenings". Its foundation stone was a riff David had composed on a stylophone, an almost childishly simple instrument described by its manufacturers as "a pocket electronic organ with a new concept in sound". (The advertisements also boasted that it was "so easy, a baby could learn to play it in fifteen minutes" – a claim supported, rather unfortunately, with photographs of the Australian singer, Rolf Harris.) It was, says Thomson, "David's toy of the moment" – and once the tune was established, "the lyrics fell into place".

In future, David was to compose many of his numbers this way, taking the germ of a musical idea and building on it with his colleagues. It was less usual for him to write the lyrics in the same manner, but in this instance, so Thomson describes, the collaborative spirit of the occasion prevailed. "We all provided lines," Thomson says. "It was very much a spontaneous thing among a group of people who were finding it fun to do what they were doing."

John Hutchinson contributed to David's success too. He was now working as a draughtsman by day and calling on David at Clareville Grove in the evening. On one such visit, David demonstrated the 'Space Oddity' tune on his stylophone, and Hutch joined in on David's twelve-string Gibson guitar. Hutch supplied "the few odd chords" and suggested that by scraping his guitar strings, David could convey the impression of a space rocket taking off. On a second visit, when the lyric had been written, David sang the words of the astronaut, while Hutch took the part of "ground control".

There were outside influences too: as David himself later acknowledged, he received a powerful stimulus from Stanley Kubrick's film *2001 – a Space Odyssey*, which also featured an astronaut who drifts into space, with instantly fatal results. Hutch identifies a second input from the Bee Gees, whose latest album he spied in the Clareville Grove flat: there was a marked resemblance between the timbre of 'Space Oddity' and the Bee Gees' 'New York Mining Disaster', both of which feature a twelve-string guitar and derive their style from American folk music. "'Space Oddity' was a Bee Gees type song," Hutch says. "David knew it, and he said so at the time. He said it was like the Bee Gees album and the way he sang it, it's a Bee Gees thing."

'Space Oddity' neatly illustrates the extent to which David looked to his colleagues for inspiration and support, and the multiplicity of sources on which, consciously or not, he tended to draw. Some jaundiced observers have called this process plagiarism, while David himself has at times engagingly confessed to the extent to which he has borrowed other people's ideas. In fact, no artists exist in a vacuum, and all soak up influences and impressions from life around them; the true test is whether, as with 'Space Oddity', the creative outcome is greater than the sum of its parts.

At first, the story of 'Space Oddity' appears straightforward enough: an astronaut, Major Tom, departs on a space journey from which he does not return. Its message, however, was more profound, for David implied that the astronaut had been so disillusioned by his distant view of earth that he did not return by choice. It was another example of David's instinct for the cross-currents eddying beneath the cultural mainstream, for this was hardly a fashionable message at a time when most people were thoroughly enthralled by the US's efforts to send a man to the moon. In retrospect, however, 'Space Oddity' appears as a rejection of the brash optimism of the 1960s and a marker for the decade to come.

The complexities of David's melody, by far the most subtle and imaginative he had yet composed, reinforced this subversive message, with its constant variation between the keys of C major and E minor, its shifts of tempo and lifts into higher keys to reflect the passage of the spacecraft, and the dialogue between the two main voices; one of Bowie's more perceptive critics called it "a kind of solo mini-opera".

By contrast, the words of 'Space Oddity' appear almost banal at first, lacking the subtlety and ambiguity of many of the lyrics of the Deram album. Major Tom takes his "protein pills" and dons his helmet; after countdown he arrives in space to find himself "floating in a most peculiar way", while

> Planet Earth is blue
> And there's nothing I can do.

Yet there *was* an alternative reading to the lyric which gives it the secondary meaning of which David was so fond. For one group of listeners was in no doubt what 'Space Oddity' meant. "As soon as I heard it," one says, "I knew exactly what it was about. It's about skag."

Skag, for the uninitiated, is slang for heroin; and, as one user explains, 'Space Oddity' precisely matches the experience of "shooting up". It begins with the careful ritual of preparation, represented in 'Space Oddity' by ground control's flat, emotionless instructions to Major Tom. There is a further indication in the countdown: "When you shoot up you start to count down from ten to twelve, and when you get to zero you suddenly feel it take effect." At this moment – paralleled in 'Space Oddity' by an ethereal swelling of the music – comes the illusion of arriving in a new dimension, precisely described by "floating in a most peculiar way", where everything looks "very different", together with the feelings of distancing and helplessness that the lyric also reproduces.

When David wrote 'Space Oddity', there were ample precedents for the use of ambiguous lyrics to convey the sensations of drug-taking. The most renowned was the Beatles' 'Lucy In The Sky With Diamonds' on their *Sergeant Pepper* album in 1967, with the song's initials, for all John Lennon's protestations, the giveaway. What was more, David later admitted that he had indulged in a "silly flirtation" with heroin in 1968 – the year 'Space Oddity' was written. And he provided a telling clue in his song 'Ashes To Ashes', released in 1980, which contains the otherwise enigmatic couplet:

> Ashes to Ashes, funk to funky,
> We know Major Tom's a junkie.

The filming of *Love You Till Tuesday*, for which 'Space Oddity' was intended, began in January, with the opening sequences shot on a wintry Hampstead Heath, and the remainder in a studio in Greenwich. They included three songs from the Deram album: 'Sell Me A Coat', 'Rubber Band', and 'When I Live My Dream'; and two numbers that David had recorded in his futile attempts to impress Decca: 'Ching-A-Ling' and 'Let Me Sleep Beside You' – its title restored to the full, pre-bowdlerised version. A sixth, 'When I'm Five', was another journey into the wish-fulfilment of David's childhood, which David sang in a suitably infantile voice.

David proved a pliant subject for Malcolm Thomson's direction,

obediently following his instructions and displaying an uncomplaining professionalism that was to mark all his later forays into
the cinema. For Hutch, the main surprise was the unexpected
insight he acquired into the character of Hermione. During 'Sell
Me A Coat', she and Hutch had to stare into each other's eyes.
"Our noses were almost touching and she said something naughty
to me," Hutch says. "I realised she wasn't just a straight lady as I
had thought."

The most original item was a mime, 'The Mask', which David
had first performed while with Feathers. Hutch had always been
impressed with it: "It was great – every time I saw him doing it I
really enjoyed it," he says. It offered a prescient comment on the
pitfalls of stardom. A young actor discovers he can make an
audience laugh by donning a magic mask but when appearing at
the Palladium (the acid test for success, be it noted, posited by Ken
Pitt) he strangles himself while trying to remove it. But newspaper
reports of the accident do not mention the mask, implying that
both it and stardom were an illusion. David emphasised his personal interest in the tale by depicting a visit to his parents, where
his father comments, in his gentle Yorkshire accent, "Oh, son, you
do make us laff – that were very good."

The film's *pièce de résistance* was 'Space Oddity' – and here
Malcolm Thomson's personal interests, revealed by his venture
into "adult movies", almost got the better of him. David, who
wore a silver lurex suit, was subjected to a partial strip-tease by
two "space sirens" wearing diaphanous dresses, one played by
Thomson's girlfriend, Susie Mercer, the other by a model, Saman-
tha Bond, who had previously achieved a measure of notoriety by
displaying her pubic hair in a Sunday colour supplement. Thomson
would like to have made more use of sex in the film. "But the
climate of the times was against it," he says. "Besides, I didn't
think Ken Pitt would approve."

By now, Pitt had become unhappy on another score: the project
was running out of money. He and Thomson had agreed on a
budget of £7,500. Pitt had made his first production payment of
£2,650 to Thomson on January 10th, with further payments in
stages thereafter. When the filming was complete, Pitt assumed
that Thomson was at work on the editing. But inexorably costs
mounted until the budget was far exceeded.

"Malcolm was coming to me for more money all the time,"
says Pitt. "Finally I said no." Then the company providing the
equipment for the film told Pitt it would not release the negative
until its charges had been paid. After some delay, Pitt managed to

raise the necessary finance, but there was nothing left to pay for the linking narrative he had intended to include.

The delay was more disastrous, Pitt felt, in another respect. When he approached the German television company, ZDF, to try to sell the film, he found that his contact, Günther Schneider, had moved on. A second German company in Munich also turned the film down. The BBC turned it down too, although a producer did helpfully suggest that Pitt should make a film with Tom Jones instead. With his bruised feelings exacerbated by the size of his financial stake, Pitt accepted defeat. "The film went up on the shelf," he says, "and there it stayed." That remained true until Pitt marketed the film as a video in 1984, recovering his investment several times over.

The failure of *Love You Till Tuesday* was matched by the collapse of another dream: David's affair with Hermione. Its deterioration had become clear to all around during the filming, with palpable tension between them and at least one overt row. When the film was over, Hermione told David that their relationship was over too.

David was to mark its brief span with impressive precision. Later that year he noted in a press release that he had fallen in love at the age of "twenty-one and three quarters" – and that, by twenty-two, he was "solo again". Far more turbulent feelings were involved than this spare summary allowed. He revealed some of them in his lyric, 'Letter to Hermione', which was racked with a painful nostalgia:

> I care for no one else but you
> I tear my soul to cease the pain.

A second lyric, 'She Shook Me Cold', which David wrote in 1971, displayed unmitigated anguish. He describes a lover who

> . . . sucked my dormant will

and

> . . . took my head, smashed it up

and

> Crushed me mercilessly . . .

His most bitter comment came in an interview published in 1976: falling in love, he said, "was an awful experience – it rotted me, drained me, and it was a disease".

At the core of David's reaction was his distress at having committed himself totally to another person who then rejected him. Among his friends, it was said that Hermione's middle-class parents had disapproved of David and had put pressure on her to break off their affair; and while Hermione herself had not been the entirely chaste creature Hutch had supposed, she had found it difficult to cope with David's physical demands.

For some time afterwards, David cherished hopes of being able to repair their relationship and made an approach to Hermione, via an intermediary, which she turned down. This left him almost inconsolable: he went back to Plaistow Grove and spent several days tearfully closeted in his bedroom. He also visited Dana Gillespie, to whom he would "pour out his tale of woe and troubles". When he had finally regained his composure, he returned, temporarily, to stay with Ken Pitt in Manchester Street.

The break-up with Hermione meant a change of David's musical plans. In place of the Feathers trio, he and Hutch formed a duo, David Bowie and Hutch. The nearest models were the Americans Simon and Garfunkel, although David strongly took the lead. "It was not a fifty-fifty thing," Hutch says. "He was quite dominant, and I thought I should fit in the best way I could."

David also acquired a liking for unsettling his colleagues in a manner that dramatically extended his camp stage performances with his former groups, such as the Manish Boys and the Lower Third. When he and Hutch were appearing at Westminster College in Battersea on March 11th, David embarked without warning on a line of patter Hutch had never previously heard. "It was a sort of gay patter, with me as a quiet straight man," Hutch says. "I was quite puzzled by it. I didn't know what to do except play guitar and sing, but it seemed to work."

David displayed the same persona to Ken Pitt. He arrived one morning in Pitt's office with his hair piled in curls and the same stagey feminine mannerisms, fluttering his eyelids and crossing his legs when he sat down. Pitt pretended not to notice.

Then David left Manchester Street again, sending Pitt a letter from 24 Foxgrove Road, Beckenham. "That," David peremptorily began, "is the new address." It was a decaying Victorian house, with a rambling garden, where a hard-working journalist, Mary Finnigan, occupied a ground-floor flat with her two young children. David first went there to meet one of his old neighbours from

Plaistow Grove, Barrie Jackson, who lived with his wife Christine on the top floor. Mary heard "someone playing the guitar and this wonderful voice", discovered that it was David, and asked all three down for coffee. David told her that he had just left his girlfriend and was looking for somewhere to stay as he hated living at home. Within a week he had moved into a spare room in Mary's flat, and within days was sleeping with her too.

The David whom Mary came to know was one of widely divergent roles. Like Natasha Kornilof, she encountered the helpless and dependent child: she would come home to find dishes piled high in the sink, empty tin cans scattered around the kitchen, and her stove covered with grease. "The place was an absolute tip," she says. "He was totally incompetent, he never cleaned up, he just didn't bother. He always wanted someone else to do it."

David could also appear in a completely contrary guise. Sometimes, on returning from a Saturday-afternoon shift in Fleet Street, Mary would find that he had cleaned the entire flat, laid the dining table with linen, flowers, and candles, and was ready to cook her a meal, accompanied by a programme of live and recorded music. "He would put on a show for me and the whole thing would be planned. I found his come-on very romantic, and it was inevitable that love-making was a part of it."

Through staying with Mary, David discovered there was life in the suburbs after all. By then the "alternative culture" had percolated to Beckenham. A confluence of the universal love proclaimed in 1967 and the protest movement of 1968, one of its key elements was the use of drugs, among them marijuana and LSD. David declined to take LSD but joined Mary in consuming copious amounts of marijuana. "He used to do incredible amounts of hash, and he used to drink a lot, barley wine, too," Mary says. The most fashionable substance was liquid tincture of cannabis, available on prescription to those who had a compliant doctor at hand. "You could take enough to cover the end of your fingernail and get stoned for eight hours," says Mary.

Buddhism was also in vogue again. Whereas neither Ken Pitt nor Tony Visconti saw any more substantial interest, on David's part, than a liking for burning joss-sticks, David talked to Mary about Buddhism with such animation that she believed him to be deeply committed to it. "It was a genuine thing," she says. "There was no farting about, he was not a butterfly at all." Under David's influence Mary become a devoted Buddhist herself, and remained one long after she and David had parted.

The most marked influence of the alternative culture was on

David's music. David had no money to pay Mary any rent, and she supported him for a month into the bargain. "We were broke," Mary says. "To make some loot, we thought we would put on a show." The landlord of the Three Tuns pub in Beckenham High Street agreed that David could perform in his back room on Sunday nights, where David's first appearance attracted fifty people and brought a profit of £10. Audiences soon passed a hundred and spilled out into the pub's back garden.

What began as a commercial venture was then infused with a more idealistic spirit. David and Mary decided to term the folk sessions an Arts Lab, to which they gave the wholesome name of Growth. In suburban Beckenham, this had a potent appeal. The audiences rose to 200 and became a focus for a range of other pursuits. There were light shows, street theatre, tie-dyeing classes, and music, mime and "free expression" for children.

Mary also helped to edit a cyclostyled bulletin which was itself entitled *Growth*. One of her editorials declared: "Growth is an Arts Laboratory, Growth is people, Growth is revolution, Growth grows at its own speed, expands according to the energy input it receives, is open to all, but closed to old ideas, clichés, destructive elements and grey thoughts . . ." The bulletin acted as a contact sheet for sympathisers, like the group of would-be communards who appealed for "houses where people of like mind can live together in Serenity, Tranquillity and Peace".

At its zenith the renown of the Beckenham Arts Lab spread so wide that it was invited to join the steering group of the Arts Lab in Britain Trust. David also received the ultimate accolade of an interview in the movement's house journal, the *International Times*. As with its senior namesake, *The Times*, David showed his facility for responding to both the concerns and the jargon of his interviewer, who on this occasion happened to be Mary Finnigan.

"There's very little compassion around," David told Mary. "I feel compassion as a source of energy, the individual is less important than the source of energy of which he is part." Writing music was "an extension of moving the energies . . . I'm playing energy games, and I've got a vibration on this posterity thing too." Here, too, Mary was utterly convinced of David's commitment. "We were all very sincere about being involved with the community," she says, "and David was too. He was very *very* sincere."

There was just one cloud to blemish this joyous firmament. By moving to Beckenham, David was perilously close to his parents' home in Plaistow Grove; when he visited them there, he sometimes met Terry too. Although he had usually concealed his anxieties from outsiders, he occasionally confided in Mary, making it clear that he regarded Terry as the yardstick of his own sanity. "He always felt he was very borderline in that respect," she says. It was also "the fact of Terry", she says, which explained his refusal to take LSD, for the drug was suspected, with good reason, of inducing states of mind similar to schizophrenia. Strongest of all, in Mary's view, was David's fear of "losing control".

As before, David's fears would soon emerge in his lyrics; as before, he could not resist spinning a small fantasy. He told Mary that his mismatched eyes, in reality the result of his schoolboy fight with George Underwood, were a sign of potential insanity. "He told me he had them from birth."

From Manchester Street, Ken Pitt contemplated the proceedings in Beckenham with distaste. He was personally averse to what he termed the "near-squalor of the so-called underground" and lamented the fact that David had not acquired a "sense of direction". Yet still he laboured on David's behalf. He arranged for David to appear in a commercial for a new ice-cream named, in the spirit of the times, Luv. He also attempted to capitalise on the asset represented by 'Space Oddity'. Despite the failure of his film, Pitt felt that 'Space Oddity' had enormous potential as a single – particularly since plans for the US moon mission, Apollo 11, were now advanced, giving the opportunity for one of the most dramatic publicity tie-ins of history.

By then there was hardly a record company in Britain which had not turned David down. Instead, Pitt looked to America. He wrote to Ahmet Ertegun, head of the Atlantic label in New York, to commend David to his attention. Ertegun was enthusiastic, and told Pitt to see his London representative, one Frank Fenter. After listening to 'Space Oddity', Fenter told Pitt that it was "not my cup of tea".

In the end, for all Pitt's efforts, it was David who finally found a US company that was prepared to offer him a recording contract. His success owed much to the unabashed pragmatism with which he conducted certain of his affairs – particularly with men. It also took him into a labyrinth of sexual relationships that made the imbroglio with Lindsay Kemp and Natasha Kornilof appear like a minor flirtation.

The most remembered aspect of Calvin Mark Lee, among those who met him in that period, is his appearance: a Chinese-American from San Francisco, he had awesomely beautiful features, with immaculate shoulder-length black hair, and a curious metallic disc, fixed to the centre of his forehead, that radiated the colours of the rainbow. Just what the disc was, and how it remained in place, nobody was quite sure. In fact, Lee explains today, it was a "diffraction grating", a reflective disc, made of metallised polyester, that breaks sunshine or white light into the colours of the spectrum. "It was a decorative element, or a love jewel," he explains. "It's self-adhesive."

Lee arrived in Britain in 1962. A pharmaceutical chemist, specialising in the structure of molecules, he had been awarded a three-year US government grant to take a post-doctoral fellowship at Chelsea College. His grant ran out in 1965 – he was then twenty-nine – but he decided to remain in Britain, where he had been ardently attracted to the world of popular music. "I was looking for beautiful, creative and intelligent people," he explains, "and you don't find too many of them in British scientific circles." Far easier, he says, to find them among musicians and artists, particularly at a time when access was far easier than now. "It was very nice to get to know these people as people," Lee says.

Lee was thus present at the ignition stage of the British popular music explosion, seeing the Rolling Stones and The Who in the earliest stages of their career, and meeting them informally in London's most modish clubs and discos, like Blaise's and the Speakeasy. His liking for them fell little short of adulation, spiced with feelings of sexual attraction experienced by any teenage groupie. One wall of the living room in his flat in Lower Sloane Street was decorated with photographs of the musicians he had met or would like to meet. He called it his "picture wall" and it was, he explains, "covered with people – well, actually, boys".

Lee first met David in 1967, and – unknown to Ken Pitt – saw him intermittently during the next two years. For a time, Calvin assisted in a boutique named Dandie Fashions in King's Road. It sold the latest, most desirable velvet clothes, and was a haunt of pop musicians, among them David. Also unknown to Pitt, it was Lee who supplied the silver lurex suit David wore while filming 'Space Oddity'.

Lee also became involved with the American record company, Mercury. The company had been founded after the second world war and by 1969 employed around fifty people at its Chicago headquarters, with its founder, Irwin Green, still at the helm. At around that time, it was in the throes of being taken over by the Philips corporation of Holland, who were gradually buying up its shares. But it still had a full-time office in London, headed by a tall, gangling American named Lou Reizner.

Reizner often saw Lee on the music industry's self-sustaining round of receptions, record launches and publicity stunts, and was impressed by the ease with which he greeted luminaries of the music world. Eventually Reizner hired Lee in the hope that he would lure his friends and contacts to the Mercury label. Lee was awarded the grandiose title of Assistant European Director and was paid a regular salary cheque, in dollars, from the US.

It so happens that at about the time Lee started working for Mercury, he and David began an affair. Lee has since pondered the question of how far David may have been motivated into doing so in the hope of advancing his career. "I liked him as a friend," Lee says. "I always wanted to help him and at that time he said, 'The time is right,' and that's fine. Maybe he needed something at that time, which was fine with me . . . I think there was a genuine feeling between us and of course one doesn't mind being used if there's feeling the other way. In fact, one wants to be used because that offers a tie."

Lee tried to be phlegmatic about the simultaneous affairs David would conduct with women. He believes that he overlapped for a time with Hermione, and he was certainly contemporaneous with Mary Finnigan. "One thing I've learned over the years is that you can't be possessive," he says. "You lose people if you start possessing them." There are grounds for believing that a further reason why Hermione Farthingale parted from David was her distaste on discovering that he also slept with men – in particular, Lee. Mary, on the other hand, was shielded from such anxieties. "David used to go off up to London once a week to spend the night with Calvin," she says, "and I never suspected a thing."

Ken Pitt, too, knew virtually none of this. But the strain of maintaining so many fictions told on David himself. "He had all these pressures because people were wanting a part of him," says Lee. "He would come over sometimes with really bad migraines."

And so Lee became convinced that Mercury should offer David a recording contract: "I could see the talent there," he says. In theory, that should not have been difficult to arrange. Lou Reizner had sufficient autonomy to make such an offer himself – he signed Rod Stewart to Mercury that same year. However, Reizner flatly disagreed with Lee's estimation of David and said that he was not willing to offer David a contract.

"I think that Lou was secretly jealous of David," Lee speculates. Lee believes that was partly because Reizner had just recorded an album for Mercury himself. "He was the Tom Jones type," says Lee. "They weren't the same market, but he may have felt, Here's competition, another male singer." Almost certainly, however, there was another component to Reizner's jealousy, stemming from the arrival of yet one more rider on the sexual merry-go-round.

Angela Barnett's advent in London was itself the result of a sexual peccadillo. Her parents lived in Cyprus, where her father, a former colonel in the US army, worked as a mining engineer. At the age of nine, she had been sent to an exclusive girls' boarding school, St George's, near Montreux in Switzerland; at sixteen, she had proceeded to Connecticut College for Women in the US. Her privileged life in Switzerland, where she had her own maids, did not fit her for a routine that entailed attending eight lessons a day and serving in the college dining hall. Her career at Connecticut was brought to a prompt and undignified end when she indulged in a very public affair with another female student, and she was expelled. Her mother then escorted her to London, where she enrolled first in a secretarial college and then went to Kingston Polytechnic to study economics and business studies. She was barred from her final exams as she had missed too many lectures but by then had been introduced to the world of popular entertainment, which offered a far greater lure.

Angie's entry to the web of relationships surrounding David began when she met Lou Reizner. Soon afterwards, Reizner introduced her to Calvin Mark Lee. Reizner, Lee observed, was "very hot" for Angie, being particularly taken with her lithe, boyish figure and her brash, noisy exuberance; Angie was less keen in response.

Between two such exotic beings as Angie and Lee, however, there was an instant attraction which was soon consummated. Then Lee showed Angie David's picture on his people wall and suggested that they meet. The new sexual equation was once uncompromisingly summarised by David in an interview: "When I met Angie, we were both fucking the same bloke." Lee is happy to confirm David's account: the bloke, he says, "was me".

David met Angie at the Speakeasy Club on April 9th, 1969 – the début of the British art rock group, King Crimson, led by Robert Fripp. Angie recalls "a lean, blond, enigmatic figure", wearing a pastel-striped sweater and mustard-coloured sailor's flares. Soon afterwards the three of them dined together at Calvin's invitation, and they became lovers the following night. "It seemed predestined," Angie declared in her memoir, *Free Spirit*. "His character cried out to be explored." David was at first more dispassionate: when he attempted to leave after their next night together, Angie – much given, like Lindsay Kemp, to the theatrical gesture – threw herself in his path. David carefully stepped over her and said he would call her the next day.

At that time, David was still living with Mary Finnigan at Foxgrove Road. Mary went away for a short holiday soon afterwards and returned to find that Angie had moved in too. "I was a bit miffed," Mary says, mildly. She nonetheless discovered that she and Angie shared a number of tastes, such as a liking for the modish radicalism of the Arts Lab, into which Angie soon sunk her unquenchable enthusiasm and energy. Angie also had an eclectic approach to sex. "David was more into women than men," says Mary. "I think men were always secondary with him. But I think she enjoyed sex with women better than with men. It was genuine with her whereas with him it was more opportunist and contrived."

It was not surprising, therefore, that Lou Reizner, having just lost Angie to David through the intervention of Calvin Mark Lee, should be so hostile to Lee's proposal that Mercury should offer David a contract. Lee now embarked on a covert lobbying operation to have David signed up by Mercury in the US. One day when Reizner was away, Lee called David to Mercury's Knightsbridge office and asked him to make an audition tape on Mercury's recording equipment. Accompanied by Hutch, David recorded nine of his songs, beginning with 'Space Oddity' and ending with 'When I'm Five', and linked with his own extempore remarks. "We've got a lot of material," David announced, "but this is the stuff we'd really like to see on an album." He apologised for several fluffs by saying, "Calvin only phoned me up about fifteen minutes ago," and boldly suggested that Mercury might sell 'When I'm Five' to "somebody hip" like Barbra Streisand or Danny Kaye.

Lee dispatched the tape to Mercury's office in New York, where he had found an ally in an Englishman, Simon Hayes, who was the company's head of product. By now, Lou Reizner had wind of Lee's campaign. He mounted a lobby in opposition, writing to Simon Hayes to warn him: "I see no potential for this artist in Britain or America." But Lee was gaining support. In Chicago, he won another convert in Mercury's publicity director, Ron Oberman.

Oberman had met David during a visit to London in April, and had at first been disconcerted by his high-camp pose: "The way he came off, the whole manner of speaking, the way he moved, I thought he might be gay. Certainly he looked different than most other artists I had worked with. But one just got a sense that if his records were as unique as he looked, he would be an artist to reckon with." On hearing David's audition tape, Oberman felt his judgment had been confirmed.

Ken Pitt, meanwhile, knew almost none of this: neither the tangled net of sexual involvements surrounding David, nor the equally fervent business machinations. His first knowledge of Mercury's interest came when David casually mentioned in a note that Simon Hayes, then in London, had told him: "America have instructed us to get you signed up." Pitt had recently become aware of the existence of Calvin Mark Lee, after reading a passionate letter Lee had sent to David at Manchester Street. But David told Pitt only that Lee worked "in a boutique I go to", and had not mentioned his links with Mercury. Pitt was inclined to see Lee as a rival for David's affections, and later termed him "the first of the predators": the vultures who, Pitt feared, would gather as David's renown grew.

Pitt was at first as dismissive of Mercury itself, but when he met Simon Hayes he was inclined to relent a little in his judgment. After all, Hayes was that rare bird, a record company executive who actually liked David's work. Pitt could hardly object when Simon Hayes told him that Mercury would like to issue 'Space Oddity' both as a single and as the title track on an album, and the two men discussed who might be a suitable producer for the records.

It was to his immense chagrin, therefore, that Pitt found himself having to negotiate the details of David's contract with Calvin Mark Lee: "Ken and I," Lee admits, "did not, as you can imagine, get along awfully well." But the terms Lee proposed appeared generous enough. Lee offered David an advance of £1,250, plus a wage of £20 a week when David was in the recording studio, in return for which David was to make at least one album and three singles a year. The contract was to run for one year, with Mercury holding two further one-year options, to be exercised at their discretion. The contract arrived from Chicago on June 16th and David signed it four days later. According to Pitt, David was both "very pleased and very relieved".

The question of who should produce David's records saw a further minor skirmish between Pitt and Lee. Pitt favoured George Martin, who had produced the Beatles' hits at EMI. After a month fruitlessly trying to speak to Martin, Pitt was eventually told by Martin's secretary that he did not like 'Space Oddity'. But by then, David and Lee had approached Tony Visconti, who said he would be delighted to produce the album.

To most people's surprise, Visconti declined to work on 'Space Oddity' itself. Ironically, he regarded it as too "commercial", and expressed himself in characteristically forthright terms. He declared it "crass and obvious" compared with David's previous work, and he also accused David of attempting to cash in on the forthcoming US moon-shot.

A willing replacement was close at hand. Occupying a cramped office in the same building was a young producer, Gus Dudgeon, a recent refugee from Decca, who had been the engineer on the Deram album. When Dudgeon heard David's demonstration tape, "it was like a total sledgehammer – it was like WOW, my mind has been expanded. I rang up Tony and said, 'It's brilliant.' He said, 'Well you go ahead and make it, and I'll do the album.'"

'Space Oddity' was recorded at the Trident studios in Soho on June 20th. Dudgeon gallantly admits that David had already done most of the hard work: "He had turned in a great demo – the ground rules were all there, I wanted to re-create the demo with the rough edges knocked off." Dudgeon was handicapped, like David, by being unable to write music, and so the musical parts were provided by Paul Buckmaster, a musician of diverse skills, among them the ability to play an electric cello.

Buckmaster played strings and flutes at the recording, while the other musicians were Terry Cox, the drummer from the folk group Pentangle, bass player Herbie Flowers, guitarist Mick Wayne, and Rick Wakeman, who played the mellotron, a keyboard instrument that reproduces the sound of strings. The orchestral parts – violins, violas, cellos, basses and flutes – were provided by classical musicians, and the recording was completed with impressive speed. "I was over the moon," Dudgeon says. "We played back the first take and it was incredible. It sounded exactly as I wanted it to be. Then we did another take and that was the one."

The B side was recorded with even greater dispatch. "I simply asked David, 'What do you want to do?'" Dudgeon says. David told him he had chosen 'The Wild Eyed Boy From Freecloud', which Dudgeon had never heard before. It told of a boy – "the wild eyed boy" – imprisoned in a village and awaiting the hangman. On the morning of his execution, an avalanche falls from the mountain above and crushes the village, but overwhelms the boy too. The recording was finished, by Dudgeon's reckoning, in little more than twenty minutes.

Although vastly overshadowed by 'Space Oddity', 'The Wild Eyed Boy From Freecloud' offered an important insight into the development of David's ideas. His own interpretation of the lyric, which he provided in a press release later that year, was of a boy who loved the mountain life and was "rather a prophet figure". David explained that while the boy was waiting to be hanged, "the mountain tries to help him by killing the village. So in fact everything the boy says is taken the wrong way – both by those who fear him *and* those who love him and try to assist."

The notion of the misunderstood prophet had natural appeal to David. But there were further undercurrents which he did not articulate. The lyric also implied that David had rejected the role of all-wise guru, like the "missionary mystic of peace/love" who, having crushed both the village and the boy, stumble back "to cry among the clouds".

More significant still, it contained one of David's first direct explorations of the question of insanity. For the villagers deem the boy to be mad; and as he awaits his execution, he utters the enigmatic cry:

> It's really Me
> Really You
> And really Me . . .

It was a cry that would be heard many times again in David's work. For it offered the key to David's exploration of himself and his sanity, as he examines himself in the mirror of those around him. Who is really sane? Himself or the wild eyed boy? Is he the wild eyed boy? Or is Terry?

There now followed one of the most bewildering months in David's life. From Chicago came further acclaim. Mercury's national product manager, John Sippel, had heard 'Space Oddity' – "it blew my mind," he says. Sippel was a hard man to please, for his first love was jazz. He had begun his career as a journalist on the prestigious jazz magazine *Downbeat* for which he had written a seminal review of Charlie Parker in 1944. "I have always had a feeling for sound," Sippel says. "The atmosphere created on 'Space Oddity' was mind-boggling."

Sippel wrote to tell David that 'Space Oddity' was "a perfect combination of the sounds of today, the thoughts of today and the music of today . . . your first record is an excellent example of great things to come." Sippel's colleague Ron Oberman was expressing himself with similar enthusiasm. He had dispatched several thousand copies of the record to journalists throughout the

US with the buoyant message: "It's one of the greatest recordings I've ever heard."

In Britain, too, Ken Pitt and Calvin Mark Lee were both — separately — hard at work. Pitt was sending copies of 'Space Oddity' to the news organisations that would be covering the moon launch, while Lee was creeping into the Mercury office after Lou Reizner had departed in the evening to mail copies to his vast range of music industry contacts. Their joint efforts appeared to pay off when 'Space Oddity' was played to the 250,000 people who had gathered at the free concert given by the Rolling Stones in Hyde Park on July 5th. Soon afterwards, *Disc* predicted that it would be "a huge hit — and knock everything senseless".

At 9.18 p.m. by British summer time on the evening of July 20th, 1969, Neil Armstrong took his first cautious steps on the dusty surface of the moon. There was a clear sky that night in London, where people alternated between watching their televisions and going into the streets to stare heavenwards in order to convince themselves that it was not all a figment of the media's imagination. For the dozen or so watchers crowded into Mary's flat at Foxgrove Road, the event was made more dramatic still when the BBC played 'Space Oddity'. According to Mary, Angie became "completely hysterical", laughing, crying and screaming. "She went completely mad," Mary recalls. "We all smoked a lot of dope and we were profoundly moved, but not as much as that."

It may have been the dope that has led Mary to believe that David was not at Foxgrove Road that night, but the photographer Ray Stevenson, a follower of the Beckenham Arts Lab, is certain that he was. At one point, Stevenson says, Angie went outside to look at the moon. When she came back she claimed — seriously, so far as Stevenson could tell — to have seen aliens or spacemen landing at the end of the street. "David humoured her," Stevenson recalls. "He said, 'Oh really, Angie?'"

Within days, the rivalries around David intensified. On July 24th, David and Ken Pitt flew to Malta, where David was to participate in the Maltese Song Festival. Pitt's main aim in going was to provide a holiday for both himself and David, which would also take David beyond the clutches of the predators, among whom he now classed Angie. They had first met when David brought her to his office in Manchester Street: Angie sat silently looking at Pitt throughout — sizing him up, he felt. Pitt concluded that she had "predacious instincts" and he also viewed her a siren, luring David on to the rocks.

Angie acknowledges today that she was very prepared to act

ruthlessly towards Pitt. He was, she says, "such a lovely man. He's a sweetheart. But all I heard about was that from David's point of view, Ken had no idea what it was he had in mind. I went and spoke to Ken and it didn't help at all. He thought I was a Jew. I guess he had the impression that aggressive dominant women were always Jewish. But one day I told him, 'Ken, you know it's not true, a lot of us Catholics are just as bad' . . . Ken was far older and he was always very sweet and he had that proper civilised manner of rising above a situation you knew you couldn't do anything about . . . I always was really fond of Ken but I couldn't bring him up to date to ride with us. I will try very hard until the point of no return but when it comes to that point you must cut . . ."

Thus when Pitt departed with David, Angie was not to be so easily outmanoeuvred. After a week in Malta, the festival moved *en masse* to the mountain resort of Monsummano-Terme in Italy, where David received an award for his recording of 'When I Live My Dream'. Angie flew to meet David there, evidently under some strain, for she was in a semi-hysterical state, weeping copiously in the departure area. She had recovered her poise by the time she reached the festival, for she staged a dramatic entrance for the benefit of both the festival organisers and Pitt. She had given David a flowing shirt to wear and had tied his hair in a bow behind his head, while she wore a see-through dress with only a brief pair of panties beneath. It was, Pitt sniffed, "like a bizarre wedding party".

Then came a bitter blow for David. While Angie flew to Cyprus to visit her parents, David returned to London. He performed confidently that evening – August 3rd – at the Three Tuns, where his audience was boosted by the release of 'Space Oddity'. Only afterwards did Mary Finnigan tell him that his father was seriously ill – and from David's enraged reaction, she knew she had erred in not warning him earlier. "It was catastrophically dreadful," she says. "He went absolutely ape."

Frail at the best of times, John Jones's constitution had been weakened by the ulcers from which he had suffered for some years. Then he contracted pneumonia, and had collapsed in the street near his office. He had been brought home to Plaistow Grove for Peggy to nurse him, while her neighbours debated whether he would have been better cared for in hospital. When David arrived he found his father weak and emaciated. David showed him the statuette he had been awarded in Italy, and his father smiled weakly. Two days later, on August 5th, David was in the Trident recording studio, having already started work on the Mercury

David with his second group, the King Bees: (left to right) George Underwood, Dave Howard, Bob Allen, Roger Bluck; one of the frustrating failures of the 1960s.

David attempts to find another winning style, this time as mod, in 1966.

Mike Weller, designer of the mysterious 'cartoon' cover of 'The Man Who Sold The World', with other designs for the Penge Artists' Collective. David first approved the cover, then disowned it.

David during a publicity session for the film 'Love You Till Tuesday', which inspired 'Space Oddity'.

Above: David performs fellatio on Mick Ronson's guitar: a rock icon, but was it artifice?

Left: David in late-Ziggy phase, with astral sphere on forehead.

Above: David as the Thin White Duke in 1976, with expressionist contrasts and skeletal cheeks.

Right: David in better shape on the 'Stage' tour, 1978.

album, when a message reached him to say that his father had died. "He cried," says guitarist Mick Wayne, "but he carried on."

The death of his father affected David more profoundly than he had ever expected. His father had been a mainstay of his ambition, offering implicit encouragement from buying David's first toy guitar to the methodical supervision he provided over the formalities of his career. David was sullen and moody for some time afterwards, arriving in Manchester Street unshaven and unwashed.

John's funeral took place at Elmers End Cemetery on August 11th, his ashes being scattered on the memorial gardens behind the cemetery chapel. Afterwards the mourners, among them several senior officials from Dr Barnardo's, repaired to a somewhat spartan reception at Plaistow Grove, where Peggy provided them all with a cup of tea. Terry was there too; so were Pat and her husband, for their venture to Australia had ended disastrously, and they had returned to Britain after little more than a year.

Pat believed that Peggy was in a state of shock at the funeral: "She was scared of what was going to happen to her," Pat says. Terry, by contrast, "was going through a good phase," and talked to John's colleagues. But David went upstairs to his bedroom, together with Lee and Angie and a number of friends. When Pat finally insisted that he come downstairs to meet his father's friends, he betrayed little emotion. "He seemed very impersonal about the whole thing, as if it wasn't his father," she says. "He may have been upset and just didn't show it. But he had no tears, no tears at all."

Five days later, the Beckenham Arts Lab staged a "free festival" at Beckenham Recreation Ground, a spacious, undulating park adjoining Beckenham Hospital, a mile south of Haddon Hall. David was the star attraction, wearing a navy blue floral blouse that Ken Pitt had given him, his curly hair tumbling around his face in an accurate reproduction of Bob Dylan's, as he performed from an ornate wrought-iron bandstand.

Among others who appeared were Bridget St John, Tony Visconti, and John Peel; there were stalls selling herbs, clothes, homemade jewellery and ceramics. David's suitors plunged into the proceedings with a will. Angie sold hundreds of hamburgers. Calvin Mark Lee had donated a collection of psychedelic posters from California which raised over £100. Mary Finnigan, who had been the main coordinator of events, was thrilled at their success.

David was the exception; the events of the previous month had taken their toll. He performed on the bandstand "like a real trouper," says Mary, but otherwise his companions found him in one of his least attractive moods. "He was in a completely catatonic state the whole of the festival," says Mary. "He was vile." David was especially abusive towards Lee. "We were ecstatic because we had made all this money, but David was absolutely foul to us," Mary adds. "He called us all 'mercenary pigs'. We actually made some money and he hated us for it and I hated him."

13

Summer's End

Throughout August 1969, the pages of the music press brought David and his supporters only despair. Each week they would scan the charts published in *New Musical Express*, *Melody Maker* and *Record Retailer*, in search of 'Space Oddity'; each week, it was nowhere to be seen.

It is a measure of Pitt's desperation for David to succeed that he resorted to underhand tactics in an effort to boost 'Space Oddity'. One evening when David was performing in Hounslow, Pitt was approached by a man in dark glasses who said that his name was "Tony Martin" and that he knew how to rig the charts. For £100, he could ensure that 'Space Oddity' reached the top thirty in the *Record Retailer* and *New Musical Express* charts, and another £50 would lift it five further places thereafter. Pitt had always dismissed such temptations before, but he now succumbed. He gave the so-called Tony Martin a total of £140, which he presumed would assist 'Space Oddity' into the high twenties in the charts.

'Space Oddity's' eventual entry into the charts was almost certainly due to more orthodox marketing methods. But the long hiatus before it arrived was yet another result of the rivalries besetting Mercury records. The takeover of Mercury by Philips had set two sets of staff at each other's throats. By retaining its London outpost, run by Lou Reizner and Calvin Mark Lee, Mercury had enraged the Philips London office, who resented Mercury's encroachment on their home territory and Mercury's penchant for signing British musicians from under their nose. But since Mercury did not have the personnel in London for a full-scale marketing campaign, the task of promoting and selling 'Space Oddity' fell to Philips. Its staff approached their task with something less than zeal.

That at any rate was the situation facing Olav Wyper, who was appointed Philips's new general marketing manager shortly after 'Space Oddity' was released. Wyper was a classical music enthusiast who had previously worked with EMI and CBS in London; on hearing 'Space Oddity', he was convinced he was going to start his new job with a hit. When he arrived at the Philips office at Marble

Arch, he found his new staff to be "depressed and dreary – I asked them what they were doing and they said, 'Nothing, really,' and then I asked about David Bowie's record, and they said, 'Well, we tried . . .'" Wyper also met David, and found him "beside himself" at the record's apparent flop.

Wyper decided to pitch his entire resources into making 'Space Oddity' into a hit – not only for the sake of David and the record, but also to revive his demoralised staff. "That was unusual," he says. "Companies don't work on just one record, and they don't work on singles, because it's not cost effective. But I had salesmen going into record shops trying to flog a single, and the promotion man only promoting that record, and the press people only working to get David Bowie in the papers."

On September 4th, 'Space Oddity' appeared at number 48 in that week's *Record Retailer*. The following week it disappeared. It returned a week later, in thirty-ninth place, and continued to rise over the ensuing six weeks, jostling for places with rivals as diverse as 'A Boy Named Sue' by Johnny Cash, 'Lay Lady Lay' by Bob Dylan, 'He Ain't Heavy' by the Hollies, and 'Je T'Aime, Moi Non Plus' by Jane Birkin and Serge Gainsbourg. It reached a high point of number five in the first week of November ('Sugar Sugar' by the Archies was top). Its heady ascent was closely matched in the charts published by the *New Musical Express* and *Melody Maker*, reaching number six in both.

Ken Pitt, for one, was feeling both delighted and relieved. His investment in the shadowy "Tony Martin" would supposedly take 'Space Oddity' only into the top thirty in the *Record Retailer* and *New Musical Express*. Since it had in fact reached the top ten in these two charts – and had done so in *Melody Maker* as well – Pitt assured himself that his £140 had done little to affect the outcome. He also felt vindicated that the verdict of the charts represented the success he and David had pursued for so long. But even in this moment of triumph, in both his lifestyle and his ambitions David was drifting further and further away from him.

In Beckenham, David reacted to the success of 'Space Oddity' in a decidedly extrovert manner. Abetted by Angie, Mary Finnigan's flat in Foxgrove Road had become the venue for a virtually continuous party. Mary herself was becoming disenchanted both with her role in the *ménage à trois* and with the disruption David and Angie were bringing to the neighbourhood. "I got fed up with people playing music and smoking dope," she says. "It was like a free festival in my flat." As an experiment she walked along Foxgrove Road one night and discovered that the noise could be heard half a mile away. Mary was therefore immensely relieved when in October David and Angie moved out.

They had decided to set up home together in a striking Edwardian house half a mile away named Haddon Hall. Its address was 42 Southend Road, and it was close to Beckenham Place Park, where David had once played baseball. David and Angie had a flat which occupied most of the ground floor, and included an ornate staircase, a stained-glass window, and a balustraded landing, known as the minstrels' gallery. The rent was just £8 per week.

According to Mary, Angie became the home-maker, seeing her role as "getting the place nice, having regular meals, giving David that kind of solid background he needed so that he could concentrate on writing his songs". The success of 'Space Oddity' had brought a marked increase in his appearance fees: he received £50 for performing locally, and up to £125 at more distant venues. David and Angie devoted much of the proceeds to imprinting their personality on Haddon Hall. They became regular visitors to local antique shops and also travelled to antique markets in Marylebone and Kensington, buying pewter and glass pieces, including art nouveau; Indian and Chinese rugs; long velvet curtains; pre-war chrome lamp standards; a twelve-foot teak sideboard, hand-carved in Burma, which had featured in a furniture exhibition at Maples in 1936; and a massive seven-foot Regency bed which David had found in pieces in a junk shop. It cost £40 and David reassembled it himself.

Angie was determined to meet the wilder aspects of David's personality too. Mary had sometimes been daunted by David's extravagant sexual demands but Angie soon proved that she was his match. Whereas Mary had been uneasy when David wanted to try on her dresses or wear her make-up, Angie encouraged him to do so: "Let it all hang out" might have been her motto. "They lived in a fantasy world," Mary says, "and they created their bisexual fantasy. They would pretend to be male or female, whichever suited them at any given moment." At times they confused even their friends from the Arts Lab: when David and Angie wore identical clothes and their hair was shorn equally close, says guitarist Greg Martin, "you couldn't tell who was who from the back."

Since the flat had several spare rooms, David and Angie invited their friends to join them. One was Tony Visconti, who moved in with his companion, Liz Hartley. Another was Nita Bowes, an eighteen-year-old school student who was one of the most devoted members of the Arts Lab. She found David and Angie "very kind and supportive to me, when they had no reason to be"; Angie, she observed, was "very practical and down to earth". Nita also found the sexual ambience of Haddon Hall to her liking, and joined David and Angie in their bed on half a dozen occasions. "It was an act of extended love and friendship," she says. "There was no great emotional scene, just reciprocal affection, and none of us thought any more about it. But it was lovely."

Angie also pursued her campaign to rid David of Ken Pitt. She complained to David that Pitt's horizons remained too limited, and told him that he should steel himself to break away. According to Mary Finnigan, David needed no persuading of Pitt's deficiencies: "He said that Pitt had completely the wrong idea about him – he was out of date and out of touch."

For the moment David was prepared to go no further, and his dexterity at switching roles left Pitt quite unaware of how far he was slipping away. Pitt continued to do his best by David, securing an appearance on the BBC's *Top of the Pops*, to which David brought his mother, and arranging for him to record 'Space Oddity' for television stations in Berlin and Zurich. David also joined a tour with the group Humble Pie, for which he was paid £50 a night, and made a brief tour in Scotland, at £100 a night.

When David visited Pitt in Manchester Street he was usually amiability itself. "He was leading this double life," Pitt says, with hindsight. "It was rather Jekyll and Hyde-ish. He put on a different hat at Haddon Hall and when he came to see me." The only hint that all was not well came from David's occasional abrupt changes of mood, which arrived "like a twist of the knife". Although they left Pitt puzzled and disturbed, he assumed they had been triggered by "something outside".

The move to Haddon Hall brought no respite from David's family preoccupations. The loss of his father was still telling on him, as he revealed to John Cambridge, a member of the Juniors Eyes group, who played at the Beckenham Free Festival and accompanied David on his brief Scottish tour. While there, says Cambridge, "David told me that for a week after his father died, the telephone rang every afternoon at 5.30. When he picked it up, there was no one there. But he told me that he knew it was his father, ringing up to make sure everything was all right."

David's mother Peggy – as her sister Pat had foretold – was feeling especially vulnerable, and showed increasing hostility to David's lovers. Mary Finnigan, who had found David's father "lovely, very gentle and unassuming", thought her "as miserable as sin". Now it was Angie's turn to incur her hostility: Peggy considered her "insincere in every way" and left David in no doubt what she thought.

Peggy believed she had scored an advantage over Angie on an occasion when David and Angie visited Plaistow Grove. When Peggy went into David's bedroom she found Angie there, stark naked. Peggy telephoned Pat to complain – Pat told her not to be a "hypocrite" – and wrote to Angie's parents in Cyprus, protesting at their daughter's morals. Since they were under no illusions, they replied that Angie's morals were her own business.

Although Pat felt little sympathy for Peggy over the incident, David's relationship with his mother gave her cause for concern. For Pat felt that David was neglecting Peggy – and feared that Terry was suffering as a result. For the previous two years, when Terry was receiving treatment at Farnborough Hospital and staying at Plaistow Grove at the weekends, Pat felt that he was in a good mental state. "He was being looked after, he had been getting attention and he felt part of the family," she says. But after the death of John Jones, things changed.

"Terry deteriorated very quickly," Pat says. "He wasn't getting the same comfort any more. My sister was upset about Angie. She was afraid that Angie was going to take David away from her. If John had lived, Terry would have been all right."

Pat resolved to confront David and demand that he pay his mother more attention. The *casus belli* was John Jones's tiny Fiat 500, which Peggy had inherited. David was using it to travel to local gigs with a pair of portable speakers strapped to the roof; Pat resolved that he should give it back to Peggy.

When Pat arrived at Haddon Hall – travelling to Beckenham from Finchley, where she now lived, by train – David opened the door. Pat pushed her way inside and started berating him. "I told him how badly I thought he had behaved at his father's funeral. I told him to give the car back immediately and I told him he had to look after his mother."

David retaliated by telling Pat she had never liked him, but he agreed to return the car. Then, further provoked, he told Pat: "I never got left anything. He never left me a thing."

That bitter row was another turning point in the family history. From then on, Pat was cast as the family troublemaker, behind whom disaster trailed: "Something bad always seemed to happen after you met her," one relative said, "like your cat being run over."

There was another way of interpreting the family's response. Pat

183

could also be seen as the bringer of unpleasant truths, unrelenting in her demands that the family meet its obligations, especially towards Terry. Pat's admonitions were still less popular for carrying reminders of the past, and she became as welcome as Banquo's ghost at Macbeth's feast.

Soon after her confrontation with David, Pat's worst fears were realised. Peggy declared that she was unable to care for Terry any more, and he became a full-time mental patient. The hospital he entered was Cane Hill.

Cane Hill occupies the crown of a wooded hill at the southern edge of Croydon, to be glimpsed rising above the trees like a gothic mansion. Built by the Victorians, and still marked on some current maps as an "asylum", the red brick and ornate towers of its entrance building give it a superficial resemblance to a railway station of the same period. But its gaunt blocks of wards, some with barred windows, make it appear more like those other monuments to the stern idealism of the nineteenth-century reformers, London's prisons.

Cane Hill formed one of the ring of homes for the insane which the Victorians built around London. Previously they had been incarcerated like animals in institutions such as the Bethlehem Hospital at the Elephant and Castle, which gave the word bedlam to the English language. The Victorians believed they were performing a kindness to the insane by installing them in the countryside. But by the 1960s their hospitals had another reputation: neglected, underfunded corners of the health service, always losing out to more glamorous areas of medicine in the competition for resources.

Although some patients left Cane Hill after short stays, many others remained there for years or decades, becoming thoroughly institutionalised in the process. Cane Hill occupied a powerful place in the demonology of South London, where schoolchildren would frighten each other by threatening: "You'll be sent to kay nill." For new patients, the feeling of entering a disjointed, Kafkaesque world could only be reinforced by the date carved in stone over the entrance, 1882, and the three clock faces on the tower above: all usually showed a different time, and all were usually wrong.

Pat concedes that there was a strong reason for Terry to leave Plaistow Grove: "I think he was getting stroppy with his mother, feeling that she was starting to reject him," she says. "But I didn't think Terry was ill enough for Cane Hill. It was a depressing, old-fashioned hospital, the food was appalling, the inmates seemed to have given up hope. Terry thought the same. He would say to me, 'Pat I can't stay here.'"

Throughout that autumn, David worked on his Mercury album at the Trident studios, with Tony Visconti as his producer. His songs were more overtly biographical than before, reflecting the events of the previous six months, such as the end of his affair with Hermione, and the Beckenham Free Festival. They also conveyed his deeper personal concerns. These were not always apparent on first sight, but were embodied in key words and references that David used again and again. They revealed the extent to which the spectre of his family's insanity was coming to preoccupy his creative life, and foreshadowed his strategy for confronting his fears.

The album began with an extended version of 'Space Oddity', taken from the session produced by Gus Dudgeon. Then came 'Unwashed And Somewhat Slightly Dazed' which David himself, in an interview after the album was released, called "a weird little song", recalling a time he was so scruffy that he was given "funny stares" in the street. He explained that it was about "a boy whose girlfriend thinks he is socially inferior", and so could have referred to either Hermione or Dana Gillespie. But it was more bitter and violent than David allowed, for he conjured disease-ridden imagery of himself as "a phallus in pig-tails" and as rotting tissue, "where the rats chew my bones". It also gave a chilling warning, the first of a similar number the album contained:

> Look out, I'm raving mad . . .

The third track was 'Letter To Hermione' – who, David explained in his interview, he had been "very hung up about" – which by David's standards ranked as one of the more moderate accounts of the end of their affair. Then came 'Cygnet Committee', which David described as a critique of the hippy movement: "It was a great ideal, but something's gone wrong with it now." David himself emerged in an unattractive light, complaining in the lyric that he had done much to help enlighten his friends, "for little pay", yet none spared him a thought now – a theme linked to that of the misunderstood prophet in 'The Wild Eyed Boy From Freecloud'.

More than any other track on the album, 'Cygnet Committee' illustrated the levels of meaning in David's work, with an overt narrative running sometimes in parallel, sometimes in counterpoint, to its underlying dynamic. The imagery was violent and disturbing – blasting guns, cesspools, slit throats, "a child laid slain upon the ground" – while there were clusters of references that revealed David's lurking fears, including "madly" and "madness" together with "father", "mother", and "brother". The lyric also contained the extraordinary menace-laden line, purportedly a slogan shouted from the crowd:

> Screw up your brother or he'll get you in the end.

Side two began with 'Janine', another portrayal of turbulent love. Although David said that it was about "his old mate" George Underwood and his girlfriend, his disclaimer could not conceal its relevance to his own fears, for there were

> . . . things inside my head
> That even I can't face.

The lyric contained another significant couplet: if Janine were to "take an axe" to him, David sang, she would

> . . . kill another man
> Not me at all.

It is a phrase Bowie devotees have puzzled over in an attempt to resolve the paradox it contained. In fact it predicted the therapeutic role-playing device David would use when creating, and then destroying, the character of Ziggy Stardust two years later.

'An Occasional Dream' was yet another valediction to Hermione, poignantly recalling their attic room and their "one hundred days" together. It also contained a potent phrase which recalled the conundrum of 'The Wild Eyed Boy From Freecloud' over who was truly mad. "In my madness," David sang

> I see your face in mine.

Although the madness was presumably a *folie d'amour*, David was finding that the idea of self-examination in the mirror of those around him was becoming more and more appealing.

Then came a new version of 'The Wild Eyed Boy From Freecloud' itself – Visconti thought it "a beautiful song" – followed by 'God Knows I'm Good', which told of an old woman caught shoplifting in a supermarket, and intended, David said, as a parable about the decline of communication between human beings in a technological age. According to Mary Finnigan, it was one of David's grass roots songs, reflecting his desire "to be with the people" and take up their cause.

'Memory Of A Free Festival' stemmed from the idealism of the past summer too, even if there was a contradiction between the foul temper he had displayed in Beckenham Recreation Ground and the happy mood he painted in his lyric:

I kissed a lot of people that day.

It could perhaps be seen as a farewell to both the summer and the decade. But it also contained glimpses of what was to come in David's writing, with his visions of space machines descending from the skies, and "tall Venusians" emerging. Before long he would explain the appeal that outer space offered as a metaphor for inner or mental space: a territory he would be exploring with increasing audacity.

The album took three months to complete, and David's collaboration with Tony Visconti bore new fruit. As well as guitarist Mick Wayne, who played on the original 'Space Oddity' session, Visconti used Keith Christmas and Tim Renwick on guitars, John Cambridge on drums, and Benny Marshall on harmonica; Visconti played bass guitar, flute and recorder himself. The greater musical impact came on the first side, beginning with 'Space Oddity' itself, moving through the hard-driving rhythm of 'Unwashed And Somewhat Slightly Dazed', where the music gradually swells to overwhelm David's disturbing imagery, offering next the gentle intimacy of 'Letter To Hermione', and culminating in 'Cygnet Committee', where the remarkable succession of discordant imagery was matched by the free-ranging harmonies and constant shifts of key.

Side two was less distinctive, and when recording 'The Wild Eyed Boy From Freecloud' Visconti was hampered by problems with the studio's new sixteen-track recording console, and the three-hour session was almost entirely lost. There was time for only two takes, and Visconti considered his attempt at a full-scale orchestral treatment had been rendered "pretty dull". David's vocal style varied throughout the album: 'Unwashed And Somewhat Slightly Dazed' and 'Cygnet Committee' showed the influence of Bob Dylan; 'Letter to Hermione' contained clear traces of Simon and Garfunkel; and the ending of 'Memory Of A Free Festival' had a repeated chorus at the end, in which the crowd supposedly joined, in the manner of the Beatles' 'All You Need Is Love'. The overall impression was of a fast-developing talent still in search of the style that would suit his urgent message.

The album was released in Britain on November 14th. Somewhat confusingly, Mercury called it *David Bowie* – the same name as the Deram album of two years before; more confusing still, it was released in the US as *Man Of Words/Man Of Music*. The cover was inspired by two of David's friends: the front bore a reproduction of a blue polka-dot design by Victor Vasarely, which Calvin Mark Lee had supplied, with a photograph of David superimposed; on the back was a painting by George Underwood showing David together with aspects of the lyrics, such as spacemen, an old woman weeping, and a portrait of Hermione. The design was credited on the sleeve to "David Bowie/CML 33"; Lee confirms that CML was him and 33 his age.

The cover did nothing to reassure Ken Pitt: on seeing the design, and the initials CML, Pitt says, his heart "sank". He considered it incohesive, "disloyal" to Vasarely, and patronising towards David. When David and Angie visited him, Pitt ventured to suggest that some of the songs were too much like Bob Dylan's, whereupon David – in a rare display of emotion – burst into tears and rushed out. Angie took the opportunity to demonstrate how far she was now in control. She told Pitt: "Leave this to me," and followed David out. When David returned a few minutes later he had regained his composure.

The album was greeted with the best reviews David had yet received. *Music Now!* called it "deep, thoughtful, probing, exposing . . . more than a record – an experience", and *Disc* predicted that David would be "a lasting talent". In the *Observer* Tony Palmer commended David's "razor-sharp observations" on "the absurdities of technological society". Despite his latest brush with Angie, Ken Pitt was hopeful that the album would help restore his stock, particularly in view of a performance David was to give at the Purcell Room of the Royal Festival Hall on November 20th, which Pitt had booked almost a year before. On the night every seat was sold, and when David sang 'Space Oddity', the audience's rapturous response made it clear he had scored a triumph.

After the performance, however, there was an unseemly row behind the scenes. A month previously, with David's acquiescence, Calvin Mark Lee had taken over all the arrangements for the concert, including press liaison, from Pitt. When David eagerly asked Pitt: "Which papers were here tonight?" Pitt told him: "Very few." David swore angrily. Just who was at fault has remained a controversial issue: Pitt is in no doubt that Lee was to blame; Lee says that is "a lie". But it was Pitt whom David held responsible.

Although by now aware, to some extent, of David's displeasure, Pitt continued to work loyally on his behalf. He began negotiations with David Platz to renew his publishing contract, and suggested to Mercury that they should pay for David to visit the US. He also calculated that in 1969 David had earned £4,094, which after deducting expenses amounted to some £60 a week – or more than double Britain's average wage at the time. But Pitt feared that the effects of the 'Space Oddity' single – which had sold around 130,000 copies by the end of the year – were beginning to fade, and suspected that instead of trying to consolidate his success, David was being diverted by the dubious pleasures of Haddon Hall. Pitt now prepared what amounted to his last throw.

Given Pitt's wary instincts, it was a brazen gamble, entailing a foray into the realm of sexual politics. When he and David were still close, they had discussed the plight of homosexuals in Britain. Pitt talked of their persecution by the law before 1967, and the prejudice and taboos that remained after the law was reformed. "Queer", "poofter", and "bent" were still the labels most commonly applied; "gay", the term many homosexuals preferred, had hardly entered the currency. Pitt believed David to be a willing listener, who had appeared to agree with his analysis.

Pitt also saw homosexuals in another light: as an untapped market for David's talents. Pitt had witnessed the adoration homosexuals directed towards such platonic idols as Judy Garland and Marlene Dietrich. Yet there was no male performer who received such adulation, and Pitt felt that David was ideally suited to that role.

And so Pitt formulated his two-pronged campaign. He believed that David should "come out" by openly proclaiming himself a homosexual, thereby presenting an image of homosexuals not as mutants or perverts, but as resolutely "normal". Commercially, it would open up a market with vast purchasing power. Ideologically, it would have an impact for homosexuals, as Pitt put it, of "Christ entering Nazareth".

There was one other benefit that would accrue: if successful, it would reassert Pitt's claim to David over the "predators" at Haddon Hall. He now included Tony Visconti among them; and he termed Angie their "high priestess".

As the first move, Pitt proposed to David that he should give an interview to the magazine *Jeremy* which – although it did not say so explicitly – was addressed to homosexuals. David apparently thought it an amusing idea, and agreed. The *Jeremy* reporter, Tim

Hughes, visited David backstage at the Palladium in December, where he was rehearsing 'Space Oddity' for a charity performance. (Hughes was pleased to find that Dusty Springfield was there too.) Then Hughes watched David perform at the Speakeasy Club. He noted the "boys in bone-tight velvet pants held up by redundant broad leather belts", whom he contrasted with the "hordes of girls with deader than dead-pan faces" who stood "in predatory clusters", and described David as "a luminous elfin face surrounded by an aureole of blond curls – he looks very vulnerable."

Hughes and a photographer also called, by arrangement, at Haddon Hall. Yet it seemed that David's heart was not in Pitt's campaign. He was out shopping when the *Jeremy* team arrived and by the time he returned it was almost too dark for photographs. Nor did he attempt to look the part that Pitt had hoped. David often distressed Pitt by his "pseudo-hippy" appearance, and this was one such day: "He looked anything but beautiful," Pitt says. The end result, with photographs showing David half-hidden by plants, disappointed Pitt enormously. "It wasn't what we had in mind," he says; David's behaviour had been "perverse in the extreme".

The truth was that although David had at first agreed to Pitt's plan, he had no wish to be portrayed as a "normal" homosexual – or a normal anything. By then his instincts, which Angie encouraged, were to become as abnormal, flamboyant and bizarre as possible. His determination to express every aspect of his personality was, in part, his search for stability; in part, his search for himself. He also told Pitt that he did not want to be part of any "cause": that would be far too committing.

In an interview with *Music Now!* just before Christmas, David also showed that he appeared to have discarded some of his recent radical attitudes. He readily admitted that he "liked money" and complained of the "hypocritical attitudes among the groups that haven't made it. They're striving like mad for some kind of commercial success . . . I've never seen so many dishonest people in my life . . ." He derided some of his companions from the summer as "apathetic", "lethargic" and "the laziest people I've met".

David's comments appeared a remarkable *volte face*, a slap in the face of those like Mary Finnigan who had believed him to be utterly sincere in his beliefs. This could, perhaps, be seen as an extension of his pattern of adopting one musical mode after another in his quest for success. Now that success had come, he was ready to step into that mode too. But the change could also be seen as part of an instinctive quest to discover himself. In the coming decade he would take on a series of new personas in an apparent attempt to discover the most effective, while also tantalising his audiences, as if defying them to identify the true David Bowie. This process would also serve as a commentary on the nature of stardom itself.

The names in the news in the closing weeks of 1969 read now like markers for the watershed between the decades. In Britain there was Harold Wilson, the ultimate pragmatist, then – as speculation about a general election presaged – approaching the end of his six years as Labour prime minister. In Africa there was General Gowon, leading Nigeria in a ruthless civil war against break-away Biafra, while the Western powers, eager for West Africa's raw materials, did all they could to help him win.

In the US there was Lieutenant Calley, a soldier who would answer charges of slaughtering 300 villagers in Vietnam by claiming that he believed the mass murder of civilians to be official US government policy. There was Mary Jo Kopechne, drowned at Chappaquiddick, whose inquest was shortly to open, fuelling suspicion about the truthfulness of politicians and ending the claims of the Kennedy dynasty to power. All of these events increased the cynicism of the young and the voiceless towards those in power, and helped disperse the ingenuous idealism of the decade about to end.

In the world of popular music, two events crystallised the transition between two eras. In August, 400,000 people gathered at a free rock festival held on farmland in upstate New York, enshrining the name Woodstock with utopian hopes of peace and harmony. Four months later came disillusion, when a festival at Altamont in California degenerated into chaos and violence, reaching a ghastly climax when Hell's Angels stabbed a spectator to death just yards from where the Rolling Stones were performing.

David's own commentary on that summer, in his lyrics and his final interview of the year, showed him to have yet another instinctive gift. In rejecting the 1960s, he was also laying a trail for the decade to come. He had not yet achieved the status of megastar; nor had he exorcised his grandmother's curse. He would achieve both objectives when his personal destiny intersected with the concerns of the new decade, and he became an emblem of his times.

14

All the Way

David began 1970 with a bold new move. For the first time since the break-up of the Buzz in 1966, he formed a group. He explained that he wanted a nucleus of musicians for live performances and recording sessions, although he was careful to reserve the right to perform solo as well: he and the group, he added, would be "two separate working units whereby we can retain our own identities". Ken Pitt, of course, had always believed that David should be a solo performer. But for David, Pitt's aspirations were by then of little importance.

For two of his musicians, David looked no further than Haddon Hall. Tony Visconti, a practised bass player, readily agreed to become a founder member of the group; and so, if more reluctantly, did John Cambridge, the drummer of the Juniors Eyes group. John, who came from Hull, where he had worked as an apprentice plasterer, was far from being the most accomplished drummer in London; but he had a lugubrious sense of humour that appealed to David, who was undoubtedly swayed by the fact that John renewed the Yorkshire connection in his life.

Like the Yorkshiremen before him, John took an uncomplicated liking to David, finding him "a real good kid – a very good sense of humour, good for a laugh". And while John, like Derek Boyes of the Buzz, found David uncondescending towards him, David by now had developed a preference for backing musicians who could be seen as the rude mechanicals of the musical world: men, like the company of artisans in *A Midsummer Night's Dream*, who could be easily persuaded to do his bidding and not challenge his authority.

David asked John to play with him at the Speakeasy on January 8th, 1970 – David's twenty-third birthday – and afterwards invited him to join his group. John told David: "There must be loads of drummers down here a lot better than me," but David assured him: "I like you as a person, and I like your drumming."

Mick Ronson might at first have been cast as another of the rude mechanicals. Outsiders who met him during his three-year partnership with David often formed a low opinion of his intellectual abilities. Americans regarded him as inarticulate; some Londoners as simply "thick". Both were reactions to his opaque, east Yorkshire accent, compounded, in England, with anti-northern prejudice. They were also misled by an intense shyness that caused him to blush merely on being spoken to. Mick was in fact an immense asset to David in more ways that one. There was, first, his overwhelming handsomeness, with startling blond hair falling about a long, Modigliani-like face. He also had high instinctive skills as a performer that were to prove a vital foil to David's.

Like John Cambridge, Mick came from Hull. His father was a storeman and the family lived in a terraced house in the style of *Coronation Street*. Mick left Maybury High School at fifteen without a single O-level to his name and went to work in the warehouse of the local Co-op. He had already shown a considerable aptitude for music: he had learned the recorder and violin at school and played the harmonium in church, and his first ambition was to become a music teacher. At the same time he watched in horror as, one by one, his old school friends married and had children while still in their teens.

"I was dying to get out," he says, not only of his home but also of the remorseless pattern of northern working-class life that predicted the same fate for him. Much like Keith Waterhouse's Yorkshire character, Billy Liar, his only escape appeared to lie in his imagination. His musical idol was the guitarist Jeff Beck, and he dreamed of emulating Beck's virtuoso style, with its screaming, distorted notes, and his fast passagework; he also pretended that he played with the Rolling Stones. "I just walked about in a dream world," Mick says.

Finally – unlike Billy Liar – Mick went to London. For a long time, it appeared that his dreams would remain unfulfilled. He found work as a garage-hand and "hung around on street corners, hoping I would meet someone". He also went to drink coffee at the Giaconda. "I never had any money and I used to sit there with one cup for five or six hours. I'd just sit there and sort of bump into someone by accident and say, 'What do you do?' I was terrified. I used to get really depressed." Finally he was enlisted by a band named Voice, sponsored by a semi-mystical organisation called Process.

After playing on a few dates with Voice, Mick went home to Hull for a weekend. When he returned to London he found that Voice and its sponsors had departed for the West Indies. He next joined a group, Wanted, that played Tamla and soul, but it soon split up, leaving Mick £100 in debt. Mick went home to Hull and took a job in a paint factory. "I was heartbroken," he says.

Mick's next move was to join a Hull group named the Rats. When the Rats arranged to play at a club in Paris for a month, Mick confidently handed in his notice at the paint factory and joined them. "This was it," says Mick. "This was definitely the big one."

The Rats had reached Grantham, eighty miles south of Hull, in their van when its engine blew up. They spent most of their savings on repairs and by the time they reached Paris they had no money at all. They also learned that their booking had been cancelled. They played for a week at an Algerian club that was constantly raided by the police and then found a new booking at a club in northern France. When they arrived, they found that the club had closed down. They headed back to Hull and had reached Grantham once more when they ran out of money. They persuaded a local club to let them play in return for enough money to buy their petrol home and a bag of chips each. Once back in Hull, Mick's parents told him it was time to settle down, and he took a job as a municipal gardener.

Somewhat to his surprise, Mick found that he liked the work. "There was something about it – cutting grass, pruning roses, I had sheep to look after too. I really enjoyed it. I thought, maybe this is what I'd end up doing."

In London, meanwhile, David was searching for a lead guitarist. John Cambridge, who had played with the Rats, urged him to give Mick a chance, and David agreed. At the end of January, John returned to Hull to fetch Mick. John found him marking out the lines on a rugby pitch. Mick had only just paid off the debts from his last bid to become a musician; since then he had bought a shirt, trousers and shoes, which he was paying for on weekly tick.

"So then John comes along and tells me to come down to London," Mick recalls. "I thought, Wait a minute, is it going to take me another two or three years to pay this lot off? I told him, 'I'm not sure about this, John.' Then I decided I had to go . . ."

Mick met David at Haddon Hall. "He was sitting playing the guitar and I just picked up a guitar and started playing with him," Mick says. David asked him to play with him on the BBC radio programme, *Top Gear*, to be recorded on February 5th. Although Mick knew none of David's songs, he did his best to play along. Afterwards David told him to go home and pack in his job and then come back to London and join his group. Mick did as David bid. "I thought, Well, here we go. I really liked David and his songs, it was real classy, it was different, I was in London, I was all set."

Mick and John Cambridge both moved into Haddon Hall, sleeping on mattresses laid out on the minstrels' gallery at the top of the stairs. In search of a name for his group, David turned briefly to Ken Pitt. He told Pitt that he hoped to launch the trio with the maximum possible publicity. "The whole thing," David said, "is just one big hype." When Pitt suggested calling the group the Hype, David agreed.

With his ear for the fashions of vocabulary, David had picked up one of the words of the moment. The Random House Dictionary gives four meanings for hype: 1) to stimulate, excite, or agitate; 2) to intensify (publicity) by ingenious or questionable methods; 3) an ingenious or questionable method used in publicity to intensify the effect; 4) a drug addict, especially one who uses a hypodermic needle. The first three meanings were all relevant (and resonances from the fourth could not be entirely dismissed). Certainly a desire to stimulate, excite or agitate, with the effect intensified by ingenious or even questionable methods, could be discerned in the Hype's first public appearance, at the Round House on February 22nd.

The ideas involved were initiated by the photographer Ray Stevenson, and were taken up with characteristic verve by Angie. Stevenson had known David since the days of Feathers, and had been photographing him ever since. He also had a sensitive feel for the rapid shifts of popular fashion, and in the autumn of 1969 sensed that changes were imminent. "That was the time of scruffy jeans and denims," Stevenson says. "But I always thought you should do the opposite of what everyone else did."

Stevenson had a passion for comic-book heroes like Superman and Captain Marvel, and on an evening spent with David and Angie, he says, "We talked of supermen and superstars." Stevenson next visited Haddon Hall one Sunday afternoon before the Beckenham Arts Lab. "They were both sitting there sewing away, making costumes for the Hype."

The costumes that Angie had designed, with the assistance of David and Tony Visconti's companion, Liz Hartley, had taken Stevenson's idea considerably further. David became Rainbowman, with lurex tights, a silky blue cape and knee-length pirate boots. John Cambridge was Cowboyman, with a frilly shirt and a ten-gallon hat. Mick Ronson wore David's silver 'Space Oddity' suit and became Gangsterman. Tony Visconti was Hypeman, with a Superman suit bearing an H on his chest instead of an S.

At first the members of the Hype were nonplussed: "I thought it was a bit naughty, a bit of a giggle," says John Cambridge, who like his predecessors among David's groups felt disturbed at the element of sexual ambiguity the costumes contained. "But when we got on stage we forgot all about it." Among the audience, the most enthusiastic response came from Marc Bolan, whose friendship with David, though never free of a competitive edge, had persisted from the days of Leslie Conn.

Bolan had entered into the spirit of the occasion by dressing as a Roman legionary, with a plastic breastplate he had bought at Woolworth's. But the rest of the audience – most of whom had in any case come to see the Fat Mattress group, who were at the top of the bill – remained decidedly unimpressed: "We died a death," David said later. Tony Visconti was more disgruntled still. His clothes were stolen from the dressing room, and he had to go home in his Hypeman suit.

The performance was nonetheless a landmark in the new styles of the 1970s, for it was the moment when glam or glitter rock was born. It was not the first time rock performers had dressed in decorative clothes: Ray Davies and the Kinks wore Regency clothes when performing 'Dedicated Follower Of Fashion' in 1966; so did the Stones, in particular Brian Jones, a year or so later. But the ambiguous sexual note that unsettled John Cambridge was new. Some chroniclers have described glam rock as a reaction to the sexual freedom of the 1960s, but the Hype's costumes were in part a projection of David and Angie's even less inhibited ideas, and a signal of their determination to push the sexual boundaries wider still.

The Round House performance was important in another respect: it marked the birth of paradox in David's work. From then on his performances would become increasingly elaborate and flamboyant, and he seemed to become the quintessential gadfly, eschewing politics or other forms of social commitment. While this led the politicised groupings who had demonstrated at Grosvenor Square in 1968 to turn away from David, others welcomed him for the same reason. In this way, David became the aptest symbol of the disenchantment of the 1970s.

Yet the staging of David's songs belied their content, for his lyrics were acquiring an ever-harder edge. But the contradiction between David's medium and his message also served his purpose. As his style became more pronounced, it diverted attention from the secret anguish of his lyrics. That formed part of David's toying with his audiences, posing an enigma which he defied them to resolve. Who was the real David Bowie? The showman or the poet? Was there a real David Bowie at all? Such questions went to the heart of David's personality and his troubled family history. But David was making sure that the answers would not be easy to find.

Ken Pitt, for one, did not approve of the new David. It had been central to his campaign, combining sexual politics with the commercial potential of homosexuality, that David should present himself in as orthodox a manner as possible; nor were flamboyance and outrageousness to his personal taste. His relationship with David was becoming more overtly acrimonious, and a dispute now broke out over which single would be best suited to follow 'Space Oddity'.

David told Pitt he wanted to make a fresh recording of 'London Bye Ta Ta' – previously turned down by Decca – together with a new song, 'The Prettiest Star'. It was, ostensibly, a tender love lyric, and David had already made a demonstration tape which he had played to Angie over the phone when she visited her parents in Cyprus at Christmas. Angie believed that David had written it for her, particularly as he called her

> . . . my rest and peace child

But David was also conjuring memories of former loves, including the familiar wish-fulfilment of his childhood imaginings, and the lost love of Hermione. David relished the rich resonances of the title, with its celestial and show-business references, and predicted that one day he and Angie would

> . . . rise up all the way

– to stardom, of course.

David recorded 'The Prettiest Star', together with 'London Bye Ta Ta', over three sessions in January. Tony Visconti's production gave it the richness it merited, so that it emerged not as a simple love ballad, but one infused with notes of regret, deepened by the lamenting tone of the lead guitar played by Marc Bolan, who had been hired as a session man.

The dispute with Pitt centred on which song should appear on the A side of David's new single. After the final recording session, David, Visconti and Pitt collectively decided – so Pitt believed – that 'London Bye Ta Ta' was the better commercial prospect, with

'The Prettiest Star' going on the B side. Shortly before Mercury released the record, Pitt discovered that 'The Prettiest Star' now occupied the A side, and 'London Bye Ta Ta' had been omitted entirely. In its place on the B side was a new track entitled 'Conversation Piece'.

Pitt was not averse to 'Conversation Piece', seeing it partly as a nostalgic reminder of David's sojourn in Manchester Street, particularly in the line: "My papers lying on the floor serve their purpose just by being there." But he was angered by the switch from 'London Bye Ta Ta' to 'The Prettiest Star', suspecting that it had been dictated by Angie; he talked darkly of doings "behind my back". Then came a further clash, when Angie insisted that David and the Hype were not to play for less than £150 per appearance; Pitt, who regarded this as hopelessly unrealistic, replied that the most he could secure was £125. For a month there was impasse, and David did not perform at all.

Both sides took encouragement from the reviews when 'The Prettiest Star' was released on March 6th. "It could do very well indeed," wrote Derek Johnson in the *New Musical Express*; "Chart cert," said Peter Jones in the *Record Mirror*; "A hit indeed," pronounced Penny Valentine in *Disc*. Decca decided to issue an album entitled *The World Of David Bowie*, containing fourteen of David's songs. Most had appeared on the 1967 Deram album but it included four tracks Decca had previously declined to release: 'London Boys', 'Karma Man', 'In The Heat Of The Morning' and 'Let Me Sleep Beside You'. In view of the disappointments Decca had caused both David and Pitt, their feelings on learning that the company had suddenly discovered his talents can best be described as mixed.

Meanwhile the battles within Mercury continued. Pitt was delighted to receive a letter from Lou Reizner disowning Calvin Mark Lee who, Reizner proclaimed, "no longer works for this firm and in no way represents Mercury as it represents our contract with David Bowie". Lee fought back, telephoning Mercury's head office in Chicago to protest about Reizner. Pitt lobbied Chicago himself, complaining of Mercury's poor communications, with the result that a Philips executive in London, Ralph Mace, who had helped to promote 'Space Oddity', was appointed to oversee David's affairs.

There were further changes in Chicago when Mercury's founder, Irwin Green, handed over to a new boss, Irwin Steinberg. Steinberg and a new head of A and R, Robin McBride, came to London in January. Although the 'Space Oddity' single had failed in the US,

Pitt found them optimistic over the imminent US release of David's first Mercury album. They also told him that they intended to take up their option on David's contract in June, and wanted David to begin work on his next album.

Then came the news that Pitt was dreading. On March 12th, David appeared at a charity performance for the mentally handicapped at the Royal Albert Hall. (David broke the £150 rule to do so, accepting a fee of £50 which Pitt had secured.) Afterwards, with Angie at his side, David announced to Pitt: "We're going to get married."

Angie has since given different accounts of why she and David decided to do anything so conventional. In *Free Spirit*, she wrote: "I was truly in love and I knew that he was in love with me." Today, she says: "When David and I married we made a deal. There was no love involved, it was a marriage of convenience, we were very good friends. He told me the day before we got married that he wasn't in love with me . . ."

The second version was closer to the explanation David offered Pitt at the time. Since Angie was no longer a student, she could only stay in Britain as a visitor and was compelled to leave at regular intervals. Marriage would give her a resident's status and the right to work. There was a major advantage for David, too, as the inhabitants of Haddon Hall realised. "Everyone knew he was marrying Angie for her green card," says John Cambridge – referring to the magic passport bestowed on the spouses of American citizens, enabling them to live and work in the US.

It was a predictably unorthodox marriage in other ways. David did not tell his mother of his plans and she only learned of the wedding the night before. She telephoned Pitt and asked if he was going. Pitt declined, pointing out with a long-suffering air that he had not been invited – although the "Haddon Hall coterie" had. David and Angie also celebrated the eve of their wedding in a suitably idiosyncratic manner. They shared a bed with a mutual friend, an art student whom Angie for one found stunningly beautiful, later describing her "incredible heart-shaped face" and her "petite but perfectly contoured body".

Angie describes this event as taking place at the friend's flat in Bloomsbury, but according to John Cambridge, the circumstances were more public than that. "It was at Haddon Hall," he says. "The three of them were in David and Angie's room. There were only thin doors and we were all outside playing darts or something like that. You could hear everything going on, it wasn't as if they were trying to hide anything, and David came out and said, 'What are you doing, lads?' and he left them in there and let them have a go. At the time I don't think I really twigged it until I sat down and thought about it, and then I thought, It's not up to me, they can do what they like."

John also disputes accounts that the three were so exhausted that they overslept and arrived at Bromley Register Office half an hour late. "We went there together from Haddon Hall," he says. "We were all sat waiting there for the registrar to arrive." David had asked John and a friend named Clare Shenstone to act as witnesses but David's mother marched briskly forward and took John's place. She had also alerted the local press, and the event was recorded by the *Beckenham and Penge Advertiser* and the *Beckenham Journal*, who photographed David and Angie with Peggy between them, her arms through theirs.

Back at Haddon Hall, the new marriage was blighted by rows over how Ken Pitt was to be disposed of. David, to Angie's impatience, was still persevering with his Jekyll and Hyde roles. Pitt believed he had found the ideal opportunity for David to broaden his performing skills when the director of the Harrogate Theatre in Yorkshire, Brian Howard, suggested that David should both act in and write the songs for a stage adaptation of Sir Walter Scott's novel, *The Fair Maid of Perth*. Nothing at that time could have been further from David's aims, but he agreed to study the script and to meet Howard in March. While David hesitated, it was Angie who insisted that Pitt be jettisoned forthwith. "She was the real backbone, making him do these things," says John Cambridge. "She was the hard one."

On March 31st, David telephoned Pitt and asked if they could meet. Later that day at Manchester Street, after some prevarication, David told Pitt: "I want to have a go at managing myself." When Pitt asked why, David said he was undertaking too many live appearances and his recording career was suffering; he also felt aggrieved at the failure of 'The Prettiest Star', which by then had sold fewer than 1,000 copies. Ken considered the criticisms unfair, particularly since he had opposed the release of 'The Prettiest Star'. David also said he was short of money, so Ken wrote him a cheque for £200.

Pitt nonetheless did his best to humour David, and promptly arranged a schedule with Tony Visconti for recording the next Mercury album. In the next two weeks, David and Visconti also recorded a new two-part version of 'Memory Of A Free Festival', which was to be issued – one part to each side – as David's next US single, instead of 'The Prettiest Star'. Pitt also agreed to make no further live bookings for David, and so hoped that he had met David's complaints.

On April 27th, however, Pitt received a letter from David. "I have been advised," it began, "that you have not performed your part of our Agreement by using your past [*sic*] endeavours to further my career thereunder . . ." He told Pitt that he no longer regarded him as his personal manager and asked him to confirm within seven days that he would no longer act in that capacity.

Although the letter was in David's handwriting, the phraseology – including the mistaken phrase "past endeavours", instead of "best endeavours" – indicated that it had been composed, however imperfectly, with the benefit of legal advice. That advice had been rendered by a former litigation clerk whose overriding ambition was to break into show business. His name was Tony Defries.

Many and delightful are the variations that have been wrought upon the name of Tony Defries. De Freece, de Freis, De Friez, De Frierz, and Desries were all among the convoluted versions on letters and telexes addressed to him in his four-year spell as David's manager. Defries affected to be irritated by them, and would complain to his secretary, the infinitely loyal Marilyn Schwartz, at the ignorance or stupidity of the people he was compelled to deal with. Yet he also regarded them with a certain wry amusement, relishing the mystery and confusion he inspired.

Those around him sometimes awarded him less flattering names: Tony de Freak, Tony Deep Freeze. Even to insiders, his personality appeared as enigmatic as that of David himself. It has been so ever since. The man who helped elevate David Bowie to megastardom remained as elusive in the 1980s as he was ten years before, and was comparable in that respect – and in others – with Howard Hughes or Elvis Presley's manager, Colonel Parker. There is not one full interview with him anywhere on record, and hardly a recognisable photograph either; and the vast newspaper library of the Press Association in Fleet Street, which files virtually every reference in the British press, has just two items under his name.

In his forties – he passed that landmark in 1983 – Defries is a trim man, with dark curly hair and a neat beard framing a face with blue-green eyes and a prominent, angular nose. He talks with a standard English accent into which more demotic strains sometimes obtrude. He divides his life between a home in a Swiss tax sanctuary near Zurich, and an apartment on the thirty-first floor of a block in central Manhattan, with one of New York's finest views of Central Park.

The apartment is adorned with mementoes of his partnership with David, and evidence of its rewards. There are numerous photographs of David, including a memorable triptych in which he is flanked at a dinner table by Mick Jagger and Lou Reed, together with the inevitable display of gold discs; there is also an opulent, if slightly ostentatious, display of furnishings and antiques. Hanging near the doorway in the narrow entrance hall is a framed original copy of *The Times* from 1805, carrying news of the funeral of Admiral Nelson after Trafalgar. In the main living room – the window overlooking Central Park occupies one entire end – is a tall, English-style portrait of a young boy, and a period French lithograph which depicts a damsel chained to a pillar and watched by a Negro slave who is holding a tray bearing a lethal knife.

There are deco-style lampstands and a selection of stylised wooden masks. Lying on a large, mirrored coffee table is a Sotheby's catalogue for an auction of watercolours by American artists, and a jewellery brochure from Cartier's; next to them is a neatly stacked pile of *Playboy* magazines. There are several items of nineteenth-century ship's furniture, including a green wardroom table inscribed "Captain Finch", and an officer's chest being a painting of a sea scene and the words "Lieutenant Pirie" and "HMS *Oak*". In a glass case alongside, its cranium inset with a sundial, is a blanched and grinning skull.

These are not solely the accoutrements of a man of leisure, for the apartment has a quiet air of purpose about it. Telephones warble at frequent intervals, and a telex machine tickers discreetly in the dining room. Ten years or more after parting from David, Defries is still involved in show-business management. He is equally preoccupied with his investments, for he has no financial need to work ever again. When he ceased to be David's manager, following a cataclysmic row, he was guaranteed a substantial portion of David's earnings for years to come. Yet the episode still touches deep and painful emotions in Defries. Ask him why he and David parted and he will say that the question is too personal, like asking a man why he has separated from his wife.

In 1970, when he replaced Ken Pitt as David's manager, Defries was not widely known in the entertainment world. Within his family, however, his background was a matter of controversy that still causes his relatives anxiety today. His ancestors, who were Jewish, came to Britain from the Netherlands province of Friesland in the nineteenth century (Friesland was also the origin of the family name). His father, Edward, was a master-builder and engineer who was almost bankrupted by the depression of the 1930s. He and his wife Lily turned to antique dealing and furniture restoring, and within ten years had established a successful business in Shepherd's Bush.

Therein lay the family controversy. In later years, Mrs Defries and the elder of her two sons, Nicholas, were angered by accounts that Edward Defries had been a stallholder, costermonger, even a rag-and-bone merchant in Shepherd's Bush market. "Do I sound like a costermonger's wife?" Mrs Defries would complain, pointing out that the family had "always owned property and had two cars". Her husband, she adds, was "extremely good-looking and an absolute gentleman".

Their anger was fuelled by their suspicion that Tony had not exactly discouraged such accounts himself. For he was not displeased by a mythology which, much like David's, gave him street credibility and accounted him a self-made man. That upset his mother still further, since she and her husband had nursed him through school and done all they could to give him a sound start in life. There was a further edge to her complaint from the fact that she had not seen Tony – or Anthony, as she always called him, regarding its abbreviation as "common" – in fourteen years, and that the rift between him and the rest of the family was almost complete.

Tony Defries almost did not survive his childhood at all. He was born in Rickmansworth, north of London, on September 3rd, 1943. When he was three months old, his mother fell ill and went to hospital. Her two other children – Nicholas, four, and Deirdre, two – were looked after by her mother-in-law. Tony was put into a wartime nursery where, his mother believes, he was not well cared for. "When I got him back I could scarcely recognise him," she says. Tony began to suffer from asthma attacks that left his mother terrified: "We used to lean over the cot to try to hear him breathing. We had a lifetime of anxiety bringing him up. Three times he nearly died."

At school, Tony's illness proved a considerable handicap. His mother had to teach him to read at the same time as her fourth child, Tina. That was the first of the problems over his education that were to set him apart from the rest of the family. "All the others were clever and passing scholarships," Mrs Defries says, "and I was worried that he might get left out." He went to a special school for delicate children and was taught breathing exercises at Hammersmith Hospital. He was also told he must avoid fights and arguments. "As he got bigger he learned to control it," Mrs Defries says, "and he learned to walk away from trouble if he could." But she fears that at the same time her son became "rather selfish and only thought about himself"; he was also "very thin".

In the early 1950s, the family moved to Croydon. Tony attended a middle-grade local authority school, Heath Clark, while his brother and sisters went to the more privileged Godolphin and Latymer. His parents were afraid to push him, and his isolation was increased by his diffidence about his chances. "He didn't want to sit exams," his mother says. "We never thought he would amount to much."

When his brother Nicholas went into the law, later becoming an estate agent, Mrs Defries wanted Tony to join a firm of solicitors too. "I had a job to get him in because he felt he couldn't do it. He said, 'I'm not Nicholas, just because Nicholas can do it doesn't mean to say that I can.' We said, 'You won't know if you don't try,' and we had to force him to try."

Defries spent almost ten years with a firm of solicitors, Martin Boston, in Wigmore Street. He never qualified as a solicitor and remained a litigation clerk, specialising in divorce work. Yet the nervous and diffident child acquired, as a young man, a remarkable compensatory self-confidence. His painful isolation gave him a determination not to be submerged by the conventions and etiquette of the business world. The techniques he acquired to survive his childhood would serve him to good purpose in adult life. And the extent to which he had been compared with his siblings grew into a fierce ambition and determination to succeed.

Defries's first contact with the entertainment world came in 1964, when the record producer Mickie Most asked Martin Boston to act for him in a dispute involving the Newcastle group, the Animals. Defries was assigned to the case, working with Most for two years and also dealing with the New York accountant and manager Allen Klein (sometimes referred to in Britain, by those who encountered his abrasive personality, as the *dreaded* Allen Klein).

Soon afterwards Defries left Martin Boston to become what he terms a "legal adviser for hire", accepting trouble-shooting commissions from a variety of clients. One was the solicitors Godfrey Davis and Batt, with offices in Cavendish Square, which Defries used as a base. While there he played a leading and controversial part in what became known as the AFAP affair. In 1969, Britain's fashion and advertising photographers formed a group which they called the Association of Fashion and Advertising Photographers, or AFAP, with some ninety members, to strengthen their hand when negotiating with advertising and model agencies.

The photographer Donald Silverstein offered to obtain a solicitor for the association, and Defries – who was not in fact a solicitor, but called himself a lawyer instead – was hired for a fee of £250 and an annual retainer of £100.

Defries soon stamped his forthright personality on AFAP's affairs. He told its members that rather than accept a flat fee they should demand a share of the copyright in their photographs. He instigated searches of publishing companies to discover who their directors were, and he lunched with leading figures of the advertising world to see if they would give their support. He proposed linking up with the militant film-workers union, the ACTT, and told AFAP that it should learn from the aggressive tactics of the print unions. As a first step, he proposed that the photographers should demand 40 per cent syndication fees from the giant International Publishing Corporation: if IPC refused, they should refuse to work for them.

At first, these tactics found favour with the photographers, and Defries's career at AFAP rapidly prospered. Defries was elected to AFAP's ruling committee, which then proposed raising the annual subscription from £10 to £50. Then the committee voted to pare itself down from eight members to three, of which Defries was one. In January 1970, the committee proposed increasing Defries's retainer to £500. In February, it published a newsletter defending the new concentration of power in the association and praising Defries's "brilliant legal brain". By then, the committee's notepaper gave its address as that of Godfrey Davis and Batt.

It was now that the rank-and-file members of AFAP decided that things had gone too far. In fact, some felt Defries's militancy was hardly apposite in a milieu where art directors, photographers and model agencies do their best to ensure that the vast sums of money swilling around in the advertising world are dispensed to the advantage of all. At the annual general meeting of the AFAP in April the three-man committee was asked to stand down. A day or so later Defries resigned from both the committee and the AFAP.

In an attempt to turn the tables on the photographers who had just dispensed with his services, Defries decided to form an association for photographers' models. Its main aim was to secure a share of the copyright of their photographs from both the model agencies and the photographers themselves.

The inaugural meeting of the proposed models' association was held over dinner at the Trattoria Terrazza in Romilly Street, on May 6th. Among those present was the show-business accountant Laurence Myers, who acted for the Animals and the Rolling Stones.

Myers had come to know Defries during the litigation involving Mickie Most and Allen Klein – Myers was a partner in one of Most's companies – and he had judged Defries to be "very eager and very bright". Defries had asked Myers what he thought of the idea of a models' association, and Myers approved. "The models were really getting screwed," Myers says, "literally and financially." Besides, any plan which entailed "having dinner with about eight or ten of the most beautiful women in London" had to be a good idea.

The meeting was not a success. Defries told the models that they should refuse to work for their agencies unless their demands for a share of the copyright of their photographs were granted. Since the models were earning up to £50 a day, almost twice Britain's *weekly* wage, the proposal that they should refuse to work lacked immediate appeal. "They were all too loyal to their agencies," says Laurence, "and anyway they burst into tears." The proposed Assocation of Fashion Models did not survive the setback. By then, in any case, Tony Defries had just found a new and potentially far more lucrative client.

In so sensitive a matter, there has been considerable dispute over who is to take the credit – or blame – for introducing David to Tony Defries. Angie claims a major share herself: "I hired Tony to break the Ken Pitt contract," she says. "I went and found Tony because I had to find an attorney who was brusque enough, who would not go for the general run-of-the-mill line that the contract was unbreakable."

For a long time, Pitt himself blamed Tony Visconti. But when he heard what Pitt was saying, Visconti denied it. In fact, the man responsible was Olav Wyper.

Wyper was the man who had revived the fortunes of 'Space Oddity' at Philips, helping both David and himself. It gave Philips its first British hit for a long time and brought Wyper promotion to general manager. Wyper had good reason to be grateful to David and had remained friendly since, lending a sympathetic ear whenever David wanted to discuss his career. In April that year, David called on him again.

"He was very disturbed and worried about his personal relationship with Ken Pitt," Wyper recalls. "He said that the friendship was getting in the way of a career, and that although he wanted to be friends with Ken, he wasn't the person to take him on to that next stage. He was unhappy, very unhappy, and kind of lost; and he felt that he was in some way bound by chains to Ken Pitt and that unless he did something to undo those chains, he'd sink without trace."

According to Wyper, he had dined a short while before with Tony Defries and Laurence Myers at the Trattoria Terrazza. Myers and Defries told Wyper that they were hoping to move into show-business management, and explained in some detail how they felt suited to such a role.

"This was about the time that Bowie had been asking me, 'What am I going to do? You must help me,'" Wyper says. "Here are two guys who ought to know. At least Bowie could go to them and check his legal position and take his contract to them. So I talked to them about David and they said they would very much like to meet him and I agreed to set up a meeting."

David visited Defries at his office at Godfrey Davis and Batt. He was, Defries once said, unshaven, hollow-cheeked, bleary-eyed and nervous, "like a refugee". Later, he gave another interpretation of David's appearance: Defries called it "playing the waif". It was a role David had played before, most notably to Hal Shaper, Natasha Kornilof and Ken Pitt.

By David's account, Defries was capable of playing a role too, that of the calm and confident figure on whom David could utterly depend. "He said, 'I can get you out of that,'" David related in 1972. "I just sat there and openly wept. I was so relieved that somebody was so strong about things."

Not for the first time, David felt trapped by a relationship and did not know how to extricate himself. When Defries told David he could "get him out of that", he was referring to David's contract with Pitt. In fact, Pitt raised little objection, but what David wanted – his words to Wyper notwithstanding – was freedom from their entire relationship.

When Pitt read David's letter, with the legalistic phrases Defries had proposed, he replied offering to discuss the "ways and means by which we might end our professional relationship". There was no reply from David; instead, Pitt received a telephone call from Godfrey Davis and Batt asking to make an appointment for David and "Mr Anthony Defries" – the first time Ken had heard his name. Defries and David arrived at Manchester Street on Thursday, May 7th.

Defries was conservatively dressed in a suit and tie, with short, tidy hair. He introduced himself as a lawyer who helped people in the music business. He did all the talking, while David perched on the edge of Pitt's chaise-longue, staring fixedly ahead. When the matter of David's contract was raised, Pitt said he would not object if David wished to end it; but he asked to be compensated for "loss of future earnings". Defries nodded sagely and said that he would have to consider the matter. When David and Defries got up to leave, David shook hands with Pitt, smiled briefly and said, "Thank you, Ken."

For Pitt, the poignancy of the parting was accentuated by his belief that, in his three years as David's manager, he had laid the foundation of his career: now, it seemed, the chance to build on that foundation would be denied him.

Pitt did not see David again for three years. From then on, their encounters proved distant and sporadic; and Pitt never gleaned any clues from David to the question he has long pondered. "To this day," he says, "I don't know why we split up."

15

Meeting the Monster

As Tony Defries and Laurence Myers contemplated the asset that
David represented, it was clear that they viewed him in notably
contrasting ways. In public at least, the difference between them
was captured by their respective explanations as to why anyone
should devote their time and energy to managing little-known
artists in the hope of producing a star.

Defries: "You're doing it because you want everyone to hear
your artist and you want everyone to feel what you feel about the
artist. That's the only reason why you do it. Why are we doing it,
Laurence?"

Myers: "For the money."

As Myers saw it, the partnership the two men formed in 1970,
in pursuit of their aim to become show-business managers, was a
suitable reflection of their views. At first Defries retained his base
at Godfrey Davis and Batt, but then moved into the offices of
Myers's company, Gem Productions, in Regent Street. Defries was
employed on Gem's staff, earning £30 a week, on the understanding
that if David proved as profitable as they hoped, he would eventually take a share in Gem's equity. Meanwhile, Myers would provide
the funds to launch – or relaunch – David's career; and Defries
would supply the *chutzpah*, the flair.

Myers candidly admits that his previous career in the dry world
of accounting had left him without a "creative background".
Where Myers's other clients were concerned, that hardly mattered.
That year he also took on the New Seekers, a group "manufactured" (Myers's word) in an attempt to repeat the formula of the
Australian group the Seekers, whose debased-folk ballads had
brought them a series of hits in the 1960s. One critic described the
New Seekers as "even more nauseatingly winsome than the first
lot", but such judgments did not embarrass Myers. "There is a
market," he says; "you package it." Soon afterwards, the New
Seekers achieved one of the most successfully packaged hits in the
history of popular music by taking a Coca-Cola advertisement to
number one in the hit parade.

But David, Myers felt, was utterly different. Myers had been impressed by 'Space Oddity' – "a spectacularly special song" – and found David friendly and personable when he met him at the Ivor Novello Awards in May, when David won a prize for 'Space Oddity'. But thereafter David resolutely refused to conform to any known precepts of packaging or marketing. "Without Defries," Myers says, "my management of David Bowie would have been a total disaster. I would have been saying to Bowie, 'You're a very good-looking guy, write some songs and stay good-looking, be a singer/composer, be very cool and laid back.' I would have been wrong."

Myers's first clue to the divide between David and his other clients came in the times they would arrive at the Gem office. The New Seekers were always there bright and early, around ten o'clock; Gary Glitter, whom Myers also took on that year, would come in around midday. David by contrast would stumble in, bleary-eyed, late in the afternoon. Later, other aspects of David's lifestyle would disturb Myers even more – but never Defries, who affected total sang-froid no matter how extravagant David's demands.

But then, by Myers's standards, Defries was most unconventional too. As Myers explains, most managers aim to preserve harmony in their relations with record companies, striking balanced deals for the sake of deals to come. But Defries, says Myers, had no regard for the etiquette of self-interest. Defries declined to go to business lunches, leaving them all to Myers, for he considered it a waste of time becoming friendly with people he had to negotiate with. "Tony didn't give a shit," says Myers. "He really, really didn't."

Defries was unusual in another respect that also impressed Myers. It became Defries's habit to describe David as "the greatest artist in the world". In the sphere of popular entertainment, such hyperbole is common: "They are *all* the greatest artists in the world," Myers explains. But Defries was different. "He absolutely *believed* that David was, and would be, the greatest star in the world, and he acted accordingly," Myers says.

As others were to find, Defries's enthusiasms could prove wildly infectious. Myers accepted that in order to make money out of David it would sadly be necessary to spend some money first. The most Myers had ever invested in a client at that time was around £5,000, and that was the amount he mentally reserved for David. His financial stake would eventually reach ten times his estimate.

And so Myers drew up a management contract for David to sign. Myers's views on the balance to be struck between artists and managers were endearingly frank: "You try to pay the artist as little as possible." In fact, David's contract was unexceptional by the standards of the music industry at that time. Gem would take 20 per cent of David's earnings. All expenses attributable to David would come from his 80 per cent share, but that was standard in the industry too.

The gloss that Defries offered David on the contract was designed precisely to meet David's needs. With the resources of Gem behind him, he explained, David could concentrate on his music, free of the financial anxiety that had plagued him before. The argument appealed readily to David, as Mick Ronson observed. "He just wanted to get signed up and get on the move," Mick says. "He didn't pinpoint things in contracts and ask, 'Right, if this means this, what is going to happen here?' He just wanted to be a star."

David's main preoccupation in the spring and summer of 1970 was to complete his next album for Mercury. His work, in fact, spanned the transition with managers, which was to prove one among a number of distractions that at times almost exhausted the patience of his colleagues. The album that emerged was a major advance in his career, and the first of a series of masterpieces that in retrospect constitute a landmark in the music of the 1970s.

First, there was a change of personnel in the Hype. On March 23rd, David and the group went to the Trident studios to make a fresh recording of 'Memory Of A Free Festival', which Robin McBride, not liking 'The Prettiest Star', had requested as Mercury's next single in the US. They also made a first attempt at recording the tune that eventually became 'The Supermen' on the forthcoming album. It included what John Cambridge describes as a "tricky little bit" which he had difficulty playing. "I just couldn't get it right and even Mick was saying, 'Come on, it's easy,' which makes you feel worse."

While David hesitated it was Angie who helped to dispose of John. David protested that John was "a mate", but Angie told him: "You've got to be ruthless." Mick produced a replacement, Mick Woodmansey – invariably known as Woody – who came from Driffield in Yorkshire, fifteen miles north of Hull. Woody had replaced John Cambridge once before, joining Mick Ronson's group the Rats when John moved on to Juniors Eyes. He was a moon-faced man with long sideburns and – unlike John – of few words. "He kept himself to himself," says John: "probably the ideal person to have in a backing band."

Although David's group was now settled, work on the new

album became, according to Tony Visconti, "a very hair-raising experience". The overriding problem was an astonishing and uncharacteristic lack of application from David. "We had a commitment to make an album," Visconti says; and yet, "this man would not get out of bed".

When the sessions began, David had supplied just one complete number, 'The Width Of A Circle', which he and the Hype had played on *Top Gear* in February, together with the melody for 'Black Country Rock'. Visconti and Mick Ronson did their best to follow their schedule by building on chords and musical phrases that they dragged out of David. In this atmosphere of crisis, Mick Ronson emerged as a force, first watching and learning from Visconti, then – with his formal musical education proving a decided advantage – contributing more and more.

This tortuous process was witnessed by the fifth participant in the album, Ralph Mace. In March, following his brief spell as the executive responsible for David's career, Mace had left Philips to join a Soho music company belonging to the giant US entertainment corporation, Gulf and Western. Mace continued to follow David's career, turning up unannounced at the recording sessions at the Trident studios, not merely out of friendship but also, Mace admits, in the hope of signing up David. "The longer time went by without a big success," Mace says, "there was always a chance one could do something with him."

Mace was an accomplished keyboard player, and when he observed Mick Ronson in difficulty with a part written for the Moog synthesiser – a versatile electronic keyboard then coming into increasing use – he volunteered to play it himself. "I said, 'I can save you a lot of time if you'll let me do that.'" In that manner, Mace adds, "I became immortal."

In general, Mace does not dispute Visconti's account of David's haphazard behaviour. Yet he is inclined to interpret it in a more charitable light, and the process he describes set the pattern which David followed, with refinements, during his subsequent recording career. "It was creation in the studio," Mace says. "They began with a basic idea from one instrument or one vocal line. They would start adding and then they would change according to their whims. They got a core of the sound and then they started over-dubbing and if it worked they kept it and if it didn't they would do it again, and it was a creative build-up, a synthesis."

Mace also saw David as a more active participant than Visconti described. "David would bounce ideas off people, there was a lot of creative interplay with all the people there," Mace says. "I thought that David knew what he wanted and what he didn't. There was often a grey area in between when he was searching, but when he was right he knew."

The music that emerged from this apparent confusion was very much of the moment. Just as David helped give birth to glam rock, he was also a midwife to the musical style known as heavy metal. The term had been current for less than two years, being taken from a novel by William Burroughs and incorporated on an album by the US group Steppenwolf in 1968. Early in 1970, its boundaries were still being defined. At its core was a pounding drum and a wailing, distorted guitar, producing a sound offensively described by one early protagonist as "woman tone"; other characteristics included reverberations, feedback, and sheer unmitigated noise.

In Britain, the first album by Led Zeppelin, dominated by the guitar of Jimmy Page, had laid down a marker for the style in 1969. Tony Visconti and Mick Ronson were in the vanguard of heavy metal too: Visconti through producing Marc Bolan, who had moved on from the florid, drug-influenced style known as psychedelia in its favour; Mick through his adulation of Jeff Beck, another of its practitioners. The recordings thus helped establish David as a style leader of the new decade. In the past he had been quick to adopt the current idiom; this time, through the musical alliances he had forged, he was among those determining what that idiom should be. Even by these new standards, however, little about the music was predictable or straightforward; here too, David time and again confounded his listeners' expectations.

If Tony Visconti had difficulty in persuading David to produce his musical ideas for the album, the task of coaxing lyrics from him was akin to that of a dentist in pulling teeth. In the past, David had arrived in the studio with a neat pile of manuscripts. This time, apart from 'The Width Of A Circle', Visconti found himself producing an album devoid of words. At the time, Visconti was inclined to blame Angie, or rather David's apparently obsessive interest in her. He was "sickened" to see David holding hands with Angie in the studio lobby, "going coo-chee coo-chee-coo". The album, he adds, "took a back seat . . . he just didn't care".

As Visconti himself later accepted, the cause of David's indecision was more profound. Marriage, with the attendant pressure from his mother, who had not relented in her dislike of Angie, was far from being the only major alteration in his life. Angie had not filled the vacuum left by the death of his father, on whom he had depended for encouragement and advice. In transition between managers, he found himself under pressure from the silent pain of

Ken Pitt and the exhortations of his peers. He was also struggling to find a style for the new decade, and to cope with the paradoxes his search presented. There was another factor too, potentially most disruptive of all: the arrival of Terry at Haddon Hall.

Although Terry had been consigned to Cane Hill, Angie was sympathetic to his plight, and invited him to stay at Haddon Hall for up to four weeks at a time. Its other inhabitants have telling memories of Terry there. Nita Bowes – still, on occasion, sharing David and Angie's bed – remembers "a wraith-like figure who always seemed on the fringe".

John Cambridge, who remained at Haddon Hall until April, recalls Terry's memory for minute sporting details, displayed in the arcane discussions the two men would hold about the composition of the Hull City soccer team. But Terry required careful attention, as demonstrated one evening when David and John took him to Beckenham High Street, where he was supposed to catch a bus back to Cane Hill. David and John repaired to a Wimpy bar opposite the Three Tuns but then discovered that Terry had disappeared from the bus queue. They found him in a nearby pub and eventually drove him back to Cane Hill themselves.

From incidents such as these, John concluded that David was far from indifferent to Terry's predicament. "I think David did care for him," John says. "He *was* bothered about him." Angie agrees. David and Terry were "very close", she says; and David was preoccupied by Terry "quite a lot". But visitors to Haddon Hall had to be on their guard against making chance remarks that could trigger David's fears. The photographer Ray Stevenson remembers being warned by Tony Visconti whenever Terry's mental condition had deteriorated. "He also told me not to make jokes about 'loonies'."

It was not merely that David had multiple distractions when working on the new album; it was also that any attempt to crystallise his thoughts would lead him into a minefield of anguish and contradiction. In the end, Tony Visconti took a decisive hand. "We had about three days left," he recalls. "I said, 'David, you're going to have to throw some lyrics on these songs and some vocals.'"

Almost miraculously, out of this maelstrom of conflict and pressure, emerged David's most remarkable lyrics yet. Some themes were familiar: the craving for affection, the yearning for the lost world of childhood, the questioning of the role of the guru, the quest for identity. But David took them in more risky directions; he also explored dangerous new areas. Another notable feature was the increasing violence and anger he displayed. But it was a controlled violence, for his writing was also more incisive: his imagery became tougher and more audacious, his use of compression and ellipsis, complexity and ambiguity, more adept. The overall impression was of a poet prepared to reveal the truth about himself: but only to those determined enough to unravel the clues that the nine lyrics contained.

David's preoccupation with the guru, seen in several lyrics on the first Mercury album, was the subject of 'Saviour Machine'. Over this song in particular, David felt the pressure of Visconti's deadline, for according to Angie he had to stay up into the early hours to complete it, with her a ministering presence by his side. What David eventually produced was the tale of a leader who rejects the unquestioning trust others place in him, with the hints of a nightmare technological future in the title reinforced by the slithering musical phrases and the fractured tempo, culminating in a despairing cacophony that fades without resolution.

There was a linked theme in 'The Supermen', which described a race of superbeings, much like the mountain giant in 'The Wild Eyed Boy From Freecloud', subject to

Nightmare dreams no mortal mind could hold

and who question the purpose of their immortality. It also displayed the speed with which David could soak up complex ideas and deploy them to his own purposes, for it contained several concepts borrowed from the German philosopher Nietzsche, whose works *Thus Spake Zarathustra* and *Beyond Good and Evil* David had been dipping into. In particular, David was attracted by Nietzsche's notion of the superman who rejects conventional morality and develops his own.

'Running Gun Blues' extended the sequence of war, death and destruction begun in 'Please Mr. Gravedigger' and 'We Are Hungry Men' in 1967. David, temporarily keeping faith with the protest movement, described a Vietnam veteran who guns down civilians in the style of several recent massacres in the US. What made it more remarkable was that, by Angie's account, David wrote it during an afternoon when both he and Visconti had to keep breaking from their work to give interviews. Musically, David portrayed the horror of the occasion through a reedy, high-pitched voice skeetering on the edge of dementia.

Equally violent imagery was to be found in 'She Shook Me Cold', even though it pursued another of David's earliest concerns, the

215

nature of love and affection. Following the bitter songs he had written in the aftermath of his affair with Hermione, there now came a culminating outburst of hatred for the woman with the "golden hair" who had "sucked my dormant will", "took my head, smashed it up", and "crushed me mercilessly". David's ferocity was intensified by his uncompromising sexual slang – "suck", "ball", "head" – together with phrases like "my young blood rising" – and the exaggerated heavy-metal guitar of Mick Ronson, doing his best to surpass even his hero, Jeff Beck.

'After All' marked a return to another of David's early themes, the desire to be immersed in the warmth and security of a fondly imagined childhood. Here once again David was able to portray himself as the insider, with adults excluded; here, too, forbidden activities could be pursued, such as

> . . . painting our faces and dressing in thoughts from the skies.

Once again, the music conveyed a sense of menace through the elaborately slow tempo which, against an ominously shifting bass part, appears on the edge of breaking down throughout the track.

Thus far, the pattern of David's thoughts was revealed not only by the ostensible narrative of the lyrics, but also by the clusters of ideas and references they contained. David's near-fixation with ideas of transience and mortality, and his tentative belief in Buddhist notions of rebirth, were shown through the frequent use of words like death, impermanence, and oblivion, together with their counterpoints in rebirth, paradise, and "endless lives". More notable still was the frequency of language and imagery connected with travelling and searching; and at least four of the lyrics directly described ascending or attaining high ground that would serve as a vantage point for David in his quests.

'Black Country Rock', for example, has usually been described solely as a parodic tribute to Marc Bolan, whose high-pitched, tremulous voice David accurately renders. It was equally significant as an account of riding on a packhorse to reach the rock of the title, a beautifully spare summation conjuring up a lonely wilderness journey.

Once on the rock, David introduced a startling new thought that brought him closer to hitherto forbidden territory:

> Some say the view is crazy,
> But you may adopt another point of view.

A third group of references took David decisively into that territory. Children, father, mother, brother: all showed the insidious pressure of his family background. A line from 'The Supermen', for example, struck the same chilling chord as the exhortation to "screw up your brother" in 'Cygnet Committee', for David sang again of "nightmare dreams" where

> Man would tear his brother's flesh . . .

And in 'After All', he told of the sudden thought –

> . . . that we're nobody's children
> At all, after all.

It appeared as a sudden insight into his illegitimacy, which he shared with Terry; it was also the archetypal cry of despair at not belonging.

In 'All The Madmen' the family theme became more stark, as David acknowledged in 1972: the song, he said, "was written for my brother and it's about my brother". David's sense of threat had been accentuated by the fate of one of his closest friends, who suffered a breakdown at about this time and was admitted to hospital too: "day after day", David lamented, his friends were being sent

> To mansions cold and grey.

When his friend returned to Beckenham, David questioned him at length about his treatment, acquiring the medical and psychoanalytical terms – "Librium", "libido", "lobotomy" – he knowledgeably deployed. But his description of a cold, grey building, with the later implication that it stood on a hill, applied equally to Cane Hill.

Then came David's key assertion. He would rather stay – and play – with "the madmen":

> For I'm quite content
> They're all as sane as me.

David thus again aligned himself decisively with the insane, including Terry, and their view of the world, by the choice he presented to his audience. Either he and Terry were insane; or both were sane, and it was the rest of the world that was out of step. David

clearly leaned to the latter, for he described those outside hospital
as "thinmen" and "sadmen". In a strange parenthetical verse –
even marked in brackets – he also complained of the "organic
minds" that are hidden "in a cellar". It echoed his complaint to
The Times the previous year that mental illness was usually hidden
away, in "the servants' quarters".

The most remarkable lyric of the album was the one with which
it began, 'The Width Of A Circle'. It too described a journey: a
journey through David's imagination, where anxiety, identity-
crisis, psychic visions and sexual ecstasy mingled and merged. It
had a powerful visual impact, with a series of scenes fading into
each other, as in a movie, but following an impressionistic rather
than sequential logic: a process David described, like a film director's imprimatur, in the line telling how his "logic" had been taken
"for a ride".

David began by rejecting the guru figures of the past, and then
embarked on his own independent quest for self-knowledge. He
met a monster, asleep by a tree – and discovered that the monster
"was me".

That led to the witty greeting:

> . . . I said hello and I said hello.

It also marked David's first encounter with a figure who would
reappear, in various guises, over the next fifteen years: the "monster", who became a potent symbol of the outsider in search of
acceptance and love.

From there, David crossed into another secret area. The next
twelve lines were larded with both implicit and explicit references
to homosexual behaviour, going far beyond the brief allusions
David had previously made in his lyrics. He was told of being
"laid" by a "young bordello" who

> Swallowed his pride and puckered his lips,

while David reached a state of sexual excitement. Now David boldly
pushed deeper into forbidden territory, to encounter a terrifying new
vision:

> . . . a cavern appeared,
> And I smelt the burning pit of fear.

It was a precise reproduction of what Terry had seen during his schizophrenic attack outside Chislehurst Caves in 1967, including the intense light that struck him to the ground, the ring of fire surrounding him, and the sheer terror he felt.

Then came the devastating climax, as David united the three main elements of his lyric – monster, schizophrenia and homosexuality – in one extraordinary couplet:

> His nebulous body swayed above,
> His tongue swollen with devil's love.

David had used the language of one clandestine activity, sexual activity between males, to help express other feelings he had long suppressed: his affection for Terry, and his sympathy for his plight.

Even more than the other tracks, the music brilliantly built up and maintained the tension of David's revelatory journey. It began with two eerie notes a full octave apart and then gradually picked up pace, with a guitar riff played against a background of increasing speed, sounding irresistibly like a departing train – an aural metaphor David was to use more explicitly on later occasions. After the first two verses, came a long musical interlude with a slowing of the tempo to reinforce the lyric's suggestion that David fell asleep and experienced his visions as a dream. Then the rhythm hardened again to match the breathtaking details of the climax.

Even now the audience could not relax. David intimated post-coital exhaustion through a line that repeated the word "breathe" three times, but then re-established the tension by describing how he was still "seething . . . waiting for you." Only at the end of a prolonged musical coda did the tempo abate, ending in a drumroll and a shout that finally faded in a shift of key, as ambiguous and mysterious as everything that had gone before.

'The Width Of A Circle' was as stunning a revelation of David's imaginative powers as the essay about a prisoner on the eve of his execution with which he had astonished his friends at Bromley Technical High School. Its implications were awesome.

First, there was David's assimilation of the identities of those he was describing. He had previously toyed with the device of role-playing, stepping briefly into his characters and out again. Now he *became* those characters – "the monster was me" – and thus presented his audiences with a series of fresh paradoxes. Was he monster or victim? Dominant sexual partner, or submissive? And – once again – himself or Terry?

The second implication of 'The Width Of A Circle' was that David had embarked on a dance with the spectre of mental illness, aiming to embrace it, and then to break away in an effort to end its thrall. It was a high-risk strategy: once in its clutches, there was no guarantee that David would be able to shake himself free. But it was the strategy that would preoccupy his creative life for the next five years.

Further clues that this was David's intention – instinctive, unconscious, but no less purposeful for that – are contained in the remaining track, 'The Man Who Sold The World'. It has gone largely ignored by other commentators, perhaps because it was based on a children's nursery rhyme:

> Yesterday upon the stair
> I met a man who wasn't there.
> He wasn't there again today,
> How I wish he'd go away.

Nursery rhymes, with their childhood associations, held a strong intrinsic attraction for David. ('The Width Of A Circle' carries an echo of the 'Teddy Bears' Picnic' in the line ". . . you'll never go down to the Gods again.") Much of their appeal, like that of fairy tales, lies in their deceptive power to evoke deep-seated fears, and this was no exception. It conjured a vision of the *doppelgänger*, the misty figure of German mythology, there and not there, who dogs a person until their death, a perpetual reminder of all they wish to forget: for David, a figure like Terry.

David's first two lines closely followed the original rhyme:

> We passed upon the stair, we spoke of was and when.
> Although I wasn't there, he said I was his friend.

David's alterations were illuminating, however, for it was not the person on the stair who did not exist, but himself. Now, it seemed, David was engaged in a *danse macabre* not only with madness, but with death itself. That sense was reinforced by the next line:

> I thought you died alone, a long long time ago.

The exchange carried the undertones of Wilfrid Owen's 'Strange Meeting', whose narrator also meets a man who calls him "friend" but also tells him:

> I am the enemy you killed.

In David's lyric, the man denies that he is dead, then adds four words that supply another key:

I never lost control.

As he embarked on his perilous strategy, staying in control – of himself, and his destiny – would be vital. At times he would appear to lose control; eventually – and at a price – he would come through.

The melody of 'The Man Who Sold The World' precisely echoed the deceptive simplicity of the words. At first, it seemed utterly obvious, almost banal: in fact, it shifted guilefully between major and minor keys, making a musical journey that conveyed the searching theme of both the track and the album. Bowie himself emphasised the significance of the track when – having delayed until the last possible moment – he selected it as the title of the album itself.

At times in his career, Bowie himself has recoiled from the implications of his album, as if its reality was more than he could bear. In an interview for BBC radio in 1976, for example, he said that making it had been "a nightmare" – and for that he blamed Tony Visconti. "It all seemed too glossy," David claimed, implying that he would have been happier with the improvisations of the Arts Lab days.

In a second interview published in 1976, David came close to disowning the album: it was, he said, "the most drug-orientated album I've made. That was when I was the most fucked up." At the time, he added, he was holding "some kind of flag for hashish".

In fact, *The Man Who Sold The World* is among the *least* drug-orientated albums David ever made. The lyrics do not contain a single reference, coded or otherwise, to drugs or drug-taking. David's companions say that he was not then using drugs to any great extent – and certainly far less than when he was living with Mary Finnigan.

"Nobody really smoked a lot of dope at that time," says John Cambridge. "I wasn't into it and David never really and Mick Ronson never. It was really casual and if I was offered I'd say, 'Nah,' and it was the same with David, he wasn't really bothered. Now and again he'd just have a drag and that would be it."

In fact, David's protestations met his aim of suggesting that enquiries into the significance of *The Man Who Sold The World* were pointless; but that he should have erected such barriers against understanding the album strongly suggests of itself how much there was at stake. Occasionally, the persistent questioner could elicit more revealing admissions from him. After complaining of Tony Visconti's over-professional approach to the album, David dropped the aside: "The subject matter was very telling for me – it was all family problems and analogies, put into science-fiction form." Later, when discussing the recording made by Lulu of 'The Man Who Sold The World' in 1974, David confessed that it might have been unfair to wish the song upon her, since it concerned the "devils and angels" within himself.

When *The Man Who Sold The World* was completed, those who appreciated it, by Visconti's count, could be numbered on one hand. "There were only four people in the world who liked that album at that time," he says: himself, Mick Ronson, Woody Woodmansey and David. "The record company," he says bluntly, "didn't."

Perversely, the album helped to cause another hiatus in Visconti's relationship with David. Visconti was feeling scarred by his battle to complete it; he was also out of sympathy with the sexual shenanigans at Haddon Hall. "I didn't mind what they did in their bedroom," he said, referring to David and Angie and their frequent nocturnal visitors. "But these people were trying to get into our bedroom as well."

Most crucially, Visconti had taken a strong aversion to Tony Defries. "He wasn't a thief," says Visconti; "I can't call him that." But Visconti does call Defries "a grasper" and "a megalomaniac". According to Visconti, Defries desperately wanted him to sign a management contract at the same time as David: "He wanted the package." Visconti was immensely wary, not least of the "blind faith" David was manifestly placing in Defries. "David was also assigning his personal power to other people . . . when he meets someone, and he falls in love – forget it. That person's the one until he's severely hurt."

The break between David and Visconti came as they stood in Regent Street after a meeting at the Gem offices. "I said to David, 'If you go with Tony Defries, I'm not going to go with you,'" Visconti recalls. David told him: "Oh no, you've got him all wrong," but Visconti was adamant. David, he said, had a "very hurt look in his eyes – and that was the last I saw of him for four years".

Visconti's departure was far from David's only problem. There were still the rivalries within Mercury to contend with, and since Calvin Mark Lee was no longer on the payroll, David was exposed to the jealousies of Lou Reizner, who made clear his distaste for *The Man Who Sold The World*.

Fortunately David had a powerful ally in Chicago in the person of Robin McBride, the new head of A and R, who had come to London with Mercury's new boss, Irwin Steinberg, in January. McBride says he was "terribly excited" when he first heard the album, and although he felt its meaning was often obscure, he judged it an "extraordinary creation in rock music". Soon afterwards he returned to Britain to take charge of the arrangements on Mercury's behalf. He was quickly aware of the tensions flickering between the various camps, but was unable, then, to identify their precise cause: his principal diagnosis was that Reizner suspected him of wanting his job. ("I didn't," McBride says.)

One consequence of the power vacuum in Britain was that the task of producing a cover for the album had been left entirely to David – an episode that has been a matter of controversy ever since. The most widely believed account is that David commissioned a cover on which he appeared wearing a dress: although that is the cover that appeared on the first British version of the album, Mercury's US headquarters were so horrified by it that they replaced it, for the American release, with a design known variously as the "cartoon" or "wild west" cover. In fact, almost precisely the reverse sequence of events occurred; and the episode is more significant for what it reveals of David's ambivalent and fluctuating attitudes towards mental illness and Terry.

To produce a cover, David turned to an artist friend, Mike Weller, who had designed posters for the Beckenham Arts Lab and was still a visitor to Haddon Hall. Weller was delighted when David asked for his help: he belonged to an artists' collective in Penge named the Artists' Union and passionately believed in the ideals of the Arts Lab and he regarded *The Man Who Sold The World* as a powerful expression of all that the Ars Lab stood for. David explained that the lyrics – in particular 'The Width Of A Circle' – were intended to portray the malevolent and oppressive forces that surrounded them. "I thought I could illustrate the mood and the feeling," Weller says.

It was Weller's idea to design a cover that depicted Cane Hill. His main impetus came from visiting a friend who was a patient there; although Weller knew that David had a brother with "mental problems", he was unaware that Terry was at Cane Hill too. Cane Hill was also part of the currency of the Arts Lab and its followers: "very much the kind of place you would finish up at if you were living at home with the problems and the pressures," Weller says. When he expounded his idea, he found David "enthusiastic – and Angie even more so".

For his reference material, Weller used a brochure about Cane

Hill which he had brought back after visiting his friend. His drawing, similar in style to posters concerning South Africa and the British police which he had designed at the Penge Artists' Union, showed Cane Hill's main entrance block, a forbidding building with its clockfaces broken and cracked. Standing in front was an unshaven figure who wore a stetson and carried a rifle wrapped in a cloth; Weller had modelled him on a photograph of John Wayne, intending him to represent David's lyric, 'Running Gun Blues'.

When Weller produced his drawings, David suggested that the gunman should have an "exploding head", a device Weller had included on many of his Arts Lab posters. He redrew the head to show a section being shot away, as if in a Sam Peckinpah movie, adding a bubble by the gunman's mouth which he filled with a few lines of speech. They included several puns on the theme of "arms" – weapons, drug-taking, and the arm of a record player. He called his drawing 'Metrobolist', after the Fritz Lang silent film *Metropolis*, whose darkly authoritarian theme Weller also wished to invoke. David, he says, was "very pleased" with the result – "or so I thought".

When Robin McBride took delivery of the recordings of *The Man Who Sold The World*, David handed him Weller's artwork. In Chicago, McBride passed the design to Mercury's art department. Shortly before the sleeve was to be printed, one of McBride's bosses at Mercury pointed out that the reference to drug-taking in the speech-bubble might not be the best way of appealing to the youth market, and the words were removed, although the bubble itself anachronistically remained. Since nobody in Mercury's Chicago offices, McBride says, "understood what the cover meant or how it related in any way in the first place, to make it more obscure was not difficult". With that, McBride believed, the question of the cover was settled.

David, evidently, believed otherwise. After McBride had returned to the US, David went into Philips's London office to meet its chief art director, Mike Stanford. "He came in to discuss a cover for *The Man Who Sold The World*," Stanford says. He particularly remembers that David had very decided views on what kind of cover he wanted, explaining that he wished to be photographed in a "domestic environment".

Stanford admits that it was not usual for a performer to tell an art director how his cover should look. But he explains that he was so struck by David's "visual charisma", feeling it to be of superstar quality, that he was happy to follow David's suggestion, and commissioned the photographer Keith Macmillan to take the picture.

Stanford was somewhat taken aback when Macmillan's photographs arrived at the Philips office a week or so later. True, David had been photographed in the "domestic situation" he had proposed. He was half-lying, half-sitting on a couch, supporting himself on the arm-rest at one end, staring quizzically into the camera. What stunned Stanford was that David was wearing a *dress*.

There was no ambiguity about it: the dress was made of a creamy satin, printed with a large blue floral pattern. What was more, David's pose, with his hips provocatively tilted, one hand raised as if toying with his hair, the other elegantly extended, lightly holding a playing card (others were scattered on the floor) was irresistibly feminine. The picture, Stanford says, was "totally unusual – and very provocative".

The dress was one of no fewer than six that David had bought at a fashionable London boutique named Mr Fish. And the idea, according to Macmillan, came from David – "very much so", he adds. "I didn't have any pre-discussion with David at all, except when and where . . . We just took loads of photographs and tried different things together."

There were a few small precedents for what David had done, most notably that of Mick Jagger when performing at Hyde Park the previous summer, when he wore a costume that appeared to be a cross between the Greek national dress and a little girl's party frock. But no one – at least to Stanford's knowledge – had gone this far.

It did not help when David explained that the photograph was intended as a parody of the Pre-Raphaelite painter, Dante Gabriel Rossetti: within Philips, there was consternation. "People blanched," Stanford says. But after agonised discussion, most centring on whether the photograph could actually be classed as indecent, Philips decided to "give David his head". There was a feeling, says Stanford, of "let's run with him, he knew what he was doing". David, he adds, was happy, and so were Philips.

There now ensued yet another instance of what can most politely be called the breakdown of communications that had bedevilled relationships between David, Philips and Mercury. For Stanford firmly believed that he was working on a cover for the British release of *The Man Who Sold The World*. David, on the other hand, had apparently become convinced that the photograph would also appear on the American version – his transactions with Robin

McBride over Mike Weller's Cane Hill design notwithstanding. For when Mercury released the record bearing Weller's design in the US in November, David – according to Tony Defries – was "appalled".

So appalled, in fact, that David was still complaining about the cover more than a year later. In September 1972, during his first US concert tour, David told a devoted fan, a guitar player named Brian Kinchy whom he met in Cleveland, that the cover was "horrible" and that he did not know where Mercury had got it from. "He was really quite pissed about it when I talked to him," Kinchy says.

By then, however, David's protests had a new ingredient. Not only did he dislike the cover; he disowned it utterly, declining to acknowledge his discussions with Mike Weller and his own enthusiasm for a picture of Cane Hill. He now told Brian Kinchy: "I don't know what that cover was all about."

Tony Defries stayed clear of the controversy over the two covers. In artistic matters, he deferred to David, trusting his own "absolute belief" in David's judgments. By the same token, he regarded himself as the expert in financial matters: that was his territory. And in the autumn of 1970 he made his first major move on David's behalf.

Not the least of Ken Pitt's distress at losing David had stemmed from the galling knowledge that at the time he was apparently free of any publishing contracts. David's contract with David Platz at Essex Music had expired in June 1969 and some unseemly haggling had then ensued. Pitt asked Platz for £2,000 to renew the contract but Platz refused. Pitt returned to Platz after the success of 'Space Oddity', this time asking for £5,000. Platz responded by offering £5,000 over three years. But as that was to be set against Essex's losses on David's previous advances, it would result in a first payment of just £416.10. Pitt – who later liked to point out that Platz had, in effect, rejected the publishing rights to four of David's finest albums – turned him down.

In the autumn of 1970, therefore, Defries viewed David's publishing rights as a major asset to be capitalised upon. They included all David's lyrics on *The Man Who Sold The World*, and six of the nine on the previous Mercury album. (The exceptions, held by Platz, were 'The Wild Eyed Boy From Freecloud', 'Memory Of A Free Festival', and 'Space Oddity'.) Defries now set about finding a publisher – although he was content to leave it to David to decide *which* publisher it should be. He sent David to meet several companies with instructions to choose whoever appeared the most sympathetic.

One of the companies David visited, together with Angie, was called Chrysalis. It had only recently started business and had three young men as partners. Two had already been dramatically successful in the performers they had engaged. One, Chris Wright, had signed Ten Years After; the other, Terry Ellis, had signed Jethro Tull; and both groups were already bringing Chrysalis highly satisfactory royalties. That left the third partner, Bob Grace, a young man of exceptionally boyish looks, anxious for a signing that would match his colleagues'.

Grace took to David at once: "We just got on like a house on fire." David played a new single, 'Holy Holy', which Mercury were about to release: Grace thought it "fantastic". David was "incredibly matey and normal. We got on so great, that was it."

Tony Defries now stepped forward. The price of David's contract, he told Grace, was £5,000 – up front. Grace was staggered and his two partners were appalled, for it was far more than they had ever paid before. Wright and Ellis asked Grace if he was "really sure". Grace replied that he was so sure that if his own father had the money he would borrow it from him. David and Defries came into the Chrysalis office on October 23rd and signed the contract, as did Grace on Chrysalis's behalf. Chris Wright drew up two cheques: in accordance with David's agreement with Gem, David took £4,000, Gem £1,000. As he signed the cheques, Wright's hand shook visibly.

Five thousand pounds may have seemed a lot of money; but equally, Chrysalis were securing the rights to a lot of songs. David was contracted to write "a minimum of 100 works" over the next five years, and of those, seventy were to be "commercially recorded". The agreement was retrospective, embracing all lyrics on David's two recent albums not covered by his previous agreement with David Platz (who had twenty-six of David's titles) or Hal Shaper (who had fourteen). Chrysalis would take 50 per cent of the revenue from the songs, David the other 50 per cent.

It seemed a straightforward agreement. However, it contained a rider which rendered it more complex than it first appeared: so complex, in fact, that there has been considerable dispute, persisting until today, over just what it meant.

The rider, which was proposed by Defries, called for a second company to be set up, Titanic Music. According to Defries, its aim was to ensure that if David became a true superstar, he was guaranteed his fair share of the proceeds. Once David had recouped his £5,000 advance, he was to receive a half-share in the copyright of his songs, and his share of the royalties was to be increased from 50 per cent to 75 per cent. This ran counter to the prevailing practice whereby publishers investing comparatively small amounts in unknown writers acquired the sole copyright to their songs, and a half-share in fortunes worth millions, as had happened to the Beatles. Defries regarded the agreement with some pride: it was, he says, "an unusual sort of deal for the time".

It must be said that this was not how Bob Grace understood the rider, either at the time or now. He believed that its main aim was to circumvent the series of agreements that Chrysalis held with its partners around the world, giving them the automatic right to Chrysalis's new signings, and stipulating the percentage they received. According to Grace, Defries argued that by setting up Titanic, Chrysalis would be able to extract a higher percentage from their overseas partners for David's songs. And it was only with misgivings that Grace agreed.

"In retrospect," he says, "it was lousy business practice and something I've never done since. But he pushed me and I was green and I didn't know any better . . . I should have told Tony it was immoral and unethical." But then Defries had a very charismatic way of arguing his case. "Powerful personalities are attractive and he had a very powerful personality," Grace says. "His self-confidence was contagious and you felt he had to be right."

Defries denies in turn that the formation of Titanic Music had either the intention or the consequence that Grace describes. But the difference of perception between the two sides contributed to a massive row that flared up within three years. The agreement also left another party aggrieved: the rival publisher, David Platz, who was still claiming that he, not Chrysalis, had the rights to David's song-writing.

Defries responded that Platz only had the right to match the Chrysalis offer, and since he did not wish to do so, any rights he might own had lapsed. Platz protested that in any case his previous contract with David was still in force because David had not yet provided him with the requisite number of songs. Defries had no sympathy with the argument. It was, he says, "a grey area – and I ignored the whole thing. I told David Platz that he didn't have a case, and if he thought he did, he should sue Chrysalis."

For David, the Chrysalis contract had a remarkably liberating effect, as if, Bob Grace says, "the finger had been taken out of the dyke and songs were pouring out of him". Grace felt as if he was standing underneath the dyke at the time. His more usual experience was of trying to coax songs out of his writers. "David was so prolific it was amazing. No sooner had he got two or three songs out than there would be more. I had never known it like that before."

It was Grace's task to arrange for David to make demonstration recordings – "demos" – of the songs that were pouring forth. Grace rented Radio Luxembourg's London studio – it was cheap because it was affected by interference from the radios of a nearby minicab firm – and went there with David at least once a week. Sometimes Grace hired a makeshift backing group; sometimes David sang to his own guitar. As David's output intensified, Grace found that he became almost "a pest in the office – I couldn't get rid of him, then he'd turn up at my flat, and then Angie would be on the phone saying, 'Darling, come over to dinner.' Then they wanted me to move to Beckenham . . ."

Grace managed to resist Angie's pleadings and remained in his own flat, near Marble Arch. But he stayed devoted to David and was thus on hand on the day in December when David arrived in the Radio Luxembourg studio with yet another new song. "He went to the piano and he was fiddling around and I said, 'What's that?' Then he got the lyrics down and I knew that was a hit."

The song in question was 'Oh! You Pretty Things', soon to become one of the most lucrative songs in the Chrysalis catalogue. The next day, Grace gave David's demo to Mickie Most, unaware of David's previous fruitless dealings with him. Most felt that David's song would be ideal to launch the solo career of Peter Noone, the former lead singer of the vastly successful 1960s group, Herman's Hermits. David played the piano part himself (not objecting, apparently, when his line "the earth is a bitch" was replaced by "the earth is a beast"). The result took Noone to number twelve in the hit parade. It also brought David and Chrysalis the promise of a healthy slice of publishing royalties.

The song provided another insight into the preoccupations shaping David's creative output. It owed its success, in part, to the mood of rebelliousness captured by the refrain, with its appeal to:

> . . . you pretty things,

who are

> . . . driving your
> Mamas and Papas insane.

Those spare lines also happened to be a powerful summation of many of the cross-currents in David's life: the intimation of bisexuality; the problems of his relationship with his own mother; and the invocation of insanity.

There were familiar themes elsewhere, too: the line

All the strangers came today

was similar to David's disturbing description of the aliens arriving from the skies in 'Memory Of A Free Festival'. Then David proposed that the strangers were the children themselves: a chill counterpoint of the theme of 'After All', where it was the adults whom David portrayed as the outsiders.

Most striking of all, David told of seeing

A crack in the sky and a hand reaching down to me.

It seemed like a further scene from a schizophrenic vision: an interpretation that David confirmed during his BBC interviews in 1976, when discussing *Hunky Dory*, the album on which his own recording of the song appeared.

"The crack in the sky, the hand coming through the crack in the sky . . . a lot of the songs in fact do deal with some kind of schizophrenia, or alternating id problems, and 'Pretty Things' was one of them . . . According to Jung, to see cracks in the sky is not, is not really quite on . . . Yes, I hadn't been to an analyst, no – my parents went, my brothers and sisters and my aunts and uncles and cousins, they did that, they ended up in a much worse state, so I stayed away. I thought I'd write my problems out."

David's halting explanation went much further than he was usually willing to go when discussing his family background. In its own way, the account he gave to Bob Grace in the Radio Luxembourg studio the day after writing the song was equally revealing. In his amazement and delight, Bob asked him where he drew his inspiration from.

"I couldn't sleep," David told him. "It was about four o'clock in the morning. I woke up and this song was going round in my head. I had to get out of bed and just play it to get it out of me so that I could get back to sleep again."

16

Changing

It was with feelings of pleasurable anticipation that Ron Oberman drove with his parents to Washington's International Airport one afternoon in January 1971. Within Mercury, the pro-David faction, led by Robin McBride, had persuaded Irwin Steinberg to pay for David to visit the US, and Oberman had been deputed, as Mercury's publicity director, to meet David on his arrival. Since Washington was Oberman's home town, that gave him the welcome opportunity to visit his parents. They had been sufficiently intrigued by his tales of David to come out to the airport too.

David's visit was timed to follow the release of *The Man Who Sold The World* and of 'All The Madmen' which Mercury had distributed as a promotional single in the US in December. The idea, Oberman says, was to "get some real good stories in the press, get some critical acclaim going".

The first omens were poor. As he waited in the arrival lounge, Oberman wondered which David he was going to meet: the "somewhat effeminate" David he had found in London the previous April, leading him to suppose that David was gay; or the seemingly domesticated David he had met at Haddon Hall on a second trip that year. On the latter occasion David "was a different person – his voice, the way he carried himself, everything". Whatever David's sexual preferences, Oberman had concluded, David was at least a "chameleon". But it now appeared that Oberman wasn't going to meet any David at all.

"The plane unloaded, everyone disembarked, and there was no David," Oberman says. "I was waiting with my parents for almost forty-five minutes. I was pretty positive he hadn't missed the plane and so I waited and waited. Finally, he got off."

The David who greeted Oberman was the David depicted on the cover of *The Man Who Sold The World* with shoulder-length hair and wearing a long blue coat. It was this, by David's account, that had caused the long delay. His appearance so alarmed US immigration officials that he had been held for questioning long after all the other passengers on the flight had been cleared. Whether he was suspected of being a drug-user, homosexual, or communist – the main categories considered as threats to the US – was not clear: perhaps it was all three. But only after a thorough interview and a search was David allowed on to US soil. David was in consequence rather subdued: the chameleon, Oberman concluded, had been "a bit shaken up" by what had occurred – "a rude introduction to this country", Oberman felt.

That was not the only impediment to David's visit. The main method by which he would win publicity, Mercury had hoped, was by performing in clubs and on radio stations in the main cities of the US. In theory, David's marriage to Angie, giving him the priceless "green card", enabled him to work in the US. But visiting musicians were subject to further controls dictated by the American Federation of Musicians – the US Musicians Union.

Although Oberman had been hoping – "up to the last minute" – that these could be overcome, they had proved insuperable, limiting David to "personal appearances" and interviews which Mercury hoped to arrange. Their target was the writers and critics who so far had ignored *The Man Who Sold The World* and the previous Mercury album, *Man Of Words/Man Of Music*. "By meeting David hopefully they would be spurred to listen to the records," Oberman explains. In that aim, David's visit had mixed results.

For David, Washington proved a suburban affair. He stayed with Oberman at his home, attended a party thrown by Oberman's brother, and dined with Oberman's parents at a local restaurant. The only interviews he was accorded were with a small underground newspaper and a local radio station. Oberman escorted David on visits to New York and Chicago, where he visited the Mercury offices and met Robin McBride. David, says Oberman, was polite and unassuming, and appeared to be taking everything in. Then Oberman put David on a plane to Los Angeles; and if the East had been wary of David, in California it was another story.

David was met at Los Angeles airport by Rodney Bingenheimer, Mercury's main promoter in southern California. Later, Bingenheimer became one of the most prominent "scenemakers" – as the jargon has it – in Los Angeles by opening a club, Rodney's English Disco, and then working as a disc-jockey with the Pasadena radio station, KROQ. He looks back on the late sixties and early seventies with nostalgia: "It was wall-to-wall people parading up and down, and a lot of night clubs happening, and there were always people twenty-four hours a day hanging out, and parties. People were more friendly then."

Changing

At first, David struck Bingenheimer as a typically reserved Englishman: "a quiet person, the kind of guy who would ask you if he wanted to go to the bathroom". David was undoubtedly suffering from the culture shock that the British experience on arriving in Los Angeles, whose familiarity from countless films and TV series induces in them the feeling that they too are part of a giant movie-set.

Bingenheimer introduced David to a fair proportion of the wall-to-wall people of Los Angeles. He arranged for him to stay at a mansion in the Hollywood hills owned by Tom Ayres, manager of the blues group the Sir Douglas Quintet. Bingenheimer borrowed Ayres's Cadillac convertible and spent a week escorting David on a tour of the music industry's most fashionable locales: the KMAC radio station at Long Beach, CIMS at Santa Anna, KET in Los Angeles, Topanga Canyon Corral, Hamburger Hamlet on Hollywood Boulevard, and the Whisky A'Gogo. At one stop, David was introduced to the 1950s rock-star Gene Vincent. David was "impressed", Bingenheimer says: "He enjoyed it all."

Bingenheimer also provided several examples of the Hollywood party, where the rich and successful mingle with the gaudy and the exotic, all vying in the nonchalance with which they affect not to desire attention. Most nonchalant of all was Andy Warhol's "superstar" Ultraviolet, who gave a series of press interviews while luxuriating, naked, in a bath filled with milk.

With such examples before him, David felt emboldened enough to appear in public in a Mr Fish dress. He did not wear it, as one myth has it, while walking past Hollywood High School ("he was wearing jeans," Bingenheimer reports) but he did put it on for a party where he sat cross-legged on a waterbed and played a selection from *The Man Who Sold The World*. Bingenheimer was surprised at seeing the sedate Englishman behave in this way, and was further confused because, despite his dress, "he wasn't coming on like a girl". Instead, David was "grabbing girls right and left. He was picking up girls hitch-hiking in the street."

Another of the wall-to-wall people observing David was Kim Fowley. He was another archetypal West Coast figure, a record producer with a host of shamelessly manufactured hits to his name, among them 'Nut Rocker' by B Bumble and the Stingers, an adaptation of the Nutcracker Suite, credited to "Tchaikovsky, arranged by Kim Fowley". A Hollywood newspaper called Fowley the "*éminence grise* of rock 'n' roll pimps . . . the reptile prince of Hollywood trash". A tall, skeletal man, with a acute feel for the technicalities of creating image and fame, Fowley later concluded that David was one of the foremost "strategists" of the music business, carefully plotting his moves ahead: "He listened more than he spoke and digested what was going on."

Fowley offers another insight into Hollywood's impact on David, illustrated with a story from his own childhood concerning the movie actor, John Garfield. In 1946, when Fowley was seven, his father returned from the war. "I had been in a semi-foster home and this was the big welcome home party," Fowley says. "My father saw me for the first time and he took me to this house and I went upstairs to my room, the first room I ever had. There was John Garfield in my bed and there was a chick putting cocaine on his cock. It was my first bedroom and it was a big moment for me, and, seeing this idiot having cocaine put on the tip of his cock, I said, 'What are you doing?' and Garfield said, 'I'm living up to my image.'"

In Hollywood, where such events – and such repartee – were commonplace, no one was likely to ask David Bowie why he was wearing a dress. Certainly not Fowley himself, who adds that in any case he already knew the answer: "He was living up to his image." Thus Hollywood conferred on David a sense of both esteem and normality: he was the centre of attention, but without having to justify his *outré* behaviour. In Hollywood, either everyone was crazy: or they were all as sane as he.

Hollywood also brought David one highly significant review. He met the *Rolling Stone* writer, John Mendelsohn, who later wrote enthusiastically of *The Man Who Sold The World* – although also warning that David's music offered "an experience that is as intriguing as it is chilling, but only to a listener sufficiently together to withstand its schizophrenia". Mendelsohn described David in his Mr Fish dress, finding him "ravishing" and "almost disconcertingly reminiscent of Lauren Bacall".

As usual, David astutely judged his audience, demonstrating to the worldly-wise readers of *Rolling Stone* that he was not deceived by the pretensions and falsehoods of rock music: "It should be tarted up, made into a prostitute, a parody of itself. It should be the clown, the Pierrot medium."

When David returned to Britain, his visits to the Radio Luxembourg studios became more frequent than ever. "He had a new song every day," says Bob Grace. "He was on the phone, 'I've written a new song, I want to do this, I want to do that' – we were forever demo-ing." Sometimes, instead of session musicians, David employed his friends from Haddon Hall: "David took whoever

was handy," says Grace. One such occasion led to the release of
two of David's songs by a group called Arnold Corns, headed by
one Rudi Valentino. The episode provided David with further
enjoyable lessons. The two songs were 'Moonage Daydream' and
'Hang On To Yourself'. David was backed by a group of Dulwich
College schoolboys, frequently to be seen at Haddon Hall, who
had formed a group called Runk. When Grace played back the
recording he was impressed: "The demo came out really good,"
he says.

Grace decided to try to market 'Moonage Daydream' as a single.
Since David was under contract to Mercury, Grace could not do
so in David's name. They turned instead to a tall, willowy dress
designer, often to be found at Haddon Hall, named Freddy Burrett:
"an incredible-looking, a beautiful-looking guy," says Grace – "if
that's what you want". Burrett had recently adopted an Italianate
version of his name, Freddi Burretti; now David proposed that he
change his name again. Freddi thus became Rudi Valentino and
Runk was renamed Arnold Corns. Under those names, Grace sold
'Moonage Daydream' to B and C records and it was released in
May.

David entered into the spirit of the enterprise with a will. Freddi
Burretti seemed wary when asked about his new career. "I'm just
a dress designer," he said. "I don't want to go anywhere rough. If
they put us on at some of those places out of London I'd get sent
up something rotten by all those butch provincial blokes." But
David showed no such caution. "I believe that the Rolling Stones
are finished and that Arnold Corns will be the next Stones," he
said, adding for good measure: "If we are to make a comparison
at all." His comments were faithfully recorded in the music press.
Yet the critics had some difficulty evaluating Rudi Valentino's
contribution to the record. His vocals, one wrote, were "virtually
inaudible". Precisely so, says Grace. "I was there every second of
the time. Freddi wasn't even there."

The episode provided David with a rich example of how to use
– and confuse – the media; how to merge image and identity; how
to play the paradox game. Another opportunity arose with the
British release of *The Man Who Sold The World* in April. The
music press reviewed it briefly, with *Melody Maker* judging it
"a surprisingly excellent album", with the production "superb",
David's songs "inventive and unusual", and "some tremendous
flashes of brilliance". The *New Musical Express* was less kind,
commenting that David was "rather hysterical" and unimagin-
atively summarising the lyrics as "a bit of horror in 'All The

Madmen', some quiet folk on 'After All', and much drive in 'The Width Of A Circle'".

It was the cover which attracted most attention, bringing David's first major national newspaper publicity since the days of Leslie Conn, for the *Daily Mirror* was sufficiently intrigued by the image of a man wearing a dress to dispatch a reporter and photographer to Haddon Hall.

David extracted full value from their visit. He posed for photographs on the lawn in the dress and offered some suitably epigrammatic quotes: "I cannot breathe in the atmosphere of convention," he said. "I find freedom only in the realms of my own eccentricity." He also refuted allegations that he was "queer and all sorts of things", asserting: "My sexual life is normal." He was rewarded with a half-page story and two-column photograph in the *Daily Mirror* of April 24th.

It all depended, of course, on what you meant by normal. By then, Bob Grace was becoming uncomfortably aware of how David was defining the word. David, it seemed, had embarked on a campaign to enlist Bob to his point of view. "He was trying to introduce me to this notion that in theory everyone was bisexual," Grace says. "I said, 'Not Mick Jagger?' and he said 'Everyone.'"

David first took Grace to see a film about a homosexual marriage. Grace found it "outrageous" and told David: "It's not for me, thanks very much." Next, David invited him to a club in Kensington High Street nicknamed the Sombrero. (Its original name was Yours And Mine but its habitués insisted on calling it after the Mexican restaurant on the first floor.) "I had never been to a gay club before," says Grace. Nor had he seen David wearing a dress, believing until then that the cover of *The Man Who Sold The World* was merely an artifice. "My jaw dropped." Angie accompanied David in a three-piece pin-stripe suit, and Freddi Burretti was there too.

What had begun as a process of intellectual seduction now went a decisive stage further. "Freddi was trying to get off with me, hand on the knee, the whole bit," Grace says. "I told him, 'Leave it out.'" Afterwards, David affected to be surprised that Grace had rejected Freddi's advances. David said, 'He's so *beautiful*.' He couldn't understand it. He was basically saying, 'If it's beautiful, give it one' – that was his philosophy. I said, 'Yes, but it doesn't make me respond in that way.'"

In retrospect, Grace believes that the incident marked a turning point in his relationship with David and Angie. "He wanted someone to be sympathetic to his wavelength, and preferably on

it. That was probably the point when he realised I was boring."
The phone calls became less frequent thereafter, the invitations to
visit Haddon Hall less insistent.

For Bob Grace, the Sombrero episode was made all the more
bizarre by virtue of the fact that Angie, in her pin-stripe suit, was
seven months pregnant at the time: it was perhaps strangest of all,
at this time, that she and David should do anything so conventional
as to have a child. Today, Angie implies that it was largely her
decision, taken to bring stability to their marriage. "David had a
wonderful relationship with his father and I had a feeling that he
should really have a son, anything to make him down to earth,
sort of realise that he's got a family at home. You must remember
that I was under the auspices of his not being in love with me . . .
and I was still very much up in the air as to the terms of our
relationship. I just thought it would be a good idea . . . I'm a very
good brood mare and I produce wonderful children."

The son Angie so confidently predicted was born at Bromley
Hospital on May 28th, 1970. His 8 pounds 8 ounces proved too
much for Angie's slim frame and the delivery cracked her pelvis.
She and David called him Zowie, to rhyme with Bowie, but
intended, according to Angie, not as a publicity gimmick but as a
male version of the name Zoë, the Greek word for "life". They
added Duncan Haywood – Haywood after David's father – in case
the adult Zowie objected to his first name.

Angie admits that, good brood mare though she might have
been, she was "also not very maternal". She dissolved into near-
helplessness when faced with the infant Zowie, and would pass
him to whoever was close by. She found a willing helper in Susie
Frost, a cheerful and dependable woman who was living with her
husband in a flat at Haddon Hall, and who effectively became
Zowie's nanny.

Angie also sought respite with Dana Gillespie. "She was a bit
freaked after the birth," Dana says. "I said, 'Come and stay with
me in Italy at my parents' place and just get over it.'" But David
evidently found it hard to manage without her. "Every day David
rang up and he was neurotic, saying 'I miss you' and 'Come back,'
" Dana says. "She flew home after a few days."

The birth of a son provided yet another creative stimulus for
David. Within twenty-four hours he had written a delightfully
sentimental song called 'Kooks', full of affectionate detail like the

. . . funny old crib on which the paint won't dry.

'Kooks' gained in irony for following so closely on 'Oh You Pretty Things', which depicted children arriving as aliens; and so David asked Zowie to stay with his parents in their "lovers' story", even if that phrase suggested that there, too, they were acting out parts. The "kooks", of course, were David and Angie themselves.

For David, the arrival of a son was a cause for optimism, as if reflecting the best of his relationship with his own father. But another incident earlier that year showed that the old family pressures could not be so easily denied. Once again, David's aunt Pat arrived to remind him of them; once again, Terry was at the centre of the crisis.

For most of his life after his first schizophrenic attack in 1967, Terry refused to accept that he was ill. According to Pat, he also "hated" Cane Hill. He often refused to take the heavy tranquillising drugs the doctors prescribed; sometimes he simply walked out. He did so for the first time one afternoon early in 1971, spending a fortnight sleeping rough before turning to Pat for help. She found him on her doorstep in Finchley in a disturbed state, "with his clothes and hair infested with lice and fleas".

Pat took Terry in and gave him a bath. She burned his clothes and replaced them from her husband's wardrobe. After a few days, Terry agreed to return to Cane Hill. But there were complications. Since Terry had discharged himself from hospital, Pat understood, he needed the recommendation of his family doctor to be readmitted. That evening, Pat's husband, Tony, drove Terry and Pat the twenty miles across London to the doctor's surgery in Beckenham. They arrived too late for anything to be done that day and were told to come back in the morning.

Instead, Pat asked Tony to take them to nearby Haddon Hall. When Angie answered the door, Pat asked if Terry could stay the night and if she and David could take him to the doctor's in the morning. Angie hesitated, explaining that they were expecting guests for dinner. Then David appeared. "I'm sorry," he told Pat, "we're busy." Pat was outraged. "It wasn't much to ask for his own brother," she says. She was not appeased when David offered to send a mini-cab for Terry the next day; David, she adds, did not even go out to speak to Terry as he sat in the car.

Events the next morning only increased Pat's anger. Rather than return to Beckenham, she took Terry to the Maudsley Hospital in Camberwell and demanded that he be readmitted to Cane Hill from there. After a three-hour wait, a nurse told her that Cane Hill was full. Pat exploded with rage, threatening to complain to the police and the press. Then she burst into tears. Five minutes later the nurse came back to tell her that a bed had been found for Terry at Cane Hill after all. Pat said goodbye to Terry and began to cry again.

The episode marked a further watershed in the family's relationships. Pat came to see it as the moment when David denied his brother: an act of rejection that confirmed David's inability to confront the family's problems directly. With Terry, Pat was rejected too, for she never met David again. But Terry – and what he represented – could not be so easily denied; and David would continue to confront him, and himself, in his songs and lyrics.

In April 1971, David's contract with Ken Pitt reached the end of its fourth year, with – in theory – one more year to run if Pitt exercised his option to that effect. Pitt's first inclination, when David asked to be released from his contract, had been to resign himself to the inevitable. But his attitude had changed on receiving a letter from Defries headed Gem Management. It was Pitt's first intimation that Defries was not merely David's "legal adviser" but intended to become his manager.

In consequence, Pitt had visited Defries at the Gem offices in December 1970. Defries's appearance amazed him: in place of his lawyer's suit, he was wearing a roll-neck pullover, a gold medallion, and an Afro-style haircut – looking, to Pitt's jaundiced eyes, like "the last of the sixties' swingers". Pitt asked Defries for compensation for his contract and repayment of what he had spent. Defries replied in a conciliatory manner: "He said he hadn't had a chance to look at the figures, but perhaps I could have a percentage of David's future earnings," Pitt recalls. But Pitt said that he did not want any of David's earnings; he wanted £2,000, from Defries and Myers, at once. Defries made no clear reply and Pitt departed. He heard nothing more in the next four months.

When April came, Pitt wrote to Defries and Myers. He formally warned them that he was still David's manager and that, in view of their silence, he would be exercising his option to extend David's contract to its fifth and final year. Defries simply ignored him.

Mercury Records were the next to encounter Defries's highly personal method of doing business. In June their contract with David was also due to expire; they too held an option to extend it, for a third year. In May, Irwin Steinberg and Robin McBride flew to London to discuss the arrangements under which, they presumed, the contract would be renewed.

McBride for one was in buoyant mood. Before leaving Chicago, he had argued to Steinberg that Mercury should offer David what would be in effect an entirely new contract, on improved terms, running for three more years. In that way, McBride hoped, all concerned could put their past errors behind them and start anew. "It was not easy for Irwin to do, because David was clearly not making a profit for the company and in many ways not cooperating." But Steinberg had agreed, believing, McBride says, that "we've done so much so far, it hasn't been enough, but let us now take a fresh view".

The meeting – their first with Defries – took place over lunch at the French restaurant of the Londonderry Hotel near Hyde Park Corner; David was there too. McBride was expecting it to be a relaxed affair, with Defries and David duly expressing their gratitude for Mercury's generosity. "I had very positive and wonderful feelings: thinking now we'll get him in a better contract, and now we've got a manager who can do things and make this whole thing happen." It thus came as a considerable shock when Defries proceeded, with a few uncompromising words, to demolish his hopes and his plans.

The onslaught, McBride recalls, came "with absolutely no warning". First Steinberg outlined Mercury's proposals. Then Defries replied. "He told Steinberg that under no circumstances would David record another note for Mercury," McBride recalls. "Irwin's reply was in that case his contract will be suspended and he will never record for anyone else. Then Defries replied that if you require David to deliver the third album under his contract, we will deliver the biggest piece of crap you have ever had. That's not a direct quote. But that's pretty much what he said."

In theory Mercury could try to hold David to his contract. But Defries had already pre-empted that move. Search as they might, there was nothing to specify that David should *not* deliver a piece of crap. Steinberg could only counter that Mercury must be repaid all it had spent on David, including advances, recording costs, artwork fees, down "to the last penny". So be it, Defries replied, knowing he had won.

McBride was devastated. "I'm sitting there with my jaw slack and hurt," he says, "because I was a greater supporter of David. I was terribly proud of the involvement I had and just thought he was an incredible person. And all of a sudden this is washing away from me." Just as when Defries had disposed of Ken Pitt, David remained almost mute throughout these exchanges. But to McBride he appeared to be "fairly confidently behind all Tony's arguments".

The ease with which Defries freed David from the Mercury contract owed much to his tactical experiments with the Associ-

Above: David with members of his first group, the Kon-Rads; (left to right) Roger Ferris and sisters Christine and Stella Gall.

Left: David plays sax – on stage with the Kon-Rads at the Hillsiders' youth club, Biggin Hill, accompanied (right) by Alan Dodds.

Medway Sound by the

Manish boys

MAIDSTONE'S FIRST GROUP TO MAKE A DISC—THE MANISH BOYS.

SHOULD you tune into one of our numerous pop shows next month, don't be surprised if you hear the Medway Sound.

Listen closely and you will discover that it is the sound of a group who call themselves The Manish Boys.

They come from Maid—

The Manish Boys, David's third group, featured in the *Kent Messenger*, February 1965. Left to right: David, Woolf Byrne, Mick White, Bob Solly, John Watson, John Flux, Paul Rodriguez.

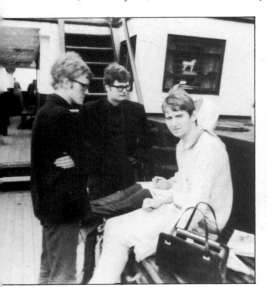

Ralph Horton (centre), David's second manager, on the Isle of Wight ferry in the summer of 1966.

Les Conn, David's first manager, today: "the most successful failure in show business."

Paul Rodriguez and Woolf Byrne of the Manish Boys today.

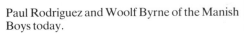

Above: David, already playing to camera, on the Isle of Wight ferry, with (left to right) Brian Pendleton and Phil May of the Pretty Things, and Denis Taylor and Phil Lancaster of the Lower Third, his fourth group.

Right: David and the Lower Third play at the Marquee's Inecto Hour in 1966; with him (left) lead-guitarist Graham Rivens and drummer Phil Lancaster.

Phil Lancaster, ex-Lower Third, today.

The faithful 'Hutch' – John Hutchinson – who played with David in three different eras, photographed here in 1969.

John Eager – 'Ego' – with memento from David's fifth group, Buzz, who offered to play with him for free.

Ken Pitt, David's third manager, at his Sussex cottage: "To this day, I don't know why we broke up."

ation of Fashion and Advertising Photographers. Before, he had achieved only limited results; this time, the "piece of crap" variant had brought dramatic success. Defries would now go in search of a new record company on whom he could exert his skills. It was time for David to return to the studio and record in earnest the songs that had so overjoyed Bob Grace.

Back in Hull, Mick Ronson was convinced that his dreams of stardom were at an end. He and Woody Woodmansey had left London when *The Man Who Sold The World* was completed, since David, in his enthusiasm for song-writing, seemed to have lost interest in live performances. Mick made a last attempt to reform the Rats, and also – calling his group Ronno – made one single, 'The Fourth Hour Of My Sleep'. "It was quite good, actually," says Mick. "But it didn't do anything." Afterwards the group effectively disbanded.

"That was the lowest point," says Mick. "I couldn't have got any lower. I was sitting there so depressed, so down, I could have committed suicide. Then I had a phone call. It was David. He said, 'Aren't you fed up with being back in Hull? Why don't you come back down?' So I said, 'Great, when?' and he said, 'Why don't you just catch the first train?' So I was really happy and I did. I met David and he said,'Let's stop messing about,' and that was it."

David told Mick that he wanted to reform his group; after a few gigs together, they would start recording his next album. Mick brought with him Woody, and, as a replacement for Tony Visconti, a third member of the Rats, Trevor Bolder, yet another inhabitant of Hull. Tall, with long black hair, Trevor came from a family with a strong local musical tradition. His father, Harry Bolder, was a trumpeter who owned a record shop in Hull, and he had several brothers who all played the guitar. To begin with, Woody and Trevor joined Mick in the commune at Haddon Hall; later, all three moved into their own flat in Penge.

Some of David's new songs received their first public airing on John Peel's *In Concert* series on BBC radio on June 5th. David – second on the bill to a group named Heron – recorded his contribution a day or so before. He brought a large group of friends with him: not only Mick, Woody and Trevor, but also Dana Gillespie, George Underwood and Bob Grace.

"This is going to be incredibly complicated," John Peel warned when he introduced David. Mick, Woody and Trevor were presented as members of Ronno; a fourth musician, Mark Carr-Pritchard, who had played on 'Moonage Daydream', was dutifully described as a member of Arnold Corns. Of David's new songs, Dana sang 'Andy Warhol'; George Underwood sang, 'Song For Bob Dylan'; and David and his band rendered 'Queen Bitch' and 'Kooks'. John Peel predicted that the new titles would appear on David's next album, which "could be very easily called *Hunky Dory*".

Peel's announcement was a shade premature, for the performance found David in diffident mood. A long time had passed since he had last appeared in public, and his high-pitched introduction to 'Song For Bob Dylan' betrayed his nerves. Worse still, his attempt to record 'Oh! You Pretty Things', ended ignominiously. "He lost his voice," says Bob Grace, "and he started panicking." In the pub afterwards, David was in tears. "He freaked out. He thought his career was over, he thought he had blown it."

Two weeks later, David was back in control. On June 20th he and most of his friends decamped to Somerset for the Glastonbury Fayre. As Dana recalls, David and Angie were at their symbiotic closest: David was wearing voluminous pink trousers and both had yellow hair. "They looked like sisters," Dana says. The Fayre was doing its best to resuscitate the spirit of the 1960s: "There were freaks everywhere, mushrooms, it was just out of it." As is traditional on such occasions, there was drizzling rain and squelching mud, causing much discomfort to Tony Defries – and amusement to the others – when he fell over in the morass.

At first it seemed that David has missed his opportunity to impress his audience. He was due to perform late at night but – as is also traditional on such occasions – there was a drastic over-run and by midnight, when the local authorities had ordered the concert to end, he had still not appeared. David was not to be so easily put off. At dawn, as spectators huddled in their tents and sleeping bags, he began to sing. He first had to overcome his audience's resentment at having their sleep disturbed. "People were waking up and they didn't expect music at this hour," Dana says. Then, as David began 'Memory Of A Free Festival', "the sun came over the hill and lit him up and everybody warmed to him. He was a huge success. He really won people over."

Days after Glastonbury, recording began at the Trident studios. David added Rick Wakeman to his band, while Tony Visconti was replaced as producer by Ken Scott, who had worked as sound engineer on both Mercury albums. Visconti's role as arranger was performed by David and Mick: "It was like me and David would go in and spend all the time in the studio," Mick says.

The composition of the new album reflected the David of the

first half of 1971. He selected the songs with the help of Scott and Bob Grace one evening at Scott's house: "We got all the demos and started going through them to decide which ones would go on the album," Grace says. While Grace pushed hard for as many as possible of David's own songs, since they would increase the revenue to Chrysalis, David, paradoxically, argued in favour of several by other writers.

Grace had also suggested the title, as trailed by John Peel. Dictionaries define hunky-dory as "satisfactory, fine", and give its origin as the middle-Dutch word *honc*. In this case, its source was a former RAF man who was landlord of the Bear, a pub in Esher, Surrey, where Grace sometimes drank. "He was one of those classic Battle of Britain types," says Grace. "His vocabulary was spattered with terms like 'prang' and 'whizzo'; another was 'everything's hunky-dory.' I told it to David and he loved it."

The title reflected the more optimistic strains of the album, to be discerned in what one critic described, if excessively, as Rick Wakeman's marzipan piano and Mick Ronson's satin-string arrangements. Musically, the album consolidated the advance represented by *The Man Who Sold The World*, rather than breaking new ground; David had also recoiled from the naked aggression of heavy metal in favour of a calmer, more reflective style. Several songs were affectionate parodies of David's American hero-figures, brought closer by his US visit.

David's fascination with the interplay between reality and image, between identity and role-playing, dominated many of the lyrics. But – belying the upbeat title – the old preoccupations were still there, redolent with menace. The album also contained two of David's pivotal lyrics: one that could serve as his anthem; and one that offered another crucial insight into his relationship with Terry, as enigmatic, audacious – and ultimately revealing – as 'The Width Of A Circle'.

The first track was 'Changes', soon to become one of the key songs in David's repertoire. It continued the rebellious mood of 'Oh! You Pretty Things', with echoes of two distinguished predecessors: Bob Dylan's 'Times They Are A-Changin'', and The Who's 'My Generation', with David also using a stutter ("Ch-ch-ch-changes") to convey the striving for self-expression in a hostile world.

Like most of the tracks on *Hunky Dory*, 'Changes' began with a brief autobiographical cameo: using hard sexual imagery, David told of his struggle for success in his career. Each time he thought he had achieved it, he found it tasted "not so sweet".

David was also recounting his parallel search for stability and identity, which had merged with the quest for fame. He described his attempts at self-examination:

> . . . I've turned myself to face me

– but these had failed. He was unable to tell how others saw him, "the faker", for he was far too fast "to take that test".

The lyric also presented the now-familiar conundrum, through the line:

> Turn and face the stranger.

Was David referring to the stranger on the stair of 'The Man Who Sold The World'? Or himself? Or were they the same person?

'Changes' was another of David's predictive songs: as well as describing David's frustration at attempting to penetrate his own dissimulating personality, it also foretold the rapid changes of style and persona that would tantalise his audiences more and more. It introduced another theme, too: the nature of transience and impermanence, emphasised in the music through the gentle shifts of key and abrupt changes of tempo.

It was in part the counterpoint to the Buddhist ideas of reincarnation that David had found wanting. It was also related to the strategy of role-playing that David was beginning to pursue – of necessity a temporary affair. That was the key to his enigmatic chorus, with its play on 'Times They Are A-Changin'':

> Time may change me
> But I can't trace time.

'Changes' was followed by 'Oh! You Pretty Things', a far more strident and declamatory version than the one recorded by Peter Noone, merging directly (the technical term is *segue*) with the gentler 'Eight Light Poem', which appeared to be a more tranquil recollection of shared experience.

Then came 'Life On Mars', which began with yet another account of his affair with Hermione – this time, a "god-awful small affair" with "the girl with the mousy hair", who was pressed by her parents to end it. The lyric posed another of the conundrums that intrigued David that year. Which of her lives was real: her day-to-day existence? Or her life as a film star, on "the silver screen"? David backed up his question with a plethora of images and allusions from the cinema and rock and roll, and told one very private joke in the line:

Oh man! Look at those cavemen go.

The line came from the 1960 hit 'Alley Oop', by the Hollywood Argyles, produced by the musical pimp of California, Kim Fowley.

The same concerns recurred briefly in 'Kooks' – "our lovers' story" – and dominated 'Quicksand' where David, himself "living in a silent film", cited comparisons with stars like Garbo and Bardot. The lyric introduced another puzzle, for David later called *Hunky Dory* a "very worried" album, without explaining why. On the evidence of 'Quicksand' and several other lyrics on the album, his principal worry in fact concerned the source and nature of his creative inspiration, and how long it could last. Given his bewilderment over how he had composed 'Oh! You Pretty Things', that was entirely understandable; and his fear was summarised in two lines of 'Quicksand':

I'm sinking in the quicksand of my thought
And I ain't got the power any more.

It was an intuitive assertion that the key to creativity lay in following the instincts and not the intellect, something that David was to articulate later in his career. 'Life On Mars' had expressed the same fears, culminating when David, using outer space to describe "inner space", posed the question:

Is there life on Mars?

An answer to these questions was to be found in 'Fill Your Heart' by Biff Rose and Paul Williams, which David had insisted on including despite the objections of Bob Grace. The lines

Forget your mind
And you'll be free

repeated the main point of 'Quicksand': creativity lies with the instincts, not the intellect. The song also recalled David's 1967 Deram album, where both love and freedom were to be found in a fantasy land. It even had "dragons".

The next three songs asked the same questions and pursued the same themes; they also celebrated three of David's American heroes: two old, one new. 'Andy Warhol' pondered the relationship between image and reality:

> Andy Warhol, Silver Screen,
> Can't tell them apart at all.

'Song For Bob Dylan', a witty impersonation of Dylan – with his "voice like sand and glue" – was also about fears of losing the muse, for Dylan had been quiescent for some time, and his audiences were impatient for his next album. But who was "the same old painted lady" who emerged "from the brow of the superbrain"? When introducing the song during his *In Concert* performance, David warned that this was "not a reference to Bob Dylan" – adding mysteriously, "you'll get the point to this song anyway . . ." The point may well have escaped his audience, for David was making an erudite classical allusion. The woman was the Greek goddess Athene, who was born from the brow of Zeus: and she was the goddess of the arts and creativity.

The third American song, 'Queen Bitch', was a tribute to the American singer Lou Reed, a member of the Velvet Underground group which had helped divert the course of popular music in the late 1960s. At the height of flower-power, Lou Reed and the Velvet Underground – who were part-sponsored by Andy Warhol – were proclaiming a new alternative culture, of drug addiction, homosexuality, sado-masochism and the reality of street life, and David, who came upon their music during his US visit, was enthralled. His fascination was heralded in 'Song For Bob Dylan' in the lines

> Here she comes
> Here she comes again

which were word-plays on the Velvet Underground songs, 'Here She Comes Now' and 'There She Goes Again'.

Although David did not mention Reed by name in 'Queen Bitch', its content made that unnecessary. In a raucous, staccato style that was close to Reed's raw, half-spoken delivery, he described members of Reed's demi-monde, the cruisers and drag queens he had seen for himself in the US. David now claimed this as his territory too, for he boasted

> . . . I can do better than that.

The lyric was also a portrait of loneliness and anxiety, with David lying on his bed gazing "at my hotel wall" and then – using a favoured sexual image – finding a taste in his mouth that was "no taste at all".

Thus far in the album, David's family problems had remained at bay. There were occasional hints that they were lurking, like the juxtaposition of "family" and "sanity" within three lines in 'Song For Bob Dylan'. They reappeared with a vengeance in the final song of the album, one of the most powerful and remarkable David ever wrote.

'The Bewlay Brothers' has always been regarded as one of the most opaque and elusive of all David's lyrics. It has an air of mystery and revelation that is enhanced by the quiet and intimate note on which it begins and the swelling crescendos it gives way to. It evidently holds strong personal significance for David, for he used it as the name of his own publishing company: Bewlay Brothers Music.

It began with the usual autobiographical reference: the rejection of prophet figures – perhaps the Buddhists – who had so beguiled David before. Then David moved abruptly into another autobiographical area:

> I was stone and he was wax
> So he could scream, and still relax, unbelievable.

David's first reference – "I was stone" – could have derived from the children's game, stone, paper, scissors. That innocent phrase then acquired sinister power by eliding into an account of homosexual sex, with David finding a precise description for successful homosexual intercourse. He reinforced the meaning with other homosexual slang, like "traders" and "marks" – both of them insiders' jargon for male sexual partners – and the unambiguous phrase

> In the crutch-hungry dark . . .

David also described cross-dressing, with "the dress" that has been "hung" and the make-up ("the Factor Max") staining his pillow. Then he moved into another secret area, that of drug-taking, citing "shooting up" and the dust that flows "thru our veins", allusions to heroin-taking that had no parallel in David's writings since 'Space Oddity'. It all comprised a portrait of clandestine activities, shielded from outsiders through its private jargon.

Then came the most startling lines of all:

> Now my brother lays upon the rocks,
> He could be dead, he could be not,
> He could be you.

David's description of a lifeless body suggested the isolation and exhaustion that follows sexual activity. Echoing 'The Width Of A Circle' and 'The Man Who Sold The World', the lines also deployed the switches of role and identity through which he examined himself and his sanity, against the yardstick of "my brother" – Terry. In conjunction with the homosexual slang and jargon David had already deployed, the effect was to conjure an image, fanciful but devastating, of Terry as David's sexual partner.

The lyric should not be taken to imply that David in fact ever had a sexual relationship with Terry. But 'The Bewlay Brothers' decisively commemorated his importance to David: as the main source of physical affection in David's childhood; as a model of manhood in David's adolescence; and as a mirror in which David could reflect upon his own sanity. David had borrowed the secret language of homosexuality and drug-taking to describe a third, illicit area of his childhood: the love which he had felt for Terry and which his father had forbidden him to express.

David has given some guidance that this is not a fanciful interpretation, for he has said in interviews that the song is about his brother, Terry. He has given no further amplification, however, and his public statements about his lyrics are not always to be trusted. But David has confirmed this interpretation in private, as an important witness describes.

When David visited New York that year, he called on someone he had not met for fourteen years: his cousin Kristina. They had last seen each other in 1957, when Kristina's mother died and she had been sent to live with her father, Kurt Paulsen, in Canada.

Several years later, Paulsen died, and Kristina moved to the US. In 1971 – after a further series of traumas – she was working as a theatrical agent and living in some comfort, as David later reported to his mother, by Central Park. David telephoned her and announced: "This is your cousin." Kristina invited him to call and David came "bounding up the stairs in high boots and long hair", she recalls. She later presented him with a Victorian velvet robe with an ermine-trimmed collar which, she felt, perfectly suited his current tastes. "He loved it."

David and Kristina soon filled in the missing years of their relationship, which they maintained, with some interruptions, over the next fifteen years. In that time, they also talked over their troubled family past. "We've gone over it a few times," Kristina says, "trying to muddle through it, make some sense of it." Among the puzzles for David was "why he was chosen and Terry was left. He could have been Terry – when you come that close to it."

On one occasion, David talked about 'The Bewlay Brothers'. "I was aware of what it took to write," Kristina says. David also told Kristina what its subject matter was: "He said it was about Terry."

In August 1971, while David was still applying the finishing touches to *Hunky Dory*, Tony Defries flew to New York. He had with him a first pressing – known as an "acetate" – of five of the songs David had been recording, including 'Changes', 'Kooks', and 'Oh! You Pretty Things'. One of his calls, after a firm of lawyers had set up an appointment, was to Dennis Katz, the head of A and R at RCA's records division at its offices on the Avenue of the Americas in Manhattan.

Katz had never heard of Defries before, and his knowledge of David was sketchy: "the guy that did 'Space Oddity', a weird guy who's a transvestite" was about all. David, he says, was "not a hot commodity in 1971".

In contrast to the pugnacious Tony Defries whom Mercury had encountered, the Defries Katz met was quiet and restrained, leaving little impression during that first meeting. What did impress Katz was the quality of *Hunky Dory*. "I was knocked out," he says. "It was theatrical, musical, the songs were excellent, there was real poetry, it seemed to have everything." Katz took the acetate home to his wife who was "completely knocked out by it" too. Katz had come to RCA only a few months before, with instructions to rejuvenate its popular music output, and David met his needs perfectly. "I wanted to sign the man," he says.

Within days, Katz had convinced his superiors at RCA that David should be offered a contract, and a memorandum sanctioning the offer arrived in his office. It was signed by three people: Mort Hoffman, a vice-president of RCA's records division; Mel Ilberman, its head of business affairs; and Rocco Laginestra, its president. Their approval had not been hard to win; but what struck Katz most of all was the ease of his negotiations with Defries.

RCA offered Defries what Katz admits was "a very inexpensive deal". At that time RCA was paying some performers between $100,000 and $200,000 an album. For David, Katz offered $37,500 an album. Later Katz heard it said that two other record companies, CBS and Elektra, had been interested in signing David, but their interest cannot have gone very far. "Nobody else seemed to be putting up resistance or giving us any competition," he says. When he pushed to close the deal, Defries did not demur. Katz was delighted. Not only was he convinced that he had just signed a major new talent for RCA; it was also one of the smoothest and most straightforward agreements he had ever made.

17

Inside the Show

In the summer of 1971, there could be no doubt which was Tony Defries's favourite book: the newly published *Elvis: A Biography*, by the American rock writer, Jerry Hopkins. Defries had a well-thumbed copy, and he liked to quote passage from it to colleagues and friends. The story Defries told most often concerned Presley's manager, Colonel Parker, who had begun his career as a fairground barker of spectacular amorality. Parker's most shameless exhibit was his Dancing Chickens, which performed a convincing high-step to the strains of 'Turkey In The Straw'. The chickens danced with such alacrity because they were standing on an electric hotplate which, as Defries loved to relate, the Colonel switched on as the music began.

Defries's fondness for the dancing chickens story does not necessarily imply that he took pleasure from cruelty to animals. But it does demonstrate a fascination for the artifices of show business that matched David's own. It also shows the pleasure that Defries took from aligning himself with Colonel Parker, contributing to his image as a huckster who could wheel and deal with all of Parker's gaudy panache. Like Parker, he was proud of his exploits, and liked to extract aphorisms from them which he would quote to his staff. One concerned the proper approach to business negotiations. "You must always," he would say, "try to *improve*."

By "improving" Defries meant that you should never feel tied down by the first offer you accept. To go shopping with him in Bloomingdale's on Lexington Avenue was an embarrassment, since he would haggle with the assistants as if that most straitlaced of stores had become an Arab souk. Improving also helped explain why Dennis Katz had found his negotiations over *Hunky Dory* so delightfully trouble-free. Defries's most important goal had been to gain a toehold at RCA: plenty of time to "improve" later on.

The Presley biography was not Defries's only reading matter that year. He was also scouring the national newspapers and American business magazines like *Fortune* and *Business Week* for all he could learn about RCA. For RCA was much in the news in

251

1971: but the wrong kind of news, for the company was torn by chaos and intrigue.

The turmoil afflicting RCA was of the kind that accompanies the ending of a dynasty. For almost forty years the Radio Corporation of America had been the personal fiefdom of its president, chairman and chief executive, David Sarnoff, known universally as "the General", even by his children. Sarnoff's story was the embodiment of the American dream: son of impoverished Jewish family in Russia arrives in New York at the age of five, starts work as an office boy earning $5.50 a week, builds the company he works for into the twenty-first largest corporation in the US.

He did so first by devoting RCA's resources to manufacturing radios and gramophones in the years between the wars, thus helping to create American consumerism's first great boom. RCA also took over the Victor Talking Machine Company, with its trademark of a fox terrier named Nipper listening to an ancient phonograph. That image, entitled His Master's Voice, helped make RCA a household name.

Sarnoff acquired his sobriquet of "the General" from serving as an officer in the US army during the second world war. When he returned to RCA he made the company a pioneer of colour television while RCA's broadcasting subsidiary, NBC, took a relentless diet of soap operas, westerns, situation comedies and ceaseless commercials into American homes. Like any Hollywood mogul, Sarnoff denied all responsibility for shaping American tastes. "Basically we're delivery boys," he would say.

By the mid-sixties, Sarnoff was old and ill. He had groomed his son Robert for the succession by installing him as the head of NBC, and in 1966 Robert began to take control of the parent corporation at its headquarters in Rockefeller Plaza. But the younger Sarnoff was not content merely to continue in his father's ways and attempted to impose his personal stamp on RCA. In a flurry of takeovers he led RCA into fields his father would not have dreamed of. RCA bought Hertz and Random House, together with companies dealing in real estate, carpets, even television dinners.

Robert Sarnoff also proved unable to impose himself on the autocratic company structure his father had created. *Business Week* later described the "Byzantine cabals, factions and schisms" that dominated the Rockefeller Plaza headquarters on the late 1960s. The *Wall Street Journal* wrote that by 1970 RCA was notorious for its "poor financial restraint, poor management, and poor planning". It was also known as the company that could be relied upon to hire staff who had been rejected elsewhere, with Robert

Sarnoff notorious for the readiness with which he awarded senior positions at RCA to men he had met while playing golf.

In the summer of 1971 all the talk was of Sarnoff's latest blunder. The previous autumn he had boasted of making RCA into a major computer manufacturer second only to IBM. In July he set up a sales and management team in London that was supposed to lead the assault on the European computer market. Just six weeks later, Sarnoff announced that RCA was pulling out of computers, at a loss of $250 million.

At its offices in the Avenue of the Americas, even though at a discreet distance from the corporate headquarters at Rockefeller Plaza, RCA's record division did not escape the confusion and intrigue. The senior Sarnoff had used the division – known formally as RCA Records and Tapes – as a loss-leader to help promote the company, which would benefit from having records emblazoned with the RCA name lying around in American homes. Now, Robert Sarnoff decreed, the division was to make a profit.

The man assigned to fulfil that task was Rocco Laginestra. For once, Sarnoff could not be accused of having made his hiring on the golf course: Laginestra's sport was tennis. Inside Records and Tapes it was an open secret that Laginestra, previously a financial controller at NBC, was being groomed for a place on the parent RCA board. No one today is quite sure why; what is certain, according to one of his former colleagues, is that Laginestra "didn't know a damn thing about the record industry".

To his credit, Laginestra was aware of that too. Soon after taking up his post as president of the division, he had hired as his principal aide Mort Hoffman, an executive with a good track record at RCA's rival, CBS. Hoffman became "vice-president, commercial operations" on the understanding that when Laginestra moved onwards in RCA, Hoffman would take over the division. While Laginestra devoted himself to RCA's internecine internal politics, Hoffman ran the division from day to day. It was Hoffman who hired Dennis Katz with instructions to revitalise the division's popular music output, until then almost solely dependent on the revenue brought in by Elvis Presley.

Laginestra's career now took an ironic turn. Largely through the efforts of Hoffman and Katz, Records and Tapes began to make the profit Sarnoff had demanded. It was Laginestra, naturally, who claimed the credit. As his reward, he was told to remain in charge of the division for the foreseeable future.

With his career path at RCA stalled, Laginestra decided to take full control over the division's affairs. He soon showed that he had little expertise in the admittedly nebulous matter of predicting which performers and which records would be a hit. And his uncertainties were most nakedly exposed when he started to take part in negotiations with RCA's artists and their managers.

One such occasion arose when RCA were due to negotiate a contract with Jerry Perenchio, a show-business manager of fearsome repute. The RCA team decided their opening position and the maximum to which they were prepared to go. According to one of the participants, Perenchio's opening demand was a "crazy, crazy figure". The response of the RCA team was to stand up as if to walk out. But Laginestra intervened and asked Perenchio if he would leave the room instead.

"I saw a smile all over Jerry's face," says the RCA man. "He knew Rocco was about to move and he knew he had it locked. RCA lost a bundle on the deal. From then on, as soon as Rocco got involved in any negotiations, everyone else walked away." Among managers the word spread: "You wanna get more money at RCA, you go see Rocco."

In public Laginestra maintained a highly favourable image. In a profile of astonishing sycophancy the rock critic Lilian Roxon of the New York *Daily News* hailed him as a "handsome, tennis-playing, happily married husband, loving father and pillar of the church back in Franklin Lakes, New Jersey". His colleagues, by contrast, saw him as devious and paranoid. He instructed his secretary to listen in to all telephone conversations with his staff, using a microphone that she kept under her desk. He also adopted what is termed a "creative" approach to his division's accounts.

One Christmas, under continuing pressure from the RCA board to maintain a profit, he ordered every record in RCA's warehouses to be shipped out to their distributors, and told his sales director to show the shipments as sales in the annual accounts. By mid-January the bemused distributors, who were unable to sell the records, began to ship them back. But by then the division's accounts had been safely presented, showing a handsome profit. "That was the kind of shit he used to pull," says a disgruntled colleague. In sum, he adds, "RCA records was not a happy place."

In 1971, not all of this was yet known to Defries. But he gradually discerned that both RCA and Laginestra were ideal for the strategy he was devising. That was also evident from his further reading of the Elvis Presley biography, for another attribute he admired in Colonel Parker was his apparent ability to induce RCA to accede to his every whim. In Parker's case, RCA had every reason to do so, for the fortunes of the record company depended on keeping him happy. Athough David was almost unknown in the US, Defries had decided to emulate Parker by making equally exorbitant demands on RCA. For he had fathomed one of the mysteries by which stardom is fashioned: the secret of becoming a star lies, above all, in knowing how to behave like one. And in London that summer, by happy coincidence, David was arriving at the same conclusion: he should act like a star.

In August 1971, London was treated to the arrival of a company of New York actors who came to perform a play named *Pork*. Only three years had passed since censorship of the British theatre had been abolished, and in that time London's bolder theatre-goers had witnessed stage nudity in plays such as *Oh! Calcutta!* and *Hair*. These were works of utter decorum compared with *Pork* which – at least according to those seismographs of national taste, the British press – conducted an onslaught against all the values that Britain held dear.

Its characters talked without embarrassment of masturbation, abortion and drug-taking. A prostitute gave herself a douche in preparation for her next client. A transsexual discussed his (or was it her?) interest in the different varieties of excrement. There were also generous measures of nudity, homosexuality and group sex – only simulated, it was devoutly to be hoped.

At the Round House, where *Pork* was to be staged, notices were posted that warned: "This play has explicit sexual content and 'offensive' language – if you are likely to be disturbed, please do not attend." London's theatre critics ignored the warning, and duly reported that they were indeed both offended and disturbed. *The Times* found *Pork* "repellently narcissistic and hopelessly parochial" and judged it a "witless, invertebrate, mind-numbing farrago". The *News of the World* asserted that *Pork* made *Oh! Calcutta!* and *Hair* look like the mythical vicarage tea-party that is always invoked on such occasions.

Pork, in fact, had a more respectable pedigree than Fleet Street allowed. It was based on conversations recorded by Andy Warhol in his New York studio, the Factory, and given dramatic form by an imaginative young off-Broadway director and playwright, Tony Ingrassia. Most of the parts were based on Warhol's gallery of "superstars". The willowy Viva was renamed Vulva and played by the transsexual Wayne County (he/she later became Jayne County); Warhol was portrayed by Tony Zanetta as a flaxen-haired voyeur, taking a salacious pleasure from the figures vying for his attention.

255

Pork was thus closely related to Warhol's work as the manipulator of popular imagery and expectations, and the *New York Times* found it a "satirical show-and-tell *fest* that is occasionally revolting but more often good dirty fun". The associations with Warhol only increased Fleet Street's outrage. Warhol was best known in Britain for his movies apparently intended to cause either sexual scandal, like *Flesh*, which the British police had seized the previous year, or terminal boredom, like his eight-hour epic, *Sleep*. Fleet Street penned its final damnations when, as the culminating insult, the actress Geri Miller exposed her mountainous breasts to photographers outside Clarence House, home of that cosy symbol of British maternalism, the Queen Mother.

All of this made it inevitable that David and *Pork* should come together. Ironically, it was the *Pork* company who sought David out, and not vice versa. *Pork*'s assistant stage director, Leee Black Childers, saw an advertisement for a forthcoming performance by David at the Country Club, close to the Round House in Haverstock Hill, on July 28th. Leee had read John Mendelsohn's article about David in *Rolling Stone* the previous April. "All I knew was that he wore dresses, so I thought this'll be interesting," says Leee; "although of course Jayne was wearing dresses all the time anyway."

The party which watched David perform included Leee, Wayne County, Tony Zanetta – known as Zee – and Cherry Vanilla, who played the title role of *Pork*, named after Warhol's superstar Brigid Polk, and who was much given, like Geri Miller, to exposing her breasts. David was accompanied at the Country Club by Angie, Dana Gillespie and Mick Ronson.

"Angela was very loud and crazy and Dana was very busty and glamorous," says Leee. "But we were all quite disappointed with David. He sat playing these little songs and it all sounded very nice and melodic. He introduced us to the audience of about twenty people and Cherry stood up and popped her tits out. He was very interested in us because we were working with Andy Warhol. At that point he was probably more interested in us than we were in him."

The *Pork* company reciprocated by inviting David to the Round House. David was entranced. He promptly invited the *Pork* company to the Sombrero, where Angie and Zee struck up an instant rapport. "They got along fabulously," says Leee, "they danced every dance. They just loved each other, they were on the phone constantly."

Between the *Pork* company and Mick Ronson, on the other

hand, there was a total culture clash. "Everyone was in love with him of course," says Leee. "Everyone thought he was gorgeous." Mick, who had not previously known that gay clubs even existed, found the attentions of the *Pork* company overwhelming. "These guys are like jumping all over me," he says. "There are hands going under the table. I'm going, 'get these people away from me' . . . I thought they were all a bunch of loonies."

David went to see *Pork* night after night, regularly meeting the cast backstage and introducing them all to Defries on his return from New York. For David, *Pork*'s brazen sexuality was a powerful magnet. So too were its uniquely American flavour and its associations with Andy Warhol. But what intrigued him above all was the complex and multi-layered role-playing involved in the cast's performances both on and off the stage.

In the first place, the actors were not the inherently outrageous characters they appeared. Wayne County, for example, came from a small rural community in Georgia, where both his parents belonged to strict religious sects. Originally Wayne Rogers, it was as a teenager that he discovered a liking for "dressing crazy" and for "confusing people"; he adopted his new name upon seeing a roadsign near Detroit that read, "You are now entering Wayne County", later adopting the name Jayne, and the female gender too.

Most of the company came from equally unlikely backgrounds. Zee was from a small town in New York state; Cherry Vanilla – originally Kathy Dorritie – was one of sixteen children from an Irish-Catholic family in New York; Leee Childers – who added the third 'e' to his name out of perversity – came from Louisville, Kentucky. For them, Zee believes, their outrageous behaviour was "the other side of repression". Most had acted with New York drama groups like Warhol's Factory and the Theatre of the Ridiculous which, Zee says, "encouraged acting out, the art of personality, playing up an aspect of your own personality and letting that be your role".

For all their delight in affronting British sensibilities, the *Pork* cast were at first bemused by their reception. That was in part due to the mistaken belief of the British press that the *Pork* cast comprised Warhol's superstars when they were merely actors playing the parts. "Once we landed in London we were all perceived as Warhol stars – we were all very pleased with that and enjoyed it," Zee says.

David was a party to the confusion too. "We immediately got on," says Zee of their first meeting. "We somehow connected. For a long time I was confused as to exactly why. Part of it I think was because I was playing Andy, and the attraction was to Warhol, the way of Warhol. I was the key to Warhol, or something like that."

Thus encouraged, Zee was happy to live up to David's expectations. "I began to get into my own fantasy of me as Warhol and people related to me as if I was," Zee says. "We were beginning to play these people, beginning to act like they did, although we were still playing ourselves. It was confusing, and it was a lot about role-playing, and David was lured in the same way, because he was in the process of doing the same thing. He was coming from the same base as we were. Which is basically an inability to be oneself and constructing a new personality in which one could act out one's fantasies and desires." In short, David was learning how to play the part of star.

In September, Defries returned to New York, this time in the company of David, Angie and Mick Ronson, together with the completed acetate of *Hunky Dory*. To Mick, this was certainly playing the role of star. "First time on a plane, first time out of the country apart from France, first time across the Atlantic, jumbo, first-class, and the night we got there we went to see Elvis Presley."

Elvis was performing at Madison Square Garden and Mick had never seen anything remotely like it before. "An orchestra, the works, sitting in the eighth row, these forty-year-old women throwing their handkerchieves about. I couldn't believe it." David told Angie that he was particularly impressed that Elvis seemed so sexy. When Angie expressed surprise that David had not realised that before, he replied: "Yes, but now I know how he does it."

The main purpose of the visit was for David and Defries to deliver *Hunky Dory* and to sign the contract with RCA, a ceremony that was accomplished in RCA's boardroom on September 9th, with Rocco Laginestra signing for RCA. The occasion was only slightly marred by a gaffe on the part of RCA's head of publicity, Herb Helman, who was so confused by his visitors' appearance that he introduced himself to Angie thinking that she was David.

The trip also brought David meetings with several of his contemporary heroes, foremost among them Andy Warhol. The introduction was secured by Zee, whom Angie had contacted as soon as they arrived. This historic encounter, which took place in Warhol's studio – the Factory – on the edge of Greenwich Village, passed in virtual silence. "Andy was never a talker," explains Zee, who was there too. "Andy waited for other people to do things around him. So did David."

David did play a recording of his song, 'Andy Warhol', to which Warhol demurely replied: "That was great – thank you very much." Warhol took a series of Polaroid photographs of David and switched on the pocket tape-recorder which had provided the raw material for *Pork*, but this appeared to inhibit David even more. Eventually Warhol ventured to admire David's caterpillar shoes and there was a brief exchange on the topic of footwear. David left after an hour, saying later that the meeting was "fascinating" because Warhol had "nothing to say at all, absolutely nothing".

RCA arranged some important introductions for David too. The company held a reception for David at Max's Kansas City, a bar and night club close to the Factory that was the most fashionable gathering place for media and show-business figures at that time, with a series of inner sancta, each more fashionable and exclusive than the last.

Among the dinner guests was Lou Reed, who told Bowie a timely joke about Andy Warhol. The Velvet Underground had once considered producing an Andy Warhol doll: when you wound it up, it did nothing at all. David enjoyed the joke, while Lou Reed was impressed upon hearing *Hunky Dory*. "I knew there was somebody else living in the same areas I was," he said later; he "especially loved" 'Queen Bitch'.

Another guest was the extraordinary figure of Iggy Pop. David had come home from his first US visit talking excitedly of a rock singer who rubbed peanut butter and raw meat over his body, cut himself with broken glass, and dived headlong into the audience. This was Pop – his true name was Jim Osterberg – who had first sung with a group named the Stooges, and had then started to perform on his own. His appeal to David, who later talked of Iggy "unleashing the animalistic parts of rock", was not hard to divine: here was someone with no apparent inhibitions, least of all when performing on stage, a state that David himself hoped to achieve.

Iggy did not arrive at Max's Kansas City until supper was over, explaining later that he had been unable to tear himself away from watching *Mr Smith Goes To Washington* on television: "James Stewart was so sincere," he said; "he was really getting to me." But Defries and David showed themselves to be considerate hosts. "They saw I was hungry and invited me to breakfast," Iggy said. "So I came up and ate about six breakfasts the next day and started hanging about with them."

That meeting was the start of one of the longest and most fruitful relationships of David's career. Not only did David draw on Iggy when creating his own stage personas; in real life too, when facing his personal nadir, he found succour in Iggy's ravaged personality. Eventually the two men made an implicit pact to rescue themselves from their plight.

By the time David returned to Britain, the more tangible rewards of his visit had begun to accrue. On September 17th, RCA made the first payment under David's contract. It was for $56,250: $37,500 as full payment for *Hunky Dory* and $18,750 as a 50 per cent advance against David's next album. Converted to sterling, it produced the highly satisfactory sum of £22,612.93. David received £4,000.

The lion's share of the RCA payment went to Gem. It was used, first, to cover the mounting debt David was incurring on his account at Gem. By October, Gem had spent £7,379.76 on David's recording activities, and a further £3,746.27 which it had paid to David directly or spent on his behalf. Against that, David had earned £2,364.61 that year, most of it from the BBC, and from the Performing Rights Society in royalties on David's songs. Gem had deducted a 10 per cent commission from most of those earnings, reducing them to £2,135.81. His debt to Gem thus stood at £8,990.22, which the RCA advance was used to cover.

Gem was also earmarking a further proportion of the RCA advance as royalties on future sales of David's records. Two-elevenths – £4,114.44 – was reserved for Gem, and one-eleventh – £2,055.72 – for the producer, Ken Scott (although when Scott would actually receive his share was to prove a controversial question). Of RCA's £22,612.93, that left a balance of just over £5,000, which for the time being went into Gem's bank account.

But David's indebtedness was steadily increasing. Gem was now paying him a regular £400 a month living expenses by standing order, which it naturally debited to his account. Gem was also making weekly payments to the rest of his band – £30 to Mick, £20 to Trevor, £15 to Woody – which were debited to David. Then Gem decided it was time to increase its share of David's performance earnings from 10 per cent to 20 per cent, and to 30 per cent where it had actually made the booking itself. This commission further increased David's debt. From its modest beginnings of just under £9,000, David's indebtedness would rise to many times that amount.

It would be a long time before David would concern himself with such financial niceties: in October 1971, he was content to enjoy the prizes of his forthcoming stardom. The £4,000 allocated to him by Gem arrived in two instalments, of £2,000 each, on September 27th and October 4th. He and Angie celebrated by going out to buy some more art-nouveau glass.

18

Give Me Your Hands

Soon after returning from New York, David contacted Ken Scott to tell him he was ready to start recording his next album. His explanation of what it would be like was strangely defensive. "You're not going to like it," he warned Scott. When Scott asked why not, David told him: "It's much more like Iggy Pop."

"I had never even heard of Iggy Pop," Scott admits today; "that didn't mean a thing to me." But David, who was not given to confiding his innermost thoughts to Scott, added only that the album would be "more rock and roll".

"I don't know how he got the impression that I didn't like rock and roll," says Scott now. When the recording began, he adds, "There was no way I could dislike it. What he'd come up with was incredible."

What David came up with was *The Rise And Fall Of Ziggy Stardust And The Spiders From Mars*. It was a work of breathtaking scope, acquiring a unity his previous albums had lacked through the creation of a central character, Ziggy Stardust. The name was a composite of Iggy Pop and an American performer, the Legendary Stardust Cowboy, who had attained the rank of celebrity through the well-intentioned awfulness of his act. The character was an alien from outer space who is received on earth as a rock and roll star, a concept that allowed David to present both a major creative work and a simultaneous commentary upon it.

It was also an intensely personal work, a *tour d'horizon* of the principal themes of David's career, flowing and merging among the lyrics, while also offering the latest instalment of his striving for stardom. It was a work of astonishing courage, too, in which David renewed his vertiginous dance with madness and death, embracing them more intimately than ever and then attempting to break free.

In depicting an alien arriving on earth, David had reversed his usual metaphor of journeying to outer space to discover the inner truths, of which 'Space Oddity' had been the prototype. Now an inhabitant of outer space had made the return journey, and by describing what he found also laid bare his own mind. In creating a character who embodied so many of his hopes and fears, it was as if David had turned to face his *doppelgänger* at last.

In musical terms, by contrast with the inspired chaos of *The Man Who Sold The World*, David arrived in the Trident studio with absolute clarity of purpose. "He knew what he wanted musically," says Scott, "and he didn't want to know any of the technicalities." In the two months that David and the Spiders spent in the studio, Mick Ronson's lead guitar emerged as a dominant force. He recorded several virtuoso solos that marked a return to the unbridled aggression of *The Man Who Sold The World*, and took all the keyboard parts as well.

The mosaic of rock styles the album contained was another pointer to the audacity of David's vision. The music darted between eras, embracing both the beginnings of rock and roll and its most modern tendencies, with stylistic glimpses of performers as diverse as Jimi Hendrix, Lou Reed and Marc Bolan. It also borrowed from other musical idioms, among them a Viennese waltz, soul music, and *West Side Story*.

The album began with 'Five Years', a song that immediately brought to the fore one of the themes that had dominated David's family mythology. The glimpses of war and destruction seen in David's earlier lyrics now became a prediction of full-scale apocalypse, five years hence. It was signalled – like the civil strife in Shakespeare's *Julius Caesar* – by omens in the streets: a woman hitting "tiny children", a soldier with a broken arm, a policeman kissing the feet of a priest, sung at first in the tone of quiet menace David had employed in 'The Bewlay Brothers', rising gradually to a note of anger mixed with despair.

The notion of Doomsday also served as an encapsulation of David's fascination with time. It gained in potency from the lyric's role as a love ballad: when David sang "We've got five years," it appeared as a cry of rage at the transience of human experience, sharpened by the culminating discordancy of the track. Significantly, David also showed his ability to distance himself from his stark message, when he stepped away from his lyric to comment: "I felt like an actor," and "don't think you knew you were in this song."

The second and third tracks – 'Soul Love' and 'Moonage Daydream' – showed, by taking up the love theme of 'Five Years', that David was as preoccupied with the nature of love and affection as he had been on the 1967 Deram album. But here the old equation was neatly reversed. Whereas the Deram album had portrayed a fantasy love which took David into a make-believe world, on *Ziggy Stardust* a fantasy figure had come to describe the reality of love and sex, told with the benefit of David's wide-ranging experiences.

In 'Soul Love', there was the innocence of "new love" between a boy and girl, speaking

> New words – that only they can share in . . .

which was also the "idiot love" that

> . . . descends on those defenceless

– as it had done on David and Hermione.

There was the pure love that parents feel, "sweeping over 'cross a baby"; and a mother's grieving love, kneeling at the graveside, for a son who has died.

'Moonage Daydream' described the love that is expressed through sexual passion:

> Make me baby, make me know you really care,
> Make me jump into the air.

Both this and the previous lyric also contained allusions to religious love, like the references to God and priest in 'Soul Love', and "the church of man, love", in 'Moonage Daydream'. The harsher lyric had its parallel in the strident rock introduction, which gave way, first, to fracturing and overlapping voices, and then a rising solo by Mick Ronson, suggesting the heavenward direction of David's imagination.

Both the music, and David's unlikely use of Christian symbolism, acted as a bridge to the more familiar figure of David's messiah or guru, who in the next lyric, 'Starman', fused with the "starman waiting in the sky". 'Starman' contained other visionary forms, such as ethereal voices and heavenly lights. Not for the first time, it linked these with another of David's most persistent themes, the harking back to childhood, expressed through the nostalgic couplet which David sang in his mock-infantile voice:

> If we can sparkle he may land tonight,
> Don't tell your poppa . . .

The lyric also reinforced the intermittent suspicion, first voiced in 'Five Years', that perhaps all of this is merely some media event: "switch on the TV," David suggests:

. . . we may pick him on channel two.

The last track on the side, 'It Ain't Easy', by Ray Davies of the Kinks, was the only song David did not write himself. Its opening words showed its appeal to David, for it told of climbing "to the top of the mountain" and looking out "over the sea", thereby reintroducing the travelling and searching theme that had dominated *The Man Who Sold The World*.

The opening track on side two, 'Lady Stardust', continued the word-play on the different meanings of "star". The lyric appeared to be a tribute to another of David's colleagues and heroes – but which one? Later, David was to perform it against a backdrop showing Marc Bolan, but the description of the character's "bright blue jeans" and "animal grace" applied equally to Iggy Pop. Whoever it was, David made clear the hidden longing he felt through the phrase "a love I could not obey", which echoed the lament of Oscar Wilde's lover, Lord Alfred Douglas, for "the love that dare not speak its name".

There was an element of parody in the exaggerated piano and bravura singing of 'Lady Stardust', and the same was true of the next track, 'Star', which hammered out a standard rock formula. The lyric used a form that David had devised in his earliest work. Like 'The Gospel According To Tony Day', it recited what had happened to David's friends. Now, one had gone to fight in Belfast, while another stayed at home "to starve". David cited his own aspirations to become "a rock 'n' roll star", which had merged with his quest for stability and selfhood; and he predicted that through taking the role of star he could achieve all that he desired: wealth and fame, affection and peace.

> I could fall asleep at night as a rock 'n' roll star,
> I could fall in love all right as a rock 'n' roll star.

The title of the next track, 'Hang On To Yourself', was a reminder to David of the importance of not losing control during his quest. The lyric was a celebration of sex as sheer sensation, in utter contrast to the romanticism of 'Soul Love', and matched by another rock formula, this time driving guitars and low, breathless choruses. David's partner was a "tongue-twisting storm" who

> Wants my honey not my money she's a funky-thigh collector.

It portrayed lovers who "don't talk much, just ball and play" and

265

who move "like tigers on Vaseline", and it contained the rock and roller's ultimate image of illicit love:

The bitter comes out better on a stolen guitar . . .

Throughout the album, David had shifted his stance constantly: sometimes it appeared he was the spaceman, Ziggy; sometimes he was watching from afar. In the next track, 'Ziggy Stardust', he could have been either. Certainly, the description of the guitarist "with God given ass" who "took it all too far" could apply to David himself. But then he appeared as a musician in Ziggy's group, torn by contradictory and violent desires towards his leader. There was a spate of homosexual allusions, with Ziggy "loaded" and "well hung"; at the same time David was envious of Ziggy – "we bitched about his fans" – and wondered whether to "crush his sweet hands".

The lyric ended with a foreboding coda. David described his process of self-examination in narcissistic terms – "making love with his ego" – and suggested that it was doomed to fail, for Ziggy became "a leper messiah" – another image of loneliness to suggest the leader or guru whom everybody shuns. Finally the earlier threat comes good: Ziggy is killed by his fans, and the band breaks up.

The penultimate track, 'Suffragette City', was equally despairing in its own way, with sexual passion reduced to an experience of the most predatory kind, framed in another expertly raucous, hard-driving rock setting. David sang of the "mellow-thighed chick" who "put my spine out of space", before disposing of her with the coarse valediction:

Wham bam thank-you ma'am!

Then came the album's astonishing climax, 'Rock 'N' Roll Suicide'. It began, to a deceptively muted guitar, with Ziggy the superstar lurching home at dawn, confused, unable to love, and contemplating suicide. Then, with the music building in a crescendo, the twin personas who have appeared throughout the album, David the performer and David the observer, merged into one. At first, David watched Ziggy from the wings; then his character became Ziggy's. Finally, David ended Ziggy's torment in an act of self-immolation. At that moment David stepped out of the character again, escaping death himself. It was a moment of release in which he discovered he could achieve love and human contact at last. It was thus an act of catharsis, with David purging all the fears that Ziggy embodied; an act of purifying psychodrama, sanctified by the audience's applause.

The *Ziggy Stardust* album was thus a breathtaking version of David's dance with death: the cautious minuet, with David taking Ziggy, the *doppelgänger*, as his partner, had become a whirling tarantella. It was also a dance with madness, with the brief cameos of 'The Width Of A Circle' amplified into a vast and overwhelming landscape. For David was acting out a new role, that of the schizophrenic, and in doing so he ventured to the edge of insanity and peered into its depths.

The monster seen in 'The Width Of A Circle' had assumed many guises: alligator, freak, space invader, transformation, wild mutation – even Ziggy himself and his band, the Spiders From Mars. There was host of "family" references throughout the album: mothers, ma, son, baby, children, together with one use of "in-sane". David depicted voices and god-like figures in the sky, flashing and glittering lights, monsters and aliens arriving on earth; he portrayed feelings of being an outsider, of being threatened by ray-guns and "'lectric eyes", of assuming the character of another person. The concept at the very heart of the album, of inhabiting the character of Ziggy, had close similarities with some schizophrenics' strategy of adopting a series of personas as if searching for one that will allow them to function and survive.

There was a further parallel at the climax of the album: many schizophrenics dislike being touched for fear of being contaminated by those around them. David appeared to confront exactly that fear in the final lines of 'Rock 'N' Roll Suicide', following Ziggy's suicide. Investing a hackneyed show-business cry with devastating new force, David implored his audience to reach out and touch him again.

> You're wonderful – gimme your hands

Applaud me, touch me, David sang; for I am free.

When the recording was over, and Ken Scott withdrew to the mixing studio, neither he nor the band were aware how far David proposed to extend the concept at the heart of the album. "We recorded *Ziggy* but we never knew what it was going to do," Trevor Bolder said later. "We just rehearsed and put the tracks down and he said, 'This is Ziggy Stardust,' and we thought, This is the end of it, that's just the name of the album." But then "David started dragging us downstairs" at Haddon Hall.

"Downstairs" meant into the basement flat occupied by Zowie's semi-official nanny, Susie Frost. She was a proficient seamstress who now joined the band of dressmakers whom David had cajoled into helping his career. And so, says Trevor, from what he had supposed was merely an album, Ziggy "slowly worked into a band with costumes".

The clothes that Trevor, Woody and Mick tried on had their origins in the costumes the Hype had worn at the Round House in 1970: lurex breeches, calf-length lace-up boots, glittering sequinned zip-up bomber jackets, and – for David – a green chequered one-piece costume much like a flying-suit. David told the band to grow their hair as long as possible, and the tumbling blond locks which the *Pork* cast had admired were soon cascading around Mick's face, while Trevor developed shoulder-length black hair and dangling fuzzy side-whiskers.

David also persuaded his band to do something he had been urging his bands to do ever since the days of the Lower Third: to wear make-up. Previously his colleagues had been put off by the bluntness of his approach; this time, a policy of stealth proved effective. "If he'd pushed it at us, we might have pulled away thinking, What's he trying to do?" said Trevor; "he just slowly did it for us." The greatest surprise, particularly to himself, was that Mick Ronson, having first regarded London as a latter-day Sodom, now discovered unsuspected corners of his personality. "I wore make-up even before David," he says. "I used to love getting into the eye-shadow and mascara stuff, loved it."

There was, however, a confusion at the heart of these developments. Was it Mick, Woody and Trevor who were dressing up? Or were they playing the parts of the Spiders From Mars, just as David was playing Ziggy? Later David implied that he was happy to leave the matter unresolved. "I liked the ambiguity of not being able to separate the personas," he said. "It's the ominous enigma of the split personality and which side is which . . ."

The band, David added, "played the part perfectly – they were a number-one spacey punk-rock band, they were absolute archetypes, everyone was right out of a cartoon book". He also suggested that the band were not astute enough to tell the difference. "They just knew they were in a band called the Spiders. They were sort of playing the part. But for them, they really were the Spiders."

It followed from what David said that he was aware himself that he was playing a part. The time would come, as it had for Tony Zanetta and the cast of *Pork*, when David would be dangerously close to confusing performance and reality. For the moment, what was significant was that David was determined to portray Ziggy as a character on stage. The birth of Ziggy, in a concert tour that began in February 1972, was to be one of the most explosive events in the story of rock music. It was also another landmark in David's personal odyssey. The cathartic gain from writing lyrics was no longer enough; now David would act out the part in a manner that would give Ziggy both life and death, and that would begin to free him out of his fears.

As the creation of Ziggy proceeded, Defries was laying his plans. What was remarkable was the extent to which they ran parallel to David's. It was as if the two men were instinctively on the same wavelength; or were growing together intellectually, in the same way as David and Angie had merged their sexual identities, resulting in an uncanny symbiosis of thoughts and goals. David had taken his band of rude mechanicals and shaped them into the image he desired. In preparation for the concert tour, Defries was surrounding himself with a youthful and innocent entourage, who knew even less about the entertainment industry than he did, and was moulding them to play their parts in the making of a star.

Among Defries's recruits was Stuey George. He was that rare being, at least for the early 1970s, a black Yorkshireman, one of only "six or seven coloured families", he says, then living in Hull. His father, a seaman from St Lucia, had settled in Hull before the war. Stuey's first aim on leaving school had been to become a motor mechanic, but he was told "we only have white boys at our garage". He worked for a time at the Hull fish docks and then joined the music business.

Stuey met Mick Ronson and Woody Woodmansey, and worked with local bands as stage manager, roadie and "gofer" (the industry's name for general factotum or dogsbody, referring to someone who will "go for" cigarettes, beer, or whatever else is momentarily required). Eventually, Mick telephoned him in Hull and summoned him to Haddon Hall. By then Stuey had a physique like an American football player: a squat, tank-like frame, with massive thighs and shoulders crowned by a bullet-like head. The role that Defries selected for him was as minder for David.

Defries began as if he was strippng down Stuey's personality in order to start anew. Defries would chair long, probing discussions whose participants were expected to reveal all there was to know about themselves. "He wanted to know *everything*," says Stuey. "Had you been in trouble, why were you in trouble, what made you do it, would you do it again, did you get satisfaction from it?" Yet Defries revealed little about himself: "All the time I was with Tony Defries, no one would turn round and say, 'I knew Tony Defries,'" Stuey relates. "Tony would only tell you what he wanted you to know. He would tell you snippets."

Then Defries began Stuey's education. "He taught you everything – anything you didn't know you got to know," Stuey says. It began with the minutiae of social behaviour – "from how you tied your shoelaces to what day you didn't wear a tie" – and embraced the principles of business management: "wheeling and dealing, style, correct manner, contracts, recording deals, the whole schmoozle".

Defries imparted some of the highly individual business precepts he had been devising, which seemed particularly appropriate to the world of show business. First, never be intimidated by the status of those you are dealing with. "No matter how much money a man's got or how much he thinks he's got," he told Stuey, "never be frightened by him."

Second, be prepared to gamble, and do so with the utter conviction – like the gambler of Dostoevsky's story – that you will win. Third, set no limit to your aspirations. "He'd tell us to go into a bank and ask to borrow a million pounds without knowing when you will pay it back and the bank will lend it to you for your sheer cheek."

Inevitably, Defries talked of Colonel Parker, relating the dancing chickens story on more than one occasion. Eventually, when he had Defries's measure, Stuey divined that he was aiming to set up a replica of "the guys" or the "Memphis Mafia", the entourage of jovial, smartly dressed young men who surrounded Elvis and humoured his every wish, but through whom Parker exerted his control. Stuey believed that Defries wanted an "inner corps" who would "match the Presley thing". He understood that he was "to look after David and keep business together while Defries wasn't there"; Defries told him that when on tour, he and David must be together "twenty-four hours a day, seven days a week".

Above all, Defries's instructions concerned the ostentatious expenditure of money. "He taught us etiquette and the rules," says Stuey. "He would take everybody out for the whole kit and have slap-up meals. He would teach you what to order, what is good, what is bad, years of wine – everything." Sometimes Defries would book David and Stuey into a West End hotel, such as the Dorchester or Brown's, where they became acquainted with the delights of room service. "He took us from stage to stage up the ladder," says Stuey. "It was like the movie days when they'd take a starlet and create a star. He said, 'When I'm ready then we'll do it for real.'"

As Defries built up his entourage, his recruits were almost invariably young men and women with little experience of the entertainment world, and ideal subjects, therefore, for the all-embracing tutelage Defries wished to impart. Will Palin, for example, was hired as a road and equipment manager on the strength of having helped to supervise a rehearsal studio in Greenwich where David went to practise. Dai Davies was a struggling freelance journalist from Wales before Defries engaged him as a publicist. When Defries asked him what salary he wanted, Davies cautiously suggested £35–£40 a week. "That's not enough," Defries told him. "You must have £100" – although Defries added that he intended RCA to foot the bill.

Many of the recruits were exposed to a technique that helps explain why Defries was so persuasive a tutor. Sometimes he adopted a soft and beguiling tone that could become almost mesmeric, as Mick Ronson, for one, discovered. "He had a really nice voice, one of those voices that are really soothing," Mick says. "He'd sit and talk and he'd got such a great voice to listen to and he seemed to know about everything. He seemed so smart and I was just a dumb kid from Yorkshire and I was really impressed. I loved it when he talked. I could have sat and listened to him all night long."

The photographer Mick Rock, who joined the entourage that year, remembers Defries's "hypnotic way of talking – quiet, reassuring – he practised that kind of hypnotism on me and it stuck in my mind".

The admiration that Defries inspired could be awesome. Another who fell under his spell was Melanie McDonald, a slim, waif-like woman, who became involved with him at this time, and remained with him for almost ten years, later giving birth to their daughter, Fleur. Defries, she says, "was the most amazing man I ever came across. He knew what he was doing all the time and he was right all the time. I've never known him to be wrong. He is right and he just knows it. He knows something's going to happen and it happens. It's amazing."

Another characteristic shared by David and Defries was the ability to present a different face to different people, as circumstances required. If Defries's intimates saw a generous and reassuring figure, those outside the entourage encountered someone very different. Soon after David had signed his contract with RCA in New York, RCA's London office received Defries's first visit. The marketing manager was Geoff Hannington, an engaging Londoner with the sense of humour vital for surviving in RCA, whose internecine conflicts could be felt even in its overseas outposts. Defries, Hannington soon found, was "a fairly bombastic character". What was more, he came into the London office in Curzon Street "with a *fait accompli*".

Hannington became acquainted with Defries and David after hearing a tape of *Hunky Dory*, which Defries had just presented to RCA's London boss, a bluff New Yorker named Ken Glancey. "I personally thought *Hunky Dory* was a work of genius," says Hannington. "The songs were so strong, I couldn't believe what I was hearing. I was listening to the tapes all day long." Hannington was responsible for deciding how the album should be marketed and at what cost, and usually had considerable autonomy. But a shock awaited him when he met Defries. "We discussed what we should do," says Hannington. "Or rather, he told me what he wanted us to do."

The *fait accompli* which Defries presented to RCA in London was neat and inescapable. During his negotiations in New York, he had asked RCA for full control over how David was to be marketed. Since Defries was prepared to accept such a modest advance – and since David was due to be launched in London anyway, which made it somebody else's problem – New York readily agreed. Now Defries had arrived to insist that RCA in London fulfil the contract to the letter. Hannington had no choice but to comply, and Defries pressed his advantage to the full. "He was a fairly demanding character," says Hannington; "although very good for his artist, I should think."

It was Hannington's task to handle the cover of *Hunky Dory*. Normally, he would have asked RCA's art department to design it; where David was concerned, he soon learned, "a sleeve for an album would be done and I would be presented with it". In the case of *Hunky Dory*, Hannington was presented with "a very strange picture of David looking like a girl".

The photograph – taken by Brian Ward – showed David staring wistfully into space and looking for all the world like Greta Garbo; to accentuate its misty, dream-like quality, the original photograph had been hand-coloured by David's friend George Underwood. Hannington says that although he had no personal qualms about the photograph, he was sure that there would be problems among RCA's distributors. "I thought it might be a drawback at a store like W. H. Smith's – the head buyer of Smith's is going to say, 'What is this?'" Hannington also admits that at that time he was at a loss to know how to sell the record. "I could never see it being pinpointed in the marketplace . . . I had no idea how to market it other than shouting from the rooftops, 'Here it is.'"

Such a plan was bound to create problems within RCA, riven by politics as it was. Among Hannington's colleagues, the most aggrieved was the head of A and R, Mike Everett, who saw no reason why RCA in London should waste its budget promoting New York's artists at the expense of those he had signed in Britain, and wasted no opportunity to say so. In the traditional RCA manner, Everett embarked on a campaign to exact revenge from the man he held responsible, Dennis Katz.

According to Katz, Everett "hated Defries with a passion – and he tried to get me fired". On his next visit to Britain, Katz confronted Everett and told him: "If you have problems working with Defries, I'm sorry, but what can I tell you? I can't get your approval of every manager of every act that we want to sign in the United States." In the end, Katz says, Everett "backed off".

It remained difficult for Hannington to carry through the marketing strategy for *Hunky Dory* that Defries demanded. With RCA's London boss, Ken Glancey, continually voicing his doubts, he found himself virtually isolated: "They were almost washing their hands of Mr Bowie and leaving it to me," Hannington says. But the combination of David and Defries proved a powerful spur. Hannington found talking to David immensely stimulating – "he was a very creative person with many ideas" – while Defries remained ever-watchful over RCA's plans, telephoning Hannington "at all hours" to check what the company was doing. "The guy," says Hannington, "was paranoid about his artist."

Almost despite himself, Hannington found that he responded by seeking to please them both, drawing up plans for a campaign centred on lavish advertising in the music press. "Somehow it generated the feeling in me that I had to do these things," Hannington says. "It was very strange."

The progress of *Hunky Dory*, however, did not ease Hannington's problems. When the album was released just before Christmas 1971, its initial sales barely reached 2,000 a month. Ken Glancey took to asking Hannington: "Why are you spending all this money on Bowie? The record's not selling."

Hannington faced further difficulties. Almost from the start of the *Hunky Dory* campaign, he knew that he would soon have to alter his tack. Defries had warned him that David would be presenting a totally different image on his next album, *Ziggy Stardust*. "Tony was already talking to us about the plans and some of the songs," Hannington says. "We knew we were in a situation where the artist was going to change like a chameleon from time to time. That was made very explicit."

By the end of 1971, much else about the launching of Ziggy was being made explicit. One evening in November, David and Angie invited the young publicist Dai Davies for dinner at Haddon Hall to discuss the forthcoming tour. Davies, who had not yet discovered just what his job involved, was unsure what to expect when he arrived. "I still felt that my appointment was pretty silly," he says. "I was so inexperienced at the time – although it was the same for everyone else."

But David appeared utterly certain of himself and what he intended to do, not only in the role of Ziggy but also in that of star. He talked of the achievements of Iggy Pop and Lou Reed, and also of the lessons of Colonel Parker. He relayed Defries's story of the dancing chickens, and told one of his own. Once Parker had run a hot-dog stand selling hot-dogs which consisted of a piece of sausage at each end and a large gap in between. Parker scattered scraps of sausage on the ground, so that if his customers complained that the middle of their hot-dog was missing, he could tell them: "You must have dropped it."

For David, as for Defries, there was a direct link between Parker's brand of chicanery and the manufacture of glamour. David showed Davies the book *Hollywood Babylon* by Kenneth Anger which told of the scandals that lay behind Hollywood's façade, and later gave Davies his own copy. David described how Marlene Dietrich insisted on being photographed from the most favourable angle, and said he intended to do the same. He also boasted that he would always expect other people to open the door for him. "After that dinner it was as if he didn't notice a door had to be opened," says Davies. "Whether he was with a man or a woman, I never saw him open a door for himself again."

David laid out plans for press coverage which, Davies assumed, had emanated from his discussions with Defries. Once the tour was under way they intended to ban all interviews and to exert as much control as they could over the coverage they received. But first they planned to make a major announcement which would guarantee massive publicity. David said that he was intending to reveal that he was bisexual: to admit, so Davies recalls, "that he liked both men and women".

At first Davies was taken aback and told David that he thought such a move could prove counter-productive. By the end of the evening he had forgotten his reservations and was only too eager to play his part in establishing David as Ziggy and as star. "David made me see things in his light," Davies says. "He convinced me he was going to be massive. I was very impressed by his plans, and flattered to be included in them."

Of David's commitment, Davies was in no doubt. "He told me he was going to *be* Ziggy." Davies believed him.

19

Wham Bam

In January 1972, Britain was in a sullen mood. The government was headed by the taut figure of Edward Heath, a bachelor who appeared to derive his main pleasure in life, when not aboard a yacht, from playing the organ. Ranged against him in the New Year were Britain's miners, whose strike filled the papers with news of violent clashes on the picket lines for the rest of the month. There was a furore at the House of Commons when the Speaker suspended a sitting because of a protest by Labour MPs at unemployment reaching the unimaginable figure of one million. The IRA exploded sixteen bombs in a day in Northern Ireland, and there were fierce battles between gunmen and British soldiers. On January 30th, as if to demonstrate that the state would brook no further challenge, British paratroopers shot dead thirteen unarmed Catholics in disturbances following a civil rights march in Londonderry.

Ironically, 1971 had seen popular music continue its retreat as a vehicle of protest; by 1972, the youth rebellion appeared to have been subdued. But it also seemed that youth was awaiting for fresh emblems to represent them in more ambiguous and subversive forms. Early that year, David Bowie stepped forward to offer himself in their cause.

In mid-January, the first reviews for *Hunky Dory*, which had been released just before Christmas, appeared in the music press. They were the best by far that David had received. *Melody Maker* considered it "not only the best album Bowie has ever done, it's also the most inventive piece of song-writing to have appeared on record for a considerable time". It judged the song-writing "sublime", called Bowie "his own caricature as a priest of high camp", and saw him as "Mick Jagger's heir". The *New Musical Express* said that *Hunky Dory* represented Bowie "at his brilliant best".

The music papers decided it was time to find out more about David. One of the reporters who met him in the Gem offices was Michael Watts, who had recently joined *Melody Maker* from a provincial newspaper. Watts took a proprietorial view of Bowie, priding himself on having discovered him ahead of his rivals on *New Musical Express*. He found David wearing a patterned combat suit, skin-tight around his legs and crotch, seductively unbuttoned at the front to display David's pale and hairless torso. David's trousers were rolled up above a pair of red plastic boots sporting platform soles that Watts guessed were three inches high. "He looked extraordinary," Watts says today. "And he was undeniably camp."

The question of David's sexual preferences was one that music reporters had been ignoring for some time; one admitted later that he avoiding asking it for fear that his readers – and David's audiences – would have profound misgivings on learning that he was "bent". In keeping to the plans he had laid with Tony Defries, David was in fact only waiting for the question to be put, and had even tried to provoke reporters by talking unprompted about his dresses. And so, impelled by David's appearance, the question popped out of Watts's mouth: 'Are you gay?" he asked. Yes, David replied – and he always had been, "even when I was David Jones".

Watts returned to the *Melody Maker* offices in Fleet Street with the excitement reporters feel on finding themselves in the right place at the right time. His editors were equally gratified and splashed his story over two pages of the issue of January 22nd, accompanied by the headline, "Oh, You Pretty Thing".

It was a remarkable confession. Although five years had elapsed since the law was reformed, homosexuals in Britain remained a subdued minority. An article in the *Guardian* a day or so later reported the sense of oppression they still felt, with MPs reluctant to champion their cause, teachers failing to break down hostility, and parents guilty of ignorance and prejudice. In that climate, many in the burgeoning gay-rights movements saw David's statement as a public "coming-out" that would help give homosexuals confidence and pride, and so it proved.

It was a decisive landmark in the erosion of sexual stereotypes and the progress of sexual liberation, encompassing both the gay and women's movements, during the rest of the decade. Homosexuals also listened with new interest to the coded messages of David's lyrics, discovering their meaning long before it became generally available. *Gay News* began regular coverage of David's performances, and published photographs of him on the front cover.

Apart from the article in the *Guardian*, however, the national press ignored David's pronouncement. But the music press hastened to catch up on the story it had missed. *Disc* carried a report headed "Why Bowie Is Feeling Butch" and the *New Musical Express* followed with an article headlined with David's quote: "I'm not ashamed of wearing dresses."

It seems that even David was taken aback at the furore he had provoked. For he was also quoted as complaining that it all "unfortunately detracted from the fact that I'm also a songwriter". Elsewhere, others shared a sense of unease. At Gem, Laurence Myers felt that David was almost beyond redemption; and at RCA, David's pronouncement did nothing to assist Geoff Hannington. But he by now was resigned to his isolation, and felt that in any case David was merely confirming the message of the cover of *The Man Who Sold The World*. "It was clear that he wasn't Frank Sinatra," Hannington says.

One man who might have been expected to feel uplifted by David's revelation was Ken Pitt. But this was far from the campaign that Pitt had planned two years before, when he had hoped that David would come out as a "normal" homosexual with whom others could safely identify. David's flamboyant posturing, Pitt says, "was not what I had in mind at all". It had all been handled in a very "vulgar" fashion; worse still, those conducting the affair were not true sympathisers, but "people on the wrong side of the fence".

The first Ziggy concert was staged at the Toby Jug, at Tolworth in the Surrey commuter belt, on February 10th. It was an inauspicious beginning. The Toby Jug is a gaunt fortress of a pub, on the edge of an underpass, that was accustomed to presenting cabaret acts for its suburban clientele. According to Stuey George, ever-present at David's side, the audience were expecting "a northern-club-type act". When David arrived, having chosen to wear one of his dresses for Ziggy's opening night, "they didn't really know how to take it – he took their breath away for a while". And when the audience did recover their voice, it was not to express universal acclaim. "There were one or two heavy guys there," Stuey recalls. "The place had never had a guy wearing a dress and we got some hostile reactions."

Tolworth proved a happy aberration. From Surrey, the Ziggy show proceeded on a zig-zag tour of Britain, encompassing the major cities of Glasgow, Manchester, Birmingham and Liverpool; suburbs like Eltham and Croydon; provincial cities and towns such as Chichester, Yeovil and Bristol; seaside venues such as Portsmouth, Southampton and Bournemouth. It left audiences dazed.

The music journalist Mick Brown, who saw Ziggy at Epsom, found it "a unique mixture of the exciting, disturbing, amusing and bizarre. The audience went wild." Jane Sinclair, a schoolgirl in Manchester, who had queued outside the Hard Rock arena from 8 a.m. to be sure of a place at the front, thought the show "fantastic – the rapport with the audience was extraordinary". Geoff Hannington, who probably saw more Ziggy concerts than anyone else, felt "amazement, absolute amazement".

The *Worthing Herald* described how "the concert ended and the audience yelled for more". A reporter in Newcastle called David the "supreme showman", praised the band's "amazing sound quality", and described how the "audience welcomed every number with wild enthusiasm", with a "genuine spontaneous standing ovation" at the end. At a concert in Croydon, one thousand fans were turned away from the doors.

At the heart of the performance was David's stage relationship with Mick Ronson. Lithe and tantalising in their satiny, sensuous costumes, they flaunted themselves at the audience and at each other, provocatively working their guitars in an overtly sexual manner and achieving an electricity, as a pair, that Bowie would never recapture until his partnership with Mick Jagger in the video 'Dancing In The Streets' in 1985.

From his hesitant start, Mick Ronson was thoroughly caught up in the enterprise. "I got into it," Mick says. "I liked dressing up and I liked doing things on stage . . . I loved it, it makes you feel totally different, it made me feel like nothing else at all." Nor did he object when David proposed that they wear dresses on stage; instead, he worried over whether his dress was straight at the back.

The immense attention to detail brought the concerts acclaim from rock audiences grown accustomed to far more shabby treatment. David experimented continually to sharpen the act, with Angie a stalwart force, goading, stimulating, encouraging, at his side. If an audience proved slow to respond she would appear on stage to spur them to applause. She also made a brilliantly apposite proposal to heighten the show's climax at the end of 'Rock 'N' Roll Suicide', suggesting that when David sang the key line "Gimme your hands", he should gesture to the audience to reach out towards him; he should then dart forward and tantalisingly brush a few of the outstretched hands. As photographs of those early concerts show, it was a stunning success, with a sea of arms waving beseechingly, confirming David in his role as the star whose aura all around wish to share.

It was Angie, too, who conferred on David a dramatic change

of appearance, bestowing on him the hairstyle that became the greatest single hallmark of the Ziggy days. Shortly before the tour began, David's hair had been cut into a tidy blond crop for the cover of the *Ziggy* album; in Brian Ward's photograph, taken in a deserted London back street at dusk, he presented an image of urban loneliness that recalled the 1950s cigarette advertisement "You're never alone with a Strand". (The advertisement won numerous prizes but did nothing to assist the sales of Strand cigarettes.) After Angie's intervention, David's hair was styled in a far more distinctive manner – although that was not exactly how it was first intended.

Towards the end of February, in a lull between concerts, Angie asked a young local hairdresser named Suzi Fussey to come to Haddon Hall to cut her hair. Suzi, who worked at the Evelyn Paget salon in Beckenham High Street, was delighted: she considered Angie "wild, wacky and wonderful – the most exciting thing to hit Beckenham before or since", and she and the other assistants would rush to the window when Angie and David passed. Suzi also knew about David from cutting his mother's hair, for Peggy talked about him incessantly. But when Suzi arrived at Haddon Hall, Angie had forgotten that she had asked her to come. On the spur of the moment, she asked Suzi to cut David's hair instead.

David was already ahead of fashion by wearing his hair short at a time when long hair remained *de rigueur*. But Suzi thought it an unimaginative "Rod Stewartish" cut and was sure it could be improved. She cropped David's hair even shorter at the crown but allowed it to fall over his neck. She cut it short at the front too, then made it stand erect by dousing it with a dandruff treatment named Guard that contained a strong setting lotion. Suzi and Angie considered the outcome most effective; David emphatically did not. "The next morning, when he woke up," Suzi reports, "he freaked out."

Angie telephoned Suzi as if there were a medical emergency – "everything was high drama with those two," Suzi says – and asked her to come back to Haddon Hall. There was little that Suzi could do as David's hair was so short already. Angie's solution was to make it more outrageous still. Since David's hair was blond, she suggested dyeing it red, and David agreed. "It's got to be the reddest red," Angie told Suzi. "So I did a lot of messing around with different colours," Suzi says, "and we came up with this red-hot colour." David declared himself satisfied, and so Ziggy's distinctive vermilion hairstyle, to be vastly emulated by David's fans, was born.

Back on the tour, David was now determined to be more audacious still; and another crucial moment in Ziggy's evolution ensued. On June 21st, the concert reached Dunstable. Without apparent warning, as the group was performing 'Suffragette City', David knelt before Mick Ronson, thrust one leg between his, clutched Mick's buttocks, and gulped at the strings of his guitar, in an unmistakable act of simulated fellatio. The moment was captured by the photographer Mick Rock, who had been following David since March. "It was just there and bang, I'd got it," Rock says.

In Mick Rock's photograph, some of the audience appear non-plussed while others are laughing; several are transfixed. Mick Rock believes that his photograph captured a pivotal moment in rock music. Hitherto it had been almost an exclusively macho affair; by taking the female role in an act of simulated fellatio – whether homosexual or heterosexual was not important – Mick Rock believes that David provided "the most potent symbol of rock and roll androgyny", even more so than the cover of *The Man Who Sold The World* or David's statement, "I am gay."

It could also be taken as a moment that signalled the new form of protest that David embodied. As audiences came to respond to his ambiguous but unashamed eroticism, they were also endorsing his attack on orthodoxy and convention. When that response combined with the feelings of loneliness and alienation that his lyrics stirred, David became, for the thousands who saw him, an emblem of his age.

By Mick Rock's account, David himself was aware of the implications of his action. As soon as the concert was over he asked Rock if he had captured it on film and asked him to process it as quickly as possible. "He was very fast, very hot to see it," Rock says. Not long afterwards, at the behest of David and Defries, RCA distributed the photograph to all and sundry as part of their publicity drive for the tour, and it has become another icon of those times. But that moment was not, as some have fondly imagined, a spontaneous one, born of the thrill of the live performance. In fact, according to Stuey George, it was conceived during the long discussions that took place – sometimes in the Gem offices, sometimes at Haddon Hall – over how the group could cause "a stir". Mick Ronson had already been emulating Jimi Hendrix by playing his guitar with his teeth: "David suggested taking it a stage further," Stuey says, "and Angie was enthusiastic." Stuey adds: "What you have to remember is that with David *everything* was choreographed."

The faithful Michael Watts apart, the music press were slow to awake to what was happening out on the Ziggy tour. Their reviewers were in consequence hard put to appreciate the special qualities of the *Ziggy Stardust* album when it was released in June, even though it went directly to nineteenth position in the *Melody Maker* chart. The *Record Mirror* hedged its bets by saying that David was "totally individual" and his albums "like no other". *Sounds*, missing the point entirely, judged that "much of it could have been the work of a competent plagiarist." The most sympathetic and accurate review came from Watts himself. "There are odd songs and references to the business of being a pop star that overall add up to a strong sense of biographical drama," he wrote; "Bowie's bid for stardom is accelerating at lightning speed."

A concert in London on July 8th at last brought David more substantial notices. When the environmental pressure group Friends of the Earth organised a concert at the Festival Hall to aid their campaign to save the world's whales, David – who was now commanding fees of up to £450 – agreed to take part for no fee and £200 expenses, most of it used on hiring equipment and staff. It was a worthwhile investment on David's part. He and the Spiders performed part of the *Ziggy* repertoire, and for the first time won appreciative notices in the weightier sections of the British press. In the *Guardian*, Robin Denselow found David "amazingly enough, a remarkable performer", and Michael Wale of *The Times* called him a "T. S. Eliot with a rock and roll beat". Best of all was *Melody Maker*, where Ray Coleman described David as "oozing with histrionic confidence", his performance exuding "glitter, panache and pace", all under the headline: 'A Star Is Born'.

The Save the Whales concert was also notable for the presence of two of the performers David most respected, and the absence of a third. David, in fact, had been consorting with all three that year, as he continued to seek the company of those performers with qualities he coveted for himself.

Iggy Pop had been in Britain since February: he had arrived at Heathrow airport with little more than the jeans and T-shirt he stood up in, and it had taken all the resources and clout of Defries and Myers to secure his entry. It was Defries's custom, in this as in other matters, to humour David's wishes, and since David said he wanted to work with Iggy, Defries persuaded CBS to pay him an advance of $25,000. It was, naturally, channelled through Gem, who reserved the customary two-elevenths royalty for themselves. Iggy was lodged at the Royal Garden Hotel in Kensington and despite some impressive bills his account with Gem was showing a marginal profit of just under £1,000 at the end of June.

For the time being, the most noticeable sign of Iggy's influence on David came early in the Ziggy tour, when during a concert at London's Imperial College, David attempted to walk out across his audience's shoulders in the manner perfected by Iggy; it was a dismal failure, for the audience was spread far too thin, and David subsided ignominiously to the floor. Later, David helped Iggy produce his album for CBS, *Raw Power*. When the album was eventually released in June 1973, it flopped; but David was to resume his relationship with Iggy two years later, to far more significant effect.

Lou Reed's collaboration with David had an equally dramatic beginning. He arrived from New York on the day before the Save the Whales concert and went directly to the studio in Greenwich where David was rehearsing. After a brief practice he consumed an impossible amount of Scotch and became, says David's equipment manager Will Palin, "somewhat inebriated".

Reed joined David on stage at the Festival Hall and performed three of his classic numbers, 'White Light/White Heat', 'Waiting For My Man', and 'Sweet Jane'. Ray Coleman found Reed "beautifully earthy, cool, and all-knowing", a judgment all the more remarkable given the condition in which Reed had reached the Festival Hall. Will Palin half-carried him on to the stage, handed him his guitar, and helped him off again afterwards. "He was absolutely out of his head," says one of those present. "I don't know if he was stoned or pissed or what . . ."

Later that year David and Mick Ronson produced Reed's album *Transformer* which was issued by RCA and contained Reed's classic number, 'Walk On The Wild Side', a passing parade of members of the Warhol *galère* in New York. From David's point of view, its most memorable aspect was the elegant and evocative solo on baritone saxophone – played by his former music teacher, Ronnie Ross.

For Ross the greatest surprise came when he discovered that the David Bowie who hired him for the session was the David Jones he had taught ten years before. "Never in a million years", he says, would he have connected the two. Ross had been telephoned and asked if he could play "West Coast jazz"; when Ross replied that he could, he was invited to play for Lou Reed, of whom he had never heard. He arrived in an empty studio, listened to the track, and added his contribution in two takes.

Then David, whom he had glimpsed in the control room, came

into the studio. "He had make-up on and it didn't register at first," says Ross; "I was amazed." Ross enjoyed talking to David and never lost his respect for him thereafter: "I think he's incredible," Ross says. "I love people who are that positive about their way of life." Ross's solo helped make 'Walk On The Wild Side' a major hit as a single in both Britain and the US; he was paid the standard session fee of the time, £9.

The third performer with whom David struck a relationship that year – and who was noticeable by his absence from the Festival Hall – was Ian Hunter of the British group, Mott the Hoople. The quality David most envied in the group was their ability to strike a rapport with their live audiences, inspired by their raw and aggressive style, and the earthy repartee of Hunter himself, their lead singer. David contacted the group and arranged to meet them backstage after a concert of theirs at Guildford. It appears that David was almost as nervous as his own fans when meeting other stars whose approval he desired.

Perhaps surprisingly too, given his own skill at playing the media game, he had been beguiled by aspects of the group's publicity. "David was trembling," says Hunter. "He had this big thing, he thought we were very heavy dudes. He used to tell people I was the head of a motorcycle gang and he had this very heavy deal about us."

The encounter left Mott the Hoople immensely suspicious in turn. At that time they were close to splitting up, since they had been quite unable to match the intensity of their stage performances when in the recording studio. To their amazement, since they could not understand why David did not want to record it himself, David offered them a song he had just written, 'All The Young Dudes'. The lyric had all of David's customary ambiguity, being an account of youth rebellion with strong sexual undercurrents. Mott the Hoople recorded it without delay at the Olympic studios, with David doing most of the producing and arranging. Hunter was delighted with the result: "It was obvious that it was a hit."

Soon afterwards David produced an album, *All The Young Dudes*, for the group, sessions that Hunter looks back on with unreserved admiration. "David was one of the few people who can walk in and there is magic in the room. He has a very inquisitive mind, he's fast, and you feel that the guy knows more than you do so you put yourself in his hands. That has never happened before or since with me."

Equipped with the recordings, Tony Defries obtained an advance of $50,000 for the group from CBS, who released 'All The Young

Dudes' as a single in July. It appealed strongly to what one reviewer termed "the solidarity of the disaffected", and was promptly adopted as an anthem, in Hunter's words, by "the closet gays". It reached number three in the singles chart, while the album reached number twenty-one. Laurence Myers meanwhile kept his customary profit-and-loss account, reserving the usual two-elevenths royalty for Gem. Mott the Hoople showed a surplus of £2,603.92 in June and a deficit of £2,017.05 in October.

But still the group remained wary of David's intentions, finding it hard to accept that he was acting from purely altruistic motives. Ian Hunter believed that by working with Mott the Hoople, David hoped to acquire the same rapport with his audiences that they had achieved. "The type of thing that Mott had that he never had was humanity," Hunter says. "I think he was upset because he never had riots. People were too polite to riot at his concerts." Hunter also believes that David did extract what he wanted from their partnership. "He sucks, like Dracula. He sucks what he can get and then he moves on to another victim."

And so, when David asked if Mott the Hoople would open the concert at the Festival Hall, Hunter declined. Feeling that their relationship was never free of a competitive edge, he suspects that David might have cast Mott the Hoople in a support role, "with a lousy sound system", for twenty minutes. "You pass like a mild irritation in the evening," Hunter adds. "I knew what the bugger was up to."

Hunter was cautious on another score too: he was being subjected to the blandishments of Tony Defries. "He'd sit and talk for hours," Hunter says. "A very fascinating guy, Tony, but when it came down to money, it was weird." Although Defries acted as the group's manager for a time, they never signed a formal agreement. Defries distributed contracts among the group, hoping, says Hunter, "that a couple of suckers would sign . . . I immediately collected them and took them home and put them under the piano stool. Now and again he'd say, 'Where's the contracts?' and I'd say somebody forgot."

Hunter had to withstand pressure from David too. "David was in love with us and wanted Tony to manage us," he says. "David said to me, 'Trust him with your life.' David also said to me, 'McGovern is going to be the next president.'"

As the tour swept on, and the performances became more polished and assured, the entourage Defries was building around David became tighter and more compact. At first it had returned to

London whenever possible; in June, it began to set up camp at hotels, commuting to the concerts within a convenient radius. The story of Ziggy now entered a decisive new stage, for this period marked the beginning of "the bubble".

For those involved, it was as if they were immured in a self-sustaining capsule where the outside world became irrelevant. One who experienced the illusion was Suzi Fussey, soon to leave the Evelyn Paget salon in Beckenham and become the group's full-time hairdresser. "We were all protected," she says. "You could try and do anything, put pins in it, but you couldn't burst that bubble, and wherever we were it was always the same."

Stuey George found himself firmly inside the bubble too. "Who paid was nothing to do with us. We were cushioned. Money — never worry about money. It was the feeling, everything was done. Defries looked after all that. If we were supposed to leave for somewhere, the tickets would arrive. You didn't have to worry. You knew that everything was taken care of."

Although Defries remained an inscrutable figure, even to those closest to him, this too seemed to form part of his plans. "Tony never talked about what he intended," says his girlfriend, Melanie McDonald. "It just happened. It was like going along in the bubble. You didn't question it."

As the bubble continued to swell, it also became a hothouse where both creative ideas and eccentricities could flourish. Later David was to admit that there had been a time when he lost control of the character he created in Ziggy. Stimulated by the balmy atmosphere of the bubble, that process began in the summer of 1972. Previously David had successfully distanced himself from the character of Ziggy. Now the distinction was becoming blurred, and in the drive for publicity David's frailties and anxieties were taken hold of and magnified.

RCA's Geoff Hannington had originally observed how David referred to Ziggy — and even, disconcertingly, himself — as "a third person, another entity". Now, at Defries's prompting, RCA issued posters proclaiming that David *was* Ziggy. At the same time, David, Angie, Defries and other members of the entourage continued to search for ways of winning publicity. Out of this came David's endlessly cited fear of aeroplanes and his vastly inconvenient decision never to fly in them again.

One account to gain credence was that David's decision followed a stormy flight he and Angie took after visiting Angie's parents in Cyprus in 1971. In fact, David was still flying with apparent aplomb in the summer of 1972, as his touring schedule became increasingly demanding. He flew to Newcastle on June 2nd and returned to Heathrow on June 9th; he made a day trip to Manchester to record a television appearance for Granada on June 15th. He even flew to New York for a weekend, leaving London on a TWA flight on June 9th to join Defries in meetings with RCA, and returning to London on June 12th. But by the time of his next visit to the US in September, as was made well known to the press, he insisted on travelling – in appropriate style – on the *QE2*.

According to Stuey George, the decision that David should not fly again emanated from another of the late-night discussions at the Gem offices. Accounts differ over just how substantial David's original fear was. "He wasn't that bothered," says Stuey. "He *was* frightened," says Angie, "so that was worked into the promotional garbage." Either way, Stuey says that the idea was crystallised by Defries. "Elvis Presley wouldn't fly," says Stuey. "So he decided David wouldn't fly or drive."

Then David's alleged dislike of flying was elaborated into a general phobia of heights: "That was all publicity too," says Stuey. At one of the Gem meetings, David mentioned that he had heard in Los Angeles that, because of the threat of earthquakes, it was safest to ask for hotel rooms near the ground floor. "That was thrown into the melting pot," Stuey recalls, "and Defries says, 'We'll make a stipulation that you don't stay above the eighth floor.'"

From there, the next step was for David to talk of a fear of dying; in an interview with Mick Rock that spring, he said that he was terrified of being assassinated on stage. By now, it was becoming hard to distinguish between David the publicity-seeker and a David who was exposing the inner workings of the character he had portrayed in Ziggy, with the further ambiguity that this might also be David himself. That process – and the bubble effect – was accentuated by a decision to increase David's isolation from the outside world.

After an initial burst of publicity at the start of the tour, all interviews with David were banned. Defries also attempted to control all photographs taken of David, demanding of editors that they should only be used once, and even stipulating the size and design of the layout; some editors, to their shame, complied. Fans were also banned from taking photographs at concerts, with intimidating notices posted at the doors and security guards seizing cameras and ripping out the film.

As Defries intended, it all helped to create a mystique that in itself was a guarantee of further publicity. Then the policy was taken a decisive stage further. So acute was David's insistence on privacy, it was said, he was no longer even to be touched; any strangers going near him were to be pulled away by Stuey George. The instruction chillingly reflected David's preoccupation over being touched that comprised the climax of 'Rock 'N' Roll Suicide'. Stuey is in no doubt where the instruction originated. "That was definitely Tony's idea."

On February 11th, 1972, the day of the first Ziggy concert at Tolworth, David's half-brother Terry got married. His wife, Olga, was another patient at Cane Hill. A sturdy woman, the daughter of a Durham miner, who retained a marked north-east accent, she was an epileptic who had been in Cane Hill for seven years. She and Terry had met at a patients' dance and became inseparable. For Terry, marriage offered the prospect of escape from Cane Hill, the stable home he had always dreamed of, and the affection he craved. Terry's aunt Pat considered Olga unworthy of Terry, and physically plain as well. But Terry was enraptured with her, and told Pat: "I could sit and look at her beauty for hours."

The wedding was held at Croydon Register Office. Among the handful of guests was Terry's old friend and protector Bill Berks, who had driven up from Cornwall with his younger brother, Jimmy, and collected Terry from Cane Hill. Terry was delighted to see him: "He was so excited about us turning up," says Berks; "we hadn't seen him for so many years." Berks was surprised to find that Terry had put on weight and had an air of "general scruffiness" about him. He was wearing a blue three-piece suit which soon became rumpled and seemed not quite to fit. On the way to Croydon they stopped at the Railway Hotel in Purley for several pints of bitter; Terry, Berks adds, was "immensely happy".

After the ceremony, the guests moved on to a reception held at the home of Olga's sister in Beckenham. "She put on a very, very good spread," says Pat. But the atmosphere was far from convivial. "I wasn't speaking to my sister at the time," Pat admits. "We had fallen out over Terry as usual." Peggy disapproved of Olga even more than Pat and did little to conceal her feelings: as they sat down to eat she muttered to Bill Berks, "This is all wrong."

Terry did his best to create an atmosphere of bonhomie, taking Olga up to Peggy several times and saying: "This is my lovely mum." But Bill Berks believes that he could discern a cause of unhappiness within him. "He was disappointed that his brother hadn't turned up," says Berks. "I don't remember him actually saying anything but knowing Terry as I did, you used to get the vibrations coming off . . . it was very sad."

David would have been hard put to attend the reception, since he was due to perform the second Ziggy concert in High Wycombe, twenty miles the other side of London, that night. But, according to Pat, he did not acknowledge Terry's wedding in any way. "My sister must have told him about it," she says. "But Terry didn't hear from him at all. I'd have known if he had, because he would have been so delighted."

After the reception, Terry and Olga moved to their new home, a large bed-sitting room in a road off Beckenham High Street. It was furnished with a bed, a dining table and chairs, and an imposing Victorian wardrobe. It was permanently damp, and clothes left in the wardrobe acquired a coating of mildew. But Olga was both hospitable and houseproud. "I must be fair," says Pat. "She always kept the place clean, and she always baked a cake or had something for you when you went round."

While Olga had been discharged from Cane Hill, Terry remained an out-patient, returning to see his doctors and to obtain prescriptions for tranquillisers. But life in a Beckenham bed-sitter was infinitely preferable to incarceration at Cane Hill, and that summer he was the happiest Pat had known him for years. "He liked just sitting there with a cigarette or a cup of tea, listening to music, and chatting," Pat says. Terry and Olga had two cats, a tabby named Boo-boo and a dappled grey cat, Wicky, which snuggled up against Terry when he lay down for an afternoon nap. "He loved that and the feeling of security he had," says Pat. "That was his idea of home."

For Terry, there was one source of dissatisfaction that could not be assuaged. He still took immense pride in David's career, which he expressed to Pat – despite the disapproval he knew she felt – when they met. He followed its progress assiduously, resourcefully telephoning RCA's London office when a new record was released, and asking them to send him a copy (they usually did). But his greatest wish was to see David in person, to talk about their childhood, to express the love he felt. In that, he was disappointed. So far as their aunt Pat is aware – and she feels certain that Terry would have told her – David and Terry did not meet for another ten years.

By the summer, Laurence Myers was increasingly uneasy about the size of his investment in David. The deficit on David's account at Gem stood at £29,062.69, although £7,844.51 of that consisted of royalties which Gem had reserved for itself. In comparison, Mott the Hoople had a surplus of £2,603.92, Iggy Pop a deficit of £5,767, and Dana Gillespie – whose career Gem was also financing – a debt of around £2,000. Myers was also unhappy at the uses to which his money was being put, which he saw as extravagance in the service of outrageousness.

"I was very aware that the meter was running," Myers says, adding, not entirely in jest, that David would persist in asking for another £5,000 for a dress made out of Liberty prints. The sales of *Hunky Dory* brought no comfort, for by the end of June, after more than six months in the shops, it had sold just 10,961 copies, a very poor figure; in the US, despite the vastly larger market, it was faring little better. "In the end," says Myers, "it got to be a choice between Liberty prints for a new dress for David Bowie and new curtains for Laurence Myers's home." He told Defries he was pulling out.

Defries received Myers's news with aplomb. He said he was determined to carry on, and asked Myers to transfer Gem's contract with David to him. Myers said he was prepared to do so: but at a price. Myers pointed out that even though David's contract was showing a loss, it was still potentially of enormous value in view of the recording agreement with RCA, which was in Gem's name. One aspect of the RCA contract now assumed particular significance.

Myers says today that his past dealings with Allen Klein had taught him one supreme lesson: "Klein told me, 'You always keep hold of the masters.'" The "masters" are the vital master recordings or blue prints from which records are pressed; they also represent the copyright in the performance which the record contains. They were in part the explanation why Myers and Defries had accepted a comparatively low price at RCA: in return, Gem retained ultimate ownership of David's master recordings, which were leased to RCA for their use. And the masters were the vital asset which Gem now possessed.

Myers told Defries that in return for the masters, he wanted his £29,000 investment to be repaid from David's earnings. That seemed only reasonable. But Myers wanted much more. If, as Defries so confidently expected, David became a superstar, then Myers wanted due reward for having helped to launch David's career: in short, a substantial sum of cash.

Since Defries had no legal stake in the contract Gem had struck with RCA on David's behalf, he appeared in a weak position. But he held a powerful card of his own. David's agreements with Gem contained a proviso – which, according to Defries, David himself had requested – that if Defries and Myers parted, the agreements lapsed. As Defries spells out, these covered David's recording, publishing, and management: "They were all void," he says, "if I were no longer with Gem."

The deal Defries and Myers struck, after some months of haggling over the finer details, reflected their respective bargaining strengths. Myers was to be paid $500,000. However, it was not "up front": he was to receive it, at a ratio of roughly one-fifth, from David's future earnings. For Defries, it was a relatively painless gamble. He would lose nothing if David failed. But if David succeeded, and Myers got rich, then everyone else should get even richer.

Little news of these negotiations reached David. He was still telling his colleagues to trust Defries implicitly, and it was in the same spirit that he learned that he would have to sign a contract with Defries to replace his agreements with Gem. The contract, however, was another example of Defries's novel business style. In comparison with Gem's 20 per cent, and Ken Pitt's 30 per cent, which included payment for Pitt's services as publicist, Defries wanted 50 per cent of David's earnings.

Defries is unabashed today about the terms: "It's very simple," he says. David needed substantial investment if he was to succeed – and "if you've got an interest of 20 per cent in something you can't afford to keep advancing money in the hope that it will reproduce enough to pay you. If you put the money in the bank you would get 12 or 15 per cent with no risk, and here you are going to advance into something with massive risk. If you are going to invest in an act that needed money to be invested then you've got to be willing to do it for a long time because even when you start earning you will not be able necessarily to survive on the earnings and in order to make that a viable possibility, you need a bigger slice of the pie."

It was not, of course, Defries who would be doing the investing: he would be relying on the advances from RCA. Nor would he be paying his own business costs, for these, together with all of David's non-personal expenses, would be deducted "off the top" – from the income, whether advances or royalties, David generated. When they learned the terms of the contract, some of David's colleagues – most notably Tony Visconti – considered them outrageous. But there was a further justification for the terms of the contract which Melanie McDonald argues on Defries's behalf. A fifty-fifty split, she says, reflected the total sharing partnership which David and Defries had embarked upon.

"They were strong because they were like two friends together or two lovers together," Melanie says. "David needed the freedom to do what he wanted . . . Tony said to David, 'You can do whatever you like and I will take care of it.' It worked as a very good partnership. It was marvellous, incredible. If David said, 'I want to go to the moon tomorrow,' Tony said, 'Fine.'"

Such explanations notwithstanding, it appears that David may not have fully comprehended the implications of his new contract. In 1971, Defries had purchased an off-the-shelf company named Minnie Bell whose purpose was "to employ authors and composers and to purchase copyrights and other rights in musical and dramatic compositions of all kinds". On June 30th, 1972, Defries altered the company's name to MainMan.

The title was taken from the unattractive phrase, "the main man", with its connotations of autocracy, influence and power, then current in the entertainment industry. Its origins were even less appealing, for it was first used as black slang for a drug dealer. Defries liked the conceit of formulating the name as "MainMan", although his insistence that it should be printed in that way was usually defeated by the unshakeably grammatical computers of the business world (the American credit-rating organisation D and B, for example, always rendered it as "Main Man".)

David's new contract was with MainMan – and several of David's colleagues believe that he assumed the "main man" to be himself. In terms of the company ownership, that was not so. Of MainMan's 100 shares, Defries owned ninety-nine; the remaining one belonged to a former accountant in Myers's office, Peter Gerber, who had recently joined the MainMan staff. Far from being the main man, David was, by virtue of his agreements with Defries, one of the company's employees. What was more, the agreement gave Defries formal control over every aspect of David's career – song-writing, recording, and performing – for ten years. It also gave him David's masters.

Mick Ronson suspects that David's single-minded desire to become a star led him, once again, to ignore the fine print of his agreements. The most powerful confirmation that this was so comes from Defries himself. He says that David was "willing to accept" that he should have "control of the environment". But the precise details, Defries agrees, may have passed David by. "The problem is, I don't think David could read or understood his own contracts."

*

The Ziggy tour meanwhile was reaching its climax. On August 19th, the final concert was due to be held at the Rainbow Theatre in Finsbury Park, North London. The promoter, Mel Bush, paid a fee of £1,000; the 3,000 seats were sold so quickly that a second night was arranged, for which Bush agreed to pay £1,250. Since Defries was now cut off from Myers's financial support, every penny was vital.

As for David, he was determined to make the last concert a triumph and spent a week rehearsing the kind of multi-media show he had dreamed of since the days of Ralph Horton's electronic console. To that end he sought the help and advice of another friend from the past, Lindsay Kemp.

Kemp was working in Edinburgh when he received a frantic call from Angie, begging him to come to London. Kemp warmed to Angie – "she had so much enthusiasm, energy, determination, not like Hermione, who was an English rose" – and agreed. He also met Defries in the fashionable studio offices in Gunter Grove, Kensington, which MainMan had moved into just two weeks before. "I adored him," says Kemp, "and he was warm and generous and loved me." Kemp listened to the *Ziggy* album and then brought down his own dance company to London. For the opening number, 'Lady Stardust', Kemp proposed that they should all wear David Bowie masks.

When Kemp met David, however, he concluded that he had changed irrevocably from the callow young man he had known. During a break in the first afternoon's rehearsal, Kemp suggested adjourning "to the caff just across the road" for a cup of tea. David said it would be better to have some tea "sent in".

"Sent in!" expostulates Kemp. "I never heard such a thing. With Fellini, Ken Russell, Margot Fonteyn, you went across the road. . . I said, 'Let's go,' but he said, 'I can't.' He wasn't that well known at the time. But he was preparing to be."

The Rainbow show gave David the triumph he sought. The presentation, with David wading on to the stage through wreaths of dry ice, was immaculate; Kemp played a stoned star-man with a joint hanging from his mouth. In *New Musical Express*, Charles Shaar Murray wrote that David had provided a "thoroughly convincing demonstration of his ascendancy over any other soloist in rock today". *Record Mirror* considered the concert a "stunning production spectacle" with a "breathtaking finale".

There were a few dissenters. *Sounds* judged that the show "didn't quite come off", and Elton John walked out before the finale saying that David had "blown it". But those on the inside had no doubts.

Will Palin says that David "created such power and charisma, you felt you understood your place on the planet, there is a purpose to what we are doing here." Lou Reed was overcome with emotion and had to be helped out of the hall by Kemp and Andy Warhol. In floods of tears, he sobbed: "I have seen my music played and it was just beautiful."

Buoyed by such tributes, and by the 6,000 seats sold at the two Rainbow shows, Defries hastily arranged a further round of concerts – not the full Ziggy repertoire, but a truncated one-hour show without the costumes – in the first week of September. By now there was a growing sense of excitement in the entourage, which was abuzz with rumours that the 'Ziggy Stardust' tour would be going to the US.

Defries in fact had been laying preparations for transporting Ziggy to the US since the time of his split from Myers. He had flown to New York in June to ask for RCA's support, the occasion when David joined him for a whirlwind weekend in the middle of the British tour. Defries had also concluded that if David and Ziggy were to succeed, it would have to be in the US: only there were the rewards commensurate with their dreams. Since Defries now had almost no capital at all, it was a monumental gamble: the gamble that would make, or break, them all.

On September 2nd and 3rd, when David was performing at the Hard Rock arena in Manchester, the entire company was lodged at the Excelsior Hotel near Manchester Airport. Will Palin discerned a new expansiveness in the air: after the first concert they were encouraged to choose whatever drinks they wanted in the hotel, at Defries's expense, and he wondered why. The following morning, all was revealed.

After breakfast, Defries summoned the entire group, most of whom were suffering from hangovers, to the hotel's conference room. "I expect you all wonder why you're here," he told them. Then he announced: "Everybody in this room will be in America in about two weeks' time."

Defries explained that the Ziggy show would be making a US tour. He did not add that there was virtually no money to pay for the tour, for the moment had come to enact another of Defries's aphorisms: the way to become a star is to act like a star. That applied not only to David, sitting at the head of the table, but also to all around him. "So far as RCA in America in concerned," Defries said, "the man with the red hair at the end of the table is the biggest thing to have come out of England since the Beatles – and possibly before the Beatles." That was manifestly not true, at least not yet. But everyone had to play their part in convincing RCA that it was.

Defries asked Will Palin: "What is the status of your equipment?" Palin explained that he was still hiring most of what was needed.

"Buy it," Defries told him.

"What about spares?" Palin asked.

"Buy two of everything."

Defries had similar conversations with most of the assembled company, leaving them in no doubt that, in the next stage of the game-plan, money was no object. They too were to help foster the illusion that Defries wished to create, as he now made even more explicit. "You've all got to learn," he told them, "how to look and act like a million dollars."

20

Rock and Roll Star

Late in the afternoon of September 15th, 1972, Gustl Breuer, an employee of the classical music section at RCA's Records and Tapes division, was looking forward to spending a weekend away from New York when he received a telephone call urgently instructing him not to leave the building. A short while later, Breuer was summoned before Rocco Laginestra. For Breuer, after an uneventful ten years at RCA, this was a dramatic moment: "I had been there that long and no one ever bothered me." He was ushered into Laginestra's office to find it "full of big shots", together with a rather overweight man he had never seen before. With the air of someone who has momentous news to impart, one of the big shots told Breuer: "You now have the great chance of working with David Bowie."

The statement did not have the impact on Gustl that those in the room had supposed. "What," he asked, "is a David Bowie?"

Thereupon the overweight stranger, who was Tony Defries, embraced Breuer and told him. "You're our man."

That Breuer should not have heard of David Bowie was less surprising than it might appear. A cultured bachelor and a Jew who had fled from the Nazi terror in Austria in 1938, he was employed as a chaperone to RCA's galaxy of classical recording stars, including Artur Rubinstein and Leontyne Price. It was the action of another of RCA's most luminary clients, Colonel Parker, which had led to Breuer's summons. On hearing of the attention being paid to a new English performer, whom some at RCA were even comparing to the Beatles, Parker had demanded that the popular music section's chief artists' relations officer, an engaging Irishman named Pat Kelleher, should fly at once to Hawaii to inspect hotels and locations for a possible concert tour. "The tour didn't exist," says Breuer, "and nobody thought it would exist. But if Colonel Parker says go, you go."

With David due to arrive in New York on the *QE2* that Sunday, and the first concert scheduled at Cleveland just five days later, Laginestra had proposed to Defries that Breuer should forsake both his weekend and his classical artists to become RCA's liaison officer for the duration of the Ziggy tour. Breuer supposed that his total ignorance of rock and roll in general and David Bowie in particular would have been an insurmountable bar. To Defries, of course, Breuer's air of innocence made him an ideal recruit.

Thus it was, two days later, that Breuer was standing on the Manhattan waterfront as the *QE2* docked. Down the gangplank, he recalls, came "Mr Bowie with very red hair and, I think, blue fingernails, and friendly and shy and amazed at the skyline, and a wife, Angela, who looked like a gentile Barbra Streisand and who was very much in command of the whole situation." Breuer escorted them to the Plaza Hotel by Central Park, settled them into their suite and told them to call him at home if they met any problems. He had just opened the door of his basement apartment on East 52nd Street when, right on cue, the telephone rang. It was Angie. "There was this incredibly angry and shrieking voice," says Breuer, "complaining that everything was fucked up."

Although Breuer could have dealt with the problem by telephone – it was "very insignificant", he says – he chose to return to the Plaza. When Angie opened the door of the suite, Breuer told her: "I just wanted to see that face that can be so abusive over the telephone." While David hovered inside the room, Angie apologised. "After that," says Breuer, "we were friends."

In the autumn of 1972, the vast mass of America, like Gustl Breuer, did not yet know what "a David Bowie" was, and the notion that he should rival the Beatles or Elvis Presley was still utterly remote. David had nonetheless made a useful start to his US career by winning the support of some of the US's most influential music writers, who were in general more perceptive about David's intentions than their British counterparts. In *Rolling Stone*, John Mendelsohn continued to champion David, describing him as "definitely an original", and *Hunky Dory* – which had been released in the US late in 1971 – as "his most engaging album musically". In *Rock*, Toby Goldstein wrote that, for an English writer, David had "an incredible feel for the rough-toughness of America".

In the *Los Angeles Times*, Robert Hilburn told of "a new singer-songwriter" whose album "contains all the humor, intelligence, irony and personal vision that one expects from our best musical minds". And Henry Edwards of the *New York Times* wrote that David was creating "a self-legend composed of legends" and described 'The Bewlay Brothers' as a "traditional psychic narrative" in the guise of "a personal and well-observed journey".

Further appreciative reviews greeted the US release of *Ziggy Stardust* in June. Lilian Roxon, who had met David during his brief weekend visit with Tony Defries, described *Ziggy* as "probably the best album to come out this year" – certainly better than the Rolling Stones' 1972 offering, *Exile On Main Street* – and predicted that it would define "what we can expect from the '70s". In *Rolling Stone*, Richard Cromelin published David's most lavish US tribute yet, saying that: the album displayed David's "employment of broadly mannered styles and deliveries, a boggling variety of vocal nuances, a verbal acumen no longer clouded by psychotic, frenzied music, and a thorough command of the elements of rock and roll". Cromelin noted the album's "parodic undercurrent" and "central duality", and articulated the "rather spine-tingling questions" it posed. How much of the rock and roll star is bluff? Is there merely a frightened and helpless figure inside?

Since most of the reviewers suffered from the handicap of never having seen David perform, Defries used his New York visit to persuade RCA to pay for a dozen of them to travel to a Ziggy concert in Britain. They included Lilian Roxon, Henry Edwards, Lisa Robinson of *After Dark*, and writers from those magazines held to be the most powerful in shaping American tastes: *New Yorker, New York, Andy Warhol's Interview, Creem,* and *Playboy*.

David staged a virtuoso performance for their benefit. The concert, on July 15th, was held at the market town of Aylesbury, near Oxford, where, before an audience ranging from provincial skinheads to loyalist gays who were now following him from venue to venue, David wore his skimpiest green jumpsuit and highest heels, with his red cockade freshly spiked by Suzi Fussey, and the Spiders From Mars in their tightest breeches and knee-length boots. David was at his most swaggering and uninhibited, and even the more blasé of the Americans were startled when, during an encore of 'Suffragette City', he performed his fellatio act on Mick Ronson's guitar.

The following day, Defries staged a press conference at the Dorchester Hotel in Park Lane, judging that its refined thirties' elegance, with its mirrored walls and subdued pastel shades, would be an appropriate setting for the further portrayal of David as star. Frock-coated waiters dispensed champagne and smoked-salmon sandwiches while David, breaking the silence of the previous four months, gave a series of interviews. Among the supporting cast were Iggy Pop and Lou Reed, both wearing eye make-up, and Reed causing a minor scandal by planting a kiss squarely on David's lips just as he was answering a question about Mott the Hoople.

But it was Angie who threatened to steal the show: having been bitten on the midriff for no apparent reason by one of Reed's roadies, she reciprocated by sinking her teeth into one of Lilian Roxon's ample breasts. It was, she says, her way of expressing her gratitude for Lilian's generous reviews: "A mere hug and a thank you is not as demonstrative of your affection as a good hard bite on the tit."

While the junket brought David further welcome publicity, the sad fact remained that the wider US audience necessary for stardom remained in ignorance of David. Sales of *Hunky Dory* were running at a dismal 5,000 a month; and although RCA shipped 150,000 copies of *Ziggy Stardust* to record stores in June, and gave it a promotional budget of $80,000, it at first fared little better. It was thus in an unpropitious climate that Tony Defries laid his plans, as the prelude to David's tour and the consequent basis of his career in the US, for transferring the headquarters of the MainMan organisation to New York.

To help him, Tony turned to those best able to play the appropriate parts. For the past year, the actor Tony Zanetta – Zee – had been helping Tony whenever he came to New York: "He would call me up and we would have dinner and he would need a copy of *Melody Maker* or need some records picked up from RCA or he'd need someone on the phone," says Zee. "It was some kind of gofer job. I was helping him get around." The scale of Defries's requests now changed: he flew Zee to London to seek his advice and asked him to find premises for MainMan in New York. Zee rented an apartment on East 58th Street and was awarded with the title of Company President, his appointment being formally confirmed when MainMan was incorporated in New York on August 31st.

The next member of the *Pork* company to be drafted was the colourful figure of Leee Black Childers, *Pork*'s stage manager, who had been so entranced by seeing some traditional English Teddy-boys during his visit to London that he had adopted their hairstyle, bleached silver-blond. Both Leee and Wayne County, who shared an apartment in New York, had been watching the favours showered on Zee with some jealousy, but had willingly helped distribute copies of *Ziggy Stardust* to New York's fashion leaders during Tony's visit in June. Leee was working as a messenger boy for *16* magazine when Tony and Zee asked him out for dinner.

"I always went out for free food," says Leee. "All during dinner I just jabbered like I jabber all the time about what I thought David should do, totally outrageous and impractical ideas, and at the end of the dinner Defries said, 'How would you like to be vice-president of MainMan?' I said OK and he turned to Zee and said, 'Arrange it, Zee,' and that was it."

Despite the appearance Defries liked to convey, not all his preparations were undertaken quite so casually. Early that summer, unknown to his new company officers, Defries telephoned the California concert promoter Jim Rismiller in Los Angeles. Rismiller was well known in British entertainment circles for having staged the Beatles' first concert on the West Coast in 1964, and for presenting successive waves of the British pop invasion during the remainder of the 1960s. It was in the same pioneering spirit that Rismiller had agreed when a booking agent suggested he stage one of the 'Ziggy' concerts at the Civic Auditorium in Santa Monica on October 20th, even though Rismiller had never heard of David before. Then came the call from Defries, which left Rismiller quite perplexed.

"I never met the man, never heard of him either, but he talked like he trusted me," Rismiller recalls. "He said, 'We're playing the Santa Monica Civic and we haven't made a deal yet, I've never made a deal in America, and I'd like you to help me structure a deal. What should David get paid?' And I'm thinking, This guy is either a total idiot or he is as smart as a fox."

Never having previously been asked by a manager how much his artist should be paid, Rismiller found himself in a pleasant dilemma. Wanting to be "very objective and honest – but not going overboard", he proposed terms that he felt were "totally straight but without being overly honest". He offered a guarantee of around $4,000 against 60 per cent of the takings from the concert, so that MainMan would receive whichever proved the greater. Defries accepted without demur.

Defries, however, had his own price for agreeing so readily to Rismiller's terms. In the next weeks and months, he called Rismiller on numerous occasions from both New York and London. Telling Rismiller, "I want you to educate me," he proceeded to seek his advice on topics ranging from concert halls and promoters to contracts and deals. At first, Defries rose in Rismiller's estimation; later, Rismiller was not so sure. "I admire someone who says, 'I don't know,'" he says. "That shows great self-confidence and security. But he kept going on and on about his lack of knowledge and how naive he was." In the end, Rismiller concluded that Defries was "totally stupid".

Stupid or not, Defries put his education to good use when

planning David's tour. The decision that it should start in the
north-eastern steel city of Cleveland, on the shore of Lake Erie in
Ohio, was shrewd. Despite its sour industrial setting, Cleveland
had a progressive reputation akin to Liverpool's. It was from
Cleveland that the radio disc-jockey Alan Freed hosted the late-
night *Moondog Rock 'n' Roll Party* that gave the words "rock 'n'
roll" to the world; twenty years later, Cleveland's disc-jockeys had
been playing tracks from *Hunky Dory* ever since its release.

Cleveland was also the home of David's first US fan club. The
founder and president of the International David Bowie Society
was the young guitar player, Brian Kinchy, who had been a fan of
David's since buying three remaindered copies of the 1967 Deram
album for 35 cents each in a junk store. When Mercury released
Man Of Words/Man of Music soon afterwards, Kinchy found
the music "incredible – then I knew I was definitely hooked". He
began to collect news clippings about David and decided to start
a club: "I thought, Maybe I'll get to meet the guy, which would
be great."

Kinchy advertised the club in the music press and was soon
exchanging cuttings with fifty or sixty other early devotees, not
only in Cleveland but also elsewhere in the US, as well as in
Australia and Japan. When David signed with RCA, Kinchy wrote
to the company's publicity office in New York, who began sending
him their press releases. Then, out of the blue, David telephoned
from Haddon Hall to thank him, Kinchy relates, "for all the things
I had been doing". David also sounded out Kinchy on the prospects
for a concert in Cleveland. Kinchy was incredulous: "When he
said we may be starting in Cleveland I thought, Jesus, and he said,
'If we do, of course I'll let you know.'"

Once Cleveland had been confirmed as the tour's starting point,
Defries applied other lessons he had learned from Jim Rismiller.
Cleveland's leading concert promoters were the Belkin Brothers –
Jules and Mike – who agreed, after consulting local disc-jockeys,
to stage America's first 'Ziggy' concert at Cleveland's Music Hall.
When it came to discussing terms, Defries showed, once again,
that he could rival David when it came to switching roles. He was
no longer the timorous figure who had sought Jim Rismiller's
advice; instead, he asked for a brazen 90 per cent of the takings,
an unprecedentedly high amount. Defries could not contain his
delight when he told everyone afterwards that the Belkins had
agreed: "Tony was very happy and very thrilled to have pulled
that off," Leee Childers recalls.

By the beginning of September, the tour's outline was clear.

Beginning in Cleveland on September 22nd, and ending in Santa Monica exactly four weeks later, it would embrace eight other major US cities: Memphis, New York, Washington, Boston, Chicago, Detroit, St Louis and Kansas. Coming just seven months after Ziggy's opening at a pub in Surrey, it was a truly audacious itinerary, on which the fortunes of both David and Defries would stand or fall. The gamble was bigger even than that, for, all appearances to the contrary, MainMan was operating on a shoestring, and had not one-tenth of the resources required to support such a tour.

Instead, Defries was relying on a combination of faith, hope, and his belief in his ability to persuade Rocco Laginestra to see things his way. But none of those qualities would avail if the opening performances flopped. By the time of the third concert in New York, Defries would know whether the gamble had succeeded; or whether he would have to return to life as a solicitor's litigation clerk, and David to the backwater of Haddon Hall.

It was with a sense of wonder that the rest of David's entourage, who included Stuey George, Suzi Fussey, Will Palin, Dai Davies and Mick Rock, joined him in New York. Most of them arrived at Kennedy Airport on Monday, September 18th, wrestling with their disbelief as they checked in at the Plaza Hotel. "When I saw the size of everything it just captivated me," says Stuey George. "It was just like the movies, it was *déjà vu*, I've been here before . . ."

Stuey's partner as bodyguard was Tony Frost, the husband of Zowie's nanny at Haddon Hall, and together he and Stuey overcame the initial trepidation they felt. "I must admit that we were a little bit frightened because we had heard about the crime, the muggings and so forth," Stuey says, "so I said the best thing we can do is go out in the street, walk five or six blocks and come back and see what we think. In a way it was like going up the Amazon and discovering a new tribe. But after that we thought, We can handle this."

By that night, the party at the Plaza numbered some two dozen: they included not only working members of the entourage but also guests whom Tony Defries had felt would contribute to the air of extravagance and *joie de vivre*. George Underwood and his wife Birgit were there; so was Mick Rock's wife Sheila. For Rock, the most remarkable feature was the nonchalance with which the party partook of the Plaza's room service, as if to the manner born. Rock was present when Tony Frost came into David's room to protest at the inadequacies of the hotel laundry. "There has been no other rock and roll tour in history," says Rock, "where a bodyguard has complained to the act that his underwear hadn't been cleaned properly."

David had other things on his mind. With just five days to go to the opening in Cleveland, he and Mick Ronson had made a radical decision over the line-up of the Spiders: they needed a pianist. The man they chose was Mike Garson, a New Yorker of broad tastes and experience, including a music degree at Brooklyn College and several years of playing jazz in the piano bars of Lower Manhattan. He had been recommended by RCA's London boss Ken Glancey, himself a jazz aficionado.

Fortunately for David, Garson was also not afraid to act on impulse, for he was giving a piano lesson in his Brooklyn apartment, with another student waiting and his baby daughter asleep in bed, when Defries telephoned to ask if he would like to join David Bowie on his forthcoming tour. Garson explained that he had never heard of David Bowie or played with a rock band either; Defries insisted that he should come for an audition at RCA right away. "So I sent one of my students home, left the other one to babysit, and went," Garson says.

While David stayed in the studio control room, Mick Ronson demonstrated some of the chords of 'Changes' and asked Garson to play them. "I must have played for eight seconds and Mick said, 'You've got the gig.'"

Afterwards Defries asked Garson how much he wanted to be paid. Garson tried to guess how much the Spiders were earning, not dreaming that it was still no more than £30 a week. "I reckoned that these guys must be on about $2,000 a week so I'll only ask for $800. So I said $800 a week and he looked a little dazed but I couldn't tell what he was thinking. But he said, 'Fine,' and I thought, What an idiot I am, I should have asked for $1,500."

The entire party, save only Tony Defries, left New York in a chartered coach for the two-day journey to Cleveland on September 20th, stopping at Erie in Pennsylvania overnight. In Cleveland, meanwhile, the concert was almost cancelled. Tony had sent Leee Childers and Dai Davies as advance men to check that all was in order. They called at the office of the Belkin Brothers and asked to inspect the Cleveland Music Hall. "Mike Belkin went to the theatre with us," says Leee. "He was very proud of it and rightly so." Leee was carrying with him a checklist of the requirements contained in the contract, forty-five in all: number 26 stated that the promoter "should provide on stage at his own expense a concert piano over six feet in length tuned to concert pitch . . ."

When Leee measured the piano at the Cleveland Music Hall, it was, so far as he recalls, some eight inches too short. "So I called Tony and he said, 'Cancel the show.'"

The Belkins were "flabbergasted", says Leee, but he insisted that Defries was serious. In desperation, the Belkins tracked down the only piano of the correct proportions in Cleveland, which belonged to the city's symphony orchestra. The orchestra declined to lend their piano for a rock concert, and Leee telephoned Defries again. This time he relented: the show, he said, could go ahead.

Leee believes now that Defries was "stirring things up" to create the maximum impact and that he did not seriously contemplate cancelling the concert on this occasion. Certainly, a policy of stirring things up in Cleveland had already proved effective. A preview in the *Cleveland Plain Dealer* spoke guardedly of David as a self-proclaimed bisexual who appeared on stage "in feminine garb" – but promised that this was not "the violent anti-sexual sham of his contemporary, Alice Cooper". Further publicity came from the activities of the local disc-jockeys, particularly Denny Sanders and Kid Leo at Cleveland's most progressive FM radio station, WMMS, who had been playing *Ziggy Stardust* almost incessantly.

The WMMS audience already knew of David through *Hunky Dory*, and Ziggy, says Sanders, "hit like a tornado". Requests for the album dominated the station's twenty-four-hour telephone line, with every track in demand. "You rarely see albums like that," Sanders says. "The Rolling Stones you could play every track, maybe The Who, and it was unusual because he was so new. But boy, when *Ziggy Stardust* came out, all of those songs were so strong. Every track went on the air, and every track hit."

The concert at the Cleveland Music Hall was a sensation. All 3,200 seats were filled, and David and the band performed as if inspired. RCA's local office had made sure that the local members of the International David Bowie Appreciation Society had good seats, with Brian Kinchy occupying pride of place next to Defries. "It was an amazing show," Kinchy says. "People were just going crazy. They were singing, they were clapping, they knew the words. He did 'Space Oddity', and he sweated and mascara ran down his face. I was in awe." Tony Defries made clear his delight in a more reserved manner. "He just smiled and said, 'Isn't he marvellous, isn't he great?'" Kinchy recalls.

Up on stage, Mike Garson was suffering from culture shock. In five days he had managed to learn a dozen of the twenty-two songs planned for the show. During his first rehearsal he had found

Above: David at the Beckenham Free Festival, August 1969 – his mother's favourite photograph.

Below: David with Hermione Farthingale, who shook him cold. Together with Tony Hill (foreground) they formed the trio Turquoise, forerunner of Feathers.

Calvin Mark Lee – wearing David's 'Space Oddity' suit but not, for once, his love jewel – in 1969.

The birth of glitter rock – David at the Round House, with Tony Visconti as "Hypeman", on February 22nd, 1970.

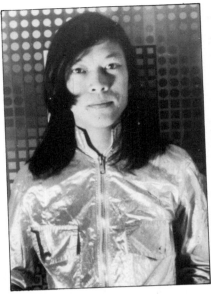

Below: David at the start of an evening at the Beckenham Arts Lab, in the back room of the Three Tuns pub, Beckenham High Street.

David enthroned at the top of the stairs at Haddon Hall.

David backstage at the Round House with Dana Gillespie and his fourth manager, Tony Defries, in August 1971.

Above: Lou Reed, Mick Jagger and David being intimate at the Café Royal party that followed the 'retirement' concert at Hammersmith in July 1973.

Below: The extrovert Angie Bowie with the more retiring Tony Defries at the Café Royal.

himself seated next to a vast stack of speakers that he assumed was the band's public-address system. "It was so loud that I stopped playing and asked for them to be turned out to the front," he says, "and they told me it was my monitor system." For the Cleveland concert he had equipped himself with earplugs, reinforced with tissues. But such was the volume of sound that neither he nor the rest of the band, including David, could hear the audience and therefore did not realise the extent of their triumph until they were greeted with a ten-minute ovation at the end.

Garson suffered again after the final encore, when the audience rushed the stage. He looked around to find that the rest of the band had disappeared, having been whisked to safety by a lift in the wings. "They had it all planned but they didn't tip me off, and meanwhile there is this whole bunch of cattle charging at the stage. Fortunately I was not their target."

After the concert, there was an exuberant reception at Cleveland's Hollanden Hotel. Angie led Brian Kinchy by the hand to David, who was sitting in a corner wearing a quilted suit and appearing, says Kinchy, "totally ecstatic". Jane Scott, the rock critic of the *Cleveland Plain Dealer*, found David bubbling with delight: "He was very pleasant and very anxious to talk," she says. She wrote later that David was "a one-man multi-media" with "an incisive, perfectionist touch" and "the sensitivity of an artist". And she concluded: "I think a star has been born."

Only Stuey George was finding it hard to enjoy himself, since so many people were approaching David, despite Tony Defries's ruling that he was not to be touched. David, savouring his triumph, declined Stuey's suggestion that he should move to another room. Around him, in their jubilation, the entourage were shedding all inhibitions. Brian Kinchy has two principal memories, apart from meeting David, of that evening. They are of Leee Childers fondling him from behind; and of a well-known children's television star asking him to go home with him that night.

The second concert, two nights later, was in the Deep South, at Memphis, Tennessee. Since Memphis was the home of Elvis Presley, and therefore regarded David as something of an upstart, it was a risky choice. In the *Memphis Commercial Appeal*, Joe E. Dove reported that David had "substituted noise for music, freaky stage gimmicks for talent, and covers it all up with volume". But Dove was compelled to admit that the sell-out audience of 4,335 at the Memphis Auditorium had not shared his view. "They loved it. They screamed. They yelled. They danced on their seats and begged for more . . ."

Four nights later, on September 28th, came New York's Carnegie Hall; and if any one venue would make or break David, this was it. RCA were still uncertain what to make of their new signing, for on his return to New York Gustl Breuer was summoned before the big shots again and asked his opinion.

"Suddenly I was very important," Breuer says, "because there was this big property and I was the only one who had seen them perform."

Knowing that Rocco Laginestra occasionally attended the opera – "he liked *Aida*", says Breuer, dismissively – he searched for an appropriate comparison. "If Elvis is a Caballé," he told them, "this one is a Callas." Breuer explained that he felt that both Elvis and the Spanish soprano Montserrat Caballé had "an incredibly sexy voice", while Maria Callas and David had "much more brain but not at all the sexiness of the voice, but to me much more interesting because there is so much intellect going into it".

While Breuer could not tell if his answer had entirely reassured RCA, the *Pork* team were in their element. They had assiduously talked up the concert to every friend and acquaintance they could find and given away countless free tickets, while simultaneously spreading rumours that they were almost impossible to come by. Each commitment attracted others, so that the event snowballed: the British actor Alan Bates promised to come, and so did Anthony Perkins, and then rock-star Todd Rundgren, and then Andy Warhol, and then Lee Radziwill, sister of Jackie Kennedy.

By the night of the concert it had become one of the social events of the year, as important to be seen there as to see: among those unable to obtain a ticket, it was improbably said, was Ahmet Ertegun, president of Atlantic Records. But every rock writer in or around New York had been invited, and mingled in the foyer of Carnegie Hall with some of New York's most glittering drag queens. From the cast of *Pork*, Geri Miller, who had added to her reputation for self-exposure by bursting naked from a birthday cake presented to Mick Jagger, arrived bearing a bunch of gladioli which she hoped to present to David on stage (whether clothed or otherwise, no one was quite sure).

Behind the scenes, David was at his most apprehensive yet. To make matters worse, he had succumbed to a wave of flu that had swept through the group. "He was very nervous and frightened that he was going to break down," says Stuey George, "plus there was the tension of playing Carnegie Hall, period."

When the concert began, David took some time to get into his stride, but by the seventh number the audience was behind him.

They were in raptures when he and the Spiders changed their costumes for the twelfth number and during the fourteenth, 'Starman', there was dancing in the aisles. When David sang 'Rock 'N' Roll Suicide', they were at his mercy, reaching out from the front rows when he sang "Gimme your hands". As the ovation burst around him, Geri Miller – fully clothed, it turned out – dashed on stage to present David his bouquet.

Not all the critics approved. *Newsday*'s Bob Christgau called David an "English fairy". *Life*'s Albert Goldman was so disenchanted by the atmosphere of hype that he wrote nothing at all although since he rarely wrote approvingly about anyone, that was probably a blessing in disguise.

There were plenty who took a different view. In the *New York Times*, Don Heckman wrote that David had overcome the suspicions aroused by the "publicity overkill", to deliver a performance of "beautiful coordinated physical movements and well-planned music"; David's promise, he concluded, was "crystal-clear". The crowning accolade came from Lilian Roxon, who had evidently forgiven Angie's act of vampirism at the Dorchester. She described David as "a great songwriter and lyricist as well as a great showman and entertainer" who had taken Carnegie Hall's "skeptical, cynical" audience by storm. "A star is born," she declared. "I have always wanted to write that in a review and now I can."

The feeling within the entourage was that a turning point had been reached: the reaction of the audience alone told them that. "They went absolutely ape-shit," says Will Palin. "The place really rocked. It was fabulous, the best. The only comparison was the Rainbow show." David himself lay in bed at the Plaza Hotel, flattened by flu. But as he perused the reviews in newspapers Stuey brought into his room, he displayed an air of new confidence. "He knew he'd got it together," says Stuey. "He knew he'd got it mastered."

21

Hollywood High

Borne on the wave of enthusiasm engendered by the first three concerts, the tour made its way through America. After playing at Boston on October 1st, it returned to New York for three days and departed again on October 6th, with concerts at Chicago, Detroit, St Louis and Kansas City in the ensuing week. Only in Kansas City was there outright financial failure when the promoter sold 250 seats in an auditorium designed for thousands, but David responded like a trouper, summoning the audience to gather round while he sat on the edge of the stage and gave them a low-key, intimate cabaret performance.

The entourage, meanwhile, was doing its best, as Defries had directed, to look and act like a million dollars. Defries set a bravura example by taking some of them to Max's Kansas City, where he liked to disembark from a limousine and saunter inside smoking an enormous Havana cigar, which carried the cachet of being forbidden to Americans by the Cuba trade embargo. "We were encouraged to drink champagne and eat huge dinners and sign everything," says Leee Childers. "We were encouraged to be as splashy and as crazy as we could."

Defries opened charge accounts at restaurants, stores and a limousine service, telling Leee: "Get the limousine to take you wherever you need to go, go shopping in it, keep it for the day." As he travelled from city to city ahead of the tour, Leee did Tony's bidding. "Limousines were taking me to and from airports, at hotels I was signing everything everywhere, all over the country."

For the British members of the entourage, young, inexperienced, unaccustomed to wealth, there could be no more potent fantasy than the one Tony had decreed. After New York, they no longer travelled by road but flew to each venue. Since it had been ordained that David was not to fly, this meant that they would while away whole days in luxury hotels as they waited for him to catch up. For Suzi Fussey, the bubble had closed around them again. "You didn't even know what day of the week it was, you were sealed and you were totally looked after," she says. "You go to a hotel and you hire a floor and it was like you were always at home."

There was one disruption to the homely atmosphere: a falling-out between Angie and Defries. Angie ascribes this today to the certain unreconstructed attitudes on Defries's part: "Tony has a chauvinist problem," she says, "and it was very difficult for him to understand that in reality my mind is just as fine as his." Others ascribe the tension to the competition between two immensely strong-willed personalities for influence over David, and believe that Defries managed to outploy Angie by asking her to undertake tasks away from the tour. "I was there and I wasn't there a lot," Angie acknowledges. "All I remember of that time was aeroplanes . . ."

David's dislike of personal confrontation led him to recoil from the rivalry between Defries and Angie, and he did not attempt to resolve it. As he maintained his stately progress around America, he too was living as if sealed from the outside world, watching the landscape slide by from the windows of his train, and learning nothing of any hitches or snags. "That was all part of the cushioning process," says Stuey George.

When David caught up with the entourage it seemed that he was some royal personage and they his courtiers awaiting his pleasure. "Everyone was very close and tight together, and it was all for David, because he was surrounded by layers of people, and they were all totally for him," says Suzi Fussey. "Everyone had a part to play and all of us would have laid down our lives, almost, for the show to go on." Only on concert nights did David venture into the outside world. After performing he would usually dine at the hotel and then, still buzzing with adrenalin, would go out with Stuey to a night club or bar, already reconnoitred by Leee or Dai Davies, until he could at last relax enough to fall asleep, usually around dawn.

As Defries had intended, the contrived impression of opulence increased the attentions of the press. When reporters in New York arrived at the Plaza Hotel to interview David they were astonished to find the entourage there too: "They'd ask, 'You're all staying *here*?'" says Suzi Fussey. They began to comment on Defries's insistence that David should live in the manner befitting a superstar, as if with access to boundless wealth. That was even more of an illusion than they guessed, for Defries and MainMan had nothing like the resources needed to sustain the lifestyle Tony had decreed, and the concert tour remained an awesome gamble.

Defries had acquired a modicum of cash by requiring promoters to pay deposits of around $5,000 in advance, while the concerts themselves were netting an average of $20,000. According to

Defries, that did not include Carnegie Hall: it was a "paper" audience, he says, for so many tickets had been given away in the bid to create a stir that there was no profit at all. Nor was the revenue from the other concerts remotely sufficient to pay for the vast cost of maintaining David and the entourage. As advance men, Leee and Dai Davies knew just how thin the resources were stretched. "I was travelling with nothing in my pocket except maybe $5," says Leee. "Every time the tour would catch up Tony would give me $100 and I'd be gone for two weeks on $100."

The crowning act of prodigality occurred when the tour reached the very home of fantasy, Hollywood. Just how it came about has been the subject of much amused discussion since: while Leee acknowledges some responsibility, he also holds Lilian Roxon to blame. She was in Los Angeles when Leee telephoned from St Louis to anounce that the tour would soon be arriving and would be staying at the Chateau Marmont Hotel. "What a shame," she told Leee. "I'm staying at the Beverly Hills Hotel – it's much nicer."

"Nice" is a minimal description of the Beverly Hills Hotel. It stands a discreet distance off Sunset Boulevard, hidden from prying eyes by lines of palm trees and a bank of lush Californian undergrowth. The impression is of a colonial mansion, embellished with arches in the Spanish style, topped with three pink domed minarets, as if from the set of an Errol Flynn desert melodrama. Its crowning features are the individual bungalows nestling among the oleanders and bougainvillaea of its gardens, like overseer's cabins in a Central American plantation, which even in 1972 cost $265 a day to rent. Virtually every cinema star of renown, from Lilian Gish to Raquel Welch, has stayed there at some time. Aristotle Onassis lived there for several years; so did Howard Hughes (he rented *four* bungalows). To Leee, it seemed that there could be nowhere more appropriate for someone acting out the role of star, and he altered the hotel booking accordingly.

By the time the group arrived at the Beverly Hills Hotel on October 16th it numbered forty-six. "It was," says Leee, "a huge mob." It had been attracting ever more members as the tour went on, among them Iggy Pop; the fabulously beautiful Cyrinda Foxe, who later married David Johansen of the New York Dolls; and Mike Garson's wife and two children. Not everyone had a bungalow – some had to make do with rooms in the main building – but the Garson family did, finding themselves flanked by Perry Como on one side and Elton John on the other. Garson still speaks of his wonder at discovering that one straightforward meal for his family cost $85 – "and that was without liquor".

By now no one had any money at all. But that in itself became an encouragement to the entourage to partake of every service the hotel could provide. They disported themselves by the side of the hotel pool and rented a line of cabanas in which to change. Unable to use taxis, since they required cash, they used limousines on the hotel account. A section of the exclusive Polo Lounge was sectioned off for their own use, with a special dispensation that they did not have to wear jackets, and they chose freely from the goods and trinkets in the hotel's shopping arcade. The most shameless of all invited chance acquaintances to dine in their rooms, charging them $10 in cash for a meal costing many times that amount.

Such a lifestyle, together with the renown of the Ziggy concerts, made them a prime target for America's notorious groupies, already renowned as the most voracious in the world (it was they who had spawned the sub-species known as plaster-casters, who liked to depart with a permanent trophy of their host's virility). Even before Los Angeles they had taken to clustering around the bus that was bearing the entourage back to their hotel, clamouring to be nominated to climb on board. David was the ultimate prize, with Stuey George commissioned, as in most other things, to act on his behalf. "If he said, 'I need two chicks,' or 'I need five chicks,'" Stuey says, "then I would try and arrange to get five chicks to spend the night with him."

For those not selected by Stuey, everyone else in the entourage, providing they were willing, was fair game. Groupies, of course, comprised another of the trappings of stardom: the only caution Defries issued was not to talk to them too much in case they were reporters in disguise. Now they gathered outside the Beverly Hills Hotel, hoping to be invited inside. All the consumption of those so favoured was added to the bill.

Defries arrived – as devoid of cash as everyone else, according to Leee – to preside over the extravaganza on October 18th. To some outsiders he did not cut a sympathetic figure. The *Rolling Stone*'s Timothy Ferris, who had been following the tour, as bemused by its profligacy as he was enthralled by the concerts, described how Defries wore tank-tops over his "lawyer-like paunch", smoked "fat black cigars" and appeared, with his pallid skin and "long pointed nose", to be a character from Dickens. To those inside, there was no need to question what was happening. "Don't forget he had spent years getting you to trust him and accept what he told you," says Stuey.

It became clear that Defries was extracting a wry pleasure from the lasciviousness around him when he issued a memorandum purporting to control the extravagance but in fact condoning it. The high level of expenditure had come to his notice, Defries grandly declared: henceforth, all groupies were to be sent home before breakfast.

Not for the first time, David himself oscillated between roles. In public he was willing to act out the part written for him (he was, after all, one of the scriptwriters). On the morning of the concert at Santa Monica on October 20th he took a limousine to the Civic Auditorium to help with the customary sound-check. Jim Rismiller was there, curious to see the protégés of the enigmatic Defries, not least because – to Rismiller's surprise – the concert had sold out "in seconds". He made to shake hands with David but was confronted by the menacing figures of Stuey George and Tony Frost, wearing white karate uniforms. "They said, 'Don't go near him, don't shake hands with him, David Bowie doesn't like to be touched,'" Rismiller recalls. (They added, for good measure, that David didn't like heights and didn't take elevators either.) David did not demur and Rismiller – accustomed to the suntanned physiques of California – recalls a "frail, chalk-white" figure. "I thought, This poor kid's a neurotic sickie."

The concert was outstanding, even by the high levels David had set, and Rismiller was deeply impressed. "The production was very good and they were very professional," he says. "The audience went crazy. And if they enjoy the show, then I enjoy the show." At the climax of 'Rock 'N' Roll Suicide', the front section of the audience reached out for David on cue, some leaving their seats to cluster around the stage. David appeared entranced by his own performance, darting forward as if to touch the outstretched hands, but then holding back; he said later that he had no recollection of seeing them at all.

It was after the concert that David revealed a different aspect of himself that also confounded some of the expectations others had of him. At a party given by the disc-jockey Wolfman Jack, he came upon Kim Fowley, whom he had met in Los Angeles in 1971. Previously, Fowley had found David quiet and inquisitive; this time, he was "another person, another creation – he was very pleased with himself, and he didn't listen as much". But David seemed unsure how to adjust to being the focus of attention. He and Fowley agreed that the party was full of "jerks", and David complained that everybody there would say they had met him that night, even though he had talked to none of them. "I'm terrified of their watching, their looking," he told Fowley.

Even in so public a place, David was not afraid of puncturing one of the illusions that Fowley shared. When Fowley saw three drag queens make a haughty and melodramatic entrance on the far side of the room, he assumed that David would want to meet them. David quickly disabused him: "Don't believe all the publicity," he said. Soon afterwards Fowley was dancing with a tall, lithe young woman when David came up to him and whispered in his ear.

"Is she with you?" he asked Fowley. "Is she your girlfriend or your wife?"

Fowley told David she was neither.

"Well, I want her," David replied.

Fowley asked the girl her name – "it was Debbie, or Donna, or Laurie" – and introduced her to David. After a perfunctory exchange, David took her by the hand and led her towards the bathroom. At that moment the three drag queens, who had been watching with unconcealed envy, pushed their way through the room and told David: "Don't go off with her." David pulled the girl into the bathroom and locked the door. The drag queens banged on the door with their high heels, yelling: "Let us in, we do it better." Fowley did not see David again that night. "He and the girl must have stayed in that room a century."

Rodney Bingenheimer met David again too. He had opened a club on Sunset Strip named Rodney Bingenheimer's Hit Club, later renamed Rodney's English Disco and renowned for its sponsorship of British records and groups. David, remembering his hospitality in 1971, made sure that he had good seats for the concert, which Bingenheimer thought "fantastic – one of the best shows I have ever seen".

David also came to Bingenheimer's club and took to the dance floor, whose décor included a wall composed of floor-to-ceiling mirrors. But David did not take a partner: "He was dancing with himself," Bingenheimer recalls. "He was dancing to the mirrors, doing certain movements, watching himself carefully, choreographing himself."

The bandwagon effect that Defries so wanted to create was powerfully increased, during the spell at the Beverly Hills Hotel, by the release of three records: one new, two old.

The new record was a single, and was directly inspired by the frenetic travelling of the early stages of the tour. On September 23rd, as their chartered Greyhound bus sped from Cleveland to Memphis, via an overnight stop at Nashville, an impromptu riff had been born. Mick Ronson was experimenting with a Les Paul gold-topped guitar he had recently acquired, connected to a pair of portable amplifiers that Will Palin had bought in New York; other guitars were produced, and most of the bus joined in. "We started this little jam," says Will Palin. "Bap bap bap *bee*-do, we're goin' bussin', bus bus *bus*, we're goin' bussin'."

David himself was well equipped for composing on the road. His baggage included several recording decks and a set of speakers which enabled him to make demonstration tapes in his hotel bedroom; he also carried a set of notepads on which he wrote lyrics, often while stretched out on the bedroom floor. Stuey George learned to withdraw when David was in one of his "pondering" moods, and fielded all telephone calls. By the time the group returned to New York for the Carnegie Hall concert David had written a lyric around the "bussin'" riff; he called it 'The Jean Genie'.

The lyric itself showed affection of two kinds: for America, and for the new words and phrases David had heard. 'The Jean Genie' spoke of the fast-moving, temporal life David had witnessed in American cities, captured in slang like "snuck off", and "strung out", and reinforced with a series of internal rhymes within each line: "lasers" and "blazers", "razors" and "waiters". The Jean Genie of the title, with its pun on the French homosexual writer Jean Genet, was a bawdy and outrageous bisexual; although some critics believed it to be based on Iggy Pop, much of it applied to David himself, like the lines in the choruses:

> Jean Genie, let yourself go

– and

> Loves to be loved, loves to be loved . . .

David and the Spiders recorded the song in the studios at RCA's Sixth Avenue offices, transforming the "bussin'" riff into a raucous shout that captured their own jubilant mood.

The release of 'The Jean Genie', backed by 'Hang On To Yourself', in the US in October coincided with the release by RCA of David's two Mercury albums. That was the result of some typically adroit manoeuvres by Defries, following his lunch with Mercury's Irwin Steinberg and Robin McBride in May 1971, when both sides had sworn their undying hatred for each other. In return for terminating David's contract, Steinberg, as he had threatened, had extracted every cent Mercury had spent on him. As spelled out in a "termination contract" dated September 27th, 1971, it came to $17,884.41.

Defries regarded the deal as a triumph. It was not just that the amount Steinberg had demanded was modest; he had also agreed to return the crucial masters of David's two Mercury albums. Defries believes that Steinberg and McBride would not have been prepared to sell the masters directly to RCA; "whereas they were willing to sell them, in effect, to Bowie".

The qualification, "in effect", was vital. Since David had signed the original contract with Mercury in June, 1969, he was responsible for securing its termination, and in consequence the crucial ownership of the masters reverted to him. But not for long. For Defries gave David a new document to sign by which he agreed to confer copyright in the masters to Gem "in perpetuity throughout the world." Defries and Myers thus leased the Mercury albums to RCA, an arrangement enshrined in a rider to the RCA contract known as the "Mercury amendment", dated December 17th, 1971.

The financial aspect of these dealings was no less ingenious. In theory, David was due to pay Mercury the $17,884.41 called for in its "termination contract". David, of course, did not have any such sum. So Defries and Myers agreed to finance the payment to Mercury on his behalf – and it was in return for providing that service that David transferred the copyright in the Mercury masters to them.

When Defries and Myers leased the masters to RCA, they received an advance of $20,000 against David's future earnings, which they used to pay off Mercury. That sum was then debited to David's account at Gem, to be repaid from his royalties in the usual way. At the end of these transactions, Gem had thus acquired, at no expense to itself, the copyright of the two Mercury albums, plus its own share in the royalties they would earn: "We got them for nothing," Myers confirms. When he and Defries parted company, the agreement was transferred from Gem to MainMan.

When RCA reissued the two albums, the first was renamed *Space Oddity* and given a new cover, showing a portrait of David. *The Man Who Sold The World* had a new cover too, a photograph taken of David during a publicity session for *Ziggy Stardust*, thereby avoiding the controversy its two previous designs – the Cane Hill and man's-dress covers – had caused. As both RCA and Defries had hoped, their release in October helped to capitalise on the success of the Ziggy concerts and album, which was now climbing the charts at last, and had just reached the top hundred in the *Billboard* listings. *Space Oddity* started to sell a creditable 15,000 copies a month and entered the *Billboard* album chart at 136 in November; *The Man Who Sold The World*, selling at half that rate, came in at 170. Out on the tour, both David and Defries joyfully brandished copies of the albums hot from the presses: David with evident pleasure at this further confirmation of his rising esteem; Defries doubtlessly inwardly smiling at the completion of another successful financial coup.

The Ziggy tour had originally been intended to end in California. In view of the success of the opening concerts, Defries had been assiduously extending it, adding dates here, subtracting others there, so that at one stage it resembled – the simile amused him – "a floating crap-game". He was still making arrangements after the Santa Monica concert, while David and the entourage languished at the Beverly Hills Hotel for almost a week. When the time came to leave, one detail remained to be attended to. The bill had soared beyond $100,000. Who would pay?

Just how RCA came to foot the bill was, according to Tony Zanetta, all a "misunderstanding" – although Zee also concedes that it was "one of the larger misunderstandings of history". For the question of the tour's finances provided a further example of Defries's mastery at turning ambiguous situations to his own advantage. RCA had agreed to make a small loan to help launch the tour, and offered help with the travel and hotel reservations. In some mysterious way, this offer became transmuted into an acceptance of full financial liability. Instead of acting as a supplicant when dealing with RCA's travel department, Leee, as Defries had instructed, had behaved in a peremptory manner: if they protested at the latest change of plans, such as switching from the Chateau Marmont to the Beverly Hills Hotel, Leee blithely assured them that it was all as Tony Defries had ordained. He also signed "RCA Records and Tapes" on every bill that was placed before him.

As RCA's representative on the tour, Gustl Breuer did not consider it one of his duties to rein in the extravagance or query the bills. Money was never his forte, he explains: "There was no sense putting me in charge." Thus when the group moved out of the Beverly Hills Hotel the magic formula "RCA Records and Tapes" was brought into play again, and the bill was forwarded to RCA's Los Angeles headquarters. Even today there is a sharp intake of breath among former RCA executives when the bill is mentioned; at the time, with the tour in full flight, there was no alternative but to settle it and hope to negotiate afterwards. That perfectly suited Defries, since it gave him another opportunity to "improve". Small wonder that out in California the cry resounded:: "RCA pay."

When the tour went back on the road, Defries made a gesture towards economy by sending some members of the entourage back to Britain, among them Dai Davies and the Underwoods. But to begin with, it appeared that he had overplayed his hand. David had a poor reception in San Francisco; at Seattle there was as meagre an audience as there had been at Kansas City; and Defries was compelled to cancel concerts at Dallas and Houston because of poor advance sales.

There were further problems in Nashville, brought about by the over-enthusiastic activities of Cherry Vanilla, who had joined Leee on the advance team. She invariably talked eagerly about the sexual activities of David and the entourage, and in Nashville, hoping to gain more publicity, she claimed that she had adopted her pseudonym while recording tapes to be distributed via the North Vietnamese government to American prisoners-of-war in Hanoi.

The news that a homosexual communist was apparently heading their way caused apoplexy among conservative groups in Nashville, and there was a demonstration outside the Municipal Auditorium on the night of the concert, November 20th. The local music establishment was as outraged as Memphis had been by the assertion that David was the "new Elvis Presley". "There is no similarity whatsoever, so far as talent is concerned," sniffed the *Nashville Banner*, which also reported that the 4,424-strong audience had been "subdued".

Once back in the north-east, however, it felt as if the tour was on home ground. It met a rapturous welcome in Cleveland, where all four RCA albums were in the local top ten and 'The Jean Genie' was selling out as soon as it reached the stores. There were two concerts in a hall holding 10,000 people: as at Carnegie Hall they became style events, and both were sold out. When the tour ended in Philadelphia, David caused a sensation. At the last encore of the final concert on December 2nd, David stirred the crowd to a frenzy and they rushed the stage. As he danced towards them he slipped and almost fell, but recovered to hook his legs over the orchestra rail, still singing as he dangled backwards: a breathtaking flirtation with disaster to match 'Rock 'N' Roll Suicide'.

Gustl Breuer returned to New York in buoyant mood: he had never thought he would enjoy himself so much. In musical terms, he felt, David would have been hard put to impress an audience at the Met, New York's opera house, since he lacked the training and voice control of operatic performers. Breuer also stood by his judgment, imparted to the big shots in September, that David lacked "out-and-out loin sex appeal". David seemed "a little bit too intellectual" – although, Breuer adds, "people can fall in love with an intellect: it's like Elisabeth Schumann against Lotte Lehmann".

The exception to his verdict – and, for Breuer the most exciting aspect of the concerts – had been the interaction between David and Mick Ronson on stage: that certainly did have loin appeal. "What happened between them was so sexy – perhaps over-sexy, but who cares?" he says. Breuer also admired David immensely as a singer who performed his own songs. Off stage, he found David shy and reserved, but interested in the friendships Breuer had struck during his long and varied career, particularly with Richard Strauss.

During the tour, there had been several occasions when the gulf between the two worlds, of classical and popular music, seemed to have narrowed. One came in Nashville, where the Guarneri Quartet was playing a Beethoven concert the night before the Ziggy concert. When Breuer announced that he was going to see "his original love", Mick Ronson and Woody Woodmansey asked if they could come too. Breuer took them backstage afterwards and introduced them to the opposition. "They spent so long discussing different string techniques," he says, "that the Guarneri missed their plane."

On the second occasion, it appeared that the superstars of the two musical worlds had much in common. The tour reached Cleveland just after a major performance of Verdi's *Requiem*, and the two camps encountered each other in a restaurant near the concert hall. On one side were such operatic giants as Placido Domingo, Martina Arroyo and Shirley Verrett; on the other, the Ziggy entourage, among them Suzi Fussey.

When Breuer crossed the floor to greet his old friends, he learned that Placido Domingo had conceived an unassuageable longing to meet Suzi Fussey. "You have to introduce me to this girl," he told Breuer; "the boobs, she is incredible."

Breuer told him not to be ridiculous; "you will have to find someone else." But Domingo persisted, until Breuer finally told Suzi that Domingo would like to meet her. He was, Breuer explained, "the greatest opera singer ever".

For once, the wishes of the greatest opera singer ever went unfulfilled. Clearly doubting Breuer's description, Suzi looked across to the other group.

"What, that fat slob?"

22

Watch the Man

Late on Christmas day 1972, Ian Hunter was fast asleep at a friend's house in Northampton when David called him from Haddon Hall. They had last seen each other in New York two weeks before, when Hunter was in the throes of an arduous tour with Mott the Hoople and David had just completed the Ziggy tour: David had played Hunter some of the songs he proposed to record on his next album, and they had parted – after Angie had insisted they all eat at an all-night deli – at 5.30 a.m. Hunter had flown home from Memphis on Christmas Eve and he and his wife Trudy had driven to Northampton for Christmas Day. Now Hunter was awoken from his sleep, born of exhaustion and jet-lag, to take David's call. There was a note of urgency in David's voice. "I want to discuss the band's future," he told Hunter. "You must come at once."

To virtually anyone else, Hunter would have responded – and frequently did – with a brief two-word epithet. But he was still in David's debt: the single 'All The Young Dudes' had sold half a million copies and had been Mott the Hoople's salvation; and when they were performing in Philadelphia, David had driven 300 miles by taxi from Pittsburgh to fulfil a promise to introduce them on stage. Assuming that David had further advice to impart, he and Trudy wearily set off from Northampton to drive to Haddon Hall.

When they arrived a surprise awaited them. Expecting David to be ready for the "urgent" talks he had proposed, Hunter found him sitting on a settee with a childish grin on his face and Freddi Burretti beside him. When Hunter asked what he wanted to talk about, David merely played peekaboo from behind a cushion and grinned again, clearly delighted at having induced Hunter so readily to drive to Haddon Hall. Angie, says Hunter, was "embarrased and upset", leaving him in a dilemma over what to do. "It was either smack him or ignore him, and I didn't really want to smack him because of Angie, so I just ignored it," he says. In some disgust, he and Trudy drove home to their flat in Wembley.

In retrospect, Hunter felt he had fallen prey to David's increasing mercuriality: "He could walk into the toilet one person and walk out another and I never knew if it was just him putting on a little charade or if it was for real." Or perhaps, Hunter wondered, it was another example of David's "chess-playing", seeking to outmanoeuvre and discomfort his rivals, even when they were also his friends.

Either way, it was clear that David had acquired all he could from Hunter: his spell as one of David's most favoured friends was over. It was a repetition of David's habit of forming intimate and creative friendships and then moving on. Now, at the end of 1972, a new colleague had been chosen for that role: the Brooklyn pianist, Mike Garson.

Their friendship had been struck towards the end of the Ziggy tour, as David began to plan his next RCA album. Late one night, when the group was winding down after a Ziggy concert, Garson started to play some jazz standards on a bar-room piano. When he struck up 'My Funny Valentine', David came across and sang with him. "He used a real straight voice, a little like Anthony Newley but his own way of doing it, and he sang it beautifully," Garson recalls. Thereafter, David displayed an obsessive interest in Garson's past among the giants of the jazz world, and listened intently as Garson talked of playing with Bill Evans, Herbie Hancock and Lennie Tristano, and accompanying Nancy Wilson and Mel Torme. In short, says Garson, "I was the star".

Like some before him, Garson was aware that he was being plundered by David; like the more astute of David's victims, he was determined to glean what he could for himself. As one of the more moral – even puritanical – musicians ever to make a rock tour, he had averted his eyes from its excesses, and was less than happy with such items as the mock-fellatio on Mick Ronson's guitar. "There were some things I couldn't support," he says. But Garson – knowing he was "in the space of a real talent" – always watched from the wings when he was not on stage. "I saw his acting and his stage presence. I knew I was around someone who was marvellous and I had the intention to learn from it."

The relationship between David and Garson deepened when David began recording his new album at RCA's New York studios in December, continuing – after a brief Ziggy tour in northern England and Scotland – at the Trident studios in London in the New Year. The Spiders were reinforced by Ken Fordham on saxophone, and there were three backing singers: Juanita Franklin; the British-born black singer Linda Lewis, then just starting her career; and MacCormack – credited as Mac Cormack – whose friendship with David went back to the days of Burnt Ash Juniors in Bromley, and who had been one of the celebrants at the Beverly Hills Hotel. But it was Garson whom David leaned on most. "Even though the Spiders were the well-known commodity, I was the one who was getting the attention," Garson says. "He was fascinated – he wanted everything I could do."

Garson remained happy to mine his experiences on David's behalf, and showed how effectively he could do so when recording a piano solo which David hoped would express the overall mood of his album. Garson first gave the solo a traditional bluesy feel and then tried a Latin beat. David was not happy with either and reminded Garson of his descriptions of the avant-garde jazz of Greenwich Village in the mid-1960s, which Garson called "dissonant, rebellious, atonal, and very *outside*". David asked Garson to play in the same style and, to emphasise his point, told him the title of the track, which he had not previously revealed. "It's called 'A Lad Insane'," David said, "and it's crazy."

Garson began with a parody of a sugary night-club style which gradually fractured into shards of modern jazz, jumping from threatening bass chords to the upper reaches of the keyboard, giving full force to the meaning of David's title. "David loved it," Garson says.

As the title itself so boldly proposed, the album once again encapsulated the principal themes of his career. As usual, there was a direct biographical input, which he obligingly signposted on the credit label by naming the place where each lyric had been written or inspired. Most sprang from the US, and showed, like 'The Jean Genie', David's fascination for the new landscape he had seen and heard, ranging from Mike Garson's jazz to the new forms of drugs and sex.

David's inner landscape was also on display, as he made clear when he told interviewers that *Aladdin Sane* – as the title-track was eventually rendered – was "really Ziggy in America". David added that he had "run into a very strange type of paranoid person" while working on the album, leaving it open that the "paranoid person" was himself. Certainly that was the implication of his further explanation that, like much of his work, *Aladdin Sane* was "just looking around – seeing what's in my head".

In keeping with the impression of turbulence and disorder, David's language and imagery were more disconnected than ever, and he sometimes succumbed to word-plays and echoes at the expense of literal sense. At the same time, his old preoccupations shone through. The nature of affection and its relationship to sex, visions of apocalypse and premonitions of disaster, the interplay between image and reality, the role and strategy of being a star; all were there. David also broached a new theme that took him into the heart of his family mythology: the horror of war.

Musically, the dominant new note was Mike Garson's piano, which showed not only Garson's jazz credentials but also the kind of versatility that David liked to deploy. The other main stylistic influence came from the Rolling Stones, and according to the producer, Ken Scott, it was this that helped to explain the album's comparative crudeness when set against the technical splendours of *Ziggy Stardust*. "We wanted to take it that much rougher," Scott says. "*Ziggy* was rock and roll but polished rock and roll. David wanted certain tracks to go like the Rolling Stones and unpolished rock and roll." Scott's explanation is valid, up to a point; but it is also true that the pressure of the Ziggy tour did not permit David to devote as much time to the *Aladdin Sane* album as he had to *Ziggy Stardust*.

The album began with 'Watch That Man', an account of a fashionable party. Although David located it in New York, its mood recalled Los Angeles: as narrator, David complained of the people "looking up to me for encouragement", just as he had told Kim Fowley of his unease at being the focus of "watching, looking" at Wolfman Jack's party; the room was also full of mirrors, like Rodney Bingenheimer's disco. The lyric was threaded with discordant, surrealistic imagery: the mirrors crack; a man paints holes in his hands and is hung up by them, as if crucified, to dry; "bodies on the screen stop bleeding", while the narrator himself is "shakin' like a leaf", unable to comprehend what is being said around him. The lyric added up to an outsider's viewpoint, unsure of himself, unable to understand, wanting to belong.

Like his previous "homosexual" lyrics, "Watch That Man' also introduced a new hidden code in David's writing. At the imagined party, David could not take his eyes off a cool, powerful figure who despite behaving "like a jerk" appeared to be in full control, disdainfully observing the lesser figures around him. He was the "man" of the title, and in the drug culture the "man" is another term denoting the dealer or supplier.

There were further clues in the song's tempo, which borrowed openly from Lou Reed's 'Waiting For My Man', an account of an addict awaiting new supplies. As usual, David was describing what he had seen. In the US of the early 1970s, cocaine, already well established among jazz musicians, was fast making inroads into the entertainment industry, and no fashionable show-business party was complete without a supply of the white powder into which a tiny spoon would be dipped for all to inhale or "snort". David had not yet partaken himself – at least, so Leee Childers believes – but had been fascinated to see the ritual acted out.

Three other lyrics on the first side of the album had similar coded references: "scored" and "snorting" in 'Drive-In Saturday'; "scored," "made a run" in 'Panic In Detroit'; "smack", "connection" in 'Cracked Actor'. These three tracks all contained other allusions to well-known ground. 'Drive-in Saturday' was subtitled 'Seattle-Phoenix', and David explained that while travelling between the two cities he had been unnerved at seeing enormous silver domes glinting in the moonlight, whose purpose he had been unable to discover. He said that they sparked a vision of "America, Britain and China, after a nuclear catastrophe", whose survivors would be unable to have children, and which David portrayed with a series of futuristic scenes, of aliens and strangers, "the strange ones in the dome", bursting arms and limbs, and "fall-out saturation".

The interplay between image and reality that had dominated *Hunky Dory* also appeared in 'Drive-In Saturday', as did the relationship between sex and affection. David depicted the familiar figure of a woman watching herself on screen: who is the real me, she asks? And do I really like my partner, even though I feel I love him? The musical setting added to the sense of questioning and otherworldliness, maintaining a tension that was never resolved by remaining tantalisingly above the tune's home key, almost like an act of unconsummated intercourse.

Similar tension ran through 'Panic In Detroit', with the title itself sung in a repeated phrase that fell and then rose, once again denying the listener the satisfaction of musical resolution. The song depicted the same urban breakdown as several of David's earlier lyrics, from the sniper in 'Running Gun Blues' to the glimpse of future nightmare in *Ziggy*. It was shot through with discordant and paranoid imagery: of guns, police sirens, screams, breaking metal, and "a trickle of strangers" who were "all that were left alive". Like *Ziggy*, it conjured scenes of the night – "the silent cars that slept at traffic lights" – and of loneliness: "I wish someone would phone." The most telling link with Ziggy came in the suggestion of a suicide, with the narrator finding a man "slumped across the table", leaving his gun and a note asking: "Let me collect dust."

'Cracked Actor', the last track on the side, with references to Hollywood High and Sunset and Vine, was firmly sited in Hollywood. It was loaded with the jargon of sex – "trick", "stiff"

— as well as of drugs — and presented a crude and strident account of a one-night stand with a partner of whom he demands an equal trade-off:

> Suck, baby, suck, give me your head.

Fittingly, for a tale of Hollywood, it also told of the selling of illusions, and of a narcissistic star, "stiff on my legend". The music was equally forthright, a raucous and uncompromising rock beat that showed that the tinsel city had not deceived David.

The second side of the album continued to explore similar themes. 'The Prettiest Star', a new recording of the single Mercury had issued in 1970, was ostensibly the most romantic track on the album, although David's presentation, with its hint of mockery and exaggeration, suggested that he was having second thoughts. 'Let's Spend The Night Together' was an impudent remake of the Rolling Stones' celebration of raw and sensual sex, with a breathless near-manic beat to rival anything the Stones themselves could have served up. David stamped his own imprint on the song with Mike Garson's discordant introduction and with the haphazard way it ended, seeming to dissipate into the ether as if David could no longer be bothered to sustain his act.

The next track, 'The Jean Genie', offered another comment through the exotic counterpoint it provided to the Stones' more orthodox approach to sex. Then came 'Lady Grinning Soul', which although attributed to London could have been written in the Beverly Hills Hotel, for its invocation of sensuous sex, with "skin sweet with musky oil", and "the fullness of her breast", and the badges of wealth: his lover wears silver and eau de Cologne, and deploys her credit card.

Mike Garson's piano enhanced the voluptuous atmosphere: "There was very romantic piano on that," he says; "a Chopin, Liszt type of attitude of the late 1800s". This also served to sustain the irony of the lyric, for the woman exerted a disdainful power over David. Still not free of Hermione, it seemed, he lamented that "she'll come, she'll go," and warned, in the last line:

> She will be your living end.

Two numbers, 'Time', which opened side two, and 'Aladdin Sane' itself, which occupied the second track on side one, appeared at first to be at odds with the rest of the album. But although they showed less of its overt themes — love, sex, affection, drugs, together with the scenes David had recollected from his travels – they stood firmly with his central preoccupations, as well as serving as David's habitual forecast of his future intentions.

'Time' staged a daring confrontation with David's old adversaries, transience and ephemerality. He placed it in New Orleans, with an introduction from Garson mimicking a 1930s "stride" pianist. "It was an almost swing or Dixieland style," Garson says, "and he liked my concept on that because it had to do with time, and I was playing in another time-zone, and he was talking about time . . ." In fact, the musical allusions were richer than Garson describes, for they also showed hints of that mocking distancing known as Brechtian, although equally the work of his composer partner, Kurt Weill.

These were reflected in the lyric, which borrowed the key metaphor of *Ziggy* in depicting time as a figure "waiting in the wings" to claim David as he played out his role. David abused time as a masturbating whore, but could not understand everything she said; he was fearful of becoming frail and old and of "the sniper in the brain", and expressed his gratitude at discovering he was still alive. At the end, in a sombre coda, David revealed his despair at the ending of relationships and the advent of loneliness and the dark. He also talked of his sorrow at discovering that by breaking up a relationship "the door to dreams was closed".

The echoes of *Ziggy*, together with David's fear that he had failed in his aim of achieving peace through fantasy, were the first suggestion that he was on the point of finishing with the Ziggy character and wanted to move on.

Further signs that this was so came in the title track, 'Aladdin Sane', and in its elusive subtitles. 'R.H.M.S. *Ellinis*' was straightforward enough: the Royal Hellenic Mail Ship *Ellinis* was the liner on which David had crossed the Atlantic at the end of the US 'Ziggy' tour. But what could (1913–1938–197?) mean?

The best answer was to be found in the lyric, which told of soldiers preparing to leave home to fight and perhaps to die. The first verse described a bouquet of dead roses, suggesting the first world war; the second verse told of the "bright young things" of Britain of the 1920s and 1930s about to be taken "away to war". Other phrases offered contrasts between celebration and suffering: "battlecries and champagne", "Paris or maybe hell", "clutches of sad remains".

Not for the first time, David had reserved his most vital message for his title song. The name itself proclaimed that he was facing the question of madness; the lyric showed that he was also prepared to confront the nature of war, the most threatening of all the themes with which previous generations of his family were burdened, and the metaphor for the family's insanity.

By mid-January, 1973, David had become a fully-fledged British media hero. His acceleration to fame was brought about, in part, by Defries's skill at playing the transatlantic game. Having persuaded RCA to pay for American journalists to see David in Britain, he now made sure that British music writers were present at his US Ziggy concerts so that they could report his success in America – in British eyes, following the renown achieved by the Beatles in the 1960s, the ultimate test.

In Britain, David began to receive national newspaper coverage, linked to the arrival of 'The Jean Genie' at number two in the hit parade, embellished by the new myths that Defries encouraged. On January 18th, the *Daily Express* reported that "a gold disc was on the way for [David's] third million-selling album"; three days later, the *Daily Mirror* also stated that *Ziggy* had sold a million copies. The claims were absurd exaggerations: by the beginning of 1973, *Ziggy* had sold precisely 95,968 copies in Britain, and roughly the same number in the US; none of his other albums had reached even half those totals.

To Defries, truth was now only of secondary importance where winning publicity was concerned: the paramount need was to create an impact. David was now proudly telling reporters that he had acquired the rights to film the science-fiction novel *Stranger in a Strange Land*, by Robert Heinlein, and that he would be both writing the score and taking the leading role. Significantly, he was making the same claim in private. One day David and Angie called on Ken Scott to find him reading *Stranger in a Strange Land*. "That's incredible," David told Scott. "I've got the lead role in the movie."

Much later Scott asked David why the film had not been made. "That was just a ploy," David told him. He explained that Defries had made the announcement so that he would be regarded as a potential actor, helping to develop his image as a man of many talents. But Scott is certain that David was originally convinced by the story himself. "David one hundred per cent believed he had the starring role in the movie, without a shadow of a doubt," he says.

On January 17th, David passed the ultimate test of national acceptance: he appeared on ITV's *Russell Harty Show*. He was, however, hard put to provide imaginative answers to questions such as "What kind of home did you come from?" ("A small one") and "Do you believe in God?"

One person who watched the programme with mounting rage, although not at the banality of Harty's questions, was David's aunt Pat, for the attention David was receiving fuelled her anger at what she saw as Terry's concomitant neglect. For that, she had principally blamed her sister Peggy but now her anger focused on David too. If he was such a star – and presumably a rich one – why could he not show more interest in Terry?

Pat excluded Angie from her strictures. Just before Christmas, Angie had telephoned to invite her for lunch at the Holiday Inn near Marble Arch, where several American members of the entourage were staying. Pat, who was working as a telephonist at the Abbey National building society in Baker Street, was delighted to accept.

When Angie and Pat met, they exchanged Christmas presents. Angie gave Pat six embroidered table mats; Pat gave Angie a bottle of Nina Ricci perfume. Angie seemed thrilled – it was, she exclaimed, her favourite scent. Over lunch, Pat talked inevitably of Terry, and complained that David never saw him any more. Angie jumped to David's defence. "Don't blame David for every-thing," she told Pat. "He always remembers how coldly he was treated as a child – and there's no love lost between him and his mother."

Then Pat explained that Terry and Olga were living on social security, receiving an "invalid benefit" which left them permanently short of money. Angie responded at once. "She went straight down to reception to get some money out and she came back and gave me £200," Pat recalls.

Pat naturally assumed that the £200 had come from Angie herself, rather than being merely added, in the usual fashion, to the hotel bill. Either way, Terry was delighted when Pat passed on the £200, which he and Olga spent on carpets. "Terry was very fond of Angie," Pat says, "because she was so kind to him."

For most of the time David spent working on *Aladdin Sane*, Tony Defries had remained in New York, where he was building up the MainMan organisation and preparing for David's next US tour. MainMan's headquarters were now established at the premises Tony Zanetta had found at 240 East 58th Street, which also contained an apartment where Defries and Melanie McDonald set up home. That brought Defries the advantage that he would not have to venture out too frequently: displaying another of the attributes he encouraged in David, he liked to be immured against the outside world.

Defries was also taking on new staff: and one person amazed to find herself in New York was Brooks Ogden, previously a hat-check girl in St Louis. She had met David and the entourage when the Ziggy concert played there, and was instantly enraptured: "They were the best-looking people I had ever met in my life," she says. Soon afterwards Melanie invited her to New York, where she became Melanie's personal assistant. Brooks was another innocent who fell under Defries's spell: "He walks into a room and tells you that orange is green and you go, 'Right, it's green.' He can explain to you why it's green, and you go away and can't quite remember how orange became green, but you know that it is."

Brooks was also astonished to discover the extent to which Defries was a workaholic, even though in the US such a condition is not necessarily regarded as a disease. Linda Palermo, who became one of MainMan's publicity officials, shared Brooks's feeling: "Working for Tony was your life and your social life," Linda says. "If you were going out of the door he'd say, 'Where are you going? Let's have a meeting.' And it would go on until two in the morning. Tony had nothing else to do and that's what he liked doing." When one staff member complained at having to work on a Sunday, Tony issued a blunt memo: "There are no Sundays at MainMan."

Tony also went to see Rocco Laginestra again. In discussions that began before Christmas and continued into the New Year, Defries broached the question of how David's tours should be financed, a topic which included the thorny matter of who would foot the bill from the Beverly Hills Hotel. Defries knew that even RCA would call a halt to expenditure on so gargantuan a scale, particularly now that the preliminary accounts of the 1972 tour had been prepared. By Defries's reckoning, the tour had produced an income of $116,260.91, which resulted in a loss to MainMan of $10,373.94. But that did not include the cost to RCA, which Tony Zanetta later estimated as close to $300,000.

From his first meeting with Laginestra, Defries went on the offensive. He brandished a sheaf of news cuttings, among them articles in *Time*, *Newsweek* and *The New Yorker*, and, best of all, a report by Timothy Ferris in *Rolling Stone*, which occupied the cover and four pages, and included half a dozen photographs by Mick Rock. Since Ferris had devoted much of his article to describing Defries's strategy for inflating David into a star, Defries could argue that here was proof that extravagance brought its own reward.

Defries had further arguments to deploy. If RCA were to insist on strict profit-and-loss accounting, deducting David's touring expenses from his record royalties, it could have a disastrous effect on this, the "critical formative period" of his career. Defries proposed instead separate accounts at RCA for tour and record revenues. He conceded that the tour account might show an initial deficit. But with almost continuous touring planned for that year, in the US, Japan, Britain, Europe, and a return to the US in the autumn, it could show a profit sooner than anyone supposed.

To this entirely reasonable proposition, Laginestra agreed. That left one detail to be settled: who would pay the bill at the Beverly Hills Hotel? Here, Defries had a formula to suggest. The touring agreement should "apply from the initial involvement"; in other words, it should be retrospective and include all expenditure on the first US tour. To that too, Laginestra agreed.

Defries did not bother to conceal the pleasure he took from dealing with record company executives. "He's really into it, he really enjoys it," says Brooks Ogden. "While you and I might go and see a Peter Sellers movie and have a good chuckle, he likes to go into a negotiation." And when he returned to the office, having achieved a coup such as this, his joy was quite unconfined. "He showed great delight," she says; "great falling-down-on-the-ground-laughing delight."

Defries once revealed to Brooks the key method he employed when impasse loomed. He liked to smoke Havana Montecristo cigars at meetings since they irritated Americans not only because of the Cuban trade embargo but also by their pungent smoke. "These are my deal-making cigars," he told Brooks. "I smoke and I smoke and I smoke, and just when I'm ready to make a deal I light another one, and they give in to anything."

Once Defries had secured Laginestra's acceptance in principle, the minutiae of the touring agreement had still to be worked out. Here, Defries did not deal solely with Laginestra, nor did he entirely have his own way. In the subsequent discussions, Laginestra's assistant, Mort Hoffman, was reinforced by Mel Ilberman, a tall and imposing man of considerable political skills who had already survived ten years at RCA, and who now began to act as backstop to the deals that Laginestra made. Ilberman considered Defries a worthy adversary. Even though he found him at times "totally unreasonable and very very difficult", he admired Defries's nerve, and conceded that he had achieved a "creative" and "novel" renegotiation of the touring finances.

It took until March 22nd to hammer out the precise terms of

the new agreement, which specified the share of the gross receipts for each side and, more fancifully, the share of the profits. It ran for five years from January 1st, 1973, although also acknowledging, in testimony to Defries's powers of persuasion over Laginestra, "that RCA has financed the Artist's United States tour, which took place in the Fall of 1972".

Defries also succeeded in reopening the terms of David's recording contract; and although those negotiations were not concluded until July 1st, they too were backdated to the start of the year. The improvement that Defries secured was less impressive than the touring agreement, at least to begin with. David's advance per album was increased from $37,500 to $60,000 in 1973, but it escalated thereafter: to $100,000 per album in 1974, $150,000 in 1975, and $200,000 in 1976. However, the royalty figures, rising to 15 per cent on sales over 750,000 copies, were generous by current standards; and Defries certainly presented the new contract as a triumph, when he claimed that it was worth $400,000.

David and Angie arrived in New York on the *QE2* on January 30th. While David applied the finishing touches to *Aladdin Sane* at the RCA studios, Defries laid the final preparations for the next series of concerts, which was due to start at New York's Radio City on February 14th. As Defries had promised RCA, the new tour would be a far tighter affair than in 1972, playing just seven cities, with several concerts in each. In deference to RCA's wishes, the supporting entourage would be virtually halved, and would do its best to behave more frugally. A respectful note from Defries to Gustl Breuer – whose services he had specifically requested – affirmed: "We would like to stay in good hotels but do not require the most luxurious." And while RCA would meet the cost of the rooms, MainMan would pay for everything else. All bills were to be signed MainMan: no longer were the words "RCA Records and Tapes" the passport to dreamland.

David's own preparations for the tour bore signs of the shift from the original Ziggy concept that the *Aladdin Sane* album hinted at. He decided to enlarge the Spiders by recruiting four extra musicians: Brian Wilshaw and Ken Fordham on saxophones; Geoffrey MacCormack as a back-up vocalist; and, on rhythm guitar, his colleague from the days of the Buzz and Feathers, the Yorkshireman John Hutchinson. Subtle changes in David's stage mannerisms were taking place too: during the short British tour in the New Year, Mick Rock observed that David appeared less camp or fey than before, and had become decisively either masculine or feminine instead.

Rock believed that David – profiting from his relationships as ever – had learned his new moves from observing Cyrinda Foxe in the latter stages of the first US tour. "He got a few moves from her, he softened up his look through her," Rock says. That, too, fitted *Aladdin Sane*, for the lyrics contained virtually none of the gay slang that marked *Ziggy Stardust*. David introduced a number of the songs from *Aladdin Sane* into his concert repertoire, although still planning to end on the cathartic 'Rock 'N' Roll Suicide'.

When the tour opened at Radio City Music Hall there were greater surprises in store for David's audience, who included Salvador Dali and the rock musicians Todd Rundgren and Johnny Winter. Several hundred fans came dressed as Ziggy, wearing high heels and Ziggy haircuts, thinking that they would be at the apogee of fashion. They found that David had already moved on, for he wore a new range of costumes, with five changes in all, the most spectacular an all-enveloping striped clown costume that was stripped from him on stage. He also took to wearing a white circle painted on his forehead, that seemed to represent an astral body and therefore related to David's use of heavenly explorations as the symbol for inner space.

The audience – the Ziggy clones apart – applauded the new David rapturously, and all 5,884 seats were sold for both Radio City performances. The most dramatic moment of the opening concert came during 'Rock 'N' Roll Suicide', when David fainted after a fan leaped on to the stage and embraced him. While most of the band hesitated, suspecting that this was yet another bid for publicity, Mike Garson abandoned his piano and rushed across to help loosen David's clothing and carry him from the stage.

David did not regain conciousness until he reached the dressing room. He stared at Garson in bewilderment and asked: "What are you doing here?" Garson presumed that David had passed out because the pores of his skin were blocked with make-up; but the incident accorded, rather too close for comfort, with the Ziggy myth itself, and with the fears David had expressed that he would be the first rock-star to be assassinated on stage.

From New York, the tour swung through Philadelphia, Nashville, Memphis, Detroit, Chicago, to Los Angeles. Seven concerts at the Tower Theatre in Philadelphia, with a capacity of 2,575, sold out in hours, and even in Tennessee, despite the continuing hostility of the press, his audiences were won over again. In Memphis, the *Press-Scimitar* reported that the audience, "in their rapt attention . . . exhibited a strange and somewhat puzzling attraction by Bowie"; in Nashville, where the music reporter on the *Nashville Banner* had made no secret of his aversion for David, proclaiming his dislike for "queers", the *Nashville Tennessean* grudgingly conceded: "Bowie really is not a bad rock musician, if one can consider him such."

Despite the compliments, even the backhanded ones, all was not quiet in the Bowie camp; among the Spiders From Mars, there were stirrings of unrest. The Spiders were unhappy that David had enlarged the band and that they were being positioned further and further away on stage; the more David's acclaim mounted, the more they felt they were being treated as a backing band.

The Spiders' dissatisfaction was not eased by a conversation between Mike Garson and Woody Woodmansey during a plane journey between venues. The two men were becoming close, particularly since Garson, who was a Scientologist, had been proselytising among his colleagues, and found Woody the most likely convert. Now Woody broached the subject that most English people regard as the great unmentionable: he asked Garson how much he was being paid.

"I was real embarrassed to tell him," says Garson, "because it was so much less than what I thought he was making." Garson had assumed Woody was earning around $2,000 a week. "So I said, '$800 a week.' His face dropped." As Woody now revealed, he and Trevor Bolder were still being paid £30 a week, plus their keep. "I was in shock," says Garson. So, it is fair to add, was Woody.

During a stop in New York, Woody, Trevor and Mick Ronson consulted Dennis Katz, the A and R man who had signed David to RCA but had since became an independent show-business lawyer. They told Katz they wanted to leave the tour, but Katz advised them that they were contractually obliged to continue. However, the Spiders now approached Tony Defries and asked for more money. Defries agreed; but like any skilful employer facing labour problems, he managed to split their forces by taking Mick Ronson on one side and promising a glowing career if he would remain loyal. Mick succumbed, and a rift developed between him and the others, never to be healed.

There was one Yorkshireman on whom these distractions did not at first impinge. He was John Hutchinson, who had been recruited to the enlarged band by Mick Ronson only days before it was due to fly to the US. Mick had given Hutch a pithy account of the delights in store. "Mick said, 'It's bloody crazy, you won't believe it, chicks, gor' . . . I was waiting to see what it was all about." For Hutch, joining the tour was like landing on another planet. "It was crazy, just crazy, from the word go."

Hutch had been told that the name of the group's hotel in New York was a closely guarded secret. When he checked in, groupies were already wandering the corridors, and one soon called him on the house phone to ask: "Can I come up?" At first Hutch was embarrassed that his desires could be gratified so easily, but he soon learned that such behaviour was considered the norm. "Groupies know they're groupies and the guys in the band just go along with it," Hutch says.

In Los Angeles, a groupie joined Hutch as he took the lift to his hotel room. "She had a bag full of grass and a pocket of cocaine. She gave me a joint and introduced me to the house detective. It was crazy." There, too, he found there was no limit to his aspirations. "I was well into it," he says. "I was quite happy to have three on the go, depending which one was there, and they all knew each other."

By the time he reached Los Angeles, however, Hutch was no longer immune to the tensions among the musicians over David's changing view of himself and their roles. At first, Hutch had hoped that despite the three-year interval, his old friendship with David could be resumed. In New York, David played him some recordings made by "a new guy he'd got to hear about", who was Bryan Ferry of Roxy Music, and they went to see a performance by the jazz bassist Charlie Mingus together. But then, says Hutch, "I gradually lost it."

Hutch found himself being cold-shouldered by the established musicians, who resented his closeness to David; one member of the entourage even warned him that he was "presuming a bit much". On stage, he was positioned so far to the side that he was sometimes almost in the wings. He suspected that David had come to feel that he was not worthy to rank among his peers; Hutch in turn became disenchanted with David in the role of star, bidding others to satisfy his whims. "With David being looked after all the time by those people, it started to give me the feeling that he was there to snap his fingers, 'get me a drink, get me a girl', and that didn't feel right to me," Hutch says.

In Los Angeles, several other people saw the changes being wrought by stardom in both David and Defries. One was Jim Rismiller, who had promoted the Ziggy concert at Santa Monica the previous autumn. This time David's concert, at the Long Beach Arena, was promoted by Pacific Presentations. Rismiller had been offered the concert, but not on the terms he had so cosily arranged when Defries was playing the innocent abroad; Defries wanted a 90/10 split of the revenue. "I said that was absolutely absurd," Rismiller says; "we passed." Rismiller felt that to accept so one-sided a deal would establish a costly precedent. "Some other promoter took it," he says. "There's always someone else who comes along."

Kim Fowley saw David again too – but only from afar. Fowley and a friend went to eat at the Rainbow Restaurant where they saw David on the first floor, flanked by Stuey George and Tony Frost. David looked down at Fowley and grimaced. "He didn't come to say hello," says Fowley. "By then his station in life didn't mean jostling through a crowd to say 'hi'."

Shortly afterwards there was a commotion as a young man made a threatening move towards David and called him a punk. Stuey bundled the man away and ushered David out of the restaurant, passing Fowley on the way. "I remember looking at David as he walked by," says Fowley. "It was a man who said, 'There is somebody here who is hostile, I have too many things to do in my life than to deal with that. Now I'll go and make my international phone call.' It was all in his face."

A third witness to the changing David was Lori Mattix; she, and a friend named Sable, both girls in their early teens, had been at the Rainbow too. Their encounter with David, by contrast, showed that even while in thrall to the rewards of stardom, he could still be sensitive to the needs of others, no matter how improbable they might appear.

Lori was slim and sprightly, with an athletic body that she instinctively knew, even at her intimidatingly young age, how to display, prancing and pirouetting while maintaining a look of smouldering innocence in her nut-brown eyes. Later, Lori achieved renown as the lover of Jimmy Page, with whom she lived for two years; while Sable was already established as one of California's most celebrated groupies.

At the Rainbow, David had spotted both Lori and Sable from afar; ironically, although it was Sable, anxious to add to her collection of rock-stars, who was more avid to meet David, it was Lori whom Stuey George invited to the hotel on David's behalf. Beside herself with jealousy, Sable insisted on coming too. "She wanted to meet him more than anything in the world," says Lori, "and she begged me to take her with me and I did."

When they arrived at David's suite, Stuey opened the door and ushered them in. Soon afterwards David came out of the bedroom. "I had this shock," says Lori, "because he had no eyebrows and carrot-red hair sticking up and two different colour eyes and he was wearing a red kimono and he was just the most amazing creature I had ever laid my eyes on. I was just in awe."

After generous servings of marijuana and champagne, David led Lori into the bathroom, where a bubble bath awaited. David asked Lori to wash his back. "So I started giving him a bath and he was sort of magnificent, this real pale creature sitting in the bath and I was really sort of turned on. He's talking to me and he's really intelligent, telling me things about himself, a real sensitive creature, and I didn't know what was going to happen and he stood up out of the bath and, ohhhhhh my God . . ."

David took Lori into his bedroom. "I'll never forget it, never, he was so gentle about the whole thing. Obviously whatever happened happened and we did it for about five or six hours. He was wonderful."

In her repose, Lori was increasingly troubled by feelings of guilt. They emanated not from her Catholic upbringing – from that point of view, she says, "it was really worth it, every minute" – but because Sable was still marooned in the sitting room. "So after David and I had sort of done things and sort of talked, I was kind of saying, 'I feel guilty over Sable.'" Although David said he only wanted to be with her, Lori insisted on returning to the sitting room to see how Sable was faring. Lori found her pacing the carpet, wearing only gloves and a pair of garters, with a coat on top to keep warm, and a joint in her hand. On the fogged-up window of the room was the inscription: "I want to fuck David".

"I really couldn't believe it," Lori says. "So I walked into the bedroom and said, 'David, I feel ever so sorry for her, she's gotta fuck you.' I knew how much it meant to her. He didn't really want to, but I said, 'I feel so bad and you gotta do it, you can't break her heart, you know.' So I brought her into the room. David was very good to her and gave her what she wanted and then we all fell asleep."

In the morning there was panic as Lori and Sable left in disarray moments before Angie was due to arrive. That night, Lori saw David perform as Ziggy at Long Beach. "From that moment," she says, "he was a star."

23

Ziggy's Band

At 4 p.m. on April 5th, 1973, the SS *Oronsay*, having crossed the Pacific from California, docked at the Japanese port of Yokohama. When David disembarked he was greeted by a gaggle of press photographers and a crowd of fans before being sped by limousine the dozen miles into Tokyo, ready for the next leg of what had now become a world tour. The other musicians and the entourage – the group was still more than twenty strong – arrived by plane the next day, to join David at Tokyo's Imperial Hotel.

As Hutch observed, the hotel lobby was thronged with eager young women. They were not, however, the ravening creatures who had vied to satisfy him in the US, but more virginal beings, swathed in kimonos, who stepped forward to proffer him a handful of Japanese coins. This was, Hutch gathered, the traditional Japanese greeting to visitors, to which he stammered out his thanks. "They wanted to welcome you and it was so polite and had a completely different feel about it," he says.

David too was captivated by the radical new culture of the East, for in coming to Tokyo he was fulfilling the dream he had nurtured ever since displaying a precocious interest in Japan to his childhood friend Dudley Chapman. What caught his attention above all were the clothes. In Tokyo he was visited by the Japanese designer Kansai Yamamoto, whose work he had first viewed on a video of a rock-fashion show Kansai had staged in Japan the previous year. David had commissioned several costumes from him for the US tour, and now Kansai arrived bearing half a dozen more.

The most alluring were those which borrowed from the traditional Kabuki theatre, whose actors donned a dozen layers of clothing which were torn away one by one by shadowy figures during the performance. One of Kansai's costumes was conveniently equipped with a line of snap fasteners so that it could be dramatically ripped off, and then re-used. David had worn something similar during the US tour, but underneath he now proposed wearing a traditional Western jockstrap, which – he argued – closely resembled the thongs worn by Japan's *sumo* wrestlers. Kansai's costumes had a further appeal for David in leading him away from the skin-tight and overtly erotic costumes of Ziggy. They also foreshadowed the range of clothing he would adopt in years to come, which through their emphasis on looseness, texture and line would make David a style-leader once again.

As for the concerts themselves – there were to be eight in thirteen days, in the cities of Tokyo, Nagoya, Hiroshima, Kobe and Osaka – David was at first anxious in case the language barrier made it harder to stir his audiences to their customary frenzy, especially given Japan's tradition of discipline and regimentation. David need not have worried. The obverse side of the shy deference he had seen in the lobby of the Imperial Hotel was a determination to break free – in the right context – of all social restrictions. Almost ritualistically, his audiences hurled themselves at the stage, where a line of policemen ritualistically hurled them back. As Hutch divined, "It was accepted in Japan that people would dive on to the stage and they would get thrown off."

Only once did matters get out of control, and for that the over-enthusiasm of Angie and Tony Zanetta was largely to blame. They had taken to encouraging the fans to rush forward – "it made for a much more exciting show", explains Leee, who was also there – but at the final performance, in Tokyo, "nothing much seemed to be getting off the ground". Angie and Zee seized some chairs and swung them around their heads. "The police scattered, the kids all ran down to the stage, and it was a wonderful show," says Leee.

The police, however, viewed this as a serious transgression of the rules. That night they complained to the RCA office in Tokyo and demanded that RCA identify the miscreants and hand them over. In the morning, believing that warrants had already been issued for their arrest, Leee hurried Angie and Zee to Tokyo Airport. On discovering that police were apparently watching all flights to London and San Francisco, he packed them off on a plane leaving for Honolulu. Almost everyone else in the party left Tokyo the same day.

That left David; and it might have seemed that through his refusal to fly he was now stranded 9,000 miles from home. Making a virtue out of necessity, he resolved to return in style. He left Japan by boat and sailed the 600 miles to Vladivostok on the south-eastern tip of the USSR. There, accompanied only by Leee, Geoffrey MacCormack and a hard-bitten US newsman named Bob Musel, he embarked on the longest train ride on earth, the Trans-Siberian Express.

The journey from Vladivostok to Moscow is almost 6,000 miles,

337

has nearly 100 stops, and lasts a week. Although David was travelling in "soft" class (the only other sort is "hard"), sharing a compartment with Geoffrey MacCormack, it had nothing of the luxury he had grown accustomed to. The single dining-car served an unvarying diet of schnitzel or boiled chicken, with semolina for dessert, supplemented with glasses of Russian tea brewed up on their samovar by the two women who acted as attendants to each carriage. Most of the soft-class passengers were Western travellers or tourists, but at each stop they joined the Russians in queuing on the snow-covered platforms for roast potatoes, boiled eggs, cans of sardines, and jars of fresh yoghurt. David pronounced the yoghurt "excellent".

Bob Musel occupied the next compartment to David. A veteran war correspondent who landed in France on D-Day plus one, he was the Moscow correspondent for the American news agency UPI, and had decided to cover this journey on the Trans-Siberian Express in the knowledge that David would be taking it too. He found David far from his stereotype of the rock-star: intelligent, inquisitive, as fascinated by philosophical questions as he was by the frozen Siberian landscape that occupied the first 2,000 miles.

Musel was also a song-writer and translator – his biggest success was the 1950s hit, 'Poppa Piccolino' – and he enjoyed hearing David sing and play his own songs, particularly the night he entertained a group of passengers in his compartment until dawn glimmered through the snow-covered firs flanking the track. Musel was also impressed, like Gustl Breuer, by the sexual prowess of this new breed of musicians. "He fucked everything that moved and quite a lot that didn't," Musel jokes.

The people of the USSR were fascinated by David too. When he disembarked during the journey, his red hair and his range of Western designer clothes made him the invariable focus of attention. For his entry into Moscow he chose orange slacks and a floppy cap. But he caused the greatest stir of all by insisting, when Musel proposed going out for a meal in Moscow, that he "wanted to eat like the Russians".

It was with considerable misgivings that Musel set off with David and Geoffrey MacCormack for the cafeteria in Moscow's main department store, GUM. As David walked through the streets wearing a silk jacket striped with green sequins, yellow trousers, and his three-inch yellow platform shoes, astonished Moscovites flocked around. Musel heard a murmur of "Bowie . . . Bowie . . ." ripple through the crowd and saw men pulling their wives away as they stopped to look.

There was further consternation among the diners at GUM when this visitation arrived. Musel recommended the dish of the day: meat balls and potatoes. All Russian eyes were on David as he raised the first helping to his mouth – and then almost gagged. "I wasn't surprised," says Musel. "I knew those meat balls tasted like glue." David's predicament was acute, for, as he confessed to Musel, he was quite unable to swallow the food down. "Everyone was still looking at him," says Musel. "I told him to empty it into his napkin. He was very upset."

Musel took charge. Telling David, "I know this town," he suggested that they abandon their meal at GUM and go to the National Hotel, reserved for visitors with hard foreign currency. There, David assuaged his hunger and his embarrassment on caviar, smoked salmon and fresh sturgeon, swilled down by several bottles of the finest Russian wine. "I don't know where the hell they put it all," says Musel.

David returned to London in triumph, even though MainMan's usual attempt to orchestrate events was undermined by his failure to catch the right train in Paris. Angie had met him there on May 3rd, and after a night at the George V Hotel they missed the boat-train which was supposed to deliver them to Victoria, where several thousand fans were milling on the concourse. When the station loudspeaker announced that David would be arriving at Charing Cross instead, there was a mass rush for the Underground, but only a hundred or so fans arrived in time to see David's train pull in. As it was, David had to make a mad dash for a limousine, with the pack at his heels and press photographers bringing up the rear.

At RCA's London office, Geoff Hannington felt that David was entitled to every accolade he got. From virtual pariah, Hannington had become a hero: all five of David's RCA albums were in the British charts. *Ziggy Stardust* had been in the top fifty ever since the previous July, to be joined by *Hunky Dory* in September and the two reissues, *Space Oddity* and *The Man Who Sold The World*, in October. Now, on the day after David's return, *Aladdin Sane* capped them all by going straight to number one.

The success of *Aladdin Sane* brought Hannington particular pleasure, not least because of the complications that had attended the design of the cover, which had made his dealings with Defries more arduous than ever.

To photograph the cover, Defries had recommended a former colleague from the stormy days of the Association of Fashion

Photographers, Brian Duffy. Duffy had recently been building his reputation by taking the photographs for the Pirelli calendar, the purest example yet achieved of soft porn elevated to the status of high art by the use of astute publicity, and was therefore of immediate appeal to Defries. When Duffy and David met, David already had the central concept in mind: "He said he wanted a flash," Duffy recalls.

Duffy believes that the origins of David's idea lay in a ring that Elvis Presley had once worn marked with a lightning flash; when it came to finding a model, Duffy turned to the nearest object at hand, which happened to be a rice-cooker made by National Panasonic and which bore that company's distinctive logo, a lightning flash. "I showed it to David and he said, 'That's what I want.'"

The lightning flash was duly applied to David's face in pink and blue stripes that crossed his temple, eye and cheek, by the make-up artist Pierre Laroche. When Duffy took the photograph, David closed his eyes, producing an image that suggested either repose or death. The ambiguity was compounded by the addition of a tiny pool of water nestling by David's collar-bone, which was air-brushed on to the photograph by the artist Philip Castle, and which was intended to convey the impression, says Duffy, "of a statue that's wet".

Of all David's albums, none had a more precisely apposite and disturbing cover than *Aladdin Sane*; by that strange semi-accidental process that surrounded so much of what he did, an image had emerged which could not have been more appropriate to the covert messages of his songs. It recalled the thunderstorms in the dreams and nightmares of his earliest lyrics, which had evolved into the hand reaching through the "crack in the sky" of 'Oh! You Pretty Things' – the song which, as David admitted, dealt with "some kind of schizophrenia".

Defries evidently considered the cover special too, for when he presented it to Geoff Hannington, he stipulated that it had to be printed *in seven colours* to achieve the full effect. Defries further insisted that since no British company was capable of performing the task, it would have to be carried out in Switzerland. Hannington had to make several journeys to Zurich to ensure that the printers were doing the job properly – and to spare himself further explosions of rage from Defries.

Defries had also induced Hannington to commit a considerable proportion of RCA's resources to advertising the *Aladdin Sane* album on television. That, says Defries, was "a bitter bone of contention" between himself and RCA, for both he and Myers had made several previous attempts to persuade Hannington's boss, Ken Glancey, to sponsor television commercials featuring David's new releases, an unprecedented move at the time. "Glancey point-blank refused," says Defries. But Defries had finally prevailed, bringing further complaints from Hannington's colleagues that he was going over the top. Hannington was therefore fully entitled to the satisfaction he felt when *Aladdin Sane* remained at the top of the album hit parade for five successive weeks.

The reviewers generally approved of *Aladdin Sane's* music and remained bemused by the lyrics, one pleading: "There are times when I feel I would like to be let in on the secret." Their reservations seemed unimportant, for David's feats in the hit parade, previously matched only by the Beatles and Tom Jones among British per-formers, guaranteed him massive press coverage as a prelude to the next British tour.

With Defries becoming over-ambitious, the tour began badly. The first concert, on May 12th, was held at Earls Court, a cavernous exhibition hall which could seat 18,000 people and would yield receipts of £27,000 (MainMan's share would be £17,000). No rock concert had ever been staged there before: the sound quality was abysmal, several thousand people at the rear were unable to see, and their shouts of protests, together with scuffles in the aisles, twice brought the show to a halt.

One person viewing the proceedings with a certain grim relish was Ken Pitt, whom David and Angie had visited, unannounced, at Manchester Street two days before. This gesture of reconciliation saw David at his most endearing: he and Angie hugged Pitt, and when David went to make some coffee, it was, Pitt later wistfully remarked, "as if he had never been away".

Pitt found David confident and self-assured, and when Angie suggested that he come to the show at Earls Court, David quickly interjected: "Yes, come and see what your boy is doing." Even before the concert began, Pitt's hackles rose at the sight of Laurence Myers walking down the aisle, a Mexican sombrero on his head, looking for all the world as if he was counting the seats. When Pitt weighed up the acoustics of the hall, he told his companion: "This is going to be a disaster." Today, he adds: "And it was." David was well aware of all that had gone wrong, and demanded that Defries cancel the return performance due later that month. Defries agreed at once.

Earls Court apart, the tour was a monstrous success. It played at 37 towns and cities in 45 days, and sold out in every one. "It seemed we were on the rampage throughout Britain," says Hutch, "creating havoc wherever we went." It won further publicity when the *Sun* reported how a young couple had sexual intercourse in the back row of the Glasgow Green Playhouse, while David – "the new god of pop 'n' rock, back on the road with the freakiest show in Britain today" – played on.

The newest member of the entourage, Jaime Andrews, could not at first comprehend what had hit him. Another of the *Pork* cast (he played Christopher Columbus), he had been recruited by Tony Zanetta at the end of April. Zee and Defries departed for the US after the Earls Court concert, leaving the tour entirely in his charge. "Zee said, 'It's just a machine, make sure the machine goes,'" Andrews recalled. "It was horrible." Not the least of Andrews's problems was that David was on such a high at his audiences' response that he wanted to stay up most of the night and talk; when David finally fell asleep, it was time for Andrews to get the rest of the group back on the road. "I didn't get much sleep for three months," he said.

The last concert of the tour was scheduled for the Hammersmith Odeon on July 3rd. But for almost everyone taking part, as Defries had spelled out on more than one occasion, the current British tour was only a prelude to yet greater things in store: after Britain, Defries had promised, there was Europe; after Europe, a return to the US.

That would be "US Tour III", which Defries and Zee were organising in New York: an itinerary was already circulating in Britain, showing that thirty-eight dates had been booked, beginning at the 17,000-seat Toronto Maple Leaf on September 1st, moving to the US with a show in Newhaven, Connecticut, on September 7th, and finishing before 10,000 people in San Antonio, Texas, on October 31st. Defries had predicted that there could be seventy concerts in all; and David had talked of going on to play China and the USSR in 1974.

It was therefore with no hint of disquiet that the band took their places on stage at Hammersmith. The audience were at their best, and the band played as if inspired to an almost continuous wall of noise. For the penultimate number, they stormed through Lou Reed's 'White Light/White Heat' and then David, after ceremonially waiting while the audience roared for an encore, stepped forward. At this juncture, Hutch usually played the introduction to 'Rock 'N' Roll Suicide' on his twelve-string guitar, but David had asked him to wait for a signal. A single light focused on David as he gripped the microphone.

"Everyone," he yelled. "This has been one of the greatest tours of our lives, and of all the shows on this tour this particular show will remain with us the longest because not only is it, not only is it the last show in the tour but it's the last show we'll ever do."

The audience were stunned. They had greeted his assertion that this was the most memorable show as a compliment to themselves, raising a cheer that had caused David to pause and repeat himself. When he announced that he was retiring from the concert stage, the cheers turned to a groan, and a perplexed cry of "Noooooo" swept through the hall. Further explanation came there none. David abruptly turned his back, throwing a brief "thank you" over his shoulder, and gestured to Hutch to start 'Rock 'N' Roll Suicide'.

If David's terse statement seemed like an act of cruelty towards his fans, to some of his band it came as a stab in the back. "I couldn't hear it too well but he said something about retiring," says Hutch. "Everybody in the band was looking at each other and saying, 'What?' Trevor and Woody seemed to take it worse because they felt double-crossed, they hadn't been told. 'What's happening?' – 'Oh fuck it.' That was the style."

Afterwards there was a party at the Café Royal that had been intended as a celebration, but now, it seemed, was to be a wake for David's career. A formidable guest list had been assembled, attesting to the heights of fashionability that David had scaled: among those who both accepted and actually turned up were Barbra Streisand, Ringo Starr, Keith Moon, Elliott Gould, Spike Milligan and Hywel Bennett. Carefully positioned alongside David at the head of the dinner table were two performers he could now safely consider his peers: Lou Reed and Mick Jagger.

Mick Rock was there too; conscious that here was another moment of rock history to be recorded, he asked the trio of superstars to kiss one another. With an obliging grin, Mick Jagger cupped his left hand around David's neck and pulled his head towards him, at the same time leaning towards Lou Reed, and there was a brief, multiple touching of lips which Rock captured. Rock approached Defries too, who had Angie sitting on his lap. While Angie waved gaily to camera, Defries shielded his face with a hand that clutched a lighter and a Havana cigar.

Although Trevor Bolder was too angry to attend the party, Hutch and Woody were there. They were still unable to discover what lay behind David's announcement. Hutch's only communication with David came when their eyes met across the dance floor. "We just nodded to each other, he looked over and said, 'All right?' and that was it."

For the following week the music press was full of the mystery but none could resolve it. The only word from MainMan was a terse press statement dated July 4th which merely confirmed that David had announced that he "was leaving the concert stage for ever". Delighted with the new publicity coup he had achieved, Defries was certainly not going to offer any amplification, even to David's own musicians. "No one," says Hutch, "ever explained what happened to the rest of the tour."

The answer, in part, lay in the byzantine politics of RCA; for in the words of Mort Hoffman, the RCA board had "wised up on Rocco". When Laginestra became head of Records and Tapes it had been a subdivision of the NBC broadcasting division, whose financial head, Aaron Rubin, was Laginestra's key supporter. But when Records and Tapes began to make a profit, thanks to the efforts of Laginestra's staff, the RCA board decided to make it a full division on its own. By being separated from NBC, Laginestra lost Rubin's protection, and his star was on the wane.

Firmly in the ascendancy was Mel Ilberman, who was fast learning how to resist the blandishments of Tony Defries. In the beginning, Defries acknowledges, "Rocco and I got on very well"; Ilberman, he adds, "thought we got on *too* well". And Ilberman, who could see Laginestra's position weakening by the day, was determined to call the shots.

Under the terms of the touring contract dated March 22nd, Defries had asked Laginestra to underwrite the autumn US tour. Under the terms of the same contract, Laginestra, heavily influenced by Ilberman, had declined. It was true that the spring tour, through concentrating on large-scale concerts in cities where David was known to be popular, had avoided the vast losses of autumn 1972. But Defries was proposing a tour that could put 1972 in the shade.

What was more, in contrast with Britain, David was still far from achieving mass appeal in the US. His three singles, 'Changes', 'Starman', and 'The Jean Genie', had sold only modest amounts – 'Changes', a pitiful 7,500 copies. In some desperation, RCA had re-released 'Space Oddity' as a single on the eve of the US tour and with sales of almost half a million it had reached fifteenth place in the *Billboard* Top 40.

But 'Space Oddity', Ilberman could argue, hardly represented the new David Bowie. The albums too were far from best-sellers. By mid-June, *Ziggy Stardust* had sold 320,000 copies, *Aladdin Sane* 260,000, *The Man Who Sold The World* 130,000, and *Hunky Dory* 120,000. In a market where success was measured in millions, these were no more than respectable numbers.

Acerbic discussions took place. Defries blamed RCA's marketing for David's poor sales; RCA responded that since Defries had insisted on full control, that was his fault; Defries riposted that RCA had not carried out his instructions. He also argued that the sales figures showed David to be poised for the breakthrough, which the next tour could achieve. But Ilberman remained adamant that RCA was not going to fund the tour that Defries proposed, and the March 22nd agreement, which they had both signed, was on RCA's side. It gave RCA "rights of approval" over seven different aspects of the tour, including its routing, budget, venues, pricing and length. RCA, said Ilberman, did not approve.

RCA did make a counter-proposal, suggesting a far smaller tour on the scale of spring 1973, concentrating on known venues, with the same attention to economy they had achieved before. But that did not fit the purposes or the ambitions of Defries: he, in turn, said no. All that remained was to salvage from the impasse what he could, which was the publicity the "retirement" announcement brought. As Jaime Andrews recalled, having been let into the secret a week before the final show, "It was a way to get press and regroup and figure out what we were going to do."

David, too, was relieved that he had time to figure out what he was going to do: once again a commercial decision had neatly coincided with his personal and artistic goals. As the lyrics of *Aladdin Sane* had presaged, he was anxious to abandon Ziggy before it was too late. The dance with death he had performed on stage was finding ominous parallels in real life; the character of Ziggy he had so readily adopted had come close to overwhelming him.

The process had been observed in New York by David's cousin Kristina. David usually looked her up when he was in the city, and had given her tickets for one of the Radio City concerts. When she met him at his hotel she felt that he was in the grip of a struggle to free himself of his part. "I would watch him when he got off stage," she says, "and afterwards I could see that he dropped the character."

Or rather, that he tried to. For Kristina also felt that he was being continually seduced by the trappings of stardom. "He was eating certain types of food and was surrounded by certain people, flamboyant people, innovative people, and that went with the Ziggy image." It was the same confusion that had befallen Zee in *Pork*, when people behaved towards him as if he really was Andy Warhol; now people were behaving in the same way, Kristina believes, "dealing with Ziggy not David".

Kristina herself had been offered a place in the entourage and a share in the fantasy, but – like Bob Grace in London – she had declined. Kristina believed that by remaining outside the entourage she could preserve the integrity of her relationship with the David she had known, and she believes that David wished to do the same. His "desperate need", she says, was for people who would "relate to him as David Jones". But each time David returned to the concert stage, Kristina could "feel the pain when he went into being Ziggy". Each time he came off stage, it was that much harder to become David Jones again.

David acknowledged much of this when he said in an interview several years afterwards: "I fell for Ziggy too. It was quite easy to become obsessed night and day with the character. I became Ziggy Stardust . . . Everybody was convincing me that I was a Messiah, especially on that first American tour. I got hopelessly lost in the fantasy." Later, he added: "I thought I might as well take Ziggy out to interviews as well. Why leave him on the stage? . . . I can't deny that the experience affected me in a very exaggerated and marked manner. I think I put myself very dangerously near the line."

By abandoning Ziggy, David had veered away from the line. Others caught up in David's fantasy found it was not so easy. After the Hammersmith concert, Woody Woodmansey spent a week with Mike Garson at the British headquarters of the Scientology movement at East Grinstead in Sussex. "Woody was bitter, and very shocked," says Garson. Woody had still received no explanation for David's announcement; then came another blow. David had already laid plans to record his next album for RCA at the Château d'Hérouville studio at Pontoise, near Paris, a week after the Hammersmith show. Entitled *Pin-Ups*, it would consist of David's own versions of the records by other performers he had most enjoyed in the 1960s, and Woody and Garson assumed they would both be taking part.

A day or so before they were due to go to Paris, Woody got married, with Garson – as an official of the Church of Scientology – presiding over the ceremony. That morning, the MainMan office telephoned Garson and asked him to tell Woody that his services were not required. Garson waited until after the wedding to impart the news. "Woody was devastated," Garson says. "This was his life and he thought he was going to the top with David."

David later claimed that he had felt unable to explain to the Spiders that they were merely playing out parts, and conceded: "It must have been very anti-climactic when I said, 'The show's all over now ... I'm going back into big melodrama, and you don't fit my scheme of things.'"

For both Woody and Trevor Bolder, life after Ziggy was indeed an anti-climax. By contrast Hutch, who had not shared the illusion and therefore did not feel betrayed, returned to Scarborough with far greater equanimity. Later that year he travelled to Hull to meet Trevor Bolder, together with another of David's rejects, John Cambridge. Toying with the idea of forming a group of their own, they spent an afternoon practising in a Scout hut, but the idea came to nothing; that evening they talked over the past at Trevor's home, a council house with a row of gold discs on the wall.

Meanwhile David, as he had promised, returned to "big melodrama". This time it would be the biggest melodrama of all. Having escaped from Ziggy, he would now attempt to play out the most dominant and burdensome of all his family themes: the threat and the horror of war.

24

Big Brother

In October 1973, David and Angie left Haddon Hall. After staying briefly in a flat in Maida Vale, owned by Diana Rigg, they moved to their new home which was a town house in an elegant early-Victorian terrace in Oakley Street, Chelsea. The rent was £600 a month, paid, as usual, by MainMan, and debited, as usual, to David's profit-and-loss account.

The move brought out Angie's home-making instincts, and she decorated and furnished the house with all the panache she could muster, and no expense spared. A visitor entering by the flight of stone steps from Oakley Street would have been struck first by the country oak dresser in the hall and the brown Wilton carpet throughout the ground floor. In the front room stood a bleached-pine dining table set with six pine chairs, an art-nouveau standard lamp, a four-foot oil painting entitled *Faces* by the versatile Lindsay Kemp, and a blue Chinese carpet woven with an intricate design of blossom and leaves.

Occupying the entire first floor was the "music room", with white painted walls, a shaggy white pile carpet, and two tall windows, stretching to the ceiling, overlooking Oakley Street. Scattered around the room was a cornucopia of musical intruments and equipment, including two pianos – one a Broadwood grand valued at almost £2,000, custom-made at Harrods – three saxophones, three guitars, a Moog synthesiser, an array of record and cassette decks and amplifiers, and more than 500 record albums.

There was a twenty-four-inch television (one of three in the house), and David's own 16mm film projector, for entertaining visitors who would lounge among blue silk cushions strewn around the room. At one end was a Persian carpet, woven in turquoise and gold, from Qum, for which David and Angie had paid £4,200. There was a collection of art-nouveau pieces, an oil painting by the promising young British artist, Kevin Whitney, and the painting of David by George Underwood which had been used in the back of the *Space Oddity* album cover. There was also a large cluster of photographs of James Dean, who had become David's current movie idol.

On the second floor were two bedrooms: one for Zowie; and one for David and Angie, with a king-size bed six feet wide, another television and a full range of video equipment. It contained a second painting by Kevin Whitney, and David and Angie's most prized art-nouveau pieces, including a pinched glass bowl by Daum and a mauve vase by Gallé. On the top floor was the spare bedroom, with a five-foot brass bedstead, and what Angie called "the office", containing two desks and an array of equipment, and a collection of gold and silver presentation albums, including six that had been mounted in a frame and inscribed to David "from his friends at RCA".

To the casual visitor, Angie's refurbishment of Oakley Street gave the appearance of refined yet cosy domesticity. But where she and David were concerned, appearances could of course be misleading, as Pat Wadsley discovered. Early in 1974, Pat, previously a receptionist at *16* magazine, was hired as a publicity officer on the MainMan staff in New York, where her job consisted almost solely of telling journalists, no, they could not have an interview with David. She was occasionally dispatched to London to perform the same task and during one stay Angie invited her to spend the evening at Oakley Street. She was pleased to find that Leee Childers, whom she had known at *16* magazine, was among the guests, and touched to see that the Bowies' son Zowie – then aged four – took his place at the dinner table too. Afterwards, the party repaired to the music room to watch television in what Pat recalls as a warm and relaxing "family atmosphere".

Pat was therefore astonished when, without warning, David put his arm around her and proposed that they return to Pat's hotel. Assuming that she had little choice in the matter, she agreed. She found David "very tender" and they spent the night together. In the morning, Pat was consumed with both guilt, since she had been brought up as a Catholic, and embarrassment, since everyone in the MainMan office knew what had occurred. For a long time afterwards she was puzzled by the episode, not least because she was at least twenty pounds overweight at the time: "I don't think David was overcome with lust," she says. She now believes that she was a "trophy" for David as he exerted control over his staff: "something he learned from Defries".

The move from Beckenham brought the Bowies more benefits than a comfortable house: Chelsea was clearly a far more appropriate setting for a rock-star to live. At one end of Oakley Street was the King's Road and its regular Saturday promenade of all that was most fashionable; at the other was the Chelsea Embankment and the River Thames. There too, on Cheyne Walk, lived Mick and Bianca Jagger, and by the precise caste system that regulates the social lives of rock musicians, the two couples could now afford to be seen together.

Having admired Jagger from afar during the 1960s, David was at first a little overawed at becoming his peer; and their relationship was never entirely free of the competitive edge Ian Hunter had seen in David. David naturally valued Jagger's views and the two men often stayed up into the small hours talking and playing music. There was also a discernible physical component to their friendship, with David going so far as to confess in an interview in November that he found Jagger "incredibly sexy and very virile". It was a measure of his desire for Jagger's esteem that David remained vulnerable to slights, imagined or otherwise, on Jagger's part. That Christmas, David munificently gave Jagger a video-cassette recorder, then still a luxury item in Britain. Jagger's present to David was far more modest – a friend remembers that it was "something like a tie," – which left David fulminating: "How cheap can you get?"

The move to Oakley Street also brought David closer into the ambit of MainMan, for the Gunter Grove office was just half a mile away along the King's Road. This, too, had a strange ambience that disconcerted those not part of the inner circle. "It had a peculiar atmosphere which I found hard to define," says the music journalist Michael Watts. "It was not the usual pop star atmosphere, with roadies and groupies, it was much more rarefied." They were, he adds, "very strange people to be around".

That was partly because most of them did their utmost to model themselves on David, with the prize, it was generally agreed, going to Defries's girlfriend Melanie, who had acquired a Ziggy hairstyle and looked more boyish than ever. "The office was peopled with Bowie clones," says Laurence Myers, who called from time to time to see how his investment was faring. "You'd walk in, they all had the same haircut, the girls looked like boys." At times Myers felt like asking, "Would the real David Bowie stand up please?"

Angie, of course, took part in the parade, dressing as provocatively as possible. Pat Wadsley particularly remembers her entrance at a hideously expensive restaurant wearing skin-tight trousers and a see-through blouse which left absolutely nothing to the imagination. "People just dropped dead when they saw her," says Pat. She also continued to play the sexual pioneer, telling an interviewer: "I don't understand this concept of faithfulness in marriage. I am not faithful in an old-fashioned way and neither is David." But while Angie tolerated, even encouraged, David's one-night stands – and David never balked at her flings with both men and women – her forbearance only lasted so long as she judged that David's affairs were not becoming a threat, at which point it gave way to old-fashioned jealousy.

The distinction became clear with the arrival in Chelsea of the slim and lively figure of Ava Cherry, a black singer and model from Chicago. Ava had first met David in New York, finding him "very much a gentleman, very sweet, very nice – I was sick of American guys, they're all so coarse, and it was refreshing to have a guy who was very gallant and that sort of thing." David was taken with her youthful vivacity – she was just eighteen – and her exotic appearance, for her close-cropped hair was dyed a platinum blonde so that she looked, as one unkind observer remarked, like a negro billiard ball.

It was not until after they had slept together that Ava discovered that David was married, when David introduced her to both Angie and Zowie at the Gramercy Park Hotel. "I was freaked out," Ava says. "I didn't want to give anyone the impression that I was in the habit of going out with married men, but David said, 'She does what she wants to do and I do what I want to do.'" David attempted to reassure her further by promising that she could join his group as a singer during his US tour in the autumn of 1973. Ava was therefore distressed to receive a telegram from MainMan telling her that the tour had been cancelled. She pursued David to Europe and confronted him in Paris, and was mollified when David apologised and gave her a plane ticket to London.

Ava arrived just as the Bowies were moving to Oakley Street. To Ava's amazement, Angie suggested that she should move in too. "David said 'Yeah, that's a great idea,' so I said, 'OK.' I was new to this whole thing, you know, wife's there, but I thought, maybe this is the way things are done in England."

At first the *ménage à trois* seemed to work. "Angie," says Ava, "was just wonderful to me." Not only were she and David sleeping together, but David made good his promise to help her career. He proposed that Ava, Geoffrey MacCormack and a US singer, Jason Carter, should form a group called the Astronettes, and spent several weeks helping them to record tracks for an album at the Olympic studios.

As willing as ever to humour David's wishes, Defries agreed that MainMan should manage the group, and set up the customary profit-and-loss account in their name. Ava even partnered David when he visited the Jaggers in Cheyne Walk. "I was in awe."

It was when Angie saw how far her position was being usurped that her liberal attitude gave way to resentment, and life at Oakley Street became distinctly less idyllic. "Angie and I were having this tension between us," Ava says. "I felt badly – I was starting to love the guy and really didn't know what to do. David would be very angry but when he wasn't there I was at Angie's mercy. Then Angie started going away and that was the best part, I was in heaven, and when she came back it would start all over again."

Defries was only too aware that all was not well in the Bowie household, particularly as Angie was bombarding him with complaints. In an attempt to restore the domestic equilibrium, he instructed the MainMan office to find Ava somewhere of her own to live, and they rented a flat on her behalf in an apartment block, Daska House, in the King's Road, five minutes' walk from Oakley Street. "Tony was very sweet," says Ava. "He said, 'That way you won't be so far from David and you can be out of Angie's hair.' Mainman took care of everything." MainMan undertook to pay a deposit of £150 and rent of £195 a month – all naturally debited to the Astronettes' account – and Ava moved in. Ignoring the conditions of her tenancy, which forbade her to alter the decorations, she celebrated by painting the flat bottle-green throughout. David commuted discreetly between the two homes and for the time being peace, of a kind, was restored.

Pin-Ups, the album David had recorded in France, was released in October. David explained that the twelve tracks were intended as a tribute to the bands he had watched at the Marquee between 1964 and 1967. "They're all very dear to me," he said. "Each one meant something to me – it's my London of the time." The reviewers greeted it with sighs of relief: here at last was an album they could understand. They nonetheless disagreed violently over its qualities: one hailed it as "as stroke of near-genius", another condemned it as a "shoddily carpentered" work that would leave "the fragile edifice of its maker's credibility tottering for some time to come".

The latter remarks certainly missed the point by a wide margin. *Pin-Ups* showed above all David's versatile skills as observer, commentator and parodist, for his versions of the songs were by turns mocking, detached, ironic and melodramatic. Yet they never lacked affection for the past he and his fellow-performers had shared, and one number in particular, The Who's 'Anyway, Anyhow, Anywhere', came across with greater power than the original. Some tracks contained interjections from David's more recent history, like the demented piano Mike Garson contributed to Pink Floyd's 'See Emily Play', and the air of despair David imparted to the Kinks' 'Where Have All The Good Times Gone?'. *Pin-Ups* succeeded perfectly as the stop-gap David intended, and was soon selling 12,000 copies a week; meanwhile David himself was, as ever, looking ahead.

With characteristically sudden passion, David had lit upon George Orwell's novel *1984*. Set in the none-too-distant future, its prediction of an oppressive, authoritarian society, with the populace controlled by the Ministry of Truth, dissidents tortured into submission by the thought police, and ubiquitous posters warning "Big Brother is watching you", accorded closely with David's preoccupations. So did the doomed character of Winston Smith, vainly struggling to maintain his belief in love and truth, until he too is crushed. David asked Defries to secure the rights to adapt *1984* as a musical, but Orwell's widow, Sonia, turned him down. Undaunted, David determined that *1984* would provide the basis for his next album and tour.

David had written several tracks by mid-October, when he performed a special show for the American television network, NBC. Pleasingly, in view of the tribute David had just paid to the venue, it was recorded over three days at the Marquee in Wardour Street. Much of his repertoire came from *Aladdin Sane* and *Pin-Ups*, including 'Time', 'The Jean Genie', The Who's 'I Can't Explain' and David's version of the Merseys' number 'Sorrow' which RCA had just issued as David's latest single.

David performed an electric duet in the old Ziggy style with Mick Ronson in 'The Jean Genie' and another, of 'I've Got You Babe', with Marianne Faithfull. David wore a spectacular range of costumes designed by Freddi Burretti, the most provocative a black fishnet leotard embellished with a pair of green lurex hands clutching at his bosom. It was Marianne Faithfull's costume which received most attention, at least for those present at the Marquee: she wore a nun's habit which was far too small and thus left an expanse of milky white flesh visible from behind.

It was the song with which David opened and closed the performance that signalled the new direction in which he was heading. It consisted of a spare four verses that warned:

Beware the savage jaw – of 1984

and alluded to the thought police, who would

. . . break your pretty cranium and fill it full of air.

The only escape, David said despairingly, lay in drugs:

You'll be shooting up as usual, like tomorrow's never there.

The song was called '1984' and the title of the programme provided another marker of David's intentions: employing another of his puns, he called it *The 1980 Floor Show*.

David continued work on the new album, *Diamond Dogs*, throughout that autumn and winter. While the influence of Orwell remained strong, he also fell under the spell of the American writer William Burroughs, following an encounter arranged by the *Rolling Stone* journalist Craig Copetas. Burroughs had assumed the status of *éminence grise* among the beat writers, with his unembarrassed descriptions of drug-taking and homosexuality, his explorations of alternative forms of consciousness, and his seemingly perverse "cut-up" method of writing, whereby he assembled his novels like an artist's collage, slicing and rejoining his text at random, incorporating fragments from authors like Shakespeare and Kafka, and encouraging his readers to start his books at any point they liked.

The meeting took place at Oakley Street on November 17th, and while Copetas's tape-recorder turned, David talked revealingly about his own creative techniques. He said that he found songwriting no longer adequate in itself, but sought the "total image" conveyed by a stage performance, where his songs took on "character, shape, body". He also admitted that he often did not know or understand what he had written about, and told Burroughs that he drew much of his inspiration from dreams, or from the dreamlike state he had learned to induce that was short of falling asleep.

David expressed enormous admiration for Burroughs's novel *Nova Express*. First published in 1966, it examined the varying states of mind and body and the fantasies they project, narrated through the vehicle of an imagined, hallucinatory interplanetary war. David told Burroughs he was astonished to find a work so akin to his own interests. He was also intrigued by Burroughs's cut-up technique, and the "wonderhouse of strange shapes and colours, tastes, feelings" it produced. Undoubtedly flattered, Burroughs returned to Oakley Street on several occasions. David was particularly interested in Burroughs's use of drugs, and fascinated when Burroughs told him that the most effective way of snorting cocaine was to clip the hairs of your nostrils beforehand.

As his work on the *Diamond Dogs* lyrics continued, David experimented with the cut-up technique too. In a later interview, he spelled out just why he found it so appealing, explaining that he aimed to "purposely fracture everything" and if his writing still made "too much sense" he would "fracture" it further. It was David's most explicit admission that he liked his lyrics to tantalise, so that their message was available only to the most loyal and persistent of his followers. He even told Burroughs, that he suspected much of his audience didn't listen to the lyrics anyway.

Certainly, where *Diamond Dogs* was concerned, David succeeded only too well in obscuring his message. When the album was released in April 1974 the critics were almost uniformly baffled and hostile. Even the admiring Chris Charlesworth could offer hardly a word of amplification, beyond saying that the album appeared to depict the aftermath of a nuclear holocaust.

Charlesworth at least had the excuse that he had heard the record in circumstances which were far from ideal. In a customary show of pomp, Defries had invited a select handful of critics to the MainMan office, where they were body-searched in case they were carrying tape-recorders, were permitted to listen to the album just once, and were not given lyric sheets. Some of the reviewers were further handicapped by the previous inadequacies of their calling, which had failed to come to grips with the intermingling of myth, illusion and personal biography running through David's work, and were therefore in no position to offer a coherent critique.

Diamond Dogs was a stunning apotheosis of David's craft, a climactic summation of all he sought to express, and the key to his own personal and artistic survival. Even more than *Ziggy*, it was a work of astonishing courage. The apocalypse he had warned against for so long had arrived, producing a war-ravaged landscape against which his characters fought to control their destiny. But they were not just his characters: they drew upon the racked generations of his family whose fate David was desperate to avoid. He did so by probing the heart of his family mythology to confront and thereby exorcise the terrors it held.

A further key to David's personal commitment to the new album was that for the first and only time in his life he attempted to produce it himself. He also arranged most of the musical parts and played many of the instruments, including guitar, saxophones, mellotron and Moog synthesiser. The musicians he employed were the drummer Aynsley Dunbar, retained from the *Pin-Ups* album, and a second drummer in Tony Newman; new recruits in bass player Herbie Flowers and guitarist Alan Parker; and the ever-present Mike Garson, making his fourth album with David.

The most notable absentee was Mick Ronson, who last performed with David on the *Midnight Special* television show. Mick says today, in his magnanimous way, that he and David merely "drifted apart", but he was far more of a victim than that, for he had fallen foul of David's increasing rival with his fellow-musicians, and of the manoeuvres of Defries.

When David withdrew from the concert circuit, Defries turned urgently to Mick as his replacement, hoping to establish him as a solo performer in his own right. Defries secured him a substantial recording contract with RCA, began to set up a tour, and accorded him the full panoply of MainMan publicity – including a six-storey billboard in Times Square, New York – to advertise his first album, *Slaughter On Tenth Avenue*. Mick's supporters – the most vociferous being Suzi Fussey, who eventually married him – believe this was far too much to expect of him. "He was pushed into it by Tony and the MainMan machine," she says. "It was a very hard thing to do after coming off something like David, and Mick wasn't ready."

Although Mick's solo career soon foundered, Ava Cherry believes that the fact that he embarked on it at all was what antagonised David. "All hell broke loose," Ava says. "Maybe David felt that Mick had betrayed him as far as he was trying to be the star. But he was very upset, very, *very* upset." Ava suspects above all that Mick threatened David's growing desire to dominate all around him.

"In those days," she says, "David had a tendency to control everyone who was around him. It was a mental control. Once he'd met them they would be his, he'd have them. He could make them do anything he wanted them to do." And so Mick, being beyond David's control, was dropped.

Certainly when recording began in the Olympic studios in Barnes, Mike Garson found that David's old friendliness had evaporated. "I just came in and played the parts and he explained some things. It was more like being a session musician."

Garson met Mick Jagger at the studio on several occasions, and is not alone in perceiving Jagger's influence on the album. "Bowie talked about him a lot," Garson says. "He was so influenced by anybody at that time that if there was someone he really respected and admired he would go to the maximum testing that out."

Garson believes that David was pushing himself to the limit too. "He didn't look good to me. I remember saying as a friend, 'You'd better watch out.' He was very thin, his face was drawn." Garson feels that the music that resulted had "a different vibe, it felt heavier, it was on the dark side"; his overall view was that the album was "macabre".

The album's introduction gave ample warning of the horrors to come. It began with the howling of the Diamond Dogs, echoing through devastated streets. Then, using his semi-recitative style, David portrayed a deserted city in the aftermath of war, with its rotting corpses, mutated scavengers and desperate bands of looters. David's use of Burroughs's cut-up technique made his bleak vision more disturbing still, for his seemingly random juxtapositions reproduced, whether by instinct or design, the broken syntax and knight's-move logic of schizophrenia: "ripping and re-wrapping mink and shiny silver fox – now leg warmers – family badge of sapphire and cracked emerald – any day now – the year of the Diamond Dogs . . ." Finally, as an audience's swelling roar was heard, he warned that this was to be no ordinary work. "This ain't Rock 'n' Roll," David proclaimed; "this is Genocide."

The first song proper, 'Diamond Dogs', prolonged the nightmare, describing a crippled survivor crawling through the alleyways in desperate fear of the marauding dogs, to a caustic and relentless setting in the style of the Rolling Stones, including an imitation of Jagger's yodelling cat-calls. David used references from the popular media, like "Browning's beast . . .", Tod Browning being the director of a cruelly explicit film featuring circus midgets entitled *Freaks*. The song introduced another of David's archetypes, whom he named 'Halloween Jack': the "real cool cat" who, like "the man" in *Aladdin Sane*, seems to have represented David's *alter ego*, watching the drama from a distance, occasionally descending from his refuge on top of a skyscraper to skirt through the debris with his "ghost-town approach".

'Sweet Thing', beginning with ghostly sounds of music recorded and played in reverse, which then gave way to the unabashed romanticism of Garson's piano, marked a return to David's obsession with love and affection, this time played out against the background of war. It told of the search for love as the antidote for loneliness, and of despairing sexual encounters in doorways of the ruined city, when love-making seemed to offer no more than

Putting pain in a stranger . . .

'Sweet Thing' merged directly with another recitative, 'Candidate', the most disjointed lyric of the album, with fearful scenes mingling from all parts of David's imagination. They included

357

public executions and slain knights; David as actor, with a set so convincing that "it even smells like a street"; David taking delight in deluding the media with their "rumours and lies"; sexual gropings on the floor, in the back of a car, or in a cellar; all ending, it seemed, in a mutual suicide, as his lovers "jump in a river holding hands".

After a reprise of 'Sweet Thing', with the music becoming richer and more complex, its rhythm and timbre changing constantly, came a hard-rock number in 'Rebel Rebel', as strident and sexually ambiguous as 'The Jean Genie'. The most accessible song on the album – it was also released as a single which reached number five in the British hit parade – it too showed a strong Rolling Stone influence, with David capturing Jagger at his most disdainful, as well as having an unmistakable autobiographical note:

> Got your mother in a whirl,
> She's not sure if you're a boy or a girl.

At the start of side two, the music struck a mellow, slow-rock note as David explored the other side of love in 'Rock 'N' Roll With Me'. It contrasted not only with 'Rebel Rebel' but also with 'Star' on the *Ziggy* album. There, David had contended that he could achieve the peace and affection he craved through playing the role of star: now he had changed his view, and viewed stardom, with its incessant demands, as a bewildering trap. Even though his fans were numbered in "tens of thousands", he would rather revert to his former self:

> When you rock 'n' roll with me
> There's no one else I'd rather be.

Like the *Aladdin Sane* number 'Time', the lyric contained a covert prediction that David would at some point be discarding the trappings of stardom, or at least rejecting those who had encouraged him to act out the part to the full.

The tenderness of 'Rock 'N' Roll With Me' continued in the next song, 'We Are The Dead'. It was nostalgic at first, with gentle opening chords from Garson, and David looking down at his sleeping lover, remembering their nights together, and hoping that their love would persist through the generations. But then, heralded by a jagged guitar, the nightmare returned to overwhelm him, and David was lost in his roles once again, uncertain whether he was real or merely acting out a part for "tomorrow's double-feature".

The disjointed syntax reappeared with a succession of ominous images and phrases whose ironic resonances David savoured. "It's a 24-hour service," he sang, invoking the delights of American consumerism; but the "service" was provided by Orwell's thought police, "guaranteed to make you tell". The sexual imagery lost its innocence, like the predators who roamed his ruined city and would "suck you while sleeping".

The final lines were the most telling of all:

> I hear them on the stairs . . .
> We are the dead.

As well as evoking memories of secret police throughout history – the footsteps on the stairs, the knock on the door – its lines directly borrowed from Orwell, for when the thought police close in, Winston Smith and his lover recite the phrase "We are the dead" in mystic recognition that although they were doomed, the knowledge they have acquired might live on.

For David, the allusions were more personal still. They echoed the key title track from *The Man Who Sold The World*, where David described his meeting with the *doppelgänger* who had trailed him through his imagination and his writings.

> We passed upon the stair . . .
> I spoke into his eyes
> I thought you died alone . . .

There, David's suggestion that it was he who had died also foretold the quest for self-knowledge he was embarking upon, with death as his companion. Now, after travelling the breadth of the world and galaxies, and crossing the landscape of his dreams and his imagination, he was at journey's end, and compelled to face the final inescapable truth:

> We are the dead.

The penultimate number was '1984', performed with far more threat and power than for American television, enhanced by an urgent guitar introduction remarkably close to the theme by Isaac Hayes for the film *Shaft*. Then, in the final lyric, came the album's stunning dénouement.

Following an apocalyptic introduction on a trumpet, David unreeled a stately succession of images linked to his earlier writings, like the "dust and roses" of 'Aladdin Sane' in memory of the war dead; or the "pulsars unreal" of imaginary space; or an asylum, made of glass, that recalled 'All The Madmen'. Then came a renewed entreaty to the messiah he had so often appealed to:

> Someone to lead us – someone to follow . . .

The phrase "some great Apollo" made clear that the figure embodied other attributes David prized, for Apollo was the Greek god of male beauty.

Now, at last, David revealed this figure's identity:

> We want you Big Brother – Big Brother

David was of course evoking Orwell's demi-god, symbol and substance of the absolute power of the state. But the coincidence it embraced was too great to be denied. Like other ambiguous references in David's deepest-felt lyrics, there was little doubt that it could also be interpreted as an appeal to his half-brother Terry. Confirmation that this was so came immediately, in the coda that ended the album, with its endlessly echoing and stifled cry:

> Bro – bro – bro – bro

David called the main lyric 'Big Brother' – and his title for the coda, a macabre reminder of the pressures that had surrounded him throughout his life, was 'Chant Of The Ever Circling Skeletal Family'.

Diamond Dogs was a *tour de force*, an achievement whose dimensions David's critics came only belatedly to recognise. Roy Carr and Charles Shaar Murray, for example, wrote later that it was "a far more powerful and coherent work than even the most perceptive of his critics realised at the time".

Few works of genius are truly original, but build upon their predecessors. In the case of *Diamond Dogs*, David had borrowed themes and techniques from artists in other fields, such as Orwell and Burroughs, and adapted them to his own. Most remarkable of all was the precision with which he had used them to re-create and confront his stricken family's mythology.

He had used the cut-up technique to reproduce not only the semblance of schizophrenia but also the random destruction of war, the very reason it had become the metaphor for his family's misfortunes, seen above all in the disjointed meanderings of his aunt Vivienne. The struggles of his characters to find love against the background of war matched the doomed liaisons of his aunts Una and Nora and, to a certain extent, his mother, Peggy.

Even the imagery David used had direct parallels in his family's tribulations. David told of "the blood of the *tricoteuses*" awaiting the next victim, and the sun that "drips blood" on the slain knights of modern warfare. It was a chilling echo of the focus of his aunt Una's derangement, as her daughter Kristina had confirmed: "She talked about blood a lot," Kristina said. "She was very concerned with blood and death."

When the recordings were complete, David embarked on the demanding task of mixing them himself. After days of effort, he finally turned for assistance to the man he had said goodbye to, with tears in his eyes, on the pavement outside the Gem office in Oxford Street three years before. Since that time, Tony Visconti had formed his own production company and was in the throes of constructing a sixteen-track studio in his home at Shepherd's Bush. Visconti had watched in horror as David became consumed by the character of Ziggy Stardust, and was relieved to find, when they met again, "underneath all the make-up and stuff, it was really my old buddy David".

As David and Visconti worked together on mixing the album, events in the real world uncannily mirrored those David had imagined and described, as both Britain and the US were gripped by political crises without parallel in modern times.

Britain's miners went on strike in a direct challenge to the pay policies of the Conservative government led by Edward Heath. The government responded by declaring a state of emergency that amounted to a siege. All through that winter, the people of Britain shivered in unheated offices and factories, stumbled home along unlit streets, and crept early to bed when all television broadcasting after 10.30 p.m. was banned.

To compound the misery, the Arab states of the Persian Gulf doubled the price of oil and then doubled it again, stoking Western inflation and producing queues and fighting at petrol stations. In February 1974, his defences crumbling, Heath called a general election to answer his question: "Who governs Britain?" The electorate replied, "Not you," and replaced him with the Labour Party and Harold Wilson.

Across the Atlantic, the greatest political cataclysm since the Civil War moved to its climax. The nation had seen a senate committee probe the evasions and deceptions of a sordid parade of the president's underlings and aides: men such as Robert Mardian and Egil Krogh and Charles Colson, who had offered to walk on his grandmother if the president wished; Maurice Stans and Howard Hunt and Attorney-General John Mitchell, who threatened that if the *Washington Post* continued its investigations into Watergate, its owner Katherine Graham would get her "tit caught in a wringer"; and H. R. Haldeman and John Ehrlichman, who said of a colleague under investigation by the FBI that he should be left to "twist slowly, slowly, in the wind".

One by one the most senior figures in the administration fell, including Mitchell and Mitchell's successor, Richard Kleindienst. America's vice-president, Spiro Agnew, had also been toppled in a separate scandal. That left President Nixon. As he struggled to avoid impeachment, he refused to hand over vital tape-recordings until compelled to do so by the Supreme Court, then sacked the prosecutor he had appointed to the case, and then lied to his successor about what the tapes contained, until finally the crescendo of calls that he should resign could no longer be denied.

That summer David would go forward to meet his nemesis too. And the act of giving *Diamond Dogs* "character, shape and body" on stage would take him to the brink of disaster.

25

Any Day Now

By 1974, MainMan had become a monster. Like David, it had been acting out its fantasies; like David, it was in danger of being overwhelmed by them. But had not Defries instructed his staff to behave as if spending money was the most natural thing in the world? Could they be blamed if they now believed that the lifestyle of the Beverly Hills Hotel was theirs by right and that it could be sustained without end?

In New York, MainMan now occupied three offices. The largest and newest was at 405 Park Avenue, a dozen blocks from one of Manhattan's most visible monuments, the Pan-Am skyscraper that bestrides the Grand Central railway terminal. Defries's room was the most sumptuous, furnished with a top-grain leather armchair and couch with hammered nail-head backs, and an imposing desk, installed with a custom-made gold-tooled leather-inlay top, and adorned with a matching silver blotter, cigar lighter and letter tray, carefully arranged.

Pictures of David in different poses and personas hung around the walls, and tidy piles of MainMan matches and MainMan notepads were conveniently placed to attract the visitor's attention. They bore the MainMan logo, a cross between the Superman emblem and a cigar band, coloured red, yellow and brown, which had been designed by George Underwood, although Defries claimed that the original idea was his.

There were separate rooms for all MainMan's senior officials: Zee was now president and corporate head, artist management; Jaime Andrews was corporate head, record production and marketing; Leee Childers, executive vice-president. With a dozen or more secretaries and assistants, the Park Avenue staff had risen close to twenty.

Cherry Vanilla meanwhile had secured an entire office suite to herself and two assistants at MainMan's former premises on 18th Street. She had become head of the MainMan film unit, which was to make or commission promotional movies for MainMan artists, and which could also lead on to full-scale feature ventures.

Defries insists today that this venture, which, he complains, has sometimes been viewed as "the very indulgent face of MainMan", was worth the "close on half a million pounds" it cost. Here, for example, originated the *Aladdin Sane* commercials which had brought such rewards in Britain: "they did a lot to make more people aware of Bowie as a commodity than they would have been, especially in England," Defries says. He believes that these also paved the way for the pop videos that are now a commonplace feature of the music world: "The fact that we were the first to do it, and that he was the first artist for whom it was ever done, I think is important".

Other members of the entourage remember the film unit more for the way Cherry Vanilla stamped her formidable personality on the 18th Street office by painting it a garish red – cherry-red – throughout. "She had the floors done cherry, the furniture, the typewriters, the telexes, everything," says Leee Childers. "It was *horrible*, it cost a fortune, and it was totally unnecessary."

The original offices in 58th Street where MainMan had been set up were still in use too, serving as a residence for Leee and Wayne County. That too was expensively equipped with a television set that projected its picture on to a full-size movie screen, and the latest video equipment. MainMan had a fourth office in Los Angeles, which Leee had been dispatched to set up early in 1973. Leee carried out his instructions with customary aplomb, renting a house just off Hollywood's exclusive Mulholland Drive in Hollywood, with extensive grounds, a swimming pool, and Errol Flynn's former home close by. Feeling the need for a car that would complete the MainMan image, he bought an enormous green Cadillac. It all reminded Leee of the line from 'There's No Business Like Show Business': "Where you get money that you don't pay back".

Leee remained in Los Angeles to run the office for six months, but while Defries talked grandly of the "West Coast operation", Leee found that his main task consisted of occupying Iggy Pop and keeping him out of trouble. Iggy had been sent to Los Angeles early in the year because Defries wanted him out of the way. David had tired of him and appeared determined, as in the case of Mick Ronson, that he should *not* become a vital star, and Defries was as anxious as ever to humour David's wishes.

"I didn't do anything except to keep Iggy from working and sit around," says Leee. To counter the boredom he would conduct costly telex conversations with Jaime Andrews in New York, who liked to transmit the most scandalous sections from the latest homosexual novel.

Leee also began a fashion for indulging in cosmetic surgery at MainMan's expense. He had long wanted a perfect set of teeth and now had every one of them capped, at a cost of $200 each, at MainMan's expense. Even this paled beside the achievement of Leee's Los Angeles assistant, Susie Ha-Ha, who told Leee that she needed an "urgent operation" that would cost $1,500. Supposing that she had a gynaecological complaint whose nature was too sensitive for him to enquire into, Leee persuaded the New York office to underwrite the cost.

After the operation, Susie Ha-Ha returned to work a new woman. "She'd gotten a tit lift," says Leee. "She was laughing and very open about what she had gotten away with. She said, 'I needed it just as much as anybody else needs all these things you all buy.' She was all fixed up and she looked great." When Defries learned what she had done, Leee says, "he just laughed".

New members of MainMan's staff were soon caught up in the air of wanton extravagance. Apart from telling journalists they could not interview David, says Pat Wadsley, "all I seemed to do was spend money". Her expectations were so quickly elevated that her first act upon checking into the Park Lane Hilton on a visit to London was to telephone the New York office to complain that her room was too small. Similarly, Jaime Andrews groused to New York of the fading décor and the snail-like service at London's Savoy Hotel at that time, and observed, in a reference to his sexual proclivities, that it was "not the kind of hotel you bring tricks to".

Back in New York, the *Pork* group took to spending their weekends in a cabin, rented at MainMan's expense, on the resort of Fire Island, opposite Long Island. Rather than face the tedious journey back to New York on a Sunday night – such a *schlapp* – they hired a seaplane to collect them for work on Monday morning. The pilot was instructed to buzz the cabin to wake them and to land by the beach ten minutes later to pick them up. It then whisked them into central Manhattan, landing at the 23rd Street seaplane terminal on East River, a convenient cab ride from the Park Avenue office.

Overshadowing them all was Angie, whose spending when she swept into New York left the others in awe. Melanie McDonald was with her when she spent $4,000 in the Park Avenue design-clothing store, Martha's, in four hours. "It was amazing," says Melanie. "I've never done that before or since."

Angie's explanation, if one was needed, was that she required the clothes for her career as fashion model, which she was pursuing under the name of Jipp Jones. But her modelling sessions were few and far between, and the fees did not remotely approach the level of her expenditure. Dana Gillespie was another partner during Angie's sprees. "I would fly off with her and we had sort of unlimited airline tickets," Dana says. "If we wanted to go anywhere a limo was there, it had a television, a bar, everything, we just travelled in fabulous luxury."

Presiding over the extravagance, with his inscrutable sphinx-like smile, was Tony Defries. Despite the distantly amused pose he liked to affect, he too seemed to have succumbed to the *folie de grandeur*. He sent urgent telexes to the London office commanding all visitors to New York to bring fresh boxes of Havana cigars, which MainMan limousines collected from Harrods. Melanie would peruse the latest copies of London fashion magazines, and ask the London office to transmit the prices so that she could choose her new wardrobe.

Defries's self-esteem had been boosted by the successful conclusion of negotiations of the kind that brought him such delight. In 1973 he had pondered David's publishing contract with Chrysalis, by which David was to receive a half-share in the copyright of his songs once he had recouped Chrysalis's £5,000 advance. That moment had arrived. Defries also interpreted the Chrysalis agreement to mean that David was entitled to an increase, from 50 per cent to 75 per cent, in his share of Chrysalis's take. Chrysalis disputed that, and a law-suit ensued. Chrysalis served a writ on fourteen separate counts, one claiming damages against Defries "for wrongful inducement of breach of contract" – in other words, that he had threatened to use the "piece of crap" ploy.

In the end, Defries got most of what he wanted. In particular, Chrysalis had to recalculate their previous payments to David. Between July 1971 and June 1973, his writing had brought them £62,747.09, of which Chrysalis had forwarded him just under half. They had now to pay him an additional £16,358.18, which MainMan received in January 1974. Under David's agreements with Defries, of course, MainMan was entitled to half that amount – and to half of his share of the copyright in his songs.

Thus emboldened, Defries talked of the greater triumphs to come. He could see no reason why MainMan should not eventually buy out RCA and merge it with Sony, and proposed that the new corporation's headquarters should be the Pan-Am building. He had a photomontage of the building made with the word "Pan-Am" replaced by "MainMan", which he hung in his office. Sometimes he lamented that it all seemed too easy. One evening a staff member came upon him in his office, drawing deeply on a Montecristo cigar, and looking down on the ant-like figures of the commuters scurrying along Park Avenue. "Why," he turned and asked, "are they all so stupid?"

By now Defries had acquired a new role model: instead of Colonel Parker he wished to be seen as Louis B. Mayer, commander of the MGM movie empire. "We had several conversations where he talked about himself as a Louis B. Mayer figure," says Leee. "He was very familiar with the whole MGM star system and he liked to think he was building something like that. He always thought of Louis B. Mayer as this fatherly figure who looked out for the best interests of the stars." Defries said more than once that MainMan had come to resemble the MGM studios at their height in the 1930s.

To David Bowie would thus be added a roster of international superstars that would make MainMan the most illustrious name in the world of entertainment. They represented another aspect of the MainMan fantasy, writ large; but they fell sadly short of Defries's hopes. They also demonstrated another less appealing attribute of David as star, taking people up, flattering them with his attentions, and then discarding them.

There was, for example, the curious case of Amanda Lear, one of the coterie of international playthings who flit from lover to lover, although Amanda invariably returned to her greatest love, the Spanish surrealist artist Salvador Dali. She also benefited from carefully fostered doubts as to her gender: was she a man posing as a woman? or a woman posing as a man posing as a woman? or a man posing as a woman posing...? David was introduced to her in London late in 1973 by Marianne Faithfull, and was predictably intrigued.

Like Ava Cherry, with whom she overlapped, Amanda did not discover that David was married until after they had slept together. She was nonplussed at the implicit encouragement Angie gave to their affair, particularly when Angie made her a present of a nightdress. Amanda found David "very demanding" and someone who "knew how to get what he wanted". He declared his love for her and also offered to help fulfil her long-cherished dream of becoming a rock-star.

Amanda helped revive one of David's earlier interests when she took him to see Fritz Lang's film *Metropolis* in Hampstead on his twenty-seventh birthday, January 8th, 1974. The next day David went out to buy every book on Lang he could find. She also talked to him about Salvador Dali, who soon became David's next passion.

Later, in New York, MainMan held a dinner in Dali's honour at the Four Seasons, then Manhattan's most expensive restaurant. Dali put his own idiosyncratic stamp on the proceedings by arriving in the company of two strangers, but no one from MainMan liked to ask why they were there. Two extra places were laid and after the meal the two men shook hands with Dali and left. At last Dali was asked who they were. "I've no idea," Dali replied. "I met them outside the restaurant and asked them if they would like to dine with me."

Meanwhile Defries dutifully attended to David's wish that Amanda should become a rock-star, arranging for her to have singing lessons in London with Florence Wiese-Norberg, who had taught David in the days of Ken Pitt. The verdict on Amanda's prospects was not encouraging. David proposed instead that Amanda should appear in a film of *Oktobriana*, an anti-Soviet cartoonstrip. A script was prepared with the usual MainMan sexual gloss: its subtitle was "the adventures of the she-devil", and Amanda was photographed in a cut-away black leotard, heavy leather belt and tall patent-leather boots. The project went little further, and Amanda returned to Salvador Dali. David, she says now, was very "capricious"; and she concluded that she had been "deceived".

While Amanda Lear never signed a formal contract with Main-Man, Wayne County did. As a transsexual who readily admits: "I was born a man but I really do feel that I should have been born a woman," Wayne was a natural object of David's curiosity. In 1973 Wayne was wearing women's clothes both on stage and off, later assuming the name Jayne and the female gender, and taking hormone pills to develop breasts. Jayne explains that although David made several sexual advances towards her they were based on a misconception on his part. "I have always been attracted to men who are more the traditional masculine men," she says. "He looked very very feminine and I was just not attracted to him." Besides, she adds, he had "knobbly knees".

Jayne's greatest grievance was that David apparently used her ideas and themes. She signed the standard fifty-fifty MainMan contract – to accord with the MGM image, it included a "morals clause", whereby she could be dismissed if her behaviour brought MainMan into disrepute – in the belief that either David or Mick Ronson would produce an album for her. David listened to demonstration tapes of her songs 'I'm Your Wonder Woman' and 'Queenage Baby', which included the line "Can't tell whether she's a boy or a girl", and soon afterwards wrote 'Rebel Rebel', with

368

Above: David "went black" in
1974. Eleven years later – in the
studio with Luther Vandross and
Chaka Khan – black music was
still a major influence.

Left: David plays sax again, this
time on the 'Serious Moonlight'
tour in 1983.

David, growing a moustache to improve his disguise, with Tony Visconti (centre) and cellist / engineer Eduard Meyer during the *Low* sessions at Berlin's Hansa Studio in 1976.

David at the Lutzower Lampe transvestite club in Berlin in 1976, alongside the proprietor, 'Carmen'. On the right is a smiling Corinne Schwab; of the others, two worked at the club, one for RCA.

Three paintings from the Brücke Museum of expressionist art, one of David's favourite places in Berlin. 'Roquairol' (left) by Erich Heckel and the self-portrait by Walter Gramatté (right) were a source for the covers of Iggy Pop's album *The Idiot* and David's album *"Heroes"*; the third, 'Lovers between Garden Walls', by Otto Mueller, helped inspire the lyric of *"Heroes"*.

David bids the audience to join him in "Heroes" during the triumphant Live Aid concert at Wembley Stadium in July 1985 – a performer at the peak of his power.

similar phrases and rhythm. "It wasn't illegal," says Jayne. "But some of my ideas went into it."

Jayne consoled herself with the belief that MainMan had agreed to produce her album, but the day before she was to fly to London she was told that the recording session had been called off. "Everything was cancelled, no album, no production by Mick Ronson, it just went 'phuttt' like that," she says. "That is when I knew beyond a shadow of doubt that I had been used."

To the despair of Leee Childers, her most loyal ally, Jayne still haunted the Park Avenue office, waiting for MainMan to promote her career. "I used to scream at her that she was being complacent," says Leee. "She would sit day after day, week after week, with nothing being done ... But she was happy enough that she was living on the Upper East Side with charge accounts everywhere."

There is general agreement that in contrast with Amanda and Wayne/Jayne, Tony Defries went to considerable lengths on behalf of Dana Gillespie, who had been his lover for a time, and signed a MainMan contract in 1973. RCA gave her a recording contract worth $60,000 for two albums in the first year, and MainMan's resources were mobilised to devise a suitable image. The outcome was typical MainMan. With a distinct note of fetishism, Dana was promoted with black basques and suspender belts, whips, and suggestions of multi-racial lesbianism. One MainMan photograph showed her in black underwear and an aggressive pose while a young black woman, similarly clad, knelt obediently at her feet.

Geoff Hannington, who had concluded Dana's agreement with RCA, found Dana's opening night at Reno Sweeney's night club in New York "the most embarrassing thing I had ever been to. There was a good upper-class audience and she was singing songs about lesbian relationships and had a friend dressed up as a maid." Hannington says now that he only signed Dana as a favour to Defries. "If I had taken a purely commercial decision I would have said no." But in David, he explains, MainMan owned RCA's most successful British artist at that time: "So what do you do?"

Dana looks back on the MainMan era with immense nostalgia and only mild embarrassment. When she was playing the minor part of Juno in *The Tempest* at London's National Theatre, she would draw up at the stage door in a rented Rolls-Royce just as Sir John Gielgud was emerging from a Mini and Arthur Lowe was arriving on foot from the Underground station. "MainMan paid for everything. Life was a glorious haze of fun and games and romping and raving, anything you wanted was there ... I was cotton-woolled, I had a secretary, BMW, great speakers, black windows, tickets all over the world . . . I was as happy as a pig in shit while I was in it, I took to it like the proverbial duck to water."

In Dana's case, there was a chastening end to the fantasy: after David and Defries had parted, she discovered that, by her contract, she virtually belonged to MainMan: "If I did a film or wrote any music or publishing royalties came in, it went to MainMan." When Dana appeared as the leading lady in *Mardi Gras* at the Prince of Wales Theatre most of her income went to MainMan – "I didn't even have enough money to tip the doorman."

Dana forfeited the BMW, too. She thought Defries had given it to her as a present, "but I discovered it was on the HP and only two years had been paid, so it was repossessed". Yet Dana's affection for Defries remains impressively undiminished. "I've always loved him and I can't ever not love him."

MainMan's most spectacular flop came when Defries decided to become a Broadway theatre producer. In the spring of 1974 the latest MainMan recruit was Tony Ingrassia, the director of *Pork*, who also signed the standard fifty-fifty contract. He had written a play about Marilyn Monroe entitled *Fame* which Defries agreed to stage in New York. With a cast of eight, including Ellen Barber, it had a week's preview at a 4th Street theatre in May 1974. Although the reviews were not encouraging, Defries decided that it should transfer to the John Golden Theatre on Broadway. There the critics were more scathing and the play was taken off after just one night, at an estimated cost of $300,000. Ingrassia's talents were thereafter employed devising publicity ideas for Dana.

Mick Ronson, meanwhile, was still being enthusiastically promoted: the Times Square billboard cost $5,000 a week and was backed up with full-page advertisements in the *Village Voice*. But his album sales were tiny, a concert tour made a loss, and his career as solo star ground to a halt. Ava Cherry had come to New York too, but the tracks she and the Astronettes had recorded in London were never released.

George Underwood was given a contract that summer, being paid a regular £465 per month as MainMan's resident designer and graphic artist, with all profits being divided, as usual, fifty-fifty; little came of it. Finally there was Annette Peacock, a jazz singer with a serious pedigree, who made one album under a MainMan contract for RCA. She was, says Leee, "pretty level-headed and a real musician". So level-headed, in fact, that she soon quit Main-Man and moved on.

*

The man on whom the MainMan fantasy depended above all was, of course, David. In 1973 his British album sales had set a record by occupying the top 50 for a total of 182 weeks, comfortably passing the previous best of 167 weeks achieved by Simon and Garfunkel in 1970. In the US, though not achieving the British heights, he had become a reliable seller. As his sales mounted, so did the advances MainMan received from RCA: $100,000 in April, $100,000 in June, $85,000 in July, and so on. They came fast enough to pay Laurence Myers the $500,000 he was due within eighteen months of the settlement agreement he had made with Defries in July 1973. Since Myers was receiving roughly one-fifth of MainMan's earnings, it meant that David brought MainMan around two million dollars in the same period.

Yet even that amount was barely enough to cover MainMan's vast expenditure: as fast as the money came in, it was pouring out again. By their contract, David and Defries were to share the profits of their venture. So far, says Defries, there weren't any. Later, the question of just who was financing the MainMan extravagance would become a matter of bitter contention but for the moment David was utterly unconcerned. All he wanted came from the MainMan fount, which was also providing spending money of £400 a month. MainMan was attending to his other obligations too, such as paying his mother £50 a month and sending her bunches of flowers.

Although, according to Defries, MainMan was not yet making a profit, Defries was using the torrent of money flowing through it to finance complex manoeuvres on the currency and commodity markets. He had set up a parent company in Fribourg, Switzerland, and opened Swiss franc accounts in banks in London and Fribourg, making substantial gains by buying and selling currency futures and juggling the RCA advances between the two accounts.

Defries was also ready to strike when the gold market was opened to US residents during this period. He believed that the price of gold would rise rapidly and urged the MainMan staff to buy as much as possible, even offering, when they proved reluctant, to do so on their behalf and deduct the investment from their salaries. "All of us said no," says Leee Childers. "But he bought into gold heavily and of course it sky-rocketed and made fortunes. He was very proud of it." Defries also boasted of the sums he made through currency specu- lation. "He was talking very very large sums," says Leee. "He wasn't talking $10,000, that would not have interested him. Anything less than $100,000 was boring to him."

Defries says that all of this was done in David's interests. "I wasn't looking at that time to make any personal fortune. I was reinvesting everything in the artists."

Despite the opulent air on which MainMan thrived, there was one group to whom there appeared to be only a thin line between profligacy and disaster. That was the MainMan London office, who spent the winter of 1973–4 – already made miserable through the cold and dark induced by the miners' strike – staving off a long series of creditors. It was not only that MainMan's resources were stretched thin, but that an aversion to paying bills appeared to be dominating Defries's business dealings. The telex lines between the London and New York offices were busy with news of creditors hammering – literally, in some cases – on the door of Gunter Grove, and the reciprocal advice from New York to stall as long as possible.

The Château d'Hérouville, where David had recorded the *Pin-Ups* album in July, had still not been paid by December, when it began to take affidavits from those who had taken part. Ken Scott agreed to give evidence, for he had not received his full producer's royalty from the albums he had worked on, and his attempts to secure his money through legal action somehow kept being snarled in the tangled web of agreements and sub-agreements surrounding Defries's settlement with Myers.

Bills totalling £300 for repairs to David's cars, one of them a Jaguar, dating from November 1973, were still unpaid four months later. At Christmas the Holiday Inn at Marble Arch was demanding payment of a bill for £2,142 incurred by Leee and Tony Ingrassia that summer. In January the Olympic studio threatened to ban David from recording there unless their bill of £4,935 was paid. The Ambassador travel agency, which made many of MainMan's airline bookings, was owed over £4,000.

By March, the London office manager, Peter Gerber, who had formerly worked at Gem, and owned one of MainMan's 100 shares, reported that the company's sterling bank account was overdrawn to the tune of £42,000. In the summer Gerber told New York that there were outstanding bills totalling £83,000, and complained bitterly that he was being used as a "handy scapegoat for the inefficiencies of others".

None of this as yet impinged on David. For he needed to live and breathe the MainMan fantasy more than anyone else. On it depended his plans for the part he was going to act out both off stage and on. For ever since completing the *Diamond Dogs* album he had been nurturing dreams of making the accompanying tour the most spectacular and extravagant in the history of rock music.

*

In April 1974 David left Oakley Street and moved to New York. He set up home in a luxurious suite in the Sherry-Netherland Hotel, by the south-east corner of Central Park; later he moved next door to the more fashionable Pierre, retaining it as his base, when he was not on tour, throughout that year.

David's companion for most of the year was Ava Cherry, who had fled from Britain in February, Angie's jealousy having mounted to the point where Tony Defries had advised it would be best for all concerned if she moved to New York. "Tony said, 'I got to get you out of England, 'cos Angie's freaking out,'" Ava says. "David was upset but he thought it was the best thing because she was giving him flak too."

Since Ava was a MainMan artist, she was first installed at the Grammercy Park Hotel. "I was ordering champagne, my phone bills were unbelievable, but that was no big deal. All those Main-Man people were going to Paris, staying at the George V, so why shouldn't an artist be doing it?"

When David arrived in New York, Ava joined him at the Sherry-Netherland; she lay low whenever Angie appeared and resumed her place beside David when Angie departed. Since Ava often signed David's room bills, she saw the extent to which he was determined not to be outstripped by the extravagance of those around him. "Dom Perignon cost a hundred bucks a bottle and we drank a lot of that."

Mick Jagger was in New York that spring, and his visits to David offered further proof that he had joined the ranks of the megastars, while also adding substantially to the room-service bill. In the belief that Jagger and assorted friends would be coming to dinner, says Ava, "David would order five or six *filet mignons*. They would come but they wouldn't eat, and so there would be bills for hundreds of dollars for just food for one night."

The Sherry-Netherland thus offered a suitable ambience as David formulated his plans for a rock tour that would out-Ziggy Ziggy and every other rock tour in history. The best token of his intentions came when he planned the set for his concert stage. He sought the advice of Jules Fisher, a slight, cultured man who was one of Broadway's most successful lighting designers and had just worked on the musical, *Jesus Christ Superstar*. When Fisher met David he was immediately impressed with the scale and clarity of his vision. "He had great ideas and he was willing to take risks," Fisher says.

David cited the films of Fritz Lang as having the distorted and exaggerated feel he sought, talking enthusiastically of *Metropolis* and other German expressionist films, like *The Cabinet of Dr*

Caligari. David also discussed the ideas of the Russian scenic designer Meyerhold, who had studied under Stanislavsky, and liked actors to perform on a forestage with an abstract backdrop.

Fisher found himself listening far more than he spoke. "The main conceptual contribution was his, not mine," he says. "He had a good awareness, he was very bright about what he was going to do and how he was going to do it, and I said, 'Fine.'" What emerged from these one-sided discussions was a mix of theatre and rock and roll on a scale never attempted before and not achieved, in Fisher's view, since. Fisher later compared David most favourably with the Rolling Stones, for whom he designed an ambitious concert set two years later. "They simply couldn't handle the kind of staging that Bowie had," Fisher says.

To put David's ideas into practice, Fisher recommended a young designer from Brooklyn, Mark Ravitz, who, though he sometimes seemed dour and over-methodical, had "the right kind of off-beat mind", Fisher felt. Fisher offered Ravitz three words of guidance to summarise what David wanted: *"Metropolis"*, "Nuremberg", and "power". When Ravitz met David at the Sherry-Netherland, he explored these concepts further. *Metropolis* closely matched the Orwellian component of *Diamond Dogs*, for, like *1984*, Lang's film portrayed a futuristic urban nightmare, where an authoritarian state is determined to quash a rebellious populace, with Lang's vision made more threatening by his quirky and distorted camera angles.

As for Nuremberg, the giant stadium where Hitler and the Nazis staged their massive rallies, that too offered disturbing imagery. "We talked about having giant banners, almost like the Nazis had," says Ravitz. Another scene that came to his mind was of the table-thumping carousing of the German beer cellars, one of the Nazis' most fertile recruiting grounds.

The concept of "power", though Ravitz did not then know it, was for David perhaps the most personal of all. In *Hunky Dory* he had revealed his fears that his creative muse would run dry — "I ain't got the power any more" — leaving him stranded and unable to express his ideas. Now, through the 'Diamond Dogs' set, he saw himself regaining, and exerting, that power to the fullest effect.

Back in his studio, Ravitz drew up lists of associations that David's ideas had sparked off. They included "tanks, turbines, smokestacks"; *"ecce homo* drawings by George Grosz, grotesque decadence, fluorescent tubing"; "state police, alleyways, cages"; and "watch towers, girders, beams, Albert Speer". Ravitz also sketched out variations on David's imagined city. One resembled an oil refinery or chemical plant, with domes and storage tanks and twisting snake-like pipes. Another looked like a giant television screen. A third showed a city of narrow skyscrapers leaning at distorted angles, and when Ravitz returned to the Sherry-Netherland, it was the third version which appealed to David most.

Gradually the set evolved. The skyscrapers were to be thirty feet high, with a bridge between two of them that would rise and fall at the touch of a button. There would be a "lunar module" that would track across the stage as if guided by unseen hands, and would then open up like a hand to reveal its mirrored interior with David inside. The most audacious idea of all, which Angie proposed, was that David should be launched out over the audience on a piece of theatrical equipment known as a cherry-picker. To complete an impression of apocalyptic doom, the décor would include tattered billboards that David could rip down, as if tearing down the city, and the walls of the skyscrapers would be painted so that they appeared to be dripping with blood.

As Ravitz pored over his plans, he realised that David had asked for nothing less than a theatrical set which would be at home on Broadway but which could also be transported from venue to venue, often with only twenty-four hours between shows. Whether that could be done remained to be seen, as did the question of whether all the complex equipment required would actually work. But if it was a mere matter of will-power, Ravitz and Fisher felt, there would be no problem. Both men had concluded that in David Bowie as rock-star they had encountered one of the largest egos they had ever known.

In musical terms, 'Diamond Dogs' represented another new departure for David, as for the first time he appointed a musical director to help organise the band. The man he chose was Michael Kamen, a stocky New Yorker with a classical piano training whose experience ranged from playing in a rock band, the New York Rock Ensemble, to writing a neo-classical ballet about the sculptor Auguste Rodin, which was performed in New York that spring. Cherry Vanilla took David to see the ballet and he was especially impressed with a moment when a dancer was frozen on stage in the beam of a giant searchlight. "We met afterwards, we talked for hours," Kamen says. He later concluded that David was "an incredibly intelligent man, one of the smartest men I've ever met on the planet".

After hiring Kamen, David consulted him continuously over the composition of the new band. Only Mike Garson survived from the 1973 tours, although the drummer Tony Newman had played on the *Diamond Dogs* album and bass player Herbie Flowers took part in the original 'Space Oddity' session. Kamen recommended two of his friends, Earl Slick as lead guitarist, and Dave Sanborn, who played alto sax and flute, and the band was completed by Pablo Rosario on percussion, Richard Grando on baritone sax and flute, and Kamen himself on keyboards. All except Newman and Flowers were American. In addition, there were two men in a dual role: Geoffrey MacCormack – who following his journey through the USSR had taken to calling himself Warren Peace – and Gui Andrisano, who were to act as both back-up vocalists and dancers.

In another move to dramatise *Diamond Dogs*, David had decided to use a choreographer to help map out his moves and those of his two dancers. He chose Toni Basil, then a vivacious young dancer with her own company, the Lockers, later to become one of the most inventive choreographers working in the US. Like Fisher and Ravitz, she found David a continuous source of ideas that kept her on her toes, in more ways than one. To begin with, she says, "I felt he was just testing me. But we just clicked, because neither of us felt that choreography was just steps. One number could have an acting premise, another could have a mime premise, another number had steps and another was more staged and choreographed. With somebody like him you don't have to be limited to one thing."

The rehearsals were held in the Capital Theatre in Rye, an hour from Manhattan in upstate New York, and it was there, over a period of four weeks, that 'Diamond Dogs' began to take shape. Mark Ravitz attempted to piece together the giant jigsaw that formed the set. Michael Kamen listened to the *Diamond Dogs* album each morning, hoping that he would "react spontaneously" to the music, before putting the band through its paces. Toni Basil wrestled with the complex tempo of David's songs, sometimes until three or four in the morning, discovering that few of them conformed to a conventional 2/4 or 4/4 beat. "It was very much like a puzzle process," she says; and David was a demanding taskmaster. "He worked terribly hard, he's very smart, and he knows as much as his choreographer does."

As yet, nobody was able to judge the full impact of what David was striving to achieve. But one thing was becoming very clear: the audience's attention would be almost exclusively on him. The two dancers would writhe and twine around him, directing their movements and gestures towards him. In dance terms their parts were undemanding, and they would even wear masks. The band would be in a clearly subordinate role, too. No longer would a Mick Ronson play off against David, sparking a mutual electricity that gave Mick his own status as star. This band was to remain in the background, half-concealed by the scenery, and invisible from many parts of the audience. This was to be David's show.

Back in Manhattan, Defries was locked in combat, once again, with RCA. His position there had been weakened by further internal machinations which had led to the final departure from Records and Tapes of Rocco Laginestra, who was "retired" by being made financial assistant to Edgar Griffiths, RCA's executive vice-president. The new head of Records and Tapes was the gruff Ken Glancey, who, as RCA's London boss, had complained to Geoff Hannington of the money he was spending on David. It was Glancey whom Defries now had to deal with in New York, together with the resolute Mel Ilberman.

The first spat was over the cover of *Diamond Dogs*. The most fashionable sleeve artist that year was the Belgian painter Guy Peellaert, whose book of airbrushed pictures, *Rock Dreams*, depicting the mythic figures of rock, had achieved the twin accolades of serialisation in the *Sunday Times* colour magazine and an exhibition at Biba's department store in Kensington High Street. David and Mick Jagger raced each other to commission an album sleeve from Peellaert, with David winning by a neck.

Peellaert's design showed David's head on the body of a dog which was being exhibited at a freak-show – 'The Strangest Living Curiosities'. As it lay upon the ground, the dog's most obtrusive feature, nestling cosily between its hind legs, was a set of canine genitals. Peellaert's picture for the inside sleeve was even more explicit. David, dressed all in black, including black leather boots and a Spanish hat, was holding a prancing Alsatian which was thrusting forward equally clear male sexual characteristics.

When Defries showed the artwork to RCA in New York, there was a massive row. Ilberman told Defries that the nation's rack-jobbers – the record wholesalers – would rise up and revolt if asked to distribute the albums to the mass-market stores of middle America. Defries remained adamant that the cover should be printed as he and David wished, and sent Leee Childers to RCA's printing plant at Indianapolis to ensure that the covers came off the presses with genitalia intact. Leee did as he was instructed and reported to Defries in New York that all seemed in order.

As soon as Leee left Indianapolis, RCA removed the printing plate and replaced it with another on which the crucial parts had been airbrushed out. Leee was convinced that he had been double-crossed, and suspected that Defries might have known that RCA would switch the offending plate. To his own amazement – "It was the most tiny little thing," he says, speaking of both the offending penis and the whole affair – Leee resigned. The episode had a sour end for Peellaert too, as he was still trying to extract his $5,000 fee from MainMan three months after completing his work.

Whether Defries had known about the change or not, the episode was a significant victory for RCA. They also dug in their heels over the financing of the 'Diamond Dogs' tour, which provided a replay of the row over the aborted tour the previous autumn. In keeping with the magnitude of David's plans, Defries intended that the tour should be the biggest yet, starting in July and lasting, with a brief respite in the middle, for six months. Once again, RCA viewed the tour as an unjustifiable gamble, and refused to back it. This time, Defries said that MainMan would both organise and finance the tour itself.

In view of MainMan's finances, it was an exceptionally bold step. But Defries did persuade Ilberman that RCA should contribute $150,000 towards the "advertising and exploitation" of David's albums that the tour would entail, and to provide extra finance by making early advances against David's royalties. With greater realism than hitherto, MainMan drew up its own budget, estimating the running costs of a twenty-week tour at $666,000. While David and a select handful could stay in de luxe hotels, the remainder would put up at Holiday Inns.

That still left some expensive items to account for, chief among them the 'Diamond Dogs' set, whose cost, including the pantechnicons required to transport it, could reach $250,000. Defries said that such a sum was no obstacle and his staff now became familiar with a new verb: to amortise. As Defries explained to most of them in turn, it meant that the cost of the set would be spread over several years. In that way, Defries triumphantly calculated, its true cost in 1974 could be as little as $50,000. The show, he announced, would go on.

26

Breaking Up

Those members of the entourage present at the opening night of the 'Diamond Dogs' tour at the Montreal Forum on June 14th, 1974, account it one of the privileges of their lives. "It was very, very exciting," says Toni Basil. "You always hold your breath because things go wrong, but it was the greatest set I have ever seen, it was the greatest rock show I have ever seen. Nobody knew if the bridge was going to crash or the pole he sat out on was going to crash. The show was phenomenal, and David was absolutely brilliant."

Fran Pillersdorf, the tour coordinator, who had come to Main-Man from a Broadway background, was spellbound. "We had this huge city in a huge arena and there was only one man in sight and he held the stage like Garland," she says. "The light came on him and it was as if he was in cabaret. He had the magnitude of the experience, but he had the stage and the environment in the palm of his hand. He was the consummate showman. We were in an arena with thousands of screaming people, he was playing against a forty-five-foot set, and it was his show."

The audiences at all three Canadian venues – Montreal was followed by Ottawa on June 15th and two shows at the O'Keefe Centre, Toronto, on June 16th – were equally awed, not least because David so totally confounded their expectations. The foyers and aisles were crowded with Ziggy and Aladdin Sane look-alikes, many of them gays or transvestites, wearing glitter outfits with enormous heels, crimson Ziggy haircuts, and lightning flashes across their faces. They were stunned to see David with a conventional hairstyle and wearing a light grey two-piece suit for his opening number, '1984'.

There followed an equally tantalising succession of changes of costume and scene. For 'Sweet Thing' David appeared on the catwalk between the two skyscrapers in a trenchcoat. He mimed a boxing match, complete with gloves and white ringside ropes, as he sang 'Panic In Detroit'. He performed 'Cracked Actor' surrounded by a battery of cameras and spotlights, as a make-up artist attended to his face. Dozens of arms reached up towards him as he swung out over the audience in the cherry-picker during 'Space Oddity'. For the final numbers, 'The Jean Genie' and 'Rock 'N' Roll Suicide', spotlights cast giant distended shadows of David and the dancers on the ruined city behind. Then, in a flash, the stage emptied, and the show was over. The spellbound Canadian audiences applauded and cheered for ten minutes or more before it was announced that there could be no encore as David had left the building.

The Canadian press was just as ecstatic. The *Winnipeg Free Press* called 'Diamond Dogs' "unique and brilliant"; the *Owen Sound Sun-Times* said it was "perfect, precision-honed showmanship"; a leading Toronto critic described it as "the most spectacular rock-show I have ever seen". Reviewers from further afield threw caution to the winds. Chris Charlesworth of *Melody Maker* almost exhausted his supply of superlatives in asserting that David's "far-reaching imagination has created a combination of contemporary music and theatre that is several years ahead of its time." 'Diamond Dogs', he added, was "a completely new concept in rock theatre – the most original spectacle in rock I have ever seen".

Only those backstage knew how fine had been the line between triumph and débâcle. Before the opening night at Montreal, the set had taken *thrity-two hours* to erect: equipment had jammed, the cat's-cradle of wiring had taken hours to unravel and connect. The moment the auditorium had emptied after the show, the road crew dismantled the set and loaded it on to trucks. They were on the road for Ottawa by dawn and at breakfast time had begun to reassemble the set. Later they divided into two teams, working alternate shifts and hot-bunking, like a submarine crew, in between. They continued almost without respite for the rest of the month, with the tour playing its first US date at Rochester, New York, on June 17th, and reaching Memphis, Tennessee, on June 30th. Only in three cities that month – Cleveland, Detroit and Pittsburgh – did the show play for more than one night, giving the team a brief rest.

Most who took part, particularly the newcomers, felt that they were at the centre of momentous events. When the band woke each morning at their latest Holiday Inn, there was excitement in the air. "We were exuberant," says Michael Kamen: "'What's happening man? Where's the buzz, man?' It was a party, a big big ball. We were surrounded by people. The tour seemed to be the focus of the entire world's attention." There were groupies, groupies, everywhere. "They'd come out of the woodwork. You'd walk out of your hotel room and they would be three deep in the hallways, waiting for a glimpse of David." The groupies would be "trawled", Kamen adds, for the benefit of all.

If in its excesses the tour seemed like a re-run of the Ziggy extravaganza, further changes were being wrought in David himself. Even from the frenzy of the Toronto auditorium, Chris Charlesworth had detected an iciness that contrasted sharply with the rapport David had previously achieved with his fans. "Not once does he address the audience or even allude to their presence, other than an odd grin," Charlesworth wrote. "Bowie comes out of this show as some kind of magical being . . . It was almost total arrogance – a MainMan star, indeed."

They were particularly perceptive remarks. In David's defence, he was under extra strain at Toronto through an attack of laryngitis, which had delayed the start of the concert by forty-five minutes. But in private, he was displaying a growing disdain for his audience, first glimpsed in the streak of cruelty he had shown at the farewell Ziggy concert at Hammersmith, now appearing as one of the least pleasant consequences of stardom: the arrogance of power.

The pre-tour incidents showed how far that process had gone. The first occurred in a meeting about the clothing and stage designs, when David discomfited a roomful of people by declaring roundly: "I'm going to show all those little kids who come in with their platform shoes and lightning across their faces. I'm going to walk out in flat shoes." One of the MainMan staff present considered the remark "shitty" and wished that David "would get back to his humanity".

The second came during discussions on the running order of the songs, when Michael Kamen told David that he disagreed with the sequence he proposed. "You're wrong," David replied coldly. "At this point all I have to do is flick my wrist and the entire audience will flip."

After seeing the first concerts, Kamen was compelled to concede that David was "dead right". But Kamen's admiration for David's professionalism was tempered by his regret that the close relationship they had enjoyed during rehearsals had all but dissipated. David, says Kamen, was fast becoming "one of those rare creatures of rock and roll – you were extremely blessed if you got close to anybody in the operation, much less David himself. 'Himself' began with a capital letter and he was being insulated, very effectively so."

The punishing schedule of the tour made it natural that David's closest companions should want to cosset him as much as possible. When David did emerge, it was to display the Jekyll and Hyde personality previously observed by Ken Pitt and Ian Hunter and now frightening in its volatility. "One minute," says Michael Kamen, "he would be a wonderful sweet friend, somebody who was easy to talk to and fool around with. The next minute he was somebody who would burn through you with their eyes. It was a quite sudden switch."

Those around David felt that the trigger of his abrupt switches of mood was plain to see: cocaine. During the Ziggy tour, David had merely watched the white powder being proffered at post-concert receptions and parties. Now, he succumbed. Dana Gillespie believes she understood why.

"David's schedule was ridiculous, and the show was so powerful and exhausting," she says. "Afterwards you're so high from the concert itself and people come round, chicks are there, people lay packets of coke on you and it's good stuff and you're up until seven in the morning and then you've got to leave at eight . . . Because there was no shortage of money, there was no shortage of coke. It was part of the whirling, flashing electric lifestyle that was going on." It was, Dana adds, "like champagne".

Ava Cherry was painfully aware of the changes the drug apparently caused. "When I first met David, he didn't do drugs," she says. "When I first went to England, he would hardly smoke a joint. His personality was altogether different, he was sweet and kind and loving, I loved him so much. When we got to America people started coming on the tours and bringing lots of coke around and of course we were all doing it. But David has an extreme personality, so his capacity was much greater than anyone else's. He would start to change his personality sometimes. It didn't affect his music or how he created, but it would affect how he would react to people, those who really liked him and cared about him."

It was Mike Garson who was the most dispassionate observer of David's decline. "I'm the only musician I know," he says, "who has never used any drug ever." What Dana saw as the "electric lifestyle" of the 'Diamond Dogs' tour appeared to Mike "like some X-rated movie – I felt the whole thing was pretty sick, to tell you the truth . . . He had a real rough time and I wouldn't have wanted to be him." Garson was even more perturbed that David seemed to be aware how far he had sunk. "At parties, when everyone was doing cocaine, he said, 'Check Mike out, I love him because he doesn't use any drugs.'" David nonetheless appeared unwilling or unable to fight what was happening to him. "He knew right from wrong. It's just that he was hooked."

Yet beneath David's need for cocaine lay more profound processes of personal disintegration. The Ziggy phenomenon was repeating itself. Just as David had been taken over by the character he created in Ziggy Stardust, he was on the brink of being overwhelmed by 'Diamond Dogs'. He was certainly not the detached observer he hoped to be seen as in the idealised character of Halloween Jack: on the contrary, the saga he was acting out on stage was enveloping him off stage as well. The dance with madness and death had taken him over once again; it seemed that the family myth he had so riskily stepped into was being played out to its inevitable end.

David's colleagues were in no doubt how close he was to disaster. Michael Kamen remembers "being struck by the idea that I was actually working with someone who under any other circumstances would be under lock and key. The fact that he was generating all these millions of dollars for various people was the only thing that kept him out." Mike Garson saw "a heavy downward spiral". David's lead guitarist, Earl Slick, says: "It was self-destruct time."

The pressures and the tensions increased as the tour continued its frenetic dash into July. On July 2nd, as the convoy carrying the stage equipment sped south from Atlanta to Tampa, a bee stung one of the drivers and his truck plunged into a rattlesnake-infested Florida swamp. While there were muted cheers from the band, who had become frustrated at being half-hidden among the scenery, David had to be begged to perform in Tampa that night. "I think he felt naked without the set," says Michael Kamen. David protested: "We can't do the show without it," but Kamen, backed up by Herbie Flowers, talked him into performing. "You have one of the greatest bands in the world," Kamen told him. "The set doesn't make any difference."

There were more serious problems when the tour reached Philadelphia on July 8th, caused this time by the abrasive business methods of Defries. Each member of the band had his own contract with MainMan, and the salaries – unknown to the musicians – varied widely. Earl Slick received $190 a week – "a pittance", he says – while the British pair, Herbie Flowers and Tony Newman, were paid around four times as much, £5,000 for a twenty-week tour. Where the contracts did agree was that these fees "did not include work other than the Tour or rehearsals, i.e., films, television, etc . . ."

When the musicians arrived at Philadelphia's Tower Theatre for the first of five nights of concerts, they discovered, in the words of Earl Slick, "extra mikes everywhere. We think, We don't use fifty mikes, what's going on?" The answer was that Defries had agreed with RCA that David should fulfil his contract by recording one of the Philadelphia concerts which would be issued as a double album.

The musicians were furious and told Defries they considered a live recording came under the aegis of "films, television, etc." in their contracts and they wanted to be paid extra. Since, they calculated, the album would earn at least $1 million, they told him they would settle for one-twentieth of that amount, namely $50,000 shared among the ten of them. Defries responded by offering them the minimum scale of around $500: "A ridiculous sum," says Slick.

With the two British musicians, Herbie Flowers and Tony Newman, assuming the role of shop stewards, the band retaliated by threatening not to perform that night. An hour before the concert, David had a furious row with Flowers in his dressing room. "I've bloody well got to go on and do a show in ten minutes," David thundered. "I don't need all this shit."

Stuey George denies the apocryphal story that David hurled a chair which narrowly missed Flowers's head. "He kicked the chair and it flew backwards," Stuey says. "It wasn't directed at any person. David wouldn't actually get physical with anybody. Verbally he could be very cutting but bodily . . . no." Finally Defries signed an agreement promising that the band would receive an extra $5,000 each. There was a familiar MainMan aftermath: "Obviously," says Earl Slick, "we didn't get paid." The musicians finally received their $5,000 after launching legal proceedings which cost them 10 per cent of their payments in lawyers' fees.

The musicians were still simmering when they went on stage that night: "All of a sudden I found myself in the midst of politics," says Slick. "It was my first slab of reality that said, 'This business is all fucked up.'" Their anger exacerbated an atmosphere already fraught with tension, which David himself likened to "vampires' teeth coming down on you".

When the critics heard the album in October, they were inclined to agree. Chris Charlesworth was puzzled that it seemed so inferior to the Toronto concert; David was "hoarse, throaty and often off-key", and Charlesworth felt that the musicians were merely going through the paces "instead of putting their all into the show". Charles Shaar Murray felt in places David moved into "outright artifice and self-parody", and concluded: "The walls seem to be closing in on Bowie."

Tony Visconti, whom David had summoned to help produce the album, and who worked on the tapes in a studio in New York that summer, called it "thin and brittle" and "one of the quickest and shoddiest albums I've ever done". At least, he acknowledged, "it was an honest live album". David later felt that the title, *David Live*, wasn't honest enough, and suggested that it should have been called 'David Bowie Is Alive And Well And Living Only In Theory'. The impression was completed with a photograph of a grinning, skeletal David, who commented later that he looked as though he had just stepped from the grave.

From Philadelphia the tour headed north for Connecticut, Massachusetts and Rhode Island, before pulling into New York, where two shows at the Radio City Music Hall on July 19th and 20th brought the tour's first phase to an end. Among the New York critics, Lilian Roxon, usually so loyal to David, was bemused by what she saw: David had performed well enough, she opined cautiously, but the show had not really worked. The *New York Times* considered that David was "gaudily fussing around" and the influential *Village Voice* headlined its report, "Dancing at Disaster's Edge".

After the Radio City shows there was a six-week break before the tour was due to resume. David returned to the Sherry-Netherland and was soon plunging further down the self-destruct spiral. "He didn't sleep very much," says Ava Cherry. "He didn't eat much either. He'd wake in the middle of the night and drink some milk or eat some cheese, that was about it. He was very thin in those days, very very thin."

When David's cousin Kristina met him she was horrified. She watched his performance at Radio City from the wings and noticed that his singing was out of synch with his musicians. She also observed how dehydrated he was from taking cocaine. "When he grimaced his lips adhered to his gums," she says. "He would turn his back on the audience to run his finger around his mouth to free them." He also took frequent gulps from the glasses of water and fruit juice he had lined up on Mike Garson's piano. "I prayed," says Kristina, "that he wouldn't die on stage."

When Kristina called on David at the Sherry-Netherland, she found that he was spending large amounts of time in his room watching television – sometimes two sets at once – and was going to bed at seven in the morning and getting up at three in the afternoon. She also saw him indulge in cocaine, but when she tried to remonstrate, David's response was to align her with others who reminded him of his responsibilities. "You're just like the rest of the family," he told her.

With David due to begin phase two of the tour in Los Angeles on September 2nd, which would take him back on the road for another three months, it seemed a moot point how long he could keep going. The nadir came sooner than that. In August, David returned to Philadelphia to record his next album. He had hired the Sigma Sound studios and recruited some extra musicians, bringing the total in his band to around a dozen.

"I'll never forget it," says Mike Garson. "He wanted some cocaine. He stopped a session, and he actually waited while someone drove over from New York because he couldn't go on and do the work until it came." The delivery took two hours and in that time David's musicians sat idle. "The clock was running," says Garson: it was late at night and the musicians were being paid double-time. "It was pathetic," Garson adds. "The worst."

It seemed that David was on the brink of destruction, both as a musician and as a human being. The implicit prophecy of *Diamond Dogs* was being fulfilled; the end had come.

But Philadelphia was also a beginning. It marked the time and place where David began to put his fears behind him and to climb out of the abyss. It was the end of the old David, the start of the new, and the moment when he began to free himself from the family curse.

27

Fame

Always before, when he wished to break with the past, David had searched for a new musical idiom with which to make a fresh start. As he discarded one group after another in the 1960s, he had moved through successive fashions of British music: blues, rhythm and blues, and the hard-rock style pioneered by The Who. Now he did so again.

The idiom David chose this time was black; and not just black music, but black everything. As Ava Cherry observed, it began with women. "He was fascinated by black people," she says. "Black girls, any girls he would sleep with when I was with him were black. It was like, 'There's another one, what a gorgeous one, over there.'" At concerts and clubs David would pick out the women he coveted and ask Stuey George, still devotedly in attendance, to arrange for them to meet him later. "I couldn't stop him," says Ava. "I used to cry but he would always say, 'You can't fence me in.' I was very faithful, and he wanted me to be. It was the old double standard: *he* didn't have to be, but *I* had to be. He was a male chauvinist – but I liked it."

From women, David moved on to music. He and Ava visited the famed Apollo Club in Harlem, where one of his earliest idols, James Brown, had appeared. They saw the Jackson Five at Madison Square Garden and went to black and Latin clubs where the newest craze was for disco music, at first a crude and monotonous sound with a thumping beat designed solely for dancing, soon to acquire a variety and vitality of its own.

David listened to the records of its most successful practitioner, the ample-framed Barry White, who was producing a stream of disco hits with titles that attested to a certain rawness in their appeal, like 'I'm Gonna Love You Just A Little Bit More Baby' and 'Never, Never Gonna Give Ya Up'. David was also much taken with the Isley Brothers, a black group who had recorded their versions of white classics like Stephen Stills's 'Love The One You're With' and Bob Dylan's 'Lay Lady Lay', and whose 1973 single 'That Lady (Part I)' sold two million copies. This was the style, David resolved, that he would employ on his next album.

Then, through Ava, David discovered the Sigma Sound studios in Philadelphia. Ava had been badgering David to fulfil his promise to assist her recording career until Defries finally intervened and asked Michael Kamen to help. Kamen took Ava to the Sigma Sound studios, located in a run-down area of Philadelphia on North 12th Street, where two black recording entrepreneurs, Kenny Gamble and Leon Huff did much of their work. Gamble and Huff seemed to have the Midas touch: 16 per cent of America's R and B hits in 1973 came from the Sigma studios, and the artists who recorded there included the O'Jays, Billy Paul, the Stylistics, the Spinners, and the Three Degrees.

Ava had just finished recording David's song 'Sweet Thing' with Kamen when David called at the studio to see how they were getting on. He was impressed with both the facilities and the studio's resident rhythm group, known as the MFSB – short for Mothers Fathers Sisters Brothers. "He met the guys, these fantastic black guys," says Kamen; "something really fundamental shifted in him." This, David decided, was where he would make his next album for RCA.

David had hoped to use Sigma's rhythm group but all except one, the percussionist Larry Washington, had commitments elsewhere and so he recruited a number of black musicians he had seen or learned of in New York. They included lead guitarist Carlos Alomar, who had played with James Brown, bass guitarist Willie Weeks, who had recorded with the Isley Brothers, percussionist Ralph McDonald, and drummers Andy Newmark and Dennis Davis. The vocal section was augmented with Robin Clark, the wife of Carlos Alomar, together with Luther Vandross, Antony Hinton and Diane Sumler.

While some of the musicians from the tour – Earl Slick, David Sanborn, Mike Garson – were retained, others were held to be surplus to requirements, including Herbie Flowers and Tony Newman, who returned to Britain, and Richard Grando. The most ironic omission from the recording sessions was Michael Kamen: having helped steer David towards his new musical style, he says, David found that he was "dispensable". It was clear by now where David's enthusiasm lay. Two days before recording was due to start, David telephoned Tony Visconti and asked him to produce the new album. "I've got the most fantastic band lined up," David told him. "I'm really into black music."

Visconti, as he had over the mixing of *Diamond Dogs*, responded to David's call for help and flew to Philadelphia the next day. He reached the Sigma studios two hours after the first session was due to begin and, like Mike Garson, found the proceedings "very strange". Sometimes David did not arrive until midnight. "He was very thin, and living kind of reversed hours, going to bed at eleven in the morning," Visconti says. It all reminded Visconti of the impromptu chaos of *The Man Who Sold The World*, with the apparent lack of organisation, David re-arranging his songs as he went on, and the album becoming "one enormous jam session".

David's later disparaging verdict on the *Young Americans* album was to call it "plastic soul". When it was released in March 1975, the British critics shared that view. Ian MacDonald described it as "a transitional piece, created in a melancholy and confused state and compounded by a generous dose of the self-pity of the privileged" with a prevailing mood of "luxurious angst" and "melancholic confusion". Michael Watts suspected it was "designed to cast our hero in the mould of soul superstar . . . I get a persistent picture of nigger patronisation as Bowie flips through his soul take-offs at Sigma Sound like some cocktail-party liberal."

Six of the album's eight songs came from the Sigma Sound sessions, and it was the confused facsimile of soul and disco, with strident saxophones, breathless vocals, a back-up chorus that sounded like a gospel choir, and clapping sounds on the off-beat, that left the British critics uneasy. Michael Watts disliked the lyrics too: "Not only are his hollow, frozen vocals weirdly out of context, but he patently lacks any deep emotional commitment to his material."

Other critics found the lyrics hard to decipher, and dismissed them as impenetrable or inaudible. David said that they were more impressionistic than anything he had done before: "It's just emotional drive, one of the first albums I've done that bounds along on emotional impact."

The most significant feature of *Young Americans* was the utter break it represented with the style of *Diamond Dogs* – and with the sequence of albums of which *Diamond Dogs* formed the climax. David also said that he had avoided philosophising in his lyrics, which were for the first time less important than the music – itself a characteristic of disco, where the voice is little more than another instrument. Certainly David's lyrics lacked their previous depth and complexity – and yet his creative instincts were not to be denied, for distinct themes still emerged to illustrate his mood and offer premonitions for the future.

The title track, 'Young Americans', was familiar David, a catalogue of sights and sounds of America, particularly black America, strewn with tags and jargon: "pimps got a Cadi", "Afro-sheeners"–

"Barbie doll", "soul train". It was also a lament for the transience
of human emotions and relationships, laced with hints of suicidal
feelings, and culminating in the anguished appeal:

> . . . ain't there one damn song that can make me
> Break down and cry?

The next song, 'Win', concerned the related themes of the deceptive
lure of sexual passion and the frail attempts of lovers to make true
human contact. 'Fascination' explored the paradox of erotic appeal
and the temptation to exploit one's sexual partners. 'Right' was
an unambiguous celebration of sexual ecstasy and gratification.

'Somebody Up There Likes Me', the opening song on side two,
also covered well-trodden territory. It portrayed the media hero,
his "smile like Valentino", as a messiah who makes a preordained
visitation to earth. This time David warned against his blandishments – he could "sell you anything" – and against the transience
of fame: "Leaders come and . . . leaders go." 'Can You Hear Me'
is another lament for true love and regret that the superstar, visiting
"sixty new cities", may only have been "faking it all".

The lyrics showed David's usual fondness for internal references
and jokes. 'Somebody Up There Likes Me' was also the title of
the movie biography starring Paul Newman as the boxer Rocky
Graziano; the line "it's harder to fall" in 'Can You Hear Me'
echoed another boxing movie, *The Harder They Fall*, starring
Humphrey Bogart – in his last movie appearance – and Rod
Steiger.

Most telling of all, and belying David's attempt to write lyrics
that were merely impressionistic, were the references in both 'Win'
and 'Fascination' to being "crazy". And two other lyrics, by
referring to "heroes", contained pointers for the future. In 'Young
Americans', a woman cries:

> . . . "Where have all papa's heroes gone?"

'Win' contains the couplet:

> Life lies dumb on its heroes,
> Wear your wound with honour, make someone proud.

There was a significant dispute, too, over the choice of title for
the album. *Young Americans*, under which it was eventually issued,
had obvious commercial appeal. According to Tony Visconti,

David's first choice had been 'The Gouster', current black argot for "a cool hip guy who walks down the street snapping his fingers". This figure was therefore recognisable as the *alter ego* seen in 'Watch That Man' and in the character of Halloween Jack in *Diamond Dogs* whom David so wished to emulate. In view of David's emotional turmoil, it was a potent piece of wish-fulfilment. And much had yet to pass before he would achieve that most desirable state.

The 'Diamond Dogs' tour resumed on the West Coast in September, with three months to run before it reached its end in the Deep South in early December. The opening concert at the Los Angeles Universal Amphitheatre on September 2nd was the first performance in California, and the *Los Angeles Times*'s Robert Hilburn, one of David's earliest supporters, saluted both him and the set. David, Hilburn wrote, was "stunning – a performer of immense style and ability"; the set and the intricate special effects were "marvellously entertaining". Further accolades greeted the show as it toured California and Arizona for the rest of the month.

In October, the tour headed for the industrial north, playing in Milwaukee, Detroit and Chicago. But the audiences there, who had already had to adjust to the new post-Ziggy David, were compelled to alter their sights again. Having won the most effusive plaudits any rock-star could expect, David performed yet another *volte face*. He abandoned the 'Diamond Dogs' set.

Inside the entourage, the effect was as if a mine had exploded. "I thought, Oh God when I first heard it," says Fran Pillersdorf; Mark Ravitz was appalled. David's decision also wrecked the arcane financial calculations of Defries: the cost of the set would have to be borne in 1974 after all. In public, Defries bore this blow with fortitude, as if this was merely another of David's whims to be favoured. "He was not happy about junking a $250,000 set," observed Jaime Andrews, mildly, "but that's what David wanted and so Tony gave in to him and said, 'OK.'" Fran Pillersdorf adopted the same stoical stance; MainMan's view, she says, was: "'If you want a new set, we'll give you another set.' As long as I knew it was in the realm of possibility, I thought, Let's do it."

Having abandoned the setting for 'Diamond Dogs', David now discarded its contents too. First, some of the people who had been most vital in creating 'Diamond Dogs' departed. The dancer Gui Andrisano took over from Toni Basil as choreographer; out went Michael Kamen too. "Fuck them," Kamen thought. "Let them do what they want."

David's choice to replace Kamen as musical director was the ever-loyal Mike Garson, the longest-surviving member of his band. That led to another row over money with Defries, for when Garson asked for $2,000 a week, Defries told him he was fired. But David insisted that Garson was reinstated. The band that Garson assembled was an amalgam of the old and the new. Four of its members, Earl Slick, Dave Sanborn, Pablo Rosario and Garson himself, had been in the original 'Diamond Dogs' line-up. Of the new recruits, guitarist Carlos Alomar and drummer Dennis Davis had taken part in the Sigma Sound sessions, while the bass player Emir Ksasan was a newcomer.

David now changed his repertoire too. Most of the *Diamond Dogs* lyrics were jettisoned along with the set, to be replaced by a range of disco and soul numbers similar to those on the *Young Americans* album; soon it was known as the 'Philly Dogs' tour. Some band members were bewildered, with Earl Slick least happy of all. "David personally is not communicating, I can't talk to him any more, all of a sudden it's all change and I become seriously unhappy," Slick says. "I thought I was important to the thing but I'm starting to feel like a fuckin' throwaway. David had gone completely in a direction I didn't like, not to mention it wasn't the way I play."

The critics hated the new show. After seeing it at the Radio City Music Hall in New York, John Rockwell of the *New York Times* said that David looked "self-consciously uncomfortable without routines to act out, and he was in hoarse voice". In the *New York Post*, Jan Hodenfeld compared the show to a sumptuous birthday cake – "made out of cardboard, with a hollow centre". Jack Hiemenz in *Zoo World* called it "a disaster . . . something like a bad night in Las Vegas . . . totally mediocre"; certainly, he concluded, it was not worth the exceptionally high prices of up to $12.50 a ticket.

Michael Kamen saw the 'Philly Dogs' show too, and was appalled. "It was horrific – a sort of third-rate gospel revivalist meeting," he says. "The stage was full of large black people going 'Halleluja' and shaking tambourines, and poor David was very thin and very white and completely out of his element."

As for the set, David persisted for a time with the four mock-skyscraper towers of Mark Ravitz's original design, before they too were discarded, to be presented to a public school (and in the United States, public school means just that) in Philadelphia. Now David appeared on virtually a bare stage, lit with spotlights against the backdrop of a simple white sheet. That too contained a clue as to the future. Later David was to say: "I stripped myself down, chucked things out, and replaced them with a completely new personality." It was a partial account of an immensely painful process that had still to run its course. But it was aptly symbolised by the white backdrop David had chosen, a *tabula rasa* on which he would begin again.

MainMan, meanwhile, seemed to be falling apart. In London the throng of creditors was becoming more strident than ever. MainMan was being sued by, among others, Island Records, Radio Luxembourg, the *Evening Standard*, IPC, and David's chauffeur. Legal action was pending from the Customs and Excise over unpaid VAT, the Post Office was threatening to disconnect the phones, the newspapers were no longer being delivered, David's Access and American Express cards were about to be withdrawn, and the gas and electricity were on the point of being cut off. The office manager, Peter Gerber, complained to Defries: "My obligations to third parties and to myself are untenuous [sic] due to your apparent unreliability," and resigned.

Gerber's successor, a resourceful woman named Diana Hanford, struggled to hold things together. She sent New York lists of MainMan's creditors divided into categories: Desperately Urgent, Very Urgent, Pushing Hard, and OK For a While. A major crisis occurred when one creditor prepared a bankruptcy petition against MainMan which London warned "will bring all the other creditors down on us"; the debt was paid only hours before the petition was due to be presented in court. But the pressure increased remorselessly. "We have had to lock and bolt the doors and not answer the phones," London told New York. "And things can only get worse."

In New York, too, the unpaid bills were mounting. The Beverly Wilshire Hotel in Hollywood, where David and Angie had stayed throughout September, was demanding payment of $29,698. In New York, the Gramercy Park Hotel, where Ava Cherry and other MainMan artists had been lodged, wanted $20,688.34 and the Pierre Hotel, where David was staying, was owed $19,077.13. The Sigma Sound studios in Philadelphia, where David had made the *Young Americans* album, wanted $3,653.56 and the Barclay Hotel, Philadelphia, where David and some of the musicians had stayed, was owed $16,328.03. Many of the debts related to the 1974 tours. Among them were Studio Instrument Rental, $8,576.67; the Hilton Inn, San Diego, $1,176.48; the Hotel St Regis, Detroit, $355.85; the William Penn Hotel, Pittsburgh, $1,042.78; Avis

Car-Rental, $17,769.23. Toni Basil was waiting for her fee of $3,500 and Jules Fisher wanted $8,437.08. CMA, MainMan's West Coast booking agency, was owed $82,000. Even MainMan's lawyers, Pryor, Cashman and Sherman, were demanding $5,000. By December, the total was $350,000, and rising.

The list of creditors was prepared by an accountant, Alice Gartman, who had been appointed MainMan's new office manager. In an attempt to impose control, she proposed a revolutionary procedure: there should be budgets. In particular, she could not understand why the Bowies' household account in London was always overdrawn and recommended to Defries that he should try to cut their personal spending. According to Jaime Andrews, David was restricted to $500 a week – much of which "he spent on coke" – and Angie was given a limit too. Then came the affair of the Ming vases.

Convinced that she had discovered a serious gap in David's life, Angie bought him a pair of Ming vases, at a cost of $1,800 each. "David couldn't care less about Ming vases," said Andrews. "Then she realised she had spent $3,600 and Defries had just put her on a budget." Defries's birthday was imminent: "So she decided to get out of it by giving them to him." Defries was quietly incensed. "I don't want these things," he told Angie, "and you shouldn't have bought them." The vases were returned to their crates and sat forlornly in the MainMan conference room. "This one," Defries added, "is the worst."

According to Andrews, the affair marked a turning point in relations inside MainMan. Defries decided that Angie was irredeemable; Angie was furious that Defries should reprimand her, and turned irrevocably against him. The terminal blow came when the Ming vases were stolen. "Someone knew they were there, and someone took them away," Andrews said. "A lot of things got screwed up in that period. The organisation was crumbling all around. No one knew what anyone was doing."

Out on the tour, David was plummeting ever downwards. In California, Fran Pillersdorf came upon him in his hotel room fast asleep in the middle of the day: "He was in this darkened room, crumpled sheets, black room, dead asleep, and I found it very depressing," she says. In Chicago, David told Bruno Stein of *Creem* magazine that while in England he had made UFO sightings "six, seven times a night for about a year . . . We had regular cruises that came over. We knew the 6.15 was coming in . . ." David explained that he had never revealed this information before as the population had been programmed by various code words to disbelieve anything of which their controllers disapproved. In Arizona, hearing a rumour that a spaceship had landed, he told his staff to monitor the local radio stations to find out all they could.

MainMan was riven with factions, with the more prescient – or calculating – members jockeying for David's favour, judging that the most profitable future lay with him. David and Defries were scarcely speaking to each other, and the man trying hardest to hold everything together was Tony Zanetta. "They had just stopped communicating and I tried to keep the thing running and keep them together and everything got out of hand," he says. "David was out of hand and Tony Defries was out of hand in a different way. The physical stress of being on the road, alcohol, drugs . . . everything was just falling apart."

That included Zee himself. "I pretended that nothing was happening to me and that I was fine. But I wasn't fine, I was falling apart too." Later Zee realised he had been close to a mental breakdown.

Then David engaged in a search for new role models and new messiahs. For a time, he lit upon Frank Sinatra. "That was his great idol, who he was modelling his whole career on," says Ava Cherry; "the clothes and everything." Ava had some of her father's zoot suits, with their baggy, tapering trousers and oversize jackets, and David incorporated similar styles in his act.

David also said that if there was ever a movie of Sinatra's life, he would like to play the leading part. It was a half-idle wish, but the MainMan rumour machine was still at work and it appeared in a show-business gossip column. Soon afterwards David and Ava went to see Sinatra perform at Las Vegas, and sent a note asking if they could meet him after his show. According to Ava, Sinatra sent back word to the effect that he didn't have time to see David and that he didn't want "some faggot" playing his life story either. "David was angry at first," says Ava. "'How dare he?' He was very hurt. Then he just never mentioned Frank Sinatra to me again."

For David, to abandon the songs and stage setting of 'Diamond Dogs' was not enough. He had been living out the fantasy of 'Diamond Dogs' on the broader stage that MainMan had provided. But MainMan was caught up in the same self-destructive illusion; MainMan must go too. A meeting with another of David's idols proved decisive. "There were only three people that he was impressed with," says Ava Cherry. "One was Mick, and one was Frank Sinatra, and one was John – most of all with John."

Four years after the break-up of the Beatles, John Lennon was living in the Dakota apartment block on the Upper West Side, New York. David visited him there in December, after the end of the 1974 tour, and Lennon called on David in his suite at the Pierre. Tony Visconti was present at their first meeting: David was "very nervous", he says. "I dominated the conversation – David was so shy, he was sitting in the corner drawing sketches, he couldn't talk to John." Even in later meetings, according to Ava, David remained "in awe" of Lennon. "David was very impressed with him," she says. "He was just glad to be in his company."

Later David said that one of their most animated conversations, which had occupied them throughout one night, concerned the penalties of success: "What it's like not having a life of your own any more," David recalled, "how much you want to be known when you aren't, and then when you are, how much you want the reverse." They had also discussed their respective managers. Lennon himself had been badly scarred, having seen his songs cynically traded among "the men in suits", and spending years extricating himself from their clutches.

For a time, Lennon and the rest of the Beatles had been managed by Allen Klein. But Klein had taken only 20 per cent of their earnings, and that only from the work he had personally secured for them, against Defries's 50 per cent of everything. According to David, Lennon told him: "You'll really go through the grind and they'll rip you off right and left – the key is to come out the other side."

One outcome of those conversations was the recording of 'Fame'. David first said he would like to record the Lennon/McCartney song, 'Across The Universe'. Lennon agreed, and so he, David and Carlos Alomar went to New York's Electric Lady studio to do so. Afterwards Lennon twanged an impromptu three notes on his guitar which Alomar enthusiastically took up and elaborated. David meanwhile sketched out the lyric in the control room, generously saying later that Lennon's ebullient presence had provided the "energy" and "inspiration" that made the adrenalin flow.

The result, which was recorded with the core of David's touring band, without Mike Garson but including two back-up vocalists in Jean Fineberg and Jean Millington, was 'Fame'. Both this song and 'Across The Universe' were added to the *Young Americans* album. 'Fame' was also released as a single, reaching number seventeen in Britain and giving David his first number one in the US.

'Fame' contained a more explicit message than any other lyric on *Young Americans*, drawing directly on David's perception of the nadir to which MainMan had brought him. Fame, David warned:

> Puts you there, where things are hollow . . .

It means that

> What you need you have to borrow.

It even

> . . . burns your change to keep you insane.

The friendship between David and Lennon did not survive for long on the same intense level, and here, according to Ava, David's unreconstructed macho attitudes were to blame. At six o'clock one morning, after they had stayed up all night talking and playing records, David told Ava to make some breakfast – "the real chauvinist trip", Ava says. Ava was quite willing to do so, but Yoko Ono was enraged.

"Why should she make your breakfast?" Yoko protested to David. "She's not your slave."

While David argued with Yoko, Lennon sat "laughing his head off", Ava says. David, rarely willing to see a joke against himself, was immensely discomfited. "I don't think they got on so well after that," Ava says.

David's conversations with Lennon had nevertheless helped to redefine his attitude towards MainMan. And what Lennon had told him compounded what he had already heard from Mick Jagger. Five years before, Jagger had discovered that after earning $17 million in three years, he had received approximately one-tenth of that amount and had been landed with an enormous tax bill as well. "Mick tried to tell David what was what," says Stuey George, "put him in the picture a little bit . . ."

Information was reaching David from other sources as a result of the factions that were forming around him within MainMan. Several promoters were feeding him figures showing what he could earn if he dealt directly with them, a process ironically stimulated by the success of Defries's gamble in financing the 1974 tours. One show at the Montreal Forum had produced well over $100,000, a sell-out at Madison Square Garden meant almost $200,000; with MainMan now able to command ninety-ten deals almost everywhere, the potential revenue was enormous. To the clamouring voices around David was added that of Angie, who asked why Defries was living in a virtual mansion in Greenwich, Connecticut when David had to make do with hotels.

Almost all of David's previous partings had focused on money. Now his attitude towards the joyous extravagance of MainMan, in which he and Angie had played their full part, changed. Prompted by Angie, David enquired further, and made a crucial discovery. Having been encouraged by Defries to accept that theirs was an equal partnership in every way, he had fondly believed that he had joint ownership of the vital masters of his own recordings. He now found this not to be so: they were owned by MainMan; and MainMan was owned by Defries.

Previously David had remained sceptical about Lennon's attacks on the virtue of all managers. Now he returned to Lennon and told him: "You were right. I've been ripped off blind."

David spent Christmas at the Pierre with Angie, Zee and Jaime Andrews, "drinking brandy", according to Andrews, "and snorting coke". Zee had partially recovered from his breakdown. "It was one of the close times with him," he says. "We spent the evening together, we stayed up all night talking." It was clear that David was preparing to leave MainMan, although David, not totally sure of his companions' allegiances, did not voice his belief that he had been ripped off.

By now the new alliances in MainMan had coalesced, and two people had emerged as David's principal supporters. One was a fresh-faced college graduate, Pat Gibbons, who had been "tour coordinator" in the latter half of 1974. The other was a former secretary from the London office, Corinne Schwab, who had joined MainMan in the US in 1974 and had gradually won David's confidence during the tour. She and Gibbons in turn enlisted a Beverly Hills lawyer, Michael Lippman, formerly of the Los Angeles agency, CMA, which had booked David's West Coast concerts.

With their guidance, David made his first move on New Year's Eve; Mel Ilberman remembers it well. "I was going to parties, going from house to house, and at every house I would get a call from David." David was anxious to know what position RCA would take if he attempted to break with Defries. After the trials

Defries had subjected him to, this was a golden moment for Ilberman, and he pledged RCA's support. "There are times when managers think that they have become bigger than they are," Ilberman says; Defries had become "too greedy" and "too important in his own eyes".

A week later David left the Pierre and moved into a rented brownstone house on West 20th Street. By now he appeared to feel under almost intolerable pressure. "That was where the really bad part of it all happened," says Ava. "He would become very upset and emotional and hysterical."

David's greatest distress, according to Ava, stemmed from his belief that he had been "ripped off". He was also intensely apprehensive in case Defries learned of his plans and launched a pre-emptive legal strike. "He felt cooped up because he had to be incognito because he didn't want Tony to sue him," Ava says. "So all of his frustration and tension and pressure was building up so it would explode on the person who was closest to him which was me."

David talked to Ava of his belief that when in Beckenham there had been "a ghost that used to follow him around all the time – this presence, this spirit, that would follow him everywhere he would go". He also told Ava that he was being pursued by "psychic vampires". The medical term paranoia would not be inappropriate to describe the state David was nearing. But even that could not account for everything that occurred. "Strange things would happen," says Ava. "The television would turn off by itself, or the stereo would turn off – I can't explain it, I just remember that weird things used to happen, things that could not easily be explained."

The most chilling incident came when David was talking again of psychic vampires. He was very distraught, and was clutching a glass in his hand. "It was thick glass," Ava emphasises. "Suddenly it just exploded in his hand. I was totally freaked out."

In his desperation to find people he could trust, David telephoned Geoff Hannington in London. Hannington had become RCA's managing director in Britain upon the promotion of Ken Glancey, and had remained in touch with David during 1974. David asked him if he could come to New York and Hannington immediately agreed. When he arrived he asked David why he was leaving Defries. "I can't take any more of this," David told him. "I've sold all these records, and I haven't got any money." He also showed Hannington his management contract. "Everything he had or did belonged to or was controlled by MainMan."

Those around Defries believe that for some time he had remained blissfully – even wilfully – unaware of David's disaffection. Defries spent the New Year on holiday on the Caribbean island of Mustique, haunt of celebrities, hairdressers, lesser British royalty, and paparazzi. At one point David had tried to contact Defries, but Defries had refused to return his calls, even when Zee had told him: "David really wants to speak to you." "I'm on holiday, Zee, I'm on holiday," Defries had replied.

According to Defries, his first intimation that all was not well came when David proposed that instead of the fifty-fifty deal, Defries should "work for him on a commission basis". Defries declined. Having worked *with* David thus far, he says, he was not prepared to start working *for* him instead.

Then David visited Defries at his house in Greenwich and told him – as he had once told Ken Pitt – that he wanted to "take charge of his own affairs". Defries says that he raised no great objection, but advised David that, rather than attempt to manage himself, he needed "a competent professional" to do so on his behalf. "I said, 'I would be very happy to talk to anyone you bring in.'" In view of their previous conversation, Defries adds, David's new request "wasn't a surprise".

David was evidently far from reassured by his conversations with Defries. On January 29th, 1975, he went to RCA's offices on the Avenue of the Americas with Michael Lippman, who had flown in from California, and met Ilberman, Hannington and Glancey. "He was trembling and he was very, very, very upset and nervous," says Glancey. "He was in a terrible state."

David was still worried whether RCA would stay loyal to him and asked for some money. Glancey had a cheque prepared for him there and then. David returned to RCA in a slightly calmer state the following day and made several further requests: he wanted a formal guarantee of financial support, office space, and a car, as he was certain MainMan would repossess his own. Ilberman promised all of these, and then asked David about the *Young Americans* album, which was planned for release in March.

RCA had already received some tapes from MainMan but David said that these were of inferior quality, and revealed that he had lodged the master tapes in a bank vault for safe-keeping. David also told Ilberman about the session with John Lennon, and said that the tapes of 'Fame' and 'Across The Universe' were still at the Electric Lady studio. Strictly speaking, only MainMan were entitled to collect the tapes, but Hannington went to the studio – "at dead of night with dollar bills" – to retrieve them.

With David's position at RCA secure, a telegram arrived that same day at the MainMan office. It was addressed to Defries, and was composed in the same legalese and with the same disregard for syntax as the telegram that David, advised by Defries, had sent to Ken Pitt almost five years before.

"On behalf of our client, David Jones, AKA David Bowie," it read, "be advised that due to various violations of your agreements including but not limited to fraud in the inducement, all agreements with you and or any companys [*sic*] owned or controlled by you are hereby terminated effective forthwith. You are further advised that said agreements are void and without force and effect for indefinateness [*sic*] and lack of mutuality. You are further advised that any purported power of attorney contained in the agreements are hereby revolked [*sic*], effective immediately. This is not an enumeration of all rights and remedies of our client in the premises." The telegram was signed: "Michael Lippman, Jay L Cooper, for Cooper, Epstein, Hurawitz and Mark, 9465 Wilshire Blvd, Suite 820, Beverly Hills, California."

Not even his conversations with David had prepared Defries for such a moment. When the telegram arrived, says Zee's secretary Mary Carol Culligan, Defries "was pretty shaken, pretty shook up".

The next day, Defries met Ilberman and one of RCA's lawyers, Myron Roth. According to Ilberman, both sides agreed that they would try to promote a settlement and – a point on which Defries was especially anxious – to keep the dispute from the press. It soon became clear that those hopes were in vain. In the coming days and weeks, it was also clear that one of the most massive legal suits in the history of show business, from which lawyers on both sides of the Atlantic would benefit, was in prospect.

Defries continued talking to Ilberman, and what emerged above all was his puzzlement that David should have acted as he did, coupled with his desperation to prevent their split from becoming public knowledge. He also asked Ilberman why he had backed David, when – so Defries argued – RCA was legally bound to deal with MainMan.

The question gave Ilberman a chance to show his true feelings. He said that in any dispute between artist and manager, RCA was bound to side with the artist.

The point is, he told Defries, "You can't sing."

28

Falling to Earth

As the rift with Defries continued to fester, not the least of the worries, for RCA and David, was to ensure the most propitious release for *Young Americans*, scheduled for mid-March. Certainly the secrecy that Defries insisted upon was in everyone's interests, for news of the split would scarcely create the kind of favourable aura the album required.

The row with Defries apart, RCA were in a bullish mood. They issued the title track, 'Young Americans', as a single in the US on February 11th, 1975, and it was soon being played by disc-jockeys throughout the US. By early March it had reached the single listings of the three main trade publications, *Billboard*, *Cashbox*, and *Record World*, with a "bullet" sign in each, showing that it was considered to have a good chance of reaching number one.

Thus encouraged, RCA allocated $200,000 to advertising and promoting the album itself, and ordered an initial 250,000 copies to be made – the largest first pressing David had yet received. By comparison, his *total* album sales in the US at that time were 480,000 copies of *Ziggy Stardust*; *Diamond Dogs*, 420,000 copies; *David Live*, 314,000; *Pin-Ups*, 258,000; *Space Oddity*, 243,000; *Aladdin Sane*, 240,000; *Hunky Dory*, 190,000; and *The Man Who Sold The World*, 120,000.

RCA's confidence in *Young Americans* soon appeared justified. Whereas the British critics saw it as a counterfeit attempt to cash in on the latest US musical trends, previews in the US trade press welcomed the album with undisguised relief that David had moved into the musical mainstream at last. David's "sophisticated soul sound," declared *Billboard*, "does not sound the least bit put on"; the album "should open up an entirely new avenue of fans". *Cashbox* hailed David as "the brightest star in the pop music constellation with this latest RCA release". *Record World* considered *Young Americans* David's "most compelling album to date".

Meanwhile RCA were continuing to support David and shield him from the worst effects of the split with Defries. They set up an office for him in the Algonquin Hotel, staffed by Pat Gibbons, and provided him with a twenty-four-hour limousine service. They were also in close touch with Michael Lippman, David's lawyer, who was based in Los Angeles and was making constant coast-to-coast flights on the notorious red-eye specials, which leave California at dusk and arrive in New York, after a truncated five-hour night, at dawn.

David himself was virtually immured in West 20th Street. Despite the best efforts of RCA, he was in constant worry, according to Ava Cherry, of how Defries might retaliate against him, "We felt cooped up," she says, "and all his frustration would build up and then explode. He would say things that were unkind, and 'Leave me alone.' I became a very nervous person at this point because I knew that something really bad was going to happen."

Something really bad soon did happen. Discussions between lawyers representing David, RCA and Defries, had dragged on through February, concentrating on one simple issue: cash. "The basic question," Mel Ilberman recalled later, "was how much money would be paid to MainMan." The negotiations seemed amiable and after a session on February 28th, Ilberman felt that "the parties seemed to be getting closer to agreement and the meeting ended on a promising note".

But then, with the suddenness of any of David's own personality changes, Defries's benevolent demeanour abruptly altered. The next round of negotiations was due to be held in the Beverly Wilshire Hotel in Los Angeles on March 11th. On the eve of the meeting, Defries made a series of extravagant demands. First, he called Ken Glancey at RCA and asked him to pay his air fare to Los Angeles. Glancey, who explained later that he simply wanted to expedite a settlement, agreed. Defries now embarked on a classic "improvement". He next demanded that RCA should pay the air fares for his lawyer and Melanie McDonald as well. Glancey agreed to that too. Then Defries stipulated that all three were to fly first-class, were to be met by a limousine, and were to stay in a first-class hotel, all at RCA's expense. Once again, Glancey agreed.

On the afternoon of March 10th Defries called Glancey again and made two fresh demands. He wanted RCA to pay $25,000 towards the cost of Mick Ronson's next tour, and to terminate its contract with Dana Gillespie; and he threatened that unless Glancey agreed to his demands, in writing, that afternoon, he would not fly to Los Angeles that evening. Trusting that this had to be Defries's final demand, Glancey duly agreed. Barely an hour before he was due to leave New York, Defries called again. This time he insisted that RCA should pay all his legal fees for the Los

Angeles trip. To that too – but feeling deeply "pissed off" – Glancey agreed.

The meeting in Los Angeles the following morning began with smiles and handshakes all round. Then came Defries's next bombshell. In mid-morning, Mel Ilberman was called to the phone. RCA's New York lawyers conveyed the devastating news that the New York Supreme Court had just granted Defries a "temporary restraining order" to prevent RCA from distributing the *Young Americans* album. Since Defries was sitting in the room in Los Angeles at the time, Ilberman realised that he must have instructed his lawyers to seek the injunction before leaving New York. The meeting broke up in disarray.

Jaime Andrews believed that Defries's tough new mood stemmed from the feeling that David had betrayed him by trying to break his contract. Defries had given "a lot" to David, said Andrews; "and then he realised his gratitude was a click of the fingers, and his appreciation the same". Defries himself blames David, his advisers and RCA for the impasse they had reached. Had David accepted his own suggestion that he should find "a competent and capable manager", he says, their differences could have been resolved amicably. But RCA's action in siding with Bowie "meant I had to sue them, which otherwise I wouldn't have done, probably".

The battle now entered its most vicious phase. The nub of Defries's case before the New York court was that RCA had broken their contract by dealing directly with David over *Young Americans*. Defries argued that since RCA's contract was with MainMan, he had full artistic control over the album and RCA should have been dealing with him.

RCA hit back, lodging affidavits with the New York court within forty-eight hours. Ilberman protested that Defries had taken out the injunction merely to pressurise RCA into paying him more money to settle the dispute. His claim to artistic control was a "bogeyman", Ilberman thundered; "MainMan's sole concern has been the amount of money it will be able to squeeze out of Bowie and RCA." Ilberman argued that the injunction was merely a ploy to force RCA into a settlement; if it were not set aside, RCA stood to lose $2 million.

David delivered an affidavit too. "The court should understand," he declared, "that my relationship with Mr Defries and MainMan absolutely is terminated and that I no longer will provide any services to them or have anything to do with them so far as my career as an entertainer and recording artist are concerned." He also disputed Defries's claim to artistic control over *Young Ameri-*

cans. "At all times I, not Mr Defries or MainMan, have controlled the artistic direction in which my career developed ... It was I, not Mr Defries, who had ultimate control of the creative concepts which were to be embodied in my albums."

Trying to shake off Defries in a law-suit was, as others had previously discovered, somewhat akin to trying to prise open the jaws of a Staffordshire bull terrier. On March 22nd, Defries swore a fresh affidavit accusing RCA of "dubious conduct and transparent double-dealing" and protesting once again that RCA had no right to deal directly with David. But in so doing, he revealed more than he might otherwise have wished of the details of his own agreements with David, hitherto a watertight secret. David's claim to effective artistic control, he contended, was bogus. "There is no provision whatsoever in any of the contracts Bowie signed with MainMan or its affiliates which grants him the slightest degree of artistic control."

Defries also revealed that he had taken steps to prevent David using one of his own favourite ploys. When MainMan's agreement with RCA had been drawn up, Defries had asked David to sign a rider which "irrevocably guarantees, absolutely and unconditionally, the full and complete performance by [MainMan] of all the terms and conditions of the agreement ... such assent and agreement shall not be subject to revocation at any time or for any reason." In other words, whether he realised it or not, David had promised never to use the "piece of crap" tactic which had proved so effective when deployed by Defries on his behalf.

In his immediate objective of preventing *Young Americans* being distributed, Defries failed, for by now the New York judge, Alfred M. Ascione, had heard enough to lift his injunction and allow the album to be released. But with further suits being prepared in Los Angeles, London and Paris, the legal battle threatened to become global in its scale and intensity. It was at this point that a somewhat unlikely *deus ex machina* arrived to resolve the dispute, in the figure of Defries's former partner, Laurence Myers.

Myers had already been acting as an intermediary between Defries and RCA, but now realised that the two principal adversaries, David and Defries, were in danger of becoming entrenched in positions from which they could never retreat. "They were taking stands," Myers says, "saying 'I will never give this and I will never give that.'" The only people likely to benefit comprised the posse of lawyers bearing down on the fray: "I thought it was very sad if they just tore each other to pieces and there was no financial sense in it anyway."

Myers proposed a fresh meeting in Los Angeles, to be held at the Century Plaza Hotel. At first David was intensely suspicious, believing that Myers was still allied with Defries. In fact, Myers had been bruised by yet another dispute with Defries over the arithmetic of their settlement; since then he had been fully paid off, and had no financial interest at all. It was nonetheless necessary, Myers recalls, to prepare for the meeting with all the attention to protocol of a summit conference between great powers. "I had to arrange for suites of equal size, limousines of equal size, the same amount of sandwiches, the same cups of coffee, and the same amounts of sugar."

What emerged from the encounter was a fifty-three-page agreement, backdated to March 1st, 1975, covering every possible contingency the highly paid lawyers representing the three sides could think of. But there was little doubt that the victor was Defries and MainMan. For his period as David's manager, from September 1972 to March 1975, Defries had preserved MainMan's full financial rights. MainMan was to be paid the full 50 per cent of all David's earnings from work accomplished in that period: 50 per cent of all future royalties on *Hunky Dory, Ziggy Stardust, Aladdin Sane, Pin-Ups, Diamond Dogs, David Live* and the two former Mercury albums, *Space Oddity* and *The Man Who Sold The World*. MainMan was also to receive 50 per cent of David's fees from all the songs he had written in that period, and even 50 per cent of David's Decca recordings, although made before Defries was David's manager. In return, MainMan no longer had sole ownership and control of the album masters, which were to be shared equally with David.

But David's contract with MainMan still had seven and a half years to run. For that period, until September 30th, 1982, Main-Man would continue to take a further 16 per cent of David's gross earnings from *all sources*, with the sole exception of David's personal appearances, from which MainMan would receive 5 per cent.

Lest there should be any misunderstanding, Defries's lawyers insisted on spelling out precisely what they meant by David's earnings. They included "fees, royalties, rents, bonuses, gifts, profits, proceeds, allowances, shares of stock and stock options . . .", and covered David's work in "television, motion pictures, radio, night clubs, vaudeville, theatres and presentation houses, legitimate theatre productions, musical shows of any kind including but not limited to Broadway and Off Broadway musicals, recordings of any kind by any means or methods whether now known or hereafter to become known, hotels, resorts, fairs, concerts, and one nighters; commercial endorsements where Bowie's name, likeness or performances are utilised; song-writing, whether as a composer or lyricist, and whether alone or in collaboration with others; musical arranging, conducting and directing; as a producer of any recordings of any kind by any means or methods whether now known or hereafter to become known; from the sale, lease, license or other disposition of literary, dramatic, musical productions, radio and/or television production shows, whether live, filmed, recorded, syndicated or in any other form . . ."

One final chilling clause spelled out the term of the agreement: it was literally without end. Defries would continue to take his percentages on David's earnings from his work between 1972 and 1982 even when 1982 had long passed. For the agreement applied "in perpetuity", so that not only would David have to go on paying Defries for the rest of their lives, but David's heirs would have to go on paying Defries's heirs.

RCA were made to pay too. In the first place, David was claiming that MainMan owed him $325,000. RCA agreed to make a further advance to MainMan so that it could pay David the $325,000 he claimed. Second, and far more costly to RCA, was the thorny question of MainMan's unpaid bills, which by March 1975 stood at $530,071.94 in the US and $57,845.16 in Britain. For these debts, Defries now blames RCA: upon siding with David, he says, "RCA had decided not to pay out any more money and we decided likewise." RCA emphatically denied responsibility for the debts; but in the end, as part of Defries's price for transferring David's contract to RCA, it agreed to give MainMan the money to settle them – not as an advance to MainMan, but as an irrecoverable payment.

Here RCA managed to insert an illuminating clause of their own. The agreement stipulated that when RCA paid MainMan the money to settle its debts, they could insist on having one of their own staff members present at the MainMan office to ensure that the cheques were actually mailed.

Few of those involved saw the financial terms of the settlement as anything other than a triumph for Tony Defries. "It was a very harsh deal for David," says Ken Glancey. Jaime Andrews believed that "Tony Defries made the best deal in history". Defries made his own view all too plain when he passed word to David that instead of asking Michael Lippman to act for him, "you should have got a shit like me".

Lippman today makes his feelings equally plain: Defries, he says, is a "prick". And he believes that, the financial details notwithstanding, David was happy that he emerged from the settlement free of all management ties with Defries and able to make his own decisions in future. "David got his freedom," Lippman says, "and I think that was the important thing for him."

There is far greater disagreement over the question of whether David was, as he so bitterly claimed, "ripped off". His grievances were manifold. He believed that the money he had generated had been used to finance the extravagances of MainMan and its unrealistic sponsorship of other performers. He had believed his partnership with Defries was equal in all respects, and yet Main-Man, not he, owned his masters. According to Kristina, it was David's belief that his trust had been abused that hurt him most of all. "David was the most trusting soul I have met, and he got badly hurt because he loved these people. He really liked Tony Defries as a friend, he cared about him . . . MainMan cost almost everything David made."

Others who had doubted Defries from the start believed their judgment had been vindicated. Tony Visconti had always thought the worst of Defries; he still thinks so today. David's mother, Peggy, came to a forthright opinion, too: "how stupid David has been putting his trust in that Jewish pig."

Yet for every one of Defries's detractors, there are others who spring to his defence. "I have from time to time been asked or comments have been made in my presence that Tony Defries ripped off David Bowie," says Laurence Myers. "And he didn't, to my knowledge."

Angie agrees. "No way," she says of David's accusation against Defries. "He never ripped him off." Defries, she adds, "was quite prepared to go anywhere, do anything to accomplish what had to be done. Someone had to take on those expenses . . . No one lacked anything, no one was suffering, no one was starving. Mortgages were taken care of, aunts, uncles, dependants were all taken care of." To complain is "looking a gift horse in the mouth and then spitting on it".

For Tony Zanetta, the suspicion that David was ripped off had been fuelled by financial confusion at the heart of MainMan over which costs were attributable to David – his contract stated that he was liable for his "personal" expenses – and which to the organisation. "There's no real answer to this question," Zee says, "because no one ever bothered to ask it. Lawyers and accountants should have been able to answer it but I don't think they can because I don't think that the right people ever asked the right question." Ergo, says Zee, the question was never answered.

Defries himself today takes, in part, a phlegmatic view of all that occurred: "I never expected David to stay around for ever," he says. Yet he admits that it was immensely disappointing for David to part at a time when he "had yet to achieve what he could achieve". It was doubly disappointing, he adds, since "David, Angela and I were very much involved in all the emotional ups and downs that you go through when a career is taking off, you have an emotional content to that relationship that cannot be easily dismissed. And it's quite traumatic for someone to say, 'I don't want to deal with you any more' or 'I don't want to talk to you any more.'"

For David's belief that he had been ripped off, Defries blames cocaine, together with David's susceptibility to the suspicions voiced by some of his companions. "If you're involved in cocaine and other things to a sufficient degree, you believe whatever anyone tells you," Defries says. "Heavy use of cocaine requires some paranoia, it has to be directed somewhere. It needed an outlet and I was the most convenient."

As for David's central complaint that MainMan owned his masters, that is, Defries agrees, "strictly speaking probably true". It was true, he says, in the sense that since RCA's agreement was with MainMan, it was to MainMan that the masters would revert when the agreement expired. But since David's agreement with MainMan gave him "a fifty-fifty interest in all the results and proceeds", Defries maintains, David would eventually have regained a half-share in the masters.

The basic problem, Defries says, stemmed from David's failure to "read or understand" his contracts. He therefore relied on the incomplete accounts others were imparting to him; but, Defries adds, it would have been almost impossible to explain the truth to him. "David never understood and probably still doesn't understand the concepts of masters and copyrights and reversions and all the elements that really make the business he's in work."

Among even those inclined to a harsh view of Defries there is considerable agreement that, whether he was deceived or not, David was culpable for not questioning MainMan's apparent extravagance at a far earlier stage. The point is made most charitably by Kristina. "David didn't want to hear gossip. He has never been a gossip-monger. He's not interested in nastiness. So to come to him without proof and say, 'I think somebody's doing this', David is not going to listen to you. And so I kept a closed mouth,

I didn't have any facts, I had intuition and that was it . . . At one point I mentioned something and David said, 'Oh they're all right.' David didn't want to believe he was being made a fool.''

David had of course played a full part in MainMan's excesses for as long as it suited him. "Dumb he wasn't," says Ken Glancey. "He just didn't want to be bothered." Or, as Mick Ronson had said, "all he wanted was to be a star". David had made a Faustian pact with Tony Defries: while Defries was given free rein to make what financial arrangements he liked, David was licensed to indulge his every whim.

MainMan had allowed him to stage 'Ziggy Stardust' and 'Diamond Dogs', at that time the most ambitious and audacious rock concerts ever mounted. MainMan had also itself become a stage where David could enact his fantasies, writ large. When David had at last questioned what he was part of, his questioning had focused on money: as at every other turning point of his career, money became the excuse, not the reason, for the parting of the ways.

There are nonetheless two interpretations possible of what Main-Man had meant to David, and whether it had been for good or ill. By one, MainMan had provided David with the means to act out his obsessions and confront his fears. By the other, MainMan had fed David's anxieties and taken him to the brink of disaster. The two interpretations can even sit alongside each other, as two sides of the same coin. Either way, it is possible to view David's behaviour at the time of his break with MainMan as similar, in some respects, to a form of schizophrenia.

Like his brother Terry, for example, David was unkempt and careless of his personal appearance and well-being. Like Terry, he believed he was visited by ethereal beings, such as the figures who followed him around, or those that threatened him, the "psychic vampires". Like Terry, his fears were tinged with paranoia. David also shared the belief with some true schizophrenics that he was a messiah, at times in a God-given role, at times in an unwilling role that others had thrust upon him. David's use of elaborate make-up and, in 'Diamond Dogs', masks, as a projection of his fantasies is another characteristic shown by schizophrenics. When he had embarked on the course he had intuitively predicted in 'The Man Who Sold The World' he had promised that he would never lose control. By the end of the 1974 tours he was on the brink of doing so. Whether for good or ill, ditching MainMan – and Defries – was an essential move if David was to regain control over his life and destiny.

*

Even after the financial settlement with Defries had been signed and sealed, David was far from achieving equilibrium. If he was truly rebuilding his character from scratch, as he said, he had barely laid the first brick. In New York, his behaviour was giving Ava immense cause for concern. David had become fascinated by the occult. He met Kenneth Anger, who was both author of *Hollywood Babylon* and a film director, making movies about sex, ritual and magic, one of them, *Inauguration of the Pleasure Dome*, concerning the neo-paganism of the decadent Victorian magician and mystic, Aleister Crowley. Anger lived in an apartment on the Upper East Side that was a shrine to Rudolph Valentino, with the blinds permanently drawn and a black shroud on the refrigerator, calling himself, in a permanent whisper, "the curator of my own museum". David's encounter with Anger and his cohorts unsettled David deeply. "He felt very strange," says Ava, "he felt all those negative vibes were after him, whatever they were."

There was a strange confrontation, too, with Jimmy Page, lead guitarist of Led Zeppelin. Page, who was living in New York and was also interested in Aleister Crowley, visited David and Ava in West 20th Street, along with Ronnie Wood, the guitarist from the Faces, shortly to join the Rolling Stones, who was proving a valuable companion to David. Between David and Page there was a furious struggle for unspoken power, as Ava observed. "David had heard that Jimmy Page was mentally very powerful and able to influence people and there was a battle of wits to prove who was the stronger. I watched their eye contact and it was very weird."

The final clash came when Page spilled some coffee over a satin cushion and Ava, hoping to defuse the situation, gallantly took the blame. "David was very angry and said to Jimmy Page, 'How could you let her take the blame for something you did?' Jimmy got upset and got ready to leave and David said, 'Yeah, why don't you take the window?'"

Even David's cousin Kristina found herself an unwitting victim of David's fears when she sent him a present of a red doll that had taken her fancy in a New York store. Invoking memories of her big sister role in Bromley, she attached a label inscribed: "A little devil for a little devil". Kristina was very disappointed when, the next time she saw David, he did not mention the gift at all. Only years later, when she plucked up the courage to ask if he had ever received it, did David tell her that he had been disturbed by it because he believed it was a satanist totem. "He was very paranoid at that time," Kristina confirms.

Towards the end of March, David moved from New York to Los Angeles. He stayed in a variety of homes, lodging for a time, *inter alia*, with Michael Lippman and then with a friend of Ava's, a former *Playboy* centrefold model, Claudia Jennings. He also rented a house at 637 North Doheny Drive, in Beverly Hills, and later another at 1349 Stone Canyon Drive, in the Bel Air district west of Beverly Hills. Still he did not find peace. In Lippman's house he would sit up half the night with Michael's wife Nancy, talking only semi-coherently of his fears. When Nancy went to bed he stayed up until dawn to paint or to create bizarre inflatable sculptures or *assemblages*, like a penis made of 3-D postcards with a Walt Disney pencil sharpener on the end.

David gave a long, disjointed series of interviews to the *Rolling Stone* reporter, Cameron Crowe, which again seemed to come close to schizophrenia in their disordered ramblings, particularly in David's obsession with himself as guru or leader. "Everybody was convincing me that I was a messiah," he said, of the first US Ziggy tour. He also felt that he would make a suitable British prime minister, or even the first English president of the United States. "I mean it," David warned. "I'll bloody lead this country, make it a great fucking nation."

Crowe was startled when David leapt to his feet in the middle of one such peroration and pulled down the blinds. "I've got to do this," David explained. "I just saw a body fall." David lit a black candle and blew it out, so that a tracer of smoke drifted upwards. "It's only protection," David told a disconcerted Crowe. "I've been getting a little trouble from the neighbours."

Ava too found herself the butt of David's imaginings. Trying to make sense of David's near-derangement, she started to confide in Claudia Jennings. When David came upon them he would ask accusingly, "Why are you whispering, talking in secret?" Ava says. "He would try to make out as though we were conspiring or something."

To David's fears was added the malign influence of Los Angeles itself. With its vast, random sprawl, its network of helter-skelter freeways, its lack of anything that could be called a city centre, its garish newness, its population of attention-seekers, its worship of the entertainment industry and all its attendant fantasies, it was perhaps the least suitable place on earth for a person to go in search of identity and stability. Later on David was to express his feelings about Los Angeles with vitriolic passion. It was, David said, "the most vile piss-pot in the whole world . . . It's a movie that is so corrupt with a script that is so devious and insidious. It's the scariest movie ever written. You feel a total victim there, and you know someone's got the strings on you."

David's first exit from Los Angeles brought him scant relief. He spent June and July in Albuquerque, New Mexico. He went there to act, at last, in a cinema feature film, a reward Defries had long promised him but which only now was fulfilled. But the part awarded David threatened only to trap him in the role from which he was so desperately seeking to escape.

David's participation in *The Man Who Fell to Earth* came about precisely because the men behind it wished to preserve him as he was. During the 'Diamond Dogs' tour David had cooperated with a production team from BBC television who had originally hoped to make a documentary about a popular performer who borrows and adapts from a host of earlier sources. The producer, Alan Yentob, saw David as a chameleon, but also someone who was "rather pretentious but always adventurous".

The chaos and increasing disintegration of both the 'Diamond Dogs' tour and MainMan reduced Yentob to following David with his camera crew and grabbing what he could. The result, a film in the BBC *Omnibus* series entitled *Cracked Actor*, was broadcast in Britain in January 1975. It showed, all too accurately, a wan and emaciated David barely clinging to his sanity. David later gave it his endorsement, telling Yentob that he had watched it "again and again". When Yentob asked why, David told him: "Because it told the truth."

Among those who saw *Cracked Actor* were the film director Nicolas Roeg and his scriptwriter, Paul Mayersberg. They had already completed the script of *The Man Who Fell to Earth* at that time. It was based on a haunting novel by Walter Tevis, the tale of an alien, Thomas Newton, who comes to earth from outer space with a range of technological secrets to impart in the hope of building a spaceship to return him to his home planet. Newton keeps his identity secret and at first all goes well; then Newton is kidnapped by sinister conspiratorial figures who hold him prisoner while probing his secrets. By the time they release him his mission has been destroyed; the film ends with Newton drowning his despair in drink.

Although Mayersberg's script had included some of David's lyrics, he and Roeg were still at a loss over whom they should cast as Thomas Newton. When they saw *Cracked Actor*, it was obvious, says Mayersberg, that David should take the part. "It was a perfect match."

Too perfect, perhaps. When Roeg asked David to appear in his film, David agreed without even reading the script. But, in the first place, Nic Roeg was a director who demanded total compliance and absolute trust, and so David had to place himself once more under another person's control. "Nic left him no alternative," says Mayersberg. David, he points out, was not a Hollywood actor: "without Nic, he was lost".

Second, the story uncannily paralleled the fantasies and preoccupations which had dragged David down. In Newton could be seen Ziggy, the "leper messiah", whose urgent truths are rejected and denied. Its end even matched one of David's family myths, the story of his grandfather Jimmy Burns, told again in 'Little Bombardier', who sought escape from his "friendless, lonely days" in drink.

Mayersberg insists that since his script was written before David was approached, all of this was coincidence. Yet, by that strange symbiotic process which occurred so often in David's career, the film evolved in a way which mirrored the symbols of his fears. Early on, Newton declines to shake hands: an echo of David's dislike of being touched which Defries had seized upon when building his public persona. Newton was also preoccupied by masks. And, as Paul Mayersberg points out, David was compelled to play a character with a divided self: "Someone who has to live a lie without being a liar, not being able to tell people he is from outer space."

Much about the circumstances of the filming contributed to the air of unreality the story required. The brilliant blue New Mexico sky, radiating from the sagebrush desert, had a reputation for yielding more sightings of UFOs than anywhere else in the United States. "You could look up into the sky and see strange things, you could see something odd, lights flashing, every day," says Mayersberg. Near the location were the Carlsberg Caverns, the home of thousands of bats that flew shrieking into the night at dusk and returned at dawn. When David visited the caves he was awe-struck and returned saying he would like to stage a concert there, "with thousands of vampire bats descending on the audience's heads".

In the most disturbing event of all, David spent two days in hospital after drinking a glass of milk in which he had seen a swirling gold liquid. Although he was diagnosed as suffering from food-poisoning, when the milk was analysed no trace of foreign substances could be found. "Six people saw this eerie mess in the milk," David said, "so I know I'm not crazy."

David's professionalism carried him through. The precise choreography he had brought to his concert performances proved invaluable on the set, to a degree that Mayersberg, accustomed to actors who vary their performances from take to take, found uncanny. "His role word for word was what was written," says Mayersberg. "He was word perfect. I don't remember seeing a fluff. It was unnerving in some ways." The most remarkable example came when David had to catch a bottle knocked over by the actress Candy Clarke. "We did that three or four times and every time he caught it in exactly the same way," says Mayersberg. "Hard things to do – but he was absolutely immaculate."

Roeg and Mayersberg also found that David had an acute awareness of where the camera was and how he would appear on screen. That, too, was a product of David's professionalism, coupled with his obsessive interest in his self-image over the years; but Mayersberg was astonished that even though David had never worked on a film set before, he seemed to know instinctively whether he was being filmed in close-up or long-shot. "He knew where he was on the screen as opposed to the set," Mayersberg says. "He had an extraordinary sixth sense for that."

The main problem David posed the film makers resulted from his skeletal physique. He developed a craving for ice-cream while making the film but was so thin that by putting on only a pound or so in weight he threatened to wreck the film's continuity. In the end, Roeg had to ask him to give up ice-cream.

David was also distracted by the stream of business callers who visited him in Albuquerque in the aftermath of the MainMan settlement. He kept himself apart from the rest of the actors and crew, and when not required on set, retired into a small mobile home which he had filled with hundreds of books. All that, too, suited Roeg. "His demeanour, his remoteness – he didn't look desperately unhappy but he looked disconcerted," says Mayersberg. "That fitted the part exactly." Others who knew David then say that the chill and uncertain alien who eventually appeared on celluloid had required very little true acting on David's part. "He would agree with that," says Mayersberg. "He has said that since. To me."

29

Searching and Searching

Two people were vital in David's rehabilitation: the first is Corinne Schwab. Yet in many quarters today Corinne – or Coco, as David calls her – arouses controversy and dislike more passionate than Tony Defries. "She lives in constant fear that I am going to kill her which makes me very happy," Angie says. "It's terrifying that she's still alive. But fortunately karma always takes care and she will suffer and she will die young because of the incarnate intensity of what she has accomplished."

Even the tolerant Tony Visconti says: "She could not get away with the way she treats people unless she was working for David. David's incredibly nice and has made a lot of goodwill around the world, and she does just the opposite." Corinne, he laughs, "should be put in a cage and thrown raw meat."

Corinne's first public appearance, unregarded at the time, was in the *Omnibus* documentary, *Cracked Actor*. In a sequence showing David being driven through the California desert, she is a cool and self-possessed figure with long curly hair, wearing a simple summer dress, sitting in the front seat with her arm stretched nonchalantly across the back.

That Corinne occupied so privileged a place in David's favours showed the ascendancy she had established as MainMan began to fall apart. She had been working for MainMan for a year, although that background is something she has not been anxious to reveal. David has said that she joined him after he advertised for an assistant, implying that this occurred after the MainMan period. In fact, Corinne began to work as a secretary and receptionist in the MainMan London office in 1973, earning the modest take-home pay of £26 a week.

One reason for her advance was her fluency in languages, invaluable to a company with the multinational aspirations of MainMan. Her prowess stemmed, as she told it, from her cosmopolitan background: her father was a photographer who lived in America, her mother a Jungian psychiatrist who worked in Switzerland. She acquired extra cachet from the circumstances of her birth, for, as she was never loth to relate, she was born in the stockroom of

Bloomingdale's in New York, her mother having gone into labour while visiting the linen department. A second reason for Corinne's progress was the manifest calmness with which she helped to stave off the phalanxes of creditors bearing down on MainMan in London.

A third reason was Angie. And since it was she and not David who gave the first boost to Corinne's career, this is something that Angie rues to this day. "This is very embarrassing to me," Angie says. "She was so exactly what I thought I needed. She spoke several languages, she had an aura of being cultured, she dressed like a slob but I knew I could straighten that out so she looked like part of what we were trying to do, a streamlined, sassy, glamorous look, and for three years she pretended to be my best friend."

The main charge of Corinne's enemies is that she obtained a privileged place in David's favour by making herself indispensable to him and then excluded almost all former friends and colleagues who had a rival claim to his affections. The more charitable interpretation of her role is that she helps to excise those people from David's life he wishes to dispose of, compensating for his lack of social skills and willingly accepting the opprobrium herself.

"There *is* no Coco," says one embittered woman who was close to David for eight years, and who believes that Corinne is merely a cypher who enacts David's wishes to the letter. "There's only David. She's the one who does all the dirty work . . . She is a very very sad case. This woman does not have her own life. She's his *alter ego*, his devil in disguise."

Certainly, when David was in the slough of despair in Los Angeles, she devoted herself to him with the dedication of a nun. Someone who recognised the role she played, since she once did so herself, was Natasha Kornilof, who met her when she resumed designing costumes for David. Natasha admires Corinne enormously and believes that she succours, above all, David's maternal needs.

"She's laid down her whole life for him," Natasha says. "David has only to utter the words, 'I'm hungry' – and, in the middle of nowhere, Coco can cook a meal over a candle and put it in front of him. He can be cold, tired, hungry – but put something warm around him, feed him, and he's happy. He just sits there receiving everything and he doesn't really care where it's coming from."

Corinne assisted David in the task of severing every possible connection with the MainMan era, a task David began as soon as he could. One of the first and most surprised victims was Mike Garson, David's pianist for the previous two years and the sole survivor through five separate albums. "The joke had been," says Garson, on reviewing the passing parade of fellow-musicians: "'When it's my time, David, just let me know.'"

Shortly before Christmas, 1974, Garson dined with David at the Hotel Pierre, and David told him: "I want you to be my pianist for the next twenty years." A day or so later Garson visited David again to exchange Christmas presents. "That was the last time I actually saw him. After that I called him fifteen or twenty times, and just never heard back."

The key to the power Corinne established lay in her control of access to David, permitting only the favoured few to reach him. Tony Visconti came to know how effective that could be. "I have been trying to phone David for three or four months," he said in 1985. "I know for a fact that Coco decides that she doesn't want David to be bothered. He doesn't know you're phoning him up."

At times David has joked about his propensity for cutting swathes through his past: "We call them his *purges*," says Kristina. Even she suffered for a time, losing contact with David for two years from mid-1975; Corinne, she says, can be "annoyingly protective". Yet Kristina's view of Corinne is the most charitable of all. "She gives him space. She fields potential headaches. She sorts through the wheat and the chaff. She's completely dedicated to him and that's what he needs."

Someone relegated from the wheat to the chaff in the summer of 1975 was Ava Cherry. At first she had found Corinne a disarming confidante. "She would tell me the little things she would do to get rid of people," Ava says. "So when she started operating on me I knew exactly what it was." Ava believes David became convinced that she was being unfaithful to him, "which was totally untrue . . . David asked me, was it true? and I said, 'No, it's absolutely not true,' and I was a bit insulted that he even asked me, because he knew how much I loved him."

Ava's relationship with David in Los Angeles stuttered through the spring, until the end came shortly before he left for New Mexico. In a last attempt to resolve their problems, Ava called on David in North Doheny Drive. Corinne was there, says Ava, "giving me the worst vibes ever. She walked out of the house while I was there, she stood outside and waited until I came out. So I just said to David, 'I'll see you.' I just said goodbye."

In the question of who really ended the relationship, Ava blames Corinne. Like Angie, Ava harbours murderous thoughts. "If there was a gun available I might have even thought of shooting her," she says. "She was really that cruel to me. She saw me coming apart at the seams . . . I could see her like a witch, standing in the shadows, hysterically laughing."

The second person who helped David back to an even keel was Iggy Pop. That process began, paradoxically, as Iggy lay in a hospital bed in Los Angeles, even more of a casualty than David.

After his enforced inactivity in 1973, Iggy had broken free from MainMan, convinced that it was Defries and not David who was responsible for stalling his career. But after the failure of *Raw Power*, the album David had helped to produce, Iggy's band broke up, and his next album was never released. Iggy declined quickly thereafter, indulging in the full gamut of drugs from amphetamines to heroin, and arriving in the Neuropsychiatric Institute at UCLA – the University of California, Los Angeles – on the verge of a mental breakdown.

David had met up with Iggy a short while before, making some tentative recordings with him in a small local studio. Although David was in little better shape, he was the only one of Iggy's friends to visit him in hospital. "I'm very grateful to him and also very fond of that person," Iggy said later. "I don't like hardly anybody but I do like him very much and I do have a place in my heart for him."

It was the beginning of a new partnership that was to persist, in varying intensity, for ten years. Like David's other partnerships, there was a strong artistic and creative element. David valued Iggy's high intelligence and breadth of reading, belying the raw, animal persona he displayed on stage, and the gruff, inarticulate quotes he served up to reporters.

There was another component too. At the core of the friendship was a therapeutic interaction that was of benefit to both. As David helped nurse Iggy back to health, through his loyalty and his diligent steering of Iggy's career, it was as if he was vicariously solving his own problems. Iggy helped David directly in turn, showing by his example that a body racked by drugs could recover its vitality and physique. The other irresistible inference was that David had found in Iggy a sufferer from mental distress whom he could help, free from the risks of confronting Terry.

When David returned to Los Angeles from New Mexico in August 1975, it was time to fulfil his obligations to RCA and make a new album. The company was worried at the reports it was receiving of David, and dispatched Geoff Hannington to California to see what he could do. Hannington visited David in Stone Canyon and found him still living topsy-turvy hours, staying up all night and sleeping all day. Hannington was followed three days later by a posse of RCA executives anxious over the fate of their investment. After Hannington had introduced them, they sat looking expectantly at David until he announced in exasperation: "I want everybody out."

"They all looked surprised," says Hannington, "because they were the record company, but then David said, 'Will you all fucking get out of here.'" Hannington himself stayed behind and dined with David that evening, finding him good company: "It was fun."

The new album was recorded at the Cherokee studio in Hollywood, with David enlisting the New Yorker Harry Maslin as his producer. Although David did not allow his aversion to RCA executives to distract him from his task, the sessions had the same appearance of desperate chaos as *Young Americans*. His musicians comprised three survivors from that album, guitarists Carlos Alomar and Earl Slick, and drummer Dennis Davis, together with newcomers Roy Bittan on piano and George Murray on bass. They found that David was still relying on amphetamines and cocaine, sometimes driving his band through exhausting twenty-four-hour sessions, sometimes behaving in complete contrast. "We show up at the studio," recalls Slick. "'Where is he?' He shows up maybe five or six hours late. Sometimes he wouldn't show up at all."

After the stylistic certainties of *Young Americans*, with its direct derivation from black American music of the moment, the new album, *Station To Station*, left the critics unsure how to respond. John Ingham saw it as "an uneasy but compelling coalition" between *The Man Who Sold The World* and *Young Americans*, with urgent guitar riffs by Carlos Alomar and Earl Slick sitting alongside the disco beat of 'Fame'. The *New Musical Express* considered it "a strange and confusing musical whirlpool where nothing is what it seems".

Not for the first time, the critics were at a loss to explain David's lyrics. Ingham concluded that the album "relies only minimally on its verbal/literary content". And while the *New Musical Express*'s reviewer called it "one of the most significant albums released in the last five years" he also admitted: "The significance of the lyrics remains elusive . . . I don't pretend to understand completely the complications and paranoia of Bowie."

In truth, the album was strikingly positive in its approach, and contained the usual clues to David's next moves. The music was inventive too, showing a refreshing determination in David to explore and fuse new styles after leaning so heavily on disco music in *Young Americans*. The reviewers were inclined to interpret the album's title, *Station To Station*, as a search along a radio waveband but it also recalled one of David's earliest images, the railway station as a point of departure, first used in 'Can't Help Thinking About Me' in 1965.

It also marked a return to his use of travelling as the metaphor for self-discovery, which had dominated *The Man Who Sold The World*. The point was reinforced in the instrumental opening to the title track, 'Station To Station', a brilliant imitation of a train at the start of a long journey, gradually picking up speed until it is rocking along to the shrill whistle provided by a guitar and driving on, David sang, "like a demon from station to station".

The travelling/exploring theme was sustained with "mountains" and "oceans" and the impassioned cry, "Got to keep searching and searching." David's interest in the occult surfaced in the words "demon" and "magic" but the other major theme, parallel to the quest for identity, was David's unending search for love. Perhaps, David wondered, he had found it at last: "Does my face show some kind of glow?" Certainly, he candidly concluded, "it's not the side effects of the cocaine".

Then David returned to the idea of travelling, ending the lyric with the prediction: "The European cannon is here." The nicely ambiguous "cannon", both as weapon of war, and – "canon" – as body of work, foreshadowed David's departure from the New World and return to the Old. As David himself later recognised, the album "was like a plea to come back to Europe for me".

The reviewers had also seen *Station To Station* as part of the bleak, alienated David, and they referred to his "cosmic anguish", "psychic turmoil", and "barely controllable hysteria". Given the speed of David's changes, it was understandable that they should persist in interpreting new albums in the light of the last. But their judgment was belied most of all by the second track, 'Golden Years'. It began as a genuflection to Stevie Wonder's 'Golden Days' and evolved into an affirmation of the value of nostalgia and of self-assertion – "walk tall, act fine". That was linked to the protective power of romantic love:

> I'll stick with you baby for a thousand years,
> Nothing's gonna touch you in these golden years.

and even of religious faith:

> I believe oh Lord, I believe all the way.

The third track, 'Word On A Wing', framed with organ music and ending with an ethereal boy chorister, continued the religious theme with phrases like "Heaven and hell", "Lord I kneel", "My prayer flies like a word on the wing," and being "born again". The images and syntax had something of the complexity of 'The Width Of A Circle' and 'The Bewlay Brothers', with visions and illusions, dreams merging with waking states, and sexual echoes to the religious invocations:

> I'll walk beside you,
> I'm alive in you.

There was a rich Bowie pun in the opening line:

> In this age of grand delusion

– which, when sung, sounded equally like "grand illusion", taken from *La Grande Illusion*, Jean Renoir's film masterpiece on the futilities of war. There was also the significant and optimistic assertion, sung again and again, that David was preparing to take control of himself:

> Ready to shape the scheme of things . . .

The fourth track was 'TVC 15', and the reviewers, in part because they were mesmerised by its title, found it the most puzzling of all. In fact it was one of the most straightforward, for it wittily reversed one of David's favourite conceits, that of the performer who descends from the silver screen, leaving David wondering which image is real. In this case, David's girlfriend had made the return journey and disappeared – "crawled right in" – into his television set. David joked:

> . . . each night I sit there pleading,
> Bring back my dream test baby, she's my main feature.

Given the inexplicable happenings witnessed by Ava Cherry in David's New York house, which included his television set switching itself on and off at will, there was a sharp frisson to David's lyric. But it was played so defiantly, driven along by a bar-room piano from the days of R and B, that all threat was removed. The remainder of the lyric was in the same joyous spirit, with David showing his fondness for the technological phrases of the moment

— "hologramic", "quadrophonic" — and his love for the assonances of the title itself.

The last original track on the album was 'Stay', a mixture of hard rock, *Shaft*-style funk, and Barry White disco, that did most to fulfil the critics' view of *Station To Station* as an album of anguish. It too was a love lyric, a lament at being separated from a new lover, suffused with regrets for the misunderstandings that beset fresh relationships. Yet it ended on a positive note:

> This time tomorrow I'll know what to do,
> I know it's happened to you.

The final track, 'Wild Is The Wind', was taken from the 1957 movie of the same name starring Anna Magnani. Its appeal fitted the romantic and nostalgic mood of the album, telling of lovers who are borne away on the wind:

> Let me climb away with you
> For my love is like the wind.

David sang it in a triumphant crescendo that picked up on the message of the opening track. He too would be going away, as far from Los Angeles as he could, in search of his rebirth.

The next person to be "purged" was Michael Lippman. He had seemed an unlikely figure from the start: "He looked rather like Tony Defries," says one MainMan insider, "but with a $400-suit and a California sheen." He was therefore inextricably part of Los Angeles; the terminal dispute centred, as usual, on money. Lippman had acted for David throughout the legal dispute with Defries; shortly before the settlement, he and David discussed their own financial arrangements but, fatally, did not draw up a formal contract. In the subsequent row, David claimed that he had promised Lippman 10 per cent of his earnings; Lippman insisted that the figure was 15 per cent.

There were worse complications to come. By the summer, Lippman decided to become a show-business manager himself with David as his first client. "I was incredibly optimistic," Lippman says. "I thought he was a genius and hoped our relationship would last a long time." Wistfully, he adds, "I was probably naive in thinking that."

When Lippman proposed to David that they form a partnership, David seemed to welcome the idea, and Lippman prepared an agreement to that effect. The laws which regulate the entertainment business in California meant that Lippman could no longer act as David's attorney. Lippman advised David to consult Stanley Diamond, a friend and colleague who had a show-business law practice in Hollywood, and show him the draft of their agreement. David did as Lippman suggested. "That is the last time," says Lippman, "I ever saw him."

What happened, as Stan Diamond confirms, is that he was so alarmed by aspects of the proposed agreement that he advised David against accepting it. He will not say precisely why; but in the subsequent legal action, the second point at issue was that Lippman had access to David's earnings, amounting to $475,000, which had been placed in trust on David's behalf. David also felt aggrieved that Lippman had failed to secure him the rights to compose the background music for *The Man Who Fell to Earth*, even after he had recorded some material in Los Angeles with his former colleague Paul Buckmaster, who had flown from London for the sessions.

Lippman flatly denies that he acted improperly in any way; "I did absolutely nothing wrong," he says. In his view, these were matters that in any case could have been resolved amicably in discussions between himself and David. He never had the chance to do so, and for that he roundly blames Corinne. "David was very weak in that way, particularly as he didn't read the paper or answer the telephone, would never do anything to communicate with the outside world, would only do what he was allowed to do by Corinne."

The news that he had been sacked reached Lippman just after Christmas from Jamaica, where David was spending two weeks relaxing and rehearsing for the new tour he was planning for early 1976. As all around Lippman could see, it left him shocked and distressed. Kristina, who had become friendly with Lippman, believes that he had erred in being overprotective at a time when David was looking for his freedom. "He absolutely loved David and was trying to do his best for him and recoup his enormous losses." When Kristina met Lippman shortly afterwards, she found him in tears.

David was almost ready to quit Los Angeles. On January 21st, he left Jamaica for Canada, where he was to begin the 1976 tour, based largely on *Station To Station*. The tour began at Vancouver on February 2nd, followed by Seattle and Portland in the north-west US on February 3rd and 4th. He was back in California for concerts in San Francisco and Los Angeles between February 6th and 12th. Then he returned to Stone Canyon Drive to help pack his belongings. A removal firm took them to Los Angeles Airport, to be freighted to Europe. On February 13th, David left Los Angeles for good.

David's new home was to be in Switzerland. In the erratic Bowie marriage, Angie was still the home-maker, and she had found a traditional-style chalet, with a verandah and steeply angled roof, in the mountains above Vevey, close to Lausanne on the north shore of Lake Geneva. Vevey is a typical Swiss town, sedate, uneventful and languorous, particularly when clouds descend from the mountains around and the landscape becomes a uniform grey. If it seemed an unlikely retreat for David, he had moved there principally on the advice of a Los Angeles accountancy firm whom Stan Diamond had consulted over how David could minimise his obligations to pay tax. It would provide a suitable European base after David's tour ended with its last concert in Paris in May.

Out on the tour, however, not everything was going to plan. Athough the American critics were enthusiastic, in Europe David was attracting some deeply hostile press reports and political notoriety of the most damaging kind. He had started to compare himself with Hitler.

The flaw lay in David's instinct that his salvation depended on creating yet another character who would embody the values he most admired. He had described that character in the opening lines of the title track, 'Station To Station':

> The return of the thin white duke
> Throwing darts in lover's eyes.

The "thin white duke" represented David's latest attempt to become the super-cool figure he had portrayed in 'Halloween Jack' of *Diamond Dogs*, in the lyric 'Watch That Man', and in the "gouster" of *Young Americans*. And the thin white duke was the character David now became as his tour proceeded from California to Phoenix, Albuquerque, Denver, Milwaukee, Cincinatti, Cleveland, Detroit, Montreal and Toronto, in February, and in the Deep South and the north-east in March, ending the US segment of the tour at Madison Square Garden, New York.

The American critics found the character to their taste. As usual, they had commented more perceptively on the *Station To Station* album than their British counterparts. Robert Hilburn of the *Los Angeles Times* called it "impressive and encouraging", its tone

"one of artistic and emotional reawakening and rediscovery". Hilburn enjoyed the concerts too: David was wearing a white dress shirt with black jacket and trousers, his hair neatly slicked back, and Hilburn found him, in comparison with the MainMan days, "happier, more confident, and relaxed".

John Rockwell of the *New York Times* liked the bare set – starker even than in the concluding phase of the 'Diamond Dogs' tour – and the white light, of "almost painful intensity", that bathed David on stage. Rockwell described David's "cool, hostile distancing" from his audience, yet still judged it the best Bowie show he had ever seen.

Much of what the US critics identified and approved of was European in origin. David, far more open about himself in interviews, had talked enthusiastically of the "Brechtian" component of his act, which led to the "distancing" Rockwell had observed. His bare set, with its acute contrasts of black and white, stemmed from his continuing interest in the German expressionist film makers. He also borrowed from Salvador Dali and the Spanish surrealist director Luis Buñuel, showing their film *Un Chien Andalou* which opens with the blood-curdling scene of a woman apparently having her eyeball sliced open with a razor. (It was filmed using a dead sheep.)

But, just like David's earlier creations, the character was not entirely within his control. In the first place, the Europeanism of which he spoke had more sinister elements. The sets and lighting for the 1976 tour were partly inspired by David's studies of Josef Goebbels, the evil genius who orchestrated Hitler's propaganda, and of Albert Speer, architect to the Third Reich. Speer helped build the Nuremberg stadium and he and Goebbels planned the special effects for the Nazis' rallies, including the *Lichtturm*, or light-tower, consisting of powerful beams from different directions converging on one commanding central figure.

David's interest in Nazism seemed to go beyond a mere technical appreciation of their presentational skills, however. There was a none-too-distant parallel between the rise of Hitler as demagogue and the power which David felt lay within a rock-star's grasp, particularly a rock-star flirting with notions of leadership and messianism. In his interview with Cameron Crowe, which appeared in *Rolling Stone* in February, David said that the impact of Ziggy had been such that he "could have been Hitler in England – it wouldn't have been hard . . . I think I might have been a bloody good Hitler. I'd be an excellent dictator. Very eccentric and quite mad."

Certainly, David's remarks were tinged with irony and self-mockery. But in a longer version of the Crowe interview published by *Playboy* later that year, David went further. "I'd adore to be Prime Minister. And, yes, I believe very strongly in fascism . . . People have always responded with greater efficiency under a regimental leadership." When David said that Hitler was "one of the first rock-stars", Crowe asked what he meant. "He staged a country," David replied.

To an extent, David was a victim of his past, since his interviews with Crowe had taken place in the summer of 1974, when his paranoia was at its most acute. He had also fallen into the notorious trap that awaits those who toy with irony, which is of being taken seriously. But the most damning interpretation of his remarks appeared to be confirmed near the end of the European segment of his tour. In Stockholm on April 26th a Swedish reporter challenged David over the quotes in *Rolling Stone*.

"As I see it," David glibly replied, "I am the only alternative for the premier in England. I believe Britain could benefit from a fascist leader. After all, fascism is really nationalism."

Among David's companions, Corinne and David's hard-nosed US publicist, Barbara DeWitt, were horrified, particularly when his remarks were picked up by the British press. In consultation with David, they decided that the best way to repair the damage would be for him to meet his fans when he arrived at Victoria Station for his British concerts on Sunday, May 2nd. Political naivety and technical ineptitude only made matters worse.

In theory, events at Victoria Station were to be coordinated between David's staff, British Rail, RCA and Capital Radio. David would make a speech from the back of a lorry, amplified by a public-address system, while police and security guards held back the expected crowds. The fans, at least, arrived on cue, several thousand of them pressing against the crush barriers surrounding Victoria's Platform 8, while reporters from the national and music press, some grumbling at missing their Sunday lunch, waited by the lorry from which David would make his speech. Everything else was a disaster.

In the first place the special four-coach train bringing David from Dover was late, delayed – so the rival reporters complained – so that David could complete an interview for Capital Radio. Next, it could be seen that the car provided to transport him the short distance to his podium was an enormous black Mercedes-Benz. Then it was discovered that the public-address system did not work.

As technicians struggled in vain to find the faulty connection, David stood up in the open-topped Mercedes-Benz to greet his fans. The photographer Chalkie Davies of the *New Musical Express* captured the moment: David, wearing a black shirt and standing in the back of a gleaming black German car, is raising his right arm at a 45-degree angle, looking as if he is giving a Nazi salute. The *New Musical Express* ran the picture over three columns, using David's Stockholm comments as the caption, and adding the headline, "Heil and Farewell".

For each person present at Victoria Station who claims that David's gesture was a fascist greeting, there is another to protest that it was a harmless wave. David insisted vehemently that it was the latter. Kristina, who later questioned David about this phase of his life, came to the middle view. "It was done tongue in cheek," she says, "or something silly like that."

The damage was done. The reviews of David's six concerts at Wembley were inseparable from his politics. In *Melody Maker*, Michael Watts wrote that he was "the only real generational leader of the Seventies". Yet the staging "raised echoes of his recent controversial comments about Fascist rule for Britain", and Watts confessed that he was "ultimately unmoved". In the *Guardian*, Robin Denselow found his image "more Nazi than futuristic".

When the tour ended in Paris on May 18th, David retreated to Switzerland. The images he left behind were not the most helpful ones. There had been a long-running newspaper story following his arrest in the US during a marijuana raid, although the charges were finally dismissed. The *Cracked Actor* documentary, showing the overwrought David of mid-1974, was shown again on BBC TV. The sniping at David in the music press over the "fascist" controversy went on.

Finally came the news that seemed to confirm all the worst suspicions anyone held. David had left his new home in Switzerland and gone to live in Berlin.

30

A New Town

David had always found a welcome in Berlin. His first visit had been in October 1969, when he went with Ken Pitt to record an appearance for a West German television pop-music programme. They stayed in a hotel just off the Kurfürstendamm, West Berlin's main thoroughfare, with its enticing arrays of luxury consumer goods to display the virtues of the capitalist West. The programme's producer escorted them on a brief tour of the city, which included a ritual excursion to the Berlin Wall, and a visit to several gay clubs. The producer had somehow arranged for the juke boxes to be playing one of David's records – 'Space Oddity' was the favourite – as David arrived. Although Pitt could as usual discern little of David's feelings, he was sure that David enjoyed the recognition he received. "Everything registered," Pitt says.

David met another appreciative audience in Berlin during the final lap of his journey on the Trans-Siberian Express in May 1973. His train stopped for forty-five minutes at West Berlin's Zoo Station where he was greeted by a small but enthusiastic group of fans. David's record sales in Germany had been pitiful, and the word reaching RCA was that he was thought to be "decadent"; but in West Berlin, at least, decadence was a virtue. Photographs of David meeting his supporters on the platform appeared in the West Berlin edition of *Bild*, whose reporter found him "intelligent, sensitive, and cultured".

David's third visit, in May 1976, came during the European leg of the 'Thin White Duke' tour. The effect of living in a walled enclave deep inside East Germany is to magnify the impact of visitors from the outside world, and David's appearance at the patriotically named Deutschlandhalle on April 10th had the impact of a visitation. Just like the first Ziggy tour in the US, the concert attained the heights of fashion, with Romy Haag, Berlin's most celebrated transsexual, capturing the pre-concert limelight when she swept to her seat with a fawning twenty-strong entourage. Many of the audience recognised the antecedents of the *Lichtturm*, its historical undertones blending unnervingly with the aura of distant sexuality created by David's appearance at the heart of the light. There was also admiration for the staging of the concert, the *Berliner Morgenpost* commenting that it unrolled "like a perfect super-machine".

David had more time to sample the delights of the city than before and to discover the theatrical possibilities they held. To celebrate Pat Gibbons's birthday, he threw a party at a restaurant on the Kurfürstendamm, with the *pièce de résistance* a giant birthday cake from which a naked woman emerged bedecked with flowers and vines. Although Mick Jagger had once staged a similar event, employing *Pork's* Geri Miller as the main protagonist, David was careful to explain that the idea – even down to the garland of vines – came first from Salvador Dali.

David also made his first excursion to East Berlin, crossing the Wall at Checkpoint Charlie in a hired Mercedes-Benz, accompanied by Corinne, Iggy Pop and the US photographer, Andy Kent. When they visited the site of Hitler's bunker David risked arrest by the East German Volkspolizei to make a quick, parodic Nazi salute for Kent's benefit. He made Kent promise never to release the photographs without his permission, thereby showing far greater political acumen than when he made his ill-fated remarks about Hitler in Sweden three weeks later.

David's return to Berlin sprang from his implicit pact with Iggy Pop. When the tour ended in France, he began work on Iggy's new album at the Château d'Hérouville, where he had made *Pin-Ups* in 1973. It was a full-blooded collaboration, David taking the musical lead while Iggy scrawled drafts of the lyrics as he crouched over large sheets of paper on the floor. The songs, rendered in Iggy's throaty growl, told of the perverse and violent beauty to be found in modern industrial landscapes, and the despair and optimism they simultaneously inspired. The first influences of Berlin could be discerned in a couplet from 'China Girl':

> I'd stumble into town,
> Visions of swastikas in my head.

The album was called *The Idiot*, from a line in the shadowy opening track, 'Sister Midnight':

> Calling Sister Midnight
> I'm an idiot for you.

After a month, David and Iggy had amassed hours of recordings but the album was far from complete. David turned to Tony

Visconti again, asking if he would help unravel and mix the material, and Visconti agreed. By now David was feeling disenchanted with the Château, especially as he and Corinne suspected that a member of the staff had leaked details of the sessions to the press. Instead, David proposed, why not finish the album at a studio of which he had heard good reports in Berlin?

The studio in question was named Hansa, with premises in several parts of the city. David, Iggy and Visconti were allocated a mixing studio in Nestorstrasse, off the Kurfürstendamm, which they found commendably efficient and businesslike. David continued to explore Berlin, discovering a twenty-four-hour city rich with nightlife, from blaring discos to friendly cafés and bars open into the small hours where he could wind down after recording sessions. In the Charlottenburg district, close to the State Opera House, he discovered a transvestite club, the Lützower Lampe, which, unlike the tourist traps on the Kurfürstendamm, had an intimate family atmosphere free of the stigma attached to such places in Britain or the US. David felt at home enough to pose for a photograph with the mistress of the house, Carmen, and two of her star performers, together with a young woman from the local RCA office and a smiling Corinne.

By the time *The Idiot* was finished, David had concluded that Berlin had far more to offer than smug, bourgeois Switzerland. He would retain the chalet in Vevey as a base and tax retreat, but would live instead in Berlin. He stayed first in the Hotel Gehrhus, housed in a former castle on the edge of the Grunewald Forest. Then Corinne found an apartment in the Schöneberg district, close to the city centre. It was at 155 Hauptstrasse, a substantial four-storey block built in the expansive days of the late nineteenth century when Berlin had just become Germany's new imperial capital. The entrance was an ornate wrought-iron doorway that opened into a hallway with a tiled floor and a staircase with a carved wooden balustrade. David's apartment, on the first floor, had seven rooms, with elegant panelled doors, high decorated ceilings, elaborate centrepieces and cornices, and French windows that gave on to a balcony above the street.

Although the flair and confidence of the décor undoubtedly appealed to David, it still seemed an unlikely home. Schöneberg was far from being the most fashionable area of Berlin: the apartment overlooked a busy dual carriageway and the shop immediately beneath sold nothing more glamorous than car spares. As David later explained, its sheer ordinariness, and the anonymity it conferred, were part of its appeal. For the first time in years he went out shopping for household goods, and could even do so without being recognised.

It was during this period of upheaval that David recorded his next album for RCA. He had committed himself to returning to the Château d'Hérouville in September, having paid a deposit of $20,000 which the studio had demanded in the light of its delayed payments in the MainMan days. The album was completed in Berlin and was thus a transitional work, embracing two cities and two moods, with, according to Tony Visconti, David's producer once again, "most of the good vibes put on in Berlin".

David's band was composed of Carlos Alomar, Dennis Davis and George Murray, who now comprised David's regular rhythm section, together with a new lead guitarist in Ricky Gardener, who came recommended by Visconti, and a second newcomer in pianist Roy Young, formerly of the British beat group Cliff Bennett and the Rebel Rousers, latterly living in Hamburg.

David's boldest choice was Brian Eno, once a member of Roxy Music, a group whose detached and ironic understatement had vastly appealed to him in the early 1970s. Since then, Eno had been pursuing an interest in experimental synthesised music, and when the two men met David was fascinated to hear Eno explain that his musical ideas were closer than might appear to disco and West Indian music, where the vocal part loses its dominance and becomes one of a number of sources "floating around", as Eno liked to put it, "coming into focus and disappearing again". With a typical burst of enthusiasm, David asked Eno to work on his next album, telling Visconti: "He's got such fantastic ideas."

David had also lit upon the synthesised music of two German groups, Kraftwerk and Tangerine Dream, and asked Visconti to listen to their records. Visconti had a trick of his own up his sleeve: he had just acquired a recording gadget known as a harmoniser, whose effect he described as "distorting the fabric of time", which appealed to David too. As he and Visconti accepted, it all added up to a colossal experiment in both musical techniques and human personalities. David even warned Visconti that the album might never be released.

It was thus in an optimistic frame of mind, in keeping with the mood of *Station To Station*, that David and his musicians assembled at the beginning of September. The mood was soon dissipated, for the return to the Château d'Hérouville could not have got off to a worse start. In Visconti's words, Corinne "read the riot act" to the studio over its former indiscretions. A day or

David with Gustl Breuer ("what is a David Bowie?") and, half-hidden, Spider Woody Woodmansey.

David plays Ziggy – taking it all too far?

Suzi Ronson

Ian Hunter

Leee Black Childers

Lori Mattix

David travels soft class on the Trans-Siberian Express, with (left) Geoffrey MacCormack ("Warren Peace") and UPI newsman Bob Musel in 1973.

Mike Garson

Jaime Andrews

Ava Cherry

Earl Slick

David returns to the stage of the Marquee Club for the spectacular '1980 Floor Show', recorded for US TV in 1973, but never shown in Britain.

Mick Ronson, the former Hull municipal gardener, on stage.

Mick Ronson in New York, today.

so later she was dismayed to discover that one of the studio assistants was a journalist.

To make matters worse, the studio's best technicians had gone on holiday, so that Visconti had to spend much of his time making his own adjustments with a screwdriver. Then there was the food: with regular monotony, it seemed, they were served rabbit, and Visconti warned that their health would suffer if they ate no salads or fresh vegetables. His warning appeared justified when both he and David were stricken with diarrhoea.

The crowning misfortune came when David became ensnared in the legal dispute that had rumbled on ever since he had fired Michael Lippman. Although the affair bordered on farce, its climax showed that David remained all too vulnerable to the pressures that had helped bring him so low the previous year. He remained intensely suspicious of anyone handling his money; and more than ever he found personal confrontations hard to handle, especially when deprived of the shield of Corinne.

In January, Stanley Diamond, who had replaced Lippman as David's lawyer, had begun a legal action in the Los Angeles courts against his predecessor for alleged breaches of contract and "fiduciary duty". Diamond complained, first, that Lippman had taken 15 per cent of David's earnings when he was only entitled to 10 per cent, and demanded that he repay the difference of $39,370.14. Second, Diamond demanded that Lippman release the $475,000 being held on David's behalf. In the grand Californian manner, Diamond also claimed "exemplary and punitive damages" of $2 million.

The proceedings soon hit a snag of David's making. He was required to make a formal deposition in the presence of lawyers from both sides. Diamond told the court that his client was unable to come to California to do so as he was on tour in Europe and had a fear of flying. The judge proved sympathetic, and said that David could make his deposition in Switzerland, provided that he paid for Lippman and *his* lawyer, Sanford Levenberg, to fly to Switzerland, and also met Levenberg's fees – a matter of $650 a day.

At the end of May four California lawyers – Lippman, Levenberg, Diamond and Diamond's assistant, James Wilson – arrived in Vevey. The proceedings, held at Vevey's Hotel Trois Couronnes, began on July 1st, and were expected to last for two days. They came to a halt after only forty-five minutes when David stormed out. After fruitless attempts to reconvene the meeting, the lawyers returned to California empty-handed.

A secondary dispute now unfolded in the Los Angeles court. Diamond claimed that David had walked out because the questioning had made him ill. Lippman counter-claimed that David had merely succumbed to a fit of pique, and demanded that he should now be compelled to come to California instead. Since David was still refusing to fly, Lippman's demand led to a further argument as to whether a suitable ship could be found to bring David to California. Lippman submitted a list of five ships which were due to cross the Atlantic in August. Diamond replied that all five were freight ships and therefore entirely unsuitable. Lippman argued in response that David had been quite happy to sail on freight ships in the past. Diamond replied that David had now arranged to record his new album at the Château d'Hérouville, and therefore could not leave Europe after all. Lippman demanded to know exactly when David had made, and paid for, the studio booking. Members of the Château staff were quizzed by transatlantic telephone but a new set of depositions proved inconclusive.

In an attempt to end the impasse, Lippman decided to fly to France. David travelled to Paris from the Château d'Hérouville to meet him, accompanied by Tony Visconti who had volunteered his support. It was fortunate that he did so. Ten minutes after being closeted with Lippman, says Visconti, David "went berserk". Visconti could hear shouting and chairs being knocked over, and then David burst out of the room. When Visconti tried to intercept him, David snapped: "You're all fucking leeches, you all want my money." Since Visconti had received only a pittance from the two Mercury albums he had produced, this touched a particularly raw nerve. "Look who you're talking to," he told David. "Not me."

In the end, according to Lippman, the dispute was resolved – "very amicably" – in a compromise: "I got some of the money, he got some of the money," Lippman says. At the time, the row left David almost speechless with rage. "He was in a coma for two days," says Visconti. "He was useless to anyone." Visconti spent a day talking to David in the grounds of the Château, "putting him back together again". But the high hopes for the sessions at the Château were irreparably tainted: all in all, says Visconti, Paris was "a horrible experience".

The effects showed all too clearly on the recordings made at the Château, with the tone set by David's choice of album title: *Low*. Musically, its mood ranged from the mildly jaunty to the utterly depressed. The lyrics were uniformly pessimistic and withdrawn, with David at times literally at a loss for words. His spare, minimal

434

lyrics offered variations on the themes of loneliness, tentative encounters and retreat, framed in discordant images of accidents and destruction — the obverse side of the optimistic themes of *Station To Station*.

The album began with a sombre and remorseless instrumental track, 'Speed of Life', dominated by a pounding rhythm section. The second track, 'Breaking Glass', more gloomy and anguished still, told of David's propensity for accidents and of his withdrawal from a lover. "You've got problems," he lamented, "I'll never touch you."

The third, 'What In The World', which included Iggy Pop as a back-up vocalist, showed David fearful of becoming involved with a new partner. It also picked up a theme from David's past. On *Ziggy Stardust*, David had wondered if he could find peace and affection as a "rock 'n' roll star"; in 'Rock 'N' Roll With Me' on *Diamond Dogs*, he concluded that he could do so only by standing back from the role of star. 'What In The World' reached the same conclusion — "wait until the crowd goes" — but added the painful question:

> What are you going to say
> To the real me?

'Sound And Vision' returned to the anxiety which dominated *Hunky Dory*, and was particularly apposite now: David's fear of losing his creative inspiration. It depicted David sitting alone —

> Waiting for the gift of sound and vision.

The music, with a simple repeated theme, enhanced by Tony Visconti's wife Mary Hopkin as a second back-up vocalist, was less despairing, implying that David knew the "gift" would always return.

There was a similar counterpoint in the next track, 'Always Crashing In The Same Car', where David again lamented that he had become accident-prone. The music sounded moderately encouraging and upbeat, and the lyric returned to the travelling theme and the need to take risks:

> . . . ev'ry chance that I take
> Take it on the road

Travelling reappeared in the next lyric, 'Be My Wife':

I've tripped all over the world

and ended with a simple plea for love and companionship:

Be my wife.

David's bleak mood had the unforeseen consequence of allowing Brian Eno a larger role than first intended. As a newcomer, Eno had been taken aback at the speed with which even a depressed David could work, stirring himself to peaks of energy and laying down tracks at breakneck speed. Since Eno was used to spending days compiling his tracks by trial and error, he was chagrined to discover that David's creative frenzies usually turned out "just right".

Originally, David had planned to float Eno's contribution over the more conventional music. When David returned from Paris almost bereft of inspiration, Eno offered to compose a track from what he called his "dreamy stuff". The result was 'Warszawa', the first of four instrumental tracks on the second side of the album.

Although David did not tell Eno at the time, the track was inspired by an excursion he had made into Eastern Europe at the end of April. He had travelled to his concerts in Finland and Scandinavia from Berlin by train, passing through Poland and the USSR en route. David's glimpses of Warsaw had conjured up images of a bleak and austere city that he hoped to translate into music, telling Eno that he wanted a slow piece with an "emotive, almost religious feel".

The two men proceeded by a combination of the cut-up technique David had learned from William Burroughs and Eno's own methods. Eno was fascinated with random events and had devised a pack of Tarot cards which he called his "Oblique Strategies": to make a decision, he drew a card and followed the course it prescribed. In this case, Eno recorded 430 finger clicks on a tape as numerical markers. He and David took different sections to work on, changing chords as the numbers dictated. The result, composed entirely on Eno's collection of electronic equipment, was a sombre and plangent track dominated by stately organ chords, with David's wordless vocals providing a chant that resembled a plainsong. Only then did David reveal to Eno the title and source of his inspiration.

David recorded a second instrumental track, 'Subterraneans', that also sprang from his initial impressions of Eastern Europe, this time his image of East Berlin as a lonely and desolate city whose inhabitants sought to escape in memories of the past. It was even more sombre than 'Warszawa', with a further range of electronic tricks to give a ghostly quality to the ponderous opening chords, its air of melancholy accentuated by wistful strings, lingering wordless vocals, and a mournful saxophone that David played himself.

By the end of September, with nine tracks recorded, David had had enough of the Château d'Hérouville. Although the studio had tried to meet the complaints over the food, relationships with the staff, says Tony Visconti, had become "really antagonistic". There was an obvious solution, which David proposed: they should complete the album at the Hansa studio in Berlin.

This time, they were able to use Hansa's main studio, housed in a seventy-year-old four-storey building in Köthener Strasse, close to the Potsdamer Platz in the centre of Berlin. They found the staff as friendly and efficient as before; but the biggest stimulus David received was from the ambience of the studio itself.

Like so many buildings in Berlin, the studio bore the scars of the murderous battles in the last days of the Third Reich, for its imposing façade was still pock-marked from shrapnel and bullets and blackened by fire. Its location bore testimony to the more recent history of Berlin, a short distance away, at the end of Köthener Strasse, ran the Berlin Wall, its white concrete slabs daubed with political graffiti, overlooked by an East German guardpost on the roof of a warehouse on the far side. The atmosphere, says Visconti, was "provocative and stimulating and frightening".

David arrived at the studio with two instrumental tracks left to record, and his surge of new energy was immediately felt. The first track, which he named 'Weeping Wall', belied the conventional associations of the title, for it began with a breezy marimba sequence which David recorded on an electronic "marimbaphone" he found at the studio. He used the same technique as on 'Warszawa', marking a tape with numbers up to 160 and then asking for the sequences to be introduced at different points, with the marimbas dominating throughout.

David also discovered Hansa's two-storey recording studio, in an ornate room that once housed the meetings and dinners of one of Berlin's craft guilds. In manifest delight, David christened it "the hall by the wall". Its unique acoustics were heard on the second new track with its spaced-out feel, bizarre echoing sound effects and a yearning cello background that was provided, almost impromptu, by the Hansa recording engineer, Eduard Meyer.

Visconti had written two cello parts, melody and rhythm, which he proposed to play himself. When Meyer revealed that he both read music and played the cello, he was enlisted in Visconti's place. The piece that evolved was as upbeat as 'Weeping Wall': beginning to relish the richness of Berlin's historical tapestry, David called it 'Art Decade' – a pun on "art decayed" and a reference to Berlin's ruined glories. He offered a further salute to Berlin in the title he bestowed on the final and notably more cheerful instrumental track on side one: 'A New Career In A New Town'.

The *Low* album thus ended as it had been intended to begin, as an assertion of progress and artistic freedom. Although David later virtually disowned the lyrics, it was a remarkably bold and innovative piece of work, and further evidence of his determination to move on. Not everybody saw it that way. So fast were his changes – as David had once warned – that he was once again trapped in the perceptions of the past, a predicament made worse by the political climate in which *Low* was released.

The news that David had moved to Berlin first appeared in the local press in August, when *Bild* reported that he was staying at the Gehrhus Hotel. In early October, both *Bild* and *Berliner Morgenpost* recorded that he had moved into the apartment at 155 Hauptstrasse, Schöneberg. They also interviewed the transsexual Romy Haag, who hinted that she had been having an affair with David. (Later, after she amplified her claim, David denied that this was so.)

Even now the British press was slow to catch on, and it was not until early 1977 that the music papers confirmed that David was living in Berlin. That discovery coincided with the release of *Low*, when Tony Visconti and Brian Eno were interviewed about their contributions to the album. The first paper to try to find David in Berlin was the *Record Mirror*, but their reporter, Jim Evans, returned empty-handed. He missed the Hauptstrasse address that the German press had already revealed, instead visiting Romy Haag's apartment and the Hansa studios, to no avail. "There are two walls in Berlin," Evans complained. "One divides the city. The other surrounds David Bowie. A wall of silence. And confusion."

It was, in part, David's elusiveness that was to blame for the adverse reception to *Low*, the most vitriolic reviews he ever received. But the critics were also reacting to a mood of crisis that had overtaken popular music at that time, as it was caught up in political issues that usually passed it by.

In 1976, the punk movement had embarked on its assault on the institutional canons of decency and good taste, initiated by the Damned, with their drummer, Rat Scabies, and taken up most enthusiastically by the Sex Pistols whose first single, 'Anarchy In The UK', had been banned by stores and broadcasters as soon as it was released. Then their bass player said "fuck" on television, the press claimed that the group vomited publicly at London Airport, and EMI cancelled the group's £40,000 recording contract. The Sex Pistols' apotheosis came when their second single, 'God Save The Queen', was released in time for Britain's Royal Jubilee. While half the nation prepared to put out bunting and hold street parties, the Sex Pistols gave an alternative view of Britain: "No future," they cried.

Parallel to punk came the growth of several neo-Nazi movements in Britain, chief among them the National Front, which was winning support among skinhead football fans and votes in the most depressed areas of the inner cities, encouraged by the opportunist utterances of the Conservative MP, Enoch Powell. Both punk and fascism were symptoms of Britain's economic decline through the latter half of the 1970s, which the Labour government under the charmless James Callaghan appeared powerless to alter. A new range of protest groups moved into the political vacuum, some springing from music itself. One of the most determined was Rock against Racism, which published a leaflet that delivered David the final retribution for his political naivety of two years before. Under the headline "Love Music – Hate Racism" it printed three heads in profile: Adolf Hitler, Enoch Powell and David Bowie.

Since David had gone to ground and could offer no explanations to assist the reviewers, they viewed the album in the light of the "fascist" controversy of the previous summer, itself largely a delayed-action result of his disjointed interview with Cameron Crowe. Although Michael Watts remained the most sympathetic to David, even he used phrases like "Hunnish" to describe the album. The most damning reviews appeared in *New Musical Express*. Ian MacDonald accused David of producing totalitarian music: "mass-production epitomized . . . for the Marching Morons of TVC 15, this is Music While You Work . . . David Bowie was last seen giving his country a fascist salute in Victoria Station."

Charles Shaar Murray was even more apoplectic: had he been a mass-murderer, David could hardly have won greater excoriation. *Low*, Murray declared, was "so negative it didn't even contain emptiness or the void . . . a totally passive psychosis, a scenario and soundtrack for total withdrawal . . . the kind of ego loss that is actually the purest complacency . . . Futility and death-wish glorified, an elaborate embalming job for a suicide's grave . . . an

439

act of purest hatred and destructiveness . . . it stinks of artfully counterfeited spiritual defeat and emptiness." The clue that Murray was reacting to more than *Low* itself came in his aside that it "comes to us at a bad time and doesn't help at all".

The most spirited response came from Brian Eno. He considered the reviewers numskulls and said: "They're so bloody thick, sometimes I could drive nails through their heads." For a long time, David himself lay low. He eventually revealed something of his bruised feelings when, after an interval of two years, he telephoned his cousin Kristina from Berlin. He told her that the political accusations against him were "nonsense". He also said, according to Kristina, "that he was getting so disgusted with everything that was going on that he wanted to buy an island and have an artistic community, with artists and writers living and working there on a basis of true democracy". Kristina adds: "It sounded a bit Utopian to me."

31

The Hero of Berlin

There was no question, in 1977, of David leaving Berlin for a desert island or anywhere else: Berlin still had far too much to offer. David and Iggy had discovered that the city's life moved in cycles from district to district, so that action was to be found, somewhere, twenty-four hours of the day. In the late morning they would descend from 155 Hauptstrasse, where Iggy had a smaller apartment of his own at the rear of the building, to take coffee in a gay bar, the Anderes Ufer, or "other side", that had opened a few doors along from the motor-spares shop. For a late supper David favoured the Ax Bax Restaurant on the corner of Leibniz-strasse and Kantstrasse in the city centre, which became crowded around midnight with minor celebrities and media people, many from the nearby television studios. David's usual choice from the short à la carte menu was thick white-bean soup, accompanied by several glasses of hoppy König-Pilsener beer.

From then until dawn, David often joined Berlin's night people as they crowded into clubs and discothèques like the Exxcess, the Harlekin, the Tolstefanz or the Dschungle – a German rendition of "jungle". At the Dschungle, David liked to sit at the far end of the balcony overlooking the bar, where he could survey the crowd and perfect his knack of using eye-contact to summon women he had taken a fancy to (an impressive proportion succumbed).

The patrons of these places included many of the gadfly people who found succour in the gaudy ambience of West Berlin, like Zazie de Paris, a French transsexual who had come to Berlin with Romy Haag, and later opened her own club near Hauptstrasse. David was intrigued by her for a time, and that, Zazie believes, is because whereas he had traversed the sexual spectrum, "I felt like a woman and lived like a woman – I had made the choice."

David also became friendly with the remarkable Rosalia di Kulessa, a fashion model who had been among the fans who greeted him at the Zoo Station in 1973. When they met again, she was a doomed and tragic figure, for she had contracted breast cancer and knew she had not long to live. She made no secret of her resolve to spend her last months in defiance of her fate. She distributed large laminated badges bearing her photograph and telephone number, and wore spectacular wigs to conceal the baldness caused by her chemotherapy treatment. She also dealt in cocaine. Both David and Iggy were fascinated, especially when, after one of her breasts had been removed, she posed with Iggy for a photograph, naked to the waist.

Even in such spectacular company, David usually went unmolested by fans to an extent inconceivable elsewhere. To make him less recognisable, Tony Visconti cut his hair short, giving him a severe, Teutonic fringe. David also grew a wispy moustache which he shaved off towards the end of 1976. Even when he was sighted, the blasé attitudes affected by young West Berliners, especially in the punk era, usually ensured that he was not troubled. When Gerrit Meijer, leader of a punk band named PVC, met David and Iggy at the SO-36 Club, Meijer pointedly ignored David and talked to Iggy instead. (He was taken aback when Iggy, whom he had never met before, asked if he had any cocaine.)

As David found, another of Berlin's attractions is that chance encounters in clubs and bars can prove delightfully fruitful. During an early visit to the transvestites of the Lützower Lampe, David met a Berliner, Artur Vogdt, who had lived in the city since the 1920s. They were soon locked in conversation, and Vogdt found David "especially interested in pre-war Berlin".

For David, Berlin's pre-war associations, including the satirical night clubs and the atmosphere of sexual decadence that had attracted writers like Christopher Isherwood, were already alluring. Vogdt described the tea-dances in the restaurants of the Kurfürstendamm, where handsome young men, known as *Eintänzer*, plied their services to lonely widows. He also told David of the rich artistic community Berlin had attracted, including George Grosz and Marc Chagall. In the 1930s, Vogdt had become restaurateur to the actors at the Berlin State Theatre, and he related how during the war he would arrive at 5 a.m. to prepare the food in the lull between air raids. When the theatre was closed in 1943, he fled to Luxembourg. He returned after the war to find the theatre in ruins – and since it lay in East Berlin, he had not been back to see it since 1957.

Vogdt also helped to deepen David's interest in German expressionism. After the war he had become proprietor of the Hotel Continental in the Kurfürstendamm, with an art gallery where he exhibited the works of the expressionist painters connected with Berlin. On that subject, says Vogdt, he and David "talked nearly the whole night". David had already discovered the Brücke Museum of

Expressionist Art in the Schmargendorf district on the edge of the Grunewald Forest, and he now returned there again and again.

The name *Brücke*, meaning bridge, stemmed from the expressionists' belief that they offered a bridge to the future for "all the revolutionary and surging elements" of early twentieth-century Germany to cross. David was drawn to the angular and asymmetrical shapes that had appealed to him in the films of Fritz Lang, as well as to the painters' direct and defiant sexuality, their choice of subject matter from the street life of Berlin, and their experiments with drugs to probe at the boundaries between sanity and madness.

David often took his friends and colleagues to the museum, among them Brian Eno, who later explained how he was struck by the evanescent note the artists had captured on the eve of the first world war, creating a "mood of melancholy or nostalgia as if they were painting something that was just disappearing", which accorded so well with the atmosphere of latterday Berlin. Eno felt that there were strong similarities with David's music, particularly in their "boldness of attack, the unplanned evolutionary mood of the images and the overall mood".

Later, David bought two expressionist works from Vogdt. One was a sketch made by Emil Nolde in preparation for his renowned painting, *The Three Kings*. The other was a woodcut of three white horses by Erich Heckel, of which the Brücke possessed another version. Vogdt took David to meet the museum's director, Professor Leopold Reidermeister. "He said the Heckel was better than theirs," Vogdt recalls. David also took up painting himself, using the same bold brushstrokes as the expressionists, and producing several works that won his friends' admiration, the most striking showing a young boy looking expectantly up an empty flight of stairs.

Inspired by the riches Berlin held, David explored further and further afield, usually in the company of Iggy and Corinne, roaming the city in the same freewheeling spirit, according to Visconti, as the trio of characters in François Truffaut's rapturous film, *Jules et Jim*. "It was like a golden period," Visconti says. "They just went everywhere together."

They often rode on the West Berlin underground railway, or U-Bahn, which also passes under part of East Berlin, clattering through ghostly closed stations whose platforms are attended only by East German guards. Sometimes they took the overground S-Bahn, which radiates into the West Berlin suburbs, sometimes selecting a destination solely because they had not been there before. They became familiar with the "Turkish" districts of Kreuzberg and Neukölln, the home of Berlin's Turkish community since before the first world war.

Gradually David's view of Berlin altered. He still owned books on Goebbels and Speer, although some had been confiscated by customs officials during his journey through Poland and the USSR in April. If anyone asked about them, he usually replied that he was researching a part in a film, although no film ever seemed to materialise. According to Zazie de Paris, however, he was no longer interested in the ideology of Nazism but rather its insignia, or outward show.

Few of the insignia of Nazism in fact remained in Berlin; instead, there were only hideous reminders of the past. Near Checkpoint Charlie was a bare plot of land with a notice proclaiming it to be the site of the Gestapo's headquarters, where countless opponents of Nazism had been tortured and killed. David would point out another monument to the chaos Nazism had brought, a solitary brick archway that was all that remained of the Anhalter Bahnhof, the largest railway station in Europe until it was devastated in the war.

East Berlin assumed new dimensions too. At first David had viewed it from the conventional Western perspective of a drab and joyless city that symbolised communist totalitarianism. Later, as a counterpoint to the air of transience that pervaded West Berlin, he savoured the illusion that East Berlin was trapped in a time warp, with the women's beehive hairstyles, and the battered and rusting cars from the 1950s, that had helped inspire his punning title, 'Art Decade'. David liked to lunch at the Ganymed restaurant, where the waiters had frock coats and the waitresses wore black ankle-length dresses and white pinafore aprons. "It was like going through a time-machine," Visconti says.

There was also a rich artistic history to be sampled, like the Brecht Theatre and Brecht's house nearby, and the remains of the Schauspielhaus, the State Theatre where Artur Vogdt had worked. The devastated building contained another message: here was a great city in ruins, its traumatic past visited on the hapless present.

On either side of the Schauspielhaus stood the skeletons of the French and German cathedrals, flanked by pitted statues untended since 1945. At the end of Unter den Linden, the broad thoroughfare laid out by Frederick the Great in the eighteenth century, rose the Brandenburg Gate, once the city centre, now marooned in the no-man's-land between East and West Berlin. On an island in the River Spree stood the Pergamon Museum, where antiquities pillaged from around the world had once proclaimed Germany's roots in the mythic past. In the 1970s, the museum's neo-classical façades were still blackened by fire, its roof open in places to the skies. Out in the suburbs, which David also visited, were mounds of rubble uncleared since the war.

Whenever David showed visitors the ruins of Berlin, the extent to which he was mesmerised by them was clear. This was a city of past splendours ravaged by twentieth-century follies, a city of myths and heroes brought low by delusions of temporal grandeur. It was the city of Ziggy Stardust and Diamond Dogs, the city where the apocalypse had occurred, the city of David's dreams and fears. No longer was it necessary to look to outer space to explore his inner mind; here was David's imagination writ large. No longer did he need to continue his spiritual odyssey in search of himself. Here was his spiritual home.

November 1976 brought the watershed in David's marriage. For much of its course it had remained as unconventional as its beginning, Angie alternating with the succession of David's lovers, whose tenure ranged from Ava's eighteen months to one-night stands. The marriage had its conventional side too. As her part in setting up a family home in Vevey showed, Angie remained the homemaker. She was fiercely proud of David's achievements, and her part in them, even when he committed *faux pas* like the Nazi salute. "I have never been cross at him for anything, even arriving at Victoria Station doing Heil Hitler stuff," she says. "I thought, *My man* was out there this afternoon."

For David too the bonds were still strong. He sometimes affected to be dismayed by Angie's excesses, particularly in the presence of Kristina, whom he still seemed to regard as his family's moral standard-bearer. The concept of the family exerted its pull on him, above all where Zowie was concerned. Zowie had a nanny who had replaced Susie Frost, and his own room in the Hauptstrasse apartment, and he went to school in Berlin.

It was this view of the family that David tried to preserve when Angie visited him in a final attempt to resolve their differences. Angie's largest grievance was the extent to which David had become dependent on Corinne. She suspected Corinne of trying to shoulder her aside, and told David that he had to choose between them. David protested that Corinne was "too useful" to him and begged Angie to withdraw her ultimatum. According to Angie, he suggested that she should "stay at home and be the wealthy wife and breed more Bowie offspring". Angie rejected his proposal, saying: "To live the rest of my life bored to death spending your money being a Swiss millionairess is not my idea of a good time."

As usual, David found the confrontation immensely painful, particularly as Corinne had made a tactical retreat for the duration of Angie's visit. The strain told when David became faint and had difficulty breathing. Afraid that he was suffering from a heart attack, Angie called the British Military Hospital in Berlin and demanded that David be admitted. Although the hospital did not normally treat civilians, Angie was so insistent that it agreed. Later the hospital denied that David had had a heart attack, saying that he had "overdone things and was suffering from too much drink". The explanation circulating among David's friends was that he had suffered from "heart asthma" – a layman's interpretation of an irregular heartbeat, produced by the stress of Angie's visit.

Angie roundly blamed Corinne for the crisis she and David had reached, believing herself to be the latest in the long line of Corinne's victims. As a parting gesture, Angie piled all the clothes she had given Corinne on the floor, soaked them with gin, and tried to set them alight. When they failed to ignite she threw them out of the window instead. She stormed out of the apartment and caught the next plane out of Berlin, a 6 a.m. Pan-Am flight that happened to be going to London.

She and David were finally divorced in 1980 with Angie receiving a settlement of some $750,000 spread over ten years. David confessed that he had escaped lightly; five years later, Angie's rage was still directed at Corinne. "If she walked in now," Angie says, "I'd shoot her."

In 1977, David resumed his guidance of Iggy's career, accompanying him on a concert tour and helping to make his next album. Following Iggy's album *The Idiot*, some observers believed that David was acting as Iggy's Svengali, manipulating him as a projection of his own goals. The description so irked David that he wrote to the music press denying that he was in any sense Iggy's manager.

Tony Visconti says that David's objection was just. The friendship was a true "creative relationship", Visconti says: "they just totally inspired each other". They were also still adhering to their implicit contract to rehabilitate themselves from the ruinous excesses of Los Angeles. "They had some kind of pact or agreement to get themselves healthy," Visconti confirms.

Iggy had become a fitness fanatic, taking up weight-training and going for ten-mile walks or runs around Berlin. His emaciated physique was gradually transformed into a body-builder's torso, with rippling pectorals and bulging forearms. David was less devoted to the task. He had always smoked heavily, like his father, and was still consuming up to forty Gitanes a day. Nor had he fully renounced cocaine. But his cheeks no longer appeared so gaunt, and his frame was filling out. On a return to Switzerland he learned to ski, and worked to improve his technique with greater persistence than his crazes usually received.

Iggy's concert tour began in Britain in early March and ended in the US in mid-April. Iggy was being hailed as "the grandfather of punk", since his early kamikaze performances predated the punks' self-immolatory violence by five years. Although his act was more restrained, it attracted large British audiences, culminating in three sell-out shows at London's Rainbow Theatre. What amazed the audiences above all was to see David playing the piano out of the limelight at the rear of the stage.

David insisted on remaining in the shadows for the rest of the tour. He would only be interviewed on condition that he was asked about Iggy, and refused to answer questions about himself. The fact that he was prepared to subordinate himself to such a degree indicated how decisively he had abandoned the delusions of the MainMan years. He had also overcome two of his most damaging phobias. The tight touring schedule of the tour meant that there was no time to travel by boats and trains, and so, after an interval of almost five years, David agreed to fly again. He also returned to California, performing with Iggy in San Francisco and Los Angeles and appearing with him on the *Dinah Shore Show* in Hollywood.

When the tour ended, David and Iggy returned to Berlin to record Iggy's next album. The musicians included Carlos Alomar and Ricky Gardener from the band David had assembled for *Low*. The engineer was the impromptu cellist, Eduard Meyer, and David produced the album himself, working with impressive confidence and speed. The album was markedly different from *The Idiot* in its buoyant and harmonious mood: the images were less discordant, the lyrics more positive, emphasising success in love and relationships. One of Iggy's most evocative tracks was 'The Passenger', a celebration of the journeys Iggy and David had made around Berlin:

> . . . all of it is yours and mine
> So let's ride and ride.

447

The title track encapsulated the evolution from *The Idiot*. Now Iggy sang:

I got a lust for life.

There was a further key to Iggy's transition, and David's part in it, in the covers of the two albums. David had designed the cover for *The Idiot* following a visit to the Brücke Museum, where he had seen a painting by Erich Heckel of a young man wearing a dark suit and a white open-necked shirt, with blue eyes and dark hair falling untidily over a broad forehead. He was standing in a garden with his arms in an awkward and disjointed pose, one held rigidly across his chest, the other at an angle by his side. Painted in 1917, it was entitled *Roquairol*, the name of a character who was incurably insane in the novel *Titan* by the nineteenth-century German romantic writer Jean Paul. In fact the painting showed Heckel's colleague Ernst Ludwig Kirchner, another of the founders of the Brücke group, who was also touched by madness; and its appeal for David undoubtedly lay in the graphic picture of dementia it so clearly represented.

At first David had suggested using the painting itself on the cover, and arranged for it to be photographed at the musuem. In the end, Iggy mimicked the pose instead, facing the camera from the same oblique angle as the figure in Heckel's painting, his head and shoulders twisted in the same awkward fashion, his left arm held tautly across his chest. There can have been no greater contrast with the photograph used on the cover of *Lust For Life*. Iggy now looked into camera with a broad smile, his eyes ablaze with confidence. The message was crystal-clear: in place of the deranged figure of *The Idiot* was a picture of physical and mental health. It may have been only a coincidence, of course, but what made the symbolism even more powerful was the undeniable similarity, in their eyes, hair and clothes, between Heckel's subject and Terry.

Soon after *Lust For Life* was completed, David returned to the Hansa studio to make his next album. RCA had been as horrified by *Low* as the critics, seeing it as irredeemably "uncommercial", and an RCA executive had suggested that David should return to Philadelphia to make a follow-up to *Young Americans*. David was vindicated when *Low* reached number two in the British album charts and number eleven in the US. He retained the core of the band which had made *Low*: the rhythm section of Carlos Alomar, George Murray and Dennis Davis, together with Brian Eno and his collection of electronics, and Tony Visconti as producer.

David's choice of lead guitarist, Robert Fripp, showed that he was still prepared to be bold. Fripp was another leading exponent of experimental music. Like Eno, his origins were in rock, when he had combined the techniques of classical guitar with a screaming heavy-metal approach for his art rock group, King Crimson. He then abandoned commercial music and produced what were in effect solo concerts, playing all the instruments himself and building up his recordings over a period of months. When David telephoned him in New York, Fripp warned that he had not played the guitar for three years. "Well," David asked, "do you think you could play some hoary rock 'n' roll?" Thoroughly disarmed, Fripp agreed.

It was in the same brash mood that the group assembled at Hansa. "The spirit was incredible," says Visconti, especially when compared with the "suicidal" mood of *Low* — "David was in better shape than I'd ever seen." David again worked at a pace that left Eno open-mouthed, for he had just spent an agonising three months working on an album of his own. "I thought, Shit, it can't be this easy," Eno said.

Eno also admired Carlos Alomar for the "lightning speed" with which he produced his distinctive melodic flourishes, and was even more amazed at the barnstorming entrance of his colleague, Robert Fripp. Less than a day after leaving New York, Fripp arrived at the Hansa studio at 11 p.m. and asked to hear the material that had already been recorded. He began to play his guitar without even knowing the correct chord sequences. "By the next day, he'd finished, packed up, and gone home," said Eno. "It was an extraordinary performance."

Virtually everything used on the album, including Fripp's contribution, proved to have been a first take. All but one track, too, had evolved in the studio, with David achieving the same kind of high creative trance that had led to his best work in the past. He and Eno would stumble back to Hauptstrasse around dawn, where David would eat little more than a raw egg which he broke into his mouth before subsiding into bed. Just how he managed to produce such inspired work in that state was, said Eno, "a mystery to me".

It was still largely a mystery to David too. Ten albums after *The Man Who Sold The World*, he was still producing lyrics by the seemingly chaotic, last-minute methods that had so annoyed Tony Visconti. The saving grace was that he now recognised that this was how he worked best and had persuaded others to accept it too.

David invariably recorded the music first, and then, says Visconti, came the "very private moment" when he sought inspiration for his lyrics. He would ask everyone bar his producer and sound engineer to leave the studio – including even Corinne. As part of his ritual of preparation, he would chat inconsequentially or scan a newspaper before crying: "I've got it." The muse had arrived: David would vanish into a recess of the studio for ten to fifteen minutes and then reappear with some lines scrawled on a piece of paper which he then recorded. He used this method, once again, on the new album, with, David later stressed, "absolutely no idea of the consequences, and no preconceptions of any kind".

The album that emerged from these mysterious processes in the summer of 1977 was a masterpiece, to rank with David's finest work from the MainMan days. Not only did it bring him the unstinted admiration of his harshest critics; it also unified some of his deepest preoccupations and brought the consummation of the most profound of all his family myths.

Four of the tracks, all on side two of the album, were instrumentals that reflected the influence of Berlin and Germany as well as some of David's key themes – travelling, arriving, cities, and war. The first, 'V-2 Schneider', used electronic effects in the same way as 'Station To Station' to create an impression of an express train at high speed. Then it introduced two raucous riffs that were repeated, with variations, throughout.

The title, also sung as a chorus near the end, was in part a salute to Florian Schneider, a member of the German group Kraftwerk which David admired. There were potent wartime associations too: the V-2 was the name of the jet-propelled rockets which Hitler had launched on Britain in 1945 and which loomed large in the collective memories of those who had lived through the war; one had fallen near the Burnses's family home in Southborough. However, although noises of a rocket taking off could also be discerned, the conjunction of the two elements of the title was merely the result of the pleasing sound they made. "We just put the two words together," says Visconti.

The second instrumental, with four ponderous piano notes against a background of sombre organ sounds, had the sense of foreboding of *Low*. Eno used his "Oblique Strategies" cards to help compose the track, and the title, 'Sense Of Doubt', seemed appropriate to its gloomily introspective air. It merged into a track of an entirely different mood, 'Moss Garden', which took David back to Japan. David played the koto, a stringed instrument six feet long dating from the seventeenth century, twanging it expertly against a suitably ethereal background. Although David explained that Moss Garden was in the Japanese city of Kyoto, there were also reminders of the city of David's imaginings to be heard in the distant howls of dogs, reverberating as if through a devastated landscape.

'Moss Garden' elided into 'Neuköln', the name of one of the Turkish districts of Berlin (the correct spelling is Neukölln but the name was misspelled on RCA's album sleeve and has been consistently misspelled since). David said that he wanted to convey the deprived and isolated conditions in which he supposed the Turks lived, and it was this track that most reminded Brian Eno of the "mood of melancholy" of the Brücke Museum.

The six tracks with lyrics also struck familiar chords. In 'Sons Of The Silent Age' and 'The Secret Life Of Arabia' David continued to explore the dilemmas posed by the images of the silver screen. The first, with its nostalgic saxophone, played by David, also appeared to be an indictment of the complacency and conformity of earlier generations:

> Stand on platforms blank looks and no books

Then David suggested, as so often before, that it was impossible to decide whether their life was real or an illusion:

> They never die just go to sleep one day.

In 'The Secret Life Of Arabia', David implied that there were secrets everywhere – behind the movie screen, behind a lover's eyes; then he joined the world of dreams and fantasy himself.

> I walk through a desert song
> When the heroine dies.

'Beauty And The Beast' was familiar territory too: David making a journey – "walking down a byroad" – which recalled the journey of 'The Width Of A Circle', when he had come upon a beast or monster. This time, in a couplet recalling his telling phrase about the "angels and devils" within him, David acknowledged the different sides of his personality:

> You can't say no to
> The beauty and the beast.

The lyric briefly revisited phases of his creative past – "slaughter in the air" and "protest on the wind" — and, like the fairy tale of the title, spun childhood memories too, telling how he wanted to be good,

> Like every good boy should.

It ended on the same positive note as *Station To Station*, with David and his partner — or perhaps the two sides of himself —

> Standing on our feet.

(One phrase in 'Beauty And The Beast' demonstrated the avidity with which David collected phrases for his lyrics, as well as the dangers of interpreting them word by word. The line

> Someone fetch a priest

was originally intended to be

> Someone fuck a priest

— which happened to be Tony Visconti's favourite oath at the time. David used it in an early version of the song but changed it when he and Visconti realised that it would further outrage the sensibilities of RCA.)

'Blackout' was closely autobiographical, incorporating scenes of Angie's visit to Berlin just before Christmas, with images of mayhem:

> The weather's grim,
> Ice on the cages.

David learns that someone is "back in town"; then comes his "blackout", followed by the cry:

> Get me to a doctor's

and ending with the same plea as 'Beauty And The Beast':

> Get me on my feet.

Some reviewers interpreted the "blackout" of the title as a reference to the night in July, 1977 when New York lost its power supplies.

In fact, like 'V-2 Schneider', it also conjured wartime memories, for the blackout was part of London's air-raid precautions, when street lights were doused and windows covered with curtains or blinds.

'Joe The Lion' was based on a newspaper item about a California "performance artist" who had persuaded his friends to nail him to the roof of a Volkswagen. Sung in a resolute crescendo, to an aggressive guitar melody by Robert Fripp, it was an image rich in violent implications: only by crucifying yourself can you discover yourself. The lyric also posed David's persistent enquiry into the nature of dreams and the waking state, illusion and reality, in the repeated phrase:

> You get up and sleep.

If the paradox seemed incapable of being resolved, it served to set up the album's title track, '"Heroes"', in which all became clear. It was one of the most romantic and optimistic lyrics David ever wrote, and a triumphant reconciliation of the main themes of his creative life. It also invoked the most alluring of his family myths, the story of grandfather Jimmy Burns.

'"Heroes"' – David later said that the quote marks denoted "a dimension of irony" – told of two lovers "standing by the wall". It was the Berlin Wall, of course, with the guns of the East German guards above the lovers' heads. These symbols of oppression were also tokens of the greater odds that lovers and all other mortals face as they struggle against transience and time.

Time and transience had always been David's enemies: now they could be beaten after all. They could be defeated by the greatness lovers attain as they suppose themselves to be kings and queens of all they survey. David explained how this could be achieved in three crucial couplets. First, the lovers could attempt to defy time:

> We could steal time
> Just for one day.

By doing so, they could imagine themselves to be immortal:

> We can be Heroes
> For ever and ever.

Immortality was impossible, of course. But now, at last, David resolved the paradox that had troubled him for so long:

We can be Heroes
Just for one day.

"Just for one day" was a telling phrase which David had first used in 'The Bewlay Brothers', when at the end of the lyric he had told of slipping away – "just for one day" – to indulge in forbidden pleasures. Now he employed it again to assert the value of role-playing, which lay at the heart of his creative endeavours, to achieve one's goals. In doing so, he stepped down from his pedestal to join everyday life. No longer was he a remote rock-star, but a mere mortal striving to fulfil his potential. And if he could do so, then so could others, provided only that they believed in themselves.

Much of this David explained when the album was released. '"Heroes"', he said, was about arriving at "a sense of compassion", about "facing reality and standing up to it", about "deriving some joy from the very simple pleasure of being alive". It was also the triumphant conclusion of his constant exploration of the nature and value of love: only in partnership with others can one's destiny be achieved.

David's closest collaborators on '"Heroes"' shared the sense of excitement David felt when the track was being composed. To Visconti, as David sang the lyrics "at the top of his lungs", in a bravura style they had dubbed "the Bowie histrionics", it was evident that he had truly "conquered the low period and felt like a hero".

Although Eno had left the studio before the lyrics had been recorded, and did not know any of the titles, he had a premonition about the '"Heroes"' track, which achieved a monumental effect through its simple but subtly varying theme repeated mesmerically against a great chordal backdrop. "It sounded grand and heroic," he said later. "In fact I had that very word – heroes – in mind." When David brought him the finished recordings and Eno first heard the words "We can be heroes . . ." he shivered – out of fear, he later supposed, and a feeling of déjà-vu.

The "*Heroes*" album was released in October 1977 with a cover that contained a hidden tribute to the Brücke Museum, particularly through its resemblance to *The Idiot*, with David posing in a stylised – but undemented – manner. (It also mimicked a photograph of another painter he had come to admire, the Austrian Egon Schiele.) The more informed reviewers were unanimous in their acclaim. Angus MacKinnon in *New Musical Express* called the songs "among the most mature and trenchant Bowie had achieved", the album his "most moving performance in years". *Melody Maker* considered it the work of "an artist who is willing to take risks but is more mature and sure of his intentions and effects" and "further evidence of Bowie's genius for dramatising the more controlled experiments of others as well as for seizing the real artistic mood of the times". *Melody Maker* also chose *"Heroes"* as its album of the year. In view of the condemnation *Low* had received, here was vindication indeed.

In contrast to *Low*, David provided copious interviews in which he talked more intimately about himself than for years. He was engagingly frank about his mistakes, and diplomatically reticent about the MainMan years. He also talked about the title track and was pressed for the source of his images and ideas. He did not disappoint his audience.

David told reporters that the lyric of the '"Heroes"' track had been inspired by a scene he had observed from the Hansa studio. He described how the studio overlooks a section of the Berlin Wall, barren and forbidding, with an East German watchtower behind, manned by armed guards. In this unlikely setting, David recounted, a young man and woman – aged nineteen or twenty – would meet every lunchtime, obviously conducting an affair. "Berlin is two-thirds woods and rivers," David told *Rolling Stone*. "Why did they choose the gun turret? I assumed their motive was guilt, thus the act of heroism in facing it."

To another US reporter David added: "Maybe they felt guilty about their affair and were drawn to the spot for that reason, to cause the affair to be an act of heroism. It seemed a very seventies incident and theme. Personal survival by self-rule – that's my only positive thought on society today."

It was a perfect story, with image and moral coinciding to provide David with the ideal theme. There was just one flaw: the story is – largely – untrue.

In 1977, the only part of the Berlin Wall that could be glimpsed from Hansa's studio two, where David was working, was a narrow section about twenty metres long some 200 metres away. The rest of the wall was obscured by an ancient factory (it is even more concealed by intervening buildings today). There *was* an East German guard post, mounted on a warehouse, and it *was* in theory possible for David's two lovers to have met each day in the precise spot visible from Hansa as David described. However, the truth is – at first sight – rather more banal.

To augment his musicians, David had hired a local session singer, Antonia Maass. One day, during a break in recording, she and Tony Visconti went for a walk by the wall, holding hands as they passed the section visible from Hansa. They were the couple David had seen. "It was us," Visconti confirms. "Coco was sitting up in

455

the control room with David, and both he and Coco said, 'We saw you walking by the wall,' and that's where he got that idea from."

That was not, however, the sole source of David's inspiration. Another came from a painting at the Brücke Museum entitled *Lovers Between Garden Walls*. By Otto Mueller, it depicted a young couple kissing as they clung to each other against a background of forbidding stone walls. The circumstances of the painting added to its poignancy. Mueller painted it in 1916, intending it to represent the dreamlike embrace of two lovers in defiance of the slaughter of the first world war. Mueller was called up into the German army soon after completing it, serving on both western and eastern fronts, miraculously surviving to the end of the war. As several people who visited the Brücke with him confirm, it was a painting which appealed strongly to David.

There were further associations for David that sprang from the central place held by heroes and heroism in his family mythology. It had begun with the story of the Military Medal awarded to his grandfather, Jimmy Burns. It was passed down through the generations by Margaret Burns, to be emphasised again when her son Jimmy won the Military Medal in the second world war and she announced: "There are two heroes in the family now."

David showed that he had absorbed the family myths when he enshrined the feats and trials of his grandfather in his earliest lyrics; later, the notion of heroism came to assume the value it had for Margaret Burns. For her it was a beacon for her family to cling to as it was assailed by misfortunes from all sides. For David, the idea of heroism eventually unlocked the conundrums that had dominated his creative life.

There was another similarity between David and his grandmother in their use of a heroic myth. Both had taken a small truth and enlarged upon it, so that the story served the purposes they required. That was the path David had followed as he created myths that served both his personal and professional needs. Both the myths and the making of them became central to the fashioning of stardom, and to David's preoccupation with the paradoxes in the relationship between role-playing and reality, fantasy and truth.

The struggle to escape those paradoxes almost destroyed David before he discovered that they could be resolved. That resolution was embodied in '"Heroes"' – and it no longer mattered whether David's account of the lyric, or Margaret Burns's tale of her husband's heroism, were the literal truth. What mattered was the poetic truth they told: the capacity for greatness lies within us all.

32

Just For a Day

The notion that the greatest art is born of conflict receives support from the course of David's career in the aftermath of '"Heroes"'. Over the next eight years he never quite reached the peak of emotional intensity and thrilling resolution that '"Heroes"' had achieved. Yet his professionalism and high technical expertise, and his unceasing quest for new idioms, ensured that he held the interest of his audience, as well as vastly increasing his earnings.

Although the lyrics of his next four albums were rarely as direct and accessible as the title track of *"Heroes"*, the familiar themes still broke through. At the same time, he began to confront and explore earlier phases of his career. His restless desire for self-knowledge also led him to examine the possibilities of other media. Here, too, his old preoccupations had an uncanny way of coming to the surface, as if he were still exorcising the ghosts of the past.

In 1978 David embarked on his biggest tour ever, which began in California in March, spent six weeks in Europe in the spring and then, after a break for the summer, resumed in the southern hemisphere, with shows in Australia and New Zealand, and concluded in Japan. The bulk of his repertoire consisted of material from *Low* and *"Heroes"* but he also delved into the MainMan era to perform six numbers from *Ziggy Stardust*. His decision stemmed from the same desire to confound his audience he had shown in the MainMan days, but without the malice: "Let's do the *Ziggy* album," he announced casually to his band during rehearsals one afternoon. "That'll surprise them."

He presented the *Ziggy* tracks with a studied understatement and what one reviewer termed a "prescient irony", as if to show that the personas of the troubled past were now firmly under control. That impression was accurately conveyed in the live double album *Stage*, recorded during his Philadelphia concerts and released in September, and David reinforced it by appearing on stage in a range of cool costumes, with baggy trousers and pastel short-sleeved shirts, that were in keeping with those in fashion that summer in London, Paris and New York.

The costumes were designed by Natasha Kornilof, who met

457

David again for the first time in five years. She found him "robust and healthy – he had filled out." The critics, while praising the concerts almost without qualification, encountered the usual problem of adjusting to the new David. Was this the real David at last? Or was it David pretending to be real? *Rolling Stone* left the enigma unresolved with its headline: "Bowie Plays Himself".

David showed his impatience to move on when he returned to the studio to make his next album, *Lodger*. He used the same key personnel as on *Low* and *"Heroes"*, and explained that the three albums comprised a triptych – a word, he said, he had always wanted to use. He worked with Brian Eno again, recording the backing tracks in Montreux in September, and adding the melody and vocals in New York early in 1979.

Newcomers like the British pianist Sean Mayes found the process bewildering, particularly when Eno used his random-choice cards to determine the chord changes, and when David asked the musicians to swap instruments and insisted on using the resultant tracks, mistakes included. But Tony Visconti suspected that David was becoming bored with experimental techniques. "I don't think his heart was in *Lodger*," Visconti says. Nor would it have been possible to match the peak of *"Heroes"*. "We were still coming down," Visconti adds.

David's restlessness showed itself in the album's title and its dominant theme, that of travelling. Four of the titles on the A side told their own story: 'Fantastic Voyage', 'African Night Flight', 'Move On' and 'Red Sails', while the fifth, 'Yassassin', linked Berlin and Turkey. (Yassassin, as the album credits obligingly explained, is the Turkish equivalent of "Viva!" or "Long Live!") The lyrics were partly inspired by the immense distances David had covered during his 1978 tour, augmented by personal diversions such as the safari-style holiday he had taken in Kenya in the spring. They also reflected his fondness for travelling as a metaphor for his psychic journeys, as several lines from the lyrics made clear.

In 'Move On' he proclaimed:

> Sometimes I feel
> That I need to move on.

In 'Yassassin', by contrast, he talked of finding roots:

> I don't want to leave
> Or drift away.

Just For a Day

In 'African Night Flight' he echoed Iggy Pop with the phrase "lust for the free life", and in 'Red Sails' he recalled his fondness for outer space as the parallel of inner space:

> We're going to sail to the hinterland

The B side also had a sense of exploration, this time of new concepts in David's view of the world. The title 'Boys Keep Swinging' suggested similarities with one of his most overtly gay lyrics, 'John, I'm Only Dancing'. In fact it showed that David had revised his former chauvinist attitudes, telling, in the form of a letter to his son, of the advantages of being male:

> Luck just kissed you hello
> When you're a boy.

The next track, 'Repetition', dealt with violence against women, portraying a suburban American household where the husband relieves his frustration and envy by attacking his wife.

The track 'Look Back In Anger' showed that David was beginning to contemplate his past. It had close similarities with 'The Width Of A Circle', particularly in the appearance of an angel who speaks to David, and the parenthetical lines:

> (Waiting so long, I've been waiting so,
> Waiting so)

– which recalled the final cry of 'The Width Of A Circle',

> Waiting for you . . .

As yet, David did not draw any conclusions about what scrutiny of the past might reveal. But he did observe that the angel who was asking him to look back seemed "very sane . . . to me".

The final number, 'Red Money', which was melodically close to 'Sister Midnight' from Iggy Pop's album *The Idiot*, depicted David searching the heavens for a sign:

> Like a nervous disease

he predicted,

> It will tumble from the sky

459

It ended with the positive assertion at the core of '"Heroes"':

> Such responsibility,
> It's up to you and me.

By the time *Lodger* was released in May 1979, David had left Berlin. He was visibly upset at leaving the Hauptstrasse apartment, but had concluded it was the moment to move on. He now divided his time between London, Switzerland and New York, where he had a spacious – and fashionable – apartment in a loft building. It was economically furnished, with a blond-coloured resined dining table, eight dining chairs and his easel; a bedroom area equipped with Japanese mats, a futon mattress, a small lamp and a bookcase; and a closet containing a modest selection of suits, kimonos, and shoes.

Zowie meanwhile went to school in Switzerland, later transferring to the Scottish public school, Gordonstoun. In apparent repudiation of the excesses of the past, he was renamed Joey, and David's friends observed the attention his father gave him, as if to preserve him from the sins and omissions of David's own youth. In another act of contrition, following the use made of Zowie in the publicity of the early MainMan days, David did his best to spare him from the predations of the press.

It was in New York that David began recording his next album, *Scary Monsters*, in February 1980. It marked another stylistic advance, a fusion of elements from the European albums with a direct rock style that showed David ready to delve again into his past. Brian Eno had departed, but Robert Fripp contributed some jagged guitar solos of astonishing force. For the fourth album in succession, the producer was Tony Visconti, who had now attained a creative closeness with David that left onlookers mystified. David invited Pete Townshend to play on the track 'Because You're Young', and Visconti awaited him with some anxiety, remembering the abandon with which he smashed equipment and instruments during The Who's heyday in the 1960s. It was Townshend who was the more intimidated on seeing David and Visconti huddled together over the control panel. "You live in your own private world," Townshend told Visconti later, "and I couldn't get in."

In the album, David attempted to stand back and evaluate both his personal odyssey and his parallel ascent to stardom. Two numbers, 'Fashion' and "Teenage Wildlife', condemned the passing parade of which he had once been part, and the styles that sprouted and withered so unfailingly:

Just For a Day

One of the new wave boys,
Same old thing in brand new drag . . .

There was a personal edge to David's complaint, for the gaudiness
he had pioneered in the early 1970s was now to be seen in the
highly coloured "new-wave" styles which had followed punk; soon
sexual ambiguity would be repeated in the androgyny of short-lived
figures like Marilyn and Boy George. They were featured in the
press as if they were utterly new, and David had never existed.
Many punks, by contrast, viewed David with something akin
to veneration, respecting him as a performer who had not com-
promised his beliefs. Yet David rejected any suggestion that he
should become a guru to the new movements. He also lamented
the loss of freedom, the hounding by fans and press, that fame
entailed.

In 'Because You're Young', which he dedicated to Joey, David
offered lessons from his youth, particularly of the love between
innocents – another subdued lament, perhaps, of his affair with
Hermione. There was a similar moral in the title track, 'Scary
Monsters (And Super Creeps)', when he warned how the failure
of love could inspire fears of the monsters which dogged his
imagination and still "keep me running scared". The warning was
backed by urgent guitar work from Robert Fripp, against a rich,
pounding background from whose menace there was no
escape.

'Ashes To Ashes' was another of David's *tours d'horizon* of his
work, beginning with 'Space Oddity' and Major Tom – "I've heard
a rumour from Ground Control" – and encompassing the end of
the MainMan era and *The Man Who Fell to Earth* with "I ain't
got no money and I ain't got no hair". David reminded his audience
of his predictions of Armageddon by referring to a "glowing"
planet and recalled his period of depression when he had reached
"an all-time low". He lamented the lack of spontaneity he had
always tried to overcome:

I've never done anything out of the blue –

and referred to his fight against drugs by saying he would "stay
clean tonight".

The fight, apparently, went on, for he sometimes succumbed to
the "little green wheels" that still pursued him.

Tony Visconti saw 'Ashes To Ashes' as an attempt by David to
dispose of the past. He interpreted the lines

461

Ashes to Ashes funk to funky
We know Major Tom's a junkie

as a bid to disown his first hit, 'Space Oddity', by which he had been defined for so long. In fact, the lyric was more an attempt to face David's past than to discard it. With considerable humility, David told *New Musical Express* that 'Ashes to Ashes' represented "a continuing, returning sense of inadequacy over what I have done". He showed his old mischievousness in calling it an "ode to childhood" and confessed to subversive pleasure in trying to smuggle drug-taking references past his old adversary, the BBC. The overall message was repeated in the final coda which asserted that the past could not be eradicated:

You better not mess with Major Tom.

The same moral could be drawn from the opening and closing track, 'It's No Game'. David told Visconti that he had written it when he was sixteen, and it contained clear notes of adolescent rebellion and alienation. It also declared that it was necessary to confront the past: far "scarier", David proposed, to "draw the blinds on yesterday". Finally David warned that no matter how frivolous the business of stardom might appear:

It's no game.

Having come close with *Scary Monsters* to matching the fervour and commitment of *"Heroes"*, David did not release another album for almost three years. That hiatus resulted in part from RCA's continuing bewilderment over how to market his albums. The despair RCA had felt on receiving *Low*, with its apparent neglect of all commercial imperatives, had been partly relieved by *"Heroes"*, but deepened again by *Lodger*. Now David had provided them with another album which seemed to defy analysis. Nor was RCA in the best position to give the album the attention it deserved, for the corporation had been going through its customary traumas, with executives toppling like trees in a gale.

In 1975, the founder's son, Robert Sarnoff, was deposed in a boardroom coup. Within a year his successor, Anthony Conrad, was forced to resign when it was discovered he had filed no tax returns for five years. Although Conrad's replacement, Edgar Griffiths, survived into 1980, his record was far from impressive. In ten years, RCA's earnings from sales were halved, and its profit margin on a turnover of $67 billion was less than $2 billion, or just 2 per cent.

There had been turmoil at Records and Tapes too, as personal fortunes rose and fell. Several executives, including Mort Hoffman, were disposed of for having been aligned with Rocco Laginestra. Astonishingly, Laginestra's career was not finished. Most people had supposed that his post of financial assistant to Edgar Griffiths, then executive vice-president, was a sinecure. When Griffiths unexpectedly became president, Laginestra found himself in a position of power again, and helped to remove Ken Glancey for the crime of having taken over from him as head of the records division. Glancey's successor, Lou Couttelenc, lasted less than a year before being replaced by Bob Summer, who lost no time on taking office in sacking several senior members of the division's promotions department.

Although Mel Ilberman was still *in situ*, his attention was frequently diverted by Tony Defries, who badgered RCA constantly for prompt payment of his share of David's revenue, and even began a law-suit against the company for alleged breach of contract in 1978. Defries nonetheless shared RCA's bleak view of David's 'European' albums, feeling that he had failed to take advantage of the commercial opportunities that he, Defries, had helped to create.

When *Scary Monsters* was finally released in September 1980, David, according to Tony Defries, had finally fulfilled the clause of his RCA contract requiring him to supply twelve albums. At that time, too, David's settlement agreement with Defries had just under two years to run. When it expired he would no longer have to earmark a proportion of his new earnings to MainMan or Fleur Music, the company Defries had set up to receive his revenue from David's lyrics. 'It was named after his daughter, who would, presumably, one day inherit Defries's unending share of David's royalties.'

David's timing was immaculate. He waited until the settlement agreement had run its course before embarking on his new album. And when he did, it was with a new record company, EMI. According to Mel Ilberman, who finally left RCA at almost the same time, David was swayed less by EMI's advance – worth, by most accounts, $17m for a five-year contract – than by his dissatisfaction with RCA. "I was told that David did not want to continue with RCA in the US," Ilberman says. He believes that RCA hoped to renew the contract but David would not do so unless US territory was excluded. "He wasn't happy with RCA in the US," Ilberman adds. "He wanted to go." David signed his contract with EMI's New York subsidiary, Capitol Records, on

January 27th, 1983, and began his next album, to be called *Let's Dance*, within a matter of days.

Outside RCA, the man most angered by David's behaviour was Tony Visconti. David had asked him to produce the album but then showed his failing of retreating from confrontations, with the slight compounded by Corinne. Shortly before he was due to fly to New York, Visconti asked David's New York office for his tickets. "Coco said, 'I'll phone back,'" Visconti says. "Coco phoned back and couldn't even tell me. She phoned my secretary and said, 'Well, he's met someone else.'"

The "someone else" was Nile Rodgers, a black American guitarist who had made some of the wittiest – and most profitable – contributions to disco music with his group, Chic, before becoming a producer with performers of the stature of Diana Ross and Paul Simon. But although *Let's Dance* had an exuberance that reflected David's new freedom, it was also more predictable than any album he had made in a long time. Its enthusiastic upbeat bordered on the monotonous, while it lacked the element of ironic fabrication that had contributed to the appeal of *Young Americans*. It left the impression that David was using his professionalism to steer him through his first offering to his new record company, producing a sophisticated disco sound that made the album accessible to an American audience on first hearing.

The lyrics were the least inventive since *Young Americans*: their mood was mostly of unqualified optimism, displayed in unaffected love songs such as 'Modern Love', 'China Girl', 'Let's Dance', and 'Without You'. The main exception was 'Ricochet', with its images, drawn from David's expressionist days, of "tramlines, factories, pieces of machinery", and its echoes of *Diamond Dogs* and '1984', set against the assertion that it was not "the end of the world". There was an intriguing personal note in David's sudden glimpse of parents who hold their children to their "heaving chests" and make promises they cannot keep; "for who," he asks, "can bear to be forgotten?"

Let's Dance was released barely a month after David had completed it, and it did everything that EMI hoped. EMI claimed that it was their fastest-selling album since the Beatles' *Sergeant Pepper*, and the single, 'Let's Dance', was top of the UK hit parade for a month, giving David only his third British number one, following the reissue of 'Space Oddity' in 1975 and 'Ashes To Ashes' in 1980. The album sold one million copies in the US in three months, compared with the ten million copies his RCA albums had sold in the previous ten years.

Above: Jules Fisher with model of the 'Diamond Dogs' set – at that time, the most extravagant set in rock history.

RCA's Ken Glancey: "why are we spending all this money?"

Mark Ravitz, set-designer for the 'Diamond Dogs' and 'Serious Moonlight' tours.

RCA's Mel Ilberman: a backstop to Rocco.

David in *The Man Who Fell to Earth* – too close to the truth for comfort.

David in title role of *Just a Gigolo* – "my 32 Elvis movies in one."

David as shark in *Yellowbeard*.

David as bicentenarian in *The Hunger*.

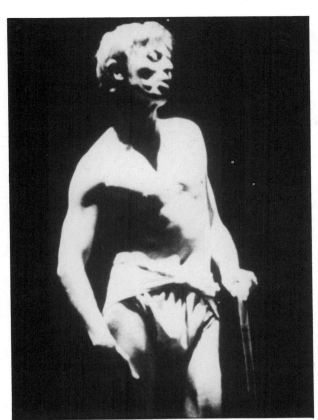

David on stage in *The Elephant Man*, winning even Broadway's praise.

David and Japanese counterpart Ryuichi Sakamoto on set for *Merry Christmas, Mr Lawrence*: chilling echoes of David's family past.

Number 155, Hauptstrasse, West Berlin: home – on the first floor, above the motor spares shop – for two years.

Berlin's Hansa Studio (right) – the "hall by the wall" – with Berlin Wall, and East Berlin beyond.

The extraordinary Iggy Pop, David's partner in an implicit pact for health.

Soon after the album was released, David embarked on the 'Serious Moonlight' tour – the phrase was from the title track, 'Let's Dance' – his first tour in five years. It brought prodigious success: it attracted 250,000 people in Britain and record receipts in North America, topped by the $1 million it earned each night in Edmonton and Vancouver. The New York critics were breathless with admiration: "a flawless show", said the *Post*; David, said the *Times*, was "subtler, more ferocious, more moving and more dazzling" than ever before.

The tour also brought reunions with figures from David's past. David commissioned Mark Ravitz, architect of the *Diamond Dogs* set, to design the backdrop for the concert stage. Ravitz, who was summoned to Switzerland at forty-eight hours' notice, produced a stunning series of light columns against a background of muted colours that, Ravitz felt, reflected the monochromes of Lake Geneva on an overcast day.

The other reunion was with Earl Slick, which required far greater magnanimity on David's part. After his disenchantment over the *Diamond Dogs* tour, Slick had been caught up in the crossfire of David's battle with Michael Lippman. Slick was quoted in the press as saying that David was "power mad", "convinced he can rule the world", and "probably the most selfish man I have ever met in my life". He had also publicly vowed never to work with David again.

Less than a week before the start of the tour, David fired his original lead guitarist, Stevie Ray Vaughan, following a row over money. Pat Gibbons, who was now sharing the management tasks with David and Corinne, called Slick and asked if he could step in. With some misgivings, Slick agreed, and spent four days closeted in a hotel room – "with coffee pot after coffee pot" – listening to tapes of David's music and doing his best to learn his part. "But that," says Slick, "didn't scare me close to meeting David again."

Slick flew to Brussels, where the tour was to start, and checked into the hotel where David and the other musicians were staying. "I was thinking, Shit, it's going to be more than embarrassing," Slick says. "But he called me up on the phone personally which is something he never used to do. I was nervous but he came in, I got a big hug and he sat down. He looked amazing, great, fit . . . It was just like nothing had ever happened."

A week later David and Slick talked through the aftermath of the 'Diamond Dogs' tour, and concluded that their disagreement had all been a misunderstanding. "Everything was straightened out," Slick says. He found the tour far happier than in 1974.

"There was communication," he says; "a lot of joking and fooling around. In the old days I'd show up at the theatre and literally not see him except for the stage part. Now it's back to normal. Business as usual."

When the tour finished, David made his next album for EMI, *Tonight*. He recorded it in Canada and produced it himself, in collaboration with Derek Bramble and Hugh Padgham. Whereas *Let's Dance* had showed his mastery over disco, *Tonight* proved his versatility in virtually any musical style he cared to try. He sang 'Don't Look Now' – one of his joint compositions with Iggy Pop – in perfect imitation of a West Indian dub record, with the refinement of a US funk big-band backing. 'God Only Knows' was rendered in the "wall of sound" manner of the Righteous Brothers. A mosaic of other styles followed, from 'Tumble And Twirl', an exercise in Latin-American and salsa rhythms, to 'Tonight', where he partnered Tina Turner in a number with the power of classic rhythm and blues, informed by a reggae beat.

The album was significant in another way. For the first time since *Pin-Ups* in 1973, it contained few original lyrics. Three of the nine were by other writers; four had been written with Iggy Pop; only two were solely David's own. Only one, 'Loving The Alien', offered any personal insights to rival the profundities of his earlier works. It told of crusaders riding to war in Arabia in order to spread a message of Christian love, a paradox to match David's inner life and his endeavours to come to terms with the monster he had feared and portrayed. The paradox was also embodied in the title and in the musical setting, a hyper-romantic string arrangement that belied the violence of the lyric.

'Loving The Alien' apart, *Tonight* left the impression that David was using his technical mastery to carry him through a comparative lack of personal involvement. Ironically, as with *Young Americans*, that same technical mastery brought him substantial sales, and helped broaden his public appeal. As a further irony, he was coming perilously close to the status of popular entertainer in the sense that Ken Pitt had aimed for and that David had once so despised. David was assisting that process in another way: while he was determined to maintain his artistic integrity, he still craved the approval of his peers, and enjoyed the feeling that he had reached the highest echelons of the show-business world.

An early landmark was the television duet of 'The Little Drummer Boy' which David recorded with Bing Crosby in 1977, and was released as a single in 1982. In short order thereafter, David narrated Prokofiev's *Peter and the Wolf* for RCA, appeared on the

Johnny Carson Show, and fraternised with superstars from Debbie Harry to Tina Turner. In 1983, he received the ultimate accolade: a cover story in *Time* magazine. Although *Time* made much of David's former status as media symbol of sexual ambiguity and the quest for identity, it suggested that he had found a new role: the teenage rebel who makes good.

Even now, however, David's old preoccupations somehow kept breaking through. His reputation as a performer with talents far beyond those of most rock-stars was boosted by his ventures into cinema, theatre and television, goals he had long talked of and was now able to fulfil. He won the admiration of his new colleagues for his devotion to the task in hand. But what was uncanny was the extent to which, as with *The Man Who Fell to Earth*, his roles mirrored his own concerns, for time and again he was cast as the misfit, outcast, or alien.

David's first film after *The Man Who Fell to Earth* was *Just a Gigolo*, which was made in Berlin shortly before he began his 1978 concert tour. The parallels with his family mythology were extraordinary: David played a German army officer who proclaims "heroism is my destiny" and who dreams of glory in the first world war. He becomes a hero by mistake, after being confused with a French soldier who had performed an act of gallantry. When he returns to Berlin he cannot find a job and makes a living as a gigolo plying his trade along the Kurfürstendamm. He is hailed as a hero again after he is killed in the crossfire of street battles between communists and fascists. Even though he had refused to take part, the fascists canonise him as their martyr.

David accepted the challenge of true acting – as opposed to the directed performance he had given in *The Man Who Fell to Earth* – with uncomplaining dedication. His colleagues had wondered whether a rock-star would prove to be a prima donna, but he soon won their respect. "He was incredibly disciplined and always prepared," says the film's assistant director, Eva Maria Schoenecker. "He never interfered, there were no quarrels, he was very friendly." One scene called on him to lie in the snow wearing little more than a pair of shorts and he was shivering violently after the inevitable series of retakes. "There was no complaining, nothing," she says. "He just did it."

The film was not a success. Its director, the British actor David Hemmings, had persuaded Marlene Dietrich to make her first cinema appearance in twenty years, but she declined to leave Paris and so all her scenes had to be shot separately. Both cast and crew became disillusioned as filming went on, with Hemmings himself commenting after one scene: "Let's commit this to celluloid before it gets any better." After it had been savagely cut by its distributors, Hemmings summarised the storyline as: "Boy comes back from the war, meets a lot of people, dies."

David virtually disowned the film too, calling it – in reference to Elvis Presley's propensity for making abysmal films – "my thirty-two Presley movies rolled into one". He endorsed that view in private when he told his cousin Kristina not to bother to see it.

David's next venture was on to the stage: the Broadway stage, at that. The play was *The Elephant Man*, the poignant story of the grotesque Victorian hunchback John Merrick, who was rescued from a freak-show circus by a compassionate London surgeon. It had already been playing in the US for several months when its director, Jack Hofsiss, asked David to take over in the title role.

To research his part, David visited the tiny museum at the London Hospital in Whitechapel where Merrick had been treated, and was immensely moved on seeing a model church that Merrick had made from cardboard, imagining his struggles to fold and glue it down. But the physical problems of the part were immense. In contrast to the film version, where the actor John Hurt was able to use elaborate make-up, David had only his body to work with. He profited greatly from his experience in mime and also had the advantage of a lean and supple physique with which to achieve a suitably deformed posture.

After previews in Denver and Chicago in August 1980, the play opened at the Booth Theatre on West 45th Street, by Broadway, on September 23rd. New York's notoriously unsmiling theatre critics were impressed. *Village Voice* wrote that David "commands the stage"; *Theater Magazine* talked of his "exquisite stillness" and "physical precision"; the *New York Times* commended his blend of innocence and scepticism; and Linda Winer of the *Daily News* praised his "restrained, tortured eloquence".

Then came an event which shook David to the core. On December 8th, 1980, John Lennon was assassinated in the doorway of the Dakota building by Central Park. Not only had David lost a friend and colleague, but Lennon's death awoke all his fears that he would be shot dead on stage. The management of the Booth Theatre took every precaution, and David used the warren of passageways that run beneath Broadway to vary his exit each night. But when Hofsiss asked David if he would extend his contract beyond January 1981, he declined.

David's next new departure was into television, when the BBC

asked him to take the leading role in Bertolt Brecht's play, *Baal*. It
was another part perfectly suited to David, particularly as he had
recorded a number of the songs Brecht composed with Kurt Weill.
Brecht's "alienation effect" appealed naturally to David, as did
Brecht's use of lyrics to comment on the action of his plays, and
the expressionist overtones of Brecht's early works, including *Baal*
itself.

Once again David was required to play the misfit and outcast:
a wandering poet adrift in Germany who abuses his women, takes
malevolent delight in the misfortunes of others, and becomes an
outlaw after stabbing his best friend in a brawl. David plunged
into the spirit of the part by allowing his hair to become greasy
and lank and growing a straggling beard. While many of his fans
found it hard to recognise David when *Baal* was broadcast on
March 2nd, 1982, his aunt Pat was in no doubt. He looked, she
said, exactly as he did during his "hippie" days at Haddon Hall.

After *Baal*, David returned to the cinema to make a science-
fiction movie, *The Hunger*, acting alongside the French star Catherine Deneuve. Both were vampire-lovers condemned to eternal life
and pretending, by nice irony, to be two of the "beautiful people"
of New York. Since David's main scene required him to age 200
years in a matter of hours, he spent a large proportion of his time
being made up. He told Kristina that the film was not worth seeing,
apart from the quality of the camera work.

Then came a film and a part of which he was proud at last. It
also struck closer to home, in its themes, than ever before. *Merry
Christmas, Mr Lawrence* was based on the story by the South
African writer, Laurens van der Post, which drew heavily on his
experiences as a Japanese prisoner-of-war between 1943 and 1945.
David was first attracted to the film by his interest in Japan and
his liking for the work of the Japanese director, Nagisa Oshima,
particularly his erotic masterpiece, *Ai No Corrida*. He finally agreed
to take part after reading van der Post's novel.

The film brought another reunion, this time with the scriptwriter
Paul Mayersberg, who had worked on *The Man Who Fell to Earth*.
Mayersberg found David a changed man. "The neurosis has largely
left him," Mayersberg said, "or gone into another area of his life
that I don't see. He doesn't seem quite as tense or hyper . . . He
has become more physical rather than mental – health rather than
disease has become interesting to him."

David's character, Major Jack Celliers, was another outsider,
both as a prisoner-of-war and as an isolated figure within that
group, a New Zealander among mostly British prisoners. The film

also had a homosexual theme, for the Japanese camp commander, played by the Japanese pop-star, Ryuichi Sakamoto, was strongly attracted to Celliers.

When David had worked on *The Man Who Fell to Earth*, the unsettling parallels between his real and screen lives were already in the script. Since the script of *Merry Christmas, Mr Lawrence* had not been completed when David agreed to take part, Paul Mayersberg was able to fashion it to suit his personality. "I definitely wrote with him in mind," Mayersberg says. "I wrote the lines thinking of David saying them and I semi-consciously changed things to suit him."

Mayersberg added a mime scene which had not been in van der Post's story because he knew David would love to play it. He included a lot of "Englishness" which he knew David would enjoy and wrote one particular line with undertones David would relish. When Celliers is being interrogated about his background he tells his captors: "My past is my business."

The most extraordinary similarity of all, which featured even more strongly in the novel than in the film, concerned Celliers's younger brother, who was a cripple. Celliers had been racked with guilt ever since he had failed to save his brother from a degrading initiation ceremony at school. He joined the army in the hope of assuaging his guilt through an act of heroism, but had ended up a captive instead. When the prisoners were threatened with mass punishment, he at last saw a way of purging his remorse. At an assembly of the entire camp, Celliers stepped forward and kissed the Japanese commander squarely on both cheeks. For that he was executed, while the rest of the prisoners were spared.

Although Mayersberg knew something about Terry, he and David never discussed the parallels between the story and David's own life. David merely told Mayersberg that he enjoyed making the film and was, in general, "very happy". The *New York Times* considered him the outstanding figure in the film, "mercurial and arresting", and outshining even the respected British actor, Tom Conti. David told Kristina she should definitely go to see it.

It was a British journalist, Hilary Bonner, who prised the most revealing remarks from David about *Merry Christmas, Mr Lawrence*, when she interviewed him at the Cannes Film Festival. "I found in Celliers all too many areas of guilt and shortcomings that are part of me," David told her. "I feel tremendous guilt because I grew so apart from my family. I hardly ever see my mother and I have a step-brother I don't see any more. It was my fault we grew apart and it is painful – but somehow there's no going back."

David's remarks were significant for confirming that the parts he played helped him to handle his own deepest feelings. They also comprised his frankest admission that he felt guilty over his family and confirmed that he was attempting to come to terms with his past, as his lyrics had indicated.

David had begun to explore his past in other ways. When in London he had taken to dropping in on his first manager Les Conn and talking over old times. He had met Dave Hadfield and asked him what he remembered of their days in the Kon-rads. He had also asked his staff to try to gather memorabilia of his early days. His London press officer offered a Croydon photographer, Richard Ward, £500 for the negatives of pictures showing him playing the saxophone with the Kon-rads. (Ward declined.)

Calvin Mark Lee agreed to lend David his own collection of photographs and tapes, forwarding them to him through his New York office. (Despite several appeals, Lee did not get them back.) David also began to trace his father's ancestral tree, later claiming that his family's true name was Bernstein, and that they were partly Jewish. He asked Kristina about their shared past, confessing that he could not remember anything before he was seven or eight.

But there was one respect in which David was not ready to face his fears, one person whom it was still too dangerous to confront. That was Terry.

As David had confessed, his relationship with his family had indeed followed a tortuous path. Soon after his father died, his mother Peggy had moved to a modern flat in Albemarle Road, Beckenham. David furnished the flat, and Peggy decorated it so lavishly with his albums, presentation discs and photographs that her sister Pat told her it looked like "a shrine". But David had almost no contact with his mother during the end of the MainMan period and the following year in Los Angeles.

Peggy complained assiduously to both Pat and Kristina of David's neglect: the last six years, she said, had been "hell". At times she blamed Angie, who had "done her utmost to cause unpleasantness between David and myself"; at times she blamed Defries. Peggy also thought that David had changed from the "gentle person" she had known to the "unhappy and guilty" figure she saw interviewed on television from Los Angeles. And she complained that David was not providing for her financially. "I owe David nothing," she said. "He owes *me*, when one looks at everything."

David's monthly standing order to his mother had in fact been cancelled when he broke from Defries, although it was later restored. But in July 1975, Peggy telephoned the *New Musical Express* to make her complaints public. When a bemused Charles Shaar Murray arrived at Albemarle Road, she told him: "My husband and I *lived* for David," adding that she only wanted him to show "a little care and sympathy".

When the interview was published, David was furious, and instructed his mother never to speak to the press again. Peggy complied. From then on David saw more of her, sending her air tickets so that she could visit him in Switzerland or the US. She became more proud of him than ever, puzzling strangers – and embarrassing companions – by announcing that she was David's mother.

For more than ten years, however, David did not see Terry at all.

In 1976, Terry and his wife Olga, together with their cats, moved from their bed-sitting room in Beckenham to a larger flat on a tidy council estate in neighbouring Penge. Although they remained happy for a time, the marriage was doomed. Olga had to contend with the hostility of Terry's family: she believed that they "thought only of their selves", and was convinced that Pat hated her.

The greatest problems stemmed from Terry's refusal to acknowledge that he was seriously ill. He neglected to take the drugs prescribed for him when he attended Cane Hill as an out-patient, and went missing from home. Sometimes he returned dirty and confused, and Olga would tell him to go back to Cane Hill. His condition worsened; he drank heavily and became violent. Eventually Olga began divorce proceedings and won a court order banning him from their home. In 1981, Terry was re-admitted to Cane Hill.

Terry was distraught. According to Pat, he loathed Cane Hill from the moment he returned. "I've lost everything," he told her. Pat detested Cane Hill too, from the all-pervading smells of disinfectant and boiled food, to the queues of patients shuffling forward in the canteen, and the hopelessness she saw in their faces. Terry was all too aware of the dangers of becoming institutionalised, accentuated by the heavy drugs he was prescribed, and was desperate to get out before it was too late. But who could help him?

Olga, his greatest comfort, had left him. Although Peggy visited him, she would insist, when Pat challenged her, that there was nothing further to be done. Pat's ability to help was limited because of the strains her devotion to Terry brought to her marriage. At first her husband Tony took her to Cane Hill by car from their North London home. But Tony came to feel that Terry was making excessive demands on Pat. Pat was sensitive to the charge, recognising that Terry tried to appeal to her sympathies when she visited him: "He tried to get under my skin because he needed attention," she says.

Then, during a visit, Tony accused Terry of expecting too much, and Terry punched him. Tony refused to visit Cane Hill again, and so Pat had to travel there by train. Certainly there was no prospect of Terry ever coming to stay with her, as Pat had once hoped. That left David.

To Terry, David remained a hero. He continued to obtain David's records from RCA and proudly told his fellow-patients whenever he heard David on the radio. David now became the focus of Terry's hopes, and he told Pat: "He could get me out of here." Pat shared Terry's view: she felt that David's money could at least ensure that Terry was settled in a private nursing home with better facilities and medical care; maybe it could even help find a cure. She wrote to David several times to ask for his help, but never received a reply.

By the summer of 1982, Terry's despair had deepened. On June 2nd, he threw himself out of a second-storey window at Cane Hill in an apparent attempt at suicide, which, he later made clear, was directed principally at Olga. He succeeded only in fracturing an arm and a leg and was taken to Mayday General Hospital in Croydon.

Pat was appalled, and decided to follow Peggy's example by calling in the press. She telephoned the *Sun* and turned all her anger on David. She complained that he was "callous and uncaring" and added that it was "time his fans knew the other side of David Bowie – and time he faced up to his responsibilities".

Pat's public intervention caused consternation in the family. Kristina's view, which she voiced after talking to David and Peggy, was that there was nothing more that could be done for Terry; "pouring money in," she said, would not help. She also believed that Pat was using Terry to "get back" at Peggy.

But Pat's complaint produced the response she had hoped for. Two weeks later, David visited Mayday Hospital. He kissed Terry and presented him with a radio-cassette player, a collection of books and some cigarettes. They discussed their childhood and then, so Terry related afterwards, David told Terry he would get him out of Cane Hill.

Terry was overjoyed. "He was full of life and happy after that,"

Pat says. "David's visit meant everything to him." Terry, she says, had at last received the acknowledgment from David he craved and a return of the love he felt. He also believed implicitly that David would be able to rescue him from Cane Hill. "He spent the next few months waiting, waiting for the promise to be fulfilled," Pat says. "He kept saying to me, 'When is David going to do it?'"

Pat now became Terry's most constant visitor, making the arduous cross-London journey once a month, leaving home at 10.30 a.m. and returning in the early evening. She brought Terry food and laundry, and drink or cigarettes from Tony. In the summer she took picnics which they ate in the hospital grounds, sometimes overlooking a cricket match. They recalled their childhood in Southborough, and Terry would ask: "Why can't we go back to how it was then?" Terry also talked of the days when he had sung in a pub, and said that with luck he could have had a professional career. Once he asked Pat: "Am I better-looking than David?"

"Of course you are," Pat replied.

According to Pat, Terry gradually realised that David's promise was not going to be fulfilled. When she visited him early in 1984 she found him markedly more despondent, particularly over his suicide attempt which had left him with a withered right arm and a limp. "I'm useless," he told Pat. "I can't look after myself any more." A patient was shouting incoherently nearby and Terry complained: "This is what I have to put up with."

Pat tried to reassure him, telling him: "I know what you're going through."

"No you don't," Terry replied. "I'm in bloody hell."

Pat telephoned Peggy after her visit and there was a furious row. Pat accused Peggy of ignoring Terry's arm. She also complained that Peggy did not visit Terry enough and that when she did, so Terry had told her, she only talked about David.

Peggy rejoined by claiming that Pat had always been "over-emotional" and accused her of having an "unhealthy attitude" towards Terry. That, Pat said later, was "a disgusting thing to say – my sister is the most tactless person I have known. She's hurtful and bitter and twisted." She and Peggy have not spoken to each other since.

In the summer of 1984, Terry's spirits were lifted when he had a brief, passionate affair with a woman who had been admitted to Cane Hill. "He had this extraordinary charisma," the woman, who has asked to be called Janet, later recalled. "He had this extraordinary kindness towards patients – he always talked so lovingly about them, he was so sweet. One of the most marvellous things is that the patients are kinder and nicer in their own way than a lot of people in the outside world. They'll give their last cigarette away at the end of the day. It's that tremendous binding strength which always comes through when I think of Terry."

Whereas Terry invariably complained to Pat about Cane Hill, to Janet he showed a far happier disposition. "I think he was trying to make the most of what we had together," Janet says. She remembers him cheering other patients with his singing and laughter; if asked what he was laughing about, Terry would reply that his "voices" had just said something funny.

Terry's doctors had warned Janet that he could be violent, but she never saw that side of him. They listened to records of Terry's favourite singers, Johnny Mathis, Nat King Cole and Frank Sinatra, as well as Tchaikovsky's First Piano Concerto, and poetry records which Janet enjoyed. On "lovely sunlit days" they would go to the pub, where Terry liked to talk to the barman. They made love among the wild flowers in the hospital grounds, Janet cradling Terry's head in her arms afterwards. "He desperately needed love," Janet believed. Terry would tell her: "I love you more than anyone else in the whole world, apart from my ex-wife, and I nearly gave my life for her."

Terry often talked about David. "He adored him," Janet says. "His face glowed with pride and he rushed to tell me every time he heard David on the radio or television." Terry would say: "I heard David again – isn't he marvellous?" He also told Janet that he believed David could get him out of Cane Hill, and that he had written to David several times without receiving a reply. "Terry's disappointment was cruelly acute," Janet says. "But I never heard him say one word against David."

Their affair ended when Janet was discharged from Cane Hill although she continued to write to him and send him money. Terry's appearance deteriorated rapidly, and sometimes when Pat visited he was soporific from drugs. In September, Pat found him depressed because Peggy had not been to visit him. He was scruffy and unshaven, his locker was untidy, and he had left cigarette butts strewn on the window-ledge by his bed.

"I'm going to stay here, aren't I?" he asked.

"You don't know what'll turn up," Pat told him. "Something might happen, you've got to have faith."

"How long do I have to have faith for?" Terry replied. "I'm going to die in here."

On November 5th, 1984, Terry's forty-seventh birthday, Peggy visited him for the first time in seven months. As Terry later recounted, Peggy gave him a present and then talked, as usual, about David. She also told Terry that David was going to help her to move to a new flat in Bromley.

"What about me, Mum?" Terry asked. "When am I going to get out of here?"

Peggy told Terry there was nothing she could do. "That's David's business," she added.

When Pat next visited Terry, on December 15th, she was relieved to see how neatly he was dressed: just like the old Terry, she thought. He was wearing a fresh white shirt open at the neck, his hair had been cut, and she was struck by how handsome he was. But he was more gloomy than ever. He told her about Peggy's visit and said: "I can't face another year in here." Once again Pat tried to encourage him, insisting that "something might turn up". Terry told Pat that he intended to go to see Olga. Pat tried to dissuade him, but Terry said: "She's my wife, and I love her."

When Pat got up to leave, Terry kissed her gently on both cheeks, and said: "Thank you for everything you have done." When Pat looked back, Terry seemed utterly dejected. "He looked very hurt, there was something indescribable about his face. I wanted to turn back but there was no point, there was nothing I could do."

After breakfast on December 27th, Terry left the hospital grounds and walked the short distance to Coulsdon South station. He waited until a train approached and lay across the rails. Just before the train reached him, he twisted between the rails and the train passed overhead. Railwaymen found him staggering along the track and he was escorted back to the hospital. He spent five days in a locked ward, lying shocked and exhausted in bed and taking no interest in his surroundings.

When Pat heard what had happened, she wrote to Terry and promised that she would come to see him again soon. She never had the chance to do so. Early on the morning of January 16th, 1985, Terry walked down the snow-covered driveway of Cane Hill, left the grounds, and once again crossed the road to Coulsdon South station. There he passed through the ticket barrier and took up a position at the end of the platform. Shortly after midday, the Littlehampton–London express came into sight, travelling towards the station at 70 m.p.h. Terry waited until the train was 200 yards away and then stepped down carefully from the platform into its path. He looked briefly towards the train, there lay down with his neck on the rail and his head turned away. The driver of the train saw Terry and braked immediately. He had no chance of stopping in time and all eight carriages passed over Terry's body before coming to a halt half a mile down the track.

Terry's funeral was held at Elmers End cemetery, a windswept burial ground in Beckenham, nine days later. Of the dozen or so people who gathered in the cemetery's spartan chapel, most were fellow-patients from Cane Hill. From Terry's family, only Peggy and Pat were there. During the brief, functional ceremony the two sisters sat on opposite sides of the chapel and ignored each other throughout.

David remained in Switzerland, where he had been when he learned of Terry's death. He sent a basket of pink and yellow roses and chrysanthemums to the funeral, together with a card that read: "You've seen more things than we could imagine but all these moments will be lost, like tears washed away by the rain. God bless you – David."

Later, Kristina said that David had not attended the funeral because he feared the attentions of fans and the press. She believed that Terry's plight had preyed on David's mind but that he had been unable to decide what he could do.

She also told how, ten days before Terry died, she had dreamed that she and Terry were in a ballroom together. Terry was wearing a suit as if to attend a funeral: whose funeral, Kristina did not know. There was a telephone on a table, and both she and Terry were waiting for a call from David. It never came.

After introducing '"Heroes"', David at first remains close to the microphone, straddling it as he sings the first verse, momentarily seeming a solitary figure even as Wembley's audience of 70,000 wills him on. Then, as the sweat from the camera lights glistens on his forehead, he pulls the microphone towards him and plucks it from its stand. He steps to the front of the stage and cups his ear to encourage the audience to repeat the chorus, then quietens them as he repeats the line himself, in almost a whisper:

We can be Heroes.

As David embarks on the verse that describes the meeting of the lovers by the wall, he takes his saxophonist, Clare Hurst, by the hand and ducks as the imaginary bullets of his lyric fly overhead. Then he builds a new crescendo, jumping down to the catwalk again, side-stepping his way along it, pointing into the audience,

477

clapping his hands above his head. The outstretched arms have become a forest, reaching to the far side of the stadium, swaying rhythmically to his call. He returns to the stage for a final chorus:

> *I said,*
> *We can be Heroes*
> *Just for a day.*

There is a noise like breaking surf as applause crashes round him. He tosses his head back and then bends forward to offer a deep bow, in ritual acceptance of the audience's acclaim. He takes the microphone to tell them: "You are the heroes of this concert." Then he walks off the stage, a performer in complete control, an artist at the peak of his power.

David Bowie's Discography

SINGLES

The vicissitudes of David's career, particularly as he searched for a record company that would take him to success in the 1960s, make attempts at a complete singles discography a complex business. For the most comprehensive listings, Bowiephiles are advised to consult the magazine *Record Collector*, which chronicles every known variation in sleeve and record-size. One example demonstrates the devotion with the magazine does so. In 1973, Decca reissued David's 1967 single, The Laughing Gnome/The Gospel According To Tony Day (giving David a surprise hit when the reissue went to number six in the hit parade). For a long time, collectors believed the two issues to be identical. *Record Collector* has now established a crucial difference: on the original version, Decca's 'matrix number', DR 39798, to be found above the catalogue number, is upside down; on the reissue, it is printed correctly.

What follows is a list of first British releases and principal reissues.

Liza Jane/Louie Louie Go Home
Vocalion POP V 9221   June 1964
Credited as Davie Jones with The King Bees
Reissued as Decca F 13807 in September 1978

I Pity The Fool/Take My Tip
Parlophone R 5250   March 1965
As The Manish Boys (David not credited)

You've Got A Habit Of Leaving/Baby Loves That Way
Parlophone R 5315   August 1965
As Davy Jones (The Lower Third not credited)

Can't Help Thinking About Me/And I Say To Myself
Pye 7N 17020   January 1966
As David Bowie with the Lower Third

Do Anything You Say/Good Morning Girl
Pye 7N 17079   April 1966

I Dig Everything/I'm Not Losing Sleep
Pye 7N 17157   August 1966

Rubber Band/The London Boys
Deram DM 107   December 1966

The Laughing Gnome/The Gospel According to Tony Day
Deram DM123   April 1967
Reissued in 1973 (see introduction above)

479

Love You Till Tuesday/Did You Ever
Have a Dream
Deram DM 135   July 1967

Space Oddity/The Wild Eyed Boy
From Freecloud
Philips BF 1801   July 1969
Issued in mono and stereo versions

The Prettiest Star/Conversation Piece
Mercury MF 1135   March 1970

Memory Of A Free Festival, Parts I
and II
Mercury 6052 026   June 1970

Holy Holy/Black Country Rock
Mercury 6052 049   January 1971

Changes/Andy Warhol
RCA 2160   January 1972

Starman/Suffragette City
RCA 2199   April 1972

John, I'm Only Dancing/Hang On To
Yourself
RCA 2263   September 1972

Do Anything You Say, I Dig
Everything/I'm Not Losing Sleep,
Can't Help Thinking About Me
Pye 7NX 8002   October 1972
Reissue of four of the 1966 Pye singles

The Jean Genie/Ziggy Stardust
RCA 2302   November 1972

Drive-In Saturday/'Round And 'Round
RCA 2352   April 1973

Life On Mars/The Man Who Sold the
World
RCA 2316   June 1973

Sorrow/Amsterdam
RCA 2424   September 1973

Rebel Rebel/Queen Bitch
RCA LPBO 5009   February 1974

Rock 'N' Roll Suicide/Quicksand
RCA LPBO 5021   April 1974

Diamond Dogs/Holy Holy
RCA APBO 0293   June 1974

Knock on Wood/Panic In Detroit
RCA 2466   September 1974

Young Americans/Suffragette City
RCA 2523   February 1975

The London Boys/Love You Till
Tuesday
Decca F 13579   May 1975
Reissued in March 1981

Fame/Right
RCA 2579   August 1975

Space Oddity/Changes, Velvet
Goldmine
RCA 2593   September 1975

Golden Years/Can You Hear Me
RCA 2640   November 1975

TVC 15/We Are the Dead
RCA 2682   April 1976

Suffragette City/Stay
RCA 2726   July 1976

Sound And Vision/A New Career In A
New Town
RCA PB 0905   February 1977

Be My Wife/Speed Of Life
RCA PB 1017   June 1977

"Heroes"/V-2 Schneider
RCA PB 1121   September 1977

Beauty And The Beast/Sense Of Doubt
RCA PB 1190   January 1978

Breaking Glass/Ziggy Stardust, Art
Decade
RCA BOW 1   November 1978

I Pity The Fool, Take My Tip/You've
Got A Habit Of Leaving, Baby Loves
That Way
EMI NUT 2925   April 1979
*EP reissue of the 1965 Parlophone
singles*

Boys Keep Swinging/Fantastic Voyage
RCA BOW 2   May 1979

D.J./Repetition
RCA BOW 3   June 1979

John, I'm Only Dancing (Again)/John,
I'm Only Dancing
RCA BOW 4   December 1979

Alabama Song/Space Oddity
RCA BOW 5   February 1980

Ashes To Ashes/Move On
RCA BOW 6   August 1980

Fashion/Scream Like A Baby
RCA BOW 7   October 1980

Scary Monsters (and Super
Creeps)/Because You're Young
RCA BOW 8   January 1981

Up The Hill Backwards/Crystal Japan
RCA BOW 9   March 1981

Under Pressure (*Queen with David
Bowie*)/Soul Brother (*Queen only*)
EMI 5250   October 1981

Wild Is The Wind/Golden Years
RCA BOW 10   November 1981

The Baal Hymn, Remembering Marie
A/Ballad Of The Adventurers, The
Drowned Girl, The Dirty Song
RCA BOW 11   February 1982
*EP with release timed to 'Baal' on
BBCtv*

Cat People (Putting Out Fire)/Paul's
Theme
MCA MCA 770   April 1982
From the film Cat People – *Bowie on
A-side only*

Peace On Earth, Little Drummer Boy
(*duets with Bing Crosby*)/Fantastic
Voyage
RCA BOW 12   November 1982

'Fashions'   November 1982
*A set of ten reissues, released by RCA
in a limited picture-disc edition of
25,000 copies:*

Space Oddity/Changes, Velvet
Goldmine   BOWP-101
Life On Mars/The Man Who Sold The
World   BOWP-102
The Jean Genie/Ziggy
Stardust   BOWP-103

Rebel Rebel/Queen Bitch   BOWP-104
Sound And Vision/A New Career In A
New Town   BOWP-105
Drive-In Saturday/'Round And
'Round   BOWP-106
Sorrow/Amsterdam   BOWP-107
Golden Years/Can You Hear
Me   BOWP-108
Boys Keep Swinging/Fantastic
Voyage   BOWP-109
Ashes To Ashes/Move On   BOWP-110

Let's Dance/Cat People (Putting Out
Fire)
EMI EA 152   March 1983

China Girl/Shake It
EMI EA 157   May 1983

*In June 1983, RCA reissued 20 singles
in new picture-sleeves:*

Drive In Saturday/Round And Round
                BOW 501
Life On Mars/The Man Who Sold The
World   BOW 502
Rock 'N' Roll Suicide/Quicksand
                BOW 503
Diamond Dogs/Holy Holy
                BOW 504
Knock On Wood/Panic In Detroit
                BOW 505
Young Americans/Suffragette City
                BOW 506
Fame/Right   BOW 507
Golden Years/Can You Hear Me
                BOW 508
TVC 15/We Are The Dead
                BOW 509
Sound And Vision/A New Career In A
New Town   BOW 510
Be My Wife/Speed Of Life
                BOW 511
Beauty And The Beast/Sense Of Doubt
                BOW 512
"Heroes"/V-2 Schneider   BOW 513
Rebel Rebel/Queen Bitch   BOW 514
The Jean Genie/Ziggy Stardust
                BOW 515
D.J./Repetition   BOW 516
John I'm Only Dancing/Hang On To
Yourself   BOW 517

Space Oddity/Changes, Velvet
Goldmine   BOW 518
Sorrow/Amsterdam   BOW 519
Breaking Glass/Ziggy Stardust, Art
Decade   BOW 520

Modern Love/Modern Love (*live
version*)
EMI EA 158   August 1983

White Light White Heat/Cracked
Actor
RCA 372   October 1983

Blue Jean/Dancing With The Big Boys
EMI EA 181   September 1984

Tonight (*duet with Tina
Turner*)/Tumble And Twirl
EMI EA 187   November 1984

This Is Not America/This Is Not
America
EMI EA 190   January 1985
with Pat Metheny group

Loving The Alien/Don't Look Down
EMI EA 195   May 1985

Dancing In The Streets/Dancing In The
Streets
EMI EA 204   August 1985
*The 'Live Aid' single, performed with
Mick Jagger*

Absolute Beginners/Absolute
Beginners
Virgin VSG 838   March 1986

Underground/Underground
(*instrumental*)
EMI EA 216   June 1986

ALBUMS

The discography of Bowie's albums is less formidable than his
singles, but is still complicated by virtue of the range of companies
he has recorded for, and the new collections that have been issued as
his renown has grown. This list is complete to June 1986. All the
first-release albums are described in the text of the book, and can be
found in the index. Some notes are included on the reissues.

DAVID BOWIE
Deram DML 1007 (mono), SML 1007
(stereo)   June 1967

Side One
Uncle Arthur
Sell Me A Coat
Rubber Band
Love You Till Tuesday
There Is A Happy Land
We Are Hungry Men
When I Live My Dream

Side Two
Little Bombardier
Silly Boy Blue
Come And Buy My Toys
Join The Gang
She's Got Medals

Maid Of Bond Street
Please Mr. Gravedigger

DAVID BOWIE
Philips SBL 7912   November 1969

Side One
Space Oddity
Unwashed And Somewhat Slightly
   Dazed
Letter To Hermione
Cygnet Committee

Side Two
Janine
An Occasional Dream
The Wild Eyed Boy From Freecloud
God Knows I'm Good
Memory Of A Free Festival

Discography

Reissued as SPACE ODDITY by RCA
(LSP 4813) in November 1972

THE WORLD OF DAVID BOWIE
Decca PA 58 (mono), SPA 58 (stereo)
March 1970

Side One
Uncle Arthur
Love You Till Tuesday
There Is A Happy Land
Little Bombardier
Sell Me A Coat
Silly Boy Blue
The London Boys

Side Two
Karma Man
Rubber Band
Let Me Sleep Beside You
Come And Buy My Toys
She's Got Medals
In The Heat Of The Morning
When I Live My Dream

Reissued by Decca (SPA 58) in 1973

THE MAN WHO SOLD THE
WORLD
Mercury 6338 041   April 1971

Side One
The Width Of A Circle
All The Madmen
Black Country Rock
After All

Side Two
Running Gun Blues
Saviour Machine
She Shook Me Cold
The Man Who Sold The World
The Supermen

Reissued by RCA (LSP 4816) in
November 1972

HUNKY DORY
RCA SF 8244   December 1971

Side One
Changes
Oh! You Pretty Things
Eight Line Poem

Life On Mars
Kooks
Quicksand

Side Two
Fill Your Heart
Andy Warhol
Song For Bob Dylan
Queen Bitch
The Bewlay Brothers

THE RISE AND FALL OF ZIGGY
STARDUST AND THE SPIDERS
FROM MARS
RCA SF 8287   June 1972

Side One
Five Years
Soul Love
Moonage Daydream
Starman
It Ain't Easy

Side Two
Lady Stardust
Star
Hang On To Yourself
Ziggy Stardust
Suffragette City
Rock 'N' Roll Suicide

ALADDIN SANE
RCA RS 1001   April 1973

Side One
Watch That Man
Aladdin Sane (1913–1938–197?)
Drive-In Saturday
Panic In Detroit
Cracked Actor

Side Two
Time
The Prettiest Star
Let's Spend The Night Together
The Jean Genie
Lady Grinning Soul

PIN-UPS
RCA RS 1003   October 1973

Side One
Rosalyn
Here Comes The Night

I Wish You Would
See Emily Play
Everything's Alright
I Can't Explain

Side Two
Friday On My Mind
Sorrow
Don't Bring Me Down
Shapes Of Things
Anyway, Anyhow, Anywhere
Where Have All The Good Times
    Gone?

DIAMOND DOGS
RCA APL1 0576   April 1974

Side One
Future Legend
Bewitched, Bothered and Bewildered
Diamond Dogs
Sweet Thing
Candidate
Sweet Thing (reprise)
Rebel Rebel

Side Two
Rock 'N' Roll With Me
We Are The Dead
1984
Big Brother
Chant Of The Ever Circling Skeletal
    Family

DAVID LIVE
RCA APL2 0771 (double album)
                    October 1974

Record One, Side One
Rebel Rebel
Moonage Daydream
Sweet Thing

Side Two
Changes
Suffragette City
Aladdin Sane
All The Young Dudes
Cracked Actor

Record Two, Side One
When You Rock 'N' Roll With Me
Watch That Man
Knock On Wood
Diamond Dogs

Side Two
Big Brother
The Width Of A Circle
Jean Genie
Rock 'N' Roll Suicide

YOUNG AMERICANS
RCA RS 1006   March 1975

Side One
Young Americans
Win
Fascination
Right

Side Two
Somebody Up There Likes Me
Across The Universe
Can You Hear Me
Fame

IMAGES
Deram DPA 3017/3018 (double
album)   May 1975
*A reissue of the 1967 Deram album,
together with other tracks which
Decca had previously declined to
release*

Record One, Side One
Rubber Band
Maid Of Bond Street
Sell Me A Coat
Love You Till Tuesday
There Is A Happy Land

Side Two
The Laughing Gnome
The Gospel According to Tony Day
Did You Ever Have A Dream
Uncle Arthur
We Are Hungry Men
When I Live My Dream

Record Two, Side One
Join The Gang
Little Bombardier
Come And Buy My Toys
Silly Boy Blue
She's Got Medals

Side Two
Please Mr. Gravedigger
The London Boys

Karma Man
Let Me Sleep Beside You
In The Heat Of The Morning

STATION TO STATION
RCA APL1 1327   January 1976

Side One
Station To Station
Golden Years
Word On A Wing

Side Two
TVC 15
Stay
Wild Is The Wind

CHANGESONEBOWIE
RCA RS 1055   May 1976
A compilation of some of David's most
"commercial" tracks

Side One
Space Oddity
John, I'm Only Dancing
Changes
Ziggy Stardust
Suffragette City
The Jean Genie

Side Two
Diamond Dogs
Rebel Rebel
Young Americans
Fame
Golden Years

LOW
RCA PL 12030   January 1977

Side One
Speed Of Life
Breaking Glass
What In The World
Sound And Vision
Always Crashing In The Same Car
Be My Wife
A New Career In A New Town

Side Two
Warszawa
Art Decade
Weeping Wall
Subterraneans

"HEROES"
RCA PL 12522   October 1977

Side One
Beauty And The Beast
Joe The Lion
"Heroes"
Sons Of The Silent Age
Blackout

Side Two
V-2 Schneider
Sense Of Doubt
Moss Garden
Neuköln
The Secret Life Of Arabia

PETER AND THE WOLF
RCA RL 12743   May 1978

Side One
Prokofiev's Peter And The Wolf,
narrated by David Bowie

Side Two
Britten's Young Person's Guide To The
Orchestra

STAGE
RCA PL 02913
(double album)   September 1978

Record One, Side One
Hang On To Yourself
Ziggy Stardust
Five Years
Soul Love
Star

Side Two
Station To Station
Fame
TVC 15

Record Two, Side One
Warszawa
Speed Of Life
Art Decade
Sense Of Doubt
Breaking Glass

Side Two
"Heroes"
What In The World
Blackout
Beauty And The Beast

LODGER
RCA BOW LP 1   May 1979

Side One
Fantastic Voyage
African Night Flight
Move On
Yassassin
Red Sails

Side Two
D.J.
Look Back In Anger
Boys Keep Swinging
Repetition
Red Money

SCARY MONSTERS (AND SUPER
CREEPS)
RCA BOW LP 2   September 1980

Side One
It's No Game (No. 1)
Up The Hill Backwards
Scary Monsters (And Super Creeps)
Ashes To Ashes
Fashion

Side Two
Teenage Wildlife
Scream Like A Baby
Kingdom Come
Because You're Young
It's No Game (No. 2)

THE BEST OF BOWIE
K-Tel NE 1111   December 1980
*A shrewdly-judged package that
reached number three in the album hit
parade*

Side One
Space Oddity
Life On Mars
Starman
Rock 'N' Roll Suicide
John, I'm Only Dancing
The Jean Genie
Breaking Glass
Sorrow

Side Two
Diamond Dogs
Young Americans

Fame
Golden Years
TVC 15
Sound And Vision
"Heroes"
Boys Keep Swinging

DON'T BE FOOLED BY THE NAME
PRT DOW 1 (10" LP)   January 1981
The three 1966 Pye singles reissued

Side One
I'm Not Losing Sleep
I Dig Everything
Can't Help Thinking About Me

Side Two
Do Anything You Say
Good Morning Girl
And I Say To Myself

Reissued by Pye as THE EARLY
YEARS (12" LP – PR NL 37122) in
1984
Reissued by Showcase as RARE
TRACKS (SH LP 137) in January 1986

ANOTHER FACE
Decca TAB 17   March 1981
Decca repackaging the Deram material

Side One
Rubber Band
The London Boys
The Gospel According To Tony Day
There Is A Happy Land
Maid Of Bond Street
When I Live My Dream
Liza Jane

Side Two
The Laughing Gnome
In The Heat Of The Morning
Did You Ever Have a Dream
Please Mr. Gravedigger
Join The Gang
Love You Till Tuesday
Louie Louie Go Home

CHANGESTWOBOWIE
RCA BOW LP 3   November 1981
A further package from RCA

Side One
Aladdin Sane

Oh! You Pretty Things
Starman
1984
Ashes To Ashes

Side Two
Sound And Vision
Fashion
Wild Is The Wind
John, I'm Only Dancing (Again)
D.J.

**THE MANISH BOYS/DAVY JONES
& THE LOWER THIRD**
Charly Records CYM 1   October 1982
*Reissue of EMI NUT 2925 EP as 10"
LP*

Side One
I Pity The Fool
Take My Tip

Side Two
You've Got A Habit Of Leaving
Baby Loves That Way

BOWIE RARE
RCA PL 45406   December 1982
*A collection of assorted B sides and
singles, some long unavailable*

Side One
Ragazzo Solo, Ragazza Sola
'Round And 'Round
Amsterdam
Holy Holy
Panic In Detroit
Young Americans

Side Two
Velvet Goldmine
Helden
John, I'm Only Dancing (Again)
Moon Of Alabama
Crystal Japan

LET'S DANCE
EMI America AML 3029   April 1983

Side One
Modern Love
China Girl
Let's Dance
Without You

Side Two
Ricochet
Criminal World
Cat People (Putting Out Fire)
Shake It

GOLDEN YEARS
RCA BOW LP 4   August 1983

Side One
Fashion
Red Sails
Look Back In Anger
I Can't Explain
Ashes To Ashes

Side Two
Golden Years
Joe The Lion
Scary Monsters (And Super Creeps)
Wild Is The Wind

A SECOND FACE
Decca TAB 71   August 1983
Yet another Decca repackage

Side One
Let Me Sleep Beside You
Sell Me A Coat
She's Got Medals
We Are Hungry Men
In The Heat Of The Morning
Karma Man

Side Two
Little Bombardier
Love You Till Tuesday
Come And Buy My Toys
Silly Boy Blue
Uncle Arthur
When I Live My Dream

FAME AND FASHION
RCA PL 84919   April 1984

Side One
Golden Years
TVC 15
"Heroes"
D.J.
Fashion
Ashes to Ashes

Side Two
Space Oddity
Changes
Starman
1984
Young Americans
Fame

LOVE YOU TILL TUESDAY
Deram BOWIE 1   April 1984
The album of Ken Pitt's ill-fated
promotional film, coinciding with its
video release.

Side One
Love You Till Tuesday
The London Boys
Ching-A-Ling
The Laughing Gnome
Liza Jane
When I'm Five

Side Two
Space Oddity
Sell Me A Coat
Rubber Band
Let Me Sleep Beside You
When I Live My Dream

ZIGGY STARDUST – THE MOTION
PICTURE
The soundtrack of the Pennebaker
film of the "retirement" concert at
Hammersmith in 1973
RCA PL 84862 (double album)
                          October 1983

Record One, Side One
Hang On To Yourself
Ziggy Stardust
Watch That Man
The Wild Eyed Boy From Freecloud

Side Two
All The Young Dudes
Oh! You Pretty Things
Moonage Daydream
Space Oddity

Record Two, Side One
My Death
Cracked Actor
Time
The Width Of A Circle

Side Two
Changes
Let's Spend The Night Together
Suffragette City
White Light/White Heat
Rock 'N' Roll Suicide

TONIGHT
EMI America DB1   September 1984

Side One
Loving The Alien
Don't Look Down
God Only Knows
Tonight

Side Two
Neighbourhood Threat
Blue Jean
Tumble And Twirl
I Keep Forgettin'
Dancing With The Big Boys

THE COLLECTION
Collector CC SLP 118 (double album)
                           January 1986

Record One, Side One
The Laughing Gnome
Rubber Band
Love You Till Tuesday
Maid Of Bond Street
Sell Me A Coat

Side Two
In The Heat Of The Morning
Karma Man
Please Mr. Gravedigger
She's Got Medals

Record Two, Side One
Silly Boy Blue
Join The Gang
Did You Ever Have A Dream
The Gospel According To Tony Day
I'm Not Losing Sleep

Record Two, Side Two
I Dig Everything
Can't Help Thinking About Me
Do Anything You Say
Good Morning Girl
And I Say To Myself

DAVID BOWIE, THE ACTOR

Between 1967 and 1986, David appeared in fourteen films, ranging from promotional documentaries to full-length features. His parts varied from a performance lasting approximately half a second in *The Virgin Soldiers* to full starring roles. He also performed on BBCtv and on the stage. In this comprehensive list, the date by each film shows the year it was released, unless otherwise indicated in the text. The list includes soundtrack albums which contain David Bowie numbers.

THE IMAGE   1967
Negus-Fancey/Border Films, director Michael Armstrong.
Starring: David Bowie, Michael Byrne.
An "art-house" movie in which David performs ably against the odds. Rarely seen or reviewed – one critic termed it "banal" – until released as a video (NME V002) in 1984.

PIERROT IN TURQUOISE   1967–1968
Starring: Lindsay Kemp, David Bowie, Jack Birkett.
David's first appearance as live actor, with events behind the scenes proving as dramatic as those on-stage. The premier was staged at the Oxford Playhouse on December 28th, 1967. There were further performances at the Rosehill Theatre, near Whitehaven, from January 3rd to 5th, 1968, at the Mercury Theatre, Notting Hill Gate, from March 5th to 16th, and at the Intimate Theatre, Palmers Green, from March 26th to 30th.

THE PISTOL SHOT   First broadcast: May 20th, 1968
BBCtv, producer Michael Bakewell
Starring: John Ronane, Peter Jeffrey, Ann Bell, Ilona Rodgers
In this story by Alexander Pushkin, adapted for television by Nicholas Bethell, David appeared briefly as a periwigged dancer, partnered by Hermione Farthingale. The back-stage drama – with Lindsay Kemp in a starring role – was once again more powerful than David's televised performance. Neither David nor Hermione were mentioned in the programme credits listed in *Radio Times*. The broadcast was repeated on December 24th, 1968.

THE VIRGIN SOLDIERS   1969
Columbia Pictures, director John Dexter.
Starring: Hywel Bennett, Nigel Patrick, Lynn Redgrave, Nigel Davenport.
In this film of Leslie Thomas's novel, only David's most devoted fans claim to be able to spot him as he flashes past the camera during a bar-room brawl.

LOVE YOU TILL TUESDAY   1969
Producer Ken Pitt, director Malcolm Thomson.
Starring: David Bowie, with Hermione Farthingale and John Hutchinson.
A revealing vehicle for David's precocious talents, made in 1969, finally released as a video (Polygram 040313) in 1984.

Alias David Bowie

ZIGGY STARDUST   1973
Producer and director D. A. Pennebaker.
Starring: David Bowie and the Spiders From Mars.
The film of David's "farewell" concert at Hammersmith in July, 1973, capturing,
despite technical deficiencies, the aura of that extraordinary occasion. Rarely seen
until released on video (TVJ 90 2113 2) in 1983. Also released as a double album
– see discography.

THE MAN WHO FELL TO EARTH   1976
British Lion Films, director Nicholas Roeg.
Starring: David Bowie, Rip Torn, Candy Clark, Buck Henry.
In the opinion of his friends, David, heavily guided by Roeg, was barely acting in
the part of the alien who arrives on earth; the distracted, skeletal figure seen on
film was painfully close to the true David in the aftermath of MainMan. The
London critic Michael Billington wrote: "Once you have pierced through its
glittering veneer, you find only another glittering veneer underneath." Was he
referring to the film – or to David?

JUST A GIGOLO   1978
Leguan Films, director David Hemmings.
Starring: David Bowie, Marlene Dietrich, Kim Novak, David Hemmings, Maria
Schell, Kurt Jurgens.
While David's colleagues admired his uncomplaining professionalism in the face
of trying circumstances, Hemmings' account of a war-hero returning to Berlin
was a dismal flop. Hemmings blamed the producers for slicing swathes out of his
film. *Time Out* commented: "it would be kinder to overlook it," and David, who
called it his "thirty-two Presley movies rolled into one," agreed.
Soundtrack album (Jambo records, JAM 1) contains 'David Bowie's Revolution
Song', by David Bowie and Jack Fishman, with David on vocals.

THE ELEPHANT MAN   1980–1981
Producer Richard Crinkley, director Jack Hofsiss.
David's stage debut set him a stern test, especially as the play, about the Victorian
hunchback John Merrick, was already a success when he took over from the
British actor Philip Anglim in the title role. He appeared in the play at the Denver
Centre of the Performing Arts from July 29th to August 3rd, 1980; at the
Blackstone Theatre, Chicago, from August 5th to 31st; and at Broadway's Booth
Theatre from September 23rd, 1980 to January 3rd, 1981. He won praise from
the toughest New York critics, *Variety* going so far as to predict that as an actor,
"Bowie has the chance to achieve legitimate stardom".

CHRISTIANE F.   1981
Solaris Film Productions, director Ulrich Edel.
Starring: Natja Brunckhorst, Thomas Haustein, Jens Kuphal. David appears as
himself.
Alternatively titled *Wir Kinder Vom Bahnhof Zoo – We Children from Zoo
Station* – the film told of prostitution and heroin addiction among young
teenagers in West Berlin. David made a deal with the producers whereby he
appeared as himself at a Berlin concert, although his performance was shot in
New York and edited into film of another concert.
The soundtrack album (RCA RCALP 3074), issued in April 1981, contains: V-2

Schneider, TVC 15, "Heroes"/Helden, Boys Keep Swinging, Sense of Doubt, Station To Station, Look Back In Anger, Stay, Warszawa.

BAAL   First broadcast: February 2nd, 1982
BBCtv, director Alan Clarke.
Starring: David Bowie
Another *tour de force*, with David proving his versatility as the wandering poet in the title role of Brecht's demanding play, while also putting his proficiency as singer to good use with his performance of Brecht's musical commentary. In an attempt to compete with Sir Laurence Olivier in John Mortimer's *Voyage Around My Father* on the rival channel, the BBC retitled the play *David Bowie in Baal*. The move backfired: with the critics, mostly unsympathetic to Brecht, comparing David against Olivier, David was the inevitable loser.

THE HUNGER   1983
MGM, director Tony Scott.
Starring: David Bowie, Catherine Deneuve, Susan Sarandon.
The story of two vampire lovers transported to modern New York called on David to look beautiful and age fast; he managed both tasks, but won little praise. The *Observer* dismissed the film as "one of the most incoherent and foolish pictures of recent months."

MERRY CHRISTMAS, MR LAWRENCE   1983
Palace Pictures, director Nagisa Oshima.
Starring: David Bowie, Ryuichi Sakamoto, Tom Conti.
As the New Zealand soldier taken captive by the Japanese in World War Two, this was David's most accomplished acting performance yet; by no coincidence, perhaps, it was also the part that had the closest parallels with his troubled family background, as David himself was to confess. The *Sunday Times* called it "a cocktail of saleable ingredients rather than genuine cinema" but for the Bowie fan it gained in appeal, like his previous film performances, for the resonances it struck with David's own personality and past.

YELLOWBEARD   1983
Orion Pictures, director Mel Damski.
Starring: Graham Chapman, Peter Cook, Marty Feldman, Eric Idle, Madeline Kahn, James Mason, John Cleese.
David agreed to play a walk-on part – as 'the Shark', with a fin strapped to his back – in this pirate spoof after meeting the Monty Python team on a beach in Mexico. The *Monthly Film Bulletin* condemned the "atrocious script, haphazard direction, and embarrassing performances from all concerned."

JAZZIN' FOR BLUE JEAN   1984
Picture Music, director Julian Temple.
Starring: David Bowie.
David's first encounter with the man who directed the Sex Pistols' epic film *The Great Rock and Roll Swindle* produced a contemporary gem. Bowie played both insider and outsider, as the insecure rock-star and the fan who is constantly turned away at the door, thereby skilfully exploiting his own media personas.

INTO THE NIGHT   1985
Universal, director John Landis.
Starring: Jeff Goldblum, Michelle Pfeiffer, Irene Papas
David takes a minor cameo role, as a small-time British crook who meets a sticky
end, in an American film that aroused little attention.

ABSOLUTE BEGINNERS   1986
Orion Pictures, director Julien Temple.
Starring: Eddie O'Connell, Patsy Kensit, James Fox, David Bowie.
David takes another cameo role in a bold and imaginative British musical tribute
to the 1950s, based on the street-life novel by Colin MacInnes. This time director
Julien Temple felt that David's previous film roles were "remote, mood
characters trading on to the myth of the earlier David Bowie" and was
determined to liberate him from the ghosts of the past. The part still had ironic
echoes: David plays Vendice Partners, the smooth ad-man whose mid-Atlantic
patter keeps giving way to authentic South London patois. It was a witty and
polished performance, with David revealing new talents as a tap-dancer. Most
reviewers, aware of its importance for the future of the British film industry, were
generous to the film, the strongest complaint being that it was like an extended
pop-video.
The soundtrack album was released – in March 1986 – in two versions: a single
album (Virgin V 2386) containing David's tracks 'Absolute Beginners' and
'That's Motivation', and a double album (Virgin VD 2514) which also included
his rendition of the 1958 hit, 'Volare'.

LABYRINTH   1986
Henson Associates/Lucas Film, director Jim Henson
Starring: David Bowie
In a film described by its producers as "a musical fantasy comedy", David plays
Jareth, leader of the Goblins, with the most of the cast consisting of puppets.
David wrote the title song and four other numbers.

VIDEOS

Characteristically, as in other fields, David Bowie has been a pioneer of promotional films and videos, showing the same skill as in music for enlisting the medium's most talented practitioners. Even his very first promotional film, Ken Pitt's 'Love You Till Tuesday' (see previous section), now appears as a project substantially ahead of its time. Three years later came an equally innovative group of films commissioned by Tony Defries and shot by the photographer Mick Rock: 'The Jean Genie', 'Space Oddity', 'John, I'm Only Dancing', made in 1972, and 'Life On Mars', made in 1973. According to Rock, however, some were made in unpropitious circumstances: 'Space Oddity' was "whacked off" at RCA's New York studios in half a day because David was due to sail for Britain that afternoon. MainMan offered 'John, I'm Only Dancing' to BBCtv's *Top of the Pops* but the BBC preferred to use its own film in which David did not appear.

David's output over the next five years remained somewhat sporadic, the numbers including 'Rebel Rebel', made as a promotional film by Dutch television, with David sporting a pirate's eye-patch; 'Young Americans'; 'Fame'; 'Golden Years', excerpted from the US *Soul Train* series; and – from the 'Berlin' period – 'Be My Wife', '"Heroes"', 'Blackout', and 'Sense Of Doubt', in which he performed further mime movements, influenced by the paintings at the Brücke museum, he had represented on the album cover of *"Heroes"*.

In 1979, David joined forces with the precocious young director, David Mallet, to make three imaginative videos to promote the *Lodger* album. In 'D.J.' he played a disc-jockey who wrecks his own studio; in 'Look Back In Anger', borrowing from *The Picture of Dorian Gray*, he acts the artist peering at himself in a mirror; and in 'Boys Keep Swinging' he audaciously appears in three different types of drag. David worked with Mallet again on 'Ashes To Ashes', 'Fashion', and 'Scary Monsters' in 1980; and in 1983 on 'Let's Dance', 'Modern Love', 'China Girl', the last achieving a minor *succès de scandale* with its sequence of David and his lover embracing naked in the surf in the manner of Burt Lancaster and Deborah Kerr in *From Here to Eternity* (Lancaster and Kerr, of course, were clothed).

In 1984, David turned to Julian Temple to make 'Jazzin' For Blue Jean' (see previous section) which was released in its full twenty-minute length and in a shorter version. A ninety-minute video of the "Serious Moonlight" tour, recorded at Vancouver (Media M441) was also released that year, and a further video of the Far East segment of the tour, entitled 'Ricochet', appeared in 1985. That year he also returned to David Mallet to make a video for 'Loving The Alien' and in 1986 he worked with a new director, Steve Barron, on a video of his latest single release, 'Underground'.

By then, David was taking a relaxed view of himself and his work, explaining, on a marathon BBCtv history of music videos, "My most important point is that I can entertain very well," and adding: "I now find I'm very comfortable as an actor and entertainer without too much all-encompassing stuff to say." Even so, his most recent videos still gave cause for thought, for they focused on some of the unsettling imagery that continued to surface in David's work.

'Loving The Alien' showed David in a surrealist set, reflecting on images of himself, watching duelling warriors, being engulfed in flames, and being submerged by an electronic nightmare. 'Underground' was even more disturbing: as David is sucked into a subterranean labyrinth of cellars and passageways, images of former personas – Ziggy, Baal, Diamond Dogs, Space Oddity among them – flash through his mind, and then he encounters the old monsters of his dreams and nightmares, beasts and hobgoblins all. It served to give dramatic impact to the coded messages of his lyric, with his lament that he felt "trapped and lonely", his plea of "Get me out of here," and the line, ambiguous and intriguing to the last, "No-one can blame you for walking away."

Acknowledgments

This book could not have been written without the help of a large number of people. First and foremost we should like to thank the interviewees who provided much of our information – although our conclusions are, of course, our own. They are:

Kristina Amadeus
Jaime Andrews
Gui Andrisano
Pat Antoniou
Tony Antoniou
Fay Baldry
Toni Basil
Dave Bebbington
Kenny Bell
Bill Berks
Madeleine Berks
Rodney Bingenheimer
John Blake
Trevor Blythe
Mel Bush
Angie Bowie
Derek Boyes
Gustl Breuer
Brian Brough
Jimmy Burns
Woolf Byrne
John Cambridge
Sheila Cassidy
Dudley Chapman
Ava Cherry
Leee Black Childers
Colin Clark
Leslie Conn
Tom Conti
Ray Cook
Jayne County
Mary Carol Culligan

Doug Davie
Dai Davies
Lily Defries
Tony Defries
Stanley Diamond
Gus Dudgeon
Brian Duffy
Shirley Dunmall
John Eager
John Edwards
Derek Fearnley
Stann Findelle
Mary Finnigan
Jules Fisher
Kim Fowley
Owen Frampton
Frederick French
Esther Friedmann
Stella Gall
Mike Garson
John Garwood
Stuey George
Dana Gillespie
Ken Glancey
Geoff Gold
Alan Gonzalez
Bob Grace
Billy Gray
Nigel Green
Dave Hadfield
Geoff Hannington
Nigel Harrison

John Hills
Mort Hoffman
Mechtild Hoppe
Ian Hunter
John Hutchinson
Mel Ilberman
Dick James
Annette Jones
Michael Kamen
Dennis Katz
Lindsay Kemp
Brian Kinchy
Natasha Kornilof
Harry Laing
Phil Laing
Phil Lancaster
Brian Lane
Pierre Laroche
Amanda Lear
Calvin Mark Lee
Michael Lippman
Robin McBride
Melanie McDonald
Clayton McDowell
Vivienne McDowell
Ralph Mace
Keith Macmillan
Toby Marris
Greg Martin
Lori Mattix
Paul Mayersberg
Sean Mayes

495

Gerrit Meijer
Eduard Meyer
Chérie Moore
Pat Mountford
Bob Musel
Laurence Myers
Ron Oberman
Brooks Ogden
David Orme
Linda Palermo
Will Palin
Zazie de Paris
Neal Peters
Fran Pillersdorf
Ken Pitt
Mark Ravitz
Jim Rismiller
Graham Rivens
Mick Rock

Christine Rogers
Mick Ronson
Suzi Ronson
Ronnie Ross
Myron Roth
Sarah Sapherson-Hine
Knut Schaller
Eva Maria Schoenecker
Marilyn Schwartz
Jane Scott
Ken Scott
Hal Shaper
Jane Sinclair
John Sippel
Earl Slick
Daniel Sloane
Mike Stanford
Ray Stevenson
Denis Taylor

Leslie Thomas
Malcolm Thomson
George Tremlett
Mike Vernon
Tony Visconti
Artur Vogdt
Pat Wadsley
Richard Ward
Ted Ward
Michael Watts
Mick Wayne
Mike Weller
Mick Whitehead
Randall Wixen
Woody Woodmansey
Chris Wright
Olav Wyper
Alan Yentob
Tony Zanetta

For memories and the history of Southborough, we are indebted to Argile Skinner, Doug Bennett, George and Kathleen Paine, and the inhabitants of Pinewood Court.

We should also like to thank the following for their advice and practical help:

John Allanson
Sheila Baird
Margaret Barratt
Tom and Tosh Barron
Paul Blencowe
Colin Boone
Pat Braybrookes
Alastair Brett
Mike Bristow
Mick Brown
Kevin Cann
Chris Charlesworth
Terry Charman
Alan Cooper
Harry Coen
Omarli Cohen
Rosie Croxford
John Davies

Pleasant Dexter
Dudley Doust
Roy East
John England
John English
Roy Evendon
Lynn Franklin
Clive Freeman
Laurence Gelber
Charlie Gillett
Danny Gillman
Seth Gillman
Anita Gornett
Nigel Green
David Haughton
Liz Kuipers
Mazher Mahmood
Russell Miller

Paul Montgomery
Philip Norman
Sean O'Connell
Sonny and Holly
   O'Connell
Ruth Polski
Thomas Porfe-Bracht
Peter Pringle
Mark Reeder
Chris Robbins
Tanya Sadourian
John Shirley
Jane Shoemaker
Chris Walker
Ian Walker
Professor John Wing
Rose Winters

496

Acknowledgments

We consulted a number of books in the course of our research. The most useful were:

David Bowie – The Pitt Report, by Kenneth Pitt (Design, 1983)
David Bowie: A Chronology, by Kevin Cann (Vermilion, 1983)
David Bowie – Theatre of Music, by Robert Matthew-Walker (Kensal, 1985)
David Bowie – The Starzone Interviews, edited by David Currie (Omnibus, 1985)
Bowie – An Illustrated Record, by Roy Carr and Charles Shaar Murray (Eel Pie, 1981)
Bowie in His Own Words, compiled by Miles (Omnibus, 1980)
The David Bowie Story, by George Tremlett (Futura, 1974)
Free Spirit, by Angie Bowie (Mushroom, 1981)
Presenting David Bowie, by David Douglas (Pinnacle, 1975)
Bowie, by Jerry Hopkins (Elm Tree, 1985)
The Guinness Book of British Hit Albums, *The Guinness Book of British Hit Singles*, *The Guinness Book of 500 Number One Hits*, all by Jo and Tim Rice, Paul Gambaccini, and Mike Read (1982 and 1983)

We should like to record our particular thanks to Ken Pitt and Kevin Cann who, although in theory our rivals, were unfailingly generous in their help; thanks too, for the same reason, to Chris Charlesworth, George Tremlett, and Tony Zanetta.

We drew on information from the following newspapers, magazines, and periodicals:

Disc, Melody Maker, New Musical Express, Record Collector, Record Mirror, Record and Tape Retailer, Sounds, Starzone.

Daily Express, Guardian, Daily Herald, Daily Mail, Mail on Sunday, Mirror, Sunday Mirror, News of the World, Evening News, Observer, Evening Standard, Star, Sun, Daily Telegraph, Sunday Telegraph, The Times, Sunday Times, Today.

Kent and Sussex Courier.

The Face, Gay News, Ritz, Time Out, Woman.

Billboard, Cashbox, Cavalier, Circus, Creem, Goldmine, Hit Parade, Moviegoer, Hit Parade, Phonograph Record, Record World, Rock Scene, Rolling Stone, Theatre Crafts, Variety, Village Voice, Zoo World.

Cleveland Plain Dealer, Denver Post, Glenside News, Los Angeles Free Press, Los Angeles Times, Memphis Commercial Appeal, Memphis Press-Scimitar, Nashville Banner, Nashville Tennessean, New York Daily News, New York Sunday News, New York Post, New York Times, New York

Sunday Times, Owen Sound Sun-Times, Philadelphia Bulletin, Philadelphia Sunday Bulletin, Philadelphia Inquirer, Rocky Mountain News, St Petersburg Independent, USA Today, Washington Post, Winnipeg Free Press.

International Herald Tribune, Newsweek, People, Playboy, Time, Vanity Fair.

Berliner Morgenpost, Bild, Die Welt.

We also consulted the files and reference shelves of public libraries at Beckenham, Bromley, Croydon, Holborn, Kingston, Lambeth, Maidstone, Southborough, Tonbridge, and Tunbridge Wells; and of the Press Association, the Goethe Institute, and the *Sunday Times* at Gray's Inn Road. In the US we consulted the New York public library and the library of the *New York Post*; and the public libraries of Memphis and Nashville, Tennessee. In Berlin, we were helped by the Axel Springer library, and by the staff of the Brücke Museum. To all of these, our thanks.

Finally, for their encouragement and support, we should like to thank Tim Anderson, Clare Bristow, Richard Cohen, Eric Major, and Jane Sinclair.

Photo Credits

The authors and publishers gratefully acknowledge all those who supplied photographs for use in this book.

Section 1 *(between pages 48 and 49)*

Pat Antoniou: page 1 top and bottom right, page 2 all, page 4 top and bottom left.
Kristina Amadeus: page 1 bottom left, page 3 top.
Chérie Moore: page 3 bottom right.

Section 2 *(between pages 112 and 113)*

Pat Antoniou: page 1 top and bottom right, page 3 bottom, page 4 top left and right.
Chérie Moore: page 1 bottom left.
Fay Baldry: page 2 bottom.
Bill Berks: page 4 bottom left.

Section 3 *(between pages 176 and 177)*

Rex Features: page 1 top, page 3 top.
Pictorial Press: page 1 bottom, page 3 bottom, page 4 top and bottom.
Dave Bebbington: page 2 bottom.

Section 4 *(between pages 240 and 241)*

Stella Gall: page 1 top.
Richard Ward: page 1 bottom.
Denis Taylor: page 2 bottom left, page 3 top.
Helen Lancaster: page 3 middle.
Ray Stevenson: page 4 top.

Section 5 (between pages 304 and 305)

Dave Bebbington: page 1 top, page 3 top.
Ray Stevenson: page 1 bottom, page 2 top right and bottom.
Calvin Mark Lee: page 2 top left.
Leee Childers: page 3 bottom.
Mick Rock: page 4 top and bottom.

Section 6 (between pages 368 and 369)

Rex Features: page 1 top and bottom, page 4.
Eduard Meyer: page 2 top.
Artur Vogdt: page 2 bottom.
Courtesy of the Brücke-Museum, Berlin: page 3 all, as follows:
Top: 'Liebespaar zwischen Gartenmauern' ('Lovers between Garden Walls') by Otto Mueller, © Cosmopress Geneva, ADAGP, Paris 6.
Bottom Left: 'Roquairol' by Erich Heckel, © Erich Heckel Estate, D-7766 Hemmenhofen.
Bottom right: 'Selbstbildnis in Hiddensoe' ('Self-portrait in Hiddensoe') by Walter Gramatté, © Ferdinand Eckhardt, Canada.

Section 7 (between pages 432 and 433)

Leee Childers: page 1 bottom, page 2 bottom, page 3 bottom.
McAlpine: page 4 main picture.

Section 8 (between pages 464 and 465)

Kobal Collection: page 2 top left and right and bottom left.
Rex Features: page 2 bottom right page 3 top and bottom.

Every effort has been made to acknowledge all those whose photographs have been used. In case of omission, we will be pleased to make the appropriate acknowledgment in any future editions.

All other photographs courtesy Peter and Leni Gillman.

Index

The titles of albums are shown in italics and the titles of individual songs are shown in quotes; thus, *Aladdin Sane* refers to the album and 'Aladdin Sane' refers to the song.

Index

Index